# ROADS TO CONFEDERATION

## The Making of Canada, 1867

Volume 2

Edited by
Jacqueline D. Krikorian, David R. Cameron,
Marcel Martel, Andrew W. McDougall,
and Robert C. Vipond

UNIVERSITY OF TORONTO PRESS
Toronto Buffalo London

Toronto Buffalo London
www.utppublishing.com

ISBN 978-1-4875-0228-7 (cloth) ISBN 978-1-4875-2189-9 (paper)

Publication cataloguing information is available
from Library and Archives Canada.

University of Toronto Press acknowledges the financial assistance to its publishing program of the Canada Council for the Arts and the Ontario Arts Council, an agency of the Government of Ontario.

Canada Council for the Arts Conseil des Arts du Canada

Funded by the Government of Canada Financé par le gouvernement du Canada

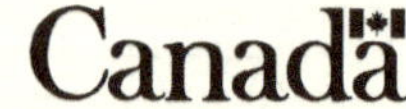

# ROADS TO CONFEDERATION

## The Making of Canada, 1867

## Volume 2

*Roads to Confederation* surveys the way in which scholars from different disciplines, writing in different periods, viewed the Confederation process and the making of Canada. Recognizing that Confederation has been traditionally defined as a process affecting only British North America's Anglophone and Francophone communities, *Roads to Confederation* offers a broader approach to the making of Canada, and includes scholarship written over 145 years.

Volume 2 of this collection focuses on three major themes. It presents research from the perspective of Canada's regions, with one chapter focusing exclusively on the competing understandings of 1867 from the perspective of Quebec. Next, it includes material pertaining to the geopolitical underpinnings of 1867 that addresses the relationship between Confederation, the U.S. Civil War and American expansionism, Great Britain, and war in the European theatre. Also included is leading scholarship by Stanley B. Ryerson, Adele Perry, Fernand Dumond, Ian McKay, and James W. Daschuk that questions whether Confederation itself was a formative event. Together with its companion volume, this is an invaluable resource for those who wish to deepen their understanding of the historical foundations on which Canada rests.

JACQUELINE D. KRIKORIAN is an associate professor in the Department of Political Science at York University.

DAVID R. CAMERON is Dean of the Faculty of Arts and professor of Political Science at the University of Toronto.

MARCEL MARTEL is a professor and Avie Bennett Historica Canada Chair in Canadian History at York University.

ANDREW W. MCDOUGALL is a lecturer of Political Science at the University of Toronto, Scarborough.

ROBERT C. VIPOND is a professor in the Department of Political Science at the University of Toronto.

*for tomorrow's Confederation scholars*

*pour les futur(e)s chercheurs et chercheuses de la fédération canadienne*

# Contents

## Volume 2

# Preface and Acknowledgments

This two-volume collection has been assembled in recognition of the country's sesquicentennial, bringing together previously published scholarship on the people, ideas, and events associated with the passage of the *British North America Act, 1867*. This interdisciplinary project aims to capture the complexities of Confederation scholarship and highlights the evolution of its interpretation over time. The historical discourses underpinning Confederation studies reflect a series of complex and contested narratives that are foundational to our day-to-day politics. The goal of this collection is to set out these debates by providing not only "classic" studies of Confederation, but also scholarly work that challenges our conventional understandings and approaches to the topic. We seek both to understand the past and to gain insights into the challenges we face today and those we need to consider for tomorrow.

Anniversaries, both personal and national, are very often fraught; the celebration associated with these moments is frequently alloyed by critical reflection, by alternative accounts that subject the conventional narrative to radical scrutiny. The alternative account that has called into question the Confederation celebrations of 2017 is the Indigenous story. For Indigenous peoples, the very idea that the "founding" of Canada in 1867 is the privileged political and constitutional moment in the lives of the peoples that live on the top of the North American continent is offensive. What about the treaties, signed by Indigenous peoples and the Crown, before and after Confederation, that sought to establish the relationship between Europeans and Indigenous peoples? What about the sorry record of treaty violation that followed thereafter? Indeed, what about the destruction of centuries-old Indigenous political and community development that was the result of European contact? For

Indigenous peoples, these are the historical moments and processes that need to be woven into our understanding of the present, and there is more of tragedy about them than satisfaction in national achievement.

We recognize that the 1867 scholarship has largely ignored both the contributions of Indigenous peoples and the hardships they have endured. For the most part, Francophone and Anglophone scholars have written the history of the making of Canada by defining it as a process affecting only British North America's two main linguistic communities. The role of Indigenous peoples and the implications of their marginalized status have not been fully explored in the scholarly literature on Confederation. It is a gap we wish to acknowledge; this collection begins to redress it.

The scholarship included in this project spans 145 years (1872–2017), involves forty-five individual and institutional authors, and includes two original and thirty-eight existing works. Published simultaneously by the University of Toronto Press and by Les Presses de l'Université Laval, the collection contains twenty-nine studies translated into either English or French for the first time. Contributions were chosen for their originality, focus, methodologies, and varying perspectives. We sought a range of competing viewpoints that reflect the richness of the approaches that both frame and underpin Confederation scholarship broadly defined. Whether originally written in French or English, this anthology aims to house some of the very best scholarship that has been published on the making of Canada.

This is a four-cornered project, involving two universities – York University and the University of Toronto – and two publishers – the University of Toronto Press and Les Presses de l'Université Laval. Our acknowledgments reflect that. When we began this project, we had no idea how complex the undertaking would be and had little appreciation for the number of tasks we would need to accomplish to achieve our goal. The list of people on whom we have relied, and whom we wish to thank, demonstrates the extent of the enterprise and the many hands that helped to make it happen.

If an army marches on its stomach, a scholarly publication advances only if there is money. We have been the beneficiaries of financial support from many quarters. At York University, we thank: the York University Canada 150 Fund; the Avie Bennett Historica Canada Chair in Canadian History; the Robarts Centre and its Director, Gabrielle Slowey; the Department of Political Science and its Chair, David Mutimer; the Faculty of Liberal Arts & Professional Studies for a Minor Research Grant

2016–17 and for support from the Book Publication Subvention Program; and the Office of Research Services for a SSHRC Research Opportunity Grant. At the University of Toronto, we thank: the U of T Canada 150 Fund; the Department of Political Science and its Chair, Louis Pauly, and its Interim Chair, Ryan Balot.

We greatly appreciate the assistance of colleagues who reviewed material for us and offered invaluable advice: Les Jacobs, Susan Kennedy, David Koffman, Tony Mauti, David McNally, Leo Panitch, Miriam Smith, and Kenton Storey.

Without the support of our research assistants, we could not have got the job done, and each has our warm thanks: Mathieu Arsenault, Julieanne Enns, Zack Goldford, Brianna Guenther, Rebecca Hellam, Geleta McLoughlin, Rebecca Rossi, Jasprit Singh, and Kate J. Winterton.

Some of the contributions in the collection had to be translated from French into English. We are in Lin Burman's debt for translating six articles into English. As part of the course work for the Advanced Translation Project/Project Management at York's Glendon Campus, a team translated the contribution of Richard Arès into English, and we thank the students for their work: Nicole Anichini, Anna Bandyk, Jillian Castelltort, Jessica Domingues, Wendy Duff, Chris Haggertay, Kim Tran, and Sally Vusi – all under the able supervision of Professor Lyse Hébert.

We also are grateful to Jennifer Brunet, Geneviève Deschamps, Lise Dufour, François Gauthier, Carmélie Jacob, Mathieu Lapointe, André Larose, and Leslie Talaga for translating a series of English contributions in the collection into French.

Wayne Herrington, Ian MacKenzie, Anne Laughlin, Breanna Muir, and Daniel Quinlan at the University of Toronto Press and Denis Dion, Jocelyne Naud, Laurie Patry, and Diane Trottier at Les Presses de l'Université Laval offered us invaluable guidance as we prepared the manuscript for publication in English and French versions. We appreciate all their efforts.

A number of people at both universities were extraordinarily helpful in moving the project forward. At York, we thank: Margo Barreto, Nadya Bloom, Janet Friskney, Helen Papacharalambous, and Associate Dean Sandra Whitworth. And at the University of Toronto: Cynthia Chandler, Mary-Catherine Hayward, Teresa Nicoletti, and Sari Sherman.

Finally, our warm appreciation to the family and friends who in many different ways helped us on our way: Randy Hesp; Don and Julie Krikorian; John and Rowena McDougall; Jonathan McKay; Dorothea

Wiens; Renée, Dominique, and Éva Choquette; Charley Rose and Max Eledam; Lauren and Cooper Elliott; Madaket and Ewan Iris; Luca L.S. Paneduro; and Andrew T. Winterton.

Jacqueline D. Krikorian
David R. Cameron
Marcel Martel
Andrew W. McDougall
Robert C. Vipond

Toronto, Ontario
July 1, 2017

# ROADS TO CONFEDERATION

## The Making of Canada, 1867

## Volume 2

# V

# From Canada East to Quebec

There is perhaps no more hotly contested question in the study of Canadian Confederation than the role that Quebec played in it. Most of Canada's francophone population lives in the province, but what it means to be a "French Canadian" has changed considerably over the years. Furthermore, what additional rights Quebec has in Canada, given that it has defined itself as the homeland of French Canadians since the 1960s, is a topic over which there is simply no agreement. There is consensus that in the century and a half since Confederation there has been a move away from the idea of "French Canada" and a stronger association with the province of Quebec by those who live there as the basis of political identity, although the former concept still has purchase nationally. Nevertheless, there is no common agreement on what Quebec's place was supposed to be in Confederation.

The five selections here examine different ways to think about Quebec's place at Canada's founding and its emergence as a separate province. In the excerpt from Eugénie Brouillet's book on the origins of the Quebec nation, its author argues that Cartier was instrumental in forcing the Fathers of Confederation to adopt federalism. For Cartier, federalism would allow various nations to coexist and at the same time permit a new common political nationality to emerge. For Brouillet, Canada became a federation in 1867 because Lower Canada politicians insisted on getting the necessary powers that would be used for the preservation of the cultural identity of French-speaking people. Similarly, Stéphane Kelly's piece focuses on the role that Sir John A. Macdonald played in Confederation and the impact that his focus on effective governance had in creating the provinces. Macdonald was particularly concerned by the governance issue. He insisted on the creation of institutions that would guarantee stability and harmony of the new endeavour, which meant that the imperial link was imperative. Indeed, relations within the British Empire should serve as a model for relations between the central government and the provinces.

Writing in the context of the country's centenary, Jean-Charles Bonenfant's piece examines what French Canadians generally thought of the pact as a whole. In his view, most French Canadians were in favour of it, faced as they were with the common commercial and defence problems of the rest of the country. In 1967, the leading journal for French-speaking historians, *Revue d'Histoire de l'Amérique française,* published an excerpt of Lionel Groulx's book on Confederation. In this journal article, Groulx insisted upon the crucial role that politicians from Lower Canada had played in the Confederation process, while minimizing the role of the Catholic Church in persuading French Canadians to support the new constitutional structure. Without Lower Canada, argued Groulx, there would have been no Confederation. Also he made an additional intellectual contribution to the two founding nations theory by arguing that there were three alliances that united the founding nations of Canada: a pact based on nationality, provincial rights, and minority rights.

Finally, Arthur Silver examines what thought was given to francophones in 1867 who lived outside Quebec, who at the time made up some 15% of the population. The answer is not much: the well-being of French in Canada was seen as being the responsibility of the Quebec government. Ottawa was an afterthought in this story and was never supposed to be the order of government responsible for their protection. One is left to wonder if more time had been spent clarifying these questions at the time much trouble would have been avoided in the century and a half afterwards.

# The French Canadians and the Birth of Confederation

## Canadian Historical Association Historical Booklet 1966

JEAN-CHARLES BONENFANT[1]

At the time of the birth of Confederation, the French Canadians formed a homogeneous group of almost a million inhabitants, representing not quite a third of the total population of the four provinces that were to form the Dominion of Canada. There were nearly 900,000 of them in Quebec, and already some 150,000 in Ontario, New Brunswick, and Nova Scotia, though the last exercised very little influence. The French Canadians of Lower Canada were nearly all Roman Catholics and the great majority of them lived in the country. Especially since 1840, they had developed their scholastic and municipal institutions; they had numerous newspapers and possessed an embryonic literature as illustrated by the Quebec literary school of 1860. What would be their reactions when faced with the events which would take place from June 1864 to 1 July 1867, and which would constitute the genesis of Confederation?

### Before 1864

For a century, theoretical projects to unite the British North American colonies in a federal union had been widely propounded. In general the French Canadians had known very little of these projects, which came for the most part from their political opponents, and to the French Canadians they often signified legislative union. However, as early as 1847, *Le Canadien* wrote, on 8 September, that "they [the French

Canadians] confidently anticipate a greater freedom of action in a federation." In 1858, a French Canadian, Joseph-Charles Taché, published the last and one of the most complete theoretical schemes of federalism, entitled *Des provinces de l'Amérique du Nord et d'une union fédérale*, a slightly revised version of thirty-three articles which he had written in his newspaper, *Le Courrier du Canada*, the preceding year. At the time of the debate on the Quebec Resolutions, in the 1865 session, the member for Lévis, Dr. Joseph S. Blanchet, quoted Taché abundantly in order to declare, with a little friendly exaggeration, that "in the division of powers between the local governments and the central government, the plan of the conference was almost word for word the work of Monsieur Taché." It was also in 1858 that Joseph-Édouard Cauchon edited in brochure form some articles which he had written in his *Journal de Québec*. As the federal system became less and less a theoretical one for the inhabitants of the British North American colonies, the French Canadians became interested in it, but they were not really called upon to make up their minds until the question became the object of political decision.

**Political Federalism**

Federalism began to become a political possibility in August 1858, when Alexander T. Galt demanded acceptance of his project of confederation before he would enter the Cartier-Macdonald ministry. George-Étienne Cartier was then converted to the idea of confederation, an important development, considering the authority that he exerted over a large number of his French-speaking compatriots. However, the mother country did not take the project seriously, and only with the political crisis of June 1864 did federalism really cease to be an academic problem. Under the patriarchal direction of Sir Étienne-Paschal Taché, who had agreed to come out of retirement in the preceding March to become premier of a Conservative government of which John A. Macdonald and George-Étienne Cartier were the real chiefs, a kind of sacred union was formed, due to the entry into the ministry of the Upper Canadian Liberal leader George Brown and some of his colleagues. The only important group which remained outside the coalition were the Liberals of Lower Canada, the "Rouges," to whom must be added some French-Canadian Conservatives who broke away from their party on this occasion, and an English-Canadian Conservative of stature, Christopher Dunkin. These Liberals were French Canadians, except for a few, including two leading figures, Luther Hamilton Holton and Lucius Seth Huntington. The serious opposition to Confederation in the united Canadas, then, was that of the French-speaking Liberals of Lower Canada, led by Aritoine-Aimé Dorion, and next to him his younger brother, Jean-Baptiste Eric, the impetuous and radical *enfant terrible*; who died suddenly on 1 November 1866, and so was spared the sorrow of witnessing the realization of Confederation.

The first act of the opponents of Confederation was to attack the coalition and to ridicule the Conservatives for becoming the friends of Brown, whom they had heretofore denounced as the greatest enemy of the French-Canadian Catholics. The struggle did not become clearly defined, however, until after the government had entered into relations with the other colonies at Charlottetown at the beginning of September 1864, and especially after the plan of federalism had been enunciated in the Quebec Resolutions at the conclusion of the Quebec Conference, which was held in October. From the social point of view in particular, the latter event was steeped in the French atmosphere of the city, but the deliberations were carried on exclusively in English and with all the pragmatism of the British. Of the thirty-three delegates who met at Quebec, only four were French Canadian: Étienne-Paschal Taché, who presided over the conference, George-Étienne Cartier, Jean-Charles Chapais, and Hector Langevin. Cartier himself seems to have been rather silent during the conference, though he must have put forward his ideas inside the cabinet of the united Canadas, which prepared the propositions which John A. Macdonald then submitted to the delegates.

## Dorion's Manifesto

By the beginning of November, although there had been no official announcement, numerous speeches and newspaper articles had made known the essential elements of the propositions adopted by the Quebec Conference, and, on 7 November, Antoine-Aimé Dorion considered it necessary to denounce them in a manifesto addressed to his constituents in the county of Hochelaga. The text of this manifesto, together with the speech which Dorion made during the winter of 1865 in the Canadian legislature at the time of the debate on the Quebec Resolutions, and the *Manifeste des vingt* of 1866, constitute a basic documentation of the struggle against Confederation in Lower Canada.

Dorion wondered, first, what independence would the provinces retain "if they were deprived of the right to regulate their own criminal and commercial laws, and if they could modify their civil and municipal laws, laws concerning public instruction, and other similar questions, only with the approval of the central government?" Theoretically Dorion was correct, for if the rights of reservation and disallowance which were written into the constitution had worked as John A. Macdonald desired at the outset, it would have been a veritable legislative union that had been created. In Dorion's eyes, the necessity of settling the problem of representation by population in the united Canada was not a sufficient reason for creating a confederation. He argued that it would have been better to grant some extra members in the assembly to Upper Canada, while preserving the equality between Upper and Lower Canada in the Legislative Council. In Dorion's opinion, the entry of the Maritime provinces into Confederation would only increase the financial drain on Upper and Lower Canada, without any compensating commercial advantages. The defense of the country would become more difficult when New Brunswick and its 500 miles of frontier with the United States was added. The Legislative Council, that is to say, the Senate, "composed of a fixed number of members appointed for life by the Crown, could impede the wishes of public opinion and paralyze all progressive legislation." And Dorion concluded with the argument which, until 1867, remained the most serious of those formulated by the opponents of Confederation when he said, "In whatever manner one views the proposed changes, there is one point on which there can be no difference of opinion, and that is that when we are concerned with nothing less than the remaking of the constitution, and the creation of new foundations for the political edifice, the people whose interest and posterity are affected, should be consulted." Although the government never succeeded in defending its attitude adequately, it was never to permit the people to express their opinion. The government claimed that it did not fear a popular consultation, but that it was unnecessary because in a number of elections the government candidates had been successful.

After Dorion's manifesto, at the end of 1864 and the beginning of 1865, the people formed ranks for battle. Meetings were held, especially in the counties of Rouville, Verchères, Iberville, Laprairie, Drummond and Arthabaska, Jacques Cartier, Chambly, Bagot, and Saint-Hyacinthe. On 7 January 1865, *Le Pays* asserted that the people were waking up in earnest and that soon the movement would embrace all of Lower Canada. "Since the present ministry," added *Le Pays*,

> does not intend to ask the people for their opinion on the constitutional changes which it is preparing for us, the people must take the initiative and prove that they are not inclined to sign this sort of death sentence without examining it very closely. Therefore, let the mayors of each village, let the prefects of each county, all set to work, and let Lower Canada, by means of public assemblies, pronounce its opinion on the plan of Confederation which is to be submitted to her representatives in Parliament in the very near future.

The assembly held at Verchères on 27 December was regarded by *Le Pays* in its edition of 29 December as "a perfect anti-Confederate triumph." The newspaper published the resolutions of the meeting, one of which was a very good summation of the arguments of the participants who were opposed to Confederation:

> 1. Because the new system would be expensive and complicated; 2. Because it would imperil the institutions and the religious faith, as well as the autonomy, of the French-Canadian nationality, guaranteed by solemn treaties and Imperial statutes; 3. Because it would impose on this province pecuniary obligations which were incumbent exclusively and by law on the other provinces of British North America, and very onerous material sacrifices, such as direct taxation, without procuring in return in this region any real or tangible benefit; 4. Because it would very probably instigate, sooner or later, throughout the said provinces, and particularly in this region, civil troubles and perhaps very serious ones.

Thus public opinion had been awakened when, at the beginning of February, the Upper and Lower Houses of the united Canadas began to study the Quebec Resolutions.

### Debate on the Quebec Resolutions

Even though Premier Taché sat in the Legislative Council, it was in the lower chamber that the principal speeches were made to praise the project as well as to fight it. Among the French Canadians, the most fervent partisans of Confederation were George-Étienne Cartier and Hector

Langevin, both members of the cabinet, and Joseph-Édouard Cauchon, who was a backbencher, but who exercised considerable influence over his fellow citizens through his newspaper, the *Journal de Québec.*

Antoine-Aimé Dorion, by virtue of his position as leader of the opposition, intervened several times, but on 16 February, he made his greatest speech, which may be regarded as the summation of the arguments of the French-Canadian adversaries of Confederation. Once again he took up the arguments of his manifesto and he defended himself successfully against the charge of having recently been in favour of a federal solution, as the Conservatives charged, when he declared that he was only "in favour of a Confederation of the two provinces of Upper and Lower Canada, but a real Confederation, giving greater powers to the local governments, and only a delegated authority to the central government." As for the problem of defense, to which was linked the construction of the inter-colonial railroad uniting Canada with the Maritime provinces, Dorion considered it impossible to regulate by means of Confederation. "What it would be better for Canada to do," he added, "would be to remain peaceful, and not give our neighbours any pretext for war." Dorion claimed also that the British railway magnates, desiring to restore the state of their finances, were the secret artisans of Confederation. He ended his speech with the words: "I greatly fear that the day when this Confederation is adopted will be a dark day for Lower Canada … I consider it one of the worst measures which could be submitted to us and, if it happens that it is adopted, without the sanction of the people of this province, the country will have more than one occasion to regret it." Eric Dorion added almost nothing to the arguments of his brother, though his style was more dramatic. After showing that the coalition of June 1864, and the project of Confederation which resulted from it, were only a manoeuvre of the Conservative party to remain in power, he repeated over and over again, "I am opposed to the project of Confederation because …"

Among the other French-Canadian opponents of Confederation were Henri-Elzéar Taschereau, Conservative representative from Beauce, who broke with his party on this occasion because, he said, he was not convinced that the proposed constitution contained "in itself sufficient guarantees for the protection of our rights," and Joseph-Xavier Perrault, member for Richelieu, who in a very long speech, after more serious arguments, took the time to revive memories of the persecutions against the Irish, the expulsion of the Acadians, and the constitutional struggles of Lower Canada, and made the assertion that on the island of Mauritius, England had not respected the clauses of the treaty which ceded that colony to her – all this to prove that the new constitution was a threat to the French Canadians.

Several votes were taken. The most revealing was that of 10 March, when the government proposal was approved by 91 votes to 33. The vote may be analyzed as follows: in Upper Canada, 54 in favour of the measure, 8 opposed; in Lower Canada, 37 in favour, 25 opposed; among the French Canadians, 26 in favour, 22 opposed. A proposal to appeal to the people before submitting the project to the imperial parliament was rejected by 84 to 35, the great majority of the latter being French-Canadian members. The Liberal newspaper *Le Pays* wrote on 14 March that the night of 10 March, the night of the most important vote, had seen "the most iniquitous act, the most degrading act, which parliamentary government had witnessed since the treason of the Irish deputies who sold their country to England for positions, honours, and gold." In an obviously different tone, the Conservative newspaper *La Minerve* had written on 11 March, "The vote in the Canadian legislature marked an important date in the history of Canada ... The union of the colonies is the consecration of our political and national existence and the guarantee of our future."

In the Legislative Council on 20 February, the Quebec Resolutions had been approved by 45 votes to 15, the latter including 8 councillors from Lower Canada. Seven of these had been elected and consequently could claim to express the sentiments of a fairly large group of public opinion. The French-Canadian voters of Lower Canada could not express their views on the project of Confederation before it was adopted, but the fact remains that a large number of their representatives in both houses were opposed to it.

From the approval of the Quebec Resolutions by the Canadian parliament to their study at the London Conference in December 1866, the plan of Confederation continued to be the object of political discussions between its partisans and its adversaries. At the beginning of March 1865, it suffered a severe blow when the government of New Brunswick, which favoured Confederation, was defeated in a provincial general election. In spite of the affirmations of Cartier and his supporters, the project seemed to have broken down and during the autumn of 1865, many people, including newspaper editors, wondered whether it might not be necessary to replace the plan for the wider union with one for the federation of the two Canadas only. However, new elections were held in New Brunswick in 1866, which returned the Confederation party to power. This made possible the London Conference in December of the same year, and finally, in 1867, the drafting and the adoption of the British North America Act.

### The Session of 1866

During this waiting period, various problems deriving from Confederation, of particular interest to the French Canadians, were discussed, and solutions were found for them during the last session of the assembly of the united Canadas in the summer of 1866. The most important debate concerned the resolutions providing for the constitutions of the future provinces of Quebec and Ontario. John A. Macdonald did not want an Upper House in Ontario, but Cartier demanded one for Quebec. The government had some difficulty in explaining this anomaly. According to Cartier, Lower Canada wanted "to give more dignity to legislative institutions," but there were further reasons for the creation of a Legislative Council. In reality, the Council was thought necessary to protect the Anglo-Saxon minority against possible legislative action by the Lower House.

At the birth of Confederation, the English and Protestant Canadians of Quebec did not wish to risk their position. They represented nearly a quarter of the population, but their real power was more considerable than their number, for, in the cities of Quebec and Montreal, they were the masters of industry, commerce, and finance, and they dominated the Eastern Townships. They were afraid that, under the new constitution, they would lose their privileged position, and that they would henceforth be at the mercy of the French-Canadian Catholic majority in the future local legislature. Their leader, Alexander T. Galt, tried to reassure them in a speech made on 23 November 1864 in the city of Sherbrooke, for which he was the member in the Legislative Assembly. He rejected the idea that the French Canadians could one day deprive their compatriots of a substantial representation in the Legislative Assembly, but even so, he had the prudence to have twelve privileged electoral districts constituted, which could not be interfered with without the consent of an absolute majority of the members who would represent them.

Galt also tried to ensure better protection for the schools of the Protestant minority in Quebec. In 1866 he was unsuccessful in his attempt to have the Legislative Assembly adopt a measure to this effect, and he resigned from the government, but, as a delegate to the London

Conference, he obtained approximately what he wanted in the final text of the British North America Act.

The problem of education for minorities at the time of Confederation, it should be remembered, was always presented from the religious viewpoint and never from the linguistic. That was no disadvantage to the Anglo-Saxon minority of Quebec, which was then identical with the Protestant minority. In the other provinces the French-Canadian population belonged to the Catholic minority, and it was only as such that it was protected. George-Étienne Cartier went so far as to say in 1866, "Upper Canada is inhabited by only one race; the same is not true of Lower Canada." Hector Langevin had made the same point in 1865: "Upper Canada has a homogeneous population professing different religions." In fact, there were nearly 75,000 French-speaking Canadians in Upper Canada, but for their compatriots of Lower Canada they were only a sort of avant-garde whose future was viewed as quite hazy. As for the Acadians, it is revealing that, during the debate on the Quebec Resolutions in the Canadian legislature, their expulsion was mentioned only twice. It was solely as Catholics that they received a meagre protection, and furthermore they were to be deprived of this protection on the morrow of Confederation. In reality, the struggle surrounding the problems of education, before as after Confederation, brought two different philosophies face to face: that of the Catholics who favoured separate schools, and that of the Protestants who, in spite of appearances, more easily accepted schools which were for all practical purposes public schools, in which the question of a specific religion was not seriously raised.

## The Final Opposition

A final assault against the project of Confederation was launched at the end of October 1866 by the drafting and publication of a manifesto signed by twenty members of the Legislative Assembly and sent to the Colonial Secretary, Lord Carnarvon. Coming after more than two years of struggle, when the die was definitely cast, the manifesto did not present any new arguments. It summed up events from the first official step towards Confederation, taken by Cartier, Ross, and Galt in 1859, to the decision which had just been made by Nova Scotia, New Brunswick, and the Canadas to send delegates to London to establish the Union. The signatories concluded,

> We have striven to prove that the initiative for the project of Confederation, and all the subsequent steps to have it adopted, are due to exigencies of the parties and not to a spontaneous and general desire of the people to make radical changes in their institutions or in their political relations.

Lord Carnarvon was unmoved by the protests which were presented to him. During the debates in the House of Lords and the House of Commons on the proposed British North America Act, the problem of the opposition which had been manifested in Nova Scotia was raised, but that of the Liberals of Lower Canada was not. Lord Carnarvon contented himself with declaring on 22 February that in the case of Upper and Lower Canada, the delegates in London had the most complete powers. For the British government, the approval of the Quebec Resolutions in 1865 constituted a definite acquiescence on the part of the two sections of united Canada. The manifesto received considerable attention in the newspapers of Lower Canada, but it left the mother country indifferent.

**The First of July 1867**

During the winter of 1866–67, Lower Canadians attentively followed the events which were taking place in London, even though the newspapers were often several weeks late in reporting the news, because the newly inaugurated transatlantic telegraph provided very little information about the conference. In the spring, the text of the act, which Queen Victoria had sanctioned on 29 March, was sent to Canada and was immediately translated into rather inelegant French. On the first of July, which was a Monday, Confederation was born, and the day was marked by great public rejoicing in the new province of Quebec. Of course its Liberal opponents accepted the new regime without enthusiasm, but it is probable that the following lines from the editorial of the *Courrier du Canada* represented more than the partisan sentiments of a Conservative newspaper:

> One hundred and six years, eight months and eighteen days ago yesterday, M. de Vaudreuil, the last of the French governors of New France, concluded a capitulation which delivered forever to his secular enemies "the most beautiful, the most French, and the most neglected" of the colonies that France possessed.... Who would have been able to foresee, we shall not say a hundred years ago, fifty or twenty-five years ago, but seven or

eight years ago, who would have been able to foresee that Lower Canada, the cradle of the French-Canadian nationality, would be, in the very near future and without ceasing to be a colony of England, governed by a French-Canadian Catholic?

## The Causes of Confederation

Even if the opposition to Confederation in Lower Canada was considerable, it cannot be assumed that the new regime had been brutally imposed on the population. Both profound causes and immediate motives led a good proportion of the French Canadians to be favourable to it.

In the birth of Confederation, several causes were intermingled, but they can be conveniently classified in this way: the economic exigencies of the time; the necessity of constructing the Intercolonial and of re-financing the railway system already in existence; fear of the United States and at the same time, to a degree, a desire to imitate them; the needs of defense; the birth in the different colonies of a common national sentiment; the consent of the mother country; and finally the desire of the Canadian government to be free of the difficulties which had for some time paralyzed the working of its political institutions.

The transformation of the economy of Great Britain in the middle of the nineteenth century considerably damaged the commerce of the colonies. A grave crisis followed, and some of the discontented English Canadians even advocated annexation to the United States. Less bound to business and industry, the French Canadians generally remained outside this movement. The Reciprocity Treaty, signed in 1854, brought a temporary prosperity to the colonies, a prosperity which became even greater during the American Civil War from 1860 to 1865, when Canadian exports increased and agriculture profited. However, the Canadians feared that the treaty would be abrogated and this in fact happened in 1866. The partisans of Confederation claimed that the problems associated with the termination of reciprocity would be corrected by the increase in commerce between the reunited colonies. Facing the economic difficulties of the time, aggravated by poor harvests, particularly in 1864, and foreseeing the greater hardship which the end of reciprocity would bring, Canadians had seen a certain degree of salvation in the new system. The French Canadians shared this hope. When in a speech to the Legislative Assembly on 9 March 1865,

Eric Dorion drew a somber picture of the farmer in the fields of Lower Canada, he was obviously exaggerating, as any opponent of the government would, but all the same his testimony revealed a recurring situation which led the people to look for a new solution, a solution such as Confederation.

Most of the French Canadians, except for some of their leaders like Cartier, were not so bound to financial and railway interests that the necessity of building the Intercolonial influenced them directly to favour Confederation, but even so, on 1 August 1867, the Conservative newspaper *Le Courrier de Saint-Hyacinthe* wrote,

> There is no doubt ... that the Intercolonial Railway will bring wealth to the part of the country through which it runs. Its first effect will be to stimulate commerce and to favour colonization greatly. The counties of Temiscouata and Rimouski which it crosses are very fertile, the immigrant will find good land there, and abundant facilities for communication with the centres of commerce.

Moreover, the construction of the Intercolonial was only one important aspect of two other factors: the fear of the United States and the necessities of defense.

Rightly or wrongly, between 1860 and 1870, the French Canadians feared annexation to the United States and viewed Confederation as the only way to prevent this. While it is true that English-Canadian politicians and newspapers sometimes invoked this argument, few attached as much importance to it as the French Canadians. Several of their political leaders and a number of their newspapers presented the alternative: "Confederation or annexation." At that time, all Canadians had serious reasons to fear the United States, and particularly the northern states who emerged victorious from the Civil War. England had shown sympathy towards the southern states, and it would have been normal for the North to take its vengeance on the British colonies of North America. Besides, the fear of the United States took a concrete form in the Fenian menace, which the politicians did not fail to exploit. In 1866, the Fenians, Irish fanatics who had been organizing in the United States and had taken advantage of the Civil War to acquire military training, attacked New Brunswick at Campobello, Upper Canada, on the Niagara peninsula, and Lower Canada at Frelighsburg. On 28 June 1866, on the occasion of the feast of Saint-Jean-Baptiste, *Le*

*Canadien* published a poem by Arthur Cassegrain entitled "The Fenian Invasion" in which he launched the appeal:

> Aux armes! fils de Jean-Baptiste
> Entendez le canon! ...
> Que votre patron vous assiste!
> Pensez à Carillon.

Moreover, the general problem of the defense of Canada was one of the important influences on the birth of Confederation in French Canada as well as elsewhere. Their politicians had made this a debating point and on 13 February 1865, *La Minerve* wrote, "It is to assure ourselves a force and sufficient means of defense that we desire a union of all the provinces destined to march under the same flag in case of war."

Several politicians and newspapers also emphasized that, at the time of Confederation, a new country was being born. The French Canadians do not seem to have been preoccupied with this idea except in so far as it concerned their survival as a group, or the possibility that union would permit them to avoid annexation. In opposing the new regime, the French-Canadian Liberals claimed, of course, that it endangered the survival of French Canada, but the *Journal de Québec* seems to have represented a large part of public opinion when it wrote on 17 December 1864,

> We want to be a nation one day, and as that is our necessary destiny and the goal to which we aspire, we prefer the political condition of which we will be a vital element, and in which we will still be in existence, rather than to be thrown into the midst of an immense people, like a drop of water lost in the ocean, where in a few years we would lose our language, our laws, and even the memory of our glorious origins.

It should be added that, at the birth of Confederation, French Canadians were happy that legal recognition was given to the use of their language in parliament and in the courts, where French had previously had only *de facto* recognition.

Finally, an examination of the causes which led to Confederation reveals that action was precipitated by the desire to escape from the political difficulties of the united province. The Union of 1840, by creating equal representation in the Lower House for Upper and Lower Canada, became eventually unjust to the Anglo-Saxon element and made representation by population one of the most important themes of political life in the united Canadas. This problem was one of the principal causes of ministerial instability, and to resolve it, federalism seemed the best solution. This was what Cartier understood, and this is what he succeeded in making a large portion of the population understand. *La Minerve* summed up the situation on 16 July 1864 when it wrote,

> Representation by population in Confederation is a completely different question from representation by population in the existing Union, since in the first case it is a safeguard and guarantee of independence and in the second case it is an infallible means to servitude and degradation.

Several days before, *La Minerve* had underlined the fact that Lower Canada could not be an obstacle to Confederation and consequently could not oppose another factor which determined the course of events, the will of London. The Conservative newspaper wrote,

> For a long time, people in England have been talking of uniting all the British possessions in America under the same legislative government. When a general movement towards Confederation develops and when this movement is perfectly motivated, can we allow ourselves to stand in the way like an insuperable barrier, at the risk of bringing about their ruin and our own?

## The Catholic Clergy

"Without Cartier and the Catholic clergy of Quebec, it would have been impossible to accomplish the union of 1867," wrote the journalist and historian Sir John Willison. The Conservative party which advocated Confederation was of course on better terms with the Catholic clergy than was the Liberal party which opposed it. The bishops and curés still exercised an influence over the electorate in political matters, which they were not to lose until the victory of Laurier in 1896. Moreover, much importance was attached to the opinion of the clergy. Cartier declared in the House during the winter of 1865,

> I will say that the opinion of the clergy is favourable to Confederation.... In general, the clergy are the enemy of all political dissension and if they

> support this project, it is because they see in Confederation a solution to the difficulties which have existed for so long.

Perhaps not all the bishops and curés were as favourable to Confederation as Cartier said. At least, this is what the Liberals claimed, but as they had never been on very good terms with the Catholic Church, it was difficult for them to boast of interpreting the sentiments of its representatives.

However, it can be affirmed that from June 1864 to the spring of 1867, the Catholic clergy, while generally favouring the Confederation project, refused to commit themselves and even felt some fear of facing the unknown. But after the new political system had been adopted by the British parliament, the five bishops of Lower Canada published pastoral letters in which they left their flock little liberty to vote against the constitution. For them, of course, it was the recognition of a *fait accompli,* the traditional acceptance by the Catholic hierarchy of established power and authority, but it was also an almost morbid fear of annexation to the United States, and a consequence of the game of bipartisanship. In effect, not to approve Confederation would have been the same as allying themselves with its opponents, who for the most part were Liberals who had broken with the clergy. Thus the bishops were only expressing publicly sentiments which they had already held for a long time, and which the public knew. The Conservatives shamelessly took advantage of this, especially during the elections which followed Confederation; the Liberals suffered from it and allowed their anger to burst forth violently in the autumn of 1867.

The French-Canadian bishop who seems to have shown the greatest enthusiasm for Confederation was Monseigneur Charles Larocque, who became bishop of Saint-Hyacinthe in March 1866. In his pastoral letter of 18 June 1867, after saying, "In our opinion, Confederation does not appear to be a danger to be feared at all," he wrote,

> Republican institutions do not suit us any better than they suit the great people from whom we are descended, the French. And the fate which would be awaiting us, if God suffered us at some future date to enter the great American republic, would be exactly comparable to that of so many tributaries which come to be swallowed up in the great, deep St. Lawrence, where they disappear without leaving the slightest trace of their existence.

After listening to such remarks, it was rather difficult for anyone who was accustomed to obeying his bishop to oppose Confederation and to vote in favour of its opponents.

### George-Étienne Cartier

Without a doubt, the great artisan of Confederation in Lower Canada, the one who succeeded in channeling all the latent forces, was George-Étienne Cartier. He was not a theorist and, if he made himself the apostle of Confederation, it was not to bring about the triumph of the system. It was because he believed that it was the only way out of the situation, favourable to Lower Canada but unjust to Upper Canada, which had been created by equal representation, and perhaps also because he was to some extent associated with railway interests. To these motives may be added the natural desire of a politician to play a role on a higher stage, and an almost morbid fear of the United States and their republican institutions. In the great speech which Cartier made on 7 February 1865 in favour of the Quebec resolutions, he declared, "The question is reduced to this: we must either have a British North American federation or else be absorbed into the American federation." When Cartier feared annexation, it was not only because it would mark a change of allegiance, but also because of something more important: Cartier, as a monarchist and a Conservative, feared republican institutions. Cartier has sometimes been criticized for not ensuring sufficiently the protection of his compatriots, and particularly for forgetting the French minorities living outside Quebec, but we must not judge a politician in the light of events which have occurred in the intervening century and which he could not have foreseen. In the sometimes difficult circumstances in which he found himself, at grips with an artful colleague like John A. Macdonald, Cartier sought concrete solutions. At the most, one can reproach him, like many other politicians after him, for having had a conception of federalism that was too simplified and too optimistic. He expressed it in 1865 in these words:

> Under the federal system, which leaves to the central government the great questions of general interest in which racial differences are not concerned, it will not be possible that the right of race and religion fail to be appreciated.

## The Elections of 1867

In attempting to understand the attitude of the French Canadians at the time of the birth of Confederation, it is necessary finally to see what happened in Quebec when the first elections were held, at the beginning of September, to elect members to the House of Commons and to the Legislative Assembly of Quebec. The Conservatives tried to transform the vote into a sort of plebiscite in favour of Confederation. At least it was easy for them to claim that their Liberal opponents, who were opposed to the new regime, were hardly likely to make it function. In another connection, as we have seen, after the new system had been adopted by the British parliament, the bishops sent out the pastoral letters in which they left their flock little liberty to vote against Confederation. The Liberals, directed by Antoine-Aimé Dorion, formed an organization not to fight against Confederation, but to "neutralize the effects of the new system." This was the Reform Association of Lower Canada, which consisted of moderate Liberals, as opposed to the young radical Liberals, often annexationists, who followed Médéric Lanctôt. As often happened at the time, the arguments of the two principal groups of opponents crystallized into two brochures, entitled, respectively, *La Confédération, couronnement de dix années de mauvaise administration* and *La Confédération, c'est le salut du Bas-Canada.*

The federal election ended in a resounding victory for the Conservatives and consequently for the supporters of Confederation. In the whole country they won 101 seats out of 181, and in Quebec, 45 out of 65. The Conservatives were also victorious in the elections for the Legislative Assembly.

## The First Session

The first session of the new federal parliament opened on 7 November and, at the very beginning, a minor incident seemed to indicate that the French Canadians who feared Confederation and claimed that it would not easily permit the realization of Canadian duality were right. After Macdonald and Cartier had proposed James Cockburn, a Conservative member from Ontario, and a Father of Confederation, as speaker, the member from Montcalm, Joseph Dufresne, opposed this choice "because Cockburn did not understand the two languages which were to be on equal footing in the House of Commons." *La Minerve* itself, while favourable to the government, did not hesitate to write, "Perhaps it was wise to present openly the rights of the French-Canadian minority in Confederation as soon as Parliament opened." This was the beginning of the difficulties which French-speaking Canadians would often meet in their attempts to participate freely in political life at the federal level, difficulties which would impel them to develop the autonomy of the province of which they would be masters because they constituted the majority.

For the moment they felt a certain pride in possessing their own institutions. When the Lieutenant-Governor, Sir Narcisse Belleau, opened the first session of the provincial legislature on 28 December 1867, he could declare,

> The constitution has entrusted you with great interests but has imposed serious obligations on you, concerning the administration of justice, public instruction, the patronage of science, the humanities, and the arts, the exploitation of public property, including our vast forests and our mines that are so important, the development of our social resources, immigration, colonization, the police, and in general, civil law and property law.

For better or for worse, the die was cast, and the legislative machinery of Confederation began to function.

**Conclusion**

Although we have no mathematical proof, it seems likely that the majority of French Canadians were favourable to Confederation during its formative stages from 1864 to 1867, and while they possessed most of the characteristics which, since the principle of nationality had developed, had led people in Europe to dream of independence, nevertheless it can be affirmed that at this time, even though the French Canadians wanted to preserve their identity, they never seriously thought of independence as a solution.

On the other hand, it appears that they understood that the political system created by the Union of 1840, even if it had become on the whole favourable to them, had to be altered because the English-speaking Canadians of Upper Canada could not agree indefinitely to a refusal of representation by population. At the time there was certainly a strong temptation of annexation to the United States, or at least the impression that this annexation would be inevitable someday, and that, after all, it would serve no purpose to fight against geographical, economic, and political imperatives, but George-Étienne Cartier and the Catholic clergy succeeded in convincing the population of the dangers which annexation would entail for them. Besides, they could believe that annexation was inevitable without wishing to take definite steps which would facilitate it.

While accepting federalism as inevitable, the French Canadians did not have a very advanced theoretical vision of it, and they would have been incapable of discussing most of the problems it poses today. They did not even suspect these problems. It could not be expected, for example, that they could imagine all the furore that lay in Paragraph 13 of Section 92 on property and civil rights. They could not have suspected that judicial interpretation would give this article such importance. They could not know all that was hidden in the words "public lands, timber and woods" of Paragraph 5 of Section 92.

The French Canadians were forced to make the best of pragmatic solutions and to foresee as well as possible the difficulties these would create. Events must not be judged in the light of later developments, with an insight which contemporaries could not possess. The French Canadians seem to have understood fairly well the powers it was necessary to entrust to the provinces so that Quebec could remain master of its institutions at the time. They thought that provincial power would be so greatly developed, especially in the case of Quebec, that they gave little thought to the possibility of a genuine Canadian duality at the federal level. However, it must not be forgotten that Confederation was accomplished at a time when Canada was an Anglo-Saxon colony and when the best government was the one which interfered to the least possible degree in the life of its people. It was therefore much less serious a hundred years ago that the federal government was almost completely Anglo-Saxon, because Canada had no international status, the state did not intervene in economic life, and there were, as yet, practically no social security measures.

However, the French Canadians of Lower Canada can be reproached for not really understanding the situation of the French minorities in Upper Canada and the maritime provinces, who from a political point of view, were not represented. At the time, the problems of education were much more centred on religion than on language, and thus the protection which was claimed for the minorities depended on the former rather than on the latter.

A majority of French Canadians favoured Confederation a hundred years ago because it was the only realistic solution which presented itself to them, and even those who opposed it were content to say that it was premature but did not offer an alternative solution. Confederation was achieved because the English Canadians needed to have the French Canadians in it, and the French could not then become independent. The great majority of nations have been formed, not by people who desired intensely to live together, but rather by people who could not live separately.

## NOTES

1 Jean-Charles Bonenfant, *The French Canadians and the Birth of Confederation*, Canadian Historical Association Historical booklet, 21 (Hull: Leclerc, 1966).

## BIBLIOGRAPHICAL NOTE

The historians who have written about the birth of Confederation have taken into account the participation of the French Canadians in the events and have briefly analyzed their attitudes, but no thorough study has been devoted to this subject as a whole. French-Canadian historians have also neglected the study of this period. The only work on the subject written by a French Canadian is *La Confédération canadienne* (Montreal, 1918), by Abbé Lionel Groulx, which the author himself admits was written too quickly, and declares "that these studies make absolutely no claim to being a definitive work." He also published in *L'Action française* (XVII, May–June 1927, pp. 282–301) a study entitled "Les Canadiens français et l'établissement de la Confédération." A chapter on the birth of Confederation is to be found in the *Cours d'histoire du Canada* by Thomas Chapais, vol. 8, 1861–1867, Quebec, 1934. It is unnecessary here to repeat a bibliography which is to be found at the end of P.B. Waite's book *The Life and Times of Confederation, 1864–1867* (Toronto, 1962), but a reference may be added to Walter Ullmann's article entitled "The Quebec Bishops and Confederation," published in the *Canadian Historical Review*, vol. XLIV, 1963, pp. 213–234. The present study has been written with the aid, in particular, of contemporary newspapers and the *Débats parlementaires sur la question de la Confédération de l'Amérique du Nord*, printed by order of the Legislature in 1865, which have been more easily consulted since 1952, thanks to the *Index aux Débats sur la Confédération, 1865* (Ottawa, Public Archives of Canada, 1952).

# "French Canadians and the Founding of Confederation"

## "Les Canadiens français et l'établissement de la Confédération"

(Translated by Lin Burman)

*Revue d'histoire de l'Amérique française*

1967

(originally published in 1927)

LIONEL GROULX[1]

The founding of Confederation depended on no other province as much as on Lower Canada. First of all, there were large numbers to be reckoned with. In the 1861 census, the population of Lower Canada was 1,111,566. This was more than the total population of the three provinces of the Gulf region, and more than a third of the total population of the future state. No federation was possible if it went against the will of those million people.

Moreover, this group had considerable political clout. In the parliament of the United Canadas, it was the foremost power and the least breakable group, and the one that, because of its cohesiveness, had just scuttled the anglicising policy of the Union, and, more than any other cause, had, under Bagot and subsequently Elgin, determined colonial emancipation. While the parliamentary group of Upper Canada was consistent only in its inconsistency, and came together and broke apart at the whim of short-lived leaders, the party of LaFontaine, Morin, and subsequently Taché treated parties and factions with disdain, allied itself in turn with one and then the other, while never ceasing to be itself and remaining identical in its principle and aspirations. The small liberal democratic faction was able to organise on its flanks and weakened it without making it a weakness. Furthermore, in 1864, the Canadian group had a born leader. Although lacking Papineau's magnetism, and a lesser character than LaFontaine and Morin, George-Étienne Cartier nevertheless wielded influence unmatched by any previous leaders over his party and fellow-countrymen. More than any of them, he possessed the forceful qualities of leadership. He dominated by authoritarian influence and a self-willed, nervous, almost despotic personality that knew how to assert itself on a people with the inherited tradition of monarchy. It was not that his race was prepared to want all that he wanted, but it did not want anything that he did not want. On this point every contemporary and historian was agreed: only one man, George-Étienne Cartier, could make his province accept the momentous political changes of 1867, in the same way that one word from this same man could make his followers stand firm in invincible opposition.

Lower Canada was thus able to hold its own for another decisive reason, its geographical situation. No doubt because it is too straightforward, historians have ignored this essential point too much. For the architects of Confederation of 1864, Lower Canada could not be anything but either the mainstay of the construct or an unknowable void. This was not only because with Montreal's harbour and the long navigable stretch of the St. Laurence, Lower Canada was the vital route of exchange and the link between the provinces and its ultimate vital artery; it was also quite simply that Lower Canada made for a contiguous territory between the maritime states and those in the centre. If the idea of politically welding provinces separated by the uncultivated lands of the Lower St. Lawrence was already considered strange and arbitrary, what kind of ingenious artifice would have cemented an alliance over a 300-mile gap? What giant arch could have covered that vast emptiness! The matter is one of *force majeure* in history and politics. Without Lower Canada, a federation of the Maritime Provinces could be formed, but certainly not a Canadian confederation. Upper Canada was faced with only three options: isolation at the other end of the country, a bipartite federation with Lower Canada, or prolongation of the regime of 1840, an unnatural coupling that was becoming increasingly intolerable day by day.

Canadian Confederation depended, in the first instance, on Lower Canada and this was, of all the provinces, the one that took the most risks. Whatever its grievances against the regime of 1841, they were no greater than those of Upper Canada. "Here we sit today seeking amicably to find a remedy for constitutional evils and injustices complained of – by the vanquished?" George Brown asked in 1865. "No," he replied, "but complained of by the conquerors!"[3] It cannot be overemphasized that the federated system, for want of anything better, does not in any way represent for peoples the perfect political state for peoples; the perfect state, strictly speaking, means the freedom to do as one wishes in total independence; hence the principles and concerns that prevail when a federation is created. Small nations federate to stabilize their political and national situation, not to make these more perilous. They take out insurance; they do not take greater risks. John A. Macdonald, in his Halifax speech in 1864, clearly set out the characteristics essential to any political federation:

> In discussing the question of political union, we must consider what is desirable and practicable; we must consult local prejudices and aspirations.... I hope that we will be enabled to work out a constitution that will have a strong central Government, able to offer a powerful resistance to any foe whatsoever, and at the same time will preserve for each Province its own identity – and will protect every local ambition; and if we cannot do this we shall not be able to carry out the object we have now in view.[4]

What special advantages, what aspirations would Lower Canada have to place under the protection of the federal state? Upper Canada had only to concern itself with political and material interests. At the very most, it kept a watch over its school system, which it jealously regarded as immutable. Similar concerns existed in the maritime colonies, which, being weaker than Upper Canada, nevertheless feared for a certain sense of political and social identity. In French Canada alone, concerns took on a sort of transcendent character. It was in a unique position. In the duel over civilization that had been taking place here since 1760, it could only apprehend a new development, one that would be more constraining than the others. After eighty years of relative isolation in which it had sustained and defended its spirit against a tiny English minority, and in a confined arena, in 1840, with the battlefield suddenly enlarged, it had had to contend with an entire British province and an entire British nation. In 1864, the battlefield was expanding to cover half the continent; Lower Canada would have to stake its destiny against four provinces instead of one. Furthermore, not only were political and economic interests and the sense of social identity at stake, but religious and moral interests as well; that is to say, its entire national being and its entire faith. A son of the Church, it could not forget that it had charge of souls and that it was up to it to obtain guarantees, not only for itself, but for every Catholic minority of the future state. For a people who had faith in Christ, nothing was as important as these responsibilities.

However, the contract that French Canada had to develop and sign with its partners in the federation was a double one: it was a political contract to preserve its full autonomy as a province and carefully define federal and provincial jurisdictions; however, it was also a contract that was national and religious in character and that, together with the rights of French-Canadian nationality, would establish the condition of religious minorities in the provinces. French Canada would alone, or almost alone, determine the very nature of the federating contract. Upper Canada, as is well known, would have preferred a simple legislative union. In the Maritime Provinces, opposition to this form of state was by no means universal, or inflexible.[5] If the alliance of 1867 became a federating pact, rather than a merger of provinces, it was because this was demanded first of all by French Canada.

Would written laws, however, have the power to calm the anxieties of a people in whom the accidents of history left no illusions concerning the inviolability of these most sacred laws? How to banish anxiety when in the very middle of the debates, both races confronted each other with such opposing attitudes and sentiments? On one side there was the desire to offer the weak a privileged situation, the desire for justice to the point of generosity, conciliation to the point of foolishness; on the other, the obstinate resolution to make the weak feel the superiority of the strong, to make Catholic and French minorities bend under the weight of rigid and mean-spirited documents. Far from rising to the ideas of the great founders of state and seeing in the diversity of races and the maintenance of their creative energies a means of stimulating and strengthening the national genius, an entire Anglo-Saxon element, the most dominant one and the most listened to, was concerned solely with affixing the arrogant signature of the lion at the bottom of the bilateral contract, and admitting any associates solely as serfs. What a harsh light the school question of 1866 was to shed on this troubling state of mind! Was Antoine-Aimé Dorion expressing something other than collective anxiety when, during the parliamentary debate of 1865, he exclaimed,

> I know that the Protestant population of Lower Canada fears that, even with the restricted powers remaining to local governments, their rights are not protected. How can we then expect Lower Canada to place great trust in the general government, which will have such vast powers over

> the destinies of their constituency? Experience shows that majorities are always aggressive and tend to be tyrannical, and it cannot be otherwise in this case.[6]

How the warning by M. Henri-E. Taschereau, Conservative member for la Beauce, and one of the few in his party who parted ways from their leaders on this point, must have resonated in the popular consciousness:

> I cannot say whether our descendants will thank us for having made it easier for them to be part of the vast empire of the English provinces of North America. On the contrary, they will soon see that this confederation is the ruin of nationality in Lower Canada, and the day this constitution is voted for, the death blow will be given to our nationality which was beginning to take root in this land of British North America.

A struggle, hitherto unequalled in violence in the history of Canada, ensued. To the bitterness of party quarrels were added underlying passions roused in the popular consciousness by an awareness of extreme danger. For the first time, and where the very survival of nationality was at stake, French Canadians were divided into two camps. It was a highly tragic situation for a small people, the greatness of whose history stemmed from the very fact that it had always held its soul and its survival to be something great. To be or not to be federalist was to betray or not betray one's race and all its hopes.[7] The day after the Charlottetown Conference, and instigated by young people, resistance to the project revived with renewed strength after the Quebec Conference because of Antoine-Aimé Dorion's forceful manifesto and the denunciations of the Union Nationale, a group that included young Conservatives, such as L.-O. David, who had broken with their party. The antifederalists were not recruited solely from the liberal democratic faction, discredited from the start by its Americanism and irreligious ideas. "We are not unaware," wrote the bishop of Saint-Hyacinthe, "that there are men filled with good faith and loyalty who fear Confederation because, in some of the details, it seems to them to present the threat of ruin for any French and Catholic influence."[8] Moreover, in the general assembly held in Trois-Rivières in the autumn of 1864, the episcopate of Lower Canada decided to let M. Clerk, editor of the Catholic newspaper *True Witness*, discuss the principles of the planned Confederation, as long as he *respected* the ministry.[9]

Spirits were raised to such an extent that, having let his newspapers promise that the electorate would be consulted on the federating project, the Canadian minister got cold feet and decided it would be wise not to do so. He skillfully manoeuvred to avoid the popular verdict, thoroughly convinced that a single incident, the smallest tactical error, could compromise everything. John A. Macdonald wrote to Leonard Tilley on 8 October 1866,

> Had we met early in the year and before your elections, the greatest embarrassment and your probable defeat at the polls would have ensued. We should have been pressed by the Opposition to declare whether we adhered to the Quebec resolutions or not. Had we answered in the affirmative, you would have been defeated, as you were never in a position to go to the polls on those resolutions. Had we replied in the negative, and stated that it was an open question, and that the resolutions were liable to alteration, Lower Canada would have arisen as one man, and good-bye to Federation.[10]

What magic power calmed this anxiety and anger and garnered the support of Lower Canada for the project of the "Fathers of Confederation"?

First of all, it was political leaders, and more than any other, George-Étienne Cartier, of whose influence we are well aware. Moreover, it was not so much the personality or prestige of these leaders, as their somewhat overstated assurances. They were careful to extend these assurances to all matters that were causing concern. First and foremost, there were the basic elements of nationality: language and faith. If the first provisions of the Quebec Confederation proved too concise for comfort, the wish to be fair and far-sighted gradually led during the debates to more extensive and precise wording. For official rights of the language, the final drafting culminated in article 133, which appeared to anticipate and protect everything; minority education rights were accommodated in the minutely detailed wording of article 93.

Such guarantees, however, could be effective only if the basic elements of the French-Canadian soul, inserted into an independent political framework, could avoid being destroyed by the unifying state, which was destructive to a sense of identity. In this regard too, Cartier and his lieutenants took a host of precautions, and ensured themselves against camouflaged federalism. Better than ghosts of the state, the provinces would be real political entities, endowed with a wide jurisdiction. At the Conference of Quebec, as at the Conference of London, the constitution was not established by the delegates' personal vote; voting was by province. To signal its ethnic and political duality, Canada had two votes. The very preamble of the new charter plainly stated that provincialism would be maintained: "Whereas the *Provinces* of Canada, Nova Scotia, and New Brunswick have expressed their Desire to be federally united ... And whereas such a Union would conduce to the Welfare of the Provinces ..." Merged into the preamble with Ontario, under the heading "Canada" we see in article 5 that Quebec recovers its distinct political entity: "Canada shall be divided into Four Provinces, named Ontario, Quebec, Nova Scotia, and New Brunswick." Cartier's term "new nationality" (today we would say Canadianism, period), which was in vogue at the time and should not be held against him, indicated a merger rather than a federation of nationalities. From that time on, the Canadian statesman, with his realistic mind, very accurately disentangled truth and falsehood, the possible and the fanciful in the dream of a new nationality. Canadian nationality, yes, in the political, but by no means the ethnic, sense of the term. "Objection is made to our project, because of the words 'a new nationality,'" Cartier remarked, "but if we unite, we will form a *political* nationality, independent of the national origin and religion of individuals." For greater clarity, he immediately added,

> Some have regretted that we have a distinction of races and have expressed the hope that, in time, this diversity will disappear. The idea of a fusion of all races is utopian; it is an impossibility.

Master of its own house, in the independent framework of its province, the French-Canadian race, according to Cartier, would also have sufficient protection in the federal context. On this more perilous battleground, he firmly indicated the only decisive tactic for his people, a tactic the abandoning of which was perhaps the cause of some of our defeats:

> When the leader for Lower Canada shall have sixty-five members belonging to his section to support him, and command a majority of the French Canadians and of the British from Lower Canada, will he not be able to upset the Government if his colleagues interfere with his recommendations to office? That is our security. At present, if I found unreasonable opposition to my views, my remedy would be to break up the Government by retiring and the same thing will happen in the Federal Government.

The speeches of Cartier and his lieutenants doubtless do not attest to much foresight. Such statements by the Conservative leader, and other similar ones by Langevin and Cauchon, would raise a smile today, if it were not for the price we paid. Were these men sincere? We believe so. Their illusion and their mistake, both great, lay in granting too much good faith to their political associates, thereby taking risky securities against the future. From what source did the men who had just lived through the belligerent history of the last quarter century claim the right to give themselves over to such optimism?

Their excuse, if such it may be termed, was to have promised nothing for which the verbal assurances of the leaders of the majority had not given grounds. What, for example, could be clearer than this statement by John A. Macdonald who, more than anyone else, was qualified to express the sentiments of his people when the federating contract was signed?

> The delegates from all the provinces have agreed that the use of the French language be one of principles on which the Confederation would be based.[11]

How could these statements not be believed, when Lord Carnarvon confirmed them from on high in the imperial parliament:

> Lower Canada, is jealous, and deservedly proud, of her ancestral customs and traditions; she is wedded to her peculiar institutions and will enter this Union only upon the distinct understanding that she retains them … And it is with these feelings and on these terms that Lower Canada now consents to enter this Confederation.

And further:

> The object of that clause [clause 93] … had been to place all these minorities, of whatever religion, on precisely the same footing, and that, whether the minorities were *in esse* or *in posse*.[12]

The words of political leaders weighed heavily on French-Canadian opinion. Would they have swept away all resistance if more august words had not been added in support? No one, we believe, could disagree that the episcopate of Lower Canada virtually held the fate of Confederation in its hands. Cartier's haste in claiming the approval of the bishops, the wrath of the democratic liberals, and the pastoral letters of 1867 show the importance attached to episcopal opinion. The bishops had no need whatsoever to take their moral influence to the opposition; their silence would have sufficed to nip the plan of the "Fathers of Confederation" in the bud.

The attitude of the bishops, let it be said from the start, was to become much more discreet than that of the political leaders. First and foremost, the bishops of Lower Canada were careful to refrain from the fervour of their colleagues in the Maritime Provinces.[13] In fact, they were worried.

> We understand the hesitation and even alarm of some of our compatriots, Mgr Cooke of Trois-Rivières will say; and it has not been without strong feeling that we ourselves have seen the daunting necessity of having to adopt a measure which is great in and of itself and in its consequences.[14]

This anxiety was felt especially in Montreal, in the entourage of Mgr Bourget, the great figure of the Canadian episcopate. When Cartier boasted in the Chamber of having for him the feeling of the bishops, M. Truteau, the vicar general of Montreal, was quick to express his reservation:

> M. Cartier ... apparently said in the Chamber that the highest Church dignitaries in every diocese of Lower Canada were in favour of Confederation. I do not know what the other Bishops think of this; however, as regards Monseigneur de Montréal, I can state positively that he has so far not wished to give an opinion on this matter. Before he left for Rome, he said he preferred to wait before taking any stand. I as a private individual sense that the country is in an exceptional position. I am quite convinced that M. Cartier has excellent intentions and that he would not wish to do anything that might be detrimental to the Church. However, I would admit that I ask God every day that, if Confederation takes place, there will be no resulting disadvantage for Lower Canada, and that we never have the misfortune of seeing our fortunate country persecuted by the Protestant part, as is unfortunately the case in Switzerland, where the Protestant cantons persecute the Catholic cantons.[15]

People in Montreal were particularly worried about the power to legislate on marriage and divorce that would be conferred on the federal parliament. M. Truteau would have wished for firm opposition by the

Catholic members of parliament to this measure, leaving "each particular legislature the right to decide on divorce." "Since it seems that the legislature of Lower Canada," he said, "will still have to comprise a majority of Catholic members, they will not provide us with the hideous spectacle presented by divorce everywhere it is allowed."[16] Every bishop in Canada found cause for alarm over minority school rights. When, in the parliamentary session of 1866, the Langevin bill appeared to ignore the minority of Upper Canada, the episcopate, in a collective plea, informed the governor-general, Lord Monck, that, "in fairness, all the rights and privileges given to the Protestant minority of Lower Canada must also be conferred on the Catholic minority of Upper Canada." A few days later, in order to back popular sentiment, the bishops, at the suggestion of Mgr de Montréal, decided to make public their plea to Lord Monck.

It was only after the vote on the federative constitution by the imperial parliament and its publication in the *Gazette officielle* of Canada, on the eve of the election of 1867, that the bishops of Lower Canada finally decided to express what they felt about the new political state. The liberal democrats furiously condemned the "interference" by the religious authorities. Was this really a skillful tactic? Given that, in spite of intervention by the bishops, the opposition decided not to back down, was not the best means of softening the blow to show the calculated discretion and extreme restraint of the praises given to the federative contract in the bishops' letters? One could search in vain for an explicit judgement about the objective value of the constitution. Let us take the time to examine this closely. To impose the charter of 1867 on the adherence of the faithful, the bishops could only come up with extrinsic motives: the need for this political form for the material development of the country, the urgency of finding a palliative against annexation to the United States, the presumed wisdom of the "work of the most eminent statesmen in each of the provinces," and lastly, and above all, after the vote of the imperial parliament and His Majesty's sanction, the duty to obey the established government. They were careful not to show any victorious guarantees for the protection of ethnic and religious rights. If they perceived any, it was in a very roundabout way, insofar as the new political state would save the country from American annexation or put an end to the intolerable regime of the Union of the Canadas. Their illusions were moderated to such an extent that everyone, faced with the future, stipulated, as an express condition of salvation, the moral and political union of French Canadians. One of them, the archbishop of Saint-Hyacinthe, who believed even in the inevitable battles, attempted to make them acceptable by showing them to be beneficial. "Doubtless," he wrote,

> under Confederation, our exceptional position which stems from our belief and customs is certainly a little perplexed and full of difficulty! Well, our very dear brothers, we tell you this with conviction: it is all the better for us that it is so, because for our people, just as for an individual, a chance to fight that is met with energy and courage is a sure way to increase our strength and earn respect!

The attitude of the venerable bishop of Montreal became even more defiant. To Cartier, who had made him hold a copy of the North America bill, Mgr Bourget had already replied with a simple acknowledgement of receipt.[17] When the time came to develop a course of action for those who depended on him, the bishop did so in a circular letter to his clergy dated 25 May 1867, and a pastoral letter of 25 July of the same year. Both of them bore the heading, not as in Trois-Rivières, Saint Hyacinthe, and Rimouski, "Pastoral letter," or "Writ of mandamus on the occasion of the new Constitution …," "Concerning the inauguration of the federal government," or "On the subject of the proclamation of Confederation," but rather "Circular on the conduct required during the coming election," and "Pastoral letter recommending public prayers on the occasion of the coming election." Unlike other episcopal documents, the circular and the pastoral letter of Montreal did not offer anything more than a plea in favour of the new regime. Occasionally, and inserted among a few principles of social morality, there was a single call to obey "any legitimately established government," and, in the pastoral letter, the example of the Church of Canada was given to reinforce the same principle.[18]

Nothing could draw the bishop of Montreal out of his reserve. The liberal democratic press, which loved a row, in vain contrasted this attitude with that of the other bishops, and in vain the bishops appealed to their colleague for a more explicit statement. He did not relent. To Mgr Larocque who wrote to him, "In such a detrimental state of affairs, could not Your Grandeur give an opinion, should you even not do so, fairly openly and publicly, to put an end to the scandal spread by malice and bad faith on the path of the weak?,"[19] Mgr Bourget made this significant reply: "I think I must state, in the sincerity of my soul, that I believe I have said, in my circular and my pastoral letter … all that

I could and should say about Confederation, for the direction of the clergy and education of the people."[20]

To summarize, the bishops of Lower Canada imposed the acceptance of the federative regime on their people, motivated by circumstance and in the name of doctrine. Out of loyalty, they refrained from doing so in the name of confidence they did not share at all. At most, like Mgr Cooke of Trois-Rivières, they vouched for the good faith of the French-Canadian "Fathers of Confederation." "We know of nothing that would lead us to think of Confederation as an act of betrayal."[21] However, among themselves, unanimity had prevailed in order to remind the faithful of the grave precept of obeisance to constituted authority. Such teaching and such lofty testimony, added to the authority of the political leaders, should destroy all opposition.[22] Voted in by parliament in 1865 by barely twenty-seven French-Canadian members against twenty-two, Confederation, which had become a *fait accompli,* rallied, in the 1867 election, fifty-three out of sixty-five Quebec ridings.

In remembering the decisive role they played in establishing Confederation, will French Canadians ask themselves on 1 July next how much notice was taken of their good will? Will our present political partners remember that our acquiescence in 1867 was given on the good faith of our religious and political leaders who, in their turn, depended on the good faith of the "Fathers of Confederation" of the majority? Do we believe that had the bishops of Lower Canada foreseen so much persecution in schools and such great breach of faith, they would have written their pastoral letters in favour of Confederation? We certainly do not deny the illusions, nor the naïve lack of foresight of the French-Canadian "Fathers of Confederation." We only make the point that if they did not demand more guarantees, it was not because they did not deem these necessary; the fact was that they did not believe that, among citizens of one and the same country, it was necessary to take away more of them.

We agree that after half a century of existence, Canadian Confederation is still an anaemic giant, containing many seeds of dissolution. In addition, it is a principle of general biology that an organic entity decays and becomes corrupted as soon as the causes that gave it its shape and constitution have ceased to act. If Canadian Confederation is not to be an artificial state, a façade on the American border, the time has come to stop opposing the forces and principles that presided over the creation of this great body politic and were to have given it the vital thrust. Everything that has been attempted in the past sixty years, and everything that is attempted in the future against the security of the French-Canadian race in this country has been attempted and will be attempted against its interests in maintaining Confederation. French Canadians did not enter Confederation to perish there, nor even to suffer diminishment; they entered in order to live there and to live there fully. This is therefore not the time to steal or to shrink the federal spirit; that spirit must be strengthened and spread across Canada all the more as contact between the two races increases. The French-Canadian race is no longer confined to the eastern part of the country; in spite of the walls erected in front of it, it has exported people to all the western provinces, as far as the Pacific coast. The reactions of these French groups as well as those of present-day Quebec against the denials of justice and the administrative mean-spiritedness should act as a warning that, even if in the past we were able to barter our membership cheaply in the federative pact, the present generation does not accept that its chances of life, any more than its right to live in dignity, were sold away.

NOTES

1 Lionel Groulx, "French Canadians and the Founding of Confederation," a translation of "Les Canadiens français et l'établissement de la Confédération," *Revue d'histoire de l'Amérique française*, 21, 3a (1967), 677–694. This work was originally published in *Les Canadiens français et la Confédération canadienne* (Montreal, Bibliothèque de l'Action française, May–June 1927), 1–21.

2 *Parliamentary Debates on the Subject of the Confederation of the British North American Provinces – 3rd session, 8th Provincial Parliament of Canada*, printed by order of the Legislature (Quebec, 1865).

3 *The Union of the British Provinces ...* (Charlottetown, 1865), 44.

4 "I know that certain members of this Chamber, and many people in Upper Canada, and the Maritime Provinces think that a legislative union would be more advantageous than a Confederation." Address by G.-É. Cartier, *Parliamentary Debates on the Subject of the Confederation*, 1865. See also Joseph Pope, ed., *Confederation: Being a Series of Hitherto Unpublished Documents Bearing on the British North America Act* (Toronto, 1895), 59, 60–61, 82, 84–95, the highly significant statements of Fisher, Whelan, and Tupper.

5 *Débats parlementaires sur la question de la Confédération*, 1865, 269. Own translation.

6 In his pastoral letter of 8 June 1867, the bishop of Trois-Rivières pointed out and deplored the particularly violent nature of the political debate: "It is with sorrow that we have seen the violence with which a few of our fellow countrymen have risen up against the project of Confederation."
7 Pastoral letter concerning the inauguration of the federal government.
8 Mgr Bourget to Mgr de Floa, 21 December 1864. *Archives de l'Archevêché de Montréal,* Lettres de Mgr Bourget, vol. XXIII: 262.
9 Joseph Pope, *Memoirs of the Right Honourable Sir John Alexander Macdonald, G.C.B., first prime minister of the Dominion of Canada* (2 vol., Ottawa, 1894), I: 306.
10 *Débats parlementaires sur la question de la Confédération,* 1865, 943. Own translation.
11 Hansard's *Parliamentary Debates,* 1867, 805.
12 Abbé Lionel Groulx, *La Confédération canadienne, ses origines* (Montreal, 1918), 116, 164–165.
13 Pastoral letter of 8 June 1867.
14 M. Truteau to M. C.-F. Cazeau, vicar general of Quebec, 20 February 1865, *Archives de l'Archevêché de Montréal,* Lettres de Mgr Bourget, vol. XXIII: 288–290.
15 M. Truteau to Mgr Bourget, 3 February and 31 March 1865, *Archives de l'Archevêché de Montréal,* Lettres de Mgr Bourget, vol. XXIII.
16 Abbé Lionel Groulx, *La Confédération canadienne,* 117.
17 "Then came the Constitution, then the union of the two provinces. The Church submitted to this and preached to its children obeisance to the constituted authority. Nowadays, it accepts the federal government without argument, because it comes from the same Authority." *Mandements, lettres pastorales,* circulars and other documents published in the diocese of Montreal since its founding (8 vol., Montreal, 1887), V: 240.
18 Mgr Larocque to Mgr Bourget, 12 October, 1867, *Archives de l'Archevêché de Montréal,* S.- Hyacinthe, Lettres 1864–1881.
19 Mgr Bourget to Mgr Larocque, *Archives de l'Archevêché de Montréal,* Lettres de Mgr Bourget, vol. XXV: 458–459.
20 The single parliamentary vote of United Canada and the ratification of this initial vote by the imperial Parliament, which, denying that it was imposing anything on the people of Canada, claimed only to ratify the work of the Conferences and the provincial Parliaments, would these suffice to make the *British North America Act* the "established government"? In other words, could the Parliaments, in a British country, change the constitution without prior consultation of the people? This involves an issue of Natural Law, which is too involved to discuss here.

21 "The Catholic clergy showed itself particularly favourable to the project of union, which must have exerted considerable influence to realise the work of a confederated Canada. Without Cartier and the Catholic clergy of Quebec, the union of 1867 could not have taken place." (Sir John Willison, *Wilfrid Laurier and the Liberal Party*, cited by John Boyd, *Sir Georges-Étienne Cartier, Baronet, sa vie et son temps* – Histoire politique du Canada de 1814 à 1873.)

# "Quebec Culture and Federalism in 1867: The Spirit and Letter of the Federal System"

## "La culture québécoise et le fédéralisme de 1867: l'esprit et la lettre du régime"

(Translated by Lin Burman)

*The Negation of a Nation: The Quebec Cultural Identity and Canadian Federalism*

2005

EUGÉNIE BROUILLET[1]

The pre-federation period has been the subject of numerous studies using historical legal and philosophical approaches. Many of these studies were written immediately following the centenary of Canadian federation, a period in which the issue of constitutional reform was clearly formulated. To this end, studying the intentions of the Fathers of Confederation was conceived of as allowing an interpretation of the constitution that respected the spirit of 1867. Many writers concluded that the original intentions were clearly centralist,[2] thereby justifying the tendency at the time to centralise power in the hands of the central government. In a more recent study, one writer has explored the intentions of the Founding Fathers with the aim of bringing out the moral dimensions of Canadian federalism.[3]

It would be futile to claim that it was absolutely essential to rely on the original intentions of federalism in order to find solutions to modern constitutional problems. The federal principle, and the systems that are its manifestations, were adopted and shaped in particular societies at a specific time in their history. Consequently, to simply try to go back to something that was devised at the end of the nineteenth century in the hope of solving present-day problems would be misguided. However, this does not mean that the past is of no use in understanding the present: the present can be correctly judged on its merits only if the past has been well understood. To progress, we must first know and understand where we come from. The same applies to constitutional matters: the dynamic nature of a constitution implies that we cannot simply dismiss the context in which it was written and adopted. Granted, a constitution must be able to evolve with time in order to adapt to new realities. However, the way in which it evolves, and the path taken in that evolution, will necessarily depend on the ideas that governed its development: "The present is the past rolled up for action, and the past is the present unrolled for understanding."[4] Our intention here is therefore to travel back to the colonial societies of the time and see to what extent the letter of the constitutional regime established in 1867 rendered the spirit that had governed its adoption, and especially to try to discover whether it addressed adequately the concerns of the Quebec nation about its identity at that time.

The pre-federation historical context, in its political, historical, and ideological aspects, is highly instructive regarding the leading role played by the issue of culture in reaching a compromise on federation in Canada. The cultural duality that characterised the groups involved was reflected first of all in the constitutions and constitutional practices before 1867. This factor also lay at the heart of differing visions of Canadian confederation defended by two of its architects, John A. Macdonald and George-Étienne Cartier. The various, more pragmatic considerations, i.e., the aggregating and segregating, or uniting and disuniting factors that drove the British colonies of North America to unite within a federation also show that cultural reality was the very basis for adopting the federal principle as the foundation of the new constitution.

[...]

## The Ideological Context

One of the differences between the concepts of "federation" and "confederation" is that the first, unlike the second, involves the creation of a new state. Adopting a federal regime involves, on the part of entities who wish to join together for certain ends, renouncing part of their sovereignty in exchange for a level of government in which they will all be represented. In that sense, the process of federation has, as its corollary, the creation of a new nationality. What was understood, in the case of the Canadian federation, by this new nationality?

Most writers who have studied the pre-federation period have lent great importance, and rightly so, to the role played by John A. Macdonald in developing the Canadian federal system. Macdonald was one of the main architects of the new system, a system that, in many respects, bears his stamp. On the other hand, there are far fewer studies devoted to another architect who also played a fundamental role in the birth of Canadian federation, particularly with regard to acceptance of the new system by the French Canadians of Lower Canada; that man was George-Étienne Cartier.

Writers who have written on the pre-federation context have almost all presented John A. Macdonald above all as a pragmatic politician.[5] Macdonald was not inclined to raise concerns before they arose: "We must above all refrain from touching the constitution, unless it is clear that the population is suffering from it."[6] In his view, it was only when dictated by political circumstance that reforms were worth undertaking. Sticking to his Conservative ideology, he therefore concentrated in his presentation of the confederation project on its tangible benefits for all the colonies, especially from the economic and military standpoint.[7]

However, it was clear that behind his defence of the project for a new constitution, Macdonald had a certain vision of the country that was proposed. Although he had not set out exactly what he meant by the creation of a new nationality, certain excerpts from his speech on the project of union before the Legislative Assembly of United Canada in 1865 may shed some light on the subject.

First of all, speaking of the initial project of uniting the Maritime provinces, he asserted, "No one yet knew whether the union should be a federal or a legislative one, but what everyone wanted was to find a course of action that would have the effect of making one single people into three different ones."[8] He went on to explain what had followed at the Charlottetown conference with regard to the project for a general union of the colonies: "We informed the delegates of our views at some length and were able to satisfy them to such a degree with our reasons and convince them so thoroughly of the advantages of a general over a specific union that they immediately put aside their own project and accepted the idea of forming a great nation and a strong government."[9] Macdonald's idea that a political union of the colonies under a strong government would allow the creation of a single people out of different peoples suggests that he presumed that the latter would gradually disappear by merging into a homogeneous whole. Further on, he outlined in more detail what he meant by this "great nation":

It must seem to the people of this country that, if we want to create a great nationality – however offensive this word might have seemed to the ears of some representatives in one of the preceding sessions –, a nationality which commands respect outside its borders and defends the institutions of which we are so proud; if we wish to have one single form of government and create a commercial union and have absolute reciprocity of trade among five colonies which are already united by a community of origin, sovereignty, allegiance, and almost of blood and descent; ... the only way to achieve this magnificent result is to subject the diverse provinces of British North America to some type of consistent organisation.[10]

By pointing out that the colonies wishing to unite already shared a "community of origin, sovereignty, allegiance and almost of blood and descent," Macdonald became the defender of the creation of a new nation, whatever that choice of sort of union might be. He subsequently gave his opinion about the form of government that should be chosen. In his view, although he would have far preferred a legislative union that would have allowed the establishing of the best, least costly, strongest, and most powerful government, he was forced to renounce it, especially because of the presence in Lower Canada of a people "speaking a different language and having a different faith from most of the people under confederation" and who felt that "its institutions, laws and national associations" could suffer from the adoption of a unitary system.[11] It was therefore only with reluctance, and because of the need for Lower Canada to be part of the projected union, that Macdonald consented to a form of federal government.

However, although he made the concession in principle, Macdonald did not change his view of what the new Canadian nation should be, i.e., a nation that was not just superimposed on those nations existing within the a new state, but one that would one day supplant them and become the sole repository of cultural identity for all its citizens. Many authors have in fact made the point, and it emerges clearly from Macdonald's speeches before the Legislative Assembly in 1865; his vision of Canadian federalism was distinctly centralist and postulated that the provinces should be in some degree subject to the central government:

The conference, finding that pure and simple legislative union is unworkable, has come to adopt a form of federal government, will have all the force of a legislative and administrative union, while at the same time, we shall preserve freedom of action for different sections. I am happy to think

> that we have come up with a plan for a government which has the advantage both of giving us the power of a legislative union and the freedom of a federal union, that is to say, protection for local interests.[12]

As regards the centralist nature of the projected federal union, he compared the project that was put to the delegates of the British colonies with the American federal system, a comparison that revealed his hopes for the new Canadian nation. In his view, the proposed project put right the mistakes made by the Americans in developing their federal system, i.e., the fact that it was too decentralised. Here is what he said in the Legislative Assembly of United Canada in 1865:

> We have had the experience of the United States to guide us. I am not one of those who regard the constitution of the United States as a failure. I believe it to be one of the greatest works ever created by human genius. But to say that it is perfect would be a mistake.... I am convinced that in the system we are submitting the people, all the defects acknowledged by experience have, in large measure, been avoided.... Before the American union was created, as we all know, the different states which were part of it were separate provinces. As is the case with us, there was no link between them other than that of their common Sovereign. Their organisation and laws were different.... By virtue of their constitution, they declared that each state was sovereign unto itself, except for the powers conferred on the general congress. Here we have adopted a different system: we have concentrated strength in the general government.... We have conferred upon it ... all the powers inherent in sovereignty and nationality.[13]

Speaking about the attribution of residual power to the federal parliament rather than the provincial parliaments, he declared, "This is what may be termed a wise and necessary provision. By this means, we shall concentrate strength in the central parliament, and we make the confederation one people and one government, instead of five peoples and five governments which are scarcely linked to one another under the authority of the home country."[14]

It would seem, therefore, in light of these excerpts from Macdonald's comments, that he hoped that the system adopted would create ever stronger identification with an overall Canadian nation. He hoped that to the citizenship and common allegiance with Great Britain, which had not allowed the Americans to develop a deep-seated common identity, there would be added deeper aspects of identity and that the unitary system, which was "unworkable" in the mid-nineteenth century, would ultimately finally prevail. For Macdonald, the great unifying symbol of the new Canadian nation would be chiefly the monarchy, the symbol needed to unite disparate elements. It was precisely the absence of a unifying symbol of this kind that, in his view, had been the root cause of the problem the Americans had had in developing a strong national identity. He described it thus: "The internecine struggles which are unfortunately raging in the United States show us that our institutions, and the principle from which they derive, are superior. May the monarchical principle long continue to guide us. Rather than turning to Washington, let us rally with the moderates to the motto: Canada United as One Province, and under One Sovereign."[15] Thus, for Macdonald, the creation of a Canadian civil or political nation that would have allowed the survival and development of specific cultural identities within it was not to be wished for, and that is why he favoured some form of federal government, granted, but still the most centralist one that the circumstances of the time permitted.

That vision of the Canadian nation favoured by Macdonald was, however, not shared by all the architects of the system, even within the ranks of those who defended the project of union. Among them was George-Étienne Cartier who, although a great defender of the projected union, did not harbour the same aspirations as his compatriot from Upper Canada with regard to the type of common nationality that would or should emerge.

In a work of political philosophy published in 1996,[16] Samuel V. LaSelva maintains that the rediscovery of the moral foundations of Canadian federalism may provide new answers to the question of coexisting multiple identities within one community of the state. To this end, he lends great importance to the role played by Cartier in developing the new constitution by shedding light on Cartier's vision with regard to a properly Canadian theory of federalism. According to Professor LaSelva, Cartier's crucial role in creating Canadian federation and his understanding of Canadian federalism have been virtually forgotten, a fact he deplores.

For LaSelva, Cartier's importance in history lies in having defended a vision of Canadian federalism that made its existence possible. For Cartier, Canada was apparently a nation in which identities and multiple allegiances could develop and flourish within a structure that gave rise to a common political nationality.[17] Cartier's theory of federalism differed from Madison's in its initial premise: Madison's theory assumed the existence of the nation and concentrated primarily on the issue of the type of government to adopt in order to achieve republican freedom; Cartier's theory had not only to demonstrate that federalism was desirable, but also that a Canadian nation could emerge and flourish. Cartier, unlike Madison, had to face the problem that there existed multiple cultural identities within the British colonies.[18] His solution was therefore to formulate a theory of federalism tailored to Canadian sociocultural and political reality, i.e., a theory based largely on the dual idea of multiple identities and one common political or civil nationality. Thus, far from assuming a nation, federalism creates one.[19] As Professor Carl Friedrich wrote, "Canadians had a very special problem to deal with which found no parallel in the American experience: this was how to arrange a federal system that would satisfy their French-speaking citizens."[20]

First of all, it was because Cartier's influence that the federal rather than the unitary form of government to which a large number of delegates inclined was chosen as the basis of the new constitution at the Charlottetown Conference in the autumn of 1864.[21] By this means, Cartier prevented the individuality of Lower Canada, and by the same token, its distinct cultural identity, from being absorbed. He shouldered enormous responsibility in this regard. In the legislative union system, he had always firmly and successfully opposed any attempts by the leaders of Upper Canada to replace the principle of equal representation of both sections of United Canada in the Legislative Chamber with representation based on population, knowing that such a concession would be fatal to the distinct cultural identity of his compatriots.[22] However, when he realised that circumstances favoured uniting the colonies of British North America, he became an ardent defender of the union of the colonies within a largely federal instead of unitary system.

At the Quebec Conference in October 1864, Cartier was called upon to play the most important role of his political career. As head of the delegation from Lower Canada, although he had had the valuable support of Hector Langevin and Thomas Chapais, Cartier had to make sure that "the interests of his compatriots were safeguarded and that the continued existence of their rights, institutions and nationality, that is to say, everything they cherished above all else, was assured in the projected union."[23] He thereby agreed to all the issues relating to the common interests of the colonies being turned over to a general government in which "there would be absolutely no reason to fear that any principle would be adopted which might harm the interests of any particular nationality."[24]

Unlike John A. Macdonald, whose vision of Canadian federalism was clearly centralist, even unitary, and assumed a degree of submission to the central government, Cartier's vision was truly federalist: provinces were sovereign in matters related to specific cultural identity, but were united within a general government that was also sovereign with regard to their common interests. As Professor Garth Stevenson asserted, "One must attribute to Cartier and his followers the fact that Canadian provinces ... were also given exclusive and substantial powers of their own."[25]

However, as is self-evident when a federal system is adopted, the vision of Canadian federalism advocated by Cartier included the creation of a nationality common to all the federated entities. In Cartier's view, federation of the colonies had become a practical necessity in order to add to their strength and ensure the perpetuation of the monarchical principle on the continent in relation to the American neighbour. This is how he spoke on the subject before the Legislative Assembly of United Canada in 1865: "The time has come for us to create a great nation, and I maintain that the confederation is necessary for our own commercial interests, our prosperity and our defence.... In British North America, we are five different peoples living in five separate provinces. We have the same commercial interests and the same desire to live under the British Crown."[26] It may be noted here that, unlike Macdonald, who spoke of merging five different peoples into one, Cartier emphasized the aspirations and interests shared by these five peoples. He later specified what he meant by that Canadian nation: "An objection has been raised to the project now under consideration, because of the words 'new nationality.' When we are united, if indeed we do become so, we shall form a political nationality independent of national origin, or the religion of any one individual."[27]

Although writers generally agree that the architects of the Canadian federation were men who were much more pragmatic than they were political thinkers, the fact remains, as Professor Samuel V. LaSelva asserted, that these men certainly had a vision of the projected country.[28] The author devotes his book to updating Cartier's vision. In his opinion, Cartier's idea behind Canadian political nationality is rooted in the ideal of fraternity, a concept that contains within it the identities and allegiances that federalism assumes.[29] In defending the creation of a new nationality, Cartier was not only rejecting assimilationist nationalism, but also foreseeing a new kind of relationship among peoples of different cultures: the Canadian federation would give rise to a new sort of nationality and fraternity. That fraternity, however, could only be partial, as it could not demand completely identical sentiments or interests between the francophone and anglophone communities. Had that been the case, the choice of a unitary system would have been more appropriate. What that Canadian fraternity assumed was that peoples with distinct ways of life or identities would show goodwill towards each other, take part in common projects, develop and maintain common allegiances, and run political institutions for the good of all citizens.[30] Professor Donald V. Smiley conceives of the Canadian political nationality in a similar fashion: "The concept of Canadian political community – or Canadian political nationality – means that Canadians have reciprocal moral and legal demands of one another which they do not have in their relations with others, and that Canadians have an ongoing determination to pool a significant number of activities in common." According to Professor Smiley, such mutual commitment first requires a vision of Canada that is nothing more than an arena in which divergent cultural, regional, and economic interests compete, and established cultural groups coexist and cooperate in a certain number of common goals without being formally separated into independent and sovereign states.[31]

Common projects are those that are linked to common themes of interest entrusted to the legislative responsibility of the federal parliament, i.e., generally the themes tied to economic and military issues. Certain common allegiances or sympathies are also necessary to create a national link: in the case of the Canadian federation, we can differentiate the rejection of the American model of government of republican democracy from the desire to perpetuate the monarchical principle, i.e., in the very terms used by Cartier, "the same aspiration to live under the British Crown."[32] The heart or bedrock of the sense of belonging to this Canadian political nation will be the sharing of citizenship common to all Canadian citizens. All the components needed for the emergence of a Canadian political or civil nationality were present. The civil nationality would superimpose itself on cultural identities within states. Cartier believed that political allegiance should not be influenced by political affiliation.[33] The Canadian "new nationality" would therefore not replace the sense of identity or pluralism but would emerge and evolve along with it.[34]

What emerges here is the concept of a dual identity or dual fraternity: the fraternity that exists between those who share the same way of life or the same cultural identity and what exists between these people and those who have a different way of life or cultural identity. Federalism, as an organising principle of the state, and to the extent that it divides the identities and allegiances of citizens, assumes that every citizen will have a dual identity.[35]

The creation of a political or civil nationality by adopting a federal regime was thus conceived as allowing and enhancing not only the survival, but also the development of new cultural identities within states. In that sense, as Professor LaSelva states, federalism's imaginative *tour de force* is to make use of a complex idea of fraternity in order to accommodate both the universal and the particular within one and the same state.[36] It is only once nationalities and cultural identities within states are assured of adequate protection that fraternity, which is vital to the survival of the federal state, can develop between those nations.

The question of identity thereby played a predominant role in the discussion that preceded the adoption of the federal system in 1867. According to Samuel V. LaSelva, not only was the issue of nationality the most divisive for the architects of the system, but it was also the concept to which nearly all the big questions about federation were linked in one way or the other.[37] What is certain is that it is because they were assured that the creation of a new Canadian nationality would not interfere with their distinct cultural identity, the French Canadians of Lower Canada and their political leaders agreed to unite with the other colonies of British North America within a federal government system. As Professor W.L. Morton wrote, "Confederation was, indeed, to be a new nationality, but it was to be a political nationality, not an absolute one which would absorb the old cultural and linguistic nationality of the French into that of the English."[38]

## The Practical Reasons for Adopting the Federal Principle in Canada

For Professor Kennedy, it is a mistake to give sole credit for finally achieving Canadian federation to the delegates taking part in the preconfederation conferences of Charlottetown, Quebec, and London.[39] The idea of uniting the British colonies by more or less federal links had taken root over the course of the century preceding its adoption as a principle of government in 1867, in various quarters.

The creator of the first project of this kind was Justice William Smith, who, at the end of 1764 and the beginning of 1765, proposed a project for confederation in order to prevent revolution in the British colonies. He proposed creating a parliament of North America, which would have brought together Quebec, Nova Scotia, and numerous other British colonies in the south, such as Florida, New York, and Georgia, and each of them would receive representation proportional to their population in the parliament thus constituted.[40]

Between 1800 and 1839, federation projects emerged in all the colonies, and even in the home country. In 1838, unlike Lord Durham, who had rejected the idea of a federal union in favour of a legislative union of the two Canadas, John Arthur Roebuck, an agent of Lower Canada in London, is reported to have opted for a federal union in order to solve the problem of the coexistence of two distinct cultures.

The question of federation really began to assert itself in Canadian politics in 1857, under a government led by George-Étienne Cartier. The project was submitted for the first time to the parliament of United Canada during the 1851 session, when William Henry Merritt, the representative for Lincoln, proposed an address to the Queen asking her to authorise the governor to organise a conference to consider the possibility of a federal union. The motion was seconded by only a handful of members of the House. In 1857, Antoine-Aimé Dorion, leader of the Liberal party of Lower Canada, suggested creating a federal union of the two provinces of Canada as a means of solving their difficulties, because of the profound differences of religion, language, and laws in the two sections of the province.[41]

In 1858, the federal project took on a more specific shape with Jean-Charles Taché. He was a French-Canadian doctor with a wide reputation as a man of learning who the previous year had founded the Quebec newspaper *Le Courrier du Canada*. He wrote a book in which he outlined the division of legal jurisdictions that would operate by adopting the federal principle as the working basis of a new government. Taché contrasted the federal principle with the unitary principle. In his view,

> Everything to do with civil laws, education, public charity, the establishment of public lands, agriculture, urban and rural police, and roads, in short, everything to do with family life, so to speak, of each province, would remain under the exclusive control of the respective governments of each, as an inherent right, as the powers of the federal government are not considered to be a cession of specially designated rights.... The attributes given by us to the federal government have to do only with external relations and with those things pertaining to the common interests of the confederated provinces.[42]

It should be noted in passing that Taché apparently reserved residual power for the provincial parliaments. His outline of a division of legislative jurisdictions between the two levels of government subsequently prompted the remark by the representative for Lévis, Joseph-G. Blanchet, during the debates on the confederation project held during the 1858 session of parliament in United Canada, that "in the distribution of powers between local governments and the general government, the project of the conference was almost word for word the work of M. Taché,"[43] with the exception of course of residual power, which was attributed to the federal parliament.

However, the political realisation of the project to federate the British colonies of North America really began only during the parliamentary session of the summer of 1858. The representative for Sherbrooke, Alexander T. Galt, proposed a motion in the Legislative Assembly of United Canada in which he presented his plan for federation as the real solution to the numerous problems experienced under the system of legislative union, despite the conventional adjustments within its working practice. His project for federation included the union of Canada West, Canada East, the Maritime Provinces, the North-West Territories, and the territories of Hudson Bay. Although his motion received hardly any backing, his entry into the new Macdonald-Cartier government as minister of finance was to turn the tide: he had entered the Cabinet on condition that it was agreed that his federation project would be raised in the Cabinet.[44] It was a definite step forward in the ultimate realisation of the federal union. In accordance with the government's programme, Cartier accompanied Alexander T. Galt and John Ross on a mission to London in the autumn of 1858. They presented Sir Edward Bulwer Lytton, the colonial secretary, with a paper recommending the union of all the provinces of British North America as the only solution to the problems between the two sections of Canada and a means of consolidating British power on the continent. The paper consequently asked the imperial government to authorise a meeting of delegates of all the colonies and both sections of Canada in order to consider a federal union and discuss the principles on which it should be based.[45] A dispatch to the imperial government was sent to London on 23 October 1858:

> It is our duty to reveal that the government of Canada is experiencing great difficulty in meeting satisfactorily the wishes of its large population. The union of Upper and Lower Canada was based on maintaining perfect

> equality between these Provinces, a condition which was all the more necessary in that they differed in language, laws and religion; and although there is a considerable English population in Lower Canada, these differences exist to such a degree that they prevent any absolute community of feeling between the two sections.[46]

London's response was negative. The adoption of a federal system for the colonies required the development of channels of communication among them by means of an intercolonial railway. At that time, however, the home country was not yet ready to release the funds required for this great undertaking.[47] Furthermore, it claimed that, although it was not opposed to a federal union of this kind, silence from the Maritime Provinces regarding the project prevented it from authorizing a conference.[48] Although the initiative of the Canadian delegates had ended in failure, it nevertheless had the effect of giving considerable impetus to the pro-federation movement.

In 1859, a meeting of delegates from Canada was held in Toronto, during which the project of an all-encompassing federal union was rejected in favour of a more restricted proposal for just the two Canadas (Ontario and Quebec). The proposal was introduced in the Legislature in 1860 and was defeated by an overwhelming majority.

During the period 1854 to 1864, another project for federal union was gradually developed in the Maritime Provinces. These provinces, New Brunswick, Nova Scotia, and Prince Edward Island, advocated the creation of federal links among them in reaction to the failure of the intercolonial railway project, which they considered essential to their economic and political survival in relation to their neighbour to the south. For them the economy was becoming increasingly linked to political unity.

In Canada, things dragged on until 1864, because the existence of successive governments was precarious: applying the rule of the double majority made governing the colony more difficult. The political crisis reached its height on 14 June 1864, when the Taché-Macdonald government was defeated in the House and the province found itself in a real deadlock. Subsequent events marked the beginning of a period that would finally lead to the adoption of the federal regime in 1867.

From the very first days of the parliamentary session of 1864, in United Canada, George Brown, the great parliamentarian of Upper Canada and zealous champion of the principle of proportional representation based on population, a position that had always pitted him strongly against Cartier, proposed creating a special committee charged with examining the relations between Upper and Lower Canada and producing a report on the constitutional changes needed to put an end to existing problems. The report was finally submitted and recommended constitutional changes "tending to a federal system, applied either only in Canada or in all the English provinces of British North America."[49]

Following the defeat in the House of the Taché-Macdonald government, a political coalition was formed, one that would finally allow the federal project to be truly set in motion. George Brown, leader of the Reformists of Upper Canada, agreed to unite with the new Cartier-Macdonald Conservative government for the sole reason that the coalition government undertook "to submit, during the next session, a measure aimed at eliminating all the current problems by introducing the federal principle in Canada with provisions which will allow the Maritime Provinces and the North-West Territories to be included in the same system of government."[50]

Whereas a coalition of parties was formed in Canada, the parliaments of New Brunswick and Nova Scotia separately adopted resolutions allowing their respective governments to begin negotiations and hold a convention in order to create a union of the Maritime Provinces. The convention thus constituted decided to meet in Charlottetown in September 1864. Informed of the conference, the government of United Canada seized the opportunity to submit its project for a federal union of all the British colonies of North America and was therefore invited to send a delegation. The federation project that had long been on the back burner both in United Canada and the Maritime Provinces was about to emerge on paper. The British North America Act of 1867 (B.N.A.) was conceived in successive stages during the three conferences at which it was developed: the Charlottetown, Quebec, and finally, London Conferences.

During the conferences and debates held in the Legislative Assembly of United Canada, following the adoption of the Quebec Resolutions, various reasons were put forward by the colonies to justify opting for the federal principle as the operating basis of the new government. The adoption of a federal system was the outcome, in the communities concerned, of the convergence of factors pushing toward union and factors requiring autonomy for certain ends.

[…]

**Lower Canada and the Federal Principle**

The legislative union of 1840, originally conceived with the avowed intent of putting an end to the problem of two coexisting cultural communities of different origin within the British colonies by assimilating the French-Canadian people, had changed in practice because of various political and cultural forces, into an embryonic federal regime. Equal representation of both sections of United Canada within the Legislative Assembly had, by the concerted action of the French Canadian representatives, allowed them to play a leading role in Canadian politics. However, the demand for proportional representation based on population by the political leaders of Upper Canada, with George Brown, leader of the opposition, at their head, was becoming increasingly insistent and it was anticipated that the imperial authorities would sooner or later follow through. In this political context, Quebec could no longer trust that federal practices would continue to exist in the margins of the formal constitution in order to ensure the survival of its distinct cultural identity.

*Le Journal de Québec* mentioned the dangers for Quebec culture of proportional representation based on population within a unitary system: for as long as there was only one legislative assembly for both Canadas, proportional representation based on population in the Chamber would place "our civil law and religious institutions at the mercy of the fanatics."[51] The adoption of a federal system, in that it entailed the existence of two sovereign orders of government in matters of exclusive jurisdictions, would eliminate such a danger by giving Quebec a provincial government in which the Québécois of French descent would be in the majority:

> Since we have this guarantee [of certain areas of exclusive jurisdiction], what difference does it make to us whether or not Upper Canada has more representatives than we in the Commons? Since the Commons will be concerned only with general questions of interest to all provinces and not at all with the particular affairs of Lower Canada, it's all the same to us, as a nationality, whether or not Upper Canada has more representation.[52]

The representative for Montcalm, Joseph Dufresne, also pointed out the threat posed by proportional representation based on population to Québécois cultural identity in the context of a unitary system:

> When we opposed representation based on population, ... was it because we feared that Upper Canada, by means of its majority, would establish a greater or lesser number of post offices, or raise the postage rates? ... No! Mr. SPEAKER, it was not for all those reasons, but because we feared, quite rightly, that when Upper Canada had more representatives than Lower Canada in the Legislature, it would trample on our rights and endanger all that we hold most dear. This is what we feared.[53]

The deep rifts between the Conservatives and Liberals of Lower Canada concerning the federation project for the colonies could not conceal their initial premise regarding Quebec's cultural identity: the autonomy of Quebec, and therefore, of the Quebec nation, was the vital element to seek in any new constitution.[54] Their divergent opinions on the federation project had to do with the manner of achieving the common objective.

For the Conservatives of Canada East, the adoption of a federal system would allow Quebec to have its own government, one that would be provided with autonomous legislative powers over all areas that were, at the time, considered essential for the survival and development of its particular cultural identity. As Me Louis-Philippe Pigeon wrote, autonomy meant "the right to be different, the right to act differently," and, for a province, "the privilege of defining one's own policies,"[55] its own standards.

It was therefore on the express condition that the union would be a federal and not a legislative one that the French Canadians of Lower Canada and their representatives agreed to unite with the other British colonies. As the historian Ramsay Cook wrote,

> The great compromise of 1867, and at the same time the great victory for the French Canadians, was the federal system of government. Had there been only one "nation" involved in the negotiations that preceded the establishment of Confederation, the proponents of legislative union would doubtless have fought harder for their viewpoint. Since there was not one nation but two, the result was federalism.[56]

This was indeed the crux of any pro-federation argument advanced by the Conservatives to the Québécois: legislative union with Ontario would be abrogated and the Québécois would have their own province with a high degree of autonomy. The prospect of a provincial legislative assembly that controlled the government by its vote, and that would be entrusted with all matters to do with their own cultural identity was what led political leaders in Quebec to agree to Quebec's entry into the Canadian federation. George-Étienne Cartier was clear concerning the choice of a federal system: "We thought that a Federation scheme was the best because these provinces are peopled by different nations and by peoples of different religions."[57] An excerpt from the newspaper *La Minerve* summed up the overall position and the expectations of the French-Canadian press with regard to the project of federation:

> The English ... have nothing to fear from the central government and are first ensuring the means of guaranteeing its proper working. It is in this government that they place their hope, and the need and the strength of action of local governments only come second for them. The French press, on the other hand, will above all place guarantees in the federal constitution for the specific autonomy of its nationality. It supports the entire system on these very guarantees; they are in the forefront, and without them, the establishment of a federal constitution will never obtain its consent.[58]

*La Minerve* maintained its position on the eve of the vote on the Quebec Resolutions in the Legislative Assembly of United Canada: "The vote in the Canadian legislature will become an important date in the history of Canada.... The union of the colonies is the consecration of our political and national existence and the guarantee of our future."[59]

The view held by the Québécois of the federation project was noticed by Arthur Gordon, the lieutenant governor of New Brunswick. He wrote to Edward Cardwell, the colonial secretary, on 12 September 1864: "'A federal union' in the mouth of a Lower Canadian means the independence of his Province from all English or Protestant influences."[60]

This analysis of the spirit that governed the Québécois' choice of a federal regime reveals that the concept of nation or culture lay at the heart of any discussion about the best system to adopt: recognition of their nation and distinct cultural identity was central to their concerns. We have already dealt with the concept of nation.[61] How did the Québécois of the pre-federation period define Quebec cultural identity? Did they confine themselves to a restricted concept of "culture" in the purely sociological sense of the term, or did they also include institutional, political, or civil aspects of identity in the word?

First of all, as Professor A.I. Silver quite rightly pointed out, in 1864 the Québécois had been long accustomed to seeing themselves as a nation and Quebec as their country: "They were scarcely aware of the existence of French-Catholic groups elsewhere in British North America. French Canada and Lower Canada were, in their eyes, equivalent terms."[62] Consequently, what the Québécois were seeking in federal union was to strengthen the Quebec nation by strengthening the powers of Lower Canada.

There was thus a strong identification between the cultural identity of the Québécois, on the one hand, and the province of Quebec, on the other. All the discussions that took place during the period 1864–1867 were based on the premise that French Canada was a geographical, as well as sociological, entity, which, in the federation, as *La Revue canadienne* pointed out, constituted "the most considerable, the most homogeneous, and the most regularly constituted population group."[63] The *Courrier de St-Hyacinthe* newspaper was of the same opinion: "The future of our race, the preservation of all that makes up our national character, will be the direct responsibility of local legislatures."[64] The *Minerve* newspaper gave a broad definition of what was understood by the expression "cultural identity": "It [Quebec] will have its own special government whose authority will extend to everything to do with the business of everyday life, of interest to the life, liberty and prosperity of its citizens … it will be master in its own house in everything to do with its social, civil and religious economy."[65] *Le Courrier du Canada* also embraced a broad concept of culture in stating that the proposed central government "would not have the right to come and interfere in our local affairs, which would remain under the control of our local legislature; since the federal legislature would not have the right to touch education, the judicial system or the internal economy of each province."[66]

The spirit underlying the division of legislative jurisdictions intended that matters of interest to all the colonies would be entrusted to a central parliament, whereas matters in which the provinces had particular interests would remain under their sole authority. These particular interests were precisely those associated with the cultural identity of the communities in question, especially the interests of the Quebec nation. As George-Étienne Cartier asserted in the language of the day, "Under the system of federation, which leaves control of the big questions of general interest, in which the differences of race have no place, to the central government, it will not be possible to disregard the rights of race or religion."[67]

Far from being confined to its sociological (linguistic and religious) aspects, the identity of the Quebec nation encompassed the institutional and civic aspects of culture: it was a territory endowed with its own political and social institutions, distinct systems of civil law, judiciary, local economy, and education system, etc. In that sense, Quebec in the pre-confederation period was a cultural nation that, while wanting to join the other British colonies, wanted to retain control over all its distinctive aspects. For the people of Lower Canada, although a particular form of association with the other colonies was necessary, the degree of integration was not to surpass the threshold required for Quebec's economic viability. As George-Étienne Cartier stated, "This is why I made sure that what was granted to the federal government was no more than the degree of authority that was strictly necessary to serve the general interests of Confederation."[68] In this federal alliance, Quebec was to be the country of the French Canadians, working with others on common projects, but still autonomous in promoting the French-Canadian nation:[69] "As a nation in the nation, we must take care of our own autonomy."[70] In contemporary terms, what the francophones concentrated in Quebec territory were seeking in the federal union of the colonies was recognition of their cultural nation within the Canadian political nation as it had been presented to them by George-Étienne Cartier.

## Upper Canada and the Maritime Provinces

It is clear from the parliamentary debates before the Legislative Assembly of United Canada in 1865 that a number of anglophone architects of the new system would have preferred a legislative to a federal union. John A. Macdonald spoke in the following terms before the Legislative Assembly: "I have stated many a time and often that if we could have had a government and a parliament for all the provinces, we would have had the best, least expensive, strongest and most vigorous government." But he continued by pointing out the unworkability of a legislative union and the reason why he felt obliged to renounce it:

> It [the system] would not meet with the approval of the people of Lower Canada, who feel that, in their particular situation as a minority, speaking a different language and professing a religion different from most people

> in confederation, its institutions, laws and national associations, for which they have a high regard, might have to suffer. This is why it has been understood that any proposal which involves absorbing the individuality of Lower Canada cannot be favourably received by its people.[71]

Antoine-Aimé Dorion, the Liberal opposition leader and fierce opponent of the federation project, which he described as a legislative union in disguise, warned the members for Upper Canada against their initial preference concerning a legislative union:

> It could be that the people of Upper Canada are of the opinion that a legislative union would be highly desirable, but I can assure its representatives that the people of Lower Canada are attached to their institutions by links that are strong enough to frustrate any attempt to take them away by such means. They will never, on any account whatsoever, consent to changing their religious institutions, their laws and their language.[72]

It seems therefore that the demand from Upper Canada in favour of the principle of representation based on population in the Legislative Assembly, as well as its commercial interests, could have been guaranteed by the adoption of a unitary system. In that sense, the political leaders of Upper Canada felt much more pressure from uniting than disuniting factors. Granted, the numerous political problems that had resulted in the legislative union of 1840 had made them realize that the existence of a different nation, concentrated in Quebec territory, made governing difficult within a unitary system. However, this was largely due to the principle of equal representation of both sections of United Canada in the Legislative Assembly. This is why conceding the principle of representation based on population would, in their case, have put an end to their grievance, and thereby brought the choice of a unitary system into line with their interests.

However, as Professor Paul Romney has shown, we must not underestimate the role played by the reformist tradition of Upper Canada in support of a large measure of local autonomy in the final choice for a federal rather than a unitary system. Since the 1820s the Reformists, led by Robert Baldwin, had been demanding greater local autonomy for Upper Canada from the imperial authorities, through recognition of the principle of responsible government.[73] We shall see later how important the part played by one of their number, Oliver Mowat, was in formulating the letter of the 1867 regime, as well in as the legal battles to defend the autonomy of the provinces in their fields of jurisdiction against the encroachment of the central government.

For Upper Canada in general, the disuniting factor that, despite everything, remained the most important one in the choice of the federal system as a working principle of the new constitution, was precisely the presence in Quebec of a different nation whose membership was essential to the realisation of the union project. The political leaders of Upper Canada knew that the only way to acquire that membership was to abandon legislative union in favour of federal union.

For John A. Macdonald, the unitary form of government was proving unworkable, not only because it was impossible for a project of this kind to gain the approval of the people of Lower Canada for cultural reasons, but also because of the refusal of the Maritime Provinces. However, unlike Quebec, the rejection of the legislative union project by these provinces was not driven mainly by cultural reasons. Granted, there were within these colonies certain local identities whose development had been made easier by the fact that each had had its own legislative assembly since 1791.[74] However, the main reason that the delegates from the Maritime Provinces were in favour of adopting a federal rather than a unitary system was that in these provinces local or municipal authorities were not well developed, and abolishing provincial authorities would have left their citizens without effective local government.[75] This is how Charles Tupper, one of the delegates from Nova Scotia who played an important role in achieving the union of the colonies, spoke at the Quebec Conference held in October 1864: "If it were not for the peculiar condition of Lower Canada, and that the Lower provinces have not municipal systems such as Upper Canada, I should go in for a Legislative Union instead of a Federal. We propose to preserve the Local Governments in the Lower provinces because we have no municipal institutions."[76]

The absence of sufficiently developed municipal institutions to deal adequately with local issues proper to each of the maritime colonies seems therefore to have been the disuniting factor that worked most strongly in favour of adopting a federal rather than a unitary system within the Maritime Provinces.

## Conclusion: The Spirit of Federalism of 1867 – A Compromise between Two Cultures

Every constitution in the history of the colonies of British North America before the adoption of a federal system in 1867 attempted, each in its own way, to respond to the bicultural reality in its communities. The response put forward in 1867, this time by colonial representatives, at first gradually took hold in the minds of certain politicians and then established itself as the only one that would solve the political problems of United Canada and was capable of satisfying the interests of the colonies, particularly Quebec's cultural identity, i.e., the adoption of a federal system. That system emerged from the confrontation of diverse ideologies, diverse visions of the new projected country, as well as from the mixing of diverse common and distinct interests that each colony sought to protect. From that confrontation, there necessarily had to emerge a compromise that was the outcome of a series of mutual concessions and one that allowed the colonies to be part of the project presented to them and, consequently, of the birth of a new nation. In that sense, the federal regime of 1867 appears to be the result of political negotiation pursued in good faith by the colonial representatives, as an agreement or a compact to which the colonial parties adhered.

What was the nature of the compact? Who were the parties to the contract? A long presentation of the ins and outs of the theory of the federal compact would be beyond the scope of this book. Besides, that exercise has been undertaken many times by many authors from various disciplines. However, it transpires from the present analysis that it was the demands for a binational compact that dictated the content of the political compact,[77] a compact that was subsequently amended by a British law. In the province of Canada, long before the pre-federation conferences, national groups were identified by the territories in which each was in the majority: French Canadians with Quebec, English Canadians with Ontario, each of these geopolitical entities being considered as the home of a distinct culture.[78] The addition of two Maritime Provinces to the federation project did not affect the cultural bipolarity, as these provinces largely shared a common cultural identity with Ontario.

Among the writers who denied the binational dimension of the federal compact, many based their conclusion on the weak protection afforded by the act of 1867 to francophone minorities outside Quebec.[79] Although there are grounds for that observation, we must in no way infer from this the absence of a pact between nationalities. The vital question here is correct identification of the parties to the contract. The two nations to which we refer when speaking of the federal compact are, on the one hand, the English-Canadian nation concentrated in three of the original provinces (Ontario, New Brunswick, and Nova Scotia) and, on the other, the French-Canadian nation, which was highly concentrated in the province of Quebec. The tendency to believe that the federal compromise was agreed upon by all French Canadians and all English Canadians, no matter in which territory they lived, is unfounded. The pre-federation negotiations were without a doubt held between territorial entities populated mostly by individuals of different cultures, not between two clans, one containing all the francophones and the other all the anglophones. The issue of protecting minority cultural rights in each of the colonies, i.e., those of the Quebec anglophones and the francophones outside Quebec, was raised only once the federal form of the constitution was assured. In that sense, the protection of the francophone and anglophone minorities was not an essential condition of the compromise that had led to the adoption of a federal system.

The main consideration of the Québécois and their political leaders concerning the proposed scheme was the adoption of the federal principle as the basis of the new system of government: it was the *sine qua non* of their membership of the new constitution and the constitutional guarantee of their survival and development as a distinct people. What they sought from federation was to strengthen their nation by taking back the powers of which they had been deprived by the system of legislative union, as Quebec was to be the only geopolitical entity within which they would have a solid majority.

The issue of Catholic minority rights in Ontario emerged in reaction to the pressing demands of the Protestant anglophones in Quebec for constitutional recognition of their religious rights. The fact was that for the first time in their history, Quebec Protestants were about to become a minority in a province governed by a majority that was culturally different from them. In exchange for recognition of their religious rights, the representatives from Lower Canada asked that the same rights be guaranteed to the Catholics of Upper Canada:

> Had we been content ... with granting the Protestants of Lower Canada the mechanisms which were first promised to allow them to attend freely the schools of their choice, and pay their school fees, the Catholics of Upper Canada would not have requested for themselves legislation that was not granted to them by the Quebec project; however, the former having insisted on new, extraordinary, privileges, the latter were fully justified in entering the arena of changes and demands, in the name of justice and equality.[80]

Thus, as A.I. Silver wrote, "Everything ... seemed to indicate that Quebec alone was to be the arena of French-Canadian national life, that within the federal alliance, Quebec was to be the French-Canadian country."[81] Quebec was to uphold, as much as it could, the rights of sister minorities, but that must never endanger the autonomy or distinct cultural identity of Quebec itself:

> Confederation was to be an association of national states called provinces, united in a federal alliance.... And in that alliance, the province of Quebec was to be the national state of the French Canadians. The province, as *the* French-Catholic province, might well be concerned to support French Catholics in other parts of the federation, but such support must never involve the acceptance of principles that would expose or endanger the autonomy of the French and Catholic character of Quebec itself.[82]

The main conditions of the federal compact were thus as follows: adoption of the federal principle was the essential condition demanded by Quebec in exchange for which it was ready to concede to Ontario and the Maritime Provinces, in the federal lower chamber, the principle of proportional representation based on population. For the Maritime Provinces, equal representation in the Senate and the construction of the intercolonial railway were the most pressing concerns.

[...]

NOTES

1 Eugénie Brouillet, "Quebec Culture and Federalism in 1867: The Spirit and Letter of the Federal System," *The Negation of a Nation: The Quebec Cultural Identity and Canadian Federalism,* a translation of material from "La culture québécoise et le fédéralisme de 1867: l'esprit et la lettre du régime," *La Négation de la nation. L'identité culturelle québécoise et le fédéralisme canadien,* Québec, Septentrion, 2005, pp. 105–106, 122–135, 140–150, 396, 399–403.

2 To cite but a few of these authors: Herbert A. Smith, "The Residue of Power in Canada" (1926) 4 *Can. Bar Rev.* 432; Vincent C. Macdonald, "Judicial Interpretation of the Canadian Constitution" (1935–36) 1 *Univ. of T.L.J.* 260; W.P.M. Kennedy, "The Interpretation of the British North America Act" (1944) 8 *The Cambridge Law Journal* 146; Vincent C. Macdonald, "The Constitution in a Changing World" (1948) 26 *Can. Bar Rev.* 21; F.R. Scott, "Centralization and Decentralization in Canadian Federalism" (1951) 29 *Can. Bar Rev.* 1095; Donald Creighton, *Towards the Discovery of Canada,* Toronto, Macmillan of Canada, 1972, p. 65.

3 Samuel LaSelva, *The Moral Foundations of Canadian Federalism*, Montreal and Kingston, McGill-Queen's University Press, 1996.
4 W. and A. Durant, *The Lessons of History*, New York, Simon and Schuster, 1968, p. 12, cited and translated in Wolfgang Koerner, *Les fondements du fédéralisme canadien*, Service de recherche, Bibliothèque du Parlement, Étude générale, Division des affaires politiques et sociales, 1988, p. 12.
5 Koerner, *Les fondements du fédéralisme canadien*, p. 10.
6 *Globe*, 12 April 1853, excerpt cited in Koerner, *Les fondements du fédéralisme canadien*, p. 11.
7 *Débats parlementaires sur la question de la Confédération des provinces de l'Amérique britannique du Nord*, 3rd session, 8th Provincial Parliament of Canada, Quebec, Hunter, Rose et Lemieux Imprimeurs parlementaires, 1865, p. 31.
8 *Débats parlementaires*, p. 28.
9 *Débats parlementaires.*
10 *Débats parlementaires*, pp. 28 and 29.
11 *Débats parlementaires*, p. 30.
12 *Débats parlementaires*, p. 33.
13 *Débats parlementaires*, pp. 33 and 34.
14 *Débats parlementaires*, pp. 41 and 42.
15 Library and Archives Canada, Macdonald fonds, vol. 158, pp. 64000 and 64012, cited in Koerner, *Les fondements du fédéralisme canadien*, p. 4. See also this latter work, p. 16.
16 LaSelva, *The Moral Foundations of Canadian Federalism*. See also Samuel LaSelva, "Federalism, Pluralism, and Constitutional Faith," *Revue d'études constitutionnelles*, 7 (2002), 204.
17 LaSelva, *The Moral Foundations of Canadian Federalism*, p. xii.
18 LaSelva, *The Moral Foundations of Canadian Federalism*, pp. 34–38.
19 LaSelva, *The Moral Foundations of Canadian Federalism*, p. xii.
20 Carl Friedrich, *The Impact of American Constitutionalism Abroad*, pp. 60 and 61.
21 John Boyd, *Sir George-Étienne Cartier*, Montreal, Libraire Beauchemin ltée, 1918, p. 21.
22 Boyd, *Sir George-Étienne Cartier*, p. 214.
23 Boyd, *Sir George-Étienne Cartier*, p. 225.
24 *Débats parlementaires* , p. 54.
25 Garth Stevenson, *Ex Uno Plures*, Montreal and Kingston, McGill-Queen's University Press, 1993, p. 8.
26 *Débats parlementaires sur la question de la Confédération des provinces de l'Amérique britannique du Nord*, pp. 55 and 58.

27 *Débats parlementaires*, p. 59.
28 LaSelva, *The Moral Foundations of Canadian Federalism*, p. 21.
29 LaSelva, *The Moral Foundations of Canadian Federalism*, p. 23.
30 LaSelva, *The Moral Foundations of Canadian Federalism*, p. 26.
31 Donald V. Smiley, *The Canadian Political Nationality*, Toronto, Methuen Publications, 1967, pp. 30 and 31.
32 *Débats parlementaires*, p. 58.
33 W.L. Morton, *The Canadian Identity*, 2nd ed., Toronto, University of Toronto Press, 1972, pp. 85 and 111.
34 LaSelva, *The Moral Foundations of Canadian Federalism*, p. 155.
35 LaSelva, *The Moral Foundations of Canadian Federalism*, p. 27.
36 LaSelva, *The Moral Foundations of Canadian Federalism*, p. 29.
37 LaSelva, *The Moral Foundations of Canadian Federalism*, p. 28.
38 W.L. Morton, *The Critical Years: The Union of British North America 1857–1873*, Toronto, McClelland and Stewart, 1964, p. 177, cited in Smiley, *The Canadian Political Nationality*, p. 9.
39 W.P.M. Kennedy, *The Constitution of Canada, 1534–1937*, London, Oxford University Press, 1938, p. 283.
40 Jean-Charles Bonenfant, *La naissance de la Confédération*, Montreal, Les Éditions Léméac, 1969, p. 25.
41 Boyd, *Sir George-Étienne Cartier*, pp. 189 and 190.
42 J.-C. Taché, *Des provinces de l'Amérique du Nord et d'une union fédérale*, Québec, Des presses à la vapeur de J.T. Brousseau, 1858, p. 181.
43 *Débats parlementaires*, p. 552.
44 Boyd, *Sir George-Étienne Cartier*, p. 191.
45 Kennedy, *The Constitution of Canada, 1534–1957*, p. 286.
46 Excerpt cited in Bonenfant, *La naissance de la Confédération*, p. 54.
47 Kennedy, *The Constitution of Canada, 1534–1937*, p. 288.
48 Boyd, *Sir George-Étienne Cartier*, p. 195.
49 Excerpt cited in Boyd, *Sir George-Étienne Cartier*, p. 202.
50 Bonenfant, *La naissance de la Confédération*, p. 57.
51 *Le Journal de Québec*, 5 July, 1864, excerpt cited in A.I. Silver, *The French-Canadian Idea of Confederation 1864–1900*, 2nd ed., Toronto, University of Toronto Press, 1997, p. 40. We have unfortunately not been able to find the original text.
52 *Réponses aux censeurs de la Confédération*, Saint-Hyacinthe, *Le Courrier*, 1867, pp. 47–49, excerpt cited in Silver, *The French-Canadian Idea of Confederation 1864–1900*, p. 40. We have unfortunately not been able to find the original text.
53 *Débats parlementaires*, p. 926.

54 Silver, *The French-Canadian Idea of Confederation 1864–1900*, p. 38.
55 Louis-Philippe Pigeon, "The Meaning of Provincial Autonomy" (1951) 19 *Can. Bar Rev.* 1126, p. 1133.
56 Ramsay Cook, *Canada and the French-Canadian Question*, Toronto, Macmillan of Canada, 1966, p. 175.
57 G.P. Browne, *Documents on the Confederation of British North America*, Toronto, McClelland and Stewart, 1969, p. 128: notes of A.A. Macdonald on the Quebec Conference, 10 to 29 October 1864.
58 *La Minerve*, 14 September 1864.
59 *La Minerve*, 11 March 1867.
60 Browne, *Documents on the Confederation of British North America*, p. 43.
61 See *supra*, part 1, chapter 1.
62 Silver, *The French-Canadian Idea of Confederation 1864–1900*, p. 218.
63 *La Revue canadienne*, IV, 1867, excerpt cited in Silver, *The French-Canadian Idea of Confederation 1864–1900*, p. 39. We have unfortunately been unable to find the original text.
64 *Le Courrier de Saint-Hyacinthe*, 28 October 1864. See also the same newspaper dated 23 September 1864 and 22 November 1864.
65 *La Minerve*, 16 July 1864, excerpt cited in P.B. Waite, *The Life and Times of Confederation: 1864–1867*, Toronto, University of Toronto Press, 1962, p. 139.
66 *Le Courrier du Canada*, 11 July, 1864, excerpt cited in Waite, *The Life and Times of Confederation: 1864–1867*, p. 139.
67 *Débats parlementaire*, p. 59.
68 Reported in *L'Union des Cantons de l'Est*, 23 May 1867.
69 Silver, *The French-Canadian Idea of Confederation 1864–1900*, p. 50.
70 *La Minerve*, 1 and 2 July 1867, excerpt cited in Silver, *The French-Canadian Idea of Confederation 1864–1900*, p. 41, note 47.
71 *Débats parlementaires*, p. 30.
72 *Débats parlementaires*, p. 268.
73 Paul Romney, "Why Lord Watson Was Right," in Janet Ajzenstat (ed.), *Canadian Constitutionalism: 1791–1991*, Canadian Study of Parliament Group, Ottawa, Queen's Printer, 1992; Paul Romney, "The Nature and Scope of Provincial Autonomy: Oliver Mowat, the Quebec Resolutions and the Construction of the *British North America Act*" (1992), 25 *Can. J. of Pol. Sci.* 3.
74 Samuel LaSelva, *The Moral Foundations of Canadian Federalism*, p. 36.
75 Smiley, *The Canadian Political Nationality*, pp. 5 and 6.
76 Joseph Pope, *Confederation: Being a Series of Hitherto Unpublished Documents Bearing on the British North America Act*, Toronto, The Carswell Co. Ltd., Law Publishers, 1895, pp. 84 and 85.

77 Richard Arès, *Dossier sur le pacte fédératif de 1867, la Confédération: pacte ou loi?* Montreal, Les Éditions Bellarmin, 1967, p. 235.

78 George F. Stanley, "Act or Pact? Another Look at Confederation," in *La Société historique du Canada*, 1956, p. 24. It is interesting to note that in the debates on the federation project that prevailed in the Legislative Assembly of United Canada in 1865, John A. Macdonald used the phrase "Lower-Canadians" or the expression "people of Lower Canada" several times to refer to the French-Canadian people, thereby emphasizing its territorial (and therefore political) attachment. See especially *Débats parlementaires*, pp. 29 and 30.

79 See especially in this regard Ramsay Cook, *Provincial Autonomy, Minority Rights and the Compact Theory, 1867–1921*, Studies for the Royal Commission on Bilingualism and Biculturalism, no. 4, Ottawa, Queen's Printer, 1969.

80 *Le Journal de Québec*, August 1866. See in the same regard, the comments of Louis-Auguste Oliver and John Sandfield Macdonald: *Débats parlementaires*, p. 19; (Antoine-Aimé Dorian and John A. Macdonald), pp. 176 and 315 (Louis-Auguste Olivier), p. 349 (Étienne Paschal Taché), pp. 417 and 25 (John Sandfield Macdonald).

81 Silver, *The French-Canadian Idea of Confederation 1864–1900*, p. 51.

82 Silver, *The French-Canadian Idea of Confederation 1864–1900*, p. 61.

# Canada and Its Aims, According to Macdonald, Laurier, Mackenzie King, and Trudeau

*Les Fins du Canada, selon Macdonald, Laurier, Mackenzie King et Trudeau*
(Translated by Lin Burman)
2001

STÉPHANE KELLY[1]

## Small and Large Federation

*Deadlock* was the term used to describe the political logjam that brought about the Great Coalition, the vehicle that led to the birth of British North America.[2] It may be recalled that at the beginning of the 1860s there were four main possible avenues for replacing the Union regime. The first was simply to repeal the Union. This involved returning to the political status quo that existed prior to the Act of Union. Lower and Upper Canada would be separate, remaining subject to the Crown. This option had supporters in both sections. The slogan "Repeal of the Union" was drawn from the one forged in Ireland by Daniel O'Connell. In Lower Canada, Liberals and Reds were sometimes tempted by this political solution. In Upper Canada, the Clear Grits subscribed to it in the 1850s in order to escape "French domination."[3] The second option was double majority.[4] This consisted of a double-headed ministry, comprising the representative of each majority in Lower and Upper Canada. It was unrealistic, according to its adherents, to try to form a purely Liberal or Conservative ministry on the scale of United Canada. Double majority would prevent laws from being passed against the wishes of the majority in one or the other section. In United Canada, moderate Liberals Denis-Benjamin Viger and Louis-Victor Sicotte backed this solution. John S. Macdonald did so in Upper Canada. Both political options had lost ground. The other two, the small federation and the large federation, became more popular. The small federation, the aim of which was to unite Lower and Upper Canada under one federal government, was popular with both Liberals and Reformists in Upper and Lower Canada. It had the advantage of being realistic and cautious, ensuring on one hand the cultural survival of the French Canadians of Lower Canada and, on the other, the immediate implementation of rep by pop, as Upper Canada wanted. The fourth political option was the large federation. George-Étienne Cartier was in favour, as were the political elite in England and the railway magnates. The four possible avenues were not the only political ideas put forward. Annexation to the United States, for example, had its adherents; John A. Macdonald, for his part, secretly cherished the hope of a legislative union (a conglomeration of the provinces). However, neither annexation nor legislative union had strong electoral support. It is nevertheless interesting to see the argument that led Macdonald to want a centralised unified regime. Since the start of the American Civil War, he had shown his concern. A few days after the Confederate attack on Fort Sumter, Macdonald pointed out that this was unfortunate proof that American federalism was too decentralised and that the republican principle led to anarchy. For its part, Great Britain was destined to expand, becoming the centre of a vast network of nations. It would soon form "an immense confederacy of free men, the greatest confederation of civilised and intelligent men that has ever had an existence on the globe."[5]

Many historians concluded from the existence of the deadlock that the political players of the day no longer had any choice. They had to reform the regime. Since the beginning of the Union regime, there had in fact been many other such inextricable situations. What triggered the process of forming a new country at that moment was the fact that the time was ripe in the minds of many key decision makers in England. The open-mindedness of the British elites helped a great deal. By the beginning of the 1860s, they had reached the point of wanting the creation of a union of all the colonies of British North America.[6] Macdonald often reminded people that creating a new regime required the assent of the imperial elites. The latter, he said, preferred a large federation. With hindsight, it is to be wondered why George-Étienne Cartier did not rally to George Brown and Antoine-Aimé Dorion in order to turn the Union regime into a small federation. After all, the Conservative Party was in the minority in Upper Canada. Cartier, Brown, and Dorion would have delivered a very large segment of the electorate behind the project. The weight of Quebec within the small confederation would doubtless have been greater than within a large one. Let us revisit the main episodes leading to the victory of that political solution.

In May 1864, when the new Taché-Macdonald ministry was formed, Brown informed his inner circle that a coalition ministry would break the political deadlock into which the Union regime was becoming mired. The Reformers, he insisted, would be well-advised to move closer to the majority of representatives of Lower Canada, led by Cartier. For the past fifteen years, the alliance with the Reds had never really borne fruit. While it is true that Brown was attached to certain Red elected representatives, there was no longer any question of considering a common future with their party. With this new strategy in mind, he decided to take action. In the Lower House, he suggested that a constitutional committee be struck to discuss possible avenues of unblocking the situation. Representatives backed the motion by 59 to 48. Opponents were more numerous in Lower Canada, but they were not toeing a party line. It should be noted that three anglophone leading lights were against the exercise: John A. Macdonald, A.T. Galt, and Luther Holton.

In the middle of June, the Brown Commission on parliamentary reform submitted its report. The main conclusion proposed the creation of a new regime, based on the principle of federation. The committee left open the question of whether the union should be limited to United Canada or extended to all the British provinces. The subject was to be put before a new commission in the next session of Parliament in the autumn. In one sense, the Brown Commission dealt a master stroke in proposing only the form of the new regime. By refusing to specify the size (large or small) of the federal union, the report received the backing of the main political leaders in the Lower House, i.e., Brown, Cartier, Mowat, Cameron, and Chapais. Three members of the commission refused to sign the report: the Clear Grit John Scoble, who wanted the principle of rep by pop to be applied uncompromisingly; John S. Macdonald, who was adamant about his solution of a double majority; and John A. Macdonald, who dismissed the federal principle and rejected the movement in favour of a constitutional amendment. There is something ironic in the fact that the future prime minister of the new regime should find himself, at that moment, among the forces resisting the constitutional process. On 14 June, Brown presented the commission's report to Parliament. By a strange coincidence, on that same day the Reformers Antoine-Aimé Dorion and William McDougall introduced a motion of non-confidence against the Taché-Macdonald government. The fourth ministry in two years had just fallen. The political impasse was termed "deadlock" in Canadian parliamentary annals. Over the course of the evening, there was much political bargaining. Brown began discussions with Conservative emissaries Alexander Morris and John Henry Pope. He swore he was ready to work with a ministry that would put an end to the impasse, on condition that his actions were governed by the conclusions of his report.

The Lower House convened the next day. The government wanted an adjournment in order to consult the governor general. On the Reformist side, John S. Macdonald was not disposed to grant one. He wished to force ministers into immediate resignation. Brown was against the idea, wanting to give the ministry time to explore scenarios for a coalition. From then on, Brown was to have the collaboration of a priceless ally, the governor, Lord Monck. In accordance with custom, after the defeat of his ministry, the prime minister went to see the governor general. Taché asked him to dissolve Parliament. Monck politely refused. He suggested instead that he consider forming a coalition ministry, which would allow the deadlock to be broken. From then on, Governor General Monck played a crucial role in the emergence of the federal Union. During discussions on a possible coalition, Monck was delighted to observe the spirit of harmony that fired Brown from then on. For his part, the Reformist leader knew that Monck was disposed to back constitutional changes. The representative of the Crown had clearly told him so in a conversation in May 1863. Monck and Brown were thus collusive and dynamic players in the constitutional process. On their side, the Liberal-Conservative leaders, Macdonald and Cartier, were taking no risks in beginning negotiations with Brown. They had been given the go-ahead by both sides at once: from Monck and from their supporters Morris and Pope, who had spoken with the Reformist leader beforehand.

On 16 June, the big unknown factor was Macdonald's attitude. His rejection of Brown's report was not simply caprice. For a long time, he had been opposed in principle to the idea of federation. As he himself admitted, he faced a terrible dilemma. He had the choice of either rallying the coalition or leaving the administration of the affairs of Upper Canada to the Reformists for the next ten years. Macdonald's members of the legislature had been in the minority in Upper Canada for a long time. He therefore took the risk of beginning negotiations with supporters of the Brown Commission's report. Galt, Macdonald, and Brown agreed to meet the following day, 17 June, at the Château

Saint-Louis (strangely, they did not see fit to invite Cartier). Right from the start of the discussion, the Reformist leader stated that he was ready to back any measure by the prime minister to break the political deadlock. He specified, however, that he did not want to be part of the next ministry. The idea of a coalition ran counter to his Liberal convictions. Galt and Macdonald insisted that he be part of it. The success of the enterprise largely depended on it. Brown asked for time to consider. The discussions then continued on the size of the new regime. Galt and Macdonald extolled their preferred option, i.e., a large federation through union of all the colonies. Brown preferred a more moderate route, a small federation. This would allow the federal principle to be combined more easily with that of rep by pop. He had been refining the idea since the Great Reform Convention of 1859. Galt and Macdonald came round to the idea that, if they could not persuade the other colonies, federation of Upper and Lower Canada would be desirable.

Unable to decide in favour of one or the other political option, they agreed to base their agreement on the Brown Commission's main recommendation, i.e., creating a federal regime that could either be restricted to United Canada (small federation) or enlarged to include all the colonies (large federation). The three men, happy to have found common ground, went on to announce it in Parliament. In the Lower House, Macdonald stated that he had followed the advice of the governor and reached an agreement with members of the opposition in order to form a huge coalition. To the surprise of many, he declared that he had convinced his old political enemy George Brown! Dorion's Reds were appalled. The following day, at the Château Saint-Louis, the three met once more. The conference then moved to the Executive Council Chamber, where Cartier joined them. The latter first made sure that Brown was not accompanied by his old enemies Holt and Dorion. He was happy to see that Brown no longer hoped to gain anything from the Reds.

On 20 June, they discussed the opportunity of first building the small confederation. Oddly enough, Cartier was fiercely opposed to the idea. The presence of the Maritime Provinces, he ventured, would diminish the clout of Upper Canada in the federation. Macdonald also defended the position. In his view, the small federation would slow the process leading to legislative union: "The sad events taking place on the other side of the border prove that federal union alone is not enough. Instead of a federal union, we must create a legislative union in fact, in principle and in practice."[7] The Union regime had been moving towards this since 1840 and he greatly regretted having to go backwards. The large federation at least had the advantage of uniting all the British colonies into one single British North America. This option, however, had to avoid the past mistake of the American Founding Fathers. They had erred in creating a federation that was too decentralized. Brown, for his part, thought it premature to build a large federation. He agreed, however, to leave the way open for enlarging the small federation to the colonies wishing to be part of it. Brown apparently tried to rally the Reds to the coalition. In their absence, he was afraid of being taken for a renegade. This is why he would have preferred to stay out of the ministry, while at the same time lending it support in its constitutional approach. As a condition of entry, Brown first asked for half the portfolios of the ministry. Did the Liberals not have a majority in the Commons? Cartier and Macdonald refused. The Lower Canada part of the ministry was already established and formed a good balance. Macdonald offered two portfolios to the Reformists, for the Upper Canada section. Brown considered the offer unfair. The Reformers enjoyed a large majority in Upper Canada. Macdonald finally agreed to give him three, i.e., half of them. Before giving his final answer, Brown consulted Governor General Monck, as well as his caucus. The latter encouraged him to accept the conditions and enter the coalition. The governor general proved very convincing. Brown came out of the conversation with the feeling that he was putting great hope in him. "Your presence," said Monck, "is vital for defending your conception of the future confederation." In the struggle for a centralized federation, Macdonald had a worthy ally in the colonial secretary, Edward Cardwell. In a letter to the British Liberal Prime Minister William Gladstone, Cardwell indicated his preference for Hamilton's ideal: "My principal fear is that the selfish interests of the men of the smaller provinces should lead them to insist on the Jefferson policy rather than that of Washington and Hamilton, on a policy which would run British North America on the rock upon which the Union has gone to pieces."[8]

**British America**

The new ministry was placed under the leadership of Étienne-Pascal Taché. The wise patriarch, respected by all, was a permanent member of the Upper House, above the fray and petty politics. For years, he had been preparing to retire from public life, but had constantly had to postpone it. Neither Brown, Cartier, Macdonald, nor Galt had enough support to assume the leadership. The Taché-Macdonald ministry had the authority, as it was made up of two strong majorities, the Conservatives of Lower Canada and the Reformists of Upper Canada. Added to this solid core were the Conservatives of Upper Canada. The opposition, made up of the Liberals of Lower Canada, was weak. When, in the Lower House, Macdonald described the negotiations, he was questioned by Dorion and Holton on the terms of the agreement. Dorion bitterly regretted that Brown, his former ally, had rallied to the idea of an enlarged federation. This political option threatened to diminish the political clout of the French Canadians. Another failing was that it presupposed the costly building of an intercolonial railway. The Reds considered these public projects to be extravagant.

On 30 June, the new Reformist ministers from Upper Canada were sworn in: George Brown was appointed president of the council, Oliver Mowat was postmaster general, and William McDougall was provincial secretary for Upper Canada. The government announced that a mission was to be sent to England and the Maritime Provinces in order to promote the federal union project. The cabinet intended to take advantage of a convention of the Maritime Provinces in Charlottetown in the autumn to propose a bigger and more ambitious project, namely the union of all the colonies. The Maritime Provinces, apprised of these intentions, willingly agreed to welcome the delegates from Canada at the Charlottetown Conference.

At the beginning of September, delegates from the various provinces travelled to the capital of Prince Edward Island. In the course of the first day, 1 September, the delegates from the Maritime Provinces agreed to consider the creation of a large federation. After a few days of deliberation, they agreed on certain basic principles. Macdonald spoke a number of times. He was careful to limit the powers of the provinces. At one point, the delegate George Coles, from Prince Edward Island, put forward a resolution: "Local legislatures have the power to legislate in all areas not specifically devolved by the Conference to the central legislature." Macdonald opposed the measure, citing the failure of American federalism: "A radical cause of weakness was going to be inserted into the new constitution of British North America. This will be our ruin in the eyes of the civilized world."[9] At the end of the conference, delegates agreed to meet in October in Quebec City in order to finalize the accord. The Founding Fathers left Prince Edward Island bound for Nova Scotia on board the *Queen Victoria*. In reference to the Confederate sympathies in England, the ship was known as "the Confederate cruiser." In Halifax, the Fathers were guests at dinner. At one point, Macdonald rose and announced that he intended to make British North America a great nation that would able to defend itself: "[Observe] the brave fight of the Confederate republic, which at present has no more than four million people, not much more than our own population. And yet, the southerners have really fought valiantly [Our aim is to] establish a great British monarchy tied to the British Empire and subject to British sovereignty."[10]

The Quebec Conference went off without a major hitch. While it is true that the delegates from Newfoundland and Prince Edward Island decided, at the end of the talks, not to join the large federation, their presence was not crucial. Demographically, they carried marginal weight; geographically, they were less needed than New Brunswick or Nova Scotia. The provincial delegates therefore adopted the Resolutions, which they intended to present to the Parliaments of the four founding provinces. Macdonald was careful to dissuade the delegates from putting the Resolutions to the nation: "A referendum is anti-constitutional and anti-British. If, after petitions and public meetings, Parliament is certain that the country does not want the project, the elected representatives will refuse to adopt it. If, on the contrary, Parliament ascertains that the country is in favour of the federation, there will be no need to appeal to the people. Submitting these complicated details to the nation is obviously absurd."[11]

Macdonald's presence during the debates on the Resolutions in the Lower House of United Canada reveals his political convictions. He opened the debate on 3 February 1865 and presented the government's actions to have the Resolutions adopted. These were in the nature of a treaty between the provinces: "These resolutions are in the nature of a treaty, and if they are not adopted in their entirety, the proceedings will have to be commenced *de novo*. If every province undertakes to change the details of the plan, there will be no end to the conferences and discussions."[12] To a member who asked him if the government intended to avoid a referendum, Macdonald gave an ambivalent answer: "I cannot give an immediate answer. If the measure is approved in the House, there will be no need for a referendum. On the other hand, if the measure is rejected, it will be up to the government to decide whether the nation is consulted."[13]

Three days later, on 6 February, Macdonald addressed an idea that was dear to him: a stable, permanent, and well-functioning political regime was imperative. Like the Loyalist elites of 1775, the Founding Father feared anarchy, political factions, unstable local governments, and tyranny of the masses. Stability of the body politic was imperative for the expansion of trade: "Antagonism between the two sections of the province and the danger of imminent anarchy, which, according to the population in Upper and Lower Canada, were the results of irreconcilable opinions on representation, presaged an unfortunate succession of governments holding weak majorities and wielding little influence, and which were therefore unable to achieve anything positive. The precarious state of our affairs, the serious apprehension of anarchy which would have ruined our credibility, destroyed our prosperity and wiped out our progress made a particular impression the members of our current Parliament."[14] The monarchical principle would ensure political stability. It presumed that Canadians were "motivated by the same loyalty to the Queen."[15] At the Quebec Conference, no delegate opposed the monarchical principle: "This resolution met with the unanimous approval of all conference members. Not one expressed the desire to break with Great Britain and not pursue our allegiance to Her Majesty."[16] The history of republics showed that the authority of the chief executive is less stable than in a monarchy:

> By adhering to the monarchical principle, we avoid one defect inherent in the Constitution of the United States. Being elected for a short period, the president is never looked up to as the head and front of the nation; he is at best but the successful leader of a party. This defect is all the greater on account of the practice of re-election; during his first term of office he is employed in taking steps to secure his own re-election, and for his party a continuance of power. We avoid this by adhering to the monarchical principle. I believe that it is of the utmost importance to have that principle recognized so that we shall have a sovereign who is placed above the region of party – to whom all parties look up; who is the common head and sovereign of all.[17]

Macdonald did not think that the prerogatives of the Crown should be merely symbolic. He wanted to give the Queen considerable leeway: "We place no restriction on Her Majesty's prerogative in her choice of representative; as it is now, so it will be if this Constitution is adopted. The Sovereign has unrestricted freedom of choice.... When in making her selection, she may send us one of her own family, a Royal Prince as a Viceroy to rule over us, or one of the great statesmen of England to represent her, we know not. We leave that to her Majesty in all confidence."[18] Later on, during the debates, Macdonald advocated the creation of a permanent army. The colonies would be called upon to play a new role in the empire. They would have to assume a greater share in the defence of the British Empire.

> The colonies are now in a transition state. Gradually a different colonial system is being developed – And it will become, year by year, less a case of dependence on our part, and of over-ruling protection on the part of the mother country, and more of a case of a healthy and cordial alliance.... Instead of looking upon us merely as a dependent colony, England will have in us a friendly nation – a subordinate, but still a powerful people – to stand by her in North America in peace or in war. And England will have this advantage, if her colonies progress under the new colonial system, as I believe they will, that, though at war with all the rest of the world, she will be able to look to the subordinate nations in alliance with her, and owing allegiance to the same Sovereign, who will assist in enabling her again to meet the whole world with arms, as she has done before.[19]

The Resolutions were not a declaration of independence. The aim was not to abandon, but to strengthen the colonial tie: "Some are apprehensive that the very fact of our forming this Union will hasten the time when we shall be severed from the mother country. I have no apprehension of that kind.... I believe that as we grow stronger,... she will be less willing to part with us than she would be now, when we are broken up into a number of insignificant colonies ... without any concerted action or common organisation of defence."[20] Later, during the debates, he would use the following phrase: "Those who dislike the colonial tie speak of it as a chain, but it is a golden chain."[21] Macdonald insisted on modelling the relationship between the provinces and the federal project on the British Empire:

> As this is to be one united province, with the local governments and legislatures subordinate to the General Government and Legislature, it is obvious that the chief executive officer in each of the provinces must be subordinate as well. The General Government assumes towards the local governments precisely the same position as the Imperial Government holds with respect to each of the colonies now.[22]

Near the end of the debates, on 13 March 1865, he reiterated his belief in Hamilton's conception of federalism: "Let us attempt to learn from that lesson [the American Civil War] and let us not break upon the same rock. Their fatal mistake, which they could perhaps not have avoided owing to the state of the colonies at the time of the revolution, was in making every State distinct and sovereign with the exception of certain cases especially reserved by the Constitution to the general government. The true principle which must serve as a basis for a confederation consists in giving the general government all the attributes and powers of sovereignty."[23] That same day, he rejected the opposition motion forcing the government to submit the Resolutions to a referendum: "An election means civil unrest."[24] And yet a number of Founding Fathers had promised a referendum after the Charlottetown Conference. At a dinner in Toronto, George Brown and Alexander T. Galt had made that promise. According to Macdonald, this was not in accordance with the British Constitution:

> We in this House are representatives of the people, not mere delegates, and by lending our support to such a law would be robbing ourselves of the character of representatives ... and the honourable member knows only too well the principle of the English constitution to support such a proceeding himself.... By what means recognised and allowed by our Constitution could we take such a vote? There is none, and to do so we would have to trample on the principles of the English constitution.... A direct appeal to the nation on a question of this kind may well be the means used by a despot, or an absolute monarch, to make his people sanction what he has usurped; this is perhaps how a despot, backed up by bayonets, can ask the nation to vote for or against the measures he proposes.[25]

The last act in establishing British North America was played out at the third constitutional conference, held in London in December 1866. John A. Macdonald tried once again to turn the federal union into a legislative one. George-Étienne Cartier blocked the initiative.[26] Macdonald also suggested naming the new country "Kingdom of Canada," but the imperial authorities feared that the monarchist-sounding name would be an insult to the American government. Instead, they adopted the suggestion of the New Brunswick Founding Father Leonard Tilley. In verse 8 of Psalm 72 in the Bible, he found an evocative phrase: "He shall have dominion also from sea to sea, and from the river unto the ends of the earth." Hence the name "Dominion of Canada."[27]

Among the Founding Fathers, John A. Macdonald was the big winner in the creation of British North America. Yet, scarcely three years earlier, he had been a vulnerable and unpopular politician who did not seem destined for a great political future. Those who thought this way, however, were forgetting the influence of the imperial elite on Canadian affairs. In fact, Macdonald had important backing in the colonial administration. Governor Monck gave him an invaluable helping hand. Aided by Denis Godley, a wily British colonial civil servant, whom Canadians nicknamed "the Almighty," Monck wrote numerous dispatches to the Colonial Office. He reported on the progress of negotiations and attended the important constitutional conferences. Monck's views were profoundly monarchist. He hoped that Canada would be made a kingdom and that his responsibility would be that of a viceroy.[28] He would thereby have become chancellor of a new Canadian order of chancery. When the time came to choose the regime's prime minister, he did not turn to the most popular or experienced man, but to the one whose opinions best espoused that British ideal, John A. Macdonald.

In March 1867, Monck informed Macdonald that he would appoint him prime minister of the new regime. There was no rule to determine who would be the lucky winner. The governor thought him the most capable of heading a ministry, given that he had masterfully presided over the London Conference: "In authorising you to undertake the task of forming the government of the Dominion of Canada, I wish to make it clear that all must fully understand that henceforth the post of Prime Minister will fall to *one* person, answerable to the Governor General for the appointment of the other ministers."[29] In fact, the title of prime minister should normally have gone to George-Étienne Cartier. His career was at its height. He was more experienced than John A. and enjoyed stronger popular support among the electorate. Not without reason, Cartier felt he had been betrayed. In the autumn of 1867, the French-Canadian Conservative leader began talks with Brown, Ontario's strongman, to lay the foundations of a new coalition party. The coalition would apparently have comprised A.T. Galt, Richard Cartwright, Thomas D'Arcy McGee, and Francis Hincks. However, Brown did not take up the offer of an alliance.[30] That same autumn, in the first election of the new regime, the Conservative Party was easily re-elected: 108 Conservatives, 72 Liberals.[31] The Conservatives achieved their best results in Quebec, winning 47 of 65 seats. The Church interfered in many ridings, but the new regime was hardly contested during the debates in political forums. Most of the opposition of 1865 had decided to give the regime a chance, and debates focused on other questions: the militia, the navy, and provincial autonomy.[32]

The regime of 1867 did not give rise to an independent country. John A. Macdonald was very clear on this point. There was no question of British North America freeing itself from the mother country. "The colonial tie," said Macdonald, "is a chain. But it is a golden chain." That vision, however, was not shared by the entire political elite. Many Liberals, especially in Quebec, wanted Canada to become an independent country. Being Canadian and being British were incompatible. The question was a divisive one among the Liberals. Those from Ontario were more attached to Great Britain. The Québécois Liberals were, for their part, more sympathetic to the United States. Those from the Montreal region in particular thought that the north-south economic axis was more likely to ensure prosperity. A pro-independence literature emerged in Montreal in the first decade of the new regime. Médéric Lanctôt, Lucius Seth Huntington, John Young, and Hector Fabre published essays on the issue. The year 1871 exacerbated resentment towards London. The signing of the Treaty of Washington between Great Britain and the United States put an end to a hundred years of wars and diplomatic struggles. Many disputes between the two countries were addressed by the treaty. Because the disputes concerned Canada, Great Britain had appointed Macdonald as negotiator. When the contents of the treaty were made public, a cry of betrayal went up throughout the country. Great Britain had, to all appearances, signed the agreement with the aim of living in peace with a threatening rival. "I admit that my first move," Macdonald acknowledged, "was to announce my resignation to Lord Grey for him to pass on to Lord Granville."[33] Once back in Parliament, he tried to minimise the seriousness of the concessions (particularly the opening up of Canadian waters to American fishermen). The damage, however, was done.

Liberal critics claimed that the "Britishness" of the prime minister had cost Canadians dear. Many Conservatives admired the fact that Macdonald was not the best defender of the country's interests. The Liberal opposition subsequently exploited nationalist sentiment. Even in Ontario, the Loyalist stronghold, there was protest against England's greed. The Canada First political movement, established in Toronto, had its moment of glory. Taking inspiration from the views of Thomas D'Arcy McGee, young authors worked to forge a national sentiment. However, the movement did not go as far as to propose breaking colonial ties.[34] Imperialists as much as nationalists, they advocated expanding Canadian territory westward as far as the Pacific. Leaders of Canada First had been at the heart of events leading up to the first Métis Red River Rebellion in 1869.[35]

NOTES

1 Stéphane Kelly, *Canada and Its Aims, According to Macdonald, Laurier, Mackenzie King and Trudeau*, a translation of material from *Les Fins du Canada, selon Macdonald, Laurier, Mackenzie King et Trudeau*, Montreal, Boréal, 2001, pp. 33–47, 261.
2 On deadlock, see Christopher Moore, *How the Fathers Made a Deal*, Toronto, McClelland and Stewart, 1997.
3 See Jacques Monet, *La Première Révolution tranquille. Le nationalisme canadien-français (1837–1850)*, Montreal, Fides, 1981; and J.M.S. Careless, *Brown of the Globe*, 2 vols., Toronto, Macmillan, 1959 and 1961.
4 See Jacques Monet, *op. cit.*
5 Donald Creighton, *John A. Macdonald. Le Haut et le Bas-Canada*, vol. 1, Montreal, Éditions de l'Homme, 1952, p. 271.
6 On the opinion of imperial elites during the years 1850 and 1859, see Ged Martin, *Britain and the Ideological Origins of Canadian Confederation*, Victoria, University of British Columbia Press, 1996.
7 15 March 1865, in Creighton, *John A. Macdonald*, p. 306.
8 Letter from Cardwell to Gladsone, 12 November, 1864, in Creighton, *John A. Macdonald*, p. 337.
9 Creighton, *John A. Macdonald*, p. 329.
10 *Globe*, 21 September 1864. Quoted in Creighton, *John A. Macdonald*, p. 321.
11 Creighton, *John A. Macdonald*, 1 December 1864, p. 335.
12 *Débats parlementaires sur la question de la Confédération des provinces de l'Amérique britannique du Nord*, Ottawa, Hunter, Rose et Lemieux, 1865, p. 17.
13 *Débats*, p. 17.
14 *Débats*, p. 27.
15 *Débats*, p. 29.
16 *Débats*, p. 34.
17 *Débats*, p. 33.
18 *Débats*, p. 35.
19 *Débats*, p. 43.
20 *Débats*, p. 43.
21 *Débats*, p. 174, 13 February 1865.
22 *Débats*, p. 42.
23 *Débats*, p. 1001.
24 *Débats*, p. 999.
25 *Débats*, pp. 1002–1003.
26 In George-Étienne Cartier, *George-Étienne Cartier (1814–1914)*, Montreal, Édition du Centenaire, 1914, pp. 81–82.

27 On this episode, consult Donald Swainson, *Sir John A. Macdonald: The Man and the Politician*, Kingston, Quarry Press, 1989.

28 On Viscount Monck, consult Elizabeth Bat, *Monck, Governor General, 1861–1878,* Toronto, Macmillan, 1976.

29 Monck to Macdonald, 24 May 1867, in Joseph Pope, *Correspondence of John A. Macdonald*, Toronto, J. Durie and Son, sine datum, p. 46.

30 J.M.S. Careless, *Brown of the Globe*, vol. 2, *Statesman of Confederation, 1860–1880*, pp. 260–283.

31 In this chapter, I use the account of the federal general election by J.M. Beck, *The Pendulum of Power*, Scarborough, Prentice-Hall, 1968.

32 On this point, see the first chapters of Marcel Caya, "La formation du Parti libéral au Québec, 1867–1887," doctoral thesis, York University, 1981.

33 Macdonald to Tupper, 27 April 1871, in Donald Creighton, *John A. Macdonald, La naissance d'un pays incertain*, vol. 2, Montreal, Éditions de l'Homme, 1981, p. 93.

34 On Canada First, see Carl Berger, *The Sense of Power: Studies in Ideas of Canadian Imperialism, 1864–1914*, Toronto, University of Toronto Press, 1976.

35 Berger, *The Sense of Power*, pp. 56–59.

# *The French-Canadian Idea of Confederation, 1864–1900*

1997

A.I. SILVER[1]

In 1864, when the Fathers of Confederation sat down to their conference table, there were about a million people of French origin in British North America, and more than 85 per cent of them lived in what would become the province of Quebec. In all other places they lived in small and scattered groups surrounded by great majorities of strangers; in Lower Canada they were a compact and organized society comprising more than three-quarters of the population. Everywhere else they were weak and without influence; in Lower Canada their language was heard daily in public life, and their values and traditions shaped the laws and institutions of the province. Thus, Quebec was the most particular homeland of the French Canadians, though it was not the sole theatre of their activities or interests.

This had always been so. Even before the Conquest, in an age when French North America stretched from the Atlantic to the Rockies, from Hudson Bay to the Gulf of Mexico, Quebec's position was always special. It was, indeed, the very centre and the heart of that empire; it alone was called Canada. On its east, Acadia guarded, perhaps, the entrance to the St Lawrence, but the tiny settlements there were of little account. They were administered separately from Canada, and that so weakly and sporadically that they were destroyed or conquered by British forces at least seven times before French diplomacy finally failed, in 1713, to return the stolen horse to the unlocked barn once more.

To the west of Canada lay the vast sweep of a wild interior: Indian country, a fur traders' and a military frontier. Exploited by Canada, traversed by Canadians, it was certainly no part of Canada itself. Those who left for the West – and by the eighteenth century they represented a small, specialized, and distinct part of the Canadian population[2] – separated themselves from the St Lawrence valley not only by distance, but also by type of environment and way of life. The world to which they went was wild and wooded, and there Indian society maintained itself. The world they left behind was settled and cultivated, covered with farms, scattered with towns and villages, organized into parishes and seigneuries. In Quebec an orderly and Christian civilization was established; at Toronto fur traders might still do the *Gan8ary*, running naked between the lodges with a keg of brandy under each arm.[3]

No wonder the moral distinction was soon made between the good people who stayed in the colony to plough their land and lead upright lives, and the bad ones who ran off to the depravities of the *pays d'en haut*.[4] No wonder, either, that men who spent years in the tramping life of the interior were never able afterwards to adapt themselves to the civilization of the St Lawrence valley.[5] And how much more was this the case when the fur trade had penetrated so far westward that return trips had become difficult for those who worked at the frontier. *Voyageurs* remained away from Quebec for longer and longer periods of time, until there were hundreds of Canadians in the West who never returned at all.[6]

Thus, differences of identity, of self-awareness between the Canadians and the other French of North America appeared during the French regime itself. Acadia and Louisiana were separated from Canada by geography, economics, and administration; the interior, though connected to Canada by commerce and by strategy, differed from it in the way of life and in the attitudes of its tiny, scattered, and largely wandering population. Above all, the vast majority of French North Americans lived in the St Lawrence valley. Throughout the French régime censuses of New France, or Canada, began with the Quebec district and never went farther west than Les Cèdres.[7]

Conquest accentuated the differences between the Canadians and the other French North Americans. But it was still the intensity of their settlement that distinguished the former from all the rest. The Acadians' sparse numbers (1,773 in Nova Scotia at the time of France's final surrender of the peninsula) had encouraged British immigration by the end of the 1740s and made possible the dramatic expulsions of the 1750s. But Quebec's 65,000 population at the Conquest ensured her a different destiny. The Quebec Act was a recognition of this numerical strength; it acknowledged that the St Lawrence valley was and would continue to be inhabited by a preponderantly French and Catholic population. True, the act included Ontario and the Ohio country in its provisions (strategic as well as commercial considerations might make this desirable), but British censuses of Quebec from 1774 to 1991 still stopped at Les Cèdres.

The success of the American Revolution only emphasized the fact that the area west of the Ottawa River was not a truly French-Canadian country. South of the Great Lakes the triumph of Anglo-American democracy precluded any possibility of a permanently constituted French fact. And while this enabled the British to persuade some of Michigan's French to cross the Detroit River, by holding up the fact that the Quebec Act still applied in Ontario,[8] the Loyalist immigration, which was a by-product of the revolution ensured that Ontario, in the long run, would be English.

The Loyalists, by the magnitude of their settlement, staked out the same claim to Ontario as had saved the French fact in Quebec. Both claims were registered in the 1791 Constitutional Act, which finally re-confined the French establishment to the old Canada of the French régime. The first session of the Upper Canadian legislature might resolve that its acts be published in French as well as in English, at a time when strategy advised the attraction of French from Detroit to Sandwich and the securing of their loyalty,[9] but clearly, the predominant character of the province was going to be English.

Thus was confirmed the distinction between the French Canadians of Lower Canada and the French minorities in the rest of North America. Henceforth, the development of French-Catholic communities outside Quebec would depend on relations with Anglo-Protestant majorities; only in Lower Canada could French Canadians hope to exert the influence of a majority in their own land.[10]

The Acadians were the oldest minority group. Estimates of their pre-expulsion numbers vary widely, as do accounts of the numbers expelled.[11] In any case, the 1767 census of Nova Scotia, taken after the deportations had ended, showed 921 Acadians among a total population of 11,779, with 147 more in the part of the province which was to become New Brunswick, and 197 on Prince Edward Island. These figures, however, certainly underrate the real numbers of Acadians still in the maritime colonies, for many were hiding in the woods, or removed to isolated regions where the British authorities would not be apt to find them.[12]

Subsequent growth of the Acadian population is not easy to follow, especially since pre-Confederation censuses did not distinguish Acadians either by language or by national origin. The Catholic bishop of Quebec, who toured the Maritimes in 1803, is reported to have found more than 8,000 Acadians there.[13] The French commentator Edmé Rameau de Saint-Père calculated there were 80,000 in 1859,[14] and the first dominion census, in 1871, announced there were 92,740 Acadians in Nova Scotia, New Brunswick, and Prince Edward Island.[15]

Increase in numbers was one thing, social development was another. Fearful both of the authorities and of the Loyalists, who poured into the Maritimes after 1783, forcing a last displacement of Acadians from the St John River in 1784, the French avoided the well-organized older regions of settlement, huddling in the wild northern and gulf coast areas. Not eager to show themselves too openly, and having, in any case, returned from exile or from hiding in small, unconnected groups, they remained isolated from each other as well as from English-speaking society.[16] They struggled for a century without the important unifying forces that promoted French-Canadian development in Quebec: Church, schools, press, and political spokesmen.

The first necessity, an Acadian clergy, was hard to acquire. The Seven Years' War had left not a single French-Catholic priest in the Maritimes, and, although the bishops of Quebec, with some help from the seminary for foreign missions in Paris, managed to send a few missionaries into the lower provinces between 1767 and 1818, they were hardly enough to establish an adequately served parish system. In any case, the Maritimes were separated from the diocese of Quebec in 1818, and from that moment, their Church was controlled by Scotch and Irish clergy. By 1844, four dioceses had been created in the Maritimes, none of which had a French-speaking bishop. After that year, there was not a single French priest in Nova Scotia,[17] though a few Quebec missionaries laboured on in New Brunswick. Even there, however, by 1860, of thirty priests at work, only seven were French-speaking, and only one an Acadian.[18] Maritime bishops often held to the theory that, in the interest of Church unity and of good relations with the Protestant majority, English should be the sole language of Catholicism in their dioceses; they tended, therefore, to name English-speaking priests even to parishes with overwhelmingly Acadian populations, and were accused of discouraging French-language life in other ways too.[19]

Under these circumstances, Acadian education developed with difficulty. A century after the expulsion, Rameau could still report that while many had learned to read and write, this was the limit of their knowledge.[20] Circumstances had opposed greater progress. A Nova Scotia law of 1766 had forbidden the operation of Catholic schools, so that lessons had to be either private or secret, given in barns, the backs of houses, and so on.[21] By the second decade of the nineteenth century, most teaching was done by itinerant instructors, who travelled through the bush giving a lesson here and a class there, for a fee – though two priests finally did open schools in 1817.[22] As late as the 1860s, the condition of Acadian education was still so bad that a French sailor who jumped ship off the coast of New Brunswick found himself the best-educated man in the village of Bouctouche, where he landed, and successfully opened and ran a school.[23]

By this time the state had begun to lend a hand. An 1841 Nova Scotia law authorized government grants to Catholic schools, where French (or German or Gaelic, for that matter) might be the language of instruction. These were not long enjoyed, however, since the province set up a non-denominational public school system in 1864, making it compulsory and universal the following year. French was eliminated, except as a subject of instruction in upper grades, and certification rules made it impossible to import teachers from the religious orders of Lower Canada.[24] Meanwhile, however, Prince Edward Island had begun granting subsidies to Catholic schools in 1852 (though French-speaking teachers apparently received 18 per cent less than English),[25] and New Brunswick began making similar grants in 1858.[26] The first Acadian secondary school opened at Memramcook, New Brunswick, in 1854, closed after a few years of financial struggle, and finally re-opened in 1864, though it was largely English in the origin of its pupils and in its language of instruction.[27]

Educational difficulties prevented the growth of other elements of national life. No French newspaper was published in the Maritimes till 1867; its first issue appeared a week after Confederation was inaugurated.[28] It had not been till 1846 that a first Acadian was elected to the New Brunswick legislature. In 1864 he was still the only Acadian MPP, and, though another was elected in 1865, the Acadians were without representation in the Maritime governments and delegations that participated in the making of Confederation.[29] Nor did their economic situation give them influence. Still mainly poor fishermen, they were little engaged in agriculture and not at all in business.[30]

In these circumstances, we need hardly be surprised to find no significant expression of Acadian opinion about the making of Confederation. Largely ignorant of its coming,[31] having had no part in its preparation, Acadians had no reason to greet it with enthusiasm.[32] They could only follow their clergy's advice to accept it passively as a *fait accompli*.[33] "Today," commented the *Moniteur Acadien* in its first issue, "there is only one thing for us to do: resign ourselves to our fate and try to make the best of it."[34]

On the other side of Quebec, the Franco-Ontarians were far more closely connected in every way with the French Canadians of Lower Canada than were the Acadians. Their old Windsor-area community had declined in relative importance since the beginning of the century, but, at the time of Confederation, their build-up of strength in eastern Ontario was still beginning. The 1861 census, on which the Fathers of Confederation had to base their considerations, showed that Canadians of French origin comprised only 2.4 per cent of Upper Canada's population, though they were close to half in the eastern counties of Russell, Prescott, and Nipissing, and a quarter of Ottawa city. In all of Upper Canada, 13 per cent of Catholics were of French origin.

Small though it was, this group was able to lead a French-Canadian life, largely because of the decentralized nature of pre-Confederation society. Especially in the frontier period, there was relatively little pressure for cultural uniformity. At a time, for instance, when schools were hard pressed to find teachers who could disseminate the elements of reading, writing, and arithmetic, there was little point in insisting on this or that language, or on conformity to this or that curriculum. Thus, in 1851, Upper Canada's Council of Public Instruction refused to challenge a local school board's hiring of a unilingual French teacher, not only on the grounds that the majority of pupils in the area were French-Canadian, but also because it was too hard to find people qualified to teach in English. The council ordered that teachers should be able to qualify for certification in French, if they chose, rather than English. This was a strictly practical decision, not a matter of natural, historical, or constitutional rights, and the facilities given to French were also allowed to German, just as the 1841 Nova Scotia law had applied to German and Gaelic as well as to French.[35]

While the language of Upper Canadian education was, thus, not a political question before Confederation, religion was one. And here the Upper Canadian Catholics were aided by the Union in 1840; though they and their allies were a minority in Upper Canada, the support of their Lower Canadian co-religionists enabled them to obtain separate school privileges. In 1855, and again in 1863, bills defining and expanding the rights of the Catholic school system in Ontario were passed against the opposition of the Upper Canadian majority, thanks to the votes of Lower Canadians in the united legislature of the two Canadas.

The important support that Franco-Ontarians received from Quebec was demographic as well as political. Beginning around 1850, emigration from Lower Canada doubled the French-Canadian population of the southwestern counties of Essex and Kent in twenty years.[36] More strikingly, it was Lower Canadian emigrants who accounted for the growing importance of French Canadians in the Upper Canadian counties that touched the Ottawa River.[37] The contact of these counties with Lower Canada meant that settlers in them formed part of a large French-Canadian bloc of population centred in Quebec, and could more easily maintain their cultural identity. Thus, the diocese of Ottawa was part of the ecclesiastical province of Quebec, and its French-Canadian bishops were ready to appoint French-speaking priests as the Maritime hierarchy were not. Again, the proximity of the east bank population made it easier to launch a French-language newspaper on the west side. Attempts were made at Ottawa in 1858 and 1861; a more successful venture began in 1865, as Ottawa was about to become the Canadian capital, and *Le Canada* was published there till two years after Confederation.[38]

Nevertheless, the Franco-Ontarians were not a political force of their own in the 1860s. There was no French Upper Canadian Father of Confederation, no Franco-Ontarian voice in the councils that planned the new régime, that wrote the new constitution. For these people there was much to be lost in the break-up of the old union of the Canadas, and they were much dependent on the French-Canadian leaders of Lower Canada to obtain what securities could be had for them in the new dominion.

Like the Acadians, the French Métis of the northwestern plains were French-Catholic cousins of the Quebeckers, but were not, properly speaking, French Canadians themselves. Descendants of old-time *voyageurs* and Indian women, they had come, by the beginning of the nineteenth century, to form, together with the English-speaking descendants of Hudson's Bay men, distinct half-breed communities, apart from both Indians and whites. In these communities the French and Catholic element slightly predominated. Censuses of Assiniboia (the Hudson's Bay Company's administrative district corresponding roughly to the Manitoba of 1870) did not note either language or national origin; but the census of 1843 showed that 54 per cent of Assiniboia's families (including the tiny minority of whites) were Catholic. The first Manitoba census, taken in 1870–1, counted 5,757 French Métis and 4,083 English Métis.[39]

The numerical importance of the French Catholics was reflected in the Company's administration of the North-West. From the time of its establishment, the bishop of St Boniface was always a member of the Council of Assiniboia, and from 1853 on, at least one French Métis was also appointed. Four years before, the council had officially sanctioned the use of French in court cases involving francophone inhabitants, and in 1850 several French magistrates had been appointed. Two years later, the council began making an annual grant to the Catholic, Anglican, and Presbyterian Churches for the support of their schools, establishing some precedent for separate Catholic and Protestant schools systems in the North-West. The French and Catholic fact had, thus, considerable institutional basis in Rupert's Land, and it is not for nothing that Assiniboia has been referred to as "a little Quebec."[40]

But the differences between Assiniboia and Quebec were at least as great as their similarities. Commercial relations between the two areas had ended with the demise of the Montreal fur trade in 1822, and if there had been a religious connection since 1818, when the first Catholic missionaries were sent from Quebec to Red River, the very establishment of that connection had been a manifestation of the difference between the two places. It was Lord Selkirk who had appealed to Quebec's Bishop Joseph-Octave Plessis to send those missionaries, when Métis, fearing that his agricultural settlement would destroy the buffalo hunt on which their livelihood depended, were led into violence. Selkirk wanted the missionaries to tame these savage Métis, to settle them down into an agricultural life like that of the French Canadians.

But agriculture was not easy to establish on the prairies. A group of French Canadians, who followed the first missionaries with the task of providing an example and a nucleus around which Métis farmers could settle, gave up within a few years and fled to the United States or back to Canada. Bishop Provencher was later to write that for six or seven years after his arrival in the North-West, though he dined at the governor's table, he never saw any bread.[41] Though churches were built and plots of land marked off along the Red River, stability was hard to achieve. Even in the late 1860s, the twice-yearly buffalo hunts still uprooted the entire community from its Red River homes and transported it across the plains for six weeks at a time. On the eve of the Canadian takeover, J.J. Hargrave was writing that one of the chief problems for the colony's future would "lie in persuading the hunting portion of the partially-civilized community to devote themselves to sedentary or agricultural labour. This is the French half-breed race."[42]

Like any great social change, in fact, the settling of the Métis was a gradual one, affecting some more quickly and more thoroughly than others.[43] The greatest degree of adaptation was found in the Assiniboia area, while those who resisted change drifted into the farther North-West. A.S. Morton sums up the situation thus: "The more sedentary portion made good farmers, but every grade of settler was found among them, down to those whose homes differed little from their former camps among the Indians, and whose livelihood continued to be hunting and fishing as of old."[44]

Not surprisingly, the Métis were unenthusiastic about joining the Canadian confederation. Fearing a sudden flooding of the plains by Canadian agricultural settlement, in the face of which their hunting life could no longer survive, they would have preferred maintenance of Hudson's Bay Company rule, if possible.[45] But if the status quo could not be maintained, they were at least determined to have a say in the conditions on which they would join the dominion. The Acadians and the Franco-Ontarians had not shared in the making of the Confederation in the 1860s; but there was an Assiniboaian revolt in 1869–70 in order to share in the making of Confederation as it affected them. And in that uprising, it was repeatedly the French Métis who took the initiatives – the section of the community still most attached to the hunt and least comfortable with agriculture.

The only French-Catholic group that played any direct part in making the original confederation, between 1864 and 1867, was French Lower Canada. Despite various challenges, this group maintained the essential numerical strength that had made it unique already in the eighteenth century. For a time after 1815, British immigration had seemed to threaten the integrity of French Lower Canada. By 1822, official estimates suggested that almost 15 per cent of Lower Canadians were living in the new townships or Protestant seigneuries. But the flood of immigration had scarcely begun. The census of 1844 showed that only 75 per cent of Lower Canadians were French-Canadian. By this time, too, a new problem had appeared to accentuate the effect of British immigration: the exodus of French Canadians from Quebec to the United States. A committee of the Canadian legislature reckoned in 1849 that 20,000 French Canadians had emigrated to the States merely in the five preceding years.[46] The movement accelerated in the following decades, as French Canadians felt increasingly the lack of good agricultural land and the absence of jobs in Quebec. By 1890, the United States census showed that there were 302,496 people born in Canada of French origin then living in the U.S.,[47] and it has been estimated that, all in all, as many as 500,000 French Canadians left Canada to live in the republic between 1851 and 1901.[48] Nevertheless, despite this exodus, and despite the lesser movement to Upper Canada, the French Canadians began slowly to regain their strength in Quebec after the middle of the nineteenth century. The 1861 census showed that they now constituted over 76 per cent of the provincial population. In 1871 the figure would be 78 per cent, and by 1901, over 80 per cent.

These facts encouraged people to continue looking on Lower Canada as a particularly French-Canadian country. It was in Lower Canada that French-Canadian nationalism emerged, in the politics and literature of Lower Canada that that nationalism expressed itself. It was not without reason that Lord Durham looked on the 1791 separation of Lower Canada from Upper as the green flag to French-Canadian national aspirations. Already in 1822, the petitions that French Canadians drew up to oppose a proposed reunion of the Canadas expressed their belief that this province had been set aside for all time as a homeland for their nationality, a territory to be characterized by their laws, their institutions, and their language.[49]

These beliefs were not extinguished by the union of 1840, for although the legislatures of the Canadas were merged, it soon became clear that the separate laws and institutions, and hence, inevitably, the separate administration and language of Lower Canada, would continue to flourish.[50] Indeed, during the very period of the union, the identity of French Canada with Lower Canada became formalized in literature, and there emerged a well-defined theory of a French-Canadian nationality in a Lower Canadian homeland.[51]

The work of Louis-François Laflèche, at the end of the Union period, was a particularly elaborate expression of this theory. Having demonstrated that the French Canadians constituted a nation, and that every nation, in order to live out its national life in accord with the will of Providence, had to have a homeland of its own, Laflèche concluded that "we have a homeland; that homeland is the land bequeathed to us by our fathers, the fine, rich valley of the St Lawrence. Providence itself gave it to our forefathers." Significantly, in defining what constituted a nation, Laflèche stressed common laws, customs, and social organization, as well as language and religion: a national homeland had to be a place where more than linguistic and religious privileges were guaranteed.[52]

Thus, on the eve of Confederation, Lower Canada stood out, as always in the past, as the most particular homeland of the French Canadians: the one place where their laws and institutions predominated, and where their elected representatives were in a position to participate fully in the making of the new regime.

In the light of what we have seen so far, we shall not be surprised to discover that the province of Quebec was the only part of the new confederation in which French-Canadian and Catholic institutions were fully and effectively established. Since Section 94 of the British North America Act provided for uniformity of civil laws in provinces other than Quebec, and since French Canadians would be able to control future legislation only in Quebec, where alone they would be a majority, there was no question of having French-Canadian laws outside that province. Section 133 established the official status of the French language, but only in Quebec and in the *federal* Parliament and courts.[53] Finally, Section 93 limited, to some degree, the provinces' powers to deprive Catholics of separate school systems once they officially possessed them – though, as the future would show, the degree of limitation was slight indeed, and official possession most difficult to demonstrate.

If these provisions did not do much to guarantee the flourishing of French-Catholic institutions outside Quebec, neither did they deprive them of any rights they had possessed before Confederation. What the new constitution did do for the minorities was to put them into the same political unit with the Quebeckers. Though the break-up of the Canadian Union deprived Franco-Ontarians of the kind of direct French-Quebec support that the united legislature had allowed, the jurisdiction of the federal Parliament was, nevertheless, sufficient to ensure that questions of the cultural rights of the minorities would come before it, and would, thus, be discussed by the French-Quebec MPs who sat in it. Moreover, the association of the British North American provinces in a single confederation might have encouraged, in some measure, either the movement of French Canadians to areas outside Quebec, where they could reinforce the minorities, or at least the idea that such a movement could be desirable.

During the first decades of Confederation the French-origin population grew at about the same rate as the Canadian population in general. It fell off only slightly, from 31.1 per cent of the total in 1871 to 31.0 per cent in 1901. But distribution of the French population throughout the dominion changed significantly in this period. While its relative importance grew in the Maritimes, Quebec, Ontario, and even British Columbia, it declined drastically on the prairies.

We have already seen that in Quebec the French-origin population grew more quickly than the non-French population, constituting 78.0 per cent of the total in 1871 and 80.2 per cent in 1901. At the same time, there was a movement of French Quebeckers into parts of the province that had previously been mainly English. Thus the French-origin population grew from 56.1 per cent of Quebec City's total in 1861 to 82.8 per cent in 1901; at Sherbrooke the increase was from 24.1 per cent in 1861 to 62.7 per cent in 1901.[54] The population of French origin thus gradually strengthened its place in the one province in which it had been a controlling majority to begin with.

The Acadian population also gained significantly in relative numbers during this period, especially in New Brunswick, where it increased from 16 per cent of the total population in 1871 to 24 per cent at the turn of the century. Acadians were a less significant part of the populations of Nova Scotia and Prince Edward Island, but there, too, their share of the total increased, from 8.5 per cent to 9.8 per cent in Nova Scotia, and, in Prince Edward Island, from 9.8 per cent in 1881 to 13.0 per cent in 1901.

This increase in Acadian strength corresponded, first of all, to a high rate of natural increase. In all three provinces, Acadian families were consistently larger than those of other Maritimers. Indeed, if one compares census figures on family size in those Maritime counties with the largest proportion of French-origin population with the figures for the Quebec counties that were most thoroughly French, one finds that the Acadians beat even the French Quebeckers in large families.

A second factor that contributed to the relative strengthening of the Acadians was the movement of the non-French population away from the Maritime provinces. New Brunswick and Prince Edward Island both experienced absolute decreases in their non-Acadian population during the 1880s and 1890s, as did Nova Scotia in the latter decade. This emigration was particularly noticeable in those counties where Acadians were most densely concentrated. For the Acadians were not spread evenly through these provinces, but were gathered together in specific regions – the southwestern tip of Nova Scotia, Cape Breton, and the northern and gulf coast areas of New Brunswick. In the last regions especially, the Acadians constituted more than half the population in three out of six counties as early as 1871, and by 1901 formed more than a third of the population in all but Northumberland County. This concentration gave the Acadians a better chance to maintain their separate language and identity than would have been expected from the general proportion in which they stood to the Maritime population as a whole. It was not surprising, therefore, that the non-French population often tended to move away from Acadian districts.

One factor that contributed very little to the growth of the French-origin population in the Maritimes was reinforcement by emigrants from Quebec. After Confederation as before, the Acadian and French-Canadian peoples remained distinct and separate from each other. In Nova Scotia and Prince Edward Island, immigration of Quebeckers was negligible, and even in northern New Brunswick, the Quebec-born element was usually equivalent to no more than 1 to 3 per cent of the French-origin population. It was only in the two counties directly bordering on Quebec that the figure ever ran above 10 per cent, and even there it was never anywhere near the proportions to be found in eastern Ontario.

As before Confederation, emigrants from Quebec continued to pour into the eastern counties of Ontario. In 1871, the Quebec-born were equivalent to more than half of the French-origin population in the four eastern counties of Glengarry, Prescott, Russell, and Nipissing. In the last, the figure ran as high as 79 per cent in 1871 and 82 per cent in 1891. Thanks largely to this kind of movement, the proportion of Ontario's population that was of French origin increased from 4.7 per cent in 1871 to 7.3 per cent in 1901. In the latter year there were 158,671 Franco-Ontarians; they had become far more numerous than any other provincial minority outside Quebec. Like the Acadians, they showed a striking rate of natural increase; families in the most densely French county, Prescott, were consistently larger than those of other Ontarians, and larger than those of French Quebeckers as well. Again, as in New Brunswick, the relative strength of the French in Ontario was boosted by the exodus of English-origin population from the areas where the Franco-Ontarians were most numerous. These areas were mainly the ones contiguous to the province of Quebec, so that the local strength of the French Ontarians was much greater than their province-wide force. Between 1871 and 1901 the number of counties whose populations were more than one-third French increased from two to six – all but Essex being in the eastern fringe. Two of the southeastern counties had French majorities.

Far different from the experience of the Acadians and of the Franco-Ontarians was that of the francophones in the North-West, for their population declined most dramatically in relative strength after Confederation.[55] Between 1870 and the end of the century, the prairie population grew at a much faster rate than that of Canada as a whole,[56] so that by 1901 the prairies had been completely transformed and the balance of the Canadian population greatly changed. The important factor, of course, was new settlement. But the lack of French-Canadian settlers left the region open to a mainly English flow of pioneers, more of whom came from Ontario than from any other place.[57] Within a decade, the French element was swamped in Manitoba and sinking in the territories. By 1891 it had dropped to a fairly permanent level: about 7 per cent of Manitoba's population and 4 to 5 per cent in the rest of the prairie region. Moreover, the French or francophone population in the West had few centres of concentration. Only in the Manitoba district of Provencher did it remain above 10 per cent of the population, running at about a third during most of our period.

Not only was French settlement on the Canadian plains meagre, but Métis families fled the census districts as white men came in, thus reducing the strength of the French-speaking community. Despite an increase in the size of the province, Manitoba's French-Métis population fell from 5,757 in 1871 to 4,369 in 1885. The desperate desire to keep up the hunting way of life had drawn Métis away from the province and into the more distant North-West. They were replaced in Manitoba by French-Canadian settlers from Quebec and the United States, and by a high rate of natural increase among the French Manitobans – a characteristic that the different French-Canadian and Acadian minorities all seem to have shared. It is interesting to note that despite the efforts of a repatriation movement that attempted particularly to go after those French Canadians who had gone to the United States, in order to bring them back as settlers in the Canadian West, the 1885 census of Manitoba indicated that more Quebeckers had been attracted there, in fact, than Franco-Americans. The Quebec-born population of Provencher, in that year, was equivalent to 62 per cent of the non-Métis French-origin community, but the American born to only 11 per cent.[58]

It was not primarily a movement of population that brought French Quebeckers into contact with the minorities after Confederation; rather, it was the social and political conflicts in which the minorities became engaged, and whose repercussions were felt at Ottawa. The first decades of Confederation saw, in fact, a dramatic succession of conflicts in which French and Catholic minorities found themselves fighting for their interests, their rights, or even, at times, their physical safety. And

French Quebeckers could not avoid becoming involved in these affairs, for again and again, the minorities appealed for help in their battles, not only to the federal Parliament, in which French Quebeckers participated, but even directly to the Quebec press and population.

The entry of the North-West into the dominion involved the first such conflict, and it dragged on long after the passing of the Manitoba Act. The question of an amnesty for participants in the Red River uprising remained unresolved until 1875, while extremists – usually from Ontario – encouraged the use of violence, especially against the French-Catholic Métis.[59] The arrest of Ambroise Lépine in 1873, and his trial the following year, for the murder of Thomas Scott, as well as Riel's expulsion from the Commons in 1874, were aspects of a continuing crisis at whose centre was the French-Catholic element. In Manitoba, press campaigns were soon launched against the separate school system and the official use of French.[60] The latter was nearly abolished in 1879 during a provincial cabinet crisis with racial overtones.

Meanwhile, the very advance of white settlement was a threat to the Métis, pushing them out of Manitoba in the 1870s and leading them to rise up, with their Indian allies, in the North-West rebellion of 1885. That rebellion, as well as the controversy surrounding the fate of its leader, Riel, provoked further expressions of anti-French feeling in Ontario and the West.

Two years later, one of a series of territorial ordinances weakened the position that federal legislation of 1875 had given Catholic schools in the territories, and this would be repeated, with increasing provocation of passions at Ottawa (where territorial ordinances were reviewed) until the establishment of the provinces of Alberta and Saskatchewan in 1905.[61]

Meanwhile, in 1890, D'Alton McCarthy's initiative in the House of Commons opened the way to the undoing of the 1877 establishment of the French language in the North-West Territories.[62] The same year saw the disestablishment of French in Manitoba and the beginning of the Manitoba schools controversy. The latter would rage with increasing ferocity, engaging the passions of French Quebeckers to an ever-greater extent, as federal politics became increasingly involved, until it was temporarily resolved by an 1896 compromise. This left the province with the common school system it had given itself in 1890, but allowed certain privileges, in practice, to the French language and Catholic religion, in school districts with sufficiently large French or Catholic enrolments. In a sense, the controversy had been far from a strictly French-Canadian question, since, by the end of the 1890s, less than half of Manitoba's Catholics were of French origin.[63] Nevertheless, the issue had become a French-Canadian national question because of the political atmosphere in 1889–90, in which the Manitoba school law had been passed at the same time as attacks were launched against the French language, and because of the unprecedented involvement of Quebec politics and opinion in the matter.

The school question, as a matter of fact, had already been raised in the first years after Confederation, when the New Brunswick government had passed a common school act, ending the 1858 practice of allowing local school boards to raise tax support for denominational schools. This law, a blow to Catholicism, did not, however, affect the position of the French language in New Brunswick schools.[64] Moreover, when it was passed in 1871, less than half of the province's Catholics were of French origin.[65] Because of this, and because the Acadians were the weakest, worst organized, and least conspicuous part of the Maritime Catholic community, the battle against the common schools was mainly waged by English-speaking Catholics.

Nevertheless, in a series of motions of 1872, 1873, and 1875, the MP John Costigan put the New Brunswick schools question before the federal House of Commons, and, thus, before the French Quebeckers, who, as Catholics, might be expected particularly to concern themselves with it. Costigan's resolutions failed to bring about either disallowance of the school law or a constitutional amendment giving greater protection to Catholic schools. Equally unsuccessful was a Catholic appeal to the courts; the Privy Council upheld the validity of the school law in the summer of 1874.

Nevertheless, Costigan had attracted Quebec's attention, and the aftermath of the Privy Council's decision excited that attention even more. Even before that decision was announced, resistance against the school legislation had led to violence, arrests, and seizures of property to pay taxes. The climax came in January 1875 in the mainly Acadian village of Caraquet. When the province tried to coerce the local school board, violence erupted. Two men were killed and several townsmen arrested.

The seriousness of the situation finally forced both sides to give in. Negotiations between prominent Catholics and the provincial government led to a compromise agreement that summer.[66]

Although the New Brunswick Catholics had appealed to Ottawa for help in their dispute, and although the Caraquet affair had brought the Acadians in particular to the attention of French Quebeckers, the

Acadians remained distinct and separate from the French Canadians. In 1881 the Acadians held their first national congress, bringing together 5,000 delegates from the three Maritime provinces. Half a century after the founding of French Canada's Saint-Jean-Baptiste Society, these Acadians set out to found a national society of their own, and in so doing, they consciously and determinedly rejected the French-Canadian identity. The congress spent much of its time trying to choose an Acadian national holiday. Two dates were proposed: June 24, Saint-Jean-Baptiste day; and August 15, the feast of the Assumption. The former would identify the Acadians with the French Canadians; the latter would distinguish them. Although speakers who favoured the identification were not lacking, it was August 15 that was chosen, after a debate that made clear the desire of the Acadians to remain a people distinct from the French Canadians.[67]

Confederation, then, did not end the ambivalence in the relations between French Quebeckers and the Métis, on the one hand, French Quebeckers and the Acadians, on the other. The one minority that did remain clearly and fully French-Canadian was the Franco-Ontarians. They, too, however, saw some diminution of their cultural privileges in the first decades after Confederation. The unilingual French schools tolerated since the early nineteenth century were rendered bilingual in 1885, and in the following years the religious and racial tensions associated with the Riel affair and the nationalist stances of the Mercier government brought increasingly loud calls for the abolition of the Ontario separate school system. Though these led to no action, pressure on the French language did continue to mount until 1912, when the Department of Education's Regulation 17 made Ontario schools unilingually English.[68]

All these changes in the position of the Acadians, Métis, and Franco-Ontarians were followed much more closely by French Quebeckers after 1867 than they had been before. Confederation, by enabling the minorities to bring their cases to Ottawa, made them, in some sense, the affairs of the French Quebeckers. But there was one more minority, not even resident in Canada, to whom the Quebeckers were also related, and whose tribulations they could also follow with regularity and interest: the Franco-Americans.

Although, as we have seen, there was some movement to Upper Canada after 1783, the old French community continued strong in Michigan after the American Revolution. As late as 1820, when the census showed Michigan had a population of 8,896, most were still French. Settlement, however, soon changed the proportions, and by 1840, five years after Michigan had attained statehood, even the most sanguine estimate could not number its French at more than 15,000 out of a total population of 220,000. In that year, the governor's speech to the legislature was, for the first time, no longer translated into French.[69]

But just as French Canadians moved into Upper Canada after 1850, so they moved, in much greater numbers, to the United States. Indeed, the movement had begun even before mid-century, as we have already seen.[70] This emigration reinforced the French communities in the American West. The Canadian-born population of Michigan grew from 14,000 in 1850 to 88,275 in 1870, and it has been reckoned that over half were French Canadians.[71] Moreover, in the early 1850s, the Abbé Chiniquy led about six or seven thousand French Canadians to Illinois, where they joined an existing French community of about eight thousand and founded a French newspaper, the *Tribune de Chicago.* At the end of the decade, Rameau de Saint-Père wrote that Wisconsin, Minnesota, and Montana were also receiving significant French-Canadian immigration from Quebec.[72]

The great bulk of French-Canadian emigration to the United States, however, was directed to New England. From the time of the Civil War, rapid industrial development created a great demand for labour, and thousands of French Quebeckers moved each year to fill the jobs in New England factory towns. Their numbers were so great that they were able to form entire French-Canadian communities, with parishes of their own, schools, and a French-language press. In the midst of the American melting pot, they kept alive their patriotism and their desire to maintain their national institutions. From 1852 on, Saint-Jean-Baptiste Societies, Lafayette Societies, and Unions Françaises sprang up throughout New England – indeed, across the United States. While British North Americans were planning Confederation, in 1865, these societies were holding the first national convention of French Canadians of the United States.[73]

One thing that helped keep alive French Canadianism in New England was the proximity of Quebec. Distances were short enough that visits could be made, ties to old friends and old places maintained. Quebeckers, too, could easily keep up with the activities of their compatriots across the border. Saint-Jean-Baptiste congresses frequently brought representatives of the two communities together, and Franco-American newspapers, whose columns were frequently reprinted in those of Quebec, also maintained the connection.

Thus, Quebeckers could follow the vicissitudes of Franco-American destinies as closely and with as much interest as those of any other minority. This was significant, because Franco-Americans experienced the same difficulties as the others. They too had their school questions, their difficulties with the English-speaking Catholic clergy, their struggle to maintain their language.[74]

There is a further discussion not on the position of the minorities, but the attitudes of French Quebeckers toward that position. To what extent did the experience of Confederation overcome the old separateness between Lower Canada and the other French-Catholic communities? Did it lead at all to a new sense of solidarity in a wider homeland than the old Lower Canada? What, in fact, were the attitudes of French Quebeckers toward Confederation and the place of their nationality in it? Was their concern for French rights in the other provinces different from their interest in the rights of Franco-Americans?

The answers to these questions will be sought mainly in the press, but also in the pamphlets, private letters, and general literature of Quebec in the first decades of Confederation. We shall look largely at reactions to those critical affairs – school questions, western uprisings, and so on – in which minority rights were so affected. But between crises as well, we shall look for expressions of feeling about the position of the minorities and about Quebec's uniqueness as a French-Canadian country. And underlying all will be the question, What place did French-Canadians see for their nationality in a bilingual Canada, in a separate Quebec?

Merely to ask this sort of question is to look for trouble. After all, are we not asking about "public opinion"? And what was public opinion in nineteenth-century Quebec? Was the ordinary Quebecker even aware of the issues that we are discussing? How much did he know or care about what parliamentarians debated: about Confederation, the New Brunswick schools, or the language question in the North-West?

In 1865, just after the Canadian legislature had debated the Quebec Resolutions, *La Revue Canadienne* had to admit that the mass of ordinary people seemed "indifferent to the project, or didn't understand anything about it. Some said, 'Oh well, I suppose it'll be a good thing!' and the others, 'I don't know – *M. le curé* hasn't breathed a word about it.'"[75] Two years later, when the Confederation project had got as far as the British Parliament, many Lower Canadians still, it seemed, did not know about it:

> There are still a lot of people, especially in the countryside, who may be completely unaware of the fact that while they go quietly about their petty domestic affairs, a new constitution is being prepared for us in the imperial parliament.[76]

Those who opposed Confederation laid much stress on the absence of any sign of mass awareness or support of it. If public opinion was characterized by a profound apathy,[77] if ignorance was widespread, it was because the government carefully avoided publicizing the project, knowing full well that if French Canadians knew what was being planned, they would exert themselves to oppose it.[78] Indeed, the opposition was convinced that there was a public opinion, that it opposed Confederation, and that if only it were consulted, it would express itself clearly enough. It was a chief complaint of the Rouge MPPs that "the people of this province have never had the chance to express their opinion about the confederation plan."[79] Let Macdonald only hold general elections, let him ask the electorate, in the way prescribed by the constitution, whether they shared his views, and he would see Lower Canadians express their opinions in the same way New Brunswickers had done when they voted Tilley out of office in 1865.[80] Would general elections in Canada have produced such results? And would election results, in any case, have proved a reliable guide to public opinion on the question of Confederation? The contrast between the Confederationists' success in Quebec in the general elections of 1867 and their catastrophic defeat in Nova Scotia, the ratification of the Confederation project by a majority of French-Canadian MPs in March 1865, and the success of Confederationists in Lower Canadian by-elections held between the summer of 1864 and the passing of the BNA Act – all this suggests that the Lower Canadian opposition had, in fact, much less support than it claimed to hold.[81] So, perhaps, does the electoral fate of the twenty-one French-Canadian MPPs who voted against Confederation in the legislature. Of those twenty-one men, seven lost their seats in the 1867 federal elections. Three more, who were not candidates themselves, saw their ridings won by Confederationists. Three were re-elected but rallied to Confederation. Only five were re-elected as anti-Confederates, with the last three seats won by new opponents of the scheme.[82]

One of the anti-Confederates who lost his seat in 1867 was J.-F. Perrault of Richelieu riding. A Rouge, Perrault had early announced his opposition to the Quebec Resolutions, and had immediately received this warning from the *Gazette de Sorel:*

> If you want to go on being the MP for Richelieu (and we'd be happy to go on giving you our support) you'll have to respect our wishes and be guided by the views and the desires of your electors ... otherwise, you'll never be re-elected in Richelieu, even though, as far as the interests of the riding itself are concerned, everyone admits that you are a zealous and useful MP.[83]

Was Perrault's defeat, then, a judgement by his electors against his anti-Confederate stand? Can one interpret the 1867 elections in general in this way? It would surely be rash to do so, for close analysis of the campaign suggests that Confederation may often not have been an issue at all.[84] And even if the voters were expressing acceptance of Confederation, would that mean that they had wanted it in the first place? The bishops had told them, after all, that whatever they had thought of the plan before it was adopted, they ought now to accept the *fait accompli* wrought by legitimate authority and to vote for men willing to accept it and make it work.[85]

No, election results are no sure guide to public opinion. If those of 1867 cannot be relied on to tell us what Quebeckers thought of Confederation, can we expect any more from later ones? How can we tell what French Quebeckers felt about the Riel affair from seeing that the Conservatives held Quebec in 1887, though they had lost power provincially as a result of elections held only a few months before? And how much ink has flowed in contradictory attempts to deduce what they thought of the Manitoba schools question from the way they voted in 1896? Elections to federal and provincial Parliaments were simply not public opinion polls – and alas, no such polls were held in the decades with which we are concerned. The claims of the Rouges that a general election on the issue would show opinion to oppose Confederation were as vain as the claims of the Sorel newspaper that voters would punish those MPPs who did not support it. It was easy for partisan editors to claim that public opinion was what they wanted it to be, but neither their own claims nor the elections to which they often appealed can be of great help to us.[86]

In inquiring into attitudes and opinions, then, we are obliged to be content, most of the time, with those that were put into writing or circulated in print. Occasionally we may find that more concrete public behaviour – mass rallies and demonstrations, migrations of thousands of people to one place in preference to another – correspond, somehow, to what was expressed or reported of mass opinion in the press or letters of the time; but in the main, we must depend on opinions that were set down on paper.

But who wrote things in Quebec in the last decades of the nineteenth century? Who read what was written? And how far did Quebeckers in general share the opinions – come to share the opinions – that were put down on paper? As late as 1901, the census reported that only 78 per cent of Quebec's school-age and older population knew how to read and write, while 18 per cent had admitted that they could do neither the one nor the other. Even this represented a considerable accomplishment, for ten years earlier the census had shown that as much as 31 per cent of Quebec's school-age and older population could neither read nor write. And at the time of Confederation, hardly more than half of French-Quebec adults were literate.[87] Apparently, the portion of French Quebeckers who read newspapers was even smaller, for the combined circulation of all French-language newspapers reported in G.P. Rowell's *American Newspaper Directory* for 1873 was equivalent to only about 33 per cent of the number of French-origin families in Quebec (given by the 1871 census). The press, at least around the time of Confederation, would seem, then, to have been read only by a certain class of people – undoubtedly the familiar élite of professionals, clerics, merchants and shop-keepers, and some well-to-do farmers.

Nevertheless, there are reasons for taking it seriously as a guide to opinion. In the first place, both literacy and newspaper circulation increased dramatically in the decades that concern us. By 1889, the total of French-language newspaper circulations reported to the *American Newspaper Directory* had become large enough to cover about 80 per cent of French-Quebec families (1891 census). Clearly, newspapers were growing enormously in this period. Before 1880, only one (*La Minerve* of Montreal) had had a press run of over 10,000. But by 1884, *Le Nouveau Monde* had set a new record with a distribution of 26,400. By the end of the decade, *Le Canadien, La Patrie, La Presse,* and probably *L'Électeur* (though this last did not report its circulation in 1889) had also passed the 10,000 mark. And the age of big circulations was only beginning; the 1890s saw the take-off of the mass-circulation daily in Quebec, as in the rest of Canada.

Moreover, the influence of the press probably did not stop with its actual circulation, for facts and opinions picked up by one reader might be spread to many other people by word of mouth. What an editor wrote one day in his paper, he (or a political colleague) might say the next (or perhaps had said the day before) at a public meeting – at a political picnic or one of those boisterous and often violent political confrontations that, as Paul Rutherford points out, were a kind of nineteenth-century equivalent of our professional hockey games. What's more, in a society in which deference to the *notables* was both a duty in the official ideology and a practice in much of the social life (note the reference to *M. le curé* in the quotation from *La Revue Canadienne,* above), it is not unlikely that what the elite read in the papers was listened to with interest later on by many non-readers.

Certainly, those who wished the support of public opinion seemed to think it important to have newspapers on their side. One has only to glance at the Beaulieu-Hamelin accounts of how papers came to be founded to see how often this politician or that bishop took the initiative in order to create a "healthy" influence on public opinion.[88] Thus, an individual paper was usually the organ of a particular political, religious, or other interest; together, the papers represented the official point of view, that is, the views of the professional-political elite that dominated French-Canadian life in the province. They put forward the ideas that that elite wanted to set before the electorate. What newspapers expressed became the body of "acceptable" ideas, to which politicians or other leaders could refer for justification or legitimation of policies or positions, and in terms of which issues were discussed – at least in so far as they *were* discussed.

In saying this, I am implying that even papers that represented positions as far apart as Rouge and ultramontane nevertheless shared certain common points of view. And indeed, the questions that we have asked of public opinion are particularly the sort to bring out common points of view. For in asking about awareness of the minorities, the sense of belonging to a homeland, feelings of solidarity with French-Catholic groups outside of Quebec, we are not as apt to be answered by party policies or platforms as by more generally held attitudes. We shall, naturally, wish to be aware of these areas of agreement, and when we find them – when we find, moreover, attitudes expressed not only in the newspapers but in the pamphlet literature, letters, novels, even poetry – we shall probably be justified in feeling that we have gotten pretty close to "French-Canadian opinion."

Nevertheless, differences – important differences – will occur, and it is important, therefore, to notice certain changes that appeared in the French-Quebec press during the third of a century that interests us. At the beginning of the period, the French-language press in Quebec was dominated by organs of the Conservative Party or by organs of Church authorities that were careful to support the Conservatives politically. At the time when Confederation was being discussed, the pro-confederation press easily dominated that of the opposition.[89] During the 1870s, the Liberals had continuing difficulty in keeping alive newspapers to compete with the disseminators of Conservative opinion. In the following decade, however, the balance of press power began to change. Thoroughgoing ultramontane-nationalist papers like *L'Etendard* and *La Vérité* achieved prominence. Though they did not support the Liberals, their rebellion against the Bleus helped weaken traditional points of view in Quebec. At the same time, important Liberal papers began to emerge, notably *La Patrie* (1879) and *L'Électeur* (1880). Thus, by the time of the Riel affair, there was a strong opposition press ready to express outrage at the federal government's conduct. In the 1890s, some of the Liberal papers were among those whose circulations soared the highest, while the same decade saw the demise of some of the great names of the old Conservative press. *Le Canadien, Le Journal des Trois-Rivières,* and *La Minerve* disappeared from the scene 1889, 1893, and 1899, to be followed by *Le Monde* and *Le Courrier du Canada* in 1900 and 1901. Even before the Liberal victory in the 1896 elections, the party's newspaper wing had scored impressive triumphs over the Conservatives.

NOTES

1 A.I. Silver, "Introduction," *The French-Canadian Idea of Confederation, 1864–1900* (Toronto: University of Toronto Press 1997), pp. 3–32.

2 Louise Dechêne, *Habitants et marchands de Montréal au XVIIe siècle* (Montreal: Plon 1974), pp. 176–83; also pp. 217–26.

3 *Histoire de l'eau de vie en Canada* (n.p., c. 1705), p. 19.

4 Marcel Giraud, *Le Métis canadien* (Paris: Institut d'Ethnologie 1945), p. 298. The evolution of the meaning of the word *habitant* in Canada during the seventeenth and eighteenth centuries is instructive. Its original signification, of course, was "inhabitant," but it came gradually to mean a "permanent settler in the colony" and finally a "farmer" or "peasant." This seems to reflect the growing distinction between the *real* "inhabitants" of Canada, who remained in the St Lawrence valley and cultivated the land, and the others, who travelled in the interior. See Konrad Fillion, "Essai sur l'évolution du mot *habitant* (XVIIe–XVIIIe siècles)," *Revue d'histoire de l'Amérique Française*, XXIV, 3 (Dec., 1970). This semantic evolution parallels a shift in the distribution of population away from the town where

the interior trade was organized and into the Quebec countryside. See Louise Dechêne, "La Croissance de Montréal au XVIIIe siècle," *RHAF*, XXVII, 2 (Sept., 1973).

5 W.J. Eccles, *The Canadian Frontier, 1534–1760* (Albuquerque: University of New Mexico Press 1974), p. 128. Also Georges Dugas, *Un Voyageur des pays d'en haut* (Montreal: Beauchemin 1890), pp. 123–4.

6 Dechêne, *Habitants et marchands*, pp. 180, 226: "Chaque voyage est un pas de plus vers cette émigration definitive."

7 *Censuses of Canada, 1665–1871* (vol. 4 of the 1871 census; Ottawa: Taylor 1876), pp. 60–1. Unless otherwise indicated, all pre-Confederation population figures in this chapter are based on the figures given in this volume. Les Cèdres is about twelve miles west of Montreal island, or halfway to the present-day Ontario border.

8 Télesphore Saint-Pierre, *Histoire des Canadiens du Michigan et du Comté d'Essex, Ontario* (Montreal: La Gazette 1895), pp. 182–4. Saint-Pierre reported, though, that by the turn of the century the Detroit parish still numbered 1,800, while Sandwich parish counted no more than 1,000 souls (p. 192).

9 Leopold Lamontagne, "Ontario: The Two Races," in Mason Wade and J.-C. Falardeau, eds., *Canadian Dualism / La Dualité canadienne* (Toronto: University of Toronto Press 1960), p. 353. The policy was not ill advised, especially since the association of British authority with the maintenance of the fur trade had already attracted the sympathies of the French traders. Thus, according to Saint-Pierre, 400 Franco-Ontarians participated in Brock's 1812 campaign against Detroit (p. 204), while the French of the Michigan interior took Michilimackinac for the British that same year (p. 201).

10 See Jacques-Yvan Morin, "Les Origines historiques du statut particulier," *RHAF*, XX, I (June, 1966). Though Morin is interested only in the *legal* status of Quebec within the context of the British Empire and British-dominated Canada, his quotation from William Pitt referring to the 1791 constitutional act (p. 8) shows clearly that legal status depended on effective occupation of territory. As for the influence of population on the authors of the Quebec Act, one need only recall, for example, the oft-quoted argument of Governor Carleton, that "barring Catastrophe shocking to think of, this Country must, to the end of Time, be peopled by the Canadian Race."

11 Emery LeBlanc, for example, in *Les Acadiens* (Montreal: Editions de l'Homme 1963), p. 19, calculates that more than 9,500 were sent to various parts of the British Empire, not counting those who escaped to the woods or made their way to Quebec. But Rameau de Saint-Père, in *La France aux colonies* (Paris: A. Jouby 1859), p. 42, claimed there were only 9,215 Acadians

altogether in Nova Scotia on the eve of the expulsion. Naomi Griffiths, in *The Acadians: Creation of a People* (Toronto: McGraw-Hill Ryerson 1973), p. 60, reckons the Acadians numbered about 10,000 in 1755, and that about 8,000 were expelled. A most detailed attempt to trace the movements of the Acadian population was made by the compilers of the 1871 census, who based their work not only on eighteenth-century censuses, but on a wide variety of documents in French and British archives. In their introduction to *Censuses of Canada, 1665–1871,* they reckoned that 18,500 Acadians lived in the Maritimes in 1755, of whom 8,200 were on the Nova Scotia peninsula, 3,000 on Cape Breton, an equal number on Prince Edward Island, and the remainder in what would become New Brunswick. The expulsion of that year hit 6,000 from the peninsula, while 1,000 more appear to have fled to Prince Edward Island and New Brunswick. By 1758, after the fall of Louisbourg, another 2,000 or even 3,000 more appear to have been expelled from Cape Breton and the Shediac district of New Brunswick.

12 Robert Rumilly speaks of this hiding-out in the woods in his *Histoire des Acadiens* (2 vols.; Montreal: Fides 1955), II, ch. 43. The authors of *Censuses of Canada, 1665–1871* reckon that the real numbers of Acadians still in the Maritimes were far higher than what the 1767 census showed. They give a total of 10,150 for the year 1765: 2,500 in Nova Scotia (of whom 800 were on Cape Breton), 1,400 on Prince Edward Island, and the rest in New Brunswick. These figures, again, are much higher than those of Antoine Bernard, who, in his *Histoire de la survivance acadienne* (Montreal: Les Clercs de Saint-Viateur 1935), pp. 30–1, estimates there were only 2,800 Acadians in the Maritimes by 1763, of whom 1,000 were in New Brunswick, 1,000 on the Nova Scotia peninsula, and 400 each on Cape Breton and Prince Edward Island.

13 LeBlanc, p. 22. Antoine Bernard, in his account of Mgr Denaut's 1803 tour of the Maritimes, reports (p. 79) that the bishop confirmed 8,800 souls in the faith, but makes no distinction between Acadians and other Catholics. It may be that LeBlanc has assumed all these Catholics were Acadians.

14 Rameau, p. 92.

15 *Census of Canada, 1870–71* (Ottawa: I.B. Taylor 1873), vol. 1; and *Censuses of Canada, 1665–1871,* p. xxvi.

16 Rumilly, II, ch. 43. On the return from exile and early isolation, see also Griffiths, pp. 73–6, and Rameau, chs. 5–6.

17 Rumilly, II, 705, 711.

18 Bernard, p. 136.

19 Rumilly, II, 794–5, 789–91, 798–9, 862–5, etc. Also see Martin Spigelman, "Race et religion: Les Acadiens et la hiérarchie catholique irlandaise du

Nouveau-Brunswick," *RHAF*, XXIX, 1 (June 1975), pp. 69–85, especially pp. 73–4 and 79–81.

20 Rameau, p. 113. In 1885, H.R. Casgrain wrote that since the expulsions the Acadians had been virtually without any means of instruction. See his *Un Pèlerinage au pays d'Evangeline* (Quebec: Demers 1888), p. 23.

21 LeBlanc, pp. 46–7; Rumilly, II, 688.

22 Rumilly, II, 688. Although most Nova Scotia restrictions on Catholic education were removed in 1786, poverty and lack of priests still retarded the establishment of Acadian schools. See G.A. Rawlyk and Ruth Hafter, *Acadian Education in Nova Scotia*, Study No. II (Ottawa: Royal Commission on Bilingualism and Biculturalism 1970), p. 6.

23 Rumilly, II, 688. Bernard, p. 148. This sailor became the first French-speaking MP from the Maritimes. He was Auguste Renaud.

24 LeBlanc, p. 47; Rumilly, II, 727–8; Rawlyk and Hafter, pp. 13–14.

25 LeBlanc, p. 47.

26 Rumilly, II, 749. The 1858 act did not actually recognize Catholic schools as such, but it left local school boards so much autonomy that in Catholic areas they were able to make their public schools Catholic in practice.

27 Ibid., p. 718. Also, Spigelman, pp. 76–7.

28 It was *Le Moniteur Acadien*, published at Shediac, N.B.

29 LeBlanc, p. 82.

30 Rameau, p. 110; Rumilly, II, 735; Bernard, pp. 99–100.

31 Rumilly, II, 735.

32 *La Revue Canadienne* (Montreal), III, 5 (May 1866), p. 316, observed that even the prospect of being united with the French Canadians did not seem to make Confederation attractive to the Acadians. Indeed, Griffiths notes (p. 80) that at Confederation the Acadians "knew nothing of 'Bas Canada, sinon qu'il y avait, à Québec et à Montréal, des Français qui s'appelaient des Canadiens.'"

33 Rumilly, II, 738.

34 *Le Moniteur Acadien*, 8 July 1867.

35 C.B. Sissons, *Bi-lingual Schools in Canada* (Toronto: Dent 1917), pp. 17–22, 30.

36 Saint-Pierre, p. 220.

37 *Census of Canada, 1870–71*, vol. 1, showed that the Quebec-born were 52 per cent of the French-origin population in Prescott county, 59 per cent in Russell, 85 per cent in Ottawa, 82 per cent in Nipissing County, and 71 per cent in Renfrew North. This is based on the assumption that in these areas, whose French-origin population was growing spectacularly, and where there was an emigration of English Canadians, virtually all the Quebec-born settlers were French Canadians.

38 André Beaulieu and Jean Hamelin, *La Presse québécoise des origines à nos jours* (vol. 2; Quebec: Presses de l'Université Laval 1975), p. 151. The last issue of *Le Canada* was followed within days by the first of a new French newspaper, and so it continued.
39 And 1,565 whites. These are probably the most frequently quoted and easily accessible census figures in Canadian history. See, e.g., G.F.G. Stanley, *The Birth of Western* Canada (London: Longmans Green 1936), p. 13; W.L. Morton, *Manitoba: A History* (Toronto: University of Toronto Press 1957), p. 145; A.G. Morice, *Histoire abrégée de l'Ouest canadien* (St Boniface 1914), p. 89, Auguste-Henri de Trémaudan, *Histoire de la nation métisse dans l'Ouest canadien* (Montreal 1936).
40 A.S. Morton, *A History of the Canadian West to 1870–71* (London: Nelson n.d.) p. 802.
41 J.-N. Provencher, *Mémoire ou notice sur l'établissement de la mission de la Rivière-Rouge* (Rome 1836), p. 2.
42 J.J. Hargrave, *Red River* (Montreal: Lovell 1871), p. 466.
43 Marcel Giraud, pp. 631–2.
44 A.S. Morton, p. 804.
45 This is expressed clearly in Louis Riel's explanation to the Council of Assiniboia of why his people had resisted the Canadian takeover. The English half-breeds, less dependent on the hunt than their French cousins, and for some time increasingly accustomed to associate with immigrants from Ontario, were less eager to block the Canadian takeover. Indeed, Frits Pannekoek argues that religious hostility toward the Catholic Métis had led them, well before 1869, to identify themselves actively with the Ontarians and to seek Canadian annexation as a desirable thing. See Pannekoek's article, "The Rev. Griffiths Owen Corbett and the Red River Civil War of 1869–70," *Canadian Historical Review*, LVII, 2 (June 1976), pp. 133–49.
46 Fernand Ouellet, *Histoire économique et sociale du Québec, 1760–1850* (2 vols.; Montreal: Fides 1971), II, 473.
47 United States Department of Commerce and Labor, Bureau of the Census, *A Century of Population Growth* (Washington 1909), p. 226.
48 Jean Hamelin and Yves Roby, *Histoire économique du Québec, 1851–1896* (Montreal: Fides 1971), p. 66.
49 Public Archives of Canada: Mouvement Anti-Unioniste, Bas-Canada, 1822–1825: Papers (MG 24, B22): Copies of petitions, especially pp. 4, 9, 19, 21–2, 93. These ideas were also repeated in the Reform polemics of the 1820s and 1830s. See, e.g., D.-B. Viger, *Analyse d'un entretien sur la conservation des établissemens du Bas-Canada* ... (Montreal: James Lane 1826), p. 31;

or Papineau's speech in *Chambre d'assemblée, vendredi, 21 février, 1834* (n.p., n.d.), pp. 32–3.

50 Indeed, the Union of the Canadas soon became a sort of semi-federalism. See, e.g., William Ormsby, *The Emergence of the Federal Concept in Canada, 1839–1845* (Toronto: University of Toronto Press 1969).

51 Expressions or reflections of this theory can be seen in the most varied sorts of works – e.g., Douze missionnaires des townships de l'est, *Le Canadien émigrant* (Québec: Coté et Cie 1851), p. 17; Stanislas Drapeau, *La Colonisation du Canada envisagée au point de vue national* (Quebec: Lamoureux 1858), p. 4; L.J.C. Fiset, *Jude et Grazia* (Quebec: Brousseau et Frères 1861), pp. 17, 24; *La St-Jean-Baptiste à Québec en 1865* (Quebec: Duquet et Cie 1865), p. 36; *Coup d'oeil sur la colonisation* (Montreal: Plinguet et Laplante 1865), p. iv, etc., etc. All these equated French Canada with Lower Canada.

52 Louis-François Laflèche, *Quelques considérations sur les rapports de la société civile avec la religion et la famille* (Trois-Rivières 1866), pp. 70, 23–5.

53 The Red River uprising of 1869–70 brought an extension of French language rights, when the Manitoba Act of 1870 applied to that province the same provisions that Section 133 had applied to Quebec. French enjoyed its official status in Manitoba, however, only until 1890. Another section of the Manitoba Act was intended to give stronger protection to Catholic separate schools than was provided by the 1867 act, but in the end it proved as frail a reed as Section 93 itself.

54 These and the following population figures come from vol. 1 of each of the appropriate federal censuses. In Montreal, the French-origin population grew from 48 per cent of the total in 1861 to 56 per cent in 1881. By 1901, in Montreal City itself, it was still 56 per cent, though in the greater Montreal urban area it was much stronger. Even in Montreal City, though, it had grown from 43,509 in 1861 to 114,245 in 1901.

55 This was also different from the experience of the French British Columbians, whose numbers increased five-fold between 1881 and 1901. Despite this growth, however, the French element in B.C. remained insignificant, constituting only 1.9 per cent of the province's population in 1881 and still only 2.6 per cent in 1901.

56 In those three decades the Canadian population grew by 52.6 per cent, from 3,485,761 to 5,318,606. In the same period the population of the Canadian prairies grew by over 1200 per cent, from about 30,000 to well over 410,000. In the single decade of the 1880s, Manitoba's population jumped by 145 per cent, and the rest of the prairies' by 158 per cent. In 1871, less than 1 per cent of Canadians lived on the prairies; by 1901, almost 8 per cent lived there.

57 The 1881 census showed that of 41,512 Manitobans who had not been born on the Canadian prairies, almost half – 19,125 – came from Ontario. A further 8,161 had been born in the United Kingdom, but only 4,085 in Quebec (including, of course, English Quebeckers). The Ontario-born were, in fact, more than twice as numerous as any other group in Manitoba, save only those born in the province itself.

58 Even considering that many who moved to Manitoba from the United States had probably been born in Quebec, the disproportion seems striking.

59 E.g., see George Taylor Denison, *The Struggle for Imperial Unity* (London: Macmillan 1909), pp. 42–3; A.G. Archibald's testimony in Canada, Parliament, *Rapport du Comité spécial sur les causes des troubles du territorie du Nord-Ouest en 1869–70* (Ottawa: Taylor 1874), p. 140; A.-A. Taché, *L'Amnistie* (Montreal: Le Nouveau Monde 1874), p. 59.

60 R.O. MacFarlane, "Manitoba Politics and Parties after Confederation," in the Canadian Historical Association, *Report*, 1940, p. 48. By 1877, Archbishop Taché had been obliged to take to print in defence of the separate schools. See A.-A. Taché, *Denominational or Free Christian Schools in Manitoba* (Winnipeg: Standard Printing 1877).

61 The use of French was similarly limited in territorial schools. The 1892 ordinance restricted it to the first two years in classes where children did not understand English. In 1930, Saskatchewan would further restrict even this much use of French. See G.F.G. Stanley's essay in Wade and Falardeau, p. 330.

62 McCarthy's bill was amended to permit a partial disestablishment of French, and the territorial council took advantage of the permission in 1892.

63 *Fourth Census of Canada*, 1901, vol. 1, showed 35,672 Catholics in Manitoba, but a French-origin population of only 16,021.

64 French-Canadian historiography has consistently, but wrongly assumed that the French language was aimed at by this legislation. But see, e.g., Maud Hody, "The Anglicising Common Schools Act of 1871: A Study in Folklore," in the Société Historique Acadienne, *19e Cahier* (Apr.–June 1968), pp. 347–9. Also Report of the Royal Commission on Bilingualism and Biculturalism, book II: "Education" (Ottawa: Queen's Printer 1968), p. 44.

65 The 1871 census showed that 47 per cent of New Brunswick's Catholics were of French origin. By 1881, the proportion had become 52 per cent.

66 This account is based mainly on Rumilly's *Histoire des Acadiens*, II, 760ff. The 1875 compromise provided that nuns and priests could obtain certification without attending the provincial teachers' college, and that they would be allowed to wear clerical costume in the classroom; formal religious instruction could be given in the classroom after normal school

hours; textbooks containing material offensive to Catholic consciences could be amended or replaced for schools in Catholic areas; and Catholic children could be allowed to attend school outside their own district if the local board of a Catholic area accepted them. Rumilly mistakenly asserts that permission to use the French language was also part of the 1875 compromise; but French, in fact, had never stopped being used. As for the men arrested at Caraquet, they were eventually released, but only after one had been convicted of murder and then had the conviction quashed.

67 LeBlanc, pp. 30–3. See also Griffiths, p. 80.

68 See Robert Choquette, *Language and Religion: A History of English-French Conflict in Ontario* (Ottawa: University of Ottawa Press 1975).

69 Saint-Pierre, pp. 206, 217–18.

70 Above.

71 Saint-Pierre, p. 221. He calculated that the French-origin population constituted about 6 per cent of Michigan's total in 1870. It is interesting to note that the 1871 census set the French-origin group at only 4.7 per cent of Ontario's population.

72 Rameau, pp. 173–4.

73 This convention saw expressions of hostility toward the project of Confederation in British North America, and calls for annexation of Canada to the United States. Such a move, by uniting Lower Canadians with their compatriots in New England, would reinforce the position of the latter by forming a large, solid, French-Canadian bloc in the northeastern United States – a bloc strong enough numerically to resist assimilation, dominate the area, and exert considerable influence even at Washington. See E. Hamon, *Les Canadiens-Français de la Nouvelle-Angleterre* (Quebec: Hardy 1891), pp. 129–30. This 1869 Detroit convention of Franco-Americans passed a series of annexation resolutions, but the idea lost support soon after, and was hurt beyond revival when one of its leading advocates, Médéric Lanctôt, publicly abandoned Catholicism. (Saint-Pierre, pp. 233–46.)

74 Robert Rumilly, *Histoire des Franco-Américains* (Montreal 1958), pp. 45, 113, 122–4, 129–30, 138, 146–7, etc.; Hamon, pp. 57–61, 75–86; G.F. Thériault, "The Franco-Americans of New England," in Wade and Falardeau, pp. 405–7.

75 *La Revue Canadienne*, 11 (1865), p. 240.

76 *Le Pionnier de Sherbrooke*, 9 March 1867.

77 *Le Défricheur* (L'Avenir), 7 Feb. 1866.

78 *L'Union Nationale* (Montreal), 8 November 1864.

79 *Représentation de la Minorité parlementaire du Bas-Canada à Lord Carnarvon, Secrétaire des Colonies …* (Montreal: Le Pays 1866), p. 3.

80 Ibid., pp. 6, 9–10. Also, *La Confédération couronnement de dix années de mauvaise administration* (Montreal: Le Pays 1867), pp. 10–13; *Le Pays* (Montreal), 27 March 1867; *L'Ordre* (Montreal), 1 July 1867.

81 The suggestion is accepted, at any rate, by J.-C. Bonenfant, e.g., in "L'Esprit de 1867," *RHAF*, XVII, I (June 1963), p. 34; also in his *La Naissance de la Confédération* (Montreal: Leméac 1969), p. 10.

82 Based on information in Jean-Paul Bernard, *Les Rouges: libéralisme, nationalisme et anti-cléricalisme au milieu du XIXe siècle* (Montreal: Les Presses de l'Université du Québec 1971), pp. 295–311; in Henry J. Morgan, *The Canadian Parliamentary Companion* (Montreal: The Gazette 1871); and in Marcel Hamelin, *Les Premières années du parlementarisme québécois* (Quebec: Les Presses de l'Université Laval 1974), pp. 17–25. The anti-Confederationists were beaten even worse in the 1867 Quebec provincial elections. Only five of the twenty-one ridings whose French-Canadian MPPs had voted against the Quebec Resolutions returned anti-Confederates, and one of the five men elected was so moderate in his opposition that he soon crossed the floor and ran as a Bleu in the following election.

83 *La Gazette de Sorel*, 21 Jan. 1865. Perrault was a candidate in the federal election only, in 1867, but his riding also elected a Bleu provincially.

84 See Marcel Hamelin, *Les Premières années*, p. 24: "L'étude de la campagne au niveau local ne nous permet pas de considérer les élections de 1867 comme un plébiscite sur la Confédération." Hamelin argues that in most ridings it was strictly local questions and not the great theme of Confederation that determined how people voted. Jean-Paul Bernard, in *Les Rouges*, contends that Confederation was, in fact, an important issue in the campaign, but so much mixed up with other issues, particularly the conflict between the clergy and liberalism, that its significance cannot be isolated. "Ainsi," he writes (p. 296), "les élections ont-elles permis de mesurer le sentiment populaire face à la Confédération et les forces relatives du clergé et des Rouges, sans qu'il soit possible de distinguer une chose de l'autre."

85 The bishops of Tloa, Trois-Rivières, St-Hyacinthe, and Rimouski, in *Nouvelle constitution du Canada* (Ottawa: Le Canada 1867), pp. 54, 61–2, 66, 78ff.

86 While Rouges claimed that opinion was against Confederation, Bleu supporters wrote with apparently equal conviction that the Lower Canadian population was mightily pleased with the scheme, or even that the very idea of Confederation arose from a groundswell of public opinion. See, e.g., *La Gazette de Sorel*, 1 Sept. 1866, and 29 June 1867; J.-C. Taché, *Des Provinces de l'Amérique du Nord et d'une union fédérale* (Quebec: Brousseau

1858), pp. iii, 7; *Le Courrier du Canada* (Quebec), 4 July 1867; *Le journal de Québec*, 2 July 1867.

87 For elaboration on the last figure and on much of what follows in this section, see Paul Rutherford, *The Making of the Canadian Media* (Toronto: McGraw-Hill Ryerson 1978), especially pp. 29–37, 48–53.

88 André Beaulieu and Jean Hamelin, *La Presse québécoise des origines à nos jours*, vol. 1 (Quebec: Les Presses de l'Université Laval 1973); pp. 113–14 on the founding of the *Mélanges Religieux*; p. 204 on the *Courrier du Canada*, vol. 2 (PUL, 1975); p. 65 on the *Journal des Trois-Rivières*; p. 106 on *Le Nouveau Monde*; pp. 188–9 on *Le National*; p. 288 on *La Patrie*, etc., etc. During the whole of the period we shall be looking at – even in the 1890s, when the mass-circulation paper financed by advertising was beginning to appear – the French-Quebec press remained highly partisan and closely connected with political or other interests that could become its patrons. Not only did newspapers often depend on government printing contracts or other forms of political patronage for their survival, but journalists often looked for appointment to public positions at the end of periods of faithful journalistic service. Frequently, journalists were also party organizers (Arthur Dansereau, for example) or even politicians. Hector Langevin, Joseph Cauchon, Wilfrid Laurier, Honoré Mercier, and Joseph-Israel Tarte were only a few of an enormous number of men who either passed from journalism to politics, or practised both professions at the same time.

89 At Trois-Rivières, Sorel, and (after the middle of 1866) Sherbrooke, pro-Confederation papers were the only ones published. At St-Hyacinthe each side was represented, but the weak anti-Confederate organ collapsed in 1868, while the *Courrier* is still published today. At Quebec City, the combined 1873 circulations of the pro-Confederation *Journal de Québec* and *Courrier du Canada* (1873 was the first year for which Rowell's directory is available) exceeded by four-to-three that of *Le Canadien*, which in any case did not oppose the principle of Confederation, but only details of the Quebec Resolutions. In the Eastern Townships, *Le Défricheur* opposed Confederation, but it collapsed in 1866 (at the age of four years) just after two new pro-Confederation papers had appeared in the area. At Montreal there were three anti-Confederate papers, *L'Ordre*, *L'Union Nationale*, and *Le Pays*, but not one of them was still publishing when Rowell's first directory appeared in 1873. In that year, in any case, the Bleu *La Minerve* had a circulation greater than all the rest of the Montreal press combined. Finally, Quebec's only review journal, *La Revue Canadienne*, also supported Confederation.

# VI

# The East, Ontario, and the West

The preamble to the *British North America Act, 1867* begins: "Whereas the Provinces of Canada, Nova Scotia and New Brunswick have expressed their desire to be federally united ..." Prosaic as they are, these words draw our attention to two fundamental characteristics of the pact of 1867. The first is the pluralism and particularity of the original initiative. Where the U.S. Constitution begins from a foundation created by a single political community – "We, the People" – the Canadian constitution stresses the heterogeneity represented by "the Provinces." The second characteristic is that these several provinces "expressed their desire," that is, they consented to be "federally united." This section of the anthology brings together scholarship that focuses on the various and different paths by which the "provinces ... expressed their desire" (or not, at least not immediately) to be part of the new Canada.

In these selections, any sense of the inevitability about Canada – in its creation, political development, and growth – is quickly lost. While it can be easy to fall into a sense of an historical tide, in which empire, capitalism, and domestic power curtail local options and bring about a country along the lines we see today, such a perspective discounts the importance of the local stories, competing visions, and even the role of chance. It was not at all clear that Prince Edward Island or British Columbia would in the end sign on to Confederation, let alone

Newfoundland. Nor was the West, initially, Canada's to govern – as it would quickly find out.

The situation in the Maritime Provinces was varied, complex, and contested. George Wilson's article, which first appeared in 1928, demonstrated how, in New Brunswick, the local governor, Albert Gordon, intervened frequently and decisively to ensure that the Confederation project went ahead, even in the face of stubborn resistance. P.B. Waite examines the politics of Nova Scotia in his book *The Life and Times of Confederation,* demonstrating how the plan had wide support in the colony but was not unanimously well received. Phillip Buckner's well-known reassessment of the Maritimes and Confederation combats head-on the myth that Maritime opposition to Confederation reflected the region's "conservatism" and risk aversion. And Waite (appearing once again), while disagreeing with a number of Buckner's conclusions, nevertheless supplies ample evidence from newspaper accounts of the sophistication of the public debate.

J.M.S. Careless's magisterial biography of George Brown provides an excellent perspective on elite opinion in Ontario at the time of Confederation. In studies of Canadian regionalism, Ontario is often excluded on the grounds that, for better or worse, Ontario does not see itself as a region but as a virtual proxy for Canada. Careless shows that, on the contrary, George Brown thought of Ontario on its own terms and in light of its own "sectional" interests. And Careless tells the story of how Ontario's participation in the Confederation pact – its "desire to be federally united" – depended crucially on calculations and decisions by a political elite led by George Brown, leader of the Grits.

W.L. Morton picks up the narrative from there to show in detail that Manitoba's accession to provincehood in 1870 had much more to do with strategic calculations about the possibility of American expansionism and negotiating the purchase of Rupert's Land from the Hudson's Bay Company than it did with any grand principle of colonial self-government in which local populations "expressed their desire" to join Canada. Indeed, he argues that it was precisely the lack of consultation with the local population – both settler and Indigenous – that led to later troubles. Here, too, there is a nice contrast with the process in British Columbia, where full responsible government and generous terms became part of the terms of B.C's accession in 1871. Doug Owram, in the excerpt from his well-known book *Promise of Eden,* tracks how the idea of expansionism to the west both captured the imagination of eastern commercial interests and profited from up-to-date scientific surveys in the 1850s.

# "Nova Scotia"

## *The Life and Times of Confederation, 1864–1867* 1962

P.B. WAITE[1]

In 1864 Nova Scotia had a population of about 350,000, which was distributed around the rocky perimeter of 4,500 miles of coast and along the great swale of the Annapolis Valley. Nova Scotia was part of the North American continent only by virtue of a neck of land twelve miles wide, and it was the classic *paenensula,* near island in shape, outlook, and attitudes. The long coastline – ten times the length of the province – nurtured an economy now approaching maturity and within two decades of obsolescence. Nova Scotian ships sailed the oceans of the globe. "In the ports of the Seven Seas and the waters thereof," wrote Frederick William Wallace, "the terms 'Nova Scotiamen' and 'Bluenose' were known to seamen of all nationalities during the 'sixties.'"[2] New Brunswick built ships and sold them: Nova Scotia built them and sailed them.[3] Wallace described one, seen in 50° south, between Cape Horn and Australia:

> … the stranger came storming up out of the west into plain sight. She was a big ship – a wooden three-master, black-hulled, heavily sparred, and deep laden – and she was forging through the long green seas with yards almost square…. This exhibition of sail-carrying in a heavy breeze, the well-set and well-trimmed masts and yards, the faultlessly stayed masts, and general spotless appearance of the ship evoked … murmured admiration…. "Hard packets these Bluenose ships. Worse than the Yankees, they say."[4]

She was a Nova Scotiaman, run like a New Englander, but flying the Red Ensign, and she was a symbol both of the origins and of the present strength of Nova Scotia.

Nova Scotia was near the zenith of her commercial prosperity. "Our province," said the *Morning Chronicle,* December 18, 1865, "is prosperous beyond example.... We are on the full tide of prosperity under the lowest tariff in America." The decades immediately following the mid-century provided a prosperity that Nova Scotia had not seen before or would again. The iron hull – the real nemesis of Nova Scotian shipbuilding – had not yet appeared; the steam engine and the screw propeller had not affected the basis of her carrying trade. The inshore and offshore banks provided the fisheries; larch, spruce, pine, and white oak, the wood; fifty or sixty snug harbours, the opportunity. The rest was up to human hands. These were not idle. "At no previous period in the history of this province has there ever been as much capital invested in shipping and ship-building, as at the present."[5] This was the opinion of the *Morning Chronicle* in 1863. By 1867 the tonnage of Nova Scotian-owned ships amounted to 350,000 – one ton for every inhabitant – and 75 per cent more than New Brunswick, Nova Scotia's nearest rival.

Nova Scotia had at that time a major role in sea communications between Britain and the United States. Ships westward bound to New York and Boston called regularly at Halifax. Ships eastward bound to Liverpool and London also called. In fact, the south shore of Nova Scotia looked out upon the whole periphery of the Atlantic. Bermuda seemed closer than Quebec. The British Empire had in consequence a meaning for Nova Scotia that it had for no other province. The empire was tangible. The forces that held it together were real and powerful. It was natural for Joseph Howe to prefer empire solidarity to visions of a continental North American domain. Where was the reality of empire in the wilderness of rock and forest that lay north and west, behind Nova Scotia? The lines of communication across the accessible ocean were broad and easy: those across the hills and distances of British North America were tortuous and remote. Surely with such a capital as London, said Howe, "we need not seek for another in the backwoods of Canada, and may be pardoned if we prefer London under the dominion of John Bull to Ottawa under the dominion of Jack Frost."[6] And, Howe asked, "Is Halifax ... so poor an outlook for an orator...?"[7]

Halifax, it is true, did not have the grandeur of London. To Dr. Charles Mackay of the London *Times,* it looked like an inferior edition of Portsmouth.[8] The houses were built of wood, often painted a dingy brown, and looked to Canadians as if mechanics might be occupying them. But then a fine carriage with a liveried coachman would drive up in front of them: "... you enquire as to its ownership and find that the person who is the subject of your interrogatory lives in the unpretending domicile of wood...."[9] Thus Charles Belford of the Toronto *Leader*. Halifax was in fact a rich city and it had a rather Georgian character. "There is a courtly air about it ... its bloods drive fast horses ... its ladies dress in the height of fashion, read the latest novels as well in the language of Madame George Sand ... as in their native tongue...."[10] Like St. John's and Charlottetown, Halifax boasted a fine Georgian legislature. Other monuments added lustre: a very expensive Government House for the governor and his entourage; a handsome round church and round clock tower that had been provided by the energy and good taste of Queen Victoria's strident father. But Halifax was still a port; its Water Street differed little from others of the same ilk in St. John's and Saint John: "... with the exception of a few good houses, the whole range of buildings is of the most filthy and inferior description; nearly all of which are petty shops, groceries, and groggeries of the lowest sort, and frequented by innumerable hordes of soldiers and seamen...."[11] The soldiers came from the companies of British artillery, infantry, and engineers who were stationed in the Citadel, a massive stone and earth fortress comprising some 50 acres which commanded the harbour and was the central point in the British defence system of the West Atlantic. Of seamen there was no end. Halifax in summer was the headquarters of both the North American and West Indian squadrons of the British Navy. A regular ship-of-the-line carried 700 men, and sometimes a dozen ships would be in port at once. The groggeries in Water Street never lacked for patrons.

Temperance legislation was still a long way in the future, and not even the Baptists – New Brunswick and Nova Scotia had the largest percentage in British North America – went so far as to seriously advocate outright abstinence in the *Christian Messenger*, which was their paper. This kind of moderation was also characteristic of the religious divisions generally in Nova Scotia. They were not as sharp or as bitter as those in other provinces. J.W. Johnston, the erstwhile Premier, Tupper, the new one, and the Conservative party as a whole had successfully cultivated the Catholic vote, and it did not appear to weaken the party with Protestant voters. Roman Catholics amounted to 25 per cent of the population; another 25 per cent were Presbyterians; Baptists, Anglicans, and Methodists, in that order, followed.

Softened asperities in religion were a concomitant of Nova Scotian political life. It is fair to say that the Nova Scotian equivalent for the Canadian rebellions of 1837 was Howe's Twelve Resolutions. Some were unkind enough to suggest that the relative mildness of the Nova Scotian reaction in 1837 was the result of a lively sense of British favours, past, present, and future. There is no doubt that the British military and naval base in Halifax exercised a chastening influence upon political and social extravagance. But perhaps the differences between Canadian and Nova Scotian political life lay also in the differences between Canadians and Nova Scotians.

In Canadian and Nova Scotian newspapers one is struck by the differences in attack and in outlook. The Canadian newspapers, notably those of Canada West, often have a rough bellicosity, a kind of frontier vehemence; in Nova Scotian papers there is a greater suavity, perhaps a little more old-fashioned dignity. It was possible to sense that Halifax was closer to London than Toronto in thought and feeling. This was not to say that Nova Scotia lacked political energy; on the contrary, as the Halifax *Evening Reporter* said, public opinion in Nova Scotia was, "if anything a little too strongly developed, stronger even than in England. The reason for this is that every man here is more or less a politician…."[12] But in Nova Scotia, politics was sustained and controlled by a rudimentary sense of fair play. Hastings Doyle, the Major-General commanding the forces in the Maritime provinces, wrote Howe in later and more troubled years, "I hope, like a true Briton, you will not kick them [the Confederation party in Nova Scotia] when they are down!" Howe replied characteristically, "The victory has been decisive but I hope it will not be abused."[13] There is no escaping the feeling of vital political energy in Nova Scotia. Even the restlessness of Nova Scotians, their dissatisfaction with the limits of provincial horizons, their search for a new and more satisfying formula of empire, British or British American, supports this. The discussion of Confederation, once started, did not abate until long after July 1, 1867. Editorials on union in all phases and shapes filled the papers; letters to the editor, public debates, and the crowds at the Temperance Hall meetings, all attest the political vitality of Nova Scotia in more spacious days.

Richard MacDonnell, the Lieutenant Governor of Nova Scotia from 1864 to 1865, remarked upon the same thing. MacDonnell never enjoyed very good report either in London or in Halifax, but his despatches, though unsympathetic to Confederation, were often shrewd and they cannot be dismissed merely as partisan opposition to a great cause. "Your ministry," he wrote Monck of Canada, early in 1865,

> ... seem not to have cared how Canadian – selfishly Canadian, they may have appeared to Bluenose who is very happy as he is ... your Ministry seem not to have suspected any rocks or shoals ahead whilst they were in reality trying to steer through a channel full of them ... don't suppose that I question in any way the good faith or ability of your Lordship's Ministers – I simply question their politic manipulation of the subject with so keen a spectator as Bluenose watching the game – [14]

It was sound advice. Nova Scotians were willing to consider union; they had been discussing the subject periodically for years, but they were not ready to be whisked into union simply because Canada was finding her own constitution too difficult to manage. Better reasons than that would have to be urged. Nothing made Nova Scotians more distrustful of Confederation, wrote MacDonnell to Cardwell, "than the strange forgetfulness of Canadian statesmen that they were speaking not merely to a Canadian Parliament but to all these Provinces."[15] If the Canadians still read Confederation in the light of Canadian politics, Nova Scotians could be excused for doing the same. The old feeling of distrust for Canadians appeared again. *Timeo Danaos et dona ferentis* (I fear the Greeks even when offering gifts): MacDonnell's quotation applied all too aptly in Nova Scotia to Canadians bearing Confederation and the Intercolonial Railway. Even Galt's Sherbrooke speech, comprehensive and searching though it was, Tupper found too much from the Canadian point of view.[16] Whelan in Charlottetown underlined the same point in a letter to Galt. "There is one drawback only to the satisfaction which I derived from the perusal of your speech: *You treat the question too much from a Canadian point of view.*"[17]

As in Newfoundland and Prince Edward Island, Confederation crossed political boundaries. In Nova Scotia there was no coalition as there was in Newfoundland in April 1865; the Nova Scotian Liberals continued to oppose the government, notably over the Pictou Railway.[18] In Nova Scotia the position was not unlike that in Prince Edward Island before December 1864; Liberals agreed to support a Conservative Confederation policy. The difference between Nova Scotia and Prince Edward Island was that in the former the Conservative government had, and continued to have, a Confederation policy; in Prince Edward

Island it had disrupted the government and caused the resignation of the premier. The Nova Scotian Liberal leaders, Archibald and McCully, supported Confederation right to the end; and while they were prepared to vote, and did vote, against the government on other issues, they never abandoned Confederation, though under considerable pressure from a wing of their party to do so. Tupper needed such support; he could never have carried Confederation without it. At the same time Archibald and McCully themselves could not have carried Confederation, and they may have believed that they had not the power to defeat it.[19]

Adams G. Archibald, leader of the Opposition in the Assembly and Howe's political heir, was remarkably deft and subtle. He had of course the warrant of an old established family name, which counted as seriously in Nova Scotia as in Boston. He never seems to have lost the respect of his Liberal colleagues, and his position in the party survived until Confederation had been passed in April 1866. Archibald had an air of sweet reasonableness about him which was singularly winning, if rather deceptive.[20] An eye witness described an interview, probably in 1866, between Howe and Archibald when Howe used all his considerable powers of argument and persuasion to get Archibald to break with Tupper. "I remember when Howe in his excitement, standing up appealing to Archibald as his (Howe's) son in political party faith, Archibald sat at the table with his head bowed between his hands as though bending beneath the storm, and, looking over at me, made a grimace and gave me an expressive wink."[21] It said much for Archibald's coolness. Perhaps it was contempt. In 1867 Howe said bitterly, "I loved him like a brother or a son."[22] One is left not so much with admiration for Archibald as sadness for Howe.

Jonathan McCully, leader of the Liberals in the Legislative Council, was much more volatile. McCully was a quick and agile debater; on his feet he was unbeatable for "strong, vigorous, downright dialectics."[23] He took up causes with ease and expounded them with facility; and, except for Howe, he was the most telling writer in the province. He had made the *Morning Chronicle,* in the six years he had been its editor, the most powerful paper in the province and its only daily. But he was not much liked or appreciated and he never had the loyal following of Howe or Archibald. He lacked the tenacity of the former and the integrity of the latter. McCully was probably sincere in his belief in Confederation, but he was facile. He lacked a solid foundation. In this respect he rather resembled his fellow Nova Scotian in Vancouver Island, William Smith

– alias Amor de Cosmos – who until 1863 owned the Victoria *British Colonist*.[24] In Windsor in 1866 Howe remarked on McCully's conversion to Confederation. St. Paul, Howe said, was converted by a flood of light; Danaë was changed from a virgin into a strumpet by a shower of gold; "You, who know the man, can judge whether McCully was converted after the fashion of Danaë or St. Paul."[25]

It was easy to allege insincerity against all three leaders, Tupper, McCully, and Archibald. Tupper, it was true, had lectured on Confederation in 1860, but he had been cool to the idea when it was first broached in the summer past by the Canadians. McCully, and probably Archibald, had been opposed. It was the events from August to October that had changed them. On November 24, the *Halifax Citizen* spoke of

> ... a few ambitious individuals, who feel our legislature too small for their capacity; and its rewards too trifling for their acceptance; who feel anxious to strut in embroidered court suits, plush breeches, silk stockings and bagwigs before a Vice Roy at Ottawa, and enjoy fat salaries, far away from the Provinces whose best interests are to be shamefully voted away in return for a fortnight's feasting and a few private promises.

William Garvie, one of the *Citizen*'s editors, poked fun at the Nova Scotia coalition on Confederation in *Barney Rooney's Letters*:

> "Tupper, alorra," sez McCully, wid a vice as soft as a tub iv Cumberland buther, "considher the claims iv the opposishun."
>
> "Troth will I, McCully mavourneen," sez Tupper, as soft as another tubful iv the same, only twice as big, "afther I look out for number one, as my way is, ye know."[26]

MacDonnell, too, was suspicious. He wrote Cardwell that he could not "allow such a measure [as Confederation] to be decided by the intrigues and influences which both Government and opposition leaders – looking for their reward to Ottawa – could bring to bear on their supporters in the present Parliament." He would have insisted on a dissolution – as Gordon was to do in New Brunswick – had he not been restrained by Cardwell.[27]

It must be said that Confederation came not inopportunely for Tupper. His school legislation of 1864 had made him unpopular. It had imposed a form of direct tax on Nova Scotians by tying school appropriations from the government to assessments levied "voluntarily" by the school districts, and, however farsighted, it was mightily resented. Confederation could serve Tupper's purpose by diverting public attention from awkward issues of provincial politics. "He would annex this Province to Canada, or to Massachusetts, or to the moon, or propose to do so," said the *Halifax Citizen,* November 5, 1864, if it would distract attention. No doubt Confederation was convenient; but it was soon clear that it would, if pressed, be a far more serious danger than the School Act of 1864. Tupper did not hesitate. There was a certain recklessness about Tupper that could be called courage. It was both physical and political, and it was one of Tupper's more endearing qualities.

To his courage Tupper joined a resolute determination and a garrulous tongue. He was an inveterate talker, and the old story of his later years – that Macdonald was the captain of the ship while Tupper supplied the wind for the sails – was only an exaggeration. The description by the Montreal *Gazette* (October 28, 1864) suited him, "forcible, keen, and emphatic," with a "suppressed temptation to sarcasm" in his voice. To Laurier, Tupper seemed "the very incarnation of the Parliamentary athlete…."[28] It took courage to pass the School Act; it was to take more courage to put Confederation through a dying legislature in the face of the probable opposition of at least two-thirds of the province. Tupper was a strong man: his curly black hair that framed his face – he affected a short and not unbecoming form of mutton-chop whiskers – gave him a resemblance to some audacious lion pertinaciously on its way forward.

Tupper and the other Nova Scotian delegates arrived in Nova Scotia early in November. McCully, Archibald, and Henry came via Portland and Saint John, Tupper and Dickey from New York. Public opinion, as in Newfoundland, was at first quiescent, not anticipating perhaps the rapidity with which the delegates were prepared to move, but by the third week in November "cat's paws" were stirring.[29] "We cannot take up a Colonial paper," said the Halifax *Evening Express* on November 14, 1864, "which is not largely occupied with … [Confederation] in some form or other." By early December the cat's paws had become a strong breeze.

As in Newfoundland and Prince Edward Island, the newspapers of the capital functioned in some respects as a metropolitan press. In Nova Scotia the easy communications by rail to Truro and Windsor – both less than three hours away – and by sea along the south shore gave the Halifax papers an important role in the public life of the province. But as in the other two Maritime provinces, the newspapers of the capital were, in respect of Confederation, distinctly misleading. In Nova Scotia there was a remarkable disparity between the Halifax papers and the country papers. The majority of Halifax newspapers supported Confederation; all but one of the country ones opposed it.

The country papers opposed to Confederation included both Yarmouth papers, the *Herald* and the *Tribune,* Conservative and Liberal respectively; the *Liverpool Transcript,* from the south shore; the *Eastern Chronicle* of New Glasgow; and the Bridgetown *Free Press* of the Annapolis Valley. Only the Pictou *Colonial Standard* supported Confederation.[30] The country papers often took the theoretical grounds for their opposition from the pages of the *Halifax Citizen,* and, by 1865, from the Halifax *Morning Chronicle.* They did not generally essay flights of constitutional argument on their own. In this respect they differed from the little Reform papers of Canada West, which stood sturdily on their own two legs in any kind of argument. The real basis of the opposition of the country newspapers to Confederation was their instinctive suspicion of change, and, be it added, of Canada. The Yarmouth papers illustrate this well.

> Are the people of Nova Scotia so discontented with their present system of Government that they are willing to change it at such a cost ...? (*Herald,* December 8, 1864)
>
> We have the trade of the world now open to us on nearly equal terms, and why should we allow Canada to hamper us? (*Herald,* December 15, 1864)
>
> Are the people of Nova Scotia prepared to yield up their flourishing customs revenue to a federal treasury in Canada, there to be squandered in jobbery and corruption? (*Tribune,* November 9, 1864)

Confederation was thought of in Yarmouth as an evil Canadian egg being hatched by politicians in Halifax. And the Intercolonial Railway, which was a long way from many centres in Nova Scotia, offered few advantages to Yarmouth.[31]

In Halifax the situation was reversed. Halifax was in fact the centre of Confederate strength in Nova Scotia. In the 1867 election, when anti-Confederates took eighteen out of nineteen seats in the Dominion House of Commons, and thirty-six out of thirty-eight seats in the Nova Scotian Assembly, it was estimated that the vote in Halifax City (as opposed to Halifax County) was almost two to one in favour of Confederation.[32] In favour of Confederation were most of the Conservative papers, the *British Colonist,* the *Evening Reporter,* and the *Evening Express* (Roman Catholic); two Liberal papers, the *Morning Chronicle*[33] and the *Morning*

*Journal;* all the religious papers, the Baptist *Christian Messenger,* the Methodist *Provincial Wesleyan,* and the Presbyterian *Witness.* That left, in opposition to Confederation, only the Liberal *Citizen,* and the Liberal *Sun,* the latter feeble with the unpopularity of its Civil War policy[34] and the age of its editor. The independent *Acadian Recorder* was uncertain of Confederation and eventually opposed it. The *Bullfrog* appeared late in 1864 edited anonymously by two of the garrison officers and was also opposed.

The most conspicuous feature of the newspaper discussion in Halifax, and to some extent in the province as a whole, was the remarkable support for legislative union of British America. Nowhere, not even in the Montreal *Gazette,* were there such persuasive arguments for the beauty of legislative union and the wickedness of federation. "We seek Union," said *the Evening Express* December 9, 1864, "because we are, in reality, one people and ought to be one nationality...." Upon this premise it was possible to speak, as the *Acadian Recorder* did, of "the superiority of ... a Legislative Union, where the central power would be absolute...." The *Evening Reporter* put it simply: "In this province public opinion has tended in favor of a Legislative Union...." A confederation seemed to the Presbyterian *Witness* "a loose business. A legislative union ... would be far more likely to prove permanently satisfactory."[35] Papers for and against Confederation sounded the same theme, but the heaviest orchestration came from the *Halifax Citizen.*

> History has now satisfactorily proved that Legislative Union is the only lasting Union. Federation is not Union.... It makes no matter that it [the Quebec plan] has given these local legislatures very little to do. The Legislatures have to meet, and having met, they will find something to do, if they have to make employment – to elaborate grievances or increase taxes.... All this is insured by the double legislature system which keeps up the barriers between the different districts of the proposed Union as rigidly as ever and prevents ... the fusion of the British American population in one actual indivisible nationality.[36]

No sooner had Tupper arrived home from New York than he found himself forced to defend the Quebec Resolutions against the charge of being a federation. The whole Confederate press took up the theme that Confederation was a legislative union in all but name. Tupper himself, in the *British Colonist,* November 22, denied that the term "federal" was really applicable.

> We have heard of late a great deal of playing upon words in the use of the term "Federation" and other cognate expressions. People are apt to be misled by words ... like these.... Consequently we, in discussing this subject, purpose dropping the use of such terms.... What the delegates on the Quebec Conference had to provide for was ... a strong Central Government, a sufficiently firm consolidation of the Provinces to insure their acting as an undivided and indivisible unit *in all cases where necessary.*

But British North America, Tupper went on, comprised a vast territory with great diversity of institutions. This made concessions to local governments necessary, even desirable. Local and private bill legislation would be so enormous that no general government could cope with it. Men sitting in the central parliament would not have sufficient local knowledge, nor feel sufficiently the local interest, to deal satisfactorily with local measures. The delegates were forced to make provision for local legislatures. But Tupper affirmed stoutly that

> ... these [local] Legislatures will not be Legislatures in the sense in which we have been used to understand the term. They will be essentially Municipal bodies; for, under the proposed Constitution, their functions will be limited and clearly defined. Nova Scotia, for instance, will be a large Municipality under the Central Government; but just as clearly a municipality as the City of Halifax now is under our Provincial Government....

This municipal nature of the provincial governments under Confederation would, Tupper said, guard against the "absurdity" of local governments assuming sovereign pretensions.

Several revealing analogies were used to develop this theme in the succeeding issues of the *British Colonist,* the most important of which was the New Zealand one. Two issues were devoted to a comparison between the New Zealand constitution of 1852 and the Quebec Resolutions. The pursuit of the same objects, said Tupper, had had the same results. Both constitutions had "endeavoured to secure *a strong General Government* whilst providing for the due protection and proper management of *local interests* by the establishing of subordinate, local, legislative organizations."[37]

Legislative union, Tupper argued, might have been the best thing in the world for British America. There was unfortunately one slight objection to it: it was impossible. "Lower Canada stands in the way. In no practicable way can the difficulty be removed." That being the case, "why babble about Legislative Union?" Federations were unpopular: Tupper admitted that. But federations were not the same everywhere. The principle showed astonishing variations. It could be "as strong or as weak as the people please," and if properly constructed could be "one of the strongest and most durable of States."[38]

Tupper was not alone in his defence of the Quebec Resolutions. He was supported by the *Evening Reporter* and *Evening Express,* both Conservative, and by the powerful Liberal daily, the *Morning Chronicle.* These followed a line similar to Tupper's, with variations. McCully, once he had resigned as the editor of the *Chronicle* and had created the *Unionist,* went even further than Tupper. Some people, McCully said, object that Nova Scotia would be swamped by Confederation. But of course Nova Scotia will be swamped, and in the central government "we hope and believe that Nova Scotia, like each and every one of the other Colonies comprised in it will be effectually swamped; that we shall then hear nothing of any local parties; that then our public men will not be known as Canadians, and New Brunswickers, and Nova Scotians, but only as British Americans."[39]

The religious newspapers supported Confederation with striking unanimity.[40] Of these the Presbyterian *Witness* was the most outspoken. It approved of Tupper's explanations and noted with particular satisfaction the power of disallowance. It was clear from this power, said the *Witness* on November 19, 1864, that "whenever there is a collision between the General and the Local Governments, the latter must always give way." Disallowance was to the *Witness* the final assurance of complete central control. It was precisely this indiscriminate use of disallowance that Christopher Dunkin was concerned about. As described by the *Witness* its use could hardly be confined, not even within the broad limits of Cartier's "unjust or unwise legislation."[41]

The support of the clerical press, and much of the clergy, was only part of the widespread support accorded Confederation by the professional classes. The opinions of the pulpit, the Bench, and the Bar were in fact constantly used as examples by the Confederate papers. The *Acadian Recorder* complained that government papers of Confederate persuasion were continually trying "to shut your mouth by invoking the name of Archbishop Connolly, Bishop Binney [Anglican], the Clergy, the Admiral, General and Governor *and the Judges and the Bar.*"[42] Even doctors were reported to anticipate an enlarged scope for their talents in Confederation.[43]

The opposition to Confederation used two arguments against it. First, Nova Scotia did not want union at all. Second, if there was to be union, federation was the worst possible kind. Howe spoke of Confederation as a monstrous thing, "unlike anything in heaven or on earth or under the earth ... neither an Empire, a Monarchy, nor a Republic."[44] McCully as well as Tupper chided the opposition with inconsistency, for saying one minute that Nova Scotia would be swamped by Confederation and the next that federation was too weak a constitution to last. But it made no difference. Both arguments were effective and both were used. Perhaps the simplest of the opposition views was that of the *Sun*. Why change? The danger it put in terms of the old saw: "I was well – I wished to be better, I took physic – and here I lie."[45]

The *Citizen* was more formidable, and its case cogent enough. Legislative union was impossible, so the *British Colonist* alleged, because of the French Canadians. But need this be? "Is everything to give place to Lower Canadian sectionalism?" Nova Scotia did not need union. She did not have to rush headlong into alliance with a province like Lower Canada, which showed such unreasoning selfishness about the first principle of union. Nova Scotia could wait if these were the conditions; she could afford to wait one year or five years, until Lower Canada outgrew her prejudices.[46] Nor was Upper Canada blameless. Confederation would merely wipe off old scores between the Canadas. Upper Canada would get her "rep. by pop.," Lower Canada her "un-British" system of local autonomy. The Maritime provinces will, however, pay the piper.[47]

The *Acadian Recorder* preached from a similar text but with additional regrets for the loss of Maritime union. If only the Quebec Conference had brought forth legislative union, all would have been well. The *Recorder* believed that "Acadia is ready and anxious to accept it...."[48] But pressure from Lower Canada for federal union was the stronger reason why the consummation of Confederation should be delayed. The division of powers seemed to the *Recorder* a peculiarly glaring example of the evils of federation. Who could have thought that British American statesmen, trained in British institutions, would have attempted "to write the duties and functions of the general government in a list," as if they were merchants making an inventory?[49] No mere stock-taking could ever be complete. The powers of responsible government were in essence unlimited, subject only in the case of the colonies, to ultimate review under the Crown.[50]

The predominant concern of the opposition, before mid-December 1864, had thus been the issue of legislative union. After that time there was a noticeable shift in emphasis. In Tupper's words, they took up "that peculiar line of argument which is perplexing to all and interesting to none": finance. "Every man of them crammed on arithmetic."[51] Tupper expressed contempt for financial arguments, but he knew perfectly well how powerful they were. His letters to Macdonald show plainly that he feared the effects of arguments that used the heavy Canadian debt, the high Canadian tariff, and the expensive double governments of federation to show that Confederation would bleed Nova Scotia white.[52] Tupper even went so far as to direct the argument to the safer levels of constitutional discussion in order to avoid taxation. The opposition should, he said, have laid "more stress … on the beauties of Legislative Union, and the evils of Federation…. The Opposition could have held before the people the example of the United States, and prophesied mourning, lamentation and woe…. The Opposition turned their backs on such resources as these, and took up Finance."[53]

The *Bullfrog* pointed the way, December 17, 1864.

> The financial portion of the Confederation scheme is its most important feature. Since no real Union is in contemplation, but rather a careful bargain between Canada and the Lower Provinces – free trade and an Intercolonial line offered by the former, and a Union which will loose Canada's political deadlock by the latter – the fiscal portion of the agreement assumes a gigantic importance.

The development of this theme began in the public meetings in December in the Temperance Hall on Starr Street. The first was on Friday, December 9, at which Tupper, Archibald, and McCully all duly glorified the powers of the central government.[54] Opposition speakers tried to control a further meeting a week later, but were voted down by the audience and retired. On Friday, December 23, however, the opposition arranged a meeting, and here not only were the familiar arguments against federation recited,[55] but calculations made, and the long battles begun over the arithmetic Tupper so much dreaded – taxation, tariffs, and exports.

The suspicions of the business community were already aroused. The *Evening Reporter* noticed with regret that "our capitalists are in the front rank of the opposition…. Many of our merchants are strenuous opponents of union because union in their estimation means more businessmen, greater competition, less profits, more trouble."[56] The leader in this issue was William Stairs, President of the Union Bank of Halifax, and he gave a major speech on the subject at the meeting on December 23. McCully in the *Chronicle* of December 18 heaped ridicule on Stairs' arguments. "He appeared before the meeting in a galaxy of figures. A Chaldean astronomer, an Egyptian astrologer, could not follow him. Gladstone would have fainted." But Stairs made his point. Basic to his argument was the Nova Scotian 10 per cent tariff that produced 80 per cent of the province's revenue. The prospect of a Canadian tariff of 20 per cent, in exchange for a mere subsidy, gave every merchant pause. Taxation and tariff was now to become too powerful to be dismissed. The *Morning Chronicle* had tried to elevate the issue on December 23: "We have no sympathy with that class of men, whose mental vision is bounded by Dartmouth on the one side, and Citadel Hill on the other. It is not the building of a Town-house we are discussing; we are engaged in laying the foundation of an Empire." But empire or not, by the end of December, joint meetings in Windsor on December 28 and Halifax on December 30 and 31 – with Temperance Hall jammed with people – had raised the issue of tariff and taxation in unequivocal terms. Opposition speakers hammered away relentlessly both at these issues and at Canada's lurid financial history. It was not long before scarcely seven merchants along the whole two miles of wharves, chandlers, and brokerages that was the Halifax waterfront were in favour of Confederation.[57] Governor MacDonnell told Cardwell that the opponents of Confederation included men "of the highest social standing here, and in fact comprise most of the leading bankers and merchants, the wealthiest farmers, and the most independent gentlemen in the Province...."[58]

At this point – January 1865 – the struggle going on behind the scenes for the control of the policy of the *Morning Chronicle* finally broke into the open. The *Morning Chronicle* had long been owned by William Annand, Liberal member for Halifax County in the Assembly and the Inspector-General in the late Howe administration. Annand had, in 1857, persuaded Jonathan McCully to take the post of editor. On July 1, 1864, Thomas Annand, a son, had turned over supervision of the paper to his brother Charles, and although the father continued, as before, to wield a strong influence, he was in England during the crucial period, August to November 1864. It was in that time that McCully, the editor, was able to use his influence to make the policy of the paper strongly Confederate. When William Annand returned he asked McCully not to compromise the paper and the Liberal party any further, but the Liberal party was already compromised, and McCully, by now as "full of glory as Lucy Neal,"[59] had no intention of abandoning Confederation.[60] At the end of December when, as a result of the Temperance Hall meetings, the differences between the two men were obvious and public, Annand went to Howe and asked Howe if he should not fire McCully. Howe would not commit himself, but Annand apparently had already made up his mind.[61] On January 10, 1865, a brief notice appeared in the *Morning Chronicle* that the proprietor, Charles Annand, was resuming full control of the paper.[62] McCully was out.[63] In a matter of two weeks McCully had bought the moribund *Morning Journal* and made it into the *Unionist and Halifax Journal*; but from this time onward the *Morning Chronicle* was the leading opposition paper in Nova Scotia. On January 11, 1865, the first of Howe's "Botheration Letters" appeared there.

Joseph Howe was at one of the most difficult points of his long career. After three years as Premier of Nova Scotia, just when he might have been expected to enjoy affluence and power, to reap the benefit of his twenty-seven years in the public service of his province, he found his taste for local politics had palled, and he had given it up in 1863. He felt the need for something grander than the petty issues of local affairs. Had he private means he might decently have retired from public life, but he had none. Howe had never cared much about money. He had been generous with it when he had it – few men more so. He "would give his last cent to relieve distress."[64] He was feckless, no doubt, but that was part of the best quality in him, the openness and warmth of his nature. He loved to love and to be loved, and he gave of himself and his means with his whole heart. Howe had looked to the imperial government to reward him according to his talents and his long public service, and he became Her Majesty's Fisheries Commissioner (pursuant to the Reciprocity Treaty) in 1863. But it was a post which, at £750 a year, he could hardly have believed decently commensurate with his capacity or his achievements. (His contemporary, Francis Hincks of Canada, had been made a Governor, first of Barbados, then, in 1862, of British Guiana.) Tired, poor, rather embittered, Howe found Confederation, coming in the circumstances it did, somewhat disconcerting. He had grown away from British North American union. He had talked about it often enough, in 1854 and in 1861. On occasion he still did, but he had grown rather disillusioned with Canadians. His attention was now directed to what he seems to have believed was the more important question of the British Empire. If for no other reason than this, Howe's attitude to Confederation was equivocal. Moreover, it was being brought to Nova Scotia by a man whose capacity was below Howe's and whom Howe regarded as an upstart doctor from Cumberland whose only major asset was sheer brass. Howe was enough of egotist to resent both Tupper and Tupper's project. There was a ring of truth in the remark attributed to him, "I will not play second fiddle to that d—d Tupper."[65] Whether he would have supported Confederation had he had an opportunity similar to Tupper's is another matter. Two contemporaries, Edward Whelan and G.M. Grant, thought he would have;[66] but reasonable doubt still remains if his interest in the whole subject was not now largely exhausted and if his public support of Confederation in August 1864[67] can be taken as anything else than alcoholic rodomontade.

Howe had been in Halifax in that month and had met Governor MacDonnell, who asked him to go to Charlottetown. But Howe's official duties prevented him.[68] Thus, while the Charlottetown and Quebec Conferences were going on, Howe was cooped up in the little 700-ton H.M.S. *Lily*, off the Labrador coast. He returned to Halifax in November to find Confederation well in train and Tupper prepared to take the question to the legislature in the spring session. Howe, who had written to Tupper in August that he would be very happy to co-operate on Maritime union, found himself in November in a very different position. The Maritime union project had metamorphosed into British American union, and that Howe was not really prepared to accept. Howe still held his hand, but by the end of December, when his old friend William Annand "had joined the opposition, and confronted the Delegates on the platform at Temperance Hall," Howe could hold back no longer.[69] He was still H.M. Fisheries Commissioner and could not come out openly, but he was also Joseph Howe and could still write. The "Botheration Letters" were the result.

Howe wrote these anonymously, but the authorship was thinly veiled, for Howe's style was recognizable. The *Evening Express* guessed: "We are not exactly certain who blows the literary bellows of the *Chronicle* now, but judging from the easy style introduced, we have a shrewd suspicion who he is."[70] The "Botheration Letters" appeared as twelve editorials in the Halifax *Morning Chronicle* between January 11 and March 2. In these Howe summed up the anti-Confederate arguments, enlivened them with the warmth of his own style, and illustrated them with reflections from his own considerable experience. Howe saw Confederation as an attempt to repeat the constitutional disasters of the first and second empires. Great Britain had tried to work local legislatures in harmony with the imperial parliament, had found the system impracticable, and had been forced to concede responsible government. Any British American parliament constituted under a federal system would encounter the same results in dealing with the local legislatures of the provinces. Sooner or later these legislatures would make their power felt in ways unknown to the letter of the Quebec Resolutions. "Why shall we try over again the experiment which the experience of the Mother Country condemns?" The only reason for federation, Howe alleged, was French-Canadian resistance to legislative union.[71] Here, with an unerring eye, Howe assessed the French position.

> Ever since the Union of the Two Provinces, the French Canadians, by sticking together, have controlled the Legislation and the Government of Canada. They will do the same thing in a larger Union, and, as the English will split and divide, as they always do, the French members will, in nine cases out of ten, be masters of the situation. But should a chance combination thwart them, then they will back their Local Legislature against the United Parliament....[72]

Union was certainly not strength under circumstances such as these.

> *Where there are no cohesive qualities in the material, no skill in the design ... unite what you will and there is no strength....* Was there strength when the new wine was united to the old bottle, or the new cloth to the old garment? Is union strength when a prudent man, doing a snug business is tempted into partnership with a wild speculator? Was Sampson much the stronger when the false Delilah got him confederated, bound him with cords and cut off his hair?[73]

In Letter No. 9 Howe spoke of the "squadron" who had helped to engineer the union of Scotland and England in 1707, and forecast a dark future for the "squadron" of Nova Scotia when they came to face the people.[74] And imperial despatches urging Confederation only compounded the felony:

> We should like to have seen Dr. Tupper making such a proposal to Simon Bradstreet Robie, or Mr. McCully trying to seduce Herbert Huntingdon into a conspiracy against the existence of our Legislature, and pleading a despatch as a reason why the people should have no voice in the matter. Robie's opinion would have been delivered with unmistakable emphasis,

> and we much mistake the man if Huntingdon's right leg, with a heavy boot at the end of it, would not have commenced a series of gymnastic responses very edifying to behold.[75]

Let the delegates blow the trumpet of union as much as they please, Howe said, "but hereafter we trust to hear no more of Imperial Despatches commanding a Union…."[76]

Howe's letters were a distinct enunciation of Nova Scotian patriotism, and they rallied opinion everywhere. In the words of one person, reporting a village Confederation debate, "A non-political community had suddenly been ushered into political existence."[77] When the discussion of Confederation began in Nova Scotia, the delegates controlled, as Howe rightly said, the most influential newspapers; they were familiar with the Quebec Resolutions and the arguments by which they might be sustained; yet within three months parties had been realigned, public meetings organized, public letters written. Howe described the change vividly.

> Nothing illustrates more finely the high spirit and intellectual resources of Nova Scotia than the rapidity with which all this was done…. Men, who had taken no share in mere party disputation, jumped upon the platform and confronted these delegates…. To its honor be it said, one portion of the independent press [the *Halifax Citizen*] sounded the tocsin of alarm from the first, other newspapers, shaking off old trammels, came into line [the *Morning Chronicle*], and the Botheration Scheme was ventilated in every part of the Province, and so far as Nova Scotia is concerned, may now be considered as dead as Julius Caesar.[78]

With Tilley's defeat in New Brunswick, four days after this was written, Confederation was to all intents and purposes just as dead as Howe said it was.

The rout of Confederation was also seen in the Assembly. "Bluster and arrogance ruled the hour until the House met, when the pin feathers of the Delegates suddenly fell."[79] The attitude in the House and in the country was distinctly threatening, and some strategic retreat might be necessary. The Speech from the Throne was non-committal. The "encomiums" of Cardwell were duly noted,[80] but the Speech asked only that Confederation be considered with care and prudence. That was on February 9, 1865. Nothing further was heard on the subject of Confederation for a month and a half. Tupper's position was in fact extremely difficult. The *Bullfrog*, as shrewd as its name, had analysed it well enough, on February 4, 1865: "The position of the ministry is precarious in the extreme: DR TUPPER has a difficult hand to play, and, although he is a cunning player ... it is just possible he may lose the game upon the issue of which he has ... risked his political existence...." The course of Confederation in Nova Scotia was largely determined by events in New Brunswick,[81] though even before the news of Tilley's defeat the adoption of Confederation by Nova Scotia was highly doubtful;[82] in any case it was clear by March 6 that Confederation had been defeated. But Tupper did not intend to lose the game. A Council meeting on March 9 resolved on Maritime union resolutions as a means of staving off an adverse vote on Confederation;[83] these were tabled on March 22 and moved on April 10.

Although the resolutions referred only to Maritime union, the debate was on Confederation. Tupper himself devoted only a fraction of his speech to the former. It was a long speech; Tupper was not famous for his conciseness. He gave the background of Confederation and much of its history, making the usual obeisance to legislative union, but he introduced little that was new. Finally he came to the resolutions for Maritime union. Owing "to circumstances over which we have no control" (well might Tupper say this), it was impossible to bring in resolutions on Confederation.[84] Maritime union was desirable in any case. Tupper admitted that the chance of persuading Prince Edward Island was slim, but he felt sure that New Brunswick would receive the proposals favourably.[85]

As in the Canadian debate on Confederation, nearly every member in the Nova Scotian House had an opportunity to express his views, and did, though usually upon Confederation rather than Maritime union. Under the circumstances it could hardly be a very distinguished debate, and it reflected little that had not already appeared in the newspapers. It dragged on until April 24. On that day, when Tupper moved resumption of the debate, Archibald rose and said it would be absurd to continue it. The resolutions for Maritime union then passed without a division. The *Morning Chronicle* of May 9 concluded in its retrospect of the session that Confederation had been "quietly shelved by the unanimous vote of the House." The *Acadian Recorder* thought so too, on April 26, and breathed a fervent, "Long may it rest."

By this time the Canadians were on the scene. Galt and C.J. Brydges were in Halifax on April 13, pursuant to an arrangement made with Tupper in Canada the previous October to consider the construction of the Truro to Moncton section of the Intercolonial.[86] They were also, with Cartier, on their way to England. Galt and Cartier, with Tilley who was also there, drove in four-horse carriages through crowded streets to a public meeting called in their honour, one which Cartier described as "vraiment magnifique."[87] The *Morning Chronicle* of April 15, 1865, called it merely a clamorous gathering of "the great unwashed." Noting the persistence of the Canadians, the *Acadian Recorder* warned, April 26, "Many a lover has succeeded by sheer dint of perseverance." As if to underline this remark the Colonial Office peremptorily ruled out Maritime union, in such terms that MacDonnell and Tupper were precluded from considering the matter any further.[88]

A mission to England by the Nova Scotian ministers, similar to that of the Canadians, would under the circumstances seem too conspiratorial if the Canadians were still in London. "It would, I fear," wrote Tupper to MacDonnell, "be just now prejudicial to the cause of Confederation here."[89] Tupper and Henry did not go to England until late in June, when the Canadians had gone home, and then ostensibly to discuss only railways and reciprocity.[90] There was rough justice in the *Morning Chronicle*'s statement of July 14: "The confederation tornado which swept across the length and breadth of British America ... has, at length, spent itself on the other side of the Atlantic."

While Confederation took Tupper and Henry eastward to London, reciprocity took Howe westward to Detroit. The abrogation of the Reciprocity Treaty, notice of which was given by the United States early in 1865, was to become effective on March 17, 1866. A variety of moves were made in the summer of 1865 to rescue the Treaty. Five hundred Americans and fifty British Americans travelled to Detroit for a convention sponsored by the Detroit Chamber of Commerce, that opened on July 11, 1865. According to the *Detroit Advertiser*, "The modesty of the Canadians was in marked contrast with the arrogance of the bristly delegation from Chicago.... They bore more than one insulting taunt of the advocates of 'the American side' with the most exemplary forbearance...."[91] Even before Howe's speech, the British Americans had won many friends, but on the last day Howe swept the convention off its feet. He spoke darkly of fortifications on the American side of the border, and appealed for peace and amity on both sides. His own son, he said, had fought for the northern cause, in the 23rd Ohio Regiment. At this the cheers were deafening, and Howe himself, never much the master of his own emotions, almost broke down.[92] For British Americans, the Detroit convention was a success, and resolutions were passed favouring renewal of the Reciprocity Treaty. But they had little effect. The New York papers boasted that two years from the end of reciprocity the British North American provinces would be forced to join the United States. This kind of triumphant leer was to appear periodically for some time to come.[93] There was truth enough in the sensible, matter-of-fact chauvinism of the *New York Herald*. All the commercial and geographical interests of the British provinces lay with the United States: Canada West with Ohio, Illinois, and Michigan; Canada East with New York and Vermont; the Maritime provinces with Maine and Massachusetts. "All other connections are to them really of no value whatever...."[94] And Washington remained adamant. Galt and Howland, in Washington while the Detroit convention was on, came home chastened and pessimistic.

Whatever might be the ultimate fate of reciprocity, it was highly desirable that measures be concerted by the British American provinces together. There was a feeling of irritation in the Maritime provinces over the way Canada pre-empted all negotiations. The free entry into the American market of flour, grain, livestock, fruit, lumber, fish, furs – in short, natural products – had benefited Canada rather than the Maritimes; the irony was that these benefits had been largely paid for by the gift of the Maritime inshore fisheries to the Americans. Earl Russell, the British Foreign Secretary, had suggested a "Confederate council" to furnish information to Her Majesty's Government on the negotiation of commercial treaties.[95] The result was another conference at Quebec, on September 15, 1865, though on a much more modest scale than that of 1864. Ambrose Shea represented Newfoundland, R.D. Wilmot New Brunswick, J.C. Pope Prince Edward Island, and J.W. Ritchie (the Solicitor General) Nova Scotia, and they met with Brown, Cartier, and Galt. Brown held a high opinion of the work of this Council[96] and he was not altogether unjustified. One concrete result was the immediate conversion of R.D. Wilmot of New Brunswick to Confederation.[97] It may also have helped to alleviate Maritime jealousy of Canadian influences in Washington and London.

The opportunity was also taken by the Canadians to extend an invitation to the Maritimers who had entertained the Canadians so warmly in August 1864, to come and visit Canada in September 1865. An estimated two hundred and forty invitations were sent out. Nova Scotia set aside $5,000 to help send visitors. The Saint John *Weekly Telegraph* of September 20 called it "return match to the great intercolonial drunk of last year," but it was in the end largely a failure. Only fifty-four actually went[98] and in the different circumstances of September 1865 not even McGee, who had charge of it, could make it a success. Confederation was at a standstill; the after-dinner speeches that rang so fervently in 1864 had a distinctly hollow note in 1865.

By this time too the Confederate cause in Nova Scotia had a hollow and empty sound. The Confederate newspapers toiled manfully at their task. The *Unionist* began a series called "Confederation Catechism" in March; the *British Colonist* a "Review of the debate on the Union of the Colonies" that occupied it through July and August; the *Evening Express*, taking a broader view, began a series on British North America from Newfoundland to Vancouver Island that lasted intermittently from July until October. The *Unionist* battled with the *Morning Chronicle* the whole summer, while the *British Colonist* took on the *Citizen* and the *Acadian Recorder*. But it was an unsatisfying business at best. On August 7 the *Express* confessed ruefully that "the feelings of a large proportion of the people of the Lower Provinces are, upon the whole, hostile to Union." The *Morning Chronicle* of September 27 commented that the "roar of artillery from the Union batteries has given place to the occasional discharge of a gun from the dismantled works."

"A nation, indeed! Say rather 'a thing of shreds and patches'" was the principal theme of the *Morning Chronicle*.[99] It elaborated in a remarkable editorial published on October 16 called "The Binomial Theory of Government," one of the most interesting criticisms of the principle of federation. Federation was described algebraically as $(x - y)^n$, where $x$ was the power of the general government, $y$ the power of the local, and $n$ the constitutional expansion. It was clear from this formula, the *Morning Chronicle* said, that the powers granted to local governments must subtract something from the simple – the otherwise simple – plenary authority of the central government. The *Chronicle* did not distinguish between the general and particular powers given to the central government in Resolution 29. It assumed, as Resolution 29, and later Section 91 of the British North America Act, assumed, that the particular powers were merely explicit illustrations of a simple and comprehensive grant of legislative authority. The *Chronicle* feared the diminution of this power. Federation, it said, deranges monarchy. It "clogs the executive function" by setting up the "derivative authority of the local Legislatures against the constituted authority of a central Government." Since the local legislatures were, by the *Chronicle*'s reasoning, derived from the central government, federation became a "second term of unknown value and an unprofitable complication in government…." The local legislatures the *Chronicle* regarded as insidious, republican devices mitigating the high authority of the Crown exercised by the central power. The local legislatures followed "the feelings and opinions of the masses; the federal principle is the consolidation of their authority...."

Another critic who had similar views was the Governor of Nova Scotia, Richard MacDonnell. He had opposed federation from the start; and although he was a chivalrous enough adversary, he distrusted both Confederation and those who had initiated it. At Quebec he remarked to Macdonald, "You shall not make a mayor of *me,* I can tell you." It was for reasons of this kind that MacDonnell was unceremoniously transferred to Hong Kong in September 1865, where he could be his own ministry, and thus avoid the conflicts that his wit, quick tongue, and critical propensities had caused in Nova Scotia. He had never been disposed, so the *Unionist* said, September 4, 1865, "to spare or spoil what he considered a joke, for a minister's sake." He was accused of being the very pivot of anti-Confederate influence; he may have been distrusted by his own Council, but not even the anti-Confederates seem to have regretted his departure.[100]

The new Governor of Nova Scotia was altogether different. Lieutenant General Sir William Fenwick Williams was a native Nova Scotian, a soldier, and a veteran of the Crimean War in which he had won fame for an honourable defence of Kars, a city in Turkish Armenia. Since that time he had been for six years Officer Commanding Her Majesty's Forces in British North America. He had no political experience. Sixty-five years of age, Williams was a fine old veteran who knew how to take orders and he was sent to Nova Scotia to put union through by every means at his disposal. The Nova Scotians were not ignorant of this purpose and they were not intended to be. On November 8, 1865, the *Royal Gazette* published Cardwell's letter to Williams, in which it was made abundantly clear that the expectation of Confederation was the reason for his appointment.

Charles Fisher's victory in the York by-election in New Brunswick in November 1865 was a cheering note for Confederates in Nova Scotia;[101] but there was, regrettably, nothing cheerful about the by-election in Lunenburg County, Nova Scotia, on December 27. The government bent all its efforts: road contracts were freely let to deserving supporters; there was a fresh despatch from Cardwell urging the wishes of the imperial government, and which was duly published on the eve of the election.[102] This despatch the *Chronicle* of December 27 represented as Canadian in origin – "the voice is Jacob's voice but the hands are the hands of Esau." But Lunenburg was lost. A seat that the Conservatives had won in 1863 by 509 votes was lost in 1865 by 686. With the reduced franchise of 1865 this was, as the government admitted, defeat by a very large majority.[103] Canadian papers commiserated, but it was not a good omen on the eve of the year 1866 when so much was expected.

However, at the same time, with the steady pressure from the British government and with Fenian alarms since October, the anti-Confederates seemed to give ground a little. On November 15, the *Morning Chronicle* suggested the possibility of a new conference on union. Perhaps this overture was the result of the York election in New Brunswick; in any case, it was greeted cordially in the government papers.[104] And just at this point George Brown arrived on the scene from Canada, his purpose being to explore the immediate prospects for union. He had had conferences with Gordon, Tilley, and Smith in New Brunswick, and he was impressed with the progress of pro-Confederation sentiment there.[105] And in Nova Scotia Brown put this question to William Annand in a long private interview at Tupper's house about November 20.

William Annand was now the leading spirit of the Nova Scotian anti-Confederates. Although he did not command the following among the Liberals that Archibald had, he had long been a close friend of Howe, and his outspoken opposition to Confederation, expressed in the *Morning Chronicle,* had given him considerable influence in the province among Liberals and Conservatives alike. Annand had been in England in the summer of 1865, where he had met A.J. Smith of New Brunswick, and, like Smith, had had a pretty frank interview with Cardwell. Apparently Cardwell made no attempt to disguise his policy; the British government "would use every means in their power, short of coercion" to induce the Maritime legislatures to accept Confederation.[106] How far Annand was sincere in his sudden interest in union in the *Morning Chronicle* was uncertain; Brown tried to find out. The Saint John *Telegraph* suspected that the real purpose was to sow discord among the supporters of Confederation.[107] Brown tried in vain to get Annand to accept Confederation as it stood; he even said that if nothing were done soon about Confederation, "Canada would seek some other mode of settling her difficulties, and leave the Maritime Provinces to their fate."[108] That Annand was much moved by this unhappy prospect was doubtful; Brown had, however, other strings to his bow. He appealed to Annand's Liberalism and held out the possibility of a British North American union under the agreeable auspices of a national Liberal party. "I have always sworn by the *Chronicle* and the

*Nova Scotian*," said Brown diplomatically. "We are all Liberals.[109] You and I have been personal friends, we have long acted together, and it is too bad at this period that I should be obliged to throw myself into the hands of our opponents to carry this measure...."[110] Brown also intimated that any support Annand might give Confederation would not go unrewarded.[111]

Annand did not commit himself, but there remained the possibility that both Annand and Smith of New Brunswick might be persuaded to support some kind of union, one cleared perhaps of the taint of the Quebec scheme. Such a proposal was not without support even in Canada. On December 8, the Conservative Ottawa *Citizen* said that the Canadian government "are prepared to listen to any proposals for the adoption of another and a better scheme." Brown and Macdonald doubtless were willing; Cartier doubtless was not. What Annand had in mind was something rather less definite and distinctly more tortuous.

In January 1866, Annand's colleague, William Miller, felt he could no longer persist in opposing union and believed the time had come for "effecting some compromise by which the objectionable features of the Quebec scheme could be got rid of."[112] Annand apparently agreed, and the result was a new editorial in the *Morning Chronicle* on January 24, 1866, urging that union be considered. Not all those who opposed the Quebec plan, said the editorial, were opposed to union; the Quebec scheme, "matured in a few weeks, amid exhaustive festivities, was not the measure to consolidate British America," and the necessity of some kind of union was becoming obvious. "The colonies cannot, in the very nature of things, always continue as they are."

The government papers welcomed these overtures. On February 2 the *Evening Express* agreed that the Quebec plan had met a storm of opposition from large and influential sections of all parties, and that some changes in it would be inevitable. The *British Colonist* tried to confine the issue to the Quebec plan, with changes in detail; the *Chronicle* insisted, however, that "the work must be commenced *de novo*."[113] By this time it was almost certain that the Nova Scotian government itself had abandoned hope of getting the Quebec Resolutions through the Legislature as they stood. They had taken too much of a battering. And union, after all, was the main issue. For union, plain union, with nothing of the Quebec taste in it, there was some sympathy in Nova Scotia. The Halifax *Sun* suggested the point on April 11, 1866: "Many had been strongly prepossessed in favour of Confederation before the completion and promulgation of the scheme which was intended to make it a fixed fact. – The vision of a vast country stretching across the continent from sea to sea, with but one Government and one Law, had in it something sublime which captivated at first sight." The great difficulty was to bring these sublimities to earth. Nova Scotians seemed to prefer to talk and dream rather than act. A great country from sea to sea was a grand conception, but the presentation of the practical means to realize it seemed depressing, perhaps even crude.[114] Before long, Tupper had grasped this point: that the question of terms could, with great advantage, be left severely alone.

Annand, for different reasons, also avoided the question. It was possible that he was considering union: what was probable was some scheme for postponing Confederation. To propose a new convention was a useful move. Anti-Confederates had no wish to appear intransigent or unpatriotic in the face of the known desires of the British government; Fenian threats made patriotism obligatory; some overt gesture toward union placed the anti-Confederates in a better tactical position. Annand, three years later, said that the whole scheme was a red herring. A new convention to discuss union from the beginning could be held in the confident anticipation that "the delegates would not agree when they met...."[115] Whatever Annand's motive, he could be, and was, "earnestly sincere in the opinion that it is better to have a new convention."[116]

Tactics were by now of some importance. The Liberal caucus met the day the legislature opened, February 22. Annand proposed that Archibald be deposed as Liberal leader on the ground of his Confederation sympathies. An anti-Confederate party, with Annand presumably at the head, would be far more effective; it could call in Conservative support, and it could propose a new union convention. But to both proposals the majority of the party appear to have been opposed. They would not depose Archibald, neither would they consider a new convention on union.[117] They were not convinced, as Annand was, of any clear and present danger from Confederation; they could not believe that anything in the nature of a *coup de main* was conceived of, and New Brunswick was surely a powerful security that nothing could be done about Confederation in Nova Scotia.

When the Nova Scotian legislature opened on February 22, to the astonishment of nearly everyone, and to the chagrin of Gordon and Monck, nothing whatsoever was said about Confederation in the Speech from the Throne. The *Chronicle* thought it extraordinary: not a syllable on Confederation in the Governor's Speech. A week later, still puzzled, it wrote, "The House of Assembly is as tranquil as a summer sea...."[118]

The Assembly without a ripple on its surface belied the frantic activity going on behind the scenes. Williams, Gordon, and Monck were in close and active communication. The telegraph did yeoman work. Two days before the Nova Scotian legislature had opened, Gordon telegraphed asking for a strong stand on Confederation in the Nova Scotian Speech. Williams replied that it was then too late to change the Speech, and that in any case he would damage the cause of Confederation in both provinces by such a statement; he could not afford to risk the possibility of a vote against Confederation. Williams for his part mightily regretted the late meeting of the New Brunswick legislature (March 8) and wired Lord Monck that Gordon must be impressed with the fact that "success depends in both Provinces entirely upon his prompt efforts."[119]

Gordon had in fact devised the stratagem of persuading A.J. Smith to accept a paragraph in the Throne Speech favouring Confederation, on the ground that Cardwell's despatch of June 24, 1865, left no alternative. Monck feared that the complete omission of any reference to Confederation in the Nova Scotian Speech would now strengthen Smith's hand, and his capacity to resist Gordon. This he wired rather tersely to Williams. Williams' telegram in reply was revealing: "Mr. Gordon knows we are in a minority here until Confederation is carried in New Brunswick. I cannot therefore see how a hostile vote here would have helped him, while it would have prevented our success after it had been carried there."[120]

About a week later, on March 7, Annand rose in the Assembly to ask what was going on. He had seen a report in the *British Colonist* of a speech of John A. Macdonald's at Cornwall, Canada West; Macdonald had said Confederation was certain to pass in a few weeks.[121] Did or did not the government of Nova Scotia have a Confederation policy? Tupper blandly replied that he was just as astonished as Mr. Annand at Macdonald's remarks. It would be "altogether futile for Nova Scotia to move at present." Annand refused to be put off. Why was it that Prince Edward Island and Newfoundland had both mentioned Confederation in their Speeches?[122] Why was Nova Scotia so very different? W.A. Henry, the Attorney General, came to Tupper's rescue. "The government," he said, "had no policy on the subject...."[123]

This was sheer evasion. Williams and the Tupper government were in an awkward position. Nearly all the ordinary business of the session would be completed in four weeks or so; the New Brunswick legislature had not met, and when it did meet, a day later on March 8, it was almost at once locked in debate over Charles Fisher's precipitate want of confidence motion.[124] In this aggravating dilemma Williams and Tupper could do nothing. Williams could only telegraph apologetically to Gordon:

> ... am sorry that my line of operations has not helped you. Hope Anti Confederate joy will soon turn to sorrow by your measures. My total abandonment of Confederation is too much like Punch even for their sincere belief. They know what I was sent here for.[125]

The same day, March 7, Canada called out the militia against the Fenians.[126] Within a few days of the receipt of this news in Nova Scotia, Williams telegraphed to Monck: "A great change here, if Gordon acts promptly for the Quebec scheme or otherwise. Pray read my message and urge him on. Nearly all our ordinary business done and Howe is away." That same day, March 12, back came Monck's answer. Could Williams possibly begin with Confederation without waiting for Gordon? It was now "morally certain" that Gordon could get Confederation through in New Brunswick, "but he may not be able to hurry matters."[127] Williams took the hint, and began.

As Lieutenant Governor, Lieutenant General Sir William Fenwick Williams had already made a good reputation in Halifax. He was a fine figure of a man and a military hero; he had made himself agreeable with an excellent table at Government House, and his geniality was a pleasant contrast to the tartness of his predecessor. But he was a soldier, and he not only knew how to take orders, but had some aptitude for executing them. On March 13, the day after Monck's telegram, he sent for William Annand. "If disengaged after breakfast, anytime after 10, should be glad to see you for a few moments."[128] Williams suggested that Annand should propose to Tupper, on the floor of the House, a new convention, to be held in London under the auspices of the Colonial Office, and which would work out the details of a plan of union. Annand could be confident that if he made such a move, Tupper would agree to it.[129] Annand hesitated. The new convention he sought was within his grasp, but he was suspicious. He asked for time to consider, and he wanted to see Smith in New Brunswick with whom he had been for some time in agreement. The aim of both was that anti-Confederates in the two provinces should "act together, adopt a common policy, and support each other."[130] Williams believed that Annand was willing,[131] and that Smith could also be brought around. On March 19 Williams telegraphed Gordon, "Annand goes today to confer with Smith and I have great hopes for our joint success – Communicate by telegraph daily in what way I can assist and push on your work...."[132]

Annand's trip was stopped, however. Gordon, for one, did not want him.[133] Gordon had his own views about how Confederation could be achieved in New Brunswick, and he was afraid Annand might stiffen Smith's resistance. In fact it was probably already too late. Smith was already dilatory and circumspect in dealing with union, and Gordon was becoming convinced that a complete change of government might be necessary. Smith, for his part, found Annand's proposal a little embarrassing;[134] and he was sure he could weather Fisher's vote of want of confidence by at least five or six votes.[135] He did not need a proposal for a new convention; union, he thought, could be defeated without recourse to that, and he was not ready to jeopardize his own position to help Nova Scotians who in any case depended heavily upon him. Besides, he was soon made aware that some of Annand's friends were not very happy about Annand's proposals. E.M. Macdonald, as soon as he got wind of them, promptly telegraphed a friend in the New Brunswick government to wire Annand to stay home.[136] Howe later remarked, "So earnest was Mr. Annand in this business that it took Killam, McLellan, McDonald, and some others of the more energetic of our party to choke him off and keep him at home."[137] Annand had to content himself with a letter to Smith. In this letter some of the efforts concerted by Nova Scotian and New Brunswick anti-Confederates, something of their mutual dependence, and some of the difficulties of their position are revealed.

Halifax, 20 March, 1866

My Dear Smith,–

I have felt very anxious since the meeting of your Parliament, as to how you would come out of the fight, and whether you would be able to hold your ground against the enemy. We have not yet heard the result of the want of confidence motion, but I was glad to see a telegram from a member of your Government on Saturday last that the Administration would be sustained, and that you were safe for the present as regards Confederation. I had made up my mind, previous to the receipt of the telegram, to visit Fredericton with the view of conferring with you, and taking such steps as might be thought advisable in the interests of both

Provinces. Like yourself, I desire no political Union with Canada, because I feel that the Maritime Provinces, in any scheme that may be matured, must be seriously injured by a connexion with a colony which must necessarily exercise a preponderating influence over all the others. But if, either through the exertions of the British Government, or change of opinion, or want of pluck, on the part of the people of the seaboard Provinces, it may be necessary to deal practically with the Union question, then I want to be in a position to make the best possible bargain under the circumstances for my own country.

Now, as long as you can rely upon your own people, there will be no necessity to move here. Large as is the Government following in our Assembly, upon the Confederation question, they are powerless, and will so continue as long as New Brunswick maintains her present attitude. But it is right you should know that, however universal the feeling in the country, the majority in the House is not to be relied on should your Province back down. I find a growing feeling among members in favor of union of some sort, and a proposition for a new Convention from our side of the House would be eagerly seized on by some of the government supporters. Now, if we are to have a Union, let it be one that has some more redeeming features than the Quebec Scheme....

My chief object in now writing is to learn if you have an idea of proposing a new Convention, because, if that policy is to prevail in the maritime provinces I would like to be in a position to take the initiative in our Assembly ... Let me know at your earliest convenience what your views are, and if necessary, telegraph on receipt of this. If we are to have a Union we must take care that it is a fair one, and this can only be done by Nova Scotia and New Brunswick acting cordially together. *Trusting that there may be no change in the POLITICAL CONDITION of these two Provinces for many a day to come,*

I am, Yours sincerely,
W. ANNAND.[138]

Mistaken in tactics Annand may have been – some of his friends thought so – but his estimate of the position of affairs was remarkably accurate.

Just three days before, on March 17, Governor Williams ordered out the Nova Scotian militia to counter the Fenian danger, 8,000 men with 2,000 in reserve.[139] Three Fenian ships were said to have left New York to attack Halifax. Militia artillery companies proceeded to man the batteries in Point Pleasant Park; war materiel was sent over to George's Island and out to McNab's at the harbour mouth. Of Fenians "nothing else was talked of during the day, and at every corner of the streets, in the principal thoroughfares, and places of public resort, anxious groups might be seen awaiting confirmation or contradiction of the news which created so much alarm."[140] On Monday, March 19, three regiments of the militia were mustered on the Common, some of them armed with the main available weapon – the Crimean muzzle-loader with its long sword bayonet.[141]

Joseph Howe arrived back in Halifax on March 27. Annand, who had wished Howe would come home,[142] now surrendered the reins to him, and then "there was an end to intrigue and editorials."[143] Annand had nibbled at union and backed away, but some of his followers succumbed. Before New Brunswick had dealt with Confederation, when, in fact, the constitutional manoeuvres of Gordon were approaching their most precarious stage, it became clear that the "growing feeling among members in favor of union of some sort"[144] had produced some definite – and as it turned out, decisive – shifts of opinion in the Nova Scotian Assembly.

NOTES

1 P.B. Waite, "Nova Scotia," *The Life and Times of Confederation, 1864–1867: Politics, Newspapers and the Union of British North America* (Toronto: Robin Brass, 2001), 209–47.
2 F.W. Wallace, *Wooden Ships and Iron Men* (London, 1924), 115.
3 *Ibid.*, 108.
4 *Ibid.*, 2–4 *passim.*
5 Halifax *Morning Chronicle*, Oct. 6, 1863.
6 *Morning Chronicle*, June 9, 1866, reporting Howe's speech at Barrington, N.S.
7 *Ibid.*
8 *London Times*, Oct. 24, 1865, report of Oct. 10 from Halifax.
9 Toronto *Leader*, Aug. 22, 1864, report of Aug. 12 from Halifax.
10 *Ibid.*, Aug. 22, 1864, report of Aug. 17 from Saint John.
11 A.L. Spedon, *Rambles among the Blue-Noses* (Montreal, 1863), 131.
12 Halifax *Evening Reporter*, Nov. 8, 1864.
13 Howe Papers, Hastings Doyle to Howe, Oct. 1, 1867 (confidential); Howe to Hastings Doyle, Oct. 5, 1867.
14 MacDonnell to Monck, Mar. 20, 1865 (private). Copy in Nova Scotia, Lieutenant Governor, General Correspondence Despatched.

15 C.O. 217, MacDonnell to Cardwell, Mar. 16, 1865 (confidential). An able despatch that well sums up the Nova Scotian attitude to Confederation.
16 W.G. Ormsby, "Letters to Galt concerning the Maritime Provinces and Confederation," *Canadian Historical Review*, XXIV, 2 (June 1953), 167–8, Tupper to Galt, Dec. 13, 1864. Also quoted *supra*, 117.
17 *Ibid.*, Whelan to Galt, Dec. 17, 1864.
18 E.g., Nova Scotia, Assembly, *Debates and Proceedings*, 1866, 182 (Mar. 30). The government won, 31 to 20.
19 Note the following from the *Halifax Citizen*, Nov. 5, 1864: "The [Liberal] opposition have not the power either to carry or defeat the Confederation scheme...."
20 Montreal *Gazette*, Oct. 28, 1864, commenting on Archibald at the Quebec Conference.
21 Related by Dr. George Johnson, and quoted by E.M. Saunders, *Three Premiers of Nova Scotia* (Toronto, 1909), 371–2.
22 *Morning Chronicle*, May 15, 1867, reporting Howe's speech at Mason Hall, Halifax, May 9.
23 *Montreal Gazette*, Oct. 28, 1864.
24 See *infra*, 341–2.
25 Halifax *Morning Chronicle*, May 19, 1866, reporting Howe's speech at Windsor of May 8.
26 [William Garvie], *Barney Rooney's Letters on Confederation, Botheration and Political Transmogrification* (Halifax, 1865), 15–16.
27 C.O. 217, MacDonnell to Cardwell, Nov. 24, 1864 (confidential). MacDonnell said he would keep no copy of this despatch. Also Cardwell to MacDonnell, Dec. 8, 1864. (See *supra*, 371n4).
28 Dominion of Canada, House of Commons, *Debates*, 1916, 585.
29 Halifax *Morning Journal*, Nov. 23, 1864; *Halifax Sun*, Nov. 23, 1864.
30 It is worth recording that the Reverend George Munro Grant (1835–1902), from 1863 minister of St. Matthew's Presbyterian Church, Halifax, and in 1877 Principal of Queen's University, Kingston, publicly supported Confederation. His general view was, "the sooner, the better." Like many Nova Scotians he disliked the federal principle, and even opposed control of the Crown lands by local legislatures. Pictou *Colonial Standard*, April 11, 1865, published his letter.
31 The Conservative *Yarmouth Herald* had criticized the Intercolonial Railway policy of the Howe government as early as 1862: "Cheapness of interest of a loan should be no inducement to undertake a railroad that cannot assuredly pay working expenses" (May 15, 1862). Its attitude to the Tupper government's Intercolonial policy was the same (Nov. 17, 1864).

32 Halifax, county and city together, was then what it is now, a two-member constituency. The vote in the 1867 Dominion election was as follows:

| | Anti-Confederation | | Pro-Confederation | |
|---|---|---|---|---|
| | Jones * | Power * | Tobin | Shannon |
| Whole constituency | 2381 | 2361 | 2158 | 2154 |
| Halifax city | 830 | 819 | 1234 | 1227 |

Sources: Halifax *Evening Reporter*, Sept. 20, 1867; Halifax *Morning Chronicle*, Sept. 23, 1867.
*Elected.

33 The *Chronicle* became anti-Confederate in January 1865.

34 The *Sun* supported the North, the only Halifax paper to do so.

35 Halifax *Acadian Recorder*, Jan. 4, 1865; Halifax *Evening Reporter*, Oct. 28, 1864; *Halifax Witness*, Nov. 5, 1864.

36 *Halifax Citizen*, Nov. 19, 1864.

37 Halifax *British Colonist*, Nov. 24, 1864 (original italics). Note the use of the New Zealand analogy by McCully at the Quebec Conference, *supra*, 105–6, by Macdonald in support of the local constitution for Canada West, *infra*, 308, and by Sir Frederic Rogers, *infra*, 351.

38 *British Colonist*, Dec. 3, 1864.

39 Halifax *Unionist*, Jan. 23, 1865. Similar views, though not so outspoken, appeared in the *Morning Chronicle*, Nov. 11, 12, 15, 19, 24.

40 The Catholic paper, the Halifax *Evening Express*, was not in this sense a religious paper. While its sympathies were undoubtedly Catholic (and Conservative), its main purpose was news, not religion.

41 *Supra*, 160.

42 Halifax *Acadian Recorder*, Apr. 18, 1866.

43 Halifax *Evening Reporter*, Dec. 10, 1864, giving a rather premature opinion.

44 Halifax *Morning Chronicle*, June 9, 1866, reporting Howe's speech at Barrington, N.S. Cf. also "hydra-headed monster" in A Farmer, *Common-Sense* (Cornwallis, 1865), 26.

45 *Halifax Sun*, Jan. 30, 1865.

46 *Halifax Citizen*, Dec. 31, 1864.

47 *Ibid.*, Nov. 24, 1864.

48 *Acadian Recorder*, Oct. 3, 1864.

49 *Ibid.*, Nov. 18, 1864.

50 *Ibid.*, Jan. 4, 1865.

51 *British Colonist*, Jan. 17, 1865.

52 "I knew that it would be excessively easy to excite our people on the question of taxation…." Tupper Papers, Tupper to Macdonald, Apr. 9, 1865.

53 *British Colonist*, Jan. 17, 1865.
54 *Morning Chronicle*, Dec. 12, 1864.
55 E.g., A.M. Uniacke: "Often have I listened with pride and pleasure to the speeches of the Hon. Mr. Howe on this subject – (loud cheers); but who ever heard him advocate a Federal Union?" (*Morning Chron*icle, Dec. 28, 1864.)
56 *Evening Reporter*, Dec. 10, 1864. A few months later it was reported in the anti-Confederate papers, by way of warning to manufacturers, that a Canadian manufacturer of boots and shoes, visiting Saint John, N.B., offered to supply men's boots at $1.90 a pair in bond. They cost $2.75 a pair wholesale in Saint John. (*Morning Chronicle*, July 26, 1865.)
57 Howe's estimate. Howe Papers, Howe to Sir John Hay, Nov. 12, 1866. Howe here recapitulates the growth of the Nova Scotian opposition.
58 C.O. 217, MacDonnell to Cardwell, Feb. 16, 1865.
59 Howe's description, after meeting McCully at the time. *Morning Chronicle*, May 19, 1866, reporting Howe's Windsor speech of May 8. Lucy Neal is a character in T.C. Haliburton's *The Old Judge* (1849); see pp. 99–185 of 1968 edition.
60 Much of this information is in the McCully-Wm. Annand correspondence, *Morning Chronicle*, Jan. 16, 1865.
61 At which Howe smiled and said to Annand, "You are very like a woman. You make up your mind first and ask counsel afterwards." Howe's account of this incident is in his Mason Hall speech in Halifax, May 9, 1867, in *Morning Chronicle*, May 15, 1867. It is later quoted by William Annand for other reasons in *Morning Chronicle*, Apr. 10, 1869.
62 Charles Annand seems only to have handled the business side of the enterprise. The responsible editor was now William Annand.
63 McCully later accused Howe of being responsible for the break between himself and Annand. (*Unionist*, Mar. 29, 1865.)
64 Rev. John Currie's recollection. John Currie (1830?–1909), a younger contemporary of Howe, was Professor of Hebrew at Pine Hill Divinity School, Halifax, from 1871 to 1908. His recollections about Howe are recorded by Archibald MacMechan, in MacMechan's copy of Chisolm's *Howe*, in Dalhousie University Library. It was Rev. John Currie who said Howe "boasted he had kissed every woman in Nova Scotia."
65 Saunders, *Three Premiers of Nova Scotia*, 371.
66 For Whelan see *supra*, 185. Grant's view is given in his *Joseph Howe* (Halifax, 1906), 73. This book was published after Grant's death, reprinted from articles Grant had published in 1875 in the *Canadian Monthly* and *National Review*.
67 *Supra*, 77.

68 Howe's account of his role at this time is given in his Windsor speech of May 8, 1866 (*Morning Chronicle*, May 19, 1866). Howe wrote Lord Russell, the Foreign Secretary, asking permission to go, but no answer was received in time, and Howe was obliged to decline, although an official invitation had already been sent to him. As it turned out, Lord Russell's decision was against Howe going to Charlottetown.
69 *Evening Reporter*, Dec. 9, 1865, letter from Howe of Dec. 7.
70 *Evening Express*, Jan. 20, 1865. Howe was invited by Annand to replace McCully as editor of the *Chronicle* at McCully's salary. Howe said he accepted no salary at all for the work he did. (*Halifax Citizen*, Apr. 8, 1869, Howe's "Letter to the Electors of Hants, No. 2.")
71 Cf. also the views of the *Citizen* and the *Acadian Recorder*, *supra*, 224.
72 *Morning Chronicle*, Jan. 13, 1865, "Botheration Letter, No. 2."
73 *Ibid.*, Feb. 8, 1865, "Botheration Letter, No. 10" (Howe's italics).
74 *Ibid.*, Feb. 3, 1865.
75 *Ibid.*, Feb. 1, 1865, "Botheration Letter, No. 8."
76 *Ibid.*, Feb. 4, 1865. Not one of the Botheration Letters, but an editorial called "Canadian Generalship," probably written by Howe.
77 *Ibid.*, Feb. 14, 1865.
78 *Ibid.*, Mar. 2, 1865, a retrospect of the session.
79 *Ibid.*, May 9, 1865, a retrospect of the session.
80 "Encomium" was not intended in any pejorative sense.
81 So Tupper told Gordon early in June, Cardwell Papers, Gordon to Cardwell, June 5, 1865.
82 C.O. 217, MacDonnell to Cardwell, Feb. 15, 1865 (confidential).
83 According to MacDonnell, this was his device. C.O. 217, MacDonnell to Cardwell, Mar. 16, 1865 (confidential).
84 Nova Scotia, Assembly, *Debates and Proceedings*, 1865, 215.
85 For Prince Edward Island reaction, *supra*, 206; for New Brunswick, *infra*, 271–2.
86 They were apparently to come in November, 1864, but their visit was postponed. Brydges sent an engineer instead to survey existing lines in Nova Scotia and New Brunswick. See P.B. Waite, "A Chapter in the History of the Intercolonial Railway, 1864," *Canadian Historical Review*, XXXII, 4 (Dec. 1951), 356–69.
87 "Mon cher Langevin:— Vous avez dû, j'espère, recevoir le télégramme de Brydges envoyé d'Halifax. La démonstration qui nous a été faite dans cette ville a été vraiment magnifique. Elle nous aidera beaucoup dans notre Mission...." Collection Chapais, Cartier to Langevin, April 22, 1865.

There were complaints in the Assembly on April 13 about the proposed use of the Volunteers to augment the celebration. (Nova Scotia, Assembly, *Debates and Proceedings*, 1865, 238–45.)

88 C.O. 218, Cardwell to MacDonnell, Apr. 1, 1865.

89 Nova Scotia, Minutes of Council, May 19, 1865, Tupper to MacDonnell, May 11, 1865.

90 Nova Scotia, Minutes of Council, June 20, 1865.

91 Detroit *Advertiser and Tribune*, July 15, 1865, quoted in the Halifax *Morning Chronicle*, July 22, 1865.

92 J. Howe, *The Reciprocity Treaty: Its History, General Features, and Commercial Results* (Hamilton, 1865), 14.

93 *New York Herald*, July 18, 1865; *New York Tribune*, July 18, 1865; for later comments, see *Erie Dispatch* quoted by Toronto *Globe*, Jan. 27, 1866.

94 *New York Herald*, Jan. 17, 1866.

95 For its constitutional significance, see N. McL. Rogers, "The Confederate Council of Trade," *Canadian Historical Review*, VII, 4 (Dec. 1926), 277–86.

96 Brown Papers, Brown to Monck, Dec. 25, 1865.

97 *Infra*, 273–4.

98 From Nova Scotia, 23; New Brunswick, 28; Prince Edward Island, 3. Even the *British Colonist* criticized some of the arrangements for the visit (Oct. 10, 1865). Also Saint John *Morning Telegraph*, Sept. 16, 1865.

99 Halifax *Morning Chronicle*, Oct. 21, 1865.

100 MacDonnell's remark to Macdonald is from Frances E.O. Monck, *My Canadian Leaves: An Account of a Visit to Canada in 1864–1865* (London, 1891), 211. The entry is dated Saturday, Nov. 26, 1864, and the information it probably drawn directly from Macdonald himself. For anti-Confederate feelings, see for example *Halifax Citizen*, Aug. 12, 29, 1865.

101 *Infra*, 275.

102 *Royal Gazette*, Dec. 23, 1865, quoting Cardwell to Williams, Nov. 24, 1865.

103 *British Colonist*, Dec. 30, 1865. Legislation passed by the Howe government reduced the franchise by 40 per cent. It became effective in June 1864.

104 Halifax *Evening Express*, Nov. 17, 1865; *British Colonist*, Nov. 21, 1865.

105 Brown Papers, George Brown to Anne Brown, Nov. 18, 1865. See *infra*, 252.

106 Annand's recollection of the conversation, given in the *Morning Chronicle*, Mar. 2, 1869; other recollections appear *ibid.*, Mar. 23, 1869.

107 Saint John *Morning Telegraph*, Nov. 18, 1865, commenting on the *Morning Chronicle*'s editorial of Nov. 15.

108 William Miller's recollection of the conversation, but at second hand, as relayed to him by Annand. Nova Scotia, Assembly, *Debates and Proceedings,* 1866, 236 (Apr. 13). Annand at first denied the truth of Miller's version, but the next day admitted it was correct, *ibid.*, 237.

109 Annand's version of the conversation, *ibid.*, 237.

110 Miller's version, *ibid.*, 236.

111 Annand alleged he was promised "money, place and preferment in Canada." Tupper promptly sent off a telegram to Brown and duly read Brown's reply to the Assembly. Brown denied making such a promise (*ibid.*, 237). Annand later claimed to have been misreported and that he had only *implied* bribery.

112 Miller's account, *ibid.*, 311 (May 1).

113 *British Colonist*, Jan. 27, 1866; *Morning Chronicle*, Feb. 1, 1866.

114 A reporter for the Montreal *Evening Telegraph*, in Nova Scotia in July 1867, reported the following conversation with what he called an "intelligent Anti": "Have you any objection to a plan of Confederation?" "No." "Well, why your objection to this one?" "I don't like it." A.G. Gilbert, *From Montreal to the Maritime Provinces and Back* (Montreal, 1867), 53.

115 *Morning Chronicle*, Mar. 2, 1869.

116 E.M. Macdonald's view, contained in a letter addressed to an unknown member of the New Brunswick government at Fredericton dated March 18, 1866. Published in the *Halifax Citizen*, Feb. 25, 1869.

117 Nova Scotia, Assembly, *Debates and Proceedings*, 1866, 311 (May 1) (William Miller). Also *Morning Chronicle*, Mar. 23, 1869.

118 *Morning Chronicle*, Feb. 23, 1866; Mar. 2, 1866.

119 Nova Scotia, Lieutenant Governor, Telegram Book, Gordon to Williams, Feb. 20, 1866; Williams to Gordon, Feb. 21, 1866; Williams to Monck, Feb. 27, 1866.

120 Williams Papers, Monck to Williams, Feb. 26, 1866; Nova Scotia, Lieutenant Governor, Telegram Book, Monck to Williams, Feb. 28, 1866; *ibid.*, Williams to Monck, Feb. 28. 1866.

121 Ottawa *Citizen*, March 2, 1866 gives a full report of Macdonald's speech of March 1. The *British Colonist*, March 6, 1866, gave only a brief report presumably of news received by telegram.

122 Nova Scotia, Assembly, *Debates and Proceedings*, 1866, 53–5 (Mar. 7). Annand said Prince Edward Island, but the legislature there had not yet met.

123 *Ibid.*, 55.

124 *Infra*, 280.

125 Nova Scotia, Lieutenant Governor, Telegram Book, Williams to Gordon, Mar. 7, 1866.

126 Note Monck's remarks: "I have called out a considerable force of Volunteers in anticipation of Fenian invasion – wh. *I* do not believe will take place…." Williams Papers, Monck to Williams, Mar. 12, 1866.

127 Nova Scotia, Lieutenant Governor, Telegram Book, Williams to Monck, Mar. 12, 1866; Monck to Williams, Mar. 12, 1866.

128 Williams to Annand, as published in the *Morning Chronicle*, Mar. 23, 1869.

129 As recounted by Annand, *Morning Chronicle*, Mar. 2, 1869.

130 *Ibid.*, May 25, 1866; Mar. 23, 1869.

131 Nova Scotia, Lieutenant Governor, Telegram Book, Williams to Monck, Mar. 14, 1866.

132 *Ibid.*, Williams to Gordon, Mar. 19, 1866.

133 *Ibid.*, Gordon to Williams, Mar. 19, 1866.

134 Letter from an unknown member of the New Brunswick government to A.G. Jones, Mar. 24, 1866, quoted by Jones in a speech, Jan. 13, 1868, *Morning Chronicle*, Jan. 16, 1868.

135 Smith to Annand, Mar. 25, 1866, referred to in *Morning Chronicle*, Mar. 23, 1869.

136 *Halifax Citizen*, Feb. 25, 1869.

137 Howe's "Letter to the Electors of Hants, No. 2," *Halifax Citizen*, Apr. 8, 1869.

138 Annand to Smith, Mar. 20, 1866, in *Morning Chronicle*, Mar. 2, 1869 (original italics). Annand reported in the paper that he had requested this letter from Smith for purpose of publication.

139 Nova Scotia, Lieutenant Governor, Telegram Book, Williams to Gordon, Mar. 19, 1866.

140 *Morning Chronicle*, Mar. 19, 1866.

141 *Ibid.*, Mar. 20, 1866.

142 Miller's report of a conversation with Annand in March 1866. (Nova Scotia, Assembly, *Debates and Proceedings*, 1866, 311 [May 1].) Annand's reply is not in the *Debates*; he alleged his speech was misreported and would not give up proofs. Annand's speech is given in the *Halifax Citizen*, May 24, 1866. Annand throws doubt on other aspects of Miller's report, but does not deny this one.

143 Howe's "Letter to the Electors of Hants, No. 2," *Halifax Citizen*, Apr. 8, 1869.

144 Annand's phrase, from Smith to Annand, Mar. 20, 1866, quoted above.

# "New Brunswick's Entrance into Confederation"

*Canadian Historical Review*
1928

GEORGE E. WILSON[1]

During the month of October 1864, representatives from the five provinces of Canada, New Brunswick, Nova Scotia, Prince Edward Island, and Newfoundland met at Quebec and drew up seventy-two resolutions, which it was hoped would serve as a basis of union. It took less than three weeks to draw up the resolutions, it took almost three years to secure their adoption. Even then the union was a union of three provinces, and not of five. Prince Edward Island and Newfoundland had dropped out.

The long delay cannot be blamed on the Canadian government. It lost no time in bringing the question of confederation before parliament. During February and March 1865, the Quebec resolutions were discussed and in the end were passed by large majorities in both the Legislative Council and the Assembly.

A much more difficult task faced Tupper in Nova Scotia and Tilley in New Brunswick. Of these colonies, Nova Scotia was much the more important by reason of history, wealth, and population. From the point of view of confederation, however, New Brunswick held a unique position. She was not only important on her own account, but important because her action largely determined the course Nova Scotia must follow. Geographical considerations made it quite feasible for New Brunswick to enter confederation with Canada even if Nova Scotia remained out; Nova Scotia, however, could not enter confederation if

New Brunswick did not come in. New Brunswick was the key province, and Tupper's political strategy in 1865 and in 1866 can be understood only by remembering how dependent he was upon events in New Brunswick, and by keeping very clearly in mind what those events were.

Although the demand was made in both Canada and Nova Scotia that the question of confederation be left to popular vote, in both provinces it was refused. Only in New Brunswick was such a vote taken. In March 1865, the Tilley government, which sponsored the new scheme, was overwhelmed at the polls, and an anti-confederate government came into office. Barely a year had gone by when that government was forced to resign, and, in the election that followed, it met with a defeat as decisive as its previous victory had been. The new government took immediate action to bring the province into confederation.

The narrative of these facts raises many questions. Why did the Tilley government appeal to the people so soon after the Quebec resolutions were made public? Was it a case of necessity or of choice? Was the question of confederation the chief issue in the election? Above all, why was the overwhelming victory of the anti-confederate government in 1865 followed by its even more decisive defeat in 1866? Was it because of the faults of the new government? Was it owing to the educative work of Leonard Tilley on behalf of federation? Did the imperial government exert any influence? Did the Canadian government play any part in the final decision? Was the change owing to the need of greater unity, which was made apparent by the threatened Fenian invasion? Or was the change one, as Campbell in his *History of Nova Scotia* suggests, for which any person acquainted with politics in New Brunswick feels it quite unnecessary to ask the reason?

However, before discussing the various lines of action open to Tilley on his return from Quebec, it is necessary to understand the position of the lieutenant-governor of the province. He was to play a part in the drama second only to that of Tilley himself. Sir Arthur Hamilton Gordon, afterwards (1893) first Baron Stanmore, held the office of lieutenant-governor of New Brunswick from 1861 to 1866. He was the son of the Lord Aberdeen who had been prime minister of England during the Crimean War. Gordon was a very active and industrious governor, intensely interested in the scheme for Maritime union and in the later larger scheme of confederation.

According to Hannay, he was a strong advocate of Maritime union because he hoped to be the first governor of the united province. He was, accordingly, very much opposed to the larger scheme of confederation, and his opposition was one of the chief factors in bringing about the defeat of Tilley's government.[2] Hannay says that it was believed that his visit to England in 1865 was the result of a summons, that in England he had to submit to a severe reproof "for his anti-constitutional meddling in a matter that did not concern him," and that he was allowed to return only on condition that he do all in his power to carry confederation. The reproof was effective, and he asserts that Gordon returned a changed man.[3] Pope, in his *Correspondence of Sir John Macdonald,* says that Gordon was later sent as governor to Trinidad because he had opposed confederation.[4]

None of these statements is entirely true. Gordon was, indeed, interested in the question of Maritime union. He accepted an invitation to Charlottetown at the time of the conference. He did so willingly, he wrote to Cardwell the colonial secretary, as he had "long taken a warm interest in the legislative and administrative union of the Lower Provinces."[5] At Charlottetown he met the Canadian ministers and had considerable conversation with them, especially with Galt, who appeared to him to be far the ablest of their number.[6] Later, when the delegates visited Fredericton, Cartier, Galt, and Brown were guests at government house, and the lieutenant-governor had another opportunity to discuss the proposed scheme of union. His opinion was clear and decisive. He was very much in favour of a legislative union of all the colonies in British North America but very much opposed to a federal union. Such a federal union as was proposed would, he thought, be useless and costly. It would leave the provincial governments much as they were, and simply add another weak government at their head.[7] He cited Lord Durham in favour of his scheme of legislative union, as well as former speeches of John A. Macdonald and George Brown. He was opposed to a federal scheme which included the separation again of Upper and Lower Canada. A federal union meant a weak and divided government, a legislative union meant a strong and united one. At the conclusion of a very long confidential despatch to Cardwell, dated October 11, 1864, Gordon stated his attitude to the proposed federal union:

> In closing this despatch I may be permitted to resume the substance of the observations it contains. I agree with Lord Durham and the other high authorities in considering all schemes of Federal Union to be clumsy and costly substitutes for legislative unity – I consider such legislative unity

impracticable at the moment, but by no means hopeless at a future and no distant day. Meanwhile if it is desired that immediate steps should be taken to bring the British North American Provinces into closer connection, I see no objection to the retention of municipal bodies invested with very large powers, provided they are, in all respects, subordinate to the central authority. I am far from wishing that the Imperial Parliament should over conscientiously scan the details of any measure such as that now contemplated or weigh too nicely the exact attributes of the central and local bodies, but if Parliament lightly sanction any plan laid before it, of which the main object seems to be to sever the union of the two Canadas accomplished in 1840, and does not insist on the adoption of one great principle of central supremacy, I fear that instead of conferring benefit on B.N.A. it will inflict a lasting injury which it will be beyond even its own powers to repair.[8]

The British government, however, was satisfied with the Quebec plan, and Cardwell wrote to Lord Monck commending it. "Her Majesty's government are anxious to lose no time in conveying to you their general approval of the proceedings of the conference." They felt that the objection urged by Gordon, that the central government had not sufficient power, was unfounded. "They are glad to observe that although large powers of Legislation are intended to be vested in local bodies, yet the principle of central control has been steadily kept in view."[9] A copy of this despatch was sent to the lieutenant-governor of New Brunswick "for his information and guidance."

Gordon replied that he would act in conformity "with Her Majesty's gracious commands" but that he had grave doubts if any such central supremacy would be established, and expressed his conviction that if the new constitution was adopted in its present form, it would inflict grave, if not irreparable injury on the social and political well-being of the different provinces of British North America. Under the circumstances, he thought it not improbable that Her Majesty's government might wish to send out another governor. Gordon accordingly tendered his resignation.[10] It was not accepted, and from this date, January 2, 1865, his whole influence was thrown on the side of the scheme which had been drawn up at Quebec, and blessed by the colonial office. Gordon's visit to England, mentioned by Hannay, took place seven months after this despatch was written, and was not the result of a summons from the colonial office but in order to attend to private business. On July 31, 1865, he wrote asking for two months' leave of absence. Two weeks later, on

August 14, he wrote saying that his need of returning to England was so urgent that he was anticipating the leave asked for, and was sailing on the next mail steamer from Halifax. On October 28, he arrived back in New Brunswick and resumed the administration.

When Tilley returned from the Quebec conference in the autumn of 1864, the problem that faced him was somewhat different from the problem that faced Tupper in Nova Scotia and the Canadian coalition government in Canada. Given parliamentary support, they could refuse to refer the question to a popular vote. It was much more difficult to avoid it in New Brunswick, as a provincial election was due in the ordinary course of events in the summer of 1865. If, however, the government so desired, one more session might be held before the election. Tilley had three choices: (i) He might dissolve parliament without calling the extra session, and fight the election on the question of confederation; (ii) he might call the extra session, and try to secure its consent to the Quebec resolutions; (iii) he might call the extra session, bring only routine business before it, and then dissolve and fight the elections on the confederation issue.

Tupper and Macdonald thought Tilley ought to call the extra session and put the resolutions through without going to the people. Public opinion in New Brunswick, however, was so strong against any scheme of rushing through confederation just before an election that Tilley and his government publicly pledged themselves not to do so.[11] It was a bad precedent, Tupper wrote to Macdonald.[12]

Tilley's own wish was to hold the extra session, dispose of current business, and then dissolve. By that time, the public would have had a better opportunity to appreciate the merit of the Quebec scheme.[13] Lieutenant-Governor Gordon, however, was opposed to this plan. It meant delay, and he thought the government ought to dissolve at once. Although the original apathy of the people to the question of federation had been replaced by a more unfriendly feeling, he had no doubts that his present government would be returned. He thought that most of the members in the Assembly, both in and out of the government, wanted an extra session in order to secure their pay before submitting to the chances of an election.[14]

On January 14, 1865, Gordon sent Tilley a letter marked "Private and confidential," in which he strongly urged the arguments in favour of an immediate dissolution. The last session is always difficult. It would be doubly so if the legislature did not know whether it was legislating for an independent province or for a small portion of a federal state. Even if the government does not ask the legislature for its approval of the Quebec scheme, who is going to guarantee that the opposition will not bring in a motion of censure? Delay is not courteous to the Canadian government. It is still more embarrassing to the government of Nova Scotia. An election will soon be due in England. More complications may arise there if New Brunswick holds up action in Canada. Gordon ended his letter by saying that, if the government insists on its policy of delay, it "will be necessary for me officially to record my opinion on the minutes of the Executive Council."[15] Gordon's letter was effective, and, on the January 23, he was able to write to the governor-general that it was his intention to dissolve the existing legislature immediately. A week later, he wrote to Cardwell that he had no doubt as to the triumph of the government. Except at St. John and in the counties of Westmoreland and York he did not think that the question of confederation would affect the result.[16] On the same day, Tilley wrote to the lieutenant-governor explaining why he had wished for delay. The people of New Brunswick had not yet time to consider the question. "We have many prejudices to overcome and much information to be given before we can expect success." Although he had consented to the election, he closed his letter with the following sentence: "I can not refrain, however, from stating that our chance of success would have been increased by adhering to our original design."[17]

Tilley's fears proved only too well founded. On March 6, Gordon wrote to the colonial secretary that the proposed confederation of the British North American provinces had met "with a most decided rejection in New Brunswick." He was not prepared, he admitted, "for such a result as that which I have now the honour to report to you." The Tilley government had been defeated by a vote of 14 to 27. Macdonald thought the result was what the New Brunswick government deserved from its unstatesmanlike action in bringing on the election.[18]

In Nova Scotia Tupper had postponed bringing the Quebec resolutions before the house so as to avoid injuring in any way Tilley's chances in New Brunswick. He himself was now on the defensive as the result of the New Brunswick election. In order to prevent a hostile motion in the Nova Scotian House, he brought in a motion to take up again the question of Maritime union, as "under existing circumstances an immediate union of the B.N.A. Provinces had become impracticable."[19] It saved the situation in Nova Scotia, although, as Tilley wrote to Galt, it certainly did not help the confederate party in New Brunswick.[20] In this same letter to Galt, Tilley explained the results of the recent election, told how the election had been brought on against his better judgment, but ended by asserting his conviction "that the day was not far distant when a majority of the electors of New Brunswick would declare in favour of a Federal Union of B.N.A."

On March 27, 1865, the Tilley government resigned. One member of that government, G.L. Hatheway, had resigned before the election as a protest against the confederation scheme. The lieutenant-governor now offered him the opportunity of forming a new government. When he declined, the governor sent for R.D. Wilmot and Albert J. Smith, and they organized the new anti-confederate government. On April 10, the governor sent to the colonial secretary an account of the various members of his new executive council. The letter was marked confidential, and is very frank. Mr. Smith, the president of the council, is a man of some ability and considerable obstinacy, "possesses the merits of honesty of purpose and resolution," is a radical, but very hostile to the United States. Mr. Allen is "a gentleman of education and position," greatly respected by all parties. Mr. Gilmor is a man of no education or ability, but his intentions are honourable and upright. Mr. Hatheway, who was now a member of the government, "is a man destitute of education and I fear of principle and altogether unfit for the position he holds." Mr. R.D. Wilmot is an honest and able gentleman. Mr. Anglin is "a man of some ability but of singularly narrow mind." Gordon concludes his despatch with a comparison between his new cabinet and the old:

> On the whole the personnel of the new government is an improvement on that of the previous council. A decided majority of its members are men of undoubted ability and two or three of their members are educated gentlemen. There is no man amongst them of the natural abilities of Mr. Tilley, but on the other hand there is no man so utterly incapable and inefficient as were some members of my late executive council.[21]

The governor, however, doubted whether the rule of educated gentlemen would last long. "It is true," he wrote, "that they have amongst their members an Irish rebel and one of the least estimable members of the late government, but I doubt whether these elements will suffice to enable them to retain the favour of the democracy."[22]

The new government, however, were determined to retain the favour of their anti-confederate supporters, and equally determined that the British government should have no illusions as to the attitude of New Brunswick on this all-important subject. On May 22, 1865, they sent a memorandum to the governor, signed by every member of the council, which they requested him to transmit to England. The document ran thus:

> Our attention has been recently attracted by a statement in the London *Times* newspaper to the effect that the confederation scheme of the B.N.A. Provinces is progressing favourably. We entertain no doubt that your Excellency's reports to the Colonial Office have placed Mr. Cardwell in possession of the real state of the public mind on that subject, but as we are anxious that no doubt should exist in the minds of the English government as to the present state of this question, we would request your Excellency at once to inform the Secretary of State for the Colonies how entirely this scheme has been rejected by the people of this province, and that we have strong reasons to believe, and do believe, that with the exception of a party in Halifax, the Legislature and people of Nova Scotia are, if possible, still more opposed to the project than those of New Brunswick. The House of Assembly in Prince Edward Island, as your Excellency is aware, has rejected it almost unanimously, and the House of Assembly of Newfoundland resolved to postpone the consideration of it until after their next election, and we venture the opinion that Canada is the only province in British America favourable to the scheme.

On June 24, Cardwell wrote a despatch to Gordon commending the scheme of federation as agreed upon at Quebec. This brought from the council another protest. They could not discover anything in the new scheme "that gave promise of either moral or material advantage to the Empire or to themselves, or that afforded a prospect of improved administration or increased prosperity." The Quebec resolutions failed to satisfy even those who desired a real union. They could find no "provisions whatever for the accomplishment of a fusion which, in the words of Mr. Cardwell's despatch, would unite in one government all the B.N.A. provinces, uniting in itself all the population and all the resources of the whole." The minute of the council concluded with the assertion that the reason the Canadians are so keen for federation is that they want to get out of their "existing difficulties." Their anxiety for federation is not nearly so great as their anxiety for the separation of Upper and Lower Canada. Unless, however, they succeed in bringing about the larger union, they cannot conceal this fact from the Imperial government.

While the New Brunswick government protested against union with Canada, it was willing to take up again the question of Maritime union. Tupper had tempered the wind to the confederation scheme in Nova Scotia by falling back on the less ambitious plan. On May 25, Smith moved a resolution in favour of appointing delegates "to confer with the government of N.S. and P.E.I. on the subject of such union." The motion carried 27 to 4.[23]

The New Brunswick government might protest its loyalty, as it did, but that did not conceal the fact that it was opposing a policy of which the imperial government approved. The lieutenant-governor might have once been a critic of the Quebec resolutions; he was now the agent of the imperial government, and, as such, a supporter of the confederate opposition against his anti-confederate advisers. His council were quite aware, Gordon wrote to Cardwell, that he would dissolve the house as soon as it was apparent that a new election would reverse the verdict of the last.[24]

He was prepared to take advantage of any difference in his cabinet. He was prepared to reverse the governor's usual role of a peacemaker. Gordon did not find his task difficult, as there were two distinct and conflicting schools of thought in his council. Some of the ministers were opposed to the union on any terms, others were in favour of union but not on the basis of the Quebec resolutions. The cabinet might be called anti-confederate, but, only in part, could it be called anti-unionist. Less than two months after the new ministers had taken office, Gordon wrote to Cardwell,

> When the session has closed, I shall endeavour to turn their difference to account, and if a union founded on an agreement of sentiment as to the necessity of closer connection between the B.N.A. Provinces could be effected between Mr. Tilley and the more respectable members of the Late Cabinet and a portion of the existing government, I think the success of the scheme tolerably certain.[25]

If responsible government means anything, it means that a governor must accept the advice of his advisers, and not plot against them with the leader of the opposition. It cannot be said that Gordon observed this rule. In his letters to the colonial secretary, he speaks time and again of having discussed the political situation with Tilley. On May 22, 1865, he writes that Tilley intends to remain quiet till November, and then begin a systematic campaign to educate the public on the question of confederation.

> He proposes to avail himself of the machinery of the Temperance Societies, of which he is a very prominent member, and to hold meetings

> at which petitions are to be adopted, praying that the Legislature will adopt measures to effect a closer union of the B.N.A. Provinces, and that in the event of their not doing so the existing Parliament may be dissolved by me.

For the time being Gordon says he and Tilley are agreed that any immediate action "would be premature and injudicious."

An opportunity to test public opinion came sooner than Gordon or Tilley expected. In September, Chief Justice Carter resigned, and the senior judge, Justice Parker, took his place. Allen, the attorney-general, and perhaps the most highly respected member in the government, was elevated to the bench. Albert Smith, president of the Executive Council, took his place as attorney-general. This change necessitated two elections. Smith had to seek re-election in his county of Westmoreland, while a successor to the former attorney-general had to be elected in the county of York. Much to Cardwell's disappointment, Smith was returned unopposed in Westmoreland.[26] At first it seemed probable that an anti-confederate would have equal fortune in York. Charles Fisher, a leading supporter of Tilley and a delegate to the Quebec Conference, decided to contest the constituency, and after a lively contest was elected. There might be some doubt whether the election indicated a real change in public opinion, as Fisher's friends did their best to keep the question of confederation out of the election, and Fisher himself gave a pledge to oppose confederation if presented to the present parliament.[27] Nevertheless, the friends of union regarded Fisher's return as a triumph for their cause. Lord Monck wrote to Macdonald that he thought it was the most important thing that had happened since the Quebec Conference.[28] He sent his congratulations to Macdonald and his colleagues. A letter of Tilley to Macdonald before the election throws light on the reason why the Canadian ministers deserved congratulations on Fisher's success. Tilley had written,

> I am quite confident Fisher can be returned under any circumstances with an expenditure of eight or ten thousand dollars. If this should be considered necessary, is there any chance of the friends in Canada providing half the expenditure, not to exceed five thousand dollars for their share?

He went on to say that although they had little chance against Smith, he considered St. John city and county theirs at any time, "if we can go into the field with a fair share of the needful."[29] On the back of this letter there is written, "My dear Galt, read this. What about the monies? J.A. MacD."

The New Brunswick government were becoming more and more conscious that, in opposing confederation, they were opposing a policy very much desired by the imperial government. On June 17, 1865, Cardwell wrote to Lord Monck that Her Majesty's government were determined to use "every proper means of influence to carry into effect without delay the proposed confederation."[30] A week later, on June 24, the colonial secretary wrote to Gordon, sending him a copy of the correspondence between himself and Lord Monck on the affairs of British North America, which correspondence Gordon was asked to communicate to the legislature of his province. "You will at the same time express the strong and deliberate opinion of Her Majesty's government that it is an object much to be desired that all the B.N.A. colonies should agree to unite in one government." The Home government felt that it had a right, and even an obligation, to urge "with earnestness and just authority" the advantage of such a union for the purpose of self-defence. Her Majesty's government, therefore, "trust that after a full and careful examination of the subject in all its bearings, the Maritime Provinces will perceive the great advantages which in the opinion of Her Majesty's Government the proposed union is calculated to confer upon them all."

Gordon not only sent a copy of this despatch to his council, but had it printed in the *Royal Gazette*.[31] It thereby became public property. No person could have any doubt as to the wishes of the Home government.

On December 4, 1865, Gordon wrote that the sentiment in favour of union had greatly increased, while the opponents of confederation had lost confidence as well as members. They felt that union was a measure "which with or without their consent is certain ere long to be accomplished, and which it is consequently useless, and it may be imprudent, any longer to resist."

So great was the change of feeling that Gordon had high hopes that his present government might itself take up the cause of union. Anglin, the most violent anti-confederate in the council, had resigned in November over a question of railroad policy.[32] Several of the remaining members, he wrote, were ready to accept the Quebec scheme with any trifling modification which would afford them a loophole for escaping from the reproach of inconsistency, while the remainder had avowed themselves by no means hostile to union apart from the details of the Quebec scheme.

> The decision of the government as a body will ultimately rest with its leader, Mr. Smith. His mind is not fully made up, but I am not at all certain that he will not yet declare himself a friend of union. Indeed at the end of a long conversation with me of several hours duration a few days ago he discussed the means by which such a measure was to be carried in a tone and spirit which led me to infer that he would finally determine to take a part in securing its adoption. Should he do so, its success is at once assured.[33]

Gordon was most anxious that union should be carried by the present House of Assembly and by the present government. Not only would the province escape the turmoil and expense of an election at a most inconvenient season of the year, but union, if carried in this way, "would not wear the character of a party triumph."[34]

In any event the lieutenant-governor was determined to force the issue. If the present ministry finally decided not to support union, they would be forced to give way to one that would. He was not going to be deceived by empty professions on the part of his council.

> Against this danger I propose to guard by compelling the adoption of a decided policy when the time for the assembly of the Legislature draws near. I then propose to submit to my council the draft of a paragraph in my speech from the throne, in which I intend to invite both branches of the Legislature again seriously to consider the question of an union of the B.N.A. Provinces, and shall express a hope that such an union will speedily be accomplished. If my government are content to adopt such language, all difficulty is at an end, and the resolutions will be adopted by both houses with trifling opposition. If, on the contrary, my council as a body decline to make themselves responsible for the enunciation of such sentiments, the time will, I think, have arrived at which a change of government may be effected and a dissolution tried.[35]

On December 4, 1865, when Gordon wrote the above despatch, he was very hopeful that his council would finally support union. Some two months later, on February 12, he wrote another long "confidential" letter to Cardwell, in which he again canvassed the situation in New Brunswick. He was now less optimistic, although still hopeful of avoiding the necessity of using drastic measures. Conditions, however, had changed for the worse, as the result of the resignation of the Hon. R.D. Wilmot from the council. Gordon had placed his chief reliance on

Wilmot to win over the government to the cause of union. He tried to persuade him to reconsider his resignation, but Wilmot felt that he had received a personal slight from the attorney-general, and refused to meet him again at the council board.

The governor then considered the possibility of using the resignation of Wilmot to force the resignation of the government. The government had originally been formed by Smith and Wilmot, and, if Gordon now refused to accept the latter's resignation, he could force the retirement of the former. The governor recognized the danger of such a measure, particularly as Wilmot was not a popular man. He was prepared, however, to take the risk if the government refused to agree to the insertion of a recommendation in favour of union in the speech from the throne. He prepared for such a refusal by ascertaining that Wilmot and Peter Mitchell, a leading member of the late Executive Council, would form an administration if necessary.[36]

Albert Smith, the head of the government, was at this time in Washington, seeking, along with the Canadian representatives, to secure the extension of the Reciprocity Treaty with the United States. Until his return, Gordon refused either to accept or refuse Wilmot's resignation. On February 14, Smith returned, and Gordon at once took up the question of Wilmot's resignation and the policy the government intended to pursue on the question of union.

In these conversations between the governor and his chief minister, it is impossible to say with certainty what exactly was promised. Smith and Gordon afterwards gave very contradictory accounts. Certain things, however, are clear. Smith found himself in a very difficult position. He suspected, with only too much justice, that the governor was in communication with the opposition and would be only too glad to dispense with his present council if the opportunity offered. He knew that the governor had the support of the colonial secretary, and had instructions from London to commend union as soon as the legislature met. He knew that, if he absolutely refused to have anything to do with union, the governor would, instead of accepting Wilmot's resignation, ask the latter to form a government.

Under the circumstances Smith and his council agreed to make some concessions. They would agree to union being commended in the speech from the throne, but not in the emphatic terms Gordon had desired.[37] They also agreed that the despatches commending union should be referred to a joint committee of the two houses. Gordon afterwards said, and so reported in his despatches to the colonial secretary, that it was understood that this committee would make a recommendation in favour of union, which the government would then take up.[38] Smith very emphatically denied that there was any such understanding. However, before anything was done, and before the meeting of the New Brunswick house, Smith asked the governor to observe the greatest secrecy for a week while he saw his friends and discovered whether they would support the government in its new policy.[39] On March 5, Gordon wrote that Smith had returned and informed him "that his party generally are willing to assent to the course which he has consented to pursue."

There might be disputes afterwards as to what that course was, but the governor had cause to be elated. If the anti-confederate government would bring about union, the great object was achieved. By failing to achieve union, the anti-confederate government would be discredited. Gordon thought they were discredited in any case. He wrote to Cardwell,

> This decision of my government enables me confidently to assert that whatever be their own fate, and I consider their retention of office under the circumstances very doubtful, the confederation scheme will, in a few weeks be acceded to by this province, and I beg to congratulate Her Majesty's government on the success of an object, the attainment of which they have so decidedly desired.[40]

The New Brunswick house met on March 8, and the speech from the throne, without definitely committing the government, expressed very clearly the wishes of the British ministry.

> I have received Her Majesty's commands to communicate to you a correspondence on the affairs of B.N.A. which has taken place between Her Majesty's Principal Secretary of State for the Colonies and the Governor-General of Canada; and I am further directed to express to you the strong and deliberate opinion of Her Majesty's government that it is an object much to be desired that all the B.N.A. colonies should agree to unite in one government.

The address in answer to the speech from the throne had been agreed to by the attorney-general and the governor before the meeting of the house. It was non-committal but not unfriendly:

> The opinion expressed by Her Majesty's government will command that respect and attention which is due to suggestions emanating from so high a source; but in any scheme for a union of the British North American Colonies which may be proposed, it is, in the opinion of this house, absolutely essential that full protection should be afforded to the rights and interests of the people of this Province; and no measure which fails to obtain these objects should be adopted.

In spite of the reservations, the governor and the public naturally expected the government to bring forward such a plan of union as would safeguard the interests of the province.

If the government was willing to take up the question of union, Gordon had hopes that an arrangement might be made with the opposition whereby the question might be taken out of the arena of party politics.[41] Smith, however, had no desire to enter into any agreement with his opponents. They, on their part, were equally anxious to miss no opportunity for attacking the party in office. The attack began at once. When the address in answer to the speech from the throne was debated, Charles Fisher moved an amendment, which was a motion of lack of confidence. The debate continued for almost a month with no apparent progress. The governor might well become impatient. He had assured the colonial secretary of the absolute certainty of the union measure passing in the Assembly, but that result seemed as far away as ever. He urged Smith to disclose his policy, but this the latter refused to do until the want of confidence resolution was disposed of. He did not desire even to appear to yield to the opposition.[42] The governor suspected that his council were deliberately prolonging the debate, and had no intention of bringing forward any measure for union.[43] If such was the case, he was determined to change his advisers. He had accepted Wilmot's resignation, so no longer had that excuse. He had also missed an opportunity when he agreed to modify the first draft of his speech from the throne.

There was still one opportunity, as Gordon wrote to the colonial secretary,

> of rendering it impossible for my government to avoid the alternative of either pledging themselves openly to an union policy, or of declaring the existence of so irreconcilable a difference of opinion between us as must necessarily lead to their resignation.[44]

The opportunity offered was when the Legislative Council came to present their address in answer to the speech from the throne. The majority in the council were in favour of union, and their address highly commended that measure. It was the usual custom for the governor to receive the addresses from the Legislative Assembly and the Legislative Council at the same time, but Gordon decided to make an exception in the present case.

He set the time for receiving the address at three o'clock on Saturday, April 7, and, without consulting his advisers, prepared the answer he intended to give. Shortly after twelve o'clock on that day, he sent a note to Smith asking him to come to Government House. Smith did not receive the note until a few minutes to three. When he arrived at Government House, the Legislative Council were already there, and they were kept waiting while the consultation took place between the lieutenant-governor and his chief minister.[45] Smith protested emphatically against the conduct of the Legislative Council in asking the imperial government to legislate contrary to the wish of the province as expressed at the recent election, and contrary to the wish of the Legislative Assembly. He protested, also, against the answer the governor had prepared and intended to give to the Legislative Council. The governor's advisers were responsible for all such official pronouncements. In the present case they had not even been consulted. The governor then suggested that Smith go down to the house and consult his colleagues, or that a carriage be sent to bring them to Government House. Smith said that they could not leave the house as the no confidence debate was in progress, and, in any case, it was a question that could not be settled in a few minutes. If the governor must receive the address that afternoon, Smith wished him to do no more than to acknowledge it.[46] He particularly objected to the concluding sentence in the governor's proposed speech:

> I rejoice to believe that the avowal of your desire that all British North America should unite in one community under one strong and efficient government, cannot but tend to hasten the accomplishment of this great measure.

In spite of Smith's protest, the governor decided to give his answer as he had prepared it. Three days later on April 10, without any further correspondence with the governor, the council sent in their resignation.[47]

They were unwilling to accept responsibility for the answer Gordon had given to the Legislative Council:

> Your Excellency had assumed to yourself the right to act and did act, in a matter deeply affecting the interest of the people of this province, without consulting your constitutional advisers, and in direct opposition to their views, thereby violating the constitution, and ignoring the principles of Responsible Government.

They also accused the governor of having consulted and advised with gentlemen of the opposition and made known to them matters which they think should be regarded as confidential.

The resignation of his advisers led to an acrimonious exchange of memoranda between the governor on the one hand, and the council and Mr. Smith on the other. The governor might protest that the Legislative Council had a right to adopt such an address as they had presented, and that there was no impropriety on his part in "expressing on Her Majesty's behalf satisfaction at the adhesion of one branch of the Provincial Legislature to a policy so emphatically recommended by Her Majesty's Government." It was difficult, however, for the governor to defend his conduct towards his Executive Council. He protested that it was an accident that prevented the council from having had an opportunity to consider his reply, but it was an accident for which his former advisers could see no adequate excuse. Even Tilley felt that the governor had been too hasty.[48]

When his council resigned, Gordon turned to Wilmot and Peter Mitchell, who had been prepared to form a government two months before. The late government were unwilling to agree to an adjournment while the new members were elected, so the governor prorogued the house.[49] Later it was decided, in spite of a telegram from John A. Macdonald against such a course,[50] to dissolve the house and once again to ask the people of New Brunswick to pass on the great question of confederation. If it were again defeated, even Gordon recognized that nothing could be done. The governor-general, Lord Monck, was indeed willing to consider the possibility of bringing New Brunswick into the union, even against the wishes of the people. Why should the imperial parliament, he wrote to Macdonald, "allow a majority in one branch of the Legislature in a small province to overbear the expressed opinion of the rest of B.N.A.?"[51]

The election turned out a triumph for the friends of confederation. In 1865 the vote had been 27 to 14 against confederation. In 1866 the vote was 33 to 8 in its favour. Gordon exulted in the fact that only two of his ex-ministers had been returned, while, of twenty-two members of the former Assembly who had signed an address protesting against his conduct, only six had seats in the new house.[52] The triumph of confederation was complete. The passing of resolutions in the new house, and the sending of delegates to England to confer with delegates from Canada and Nova Scotia on the bill to be laid before the imperial parliament, followed as a matter of course.

Before closing, something must be said regarding the various factors that led to the triumph of the confederate cause in the election of 1866, and that in spite of the fact that the governor's action had enabled his ex-ministers to appeal to the electors as defenders of the great principle of responsible government.

One cause was the decline in popularity of the Smith administration. The election of Fisher in York in 1865 was, apparently, only an indication of a fairly general feeling. So convinced was Gordon of the government's growing unpopularity that, if time had allowed, he said he was willing to trust to the defeat of the government in the session of 1866.[53] The letters of Fisher and Tilley to the Canadian ministers bear out this judgment of the lieutenant-governor. This unpopularity was not wholly to the government's discredit. Much of it was due, Gordon admitted to the colonial secretary, to the fact that they had refused to act "with the injustice and partiality required by their supporters."[54]

Then, again, the supporters of confederation appealed to the electors in favour of a policy strongly endorsed by the imperial government. In 1865, the electors might think that the Quebec scheme was a trap laid for them by the Canadians. In 1866, it became almost a patriotic duty to vote for a measure so emphatically recommended by Her Majesty's ministers. The province founded by the Loyalists could not be lacking in loyalty. Moreover, the Smith government was fatally weakened in its opposition to confederation in the election of 1866 because it did not appeal to the electors with an unblemished record. It might denounce the Quebec resolutions as much as it liked, but the public knew that the government itself had professed its willingness to sponsor some form of union of its own. The speech from the throne could not be forgotten. If Gordon had failed in his plan of passing union as a non-partisan measure, he had at least succeeded in discrediting the anti-union party.

The supporters of confederation were also fortunate in the events of the spring of 1866. It was the time of the threatening Fenian invasion of the province. The whole population was deeply concerned. Frontier towns like St. Andrews and St. Stephen were threatened with destruction. The militia was called out and regular troops were sent from Halifax. No event could have more dramatically brought to the attention of the province its present weakness, or proved more conclusively the arguments of the colonial secretary that the confederation of the British North American provinces was needed for their protection. Excited anti-confederates even accused the Canadians of sending the Fenians in order to further their own nefarious schemes.[55]

Elections are not won by prayers. Campaign contributions were needed, and the leaders of the confederate party in New Brunswick turned to Canada. The Canadian government could not see the cause fail from lack of funds. On April 14, four days after the resignation of the Smith government, Tilley wrote to Macdonald, "We must have the arrangement carried out and without delay that was talked of when I met you at Quebec. Telegraph me in cypher saying what we can rely upon." Three days later Tilley wrote again in the same strain. The constitutional issue makes the election uncertain. "Assistance must be had of a substantial character." He thinks some forty or fifty thousand dollars will be required for the election.[56] Gordon wrote to Lord Monck that as much help as possible ought to be sent as it might be needed.[57] On April 20, Tilley wrote to Macdonald again with still greater frankness:

> I think we can, with good management and with means, carry a majority in the province, outside of St. John, in favour of resolutions such as were passed in N.S., but St. John is a very important constituency and ought to be carried if possible, – and to be frank with you the election in this province can be made certain if the *means are* used. It will remain for the friends in Canada to say how the arrangements are to be made. It must be done with great caution and in such a way as not to awaken suspicion.[58]

Tilley suggested that a leading citizen of St. John, a large ship-owner worth at least £100,000, might go to Portland, and there meet Mr. Brydges or anyone else without arousing suspicion.[59] Mr. Brydges was manager of the Grand Trunk Railway.

One cause that must not be overlooked in accounting for the victory of confederation in 1866 was the educational work of Tilley himself. He might not have been the head of the government, but he was its real leader. No one could compare with Tilley in the work that he had done on behalf of union. He had spent the past year very largely in a campaign, the purpose of which was to remove the prejudices and misconceptions which he was convinced explained the defeat of 1865. The victory of 1866 was a personal triumph as well as the triumph of the cause he had so much at heart.

NOTES

1 George E. Wilson, "New Brunswick's Entrance into Confederation," *Canadian Historical Review*, 9, 1 (1928), 4–24.
2 James Hannay, *Sir Leonard Tilley* (Toronto, 1926), p. 97.
3 *Ibid.*, p. 98.
4 Sir Joseph Pope, *Correspondence of Sir John Macdonald* (Toronto, n.d.), p. 29, note.
5 Canadian Archives, *New Brunswick Despatches*, Gordon to Cardwell, Sept. 12, 1864.
6 *Ibid.*
7 *Ibid.*, Gordon to Cardwell (confidential), Oct. 11, 1864.
8 *Ibid.*
9 Canadian Archives, *Series G*, vol. 172, p. 382.
10 *N.B. Despatches*, Gordon to Cardwell, Jan. 2, 1865.
11 Canadian Archives, *Macdonald Papers*, VI, Tilley to Macdonald, Nov. 23, 1864.
12 *Ibid.*, VI, 53, Tupper to Macdonald, Dec. 13, 1864.
13 *Ibid.*, VI, Tilley to Galt, undated.
14 *N.B. Despatches*, Gordon to Cardwell, Jan. 16, 1865.
15 *Ibid.*, Gordon to Tilley, Jan. 14, 1865.
16 *Ibid.*, Gordon to Cardwell (confidential), Jan. 30, 1865.
17 *Ibid.*, Tilley to Gordon, Jan. 30, 1865.
18 Pope, *Correspondence of Sir John Macdonald*, p. 23, Macdonald to Hon. John Hamilton Gray, Mar. 24, 1865.
19 Nova Scotia *Journals*, 1865; resolution moved April 11, 1865.
20 *Macdonald Papers*, VI, 80, Tilley to Galt, undated.
21 *N.B. Despatches*, Gordon to Cardwell, Apr. 10, 1865.
22 *Ibid.*, Gordon to Cardwell (confidential), May 8, 1865.
23 Journal of the House of Assembly of the Province of New Brunswick, p. 174.
24 *N.B. Despatches*, Gordon to Cardwell, May 22, 1865.

25 *Ibid.*
26 *Macdonald Papers*, VI, 174, Monck to Macdonald, Nov. 22, 1865.
27 *N.B. Despatches*, Gordon to Cardwell, Nov. 20, 1865.
28 *Macdonald Papers*, Monck to Macdonald, Nov. 22, 1865.
29 *Ibid.*, Tilley to Macdonald, Sept. 13, 1865.
30 Canadian Archives, *Series G*, vol. 174, p. 54, Cardwell to Monck, June 17, 1865.
31 *N.B. Despatches*, Gordon to Cardwell, July 15, 1865.
32 *Ibid.*, Nov. 20, 1865.
33 *Ibid.*, Gordon to Cardwell, Dec. 4, 1865.
34 *Ibid.*
35 *Ibid.*
36 *Ibid.*, Gordon to Cardwell, Feb. 12, 1866.
37 *Ibid.*, Gordon to Cardwell, Mar. 12, 1866.
38 *Ibid.*, Feb. 12, 1866.
39 *Ibid.*
40 *Ibid.*, Gordon to Cardwell, Mar. 5, 1866.
41 *Ibid.*, Feb. 21, 1866.
42 *Ibid.*, Gordon to Cardwell, Mar. 25, 1866.
43 *Ibid.*, Apr. 23, 1866.
44 *Ibid.*
45 *Macdonald Papers*, Tilley to Macdonald, Apr. 14, 1866.
46 *N.B. Despatches*, Gordon to Cardwell (confidential), Apr. 23, 1866.
47 *Ibid.*
48 *Macdonald Papers*, VI, 227, Tilley to Macdonald, Apr. 14, 1866.
49 *N.B. Despatches*, Gordon to Cardwell, Apr. 16, 1866.
50 *Macdonald Papers*, VI, 273, Tilley to Macdonald, Apr. 21, 1866.
51 *Ibid.*, VI, 242, Monck to Macdonald, Apr. 17, 1866.
52 *N.B. Despatches*, Gordon to Cardwell (confidential), June 19, 1866.
53 *Ibid.*, Gordon to Cardwell, Feb. 12, 1866.
54 *Ibid.*, Dec. 4, 1865.
55 *Macdonald Papers*, Tilley to Macdonald, Apr. 21, 1866.
56 *Ibid.*, Tilley to Macdonald, Apr. 17, 1866.
57 *Ibid.*, Monck to Macdonald, Apr. 18, 1866.
58 *Ibid.*, Tilley to Macdonald, Apr. 20, 1866.
59 *Ibid.*

# "The Maritimes and Confederation: A Reassessment"

*Canadian Historical Review*
1990

PHILLIP BUCKNER[1]

A number of years ago Ernie Forbes in an important article challenged the stereotype of Maritime conservatism and attempted to show how it had distorted the way in which the history of the Maritimes has been portrayed in the post-Confederation period.[2] Yet it can be argued that this stereotype has also influenced our interpretation of the pre-Confederation era in a variety of ways. Nowhere is this truer than in studies of the role of the region in the making of Confederation. The failure of the Maritime colonies to respond enthusiastically to the Canadian initiative for Confederation in the 1860s has come to be seen as yet another example of their inherent conservatism. The impression that emerges from the literature is of a series of parochial communities content with the status quo and trapped in intellectual lethargy who were dragged kicking and screaming into Confederation. This stereotype leads to several misleading conclusions. First, it encourages historians to underestimate the degree of support which existed within the Maritimes for the ideal of a larger British North American union and to exaggerate the gulf that divided the anti-confederates from the pro-confederates. Second, it oversimplifies and trivializes the very real and substantive objections which many Maritimers had to the kind of union that they were eventually forced to accept. Recent American historiography has led to a substantial rethinking of the debate that took place in the United States over the ratification of the American constitution in the 1780s, and a similar reassessment of the debate over the Quebec Resolutions in the Maritimes in the 1860s is long overdue.

The first studies of Confederation, in fact, devoted little time to this issue. Reginald George Trotter in *Canadian Federation: Its Origins and Achievement* (Toronto 1924) barely mentions the debate over Confederation in the Maritimes, and M.O. Hammond in *Confederation and Its Leaders* (Toronto 1917) simply ascribed the views of anti-confederates such as Albert Smith to their "opposition to change of any kind" (237). In the first scholarly article on New Brunswick's entrance into Confederation, George Wilson assumed as a given New Brunswick's hesitancy and focused on the factors – the loyalty cry, Canadian campaign funds, and the "educational work of Tilley" (24) – which he saw as critical in persuading New Brunswickers to vote for union.[3] D.C. Harvey also concentrated on the idealism of the expansionists in his paper, "The Maritime Provinces and Confederation" in 1927.[4] Writing at a time when there was a feeling in the Maritimes that Confederation had not delivered what had been promised,[5] Harvey stressed that union could have been accomplished relatively easily if the "factious" opponents of federation had not been "able to whip up an opposition that caused no end of trouble to the unionist statesmen and left behind a legacy of suspicion and which has been like an ulcer in the side of the Dominion" (44). Harvey called for Maritimers to "recapture" the initial enthusiasm of the pro-confederates and to abandon the tendency to blame Confederation for their problems. By implication, then, the critics of Confederation both in the 1860s and the 1920s lacked vision and statesmanship.

This perspective was also implicit in William Menzies Whitelaw's *The Maritimes and Canada before Confederation.*[6] In his preface, Whitelaw declared that he had focused the book upon "the struggle between an incipient nationalism and a rugged particularism" (xix). The book was published in 1934 after the collapse of the Maritime Rights Movement and the onset of the Great Depression, at a time when most Canadian historians were beginning to see the advantages of a strong central government and Maritimers were again discussing the chimera of Maritime Union. Not surprisingly, Whitelaw approached the topic with a strong bias in favour of Confederation and preferably a highly centralized federal system. From the beginning the emphasis of the book was on the relative backwardness of the Maritimes and the persistence there of "early particularism," the title of one of the first chapters. Whitelaw ended his study in 1864 with an insightful chapter,

"Maritime Interests at Quebec," which showed how the Canadians manipulated the Quebec Conference and out-manoeuvred the divided Maritimers.[7] Interestingly, he did not discuss the actual debate over the Quebec Resolutions but concluded with a brief lament over the decision to abandon Maritime Union. In his review of the book in the *Canadian Historical Review,* Chester Martin with some justification declared that Whitelaw "leaves an impression not only of 'particularism' but of parochialism: of particularism run to seed, too inert to defend or even to discern their own interests in the presence of the expansive forces then abroad in Canada and the United States."[8]

In the 1940s, A.G. Bailey contributed two important articles to the small corpus of serious scholarly literature on the Maritimes and Confederation.[9] In "Railways and the Confederation Issue in New Brunswick, 1863–1865," he focused rather narrowly on the debate over the western extension, which he argued was the "most potent" factor behind the opposition to Confederation in the colony (91).[10] The problem with explaining the debate in New Brunswick in these terms is that many pro-confederates wanted the western extension, not a few anti-confederates wanted the Intercolonial, and a large number of New Brunswickers wanted both, although they could afford neither.[11] In "The Basis and Persistence of Opposition to Confederation in New Brunswick," Bailey adopted a broader approach. Although starting from the assumption that "in the early stages of the union movement there was a misapprehension of its significance, together with some degree of apathy, rather than a reasoned opposition" (93), he went on to explore with some subtlety the roots of anti-Confederation sentiment. The rapid collapse of the anti-confederate government he again ascribed primarily to its failure to complete the western extension, but he also emphasized mounting pressure from the imperial government, as well as "the exaggerated menace of Fenian invasion" (117) and Canadian campaign funds. He also recognized that many of those who opposed union "directed their attacks not so much against the principle of Confederation as against the specific terms of union which had been embodied in the Quebec Resolutions" (115). Indeed, the failure of the pro-confederates to make substantial alterations in those resolutions in London accounted, he suggested, for "the remarkable persistence of opposition" to Confederation after 1866 (116). But he did not emphasize this point, which is made as a kind of aside in the conclusion of the article.

The next major study of Confederation came from Chester Martin. In *Foundations of Canadian Nationhood* (Toronto 1955), he dismissed the opposition to Confederation in the Maritimes as "too general to be the result of personalities or sheer parochialism" (347). This insight might have provided the basis for a fundamental reassessment of the debate in the Maritimes, but Martin quickly reverted to the stereotype of Maritime conservatism. Indeed, one of the major subthemes in the book is that the original decision to partition Nova Scotia into a series of smaller units had inevitably promoted parochialism: "Where local division had been deliberately planted and thriven for three-quarters of a century, provincialism was only too apt to degenerate into sheer parochialism" (290). Because he saw Confederation as forced upon the British North American colonies by (in what was the *leitmotif* of this section of the book) "events stronger than advocacy, events stronger than men" (291) and the opposition to it as a natural instinct (see 297), Martin also accepted that "there were solid reasons for resistance based upon conflicting interests and a long train of policy" (355). Nonetheless, the clear implication of his approach was that the fundamental motivation behind the widespread Maritime opposition to the Quebec Resolutions was the deep-seated conservatism of the region.

During the early 1960s, writing on Confederation became a growth industry as Canada approached its centennial. Since most Canadian historians were still influenced by the consensus approach, which minimized the significance of internal conflicts by focusing on the things which united Canadians and distinguished them from other people, they tended to downplay regional concerns and to interpret the making of Confederation as a success story of which all Canadians should be proud.[12] The best of these studies was P.B. Waite's *The Life and Times of Confederation 1864–67*, and it is a tragedy that it has been allowed to go out of print.[13] Although Waite does not indicate that he was directly influenced by Chester Martin, there are a number of parallels in their interpretations. Like Martin, Waite saw Confederation as forced upon the British North Americans by external pressures. Although he was less deterministic and did not see Confederation as an inevitable response to these pressures, he concluded that Confederation was "imposed on British North America by ingenuity, luck, courage, and sheer force" (323). Like Martin, he argued that the opposition to Confederation was rooted in the "innate conservatism" of the smaller communities across British North America (14) and that this conservatism was particularly strong in the Maritimes. But reflecting the spirit of the 1960s, Waite also saw the tentative stirrings of a sense of Canadian nationalism in the 1860s. By 1864, he concluded, "Whether for good or ill, there was a national spirit stirring in the Maritime provinces" (72); in fact, the Maritime pro-confederates were even more eager than the Canadians to escape from "the littleness of provincial pastures" (89).

Since Waite clearly accepted that Confederation was necessary and desirable and that the Quebec Resolutions were an imaginative and ingenious recipe for union, he had limited patience with the anti-confederates who are seen as "men of little faith."[14] His impatience with their unwillingness to accept the Quebec terms is revealed in his treatment of the "poor, tired, rather embittered" Joseph Howe, who might "have supported Confederation had he had an opportunity similar to Tupper's" (210). And it is even more clearly revealed in his assessment of L.A. Wilmot: "It may have been that Wilmot was perfectly genuine in his conversion to Confederation. But if so, it was not his main motive. With Wilmot perquisites usually triumphed over policies" (256). Waite accepted that Nova Scotians had some reason for resentment, since the Quebec Resolutions were imposed upon them against their will, but he did not extend the same sympathy to New Brunswick and Prince Edward Island, which he described as totally mired in an all-pervasive parochialism: "Of both Fredericton and Charlottetown Goldwin Smith's unrepentant aphorism is not altogether inappropriate: 'The smaller the pit, the fiercer the rats'" (233).[15] It was the "ferocity of politics" which accounted for the "primeval character" of the discussion of Confederation in New Brunswick (233–4). As for Prince Edward Island, their opposition is more simply explained. Most Islanders had never been away from the Island in their lives (at least according to George Brown) and they had "had little opportunity to cultivate larger loyalties." "Like the Acadians a century before, they simply wanted to be left alone" (180–1).

Waite's emphasis on the parochialism and conservatism of New Brunswick and Prince Edward Island was reinforced by two more specialized studies which appeared in the early 1960s. There was always a curiously ambivalent attitude in the work of W.S. MacNutt towards his adopted province. Because he was disappointed with the province's performance in the post–World War II era, he took up the cause of Maritime unity in the 1950s and railed against those local politicians who were obsessed with the distribution of local patronage and lacked a vision of grandeur.[16] In *New Brunswick: A History: 1784–1867* (Toronto 1963), he projected this anger backwards, and his impatience with the provincial politicians shines through. Although MacNutt felt it was "difficult to allow very much praise for the politicians" of the province

(460), at least "a few leaders of imagination and daring had made themselves the instruments of the grand idea that was British North America's response to the problems of the time, the urge for mergers and the manufacturing of great states" (454). Francis W.P. Bolger adopted a not dissimilar approach in *Prince Edward Island and Confederation 1863–1873* (Charlottetown 1964). During the years that Confederation was discussed, Island politics, he noted, "remained personal, parochial, and violent" (14), and it was inevitable that the Island would resist with all its might the pressures for union.[17]

It is difficult not to come away from these works with the impression that there was virtually no support for Confederation in the Maritimes, except for a handful of prescient individuals who had the imagination to accept the leadership of the more far-sighted and progressive Canadians. Yet all three studies revealed very clearly that anti-Confederation sentiment in the region was generated as much by the unpalatability of the Quebec Resolutions as by opposition to the idea of Confederation itself. All three historians also accepted that the terms adopted at Quebec City reflected Canadian needs and Canadian priorities, and, like Whitelaw, they clearly assumed that the Maritime delegates to Quebec had failed to secure better terms because of the superior acumen and organization of the Canadian delegation. It is, of course, true that the exigencies of Canadian politics forced the members of the Great Coalition to adopt a relatively united front on the constitutional issues under discussion at a time when the Maritime delegations were divided both internally and amongst themselves at Quebec. But one could as easily attribute the failure of the Maritime delegates to their realism and to the extent of their desire for some kind of union. Their basic problem was that the two regions were of such unequal size. At Philadelphia in 1787 the Americans were forced to resort to equal representation in the Senate, not solely to appease the small states but also for reasons of "*regional* security," in order "to safeguard the most conspicuous interests of North and South."[18] In the end it was the comparative equality of the two regions which compelled the delegates at Philadelphia to agree to the "Great Compromise." No such pressure existed at Quebec in 1864. Because of the uneven size and power of the two regions, the Maritime delegates were compelled to agree to union on Canadian terms, if they wanted union at all.

The leading Maritime politicians at Quebec had no illusions about the limited room they had for manoeuvre. Even at Charlottetown, Samuel Leonard Tilley and W.H. Pope opposed the suggestion that Maritime

Union should precede Confederation, on the grounds that the Maritime provinces would be able to arrive at better terms with Canada by negotiating separately rather than united.[19] Indeed, Charles Tupper believed that the gradual withdrawal of Britain had made the subordination of the Maritimes to Canada inevitable and that the goal of the Maritime delegates at Quebec must be to gain the best terms of union that they could.[20] The Maritimers did try to offset their weakness in the House of Commons by insisting on sectional equality in the Senate, and the majority of them also sought to ensure that the provinces would be left with control over those local matters of most immediate concern to their constituents. Although Jonathan McCully failed in his attempt to have agriculture removed from the list of federal responsibilities, Tilley persuaded the delegates to transfer control over roads and bridges to the provinces.[21] Indeed, upon returning to New Brunswick, Tilley worked out that only five of the fifty-nine acts passed by the New Brunswick legislature in the previous session would be found *ultra vires* of the provincial government under the proposed division of powers.[22] And both Tilley and Tupper pointed out forcefully at the London Conference that their intention had not been to create a "Legislative Union."[23] Yet even after it became clear to them how unpopular the Quebec Resolutions were, the pro-confederate leadership recognized that there were limits to the concessions the Canadians could make without destroying the fragile unity of the great coalition. Reluctantly, therefore, they accepted that, if Confederation was to take place in the 1860s, "it is the Quebec scheme & little else we can hope to have secured."[24]

Although the pro-confederate leadership was probably right in this assumption, the Quebec Resolutions weakened the potential support for union in the region. Many of those sympathetic to the ideal of Confederation felt that a second conference should be called to renegotiate the terms of union.[25] Both Bailey and MacNutt attributed much of the lingering resentment to Confederation in New Brunswick after 1866 to the failure of the efforts of the New Brunswick delegates at the London Conference to make substantial alterations in the unpopular Quebec plan.[26] Bolger also accepted that the Island rejected the initial proposals because they were not "sufficiently attractive."[27] Much of the debate in the Maritimes revolved not upon the issue of whether union was desirable but whether the Quebec Resolutions adequately met Maritime needs and concerns. The strength of the anti-confederate movement throughout the region was that it could appeal both to those whom Waite describes in Canada West as the "ultras," who opposed

Confederation on any terms, and the "critics," who had specific objections to the Quebec scheme, although they were not opposed to Confederation on principle.[28] In Canada West, most of the critics were easily convinced to put aside their objections; in the Maritimes, the proponents of the Quebec Resolutions had an uphill battle to bring the critics on side. Unfortunately, Waite does not present the struggle in the Maritimes in quite these terms but lumps the critics together with the ultras, thus creating the impression that die-hard opposition to union was stronger than it was. He therefore concludes that "New Brunswick was pushed into Union, Nova Scotia was dragooned into it, and Newfoundland and Prince Edward Island were subjected to all the pressure that could be brought to bear – short of force – and still refused."[29] In a literal sense these comments are true, but they gloss over the fact that what the Maritimes were pushed, dragooned, and in the case of PEI "railroaded" into was a union on Canadian terms.[30] MacNutt and Bolger also admitted that there were severe imperfections in the Quebec Resolutions from the perspective of the Maritimes, but they too ignored the implications of this argument and bunched together all anti-confederates as conservatives who lacked foresight.

This was also the conclusion of Donald Creighton in *The Road to Confederation: The Emergence of Canada 1863–1867* (Toronto 1964). As in all his works, Creighton's writing was infused with a strong moral tone and a rigid teleological framework which emphasized that Confederation was the logical destination at the end of the road. Those who stood in the way of his vision of what was both right and inevitable were dismissed as narrow-minded obstructionists, and he began his book by approvingly paraphrasing Arthur Hamilton Gordon's description of the Maritimes as "half a dozen miserable fragments of provinces" where the "inevitable pettiness and the lack of talented and devoted men in public life could not but make for parochialism, maladministration, and low political morality in every department of provincial life" (8). Throughout the book, Creighton contrasted "the lofty nationalist aims of the Canadians" (154) with the parochialism of the Maritimers. "If the Charlottetown Conference was likely to end up as an open competition between confederation and Maritime union," he wrote scornfully, "the Maritimers seemed placidly unaware of the prospect, or disinclined to get excited about it. They appeared to be simply waiting without much concern, and even without a great deal of interest, to see what would turn up" (91). To Creighton, the opposition of the Maritimers to Confederation was almost incomprehensible. Since "Maritimers showed, again and again, that they could not but feel their ultimate destiny lay in North American union" (75), their opposition could only be based upon a natural lethargy. A much more sophisticated study of the Confederation era was W.L. Morton's *The Critical Years: The Union of British North America, 1857–1873* (Toronto 1964). But Morton too had limited sympathy with the Maritimers' failure to see what he described as the "moral purpose of Confederation" (277). New Brunswick's opposition he ascribed to the lack of moral integrity of its politicians and the lack of principle of its electorate, which "was largely composed of individuals who were politically indifferent, or took no interest in politics except to sell their votes" (172).

The later 1960s and the 1970s also saw a considerable number of more specialized studies, mainly by academics coming from or living in the Maritimes, and they usually took one of two forms. On the one hand, some of these historians attempted to show that Maritime pro-confederates had played a more significant role in the Confederation movement than had previously been assumed, although they did not question the view that the pro-confederates possessed a larger vision than the vast majority of the inhabitants of the region.[31] Del Muise in his study of the debate over Confederation in Nova Scotia took a different and much more significant tack. Moving beyond the narrow political boundaries in which the whole debate had come to be cast, he argued that the battle over Confederation was between the proponents of the old maritime economy of "wood, wind and sail" and the younger, more progressive members of the regional elites who were prepared to make the transition to a continental economy based on railways and coal and committed to industrialization.[32] Muise's interpretative framework was particularly convincing in explaining – really for the first time – why pro-confederates such as Tupper, who were from areas with the potential for industrialization, were prepared to support union even on the basis of the somewhat unpalatable Quebec Resolutions, and he successfully established that "certain regions and interests in the Province wanted and carried Confederation."[33] Muise's thesis also helped to explain why those most committed to an international economy based on shipping and shipbuilding were so vehemently opposed to Confederation on almost any terms. By rescuing the debate from a narrowly political framework and focusing on the economic interests of the participants, Muise challenged the stereotype that most Maritimers were motivated by a rather simple-minded conservatism. Yet he also fell into the classic trap by identifying the pro-confederates as younger men while their opponents come across as conservatives resisting the forces of change. The work of the Maritime History Group has undermined this fallacious dichotomy, for they have shown that those who remained committed to the traditional economy – or at least to the shipping and shipbuilding industries – were among the most dynamic economic entrepreneurs in the region and that they were motivated not by a misplaced conservatism but a sensible analysis of the economic benefits still to be derived from investing in the traditional sectors of the economy.[34] Although it was not his intention, by portraying the division of economic interests in the province in terms of the old versus the young (and by implication those representing the future against those wedded to the past), Muise's thesis thus inadvertently reinforced the stereotype that the anti-confederate forces were motivated by parochialism and unprogressive attitudes.

Moreover, the attempt to divide the whole province into pro-confederates and anti-confederates on the basis of their commitment to the economy of wood, wind, and sail was too deterministic. By the 1860s there was a growing desire to participate in the evolving industrial economy, but, as Ben Forster has pointed out in his recent study of the rise of protectionist sentiment in British North America, the Saint John manufacturing interests "had divided opinions as to the value of Confederation." Pryke makes the same point about Nova Scotian manufacturers.[35] Public opinion in those communities tied to wood, wind, and sail was also more deeply split than Muise's thesis allowed. After all, as he admitted, when Stewart Campbell introduced his resolution against Confederation in March 1867, only nine of the sixteen members of the Nova Scotia legislature who supported it were from areas committed to the traditional economy, and while twenty-five of the thirty-two members who supported it represented areas "with at least some commitment to the emerging economy of coal and railroads," the degree of that commitment varied considerably.[36]

Although Muise's approach was extremely valuable in helping to explain the extremes of opinion – the views of the ultras on both sides – it could not adequately explain the motives of the large body of men who were prepared to consider union with Canada but who disliked the Quebec Resolutions. We do not know precisely how many Maritimers fell into this category and we may never know, since the issue of accepting or rejecting the Quebec Resolutions temporarily forced most Maritimers to identify themselves as pro- or anti-confederates on that basis. What is certain is that a variety of interests and ideological and cultural perspectives were represented in both camps. Years ago, Bailey pointed out that in New Brunswick, "the cleavage of opinion seems not to have followed either occupational or class lines," and suggested that there were strong ethnic and religious overtones to the struggle.[37] Subsequent studies of New Brunswick have reaffirmed Bailey's insight and have emphasized cultural over economic factors, and similar patterns can be found in the other Maritime provinces. Traditionally, Canadian historians have emphasized the growing independence of the British North American colonies after the grant of responsible government. Yet these were also decades when, in a variety of ways, the colonies were becoming increasingly Anglicized.[38] The Quebec Resolutions, which so clearly sought to follow imperial and British institutional models, appear to have been most strongly supported by those who welcomed movement in this direction and particularly by the British-born; they were less enthusiastically endorsed by the native-born, of whom there was a much larger number in the Maritimes than in Canada West, and were viewed with greatest suspicion by cultural minorities such as Irish Catholics and Acadians. Nonetheless, as William Baker has shown, "the whole idea of a monolithic response by Irish Catholics to Confederation is highly questionable."[39] Desirable as it may be to come up with matching sets of dichotomous interests or ethno-religious categories, one can do so only at the risk of obscuring the diversity that existed on both sides in the struggle.

The second major emphasis of the more recent scholarship has been on analysing the position of those Maritimers who opposed union. J. Murray Beck spent most of a life-time trying to correct the negative image of Howe embodied in the literature, although he did not deny that Howe "set store by the wrong vision."[40] Similarly, Carl Wallace dissected the motives of Albert J. Smith, who, he claimed, "exemplified the true mentality of New Brunswick 'in this era' and who, like New Brunswick, turned to the past, unable to adjust to the changing present."[41] Other historians, strongly influenced by the debate over the continuing underdevelopment of the region and a feeling that Maritimers may have made a bad deal when they entered Confederation, produced a series of studies that were more sympathetic to the anti-confederate position. Baker wrote a finely crafted book on Timothy Warren Anglin, pointing out that "in his original criticism of Confederation Anglin had been correct on many counts."[42] Robert Aitken supplied a sympathetic portrait of Yarmouth, that hotbed of anti-Confederation sentiment.[43] David Weale resurrected Cornelius Howat as the symbol of the desire of Prince Edward Island to retain control of its own destiny and, in *The Island and Confederation: The End of an Era,* produced with Harry Baglole a lament for the decision of the Island to enter Confederation.[44] Ken Pryke contributed an extremely balanced and very sophisticated study of *Nova Scotia and Confederation* (Toronto 1979). Although he argued that Nova Scotians "had little alternative but to acquiesce" in a plan of union designed to meet Canadian needs, he explained the willingness of Nova Scotians to accept their "unwelcome subordination" to Canada by factionalism among the anti-confederates and imperial pressure. His conclusion was that "by default, then, Nova Scotia entered into and remained in Confederation" (xi). Whereas earlier historians had consigned the Maritime anti-confederates to the dust-basket of history, the revisionists rescued them from obscurity and emphasized that they were the true standard-bearers of the wishes of the majority of the population. Unfortunately, revisionism carries its own risks, for this approach often portrays the most vehement of the die-hard anti-confederates as the legitimate voice of the Maritimes. Moreover, once again inadvertently, the revisionists also tended to reinforce the image that Maritimers were motivated by an all-pervasive parochialism and stubborn conservatism which explained the depth of anti-confederation sentiment in the region.

It is time to challenge this stereotype. If one turns the traditional question on its head and asks not why were so many Maritimers opposed to Confederation but why so many of them agreed so easily to a scheme of union that was clearly designed by Canadians to meet Canadian needs and to ensure Canadian dominance – which virtually everybody who has written on the subject agrees was implicit in the Quebec scheme – then the Maritime response to the Canadian initiative looks rather different. It may be true that there had been little discussion of the idea of an immediate union before the formation of the Great Coalition made Confederation an issue of practical politics, but the idea of British North American union, as Leslie Upton pointed out years ago, had been in the air since the arrival of the Loyalists.[45] In an unfortunately much neglected article written in 1950, John Heisler concluded in "The Halifax Press and British North American Union 1856–1864" that "it seems unlikely that a sense of British North American Unity had ever been wholly obscured."[46] Many Maritimers appear to have thought like the anonymous correspondent to the *Provincial Wesleyan* who, in 1861, referred to "our home" as "Eastern British America," thus implying some sense of a common destiny with Canada.[47] As Peter Waite pointed out, the initial response of the Maritimers at Charlottetown and in the regional press was certainly not unfavourable to the idea of union. Even Anglin, perhaps the most committed anti-confederate elected to the New Brunswick legislature, admitted that he did "not know of any one opposed to union in the abstract."[48] Indeed, Anglin himself believed union was desirable as a future goal, though on terms so favourable to New Brunswick that they were undoubtedly impracticable.[49]

It was the terms agreed upon at Quebec which hardened Maritime attitudes as the ranks of the ultras swelled with support from the critics of the Quebec scheme, to use Peter Waite's terminology. Even then, what is surprising is how much support the pro-confederates had. In New Brunswick, the only province in which the issue was put to the electorate, the supporters of the Quebec plan were initially defeated at the polls but, for their opponents, it proved to be a pyrrhic victory.[50] From the beginning the new government included a large number of men who were sympathetic to the idea of Confederation, if not the Quebec Resolutions, and who were converted fairly easily into pro-confederates, once it became clear that union was not possible except on the basis of those resolutions. The attitude of the premier, A.J. Smith, towards Confederation was somewhat ambiguous, and he was surrounded by others like R.D. Wilmot who were even more clearly critics of the Quebec scheme rather than die-hard opponents of union.[51] Ultra sentiment may have been more widespread in Nova Scotia than in New Brunswick, but the victory of the anti-confederate forces at the polls in 1867 was roughly of the same dimensions as in New Brunswick two years earlier. This result may have been distorted by the legitimate feeling of outrage that many Nova Scotians felt against the undemocratic way they had been forced into the union and by the fact that the Nova Scotia election took place after it had become certain that there would be no substantial alterations in the Quebec plan.[52] In any event, any anti-confederate government in Nova Scotia would have suffered from the same internal divisions as did the Smith government in New Brunswick and would probably have met much the same fate in much the same way. At least that is a viable reading of Pryke's study of what happened to the deeply divided anti-Confederation movement after Confederation. Indeed, Pryke suggests that those who advocated "an extreme stand towards union during the election represented a small minority of the anti-confederates."[53]

Even Prince Edward Island's opposition is easily exaggerated. There is in Island historiography a powerful tradition of Island "exceptionalism" and there is undeniably some justification for this approach. Prince Edward Island was small, its future on the edge of a large continental nation was bound to be precarious, and opposition to the idea of union was stronger than on the mainland. Yet it is doubtful whether the Islanders' commitment to the protection of local interests differed more than marginally from a similar commitment by other British North Americans.[54] After the Charlottetown Conference, the majority of the Island's newspapers came out in favour of a federal union "upon terms that the Island may reasonably stipulate for," and at Quebec the PEI delegates never opposed the principle of union.[55] Of course, the support of the Island elite for union was not unconditional and the forces favouring Confederation would have faced a difficult battle in persuading the majority of Islanders that Confederation was necessary in 1867. But what appears to have decisively swayed Island opinion was the failure of the Quebec Conference to respond sympathetically to any of the Island's needs.[56] Thanks to the resistance of the French Canadians and the Maritimers, the preference of some of the delegates for a legislative union was abandoned. But to the Islanders' requests for changes in the composition of the Senate and an additional member of the House of Commons (or even for a larger House in which the Island would have six representatives), for a recognition of the peculiar financial position of the Island with its very low debt and limited sources of potential revenue, and for financial assistance to resolve permanently the land question, the delegates from the other colonies turned a deaf ear. It is easy to dismiss the Island's demands, particularly the desire for adequate representation in the new federal parliament, as unrealistic. But during the discussions at Quebec, Alexander Tilloch Galt offered an alternative system of representation in the House of Commons that would have given the Island the six federal representatives they wanted, and an additional senator for the Island was surely not a radical demand.[57] Indeed, after Confederation, the principle of "rep by pop" was abandoned to meet the needs of the west.[58] It was the obduracy of the Canadians and the refusal of the other Maritime delegations to support PEI's demands, not the latter's unwillingness to compromise, that isolated the Islanders and delayed the Island's decision to enter Confederation.

Not surprisingly, the Islanders refused to consider the degrading terms which were offered to them and defiantly declared in the famous "no terms" resolution that they would never enter Confederation. Although in 1869 they again rejected a set of marginally better terms offered by the Macdonald administration, they found themselves inevitably drawn within the orbit of Canada. They adopted the Canadian decimal system of coinage and were forced to follow Canadian policy in regulating the Atlantic fisheries.[59] Unable to negotiate reciprocity on their own and eager for an infusion of money to resolve the land question, the Island leadership did not abandon negotiations with Canada. Undoubtedly the financial crisis generated by the building of an Island railway explains the timing of Confederation, but, as the debate in 1870 when the legislature rejected Canada's 1869 offer shows, the number of MLA's prepared to accept Confederation if the terms were fair was growing steadily even before the Island approached insolvency. When the Canadian government offered "advantageous and just" terms in 1873, giving the Island much of what it had demanded at Quebec in 1864, the opposition to Confederation evaporated.[60] If Cornelius Howat was the authentic voice of the ultras on the Island, his was very much a voice in the wilderness by 1873.

From a longer perspective, what is remarkable is not that there was opposition to Confederation in the Maritimes but how ineffectual it was. In Ireland, the union with Britain was never accepted and ultimately resulted in separation and partition. Even today there are secessionist movements in Scotland and in Wales. The imperial government was so impressed with the success of the Canadian experiment that it would try to reproduce it elsewhere, but except for Australia and South Africa – and in the latter it was imposed by force – few of the federations it created survived for long. In fact, unlike other areas of the world forced into federation on terms considered unjust, the Maritime opposition to Confederation was remarkably weak and evaporated remarkably quickly. Although there remained pockets of secessionist sentiment, Maritime separatism has never been a potent force.[61] Of course, the simple explanation of this phenomenon is the willingness of the Maritime leadership to sell their birthright for a mess of Canadian pottage. But the assumption that Maritime politicians and the Maritime electorate were more venal and more corrupt than politicians elsewhere is an assumption which cannot be sustained. Historians have for too long quoted enthusiastically the comments of Arthur Hamilton Gordon and other imperial visitors to the colonies. Inevitably, they were critical of what they saw, since they came from a more patrician political culture controlled by an elite who feared any movement in the direction of democracy.

But much of what they disapproved of – the scrambling of different interest groups, the narrow self-promoting nature of much of the legislation, the continual catering to popular demands – is what popular politics is all about. The ideal of the disinterested gentleman-politician made little sense in colonies where there were virtually no great landed estates, limited inherited wealth, and no hereditary ruling caste. Much of the opposition to the Quebec scheme seems to have come from those who feared, legitimately, that it was designed to create just such a caste and to place power in the hands of an elite which professed the ideal of disinterestedness while lining their own rather larger pockets.[62]

The belief that politics in the Maritimes was individualistic and anarchic is also mythical. During the transition to responsible government, the Maritime provinces had begun to evolve parties in the legislatures at pretty close to the same pace as they evolved in Canada. In the decades before Confederation, all these provinces were in the process of developing party systems with roots deep in the constituencies, even New Brunswick.[63] If Confederation disrupted this development and brought about a major political realignment and considerable political confusion, it was because of the far-reaching implications of the measure, not because of the inherent pliability or lack of principle of Maritime politicians. It had the same effect in Ontario and Quebec, which also had their share of loose fish. Similarly, the belief that Maritimers were either by nature or because of the scale of their political structures more susceptible to patronage and corruption should be challenged. Gordon Stewart has advanced the claim that the Canadian political system before Confederation was more corrupt and more patronage-ridden than in the Maritimes, since Canadians had adopted the spoils system with greater enthusiasm and consistency during the transition to responsible government.[64] In fact, there may be a reverse correlation between size and patronage in pre-industrial societies. In a larger political unit, politicians are more remote from the people they serve and less likely to be drawn from a clearly defined local elite. They cannot command the same degree of deference and therefore require access to a larger fund of patronage to cement the more impersonal bonds of party loyalty. Certainly those Maritime politicians who held posts in the new federal administration, Tilley and Tupper for example, claimed to be appalled by the ruthlessness of the Canadians in distributing patronage along party lines, although they soon began to pursue similar policies to ensure a fair distribution for their own constituents and their own re-election.[65] By proving that the system was not totally biased in favour of the Canadians, the Maritime political leadership did something to dissipate the lingering fears that the new political system would be dominated by Canadians and Canadian needs. But this evidence cannot be used to explain the success of the pro-confederates in the first place, nor does it adequately explain the rapidity with which integration took place.

The degree of support for Confederation in the region can only be explained by abandoning the notion that all but a handful of Maritimers were inherently parochial and conservative. Maritimers did not live in a dream world. Although they had experienced a period of rapid economic and demographic growth, they were aware of the changes taking place around them. They were acutely aware that external events had made some form of larger union desirable in the 1860s. British pressure, the American Civil War and the cancellation of reciprocity, and the Fenian raids helped to drive home this message, as they did in the Canadas. But no external pressures could have compelled the Maritimes to join Confederation if, ultimately, they had not been convinced that it was in their own interests to do so. That is the lesson which can be drawn from the failure of the earlier initiatives on Confederation in the 1830s and 1840s.[66] In all these cases, despite the strong advocacy of the Colonial Office and enthusiastic support from British officials in the colonies, the union movement collapsed because of lack of colonial support. Similarly, the Maritime Union movement, despite strong imperial pressure, collapsed because of lack of colonial enthusiasm. Undoubtedly imperial support helped to sway the more conservative groups in the colonies, such as the hierarchy of the Catholic church.[67] But imperial interference could also unleash a colonial reaction. As allies, men like Gordon were a mixed blessing, and it is quite possible that the pro-confederates won their victory in New Brunswick in 1865 despite, not because of, Gordon's interference in the politics of the province.[68] The combined pressures generated by the American Civil War and the British response to it were critical factors in the timing of Confederation. Without those immediate pressures, union might not have come about in the 1860s and it would certainly not have come about on the basis of the Quebec Resolutions, since it was those pressures which persuaded so many Maritimers to accept union on those terms. But since the idea of Confederation does seem to have had widespread and growing support, at least from the elites in the region, it does not follow that in the

1870s negotiations between the Canadians (now presumably united in their own federal union) and the Maritimers could not have been successful, albeit on a somewhat different basis.

By the 1860s, a variety of indigenous forces were, in fact, leading an increasing number of Maritimers to the conclusion that some form of wider association was desirable. The restlessness of provincial elites may have been, as Waite suggested, part of the reason for the enthusiasm for a larger union, but this restlessness cannot be related solely to their political ambitions and their immediate economic self-interest. Support for the idea of union was, indeed, too widespread for it to be simply the result of individual ambition. Clearly there must have been some correlation between an individual's socio-economic position and his response to the Confederation issue, but it would be foolish to revert to the kind of Beardian analysis which American historians have come to find less and less useful.[69] In any event, without the support of a wide cross-section of the articulate public, any effort at union would have been pointless.

It can hardly be denied that much of the support for a larger union came from those who equated consolidation with material progress and modernization, as most historians have recognized. What they have been less willing to accept is that these intellectual pressures were growing stronger in the Maritimes as in the Canadas and affected many of the opponents of the Quebec scheme as well as its advocates. Even prior to Confederation, governments in the Maritimes took on new responsibilities as the nineteenth-century revolution in government filtered across the Atlantic.[70] Maritimers shared with other British North Americans an enthusiasm for railways, for expanded and more highly centralized school systems,[71] for improved social services, and for governments with enhanced access to credit. In *Inventing Canada: Early Victorian Science and the Idea of a Transcontinental Nation* (Toronto 1987), Suzanne Zeller has argued that the diffusion of early science was another of the pressures encouraging the establishment of larger units of government, and that the inventory methods of Victorian science "laid a conceptual and practical foundation for the reorganization of British North America" (9). Unfortunately, Zeller focuses almost exclusively on developments in the United Province of Canada. But the Maritimes had its share of scientists influenced by similar notions and a wider political community similarly affected by the diffusion of scientific knowledge, and it seems likely that the same developments were occurring there.[72] Nonetheless, Zeller's book points to the direction which studies of the movement for Confederation must now take. What is required are detailed analyses of the intellectual milieu in which literary figures and the growing number of professionals functioned, of clerical thought, and indeed of changing views of the role and function of the state held by entrepreneurs and by other groups in society. One suspects that such studies will reveal support, in the Maritimes as elsewhere in Canada, for the emergence of larger and more powerful institutional units of government.

Yet it does not follow that all of the supporters of Confederation were on the side of an expanded role for government and material progress, while all of those who opposed the Quebec scheme were not. The most vehement opposition to Confederation in the Maritimes came, as Muise correctly pointed out, from those whose economic interests seemed most directly threatened by union with Canada. It is, however, far from self-evident that they were opposed to the other changes that were taking place in their colonial societies. Some of the opposition to Confederation in the Maritimes, as in the Canadas, probably did come from those whose social ideal was reactionary and anti-modern in several respects, but not all anti-confederates, perhaps not even a majority, opposed commercial development or technological change. There does appear to have been an overlap between those who resisted government intervention, feared increased taxation, and resented outside interference with community institutions and those who opposed Confederation. Yet many pro-confederates shared these concerns. In summarizing the vast literature dealing with the politics of the early American republic, Lance Banning points out the futility of trying to describe the Republicans and Federalists as liberal and conservative and their opponents as conservative and reactionary: "If revisionary work has taught us anything, it has surely taught us that both parties were a bit of each."[73]

It has long been known that the Fathers of Confederation were not democrats and that they were determined to secure the protection of property and to create barriers against the democratic excesses which, in their minds, had led to the collapse of the American constitution and to the American Civil War.[74] For this reason they limited the size of the House of Commons so that it would remain manageable, chose to have an appointed rather than an elected second chamber, and sought to ensure that both houses of the proposed federal legislature were composed of men who possessed a substantial stake in society. Most of the Maritime delegates at the Quebec Conference shared these anti-democratic and anti-majoritarian objectives. So, of course, did many of the most prominent anti-confederate leaders – even that tribune of the people, Joseph Howe. Ironically, a considerable part of the initial opposition to the Quebec Resolutions came from those – for instance, Howe and Wilmot – who, like the leading pro-confederates, were wedded to British constitutional models but who rejected the Quebec plan for not establishing a legislative union or because they feared it might lead to the disruption of the empire. But once convinced that legislative union was impracticable, primarily because of the determined opposition of the French Canadians, and that Britain was solidly behind the Quebec scheme, many of these critics were converted fairly easily into supporters of union, although they continued to ask for marginally better terms for their provinces.

The more serious and determined opposition came from those who believed that the Quebec plan would create a monster, an extraordinarily powerful and distant national government, a highly centralized federal union in which Maritimers would have limited influence. It is easy to dismiss these arguments as based on paranoia, irrational fears, or perhaps some kind of psychological disorder, particularly since the worst fears of the anti-confederates were not realized. But the opposition to centralizing power in a distant and remote government was deeply rooted in Anglo-American political thought. Elwood Jones has described this attitude as "localism," as a world view that was held by many articulate conservatives and reformers on both sides of the Atlantic and was "an integral part of the British North American experience."[75] This approach has the merit of indicating the considerable overlap between those who supported and those who opposed the Quebec Resolutions. Those resolutions were capable of more than one interpretation, and many of the Canadian pro-confederates supported Confederation because it promised more, not less, autonomy for their provinces.[76] Nonetheless, the term "localism," with its implication of parochialism, to some extent distorts the nature of the opposition to the Quebec Resolutions. It reinforces the notion that the pro-confederates were drawn from the men of larger vision, usually described in American historiography as the cosmopolitans, while their opponents were men of more limited experience and a more local, and thus more limited, frame of reference.[77] In American historiography, however, the "men of little faith" are now taken more seriously than they used to be and it is time to reassess the criticisms made by those who fought hardest against the Quebec scheme.[78]

Only a minority of the Maritime anti-confederates appear to have denied the need for some kind of a union, but since the Maritimers were not, like the Canadians, trying simultaneously to get out of one union while creating another, they were less easily convinced of the merits of the Quebec Resolutions. Following the Charlottetown Conference, the *Acadian Recorder* expressed the belief that when "the delegates ... have to let the cat out of the bag," it would be found that the cat was "a real sleek, constitutional, monarchical, unrepublican, aristocratic cat" and that "we shall ask our friends the people to drown it at once – yes to drown it."[79] It will not do to create yet another over-simplified dichotomy, pitting democratic anti-confederates against aristocratic pro-confederates. Yet clearly the anti-confederates did attract to their cause those who were suspicious of the aristocratic pretensions of the designers of the new constitution. Whether such critics were true democrats or simply adherents of an older classical republican tradition, whether they drew upon English opposition thought, classical liberalism, or Scottish common-sense philosophy, or whether they simply drew eclectically upon the host of Anglo-American intellectual currents available to them, cannot be established until more detailed studies have been completed of their rhetoric.[80] But it does seem likely that it is on the anti-confederate side that one will find most of those who were most sympathetic to wider popular participation in government and to the movement towards democracy already underway in the Maritimes.[81] And such men surely had good reason to be suspicious of the ideological goals of those who had drafted the Quebec Resolutions.

The critics of the Quebec Resolutions were also surely correct to believe that the proposed constitution went further in the direction of centralization than was necessary or desirable in the 1860s. The real weakness in the analysis of most of what was written in the 1960s, and it is particularly apparent in the work of Morton and Creighton, is that it focuses too much on the twentieth-century *consequences* of what was done rather than on the more immediate *context* of the late nineteenth century.[82] The Quebec plan, after all, never worked out as the far-sighted Macdonald and his associates hoped. Despite Macdonald's expectations, the provincial governments did not dwindle into insignificance after Confederation. Because of pressure from the provinces and the decisions of the Judicial Committee of the Privy Council, as well as Macdonald's own retreat from an extreme position on such issues as the use of the power of disallowance, the power of the federal government to interfere with the activities of the provinces was constrained in the late nineteenth century and the constitution was effectively decentralized. This decentralization made considerable sense at a time when, by our standards, the people and politicians had a remarkably limited concept of the role of government in society, particularly of the role of a remote federal government.[83] Twentieth-century historians such as Creighton and Morton may, for very different and to some extent contradictory reasons, lament the fact that those who lived in the late nineteenth century were not prepared to accept a twentieth-century role for the federal government, but it does not alter the reality. In fact, Macdonald shared with his contemporaries this limited conception of the role of the federal government. He did not wish a highly centralized federal system, either to introduce the degree of control over the economy that Creighton longed for in the 1930s or because of any commitment to the nation-wide bilingualism and biculturalism policy that Morton espoused in the 1960s when he was converted to a Creightonian conception of Confederation. It is time to abandon the Creightonian myth that Macdonald and the other advocates of a federal union that was a legislative union in disguise were simply practical politicians engaged in the necessary work of building the Canadian nation.[84] Confederation certainly did not require that the federal government should attempt to "treat the provinces more 'colonially' than the imperial authorities had latterly treated the provinces" through its control over the lieutenant-governors and the resurrection of the anachronistic power of reservation.[85] The Fathers of Confederation were not philosopher-kings, but neither did they live in the intellectual vacuum that much of the traditional literature seems to assume existed throughout British North America, particularly in the Maritimes. In fact, the roots of the thought of the exponents of centralization emerged not out of a vacuum but out of a body of conservative thought that was deeply suspicious of democracy, and their opponents were surely correct to place little faith in the motives of such men and the scheme they proposed. Many of the anti-confederates were clearly marching to a different drummer.[86]

Ideological and sectional considerations did not take place in isolation from each other, and what initially united the Maritime anti-confederates, regardless of their ideological differences, was their feeling that the Quebec Resolutions did not adequately protect their sectional interests. As the anti-confederate newspaper, the *Woodstock Times,* noted, "Union is one thing and the Quebec scheme is quite another."[87] The scheme that emerged out of the Quebec Conference was designed to mollify its potential critics in two ways: by ensuring that sectional interests would be protected through federal institutions such as the cabinet and the Senate, and through the creation of a series of provincial legislatures with control over local matters. Yet those critics who argued that the Senate would be too weak and ineffectual to defend regional interests would be very quickly proved correct after Confederation. Indeed, by making the Senate an appointed body, the Fathers of Confederation had intentionally ensured that the decision-making body in the new federal system would be the House of Commons. This was no accident, for, as Robert MacKay pointed out, Macdonald's intention was to grant "the forms demanded by sectional sentiments and fears," while ensuring "that these forms did not endanger the political structure."[88] Traditionally, Canadian historians and political scientists have laid great stress on the principle of sectional representation in the cabinet as one of the primary lines of defence for the protection of regional interests. Yet this argument ignores the fact that, however important individual ministers may be, the policies that emerge from the collective decisions of the cabinet must inevitably reflect the balance of power in the House of Commons. The fears of the Maritime critics of the proposed constitution were undoubtedly exaggerated, but they were surely correct to believe that in the long run there was no effective guarantee that their vital interests were adequately protected at the federal level.[89]

Similarly, they were surely correct to be suspicious of federalism as it was presented to them in the 1860s. The question of whether the anti-confederates leaned towards a different and less centralized model of federalism than the supporters of the Quebec scheme is a controversial and ultimately unanswerable one, since it depends upon which group of anti-confederates one takes as most representative. In Halifax, as Peter Waite showed, there was considerable support for a legislative union, at least as reflected in the city's newspapers.[90] But outside of Halifax and in New Brunswick and Prince Edward Island there seems to have been considerably more sympathy for the federal principle.[91] Federalism was viewed suspiciously by conservatives who believed that it would leave the government without the power to govern, and such fears were expressed by both sides in the Confederation debate. They were, however, most forcefully expressed, in Halifax and elsewhere, by the pro-confederates, and the Quebec Resolutions went a long way to pacifying most of those who wanted a purely legislative union. But the Quebec Resolutions did little to mollify those who feared that the proposed provincial legislatures would be nothing more than glorified municipal institutions and that all real power would be concentrated in the federal parliament. As Richard Ellis points out, during the debate over the American constitution, the supporters of ratification "preempted the term 'Federalist' for themselves, even though, in many ways, it more accurately described their opponents."[92] Until detailed studies of the Confederation debate in the three Maritime provinces have been completed, it would be premature to assume that the Maritime anti-confederates anticipated the provincial rights movement of the 1880s and argued for a form of co-ordinate sovereignty. But many of the critics of the Quebec Resolutions in the region clearly believed that their provincial governments would be left with inadequate powers and resources. In this regard they were also more prescient than the pro-confederates. The Maritime governments required special grants to cover their deficits in the later 1860s and 1870s and were forced to turn time and again to the federal government for financial assistance. We know little about how Maritimers responded to the provincial rights movement of the 1880s, since the literature assumes that Ontario and Quebec were the key players while the Maritimers were motivated solely by the desire for larger subsidies, but it is plausible to assume that the movement was supported in the region by many of those who had resisted the Quebec scheme of union.

If the enthusiasm of Maritimers for Confederation upon the basis of the Quebec Resolutions was less pronounced than in Canada (or at least in Canada West), it was, then, not because they lagged behind intellectually but because they obviously had more to lose in a federation which was not designed to meet their needs. It was not an obtuse conservatism which led to many Maritimers to oppose the terms that were initially offered to them in 1864 but a feeling that those terms were patently unfair. They were motivated not by an intense parochialism which manifested itself in separatist tendencies but by a desire to find a place for themselves in a union which protected their interests. Under the pressure of events the majority, at least in New Brunswick and Prince Edward Island, did agree to union on terms which they did not like.[93] But what most Maritimers sought in the Confederation era was not a future for themselves outside of Confederation but a more equitable union than seemed to be promised by the Quebec Resolutions.[94]

NOTES

1 Phillip Buckner, "The Maritimes and Confederation: A Reassessment," *Canadian Historical Review* (*CHR*) 71, 1 (1990): 1–30.

2 E.R. Forbes, "In Search of a Post-Confederation Maritime Historiography, 1900–1967," *Acadiensis* 8 (2) (autumn 1978): 3–21.

3 *CHR* 9 (March 1928): 4–24.

4 Canadian Historical Association, *Annual Report*, 1927: 39–45.

5 The roots of this sentiment are discussed in E.R. Forbes, *Maritime Rights: The Maritime Rights Movement, 1919–1927* (Montreal 1979).

6 I have used the reprint edition, which contains a valuable introduction by Peter Waite (Toronto 1966).

7 Whitelaw pointed out that there was only one recorded vote at Quebec on which Canada was outvoted by the four Atlantic provinces voting together. See *The Maritimes and Canada before Confederation*, 240.

8 *CHR* 16 (March 1935): 72, cited in Waite's introduction to *The Maritimes and Canada before Confederation*, xv. Waite includes this excerpt as "an illustration of the best and the worst of Chester Martin – that is, of the comprehensiveness of Martin's thinking and his inability to change it." Yet it seems to me a fair interpretation of Whitelaw's perspective.

9 One might include James A. Roy, *Joseph Howe: A Study in Achievement and Frustration* (Toronto 1935) as a serious study, but it is a perverse work that simply reiterates the myths about Howe perpetuated in earlier studies. For a critique of the book, see J. Murray Beck, "Joseph Howe and Confederation: Myth and Fact," *Transactions of the Royal Society of Canada*, 1964, 143–4. Perhaps because the issue of Confederation was not put to the electorate in Nova Scotia as it was in New Brunswick, the early writing on Nova Scotia focused almost exclusively on the perversity of Howe in opposing Confederation.

10 "Railways and the Confederation Issue in New Brunswick, 1863–1865" and "The Basis and Persistence of Opposition to Confederation in New Brunswick" first appeared in the *CHR* 21 (1940): 367–83, and 23 (1942): 374–97, and both are reprinted in Bailey's *Culture and Nationality* (Toronto 1972), from where the quotations in the text are drawn.

11 For example, Timothy Warren Anglin was not opposed to the Intercolonial, although he thought the western extension should be the priority. See William M. Baker, *Timothy Warren Anglin 1822–96: Irish Catholic Canadian* (Toronto 1977), 54. Baker also notes that many pro-confederates supported the western extension, although frequently as a second choice (55).

12 The concept of a consensus approach is, of course, taken from American historiography but, as I have tried to argue elsewhere, it seems to be applicable to Canadian historiography. See my "'Limited Identities' and Canadian Historical Scholarship: An Atlantic Provinces Perspective," *Journal of Canadian Studies* 23 (1 & 2) (spring–summer 1988): esp. 177–8.

13 I have used the second printing (Toronto 1962), which contains "a few minor corrections" (preface, vi). As will become apparent, I have drawn heavily upon Waite's sources in the discussion which follows.

14 I do not know if Waite had read Cecelia M. Kenyon, "Men of Little Faith: The Antifederalists on the Nature of Representative Government," *William and Mary Quarterly*, 3d ser., 12 (1955): 3–43, but his approach was certainly in line with the American historiography of the period.

15 I attempted to trace the context of Goldwin Smith's remark, but Waite's source was G.M. Wrong, "Creation of the Federal System in Canada," in Wrong et al., *The Federation of Canada, 1867–1917* (Toronto 1917), 17, and Wrong does not indicate his source. It seems likely, however, that the quote referred to Canadian politics in the post-Confederation era and reflected Smith's somewhat biased view of his adopted home.

16 Forbes makes the same point about J. Murray Beck in his "In Search of a Post-Confederation Maritime Historiography," 55.

17 Bolger also contributed the chapters on Confederation to *Canada's Smallest Province: A History of Prince Edward Island* (Charlottetown 1973), where his larger work is synthesized.

18 See Jack N. Rakove, "The Great Compromise: Ideas, Interests, and the Politics of Constitution Making," *William and Mary Quarterly*, 3d ser., 14 (July 1987): esp. 451.

19 See G.P. Browne, ed., *Documents on the Confederation of British North America* (Toronto 1969), 38–9.

20 See Ken Pryke, *Nova Scotia and Confederation* (Toronto 1979), 190.

21 See Browne, *Documents*, 77–8.

22 Ibid., 171.

23 Ibid., 211. Tupper personally supported the idea of a legislative union, but he was undoubtedly influenced by the knowledge that this position was not shared by most Nova Scotians.

24 McCully to Tilley, 8 June 1866, quoted in Pryke, *Nova Scotia and Confederation*, 28.

25 See Pryke, *Nova Scotia and Confederation*, 22–3, 26.

26 Bailey, "The Basis and Persistence," 16; MacNutt, *New Brunswick*, 456–7.

27 Bolger, *Prince Edward Island and Confederation*, v, 293.

28 See *Life and Times of Confederation*, 122.

29 Ibid., 5.

30 "Railroaded" is the clever aphorism used by Peter Waite in his chapter in Craig Brown, ed., *The Illustrated History of Canada* (Toronto 1987), 289.

31 See Alan W. MacIntosh, "The Career of Sir Charles Tupper in Canada, 1864–1900" (PhD thesis, University of Toronto, 1960); and Carl Wallace, "Sir Leonard Tilley: A Political Biography" (PhD thesis, University of Alberta, 1972). MacIntosh presents a very traditional portrait of Tupper, who is seen as accepting and following the overweening vision of Macdonald. Wallace makes a more successful effort to place Tilley in a regional context, but he too believes that "a good argument can be put forward to prove that Confederation was little more than a smokescreen for a diversity of local issues" (209).

32 This argument is presented in "The Federal Election of 1867 in Nova Scotia: An Economic Interpretation," *Collections of the Nova Scotia Historical Society* (1968): 327–51, and developed at greater length in "Elections and Constituencies: Federal Politics in Nova Scotia, 1867–1878" (PhD thesis, University of Western Ontario, 1971).

33 Muise, "Elections and Constituencies," iv. For an application of the Muise thesis, see Brian Tennyson, "Economic Nationalism and Confederation: A Case Study in Cape Breton," *Acadiensis* 2 (1) (autumn 1972): 38–53.

34 This argument is developed in a variety of works published by members of the group but most recently and fully in Eric W. Sager and Gerry Panting, "Staple Economies and the Rise and Decline of the Shipping Industry in Atlantic Canada," in Lewis R. Fischer and Gerald E. Panting, eds., *Change and Adaptation in Maritime History: The North Atlantic Fleets in the Nineteenth Century* (St John's 1985). For an interpretation that incorporates this approach, but one that builds upon Muise's insights, see John G. Reid, *Six Crucial Decades: Times of Change in the History of the Maritimes* (Halifax 1987), esp. 113–16.

35 Ben Forster, *A Conjunction of Interests: Business, Politics, and Tariffs 1825–1879* (Toronto 1986), 62. On Nova Scotia see Pryke, *Nova Scotia and Confederation*, 107, 190–2.

36 Muise, "The Federal Election of 1867 in Nova Scotia," 337–8.

37 Bailey, "The Basis and Persistence," 99. Peter Toner emphasizes "the Irish threat, real and imagined" in his discussion of the politics of Confederation in New Brunswick in "New Brunswick Schools and the Rise of Provincial Rights," in Bruce W. Hodgins, Don Wright, and W.H. Heick, *Federalism in Canada and Australia: The Early Years* (Waterloo 1978), esp. 126–7.

38 The increased Anglicization of the Thirteen Colonies in the decades prior to the American Revolution is a major theme in Jack P. Greene, "Political

Memisis: A Consideration of the Political Roots of Legislative Behaviour in the British Colonies in the Eighteenth Century," *American Historical Review* 75 (1969–70): 337–67. It is a theme which has yet to be adequately explored in the evolution of *British* North America in the mid-decades of the nineteenth century.

39 Baker, *Anglin*, 79.

40 "Joseph Howe and Confederation: Myth and Fact," 146; and *Joseph Howe: II: The Briton Becomes Canadian 1848–1873* (Kingston and Montreal 1983), 211.

41 Carl Wallace, "Albert Smith, Confederation and Reaction in New Brunswick: 1852–1882," *CHR* 44 (1963): 311–12. An extended version of this argument is contained in "The Life and Times of Sir Albert James Smith" (MA thesis, University of New Brunswick, 1960), which concludes with the statement that "he lacked the depth and vision to be a great statesman" (210).

42 Baker, *Anglin*, 116.

43 Robert M. Aitken, "Localism and National Identity in Yarmouth, N.S., 1830–1870" (MA thesis, Trent University, n.d.).

44 David Weale, *Cornelius Howat: Farmer and Island Patriot* (Summerside 1973); and David Weale and Harry Baglole, *The Island and Confederation: The End of an Era* (n.p., 1973).

45 L.F.S. Upton, "The Idea of Confederation, 1754–1858," in W.L. Morton, ed., *The Shield of Achilles: Aspects of Canada in the Victorian Age* (Toronto 1968), 184–204.

46 *Dalhousie Review* 30 (1950): 188.

47 *Provincial Wesleyan*, 16 Jan. 1861. I am grateful to John Reid for supplying me with this reference.

48 Baker, *Anglin*, 103. I am grateful to a student in one of my seminars, Mary McIntosh, for supplying me with this reference.

49 See ibid., 58, 64–5.

50 Historians remain divided over the scale of the victory. Waite suggests in *The Life and Times of Confederation*, 246, that the election results were comparatively close, but Baker in *Anglin*, 75, argues that the anti-confederates won at least 60 per cent of the popular vote.

51 Once again historians are not agreed on whether Smith did convert to Confederation prior to the defeat of his government. Baker in *Anglin*, 102, argues that he did not, but Wallace feels that Smith was willing to lead the province into union. See "Albert Smith, Confederation and Reaction in New Brunswick," 291–2. In his "Life and Times of Smith," Wallace points

out that as early as 1858 Wilmot had indicated his belief in the inevitability of British North American union (see 23).

52 Del Muise points out that about 60 per cent of the Nova Scotia electorate voted for anti-confederates in 1865, which is roughly comparable to Baker's figure for New Brunswick.

53 See *Nova Scotia and Confederation,* 49.

54 For a different point of view, see Weale and Baglole, *The Island and Confederation.* I have two major disagreements with the authors. First, they create an image of harmony and unity on the Island that ignores the very real ethnic, religious, and class divisions which existed and thus postulate a unified response to Confederation. Second, they imply that Islanders had developed a strong desire to be separate that almost amounted to a sense of Island nationalism. But the Island had never been an independent and autonomous state and there is no evidence that any sizeable number of Islanders ever wanted it to become one. Indeed, the tendency to equate resistance to Confederation in the Maritimes to a kind of "provincial nationalism" is, I believe, utterly wrongheaded. What most Maritimers wanted, and Prince Edward Islanders were no exception, was to protect the corporate identities of their long-established assemblies. For a development of this theme in American historiography, see Jack P. Greene, *Peripheries and Center: Constitutional Development in the Extended Politics of the British Empire and the United States, 1607–1788* (Athens, GA 1987).

55 Bolger, *Prince Edward Island and Confederation,* 59, 61, 86.

56 Unfortunately, most of the literature on Confederation, including Bolger, simply dismisses the Island's needs as irrelevant. See ibid., 68ff.

57 For Galt's plan and the discussion of the extra senator, see Browne, ed., *Documents,* 106. Today we accept much wider departure from the principle of rep by pop than PEI requested in 1864.

58 David E. Smith, "Party Government, Representation and National Integration in Canada," in Peter Aucoin, ed., *Party Government and Regional Representation in Canada* (Toronto 1985), 14.

59 See Frank MacKinnon, *The Government of Prince Edward Island* (Toronto 1951), 132.

60 Bolger, *The Island and Confederation,* 210, 262.

61 The only serious expression of separatist sentiment was the repeal movement of the 1880s. It was in part, indeed perhaps in large part, simply a strategy for better terms. See Colin Howell, "W.S. Fielding and the Repeal Elections of 1886 and 1887 in Nova Scotia," *Acadiensis* 8 (2) (spring 1979): 28–46.

62 I have drawn for inspiration in these comments on Gordon S. Wood, "Interest and Disinterestedness in the Making of the Constitution," in Richard Beeman, Stephen Botein, and Edward C. Carter II, eds., *Beyond Confederation: Origins of the Constitution and American National Identity* (Chapel Hill and London 1987), 69–109.

63 See Gail Campbell, "'Smashers' and 'Rummies': Voters and the Rise of Parties in Charlotte County, New Brunswick, 1846–1857," *Historical Papers*, 1986: 86–116.

64 Gordon Stewart, *The Origins of Canadian Politics: A Comparative Approach* (Vancouver 1986), 88–9.

65 The latter statement is based upon an examination of the patronage files in the Tilley and Tupper papers held in the National Archives of Canada, during the 1870s. I discuss the question of patronage at more length in "The 1870s: The Integration of the Maritimes," in E.R. Forbes and D.A. Muise, eds., *The Atlantic Provinces in Confederation* (in press).

66 On the earlier attempts to achieve Confederation, see Ged Martin, "Confederation Rejected: The British Debate on Canada, 1837–1840," *Journal of Imperial and Commonwealth History* 11 (1982–3): 33–57; and B.A. Knox, "The Rise of Colonial Federation as an Object of British Policy 1850–1870," *Journal of British Studies* 11 (1971): 91–112. My interpretation of Ged Martin's "An Imperial Idea and Its Friends: Canadian Confederation and the British," in Gordon Martel, ed., *Studies in British Imperial History: Essays in Honour of A.P. Thornton* (New York 1985), 49–94, is that while British support was essential for Confederation, it was the circumstances within British North America which gave the British something to support.

67 For example, Bishop MacKinnon wrote to Tupper, "Although no admirer of Confederation on the basis of the Quebec Scheme, yet owing to the present great emergency and the necessities of the times, the union of the Colonies upon a new basis, we receive with pleasure" (Pryke, *Nova Scotia and Confederation*, 27). MacKinnon's reservations are not spelled out, but they were likely similar to those of Archbishop Connolly, who wrote that "the more power that Central Legislature has the better for the Confederacy itself and for the Mother Country and for all concerned." Connolly to Carnarvon, 30 Jan. 1867, in Browne, ed., *Documents*, 262. See also K. Fay Trombley, *Thomas Louis Connolly (1815–1876)* (Leuven 1983), esp. 302–44.

68 Wallace, "Life and Times of Smith," 47.

69 The reference here is, of course, to Charles Beard's economic interpretation of the making of the American constitution. As Richard Beeman notes in his introduction to *Beyond Confederation*, 14, the prolonged

historiographical debate over Beard's interpretation has come to be seen as important by "ever-decreasing numbers" of American historians.

70 See Rosemary Langhout, "Developing Nova Scotia: Railways and Public Accounts, 1849–1867," *Acadiensis* 14 (2) (spring 1985): 3–28.

71 As Ian Robertson points out, Prince Edward Island claimed to be the first place in the British Empire to introduce "a complete system of free education" with the adoption of the Free Education Act of 1852, and Nova Scotia was the next British North American colony to follow suit, in 1864. See "Historical Origins of Public Education in Prince Edward Island, 1852–1877," unpublished paper given at the Atlantic Canada Studies Conference, University of Edinburgh, May 1988, 3, 5.

72 A.G. Bailey points out that the Maritime universities, like the central Canadian universities, "tempered their concern for the classics with a lively concern for the sciences" during the Confederation period. See "Literature and Nationalism in the Aftermath of Confederation," in Bailey, *Culture and Nationality*, 66.

73 Lance Banning, "Jeffersonian Ideology Revisited: Liberal and Classical Ideas in the New American Republic," *William and Mary Quarterly* 43 (1) (Jan. 1986): 14.

74 See Bruce Hodgins, "Democracy and the Ontario Fathers of Confederation," in *Profiles of a Province: Studies in the History of Ontario* (Toronto 1967); and "The Canadian Political Elite's Attitude toward the Nature of the Plan of Union," in Hodgins et al., eds., *Federalism in Canada and Australia*, 43–59.

75 Elwood H. Jones, "Localism and Federalism in Upper Canada to 1865," in Hodgins et al., *Federalism in Canada and Australia*, 20.

76 See Arthur Silver, *The French-Canadian Idea of Confederation 1864–1900* (Toronto 1982), 33–50; and Robert Charles Vipond, "Federalism and the Problem of Sovereignty: Constitutional Politics and the Rise of the Provincial Rights Movement in Canada" (PhD diss., Harvard University, 1983), 82–7.

77 In American historiography, the notion of the federalists as cosmopolitans and the anti-federalists as provincials, found for example in Jackson Turner Main's *The Antifederalists: Critics of the Constitution, 1781–1788* (Chapel Hill, NC 1961) and *Political Parties before the Constitution* (Chapel Hill, NC 1973) has been challenged by Wood in "Interest and Disinterestedness in the Making of the Constitution."

78 See, for example, James H. Hutson, "County, Court and Constitution: Antifederalism and the Historians," *William and Maly Quarterly*, 3d ser., 38 (3) (July 1981): 337–68; Isaac Kramnick, "The 'Great National Discussion': The Discourse of Politics in 1787," ibid. 45 (1) (Jan. 1988): 3–32; and

Richard E. Ellis, "The Persistence of Antifederalism after 1789," in Beeman et al., eds., *Beyond Confederation*, 295–314.

79 *Acadian Recorder*, 12 Sept. 1864, quoted in R.H. Campbell, "Confederation in Nova Scotia to 1870" (MA thesis, Dalhousie University, 1939), 80.

80 I am, of course, calling for the kind of intellectual history associated with American scholars such as Bernard Bailyn and Gordon S. Wood and British scholars such as J.G.A. Pocock. The only serious attempts to apply this approach to the Confederation era have been by Jones, "Localism and Federalism"; and by Peter J. Smith, "The Ideological Origins of Canadian Confederation," *Canadian Journal of Political Science* 20 (1) (March 1987): 3–29. Unfortunately, both efforts seem to me flawed by the effort to deal with too wide a time frame and to apply to the mid-nineteenth century categories developed for the eighteenth century.

81 It is worth noting that the Maritimes were at least as far, if not further, advanced in this direction than the Canadas. According to John Garner, *The Franchise and Politics in British North America, 1755–1867* (Toronto 1969), Nova Scotia had been "the first colony in North America to introduce manhood suffrage" (33). Although Nova Scotia subsequently drew back from the experiment, all of the Maritimes had wide franchises and Prince Edward Island had virtually universal male suffrage by the 1860s. After Confederation, when the federal government decided against vote by ballot, there was an outcry from New Brunswick, which had adopted the ballot in 1855. Indeed, it was this increasingly democratic climate that annoyed men like Gordon and that perhaps accounts, at least in part, for the desire of some members of the colonial elites for a wider, and preferably a legislative, union.

82 I have been influenced here by Beeman, Introduction, *Beyond Confederation*, 5–8.

83 There has been a heated debate over the role of the Judicial Committee of the Privy Council, but much of the controversy centres upon the consequences in the 1930s of the decisions taken under very different circumstances in the 1880s and 1890s. For a summary of the recent literature, see Frederick Vaughan, "Critics of the Judical Committee of the Privy Council: The New Orthodoxy and an Alternative Explanation," *Canadian Journal of Political Science* 19 (3) (Sept. 1986): 495–519. Unfortunately, Vaughan is also primarily concerned with the implications of the decisions, this time in the 1980s, and expresses the fear that the JCPC "left us with a federal system that is seriously lacking an institutional body by which to bind the several provinces at the centre so as to ensure the continued existence of Canada as one nation" (505).

84 This point is also made in Smith, "The Ideological Origins of Canadian Confederation," 3–4.

85 Vipond, "Federalism and the Problem of Sovereignty," 128–9.

86 James H. Hutson in "Country, Court and Constitution" has suggested that the division over the constitution in the United States in the 1780s was between those committed to a Country and a Court ideology. The Court party supported commercial expansion and was profoundly statist in orientation, while their Country opponents defended agrarian interests and feared any substantial increase in state power. These categories have some value, but British North America in the 1860s was not the United States in the 1780s. There were very few self-sufficient agricultural communities, even in the Maritimes in the 1860s, and it is doubtful whether the majority of the anti-confederates were any less market-oriented than their opponents. Ideological determinism is as distorting as any other kind, and there is the danger of turning all the pro-confederates into Hamiltonians and all of the critics of the Quebec resolutions into Jeffersonians.

87 Quoted in Waite, *The Life and Times of Confederation*, 252.

88 See Robert A. MacKay, *The Unreformed Senate of Canada* (rev. ed., Toronto 1963), 43.

89 This is one of the major themes in Forbes, *Maritime Rights,* and is implicit in T.W. Acheson, "The Maritimes and Empire Canada," in David Bercuson, ed., *Canada and the Burden of Unity* (Toronto 1977).

90 See "Halifax Newspapers and the Federal Principle, 1864–1865," *Dalhousie Review* 37 (1957): 72–84.

91 See Waite, *Life and Times of Confederation,* 238–9, on New Brunswick. Vaughan in "Critics of the Judicial Committee of the Privy Council" argues that the main anti-confederate alternative to Confederation in the Maritimes was an imperial union (510), but then admits a few pages later that an examination of the Confederation debates in the Maritimes shows that much of the resistance there was based on a clear perception of the centralist philosophy which lay behind the Quebec Resolutions (512).

92 Ellis, "Persistence of Antifederalism," 302.

93 In his study of the persistence of sectionalism in Britain, *Internal Colonialism: The Celtic Fringe in British National Development, 1536–1966* (Berkeley and Los Angeles 1975), Michael Hechter concludes that "the persistence of objective cultural distinctiveness in the periphery must itself be the function of the maintenance of an unequal distribution of resources between core and peripheral groups" (37). That periodic outbursts of regional discontent in the Maritimes are rooted in such an unequal distribution seems unquestionable, but the very ease with which the Maritimes was integrated into

Canada and the weakness of secessionist movements seems to me to imply that most Maritimers have always seen and continue to see themselves as a part of the core rather than the peripheral group in Canada.

94 I have not dealt with Newfoundland in this paper because it seems to me that it was the one place where, for a variety of historic reasons, these generalizations may not apply.

# "The Maritimes and Confederation"

*Canadian Historical Review*
1990

P.B. WAITE[1]

Philip Buckner's spacious survey of the historiography and argument of Confederation is refreshing. However, if some old books are not wholly anachronistic, the authors are apt to be. There is some irony in being asked to review an article that reveals Professor Buckner's grasp of the field and this author's failure to keep steadily up with it.

The most telling argument in Buckner's article is his turning the usual thesis inside out. Instead of asking why so many Maritimers opposed Confederation, he asks why so many agreed to accept it and, especially, a union that so clearly reflected the exigencies of the Province of Canada. Professor Buckner has cast his mind over the Maritime region and pulled diversities together. In other words, he says, if anti-confederates won 58.1 per cent of the popular vote in Nova Scotia and 50.8 per cent in New Brunswick, it is also true that confederates won 40.9 per cent in the former and 46.7 per cent in the latter.[2] It is a position not to be underestimated.

Nevertheless, there is no use in blinding oneself to the bitterness of the time, whatever the outcome in the long run. Perhaps it might all have been less traumatic had there been, after 1 July 1867, healing and hope from the new dominion government in Ottawa over the heart-burning in Nova Scotia and in New Brunswick. There wasn't. The Maritimes had but 33 seats in the Canadian House of Commons of 181 (in 1872 it was 37 in 200), and that elemental datum helped determine

Macdonald's still limited perspective. The Maritimes also discovered that Canadian administrators were both tougher and more efficient at administering what were now Canadian laws. This was not only true of administration of the Customs; the criminal law was tightened; offences that Maritimers had been inclined to treat in a milder fashion were dealt with more rigorously by Ottawa. New and more onerous tariffs also bedevilled the Maritimers' first years in Confederation.[3]

It seemed to prove that the Canadians had learnt little from the tumultuous process of Confederation, other than the clear recognition of their own needs and a determination to realize them. For the "pacification of Nova Scotia" – Creighton's expression in his *Macdonald,* volume 2 – began with Tilley, not Macdonald. It was Tilley who wrote, from Windsor, NS, in July 1868 these stern lines: "I am not an alarmist, but the position can only be understood by visiting Nova Scotia. There is no use crying peace when there is no peace. We require wise and prudent action at this moment; the most serious results may be produced by the opposite course."[4] The plain good sense of that letter Macdonald did, indeed, pay attention to.

This judicious review by Buckner, while it redresses a balance long in need of it, does not quite translate the anger and frustration in Nova Scotia and New Brunswick before and after 1867. That was not going to simmer down for some time. Anti-Confederation in Nova Scotia, and to some degree in New Brunswick too, was like malaria: whenever the patient became run-down or weak, the disease would surface; the patient would develop a temperature and have fevered visions of Maritime union, Greater Nova Scotia, or fighting Ottawa. It was endemic. W.S. Fielding eventually became Canadian, after 1896; but in 1892 he felt constrained to refuse, politely enough, an invitation to a July 1st celebration at Canada House, London, because there would be toasts that he would be obliged, publicly, to disagree with. There was the old man in Halifax whom George Wilson remembered in the federal election of 1925 who got up and exclaimed, "I voted against Confederation and the Tories in 1867 and, by God, I'll do it again!"

Something of this, and Wilson's delight in pulling away illusions, was in his article on New Brunswick and Confederation in 1928. There was ruthlessness, and some *Schadenfreude,* in exposing the machinations in New Brunswick to a Canada recently filled with the rhetoric of the 60th, Diamond, Jubilee of Confederation in 1927. What won New Brunswick, Wilson was saying in 1928, was power and manipulation. Arthur Gordon used both, with the British government and the Canadians backing him to the hilt. Wilson's article was a blockbuster and it was intended to be. Of course Buckner is right in saying that there was no use in Great Britain's commanding a British North American union if there did not exist the local will, and acceptance, to realize it. That difficulty was well known at the Colonial Office and was illustrated in Prince Edward Island and Newfoundland. The Fenians, and Canadian cash, had not reached either.

One need not accept Buckner's ingenious explanation of the allegedly superior skill of Canadians (West and East) at patronage. In the Atlantic provinces we had a 100-year running start at it even before Confederation, and there are delicious examples. A.H. Gillmor of Charlotte County, NB ("goes for Charlotte," as he delicately put it); or the great five-cent stamp escapade (also in New Brunswick), where the postmaster general thought patronage of himself was superior and put his visage eloquently on the new New Brunswick stamp; and, of course, both before and after Confederation we have those native geniuses out of Cumberland County, NS, the Charles Tuppers, senior and junior. Even Sir John A. Macdonald, hardened as he was, blanched at the full range of Charles Hibbert Tupper's exigencies in Pictou County.

As to Professor Chester Martin, it is proper to say that those graduate students who took his seminar on Canada, 1760–1867, were impressed with his scholarship; the trouble was it seemed twenty-five years, or more, old. Martin had done tremendous work in his time; but when a graduate student's paper came on that broached a new view of one of Martin's favourite themes, out would come those dog-eared notes from his inside pocket, and he would prove to his own certain satisfaction that you were wrong and he was right. You had not got the balance right, or had not put the right weight on the right documents. The granite of his face revealed the rock-like character of his mind. Both had been set many years before.

Donald Creighton was not like that, at least not in the 1950s when he was at the height of his powers. Few historians were more conscientious with their sources. There may be historians now who take their page proofs to the archives to check the accuracy of quotations, but I personally don't know of any. In seminar, unlike Martin, Creighton would accept anything if you could properly document it. The only occasion I saw him bulldoze a student was in the face of simple incompetence of research. His supervision of more than one PhD thesis was constant, conscientious, patient, impeccable, even when he was away from Canada. And there is something else. It was well known by the early 1950s that as soon as he had finished *Macdonald* he was going to do a major new history of Confederation. My thesis was squarely across his project; yet he was the first to urge me to get it published. Not all professors would be high-minded enough to encourage that or avoid stealing some of it. There was never repining from him when *The Life and Times of Confederation* came out only two years before the appearance of his book on virtually the same field. Still, his *Road to Confederation* of 1964 deserves Buckner's strictures.[5]

There is one weakness in the historiography of the period that Phillip Buckner does not comment on: the absence of any detailed studies of the first real round of Confederation talk, 1857–60. One still has to assume that the difference between the Confederation movement of 1858 and that of 1864 was due to the shift of a whole set of variables in those six years, some domestic, others external: the grid-lock of the political system of the Province of Canada; the American Civil War; and not least Cardwell and the British government, whose relentless policy was sustained across three successive ministries. It is a pity more has not been done to develop or criticize that argument, those assumptions.

Professor Buckner is generous to the *Life and Times of Confederation,* but he gives me credit for more sophistication than I had. He suggests that I may have been influenced by Cecilia Kenyon's 1955 article, "Men of Little Faith" in the *William and Mary Quarterly.* I had heard of the quarterly, but that much only is true. Indeed, aside from reading a great deal of American history for my Dalhousie classes, I deliberately avoided reading American learned articles. They carried the taint of American thought. My peculiar frame of mind derived from the fact that Confederation in its political ideology was in many ways a revolt against American ideas and American influences. I wanted my history pure; right or wrong, I was imbued with a strong determination to let the argument of the thesis (and the book) grow out of the vast and multifarious native sources that were available, the newspapers of the time. I did not want to be influenced by secondary literature. Frankly, I was afraid of it, of being turned by it, of having the raucous voices in the newspapers that came so vociferously muted by reflections engendered by modern minds, especially American ones. I wanted to be soaked in the British North America of the 1860s and to make myself, if that ever could be possible, the means by which that world might be transmuted into the 1960s.

That was, of course, romantic and naïve. But then so were the 1860s as they came through the newspapers. What was overwhelming was the exhilaration of it. One was driven to the newspapers, to the Parliamentary Library, to the St John's library, to the hot little sheds on Pinnacle Street, Belleville, Ont., not by the exigencies of a PhD, but by adrenalin.

For there was the nationalism of it, as well. That, I suppose now, is where one's historian's control slipped a little. One slackened the reins and the powerful steed took over. One was caught, as the newspapermen of the time were, by the sheer magnitude of Confederation, of colonials meeting and greeting each other for the first time, a bit star-struck some of them, the way the writer was, who'd caught it too. It made for peculiar history, nationalism reined in with difficulty by the historian's discipline, a discipline furnished, it is right to say, by the unrelenting intellectuality of D.J. McDougall and others, who ministered to that PhD at the University of Toronto.

And there may be, *horribile dictu,* a philosophical question in all of this. Who, what, made the running in 1864? Was it men? Or was it events, according to Chester Martin, "stronger than advocacy, stronger than men"? Abraham Lincoln would have agreed with Martin. "I claim," Lincoln said in 1864, "not to have controlled events but confess plainly that events have controlled me." That view of life, history, and the Civil War, reminiscent of Tolstoy in *War and Peace,* may be reasonable enough, from the White House, with telegraphs, interviews, letters, streaming in upon one's consciousness. Still, it underestimates Lincoln's use, adaptation, of events, which in some critical cases was far from being passive. That small, low island in the roadstead of Charleston, South Carolina, is a case in point. Lincoln's move to notify Governor Pickens of South Carolina at the end of March 1861 that the federal government would supply Fort Sumter with provisions only, not with arms, was brilliant. It was carefully weighed and pondered. It forced the South to make war first.

Does the Confederation movement suggest that men shape their own destinies? Does it argue, for example, that without George Brown Confederation might not have happened when and how it did? Or that without Anne Nelson Brown, George would not have offered coalition in June 1864? Is Frank Underhill's suggestion of the "Mother of Confederation" merely ironic?

These are questions that certainly I did not ask, and that one thinks of now. Confederation is susceptible to interpretation as dialectic between men and events, to prove (disprove) that action is possible. Different positions on that question might well have been taken by Tupper (who probably believed he could do anything), by Macdonald, or by Tilley.

Perhaps it could be said that all men in political life prefer to live and work with the fundamental assumption that not only is action possible, but that it matters. Probably the basic apposition of men *vs* events is too crude. Wilhelm Dilthey fairly meets something of this difficulty: "The historian must therefore understand the whole life of an individual as it asserts itself at a certain time and at a certain place. It is also the whole clutch of connections that goes from individuals ... to the cultural systems and communities and eventually to the whole of mankind, which makes up the character of society and history. Individuals are as much the logical subjects of history as communities and contexts."[6]

NOTES

1 P.B. Waite, "The Maritimes and Confederation," *Canadian Historical Review*, 71, 1 (1990), 30–35.

2 The figures are from J.M. Beck, *Pendulum of Power* (Toronto 1968), 12; for a more extended analysis see Del Muise, "The Federal Election of 1867 in Nova Scotia: An Economic Interpretation," Nova Scotia Historical Society, *Collections* (1968): 327–51.

3 P.B. Waite, "Becoming Canadians: Ottawa's Relations with Maritimers in the First and Twenty-first Years of Confederation," in R. Kenneth Carty and W. Peter Ward, *National Politics and Community in Canada* (Vancouver 1986), 153–68.

4 Tilley to Macdonald, 17 July 1868, cited in Joseph Pope, *The Memoirs of Sir John A. Macdonald*, vol. 2 (Ottawa 1895), 27–8.

5 The powerful drama of *Road to Confederation* helps disguise its teleology. Opponents of Confederation were nearly always wrong-headed. Joseph Howe, for example, is described as "tired, disappointed, unfulfilled, troubled by a haunting sense of lost causes and unused abilities, he had to look on enviously" (225).

6 Wilhelm Dilthey, *Gesammelte Schriften*, vol. VII (Stuttgart 1961), 135. The German is as follows: "Der Historiker muss daher das ganze Leben der Individuen, wie es zu einer bestimmten Zeit und an einem bestimmten Ort sich äussert, verstehen. Es ist eben der ganze Zusammenhang, der von den Individuen ... zu Kultursystemen und Gemeinschaften, schliesslich zu der Menschheit geht, der die Natur der Gesellschaft und der Geschichte aumacht. Die logischen Subjekte, über die in der Geschichte ausgesagt wird, sind ebenso Einzelindividuen wie Gemeinschaften und Zusammenhänge."

# "George Brown"

*Dictionary of Canadian Biography*
1972

J.M.S. CARELESS[1]

[...]
In short, within a few years of establishing his newspaper, George Brown had moved it from the day of personal journalism to the era of big newspaper business in Canada. He made himself a leading Toronto businessman in the process and also shaped a formidable political power. But though he was to enter politics himself, his strongest concern would always remain with the *Globe*, just as it did at its beginning, in March 1844.

He gave his first significant political speech in that very month on 25 March, to the Reform Association of Canada, at a meeting held in Toronto to protest Sir Charles Metcalfe's attempt to carry on government with but a trio of ministers, W.H. Draper, Dominick Daly, and Denis-Benjamin Viger, who had not yet managed to fill up the other ministerial offices. The young *Globe* editor's ringing denunciation of such an un-British and illiberal practice roused warm response. From that time onward, his fervent, powerful oratory was often called upon at party gatherings and public meetings. Meanwhile, he vigorously engaged the *Globe* in the Reformers' battle against Metcalfe and the Tory-Conservative forces that were rallying to the governor general's side. There was, indeed, a growing reaction in English-speaking Canada against what seemed excessively partisan Reform insistence on removing the governor's power over patronage. Hence, in the elections held that autumn, pro-Metcalfe forces carried Canada West (popularly still called Upper Canada), though the victory of La Fontaine's Liberals in Canada East, the largely French-speaking Lower Canadian section, meant that the new Conservative ministry had only a bare majority over all.

[...]

Another measure of the session further aroused his concern about Catholic influence on government policy. This, the Upper Canada school act introduced by Hincks, enlarged provisions for separate denominational schools in the western system of public education, so that Catholic schools, specifically, could more readily be organized to receive state support. Brown saw this enlargement as an alarming inroad into the maintenance of one non-sectarian public system. His *Globe* called it "the entering wedge." Then, as he and other voluntaryists were becoming increasingly exercised over "state church" influences on public affairs, the papal aggression question burst in England in the fall of 1850.

The root of the issue was a papal brief recreating a Roman Catholic hierarchy in England for the first time since the Reformation. The brief was at least unwise in declaring this realm of Anglicanism, Puritanism, and Methodism to be now returned to an "orbit" around Rome. There was strong response from Protestants, already reacting to the resurgent ultramontane and anti-liberal zeal of the papacy under Pius IX. Brown's *Globe* was only one of numerous liberal or voluntaryist-minded journals in Canada that commented severely on these papal and Catholic presumptions, but its power and vehemence involved it in a bitter exchange of doctrinal arguments and name-calling with the local Catholic press. Inevitably, by the spring of 1851, Brown had emerged as either a potent voluntaryist champion or an arch anti-Catholic in a country deeply divided by religious passions.

Meanwhile he had decided to try for parliament himself, to strengthen the cause there of non-sectarian public education and the separation of church and state. He stood in a by-election for Haldimand County in April 1851. His chief opponent was William Lyon Mackenzie, now back, amnestied, from his long American exile and a rather obstreperous ally of the Grit radicals. The power of Mackenzie's name among western Grit farmers, the half-hearted support which the Reform leaders gave their own somewhat troublesome candidate, Brown, and, in particular, a powerful Catholic appeal to Irish Reformers to reject the sworn enemy of their faith, all combined to give the victory to Mackenzie.

Brown's growing breach with the ministry widened and his concern over Catholic influence in politics was only reinforced.

[...]

Sectionalism had been embedded in the very constitution of the union, since the two Canadas had been given equal representation in its parliament. Underlying this political division, however, was the deeper division between two cultural communities: that of Upper Canada, English-speaking and mainly Protestant; that of Lower Canada, largely French-speaking and Roman Catholic. The distinction could only be sharpened by the different aims of zealous western voluntaryism, striving to end state support and recognition of religion, and equally zealous French-Canadian Catholicism, seeking to establish new religious corporations for educational and welfare purposes or to back demands from the Upper Canadian Catholic minority for further separate school rights. Sectional strains mounted when the reserves question and ecclesiastical corporations bills came up, and when a new separate school measure for the west was carried through by Lower Canadian votes. It was charged that a "French domination" was imposing its will on Upper Canada. George Brown was in the forefront of debate, clearly representing a broader constituency in the west than just his own riding of Kent.

As parliament went on into 1853, he made himself still more prominent in Upper Canada by moving a resolution in March for representation by population. This would give the western section a preponderance of parliamentary seats, for its population had now outstripped the east's. French Canadians naturally feared being swamped by a western, English ascendancy, and held to the bulwark of equal sectional representation. In any case, Brown's motion did not win many adherents as yet in English Canada, which was more divided politically between Reform and Tory parties than the more compact, ethnically united French-Canadian minority. The idea of "rep by pop," not originally Brown's, would become strongly associated with him, and would increasingly gain western support as sectional strife continued in the union.

Indeed by 1854 it threatened to break up the Reform party and topple the Hincks-Morin government. In June the failure of that government to settle the reserves – though they now had imperial authorization to act – was a major factor in creating a sudden combination of dissentient groups that defeated Hincks in parliament and led to elections that summer. Brown was handily returned for Lambton, a constituency newly divided off from Kent. Out of the party turmoil he hoped to shape a new alignment to advance voluntaryism and secularize the reserves, composed of non-radical Reformers and moderate Conservatives, many of whom were now ready to support secularization.

The governing coalition that emerged when parliament met in September dashed Brown's hopes. It combined Hincks' former following of moderate Liberals and the French-Canadian group still under Morin with the Tory-Conservative forces led by Sir Allan MacNab. In this new MacNab-Morin regime, Tories and Conservatives would accept the need to abolish the reserves; and they and the followers of Hincks could foster railway development in the alliance, which upheld the French Canadians' cultural interests. In short, this Liberal-Conservative coalition represented a fresh attempt to bridge sectional divisions, leaving in opposition George Brown and some western voluntaryists, the Clear Grit radical wing, and the smaller, largely French-Canadian eastern radical faction, termed the Rouges, under Antoine-Aimé Dorion.

Among these fragments of Reform there was no recognized opposition leader, but Brown increasingly took a prominent role, thanks to his parliamentary prowess and the strength of the *Globe*. When the government's promised measure to abolish the reserves came up in October 1854, he and his former Clear Grit foes could vote together in criticizing loopholes in the bill, though they accepted its main tenor. Brown could also at least cooperate with the Lower Canadian Rouges in attacking alleged governmental waste and corruption in railway schemes, especially in regard to the costly Grand Trunk then building the main line across the province. In fact, he also might reach common ground with Rouges on many "state church" issues, since they had inherited the French-Canadian strain of anti-clericalism. Nevertheless, any Liberal opposition front could only be a loose working alliance of sectional elements at best, and Brown's prime effort was to form a coherent Reform party within the western half of the union.

He achieved a good deal of progress during 1855. The *Globe* made overtures to the Clear Grits, urging the need for Reform unity. Leading Grit radicals were ready to sink their differences with Brown and put by their hopes of sweeping elective constitutional reforms in the more urgent need to fight revived Conservative power and the dangers of "French Catholic domination." It was an important sign, therefore, when Brown bought out the Grit *North American* in February, and its editor, McDougall, joined the *Globe* staff. Then in May a new bill for Upper Canadian separate schools brought still more important developments. The act of 1855 introduced by Étienne Taché was suddenly put through parliament in its last days at Quebec, when many Upper Canadian members had left for home. It was passed, moreover, by an eastern majority over the votes of those westerners still on hand, including Brown. This event seemed hard proof of Lower Canadian domination of the union, and of the Liberal-Conservative ministry's connivance in that domination.

In the indignation that swept Upper Canada, many Grit adherents called for dissolution of the union. But Brown, the Toronto businessman, was perhaps more conscious of the commercial values of the Canadian union than embattled western farmers. He and the *Globe* argued for representation by population instead: to remake rather than destroy the union, assure justice for Upper Canada but maintain the unity of the St Lawrence transport system and the broad economic development that would be lost by separation. They waged a campaign for rep by pop through Upper Canada in the summer of 1855. By autumn Grittism had been largely won to it, and Brown had supplied a powerful policy on which to focus the reunification of Upper Canadian Reform.

He made further gains the next year. In parliament in the spring of 1856, the Liberal-Conservative regime, facing sectional discords and internal divisions itself, lost some of its Liberal supporters to the Reform forces in opposition. The ministry was reconstructed in May, when MacNab was replaced by the far more able John A. Macdonald as western leader – and still only narrowly avoided defeat in the assembly. During heated debates earlier in the session Brown and Macdonald had had a sharply significant personal encounter. Macdonald, who had always supported the cause of an old family friend, Henry Smith, the ex-warden of the Kingston penitentiary, was carried away in anger to accuse Brown as secretary of the 1848–49 commission of having falsified evidence and suborned witnesses. The committee of inquiry, which the latter immediately requested, heard a mass of testimony that palpably exonerated Brown; but it produced only a non-committal verdict, being politically weighted against him. A proud and sensitive man, he was left with the grave charges unretracted, which put more than political barriers between him and his great Conservative rival.

In August 1856, Brown began a new campaign through the *Globe*, calling for the annexation to Canada of the vast British territories beyond the Great Lakes, still the preserve of the fur-trading Hudson's Bay Company. He had long been interested in the potentialities of the North-West. Now they were attracting widespread attention in Upper Canada, both from land-hungry farmers seeking new frontiers to settle and from Toronto businessmen hoping to direct new flows of trade to their fast rising metropolis. Brown and his brother Gordon were closely identified themselves with Toronto efforts to open communications with the North-West. And northwestern expansion was another powerful policy for a resurgent Upper Canadian Reform party, on which commercial and agrarian interests could unite. The time seemed ripe to cement party unity, when in December 1856 the emerging Toronto business and professional leadership group (with George Brown at its core) issued a call for a Reform convention to gather in the city.

The convention held on 8 January 1857 brought together 150 Brownites, Clear Grits, and Liberals who had formerly followed Hincks. It readily adopted a platform that marked successful Reform reunion and included representation by population, annexation of the North-West, national non-sectarian education, and free trade. It was Brown's platform; he dominated the proceedings and his friends the central party structure. He had remade the party in a Brownite image. Its opponents still might dub it "Clear Grit" – and "Grits" the Brownite Liberals would long be termed. But the old Clear Grit radicalism of American elective democracy had really been submerged within Victorian British parliamentary Liberalism.

The reorganized party faced its test when elections were announced in November by the government, now led by Macdonald and his powerful French-Canadian ally, George-Étienne CARTIER. Brownite Reform forces won a clear majority in Upper Canada, and Brown himself was triumphantly returned for both Toronto and North Oxford, but in Lower Canada the Rouges under Dorion were decisively defeated by Cartier's large Bleu Conservative contingent. Hence the Macdonald-Cartier regime was able to continue in office when the new parliament opened at Toronto in February 1858. But Brown pressed hard on the ministry's weakness in Upper Canada; by midsummer it was in trouble, meeting dissension in its ranks and minor defeats in the house. Accordingly, the Macdonald-Cartier cabinet decided to resign when a vote of 28 July rejected the choice of Ottawa as future permanent capital, a choice with which the cabinet was identified.

The governor general, Sir Edmund Head, called on Brown as the leading figure in the opposition to form a new government. The danger for Brown was obvious, since his side had no real majority in the house. Yet if he refused, he would virtually endorse the constant Conservative charge that he was a "governmental impossibility." He worked closely with Dorion, and succeeded in constructing an able cabinet, dedicated to establishing representation by population, but with constitutional guarantees for French Canada. As might be expected, this Brown-Dorion ministry was nevertheless defeated when it met parliament on 2 August; but Brown had then hoped to go to the country and win a new general election. Head refused his request, on the ground that elections had been held so recently. Brown could only resign, as he did on 4 August.

[...]

In 1862, with his health still uncertain, he decided to take a long recuperative holiday in Great Britain. He landed in Liverpool on 23 July, his first return in 25 years. After a month in London, he moved on to Edinburgh, and there saw such old friends as William and Thomas Nelson, of the Nelson publishing family, who had been his school mates at the High School. Above all, he met their sister, Anne Nelson, lively, intelligent, and cultivated. He fell deeply in love at 43, and on 27 November, he and Anne were married at Abden House, the Nelson home.

They returned to Canada in late December, to receive a tumultuous mass welcome in Toronto. But soon, despite George Brown's wholehearted affection for his new domestic life, he felt the pull of unfinished political business. With his health fully restored and his horizons undoubtedly broadened by viewing colonial sectional politics from the centre of empire, he decided on another try: a man no less vigorous and resolute than before, but somehow more detached and judicious – perhaps the mellowing result of marriage.

Brown easily won a by-election in South Oxford in March 1863. He found himself in a parliament both altered and much the same. A moderate Liberal government under Sandfield Macdonald had replaced a crumbling Conservative regime in 1862, but Sandfield's ministry was just one more attempt to keep the existing union running without dealing with underlying sectional and constitutional problems. Sandfield, in fact, had pinned his faith to the double majority principle, whereby neither section of the union would be governed against the will of its own parliamentary majority. But that principle had foundered shortly before Brown rejoined parliament at Quebec in April, when another separate school bill had been passed for Upper Canada without having received western majority support. The discredited government was thereupon recast to give it a firmer Reform character, Brown playing a prominent part as he reasserted his old influence in his party even though he preferred to stay outside the ministry. Dorion and his Rouge friends replaced moderate eastern Liberals in the cabinet; associates of Brown, such as Oliver Mowat, entered its western half. This new Macdonald-Dorion ministry then went to the polls in July 1863. The Reformers won in Upper Canada emphatically (as Brown again did in South Oxford), but Cartier's Conservatives equally swept the east. The two sides were practically in balance. Deadlock was approaching.

The fruitless power struggles in parliament that autumn showed that no real change had been made in the political situation. Brown, however, acting as a private member, disclosed a significantly new approach. He announced his intention to move for a select committee to inquire impartially into the sectional problems of Canada and report on the best means of remedying them. It was a constructive proposal, carefully worded to be non-partisan. But his motion did not come to a vote until the spring session of 1864, as the house battled on through more bitter, barren factional contests. The Sandfield-Macdonald ministry, unable to govern, gave up in March. The Conservative cabinet that replaced it, under John A. Macdonald and Sir Étienne Taché, had no greater chance of achievement, or even survival. Brown's single-minded aim was to settle the constitutional impasse and retire from the burden of parliament to the warm family world he longed for – his first child, Margaret, had been born that January. Finally, on 19 May 1864, his motion passed. He became chairman of a select committee drawn from leading members of all parties; he put it industriously to work. And on 14 June it reported to parliament "a strong feeling" in favour of "a federative system."

This was only a general statement in a brief progress report. Yet it supplied the essential basis for a way out when, on the very day of that report, the Macdonald-Taché government collapsed. Brown moved decisively to use this latest crisis: he let the Conservative leaders know that he would support their ministry, or any other, if they would act to solve the constitutional problem. They were ready to respond. On 17 June, John A. Macdonald and Alexander Tilloch Galt, a leading proponent of British North American federation, met with Brown in his room at the St Louis Hotel. Cartier later joined the discussions. It was soon decided that the only solution lay "in the federative principle suggested by the report of Mr. Brown's committee," and that an approach should first be made to the Atlantic provinces to seek a general British American federal union. Brown had looked ultimately toward this larger goal, but he had deemed earlier Conservative advocacy of it to be premature and mainly used as a red herring to evade action on Canada's own internal constitutional problem. But since the Conservatives had now agreed to federate the Canadian union, he could only see a great gain if the other colonies could also be included. He agreed, though reluctantly, to enter the government with two Reform supporters. The new coalition to seek a confederation would thus have overwhelming strength in the house, backed both by the Brownite Grit western majority and Cartier's Bleu eastern majority. Deadlock was over. George Brown had initiated the breakthrough, and the movement to a whole new union.

On 22 June 1864 the "Great Coalition" was announced to a wildly jubilant house. Brown joined Macdonald and Cartier and their colleagues in the cabinet as president of the council, along with Mowat and McDougall as his Reform associates, all under Taché as prime minister. During the summer this strong new government developed the outlines of a federal scheme to lay before representatives of the Maritime provinces at a meeting in Charlottetown in September. Among the eight Canadian cabinet members who went to the Charlottetown conference, Brown took an important role, on 5 September presenting to it the constitutional structure proposed for federal union. After the conference unanimously endorsed confederation in principle, he went on to meetings at Halifax and Saint John.

In October came the larger Quebec conference to work out detailed terms for confederation. Again Brown took a leading part in this critically important gathering – being, after all, the strongest representative there of the most powerful provincial interest, that of the future Ontario. Yet his own interest was not just sectional, but national. For example, it was he who moved the essential resolution stipulating central and provincial governments for the union, with provision for the admission of the North-West, British Columbia, and Vancouver Island. He took a stand against an elected senate in the new federal parliament, as he had previously against the elective upper house introduced in the province of Canada, because of the problem of basing British responsible government on the confidence of two representative bodies, particularly if they were of different party complexion. And he wanted simple, non-political new provincial authorities, since they were to be left only "insignificant" matters to deal with. Brown believed that the establishing of representation by population in the central government (another resolution which he moved) would give Upper Canada its due voice in important national matters, and that the provincial regimes would take the divisive, but essentially local, sectional issues out of high politics. It was a clouded vision, but at least a well-meaning one for this "sectional" politician to become a confederation statesman.

After the conference closed, Brown was one of the spokesmen who first presented the actual plan for confederation embodied in the 72 Quebec resolutions to the Canadian people, in his case, through a major speech in Toronto on 3 November. Later that month he set out for England. He had been chosen to open discussions with the imperial government on the project of union, and also to discuss the transfer of the North-West from the HBC to this grand new design. During December he went into these questions with British government and opposition leaders in London, as well as the question of British North American defence, made urgent by strained relations with the United States arising out of the Civil War, now hastening towards a northern victory. He returned early in 1865, sure of imperial approval for the confederation project, hopeful of progress on the transfer of the North-West, but worried by apparent British readiness to see the still weak colonies "shift for themselves" in the face of American danger.

The Canadian parliament met again in February, to debate the Quebec conference scheme and to give the approval to be expected from the government's big majority. Still, the confederation debates of 1865 were no mere rubber stamp; they expressed doubts and penetrating criticism, national hopes and powerful arguments for union. In the latter regard, Brown's own speech of 8 February was perhaps his greatest, and one of the strongest in support of confederation. Before the vote was taken, however, the plan had met reverses in the Maritimes, where the pro-confederation government of Samuel Leonard Tilley had lost an election in New Brunswick in March, and the Charles Tupper regime had not even dared to introduce the Quebec scheme in the Nova Scotian assembly.

Another Canadian mission was accordingly sent to England to discuss the future of confederation, this time composed of Brown, Macdonald, Cartier, and Galt. After busy meetings and much social life in London in May and June, they succeeded handsomely, gaining imperial assurance of cooperation in forwarding the project and of the defence of Canada in event of war, though now that the Civil War had ended any American military threat seemed fast receding. The British government also promised aid in negotiating a new trade agreement with the United States, since the existing reciprocity treaty was to end the following year. While in Britain, Brown was fully involved in the working out of these vital concerns of the confederation movement. The remaining essential was winning back the Maritimes. After the mission returned he played a part here also.

In September 1865 he and Galt represented Canada at the Confederate Trade Council in Quebec, a smaller meeting of the provinces to consider their commercial future now that their reciprocity agreement with the United States was to be terminated. The common approach to trade the council sought, and the Maritime contacts Brown made, stood him in good stead afterwards when the Canadian government sent him to the Maritimes to try the climate anew on confederation. He marked a hopeful trend in New Brunswick, and dealt with Tilley and Lieutenant Governor Arthur Hamilton Gordon on ways to advance it. On his return in mid-November, however, he found the Canadian government had decided on a policy of their own for seeking reciprocity with the United States, by joint legislative action rather than by treaty, and this he firmly opposed.

Brown had long upheld reciprocity, as an economic liberal seeking to remove, not raise, the barriers of tariffs, and as an Upper Canadian who had seen his own section benefit from it. But he did believe its price might come too high. Legislative reciprocity, virtually open to change at the will of an American congressional lobby, would, he thought, place Canadian prosperity at the mercy of American dictation. He fought the proposal through tense cabinet discussions, yet failed to convince his colleagues. At length, on 19 December, he resigned. There is no doubt that the issue was crucial to Brown, though it is also true, of course, that strains had long been rising in the cabinet between two strong chieftains and old opponents, Macdonald and himself. Moreover Brown was still uneasy in a coalition, however great its purpose, and felt he was unduly committed in an old game of power-building and office-dealing. Hence he was emotionally ready to resign over an issue as important as reciprocity. There was meaning in the telegram he sent his wife: "I am a free man once more."

In any case, confederation now was well in train. Brown continued wholeheartedly to support it, in the *Globe* and at the next session of parliament in 1866. He had the satisfaction of seeing New Brunswick elect Tilley's pro-confederates in the spring, and Nova Scotia reopen the quest for union – not to mention, meanwhile, the failure of the legislative reciprocity approach to a scarcely interested United States. Towards the close of the year the final confederation conference met in London to draft the imperial bill, still fundamentally embodying the Quebec resolutions Brown had helped to formulate. It was passed as the British North America Act in March 1867.

[...]

NOTES

1 J.M.S. Careless, "George Brown," 93–101. *Dictionary of Canadian Biography*, 10 (1871–1880). Toronto: University of Toronto Press 1972.

# The West and Confederation

## Centennial Historical Booklet 1967

W.L. MORTON[1]

### The West in 1857

In 1857 the present Canadian West was not part of Canada. As territory of the British Crown it was a portion, by far the largest portion, of British North America. It was itself made up of three parts. On the Pacific coast was the Colony of Vancouver Island, created in 1849. The Pacific slope between the 49th parallel and Alaska eastward to the divide of the Rockies, and the Arctic watershed down to the northern coast, was "the Indian Territory." To the east lay the enormous tract known as Rupert's Land. At fullest extent, Rupert's Land extended from the divide of the Rockies across British North America to Hudson Bay and around to the coast of Labrador. The boundaries between Rupert's Land and the Province of Canada had never been authoritatively fixed. The limits of Rupert's Land, wherever they lay, were to be found in the broad terms of the Hudson's Bay Company's Charter of 1670, except as those might have been modified by international treaty or by British statute.

Over all this territory, from the Colony of Vancouver Island to the wastes of Ungava, the governing power was the Hudson's Bay Company. The Company, a relic of the colonial regime of the seventeenth century, was at once a commercial corporation and a colonial government, created by the Crown of England.

The Company traded and governed in Rupert's Land by virtue of the Charter of 1670. However, its authority had been strengthened there, and at the same time extended over the Indian Territory, by Licence granted in 1821 for a term of twenty-one years. The grant was made under the Act passed that year to regulate the fur trade after the union of the North West and Hudson's Bay Companies. In 1838 the Licence was renewed for a further period of twenty-one years, to run until 1859. In 1857, therefore, the question of its renewal was to the fore in the minds of the Company and of the Imperial Government.

### New Forces in the North West

Had the circumstances of 1857 been those of 1838 or 1821, there can be little doubt that the Licence would have been renewed for a further term. Circumstances had altered greatly, however, and were in 1857 rapidly altering still more. The isolation of North West British America was ending; the very concept of that North West as a fur trader's preserve was being challenged and overthrown. And within the territories of the Company, changes were proceeding which threatened both its commercial monopoly and its political authority.

The North West was, in fact, an area on which forces widely scattered in their origin were beginning to converge. A new view of the climate of much of its area had been advanced in 1856, and was being widely publicized. The view was that the summers of the North West were much warmer than was commonly thought. It was expounded in Lorin Blodget's *Climatology of the United States.* Blodget had found much data for his thesis in the reports of the survey parties for a Pacific railway in the United States. Further data were provided by the discovery of the warm Japanese current of the North Pacific, made by the squadron of Commodore Matthew C. Perry returning early in 1854 from the famous "opening" of Japan. In two factors, the effect of the continental land mass on extremes of temperature and the influence of the warm current on the North West coast, Blodget found an explanation for the fact that in summer the North West was warmer than its latitude would suggest and moister than the character of the southern plains of the United States would imply. Information obtained from fur traders' journals and narratives and reports from posts of the Hudson's Bay Company from Red River to the Mackenzie were the basis for his finding, much celebrated in its day, of the northwestward swing in summer of the lines of equal temperature: "... the spring opens," he asserted, "at nearly the same time along the immense line of plains from St. Paul's to Mackenzie's River." Here then was a region which, contrary to accepted belief, was suitable for agricultural settlement and the building of a Pacific railway.

Political circumstances, as well as scientific, were working to bring the North West out of its long obscurity. The first of these was, odd though it may seem, the Crimean War. Alaska had been Russian since the seventeenth century, as Rupert's Land had been British. In 1825 the boundary between the Russian and the British claims in the far North West had been defined by treaty. The agreement ended Anglo-Russian difficulties in the Pacific North West, but during the Crimean War a British ship-of-war or two might well have garnered in the Russian empire in America had the effort seemed worth while. It did not, however, and by mutual and tacit agreement the region was in fact neutralized during the conflict.

The war, however, had two effects on Russian policy in the Pacific. One was to reveal the slender thread by which Russia's American possessions hung and so prepare the way for the sale of Alaska to the United States in 1867. Another was to cause a lessening of Russia's activity on its European borders and a forward movement on the Pacific. In 1857 Russia became active in the lower Amur Valley, occupied since 1689, and so began its approach to a warm water port on the Pacific. Thus the emergence of the United States as a Pacific Power in 1848 was followed by this ominous stirring of Russia in 1857. As the North Pacific ceased to be a power vacuum, the continental North West must also cease to be a diplomatic void.

Far more pressing, however, than faint echoes of Russian movements on the Amur was the interest of two regions of the United States in the territory north of the international line. One was the territory of Minnesota and its ambitious capital, St. Paul; the other was the Pacific slope where the prospectors were working along the mountain streams eastward and northward. The interest of San Francisco and the American Pacific slope in the North West was entirely novel, and first aroused only with the Fraser gold rush of 1857. But the interest of St. Paul in Red River had been active for some years and was already fed with dreams of regional empire. It had begun with Norman W. Kittson's visit to the Red River Settlement in 1843. An outburst of free trading followed, which grew steadily year by year. The interest of St. Paul in the North West grew with any new prospect over the boundary, such as Blodget's *Climatology* painted, with its argument that the northern route was the best for the Pacific railway and its conviction that the North West was suitable for settlement.

The sovereign power in the North West, the United Kingdom, had no such interest. The Hudson's Bay Company had been the sole occasion for British interest in the possession of the North West. From Canada to the Gulf of Georgia the British Government maintained not a single commissioned officer, governmental, judicial, or military.

Yet there was at issue, with American interest in the North West growing, and with Russian power in the Pacific increasing, the balance of power in North America established by the diplomatic events of 1817–1825. The Rush-Bagot agreement of 1817, by neutralizing the Great Lakes, recognized the fact that American military power on the continent was offset by British naval supremacy on the Atlantic coast. The Monroe Doctrine had had the effect of checking Russian expansion on the continent, and the Anglo-Russian treaty of 1825 had in effect balanced the two imperial powers to the advantage of the United States. Now the new continental dimensions of the United States threatened the diplomatic fabric of 1817–1825, except as the potential power of the United States was checked by the internal balance of North and South, of free soil and slave soil. The Imperial Government was therefore bound, as during the Oregon crisis, to deal gently but firmly with the American pressure, in such a way as to maintain the equilibrium of 1817–1825 without provoking a collision with the United States. Britain was thus committed to playing some definite part in changes affecting the North West, at once as the sovereign of the Hudson's Bay Company and also as trustee for the Canadian interest in the North West.

That interest was definite and of long standing, even if since 1821 it had been dormant. The French regime and the North West Company had left behind them a connection between Canada and the North West which the undefined boundaries of Rupert's Land might allow Canada to erect into a claim to the southern portion of the territory governed by the Hudson's Bay Company. Nor was Canada's lack of interest in the North West since 1821 as great as it seemed, or as it is customarily stated to have been. There were many bonds, none of them insignificant. The Southern Department of the Hudson's Bay Company included much Canadian territory; its posts looked out from the foot of the Laurentian escarpment over the Lakes, the Ottawa valley and the St. Lawrence. They were scattered through much of the territory of the present-day northern Ontario and Quebec. The Company still recruited some French Canadians as *voyageurs*. The headquarters of the Company in America, except for the early summer months, was from 1833 the residence of Governor George Simpson at Lachine. The French colony at Red River and the Roman Catholic missions in the North West furnished another vital connection. And a number of ex-officers and servants of the Company had retired, not to Red River, but to Canada. In them was the seed of a new North West Company.

Even more important than these connections with the North West were certain developments in Canada itself. Canada West, or Upper Canada as it was still called, was at the peak of the great boom of the 1850's. This had been stimulated by California gold, the Reciprocity Treaty, the Crimean War, and the building of the Grand Trunk and other railways. A great inflow of capital and immigrants, coupled with good crops and good markets, had resulted in a feverish exploitation of the forests and soil of western Canada. The Reciprocity Treaty stripped off the white pine stands for the building of American cities, the St. Lawrence canals and the railways pulled the grain and other farm produce to the British and American markets. As a result, there was capital and enterprise; as a result, there was a quest for new timber stands, farm lands, and richer mines. For new land there was not only a quest but a positive need, as the farm lands of Upper Canada had, practically speaking, been occupied. That there was trade to be won and land to be taken up in Red River was news that would find hearers in Upper Canada.

**The Select Committee of 1857**

Such was the situation of the Canadian West at the beginning of 1857, when the British Colonial Secretary, Henry Labouchere, decided that a Select Committee of the House of Commons should be set up to enquire into the desirability of renewing the Company's jurisdiction.

The Committee began its sittings in February 1857. Even if there was some disposition in the Government to pre-judge the issue, a very full hearing was held, and much testimony was heard and recorded. Canada, as an interested party and a potential heir of the Company's regime, was invited to make its views known. A major result of the enquiry was an awakening of interest in Canada in the future of the North West.

The Canadian Government, the Taché-Macdonald administration formed in 1856, took up the matter promptly but with caution. The ministry was dependent on Lower Canadian members for its strength and was closely associated with the Grand Trunk Railway. The French of Lower Canada were not, as a group, interested in the North West. Montreal and the Grand Trunk had as their main enterprise the attraction of the trade of the American Middle West. They could not be interested in the remoter, less promising trade of a Canadian West. On the other hand, the Government could not ignore the quickly vocal interest of Upper Canada in the Red River valley and the Saskatchewan.

The Government also had in its own ranks an eloquent advocate of Canadian expansion. This was Joseph Cauchon, Commissioner of Crown Lands, a Quebec journalist and member of Parliament from Lower Canada, who was to prove himself an ardent protagonist of westward expansion and of the confederation of British North America. But in this particular work he was aided, it may be was inspired, by an official of the Provincial Secretary's department, A.R. Roche, who had made a special study of the North West and of Canada's claims to the region. It seems apparent that it was Roche's ideas which informed a memorandum Cauchon prepared for the cabinet. That document asserted Canada's right to the North West as far as the Pacific, and urged immediate annexation by Canada to give government to Red River, where discontent existed, and to forestall absorption by the United States. "It is of incalculable importance," the memorandum concluded, "that these measures should be most forcibly pressed upon the Imperial Government at the present juncture, for on their solution depends the question whether this country shall ultimately become a Petty State, or one of the Great Powers of the earth; and not only that, but whether or not there shall be a counterpoise favourable to British interests and modelled upon British institutions to counteract the preponderating influence – if not the absolute dominion – to which our great neighbour, the United States, must otherwise attain upon this continent."

The Government, whatever its impression of the memorandum, could not let Canada's claims go by default, and could do no less than lay the Canadian claims before the Select Committee, in however moderate and legalistic a manner. But events had already begun which gave rise to a vigorous public demand in Upper Canada for the annexation of the North West.

In the summer of 1856, a troop of American cavalry appeared on the plains south of the border and warned the Red River Métis to desist from running buffalo on American territory. It was feared by Governor Sir George Simpson that this heralded the establishment of a military post on the border, which would become a focus of Métis settlement and of free trade activity below the border which the Hudson's Bay

Company would be unable to control. He therefore obtained the despatch of a detachment of the Royal Canadian Rifles to Fort Garry, on the pretext of danger from the American military post, but really as a means of overawing the Métis and the free traders whom the post would encourage.

He may well have known also that the danger to the Company's trade and government came not only from a free trade stimulated from St. Paul, but also from one begun from Canada. For in the winter of 1856–1857, a group of Toronto businessmen, inspired by old Hudson's Bay men, formed the North West Trading and Colonization Company to open communications and trade with the North West. A principal agent in the affair was George Gladman, once a chief trader in the Company and now a hostile critic of it. Gladman was in contact on the one hand with A.R. Roche and on the other with George Brown, editor of *The Globe* and just about to become the mouth-piece of Canadian interests in the North West. These men in January 1857 sent William Kennedy to Red River as their agent. Kennedy, a North West half-breed, had connections in Red River and was sent to make arrangements for trade and to inspire a demand for union with Canada. Simpson knew of his departure, and it was no doubt to contain the trouble Kennedy might cause as much as that an American military post might inspire that he had sought the despatch of a detachment of troops to Fort Garry.

The Canadian Government had no reason to be ignorant of the interest in the North West which the above events were arousing. In the session of the Canadian Legislature begun in the new year George Brown obtained the appointment of a committee to investigate the Canadian claims to the region and to report on the desirability of Canada seeking to obtain possession of the West.

### Canada before the Committee

When therefore the Government accepted the Colonial Secretary's invitation to be represented before the proposed Select Committee in London, it had cause to see that the opportunity was not missed and that a strong case was made. But it did not share the hostility to the Hudson's Bay Company and the strident enthusiasm for westward expansion which were being worked up in Upper Canada. Its attitude was perhaps reflected in the balanced appointments of Chief Justice William Draper as Canadian representative, and of A.R. Roche as his assistant. Draper naturally took a cautious and lawyer-like approach to a problem which bristled with legal difficulties, while Roche held sweeping views on the resources of the North West and the nature of Canada's claims.

Canada's official claim, as stated by Draper, was in effect a request that the boundaries be determined. He had previously informed Labouchere privately that in his considered opinion this would result in all the southern territory being surrendered to Canada. As this was not clear from his testimony, he and the Government were at once assailed by *The Globe* for failing to claim the whole territory on the ground that the Charter was invalid and for being indifferent, if not actually hostile, to westward expansion.

But Canada had made an indirect claim to the North West, and much of the evidence given before the Committee was unfavourable to the continuation of the Company's privileges and power. In consequence, the Committee could not simply recommend a renewal of the Licence and sought a compromise. One was found in recommending that Vancouver Island be no longer a colony of the Company, and that a colonial government be erected on the mainland west of the Rockies. East of the Rockies an arrangement should be sought with Canada for taking over the administration of the southern regions where settlement was possible. To the north of such districts the Licence should be renewed. If no arrangement could be made with Canada for the administration of the southern districts, then thought should be given to the establishment of some separate government.

The need for an enquiry had convinced the Colonial Secretary that there was also a need for more information on the North West. Labouchere, at the suggestion of the President of the Royal Geological Society, had already determined to despatch an exploring party under Captain John Palliser.

The Committee's report, dated July 31, 1857, gave no satisfaction to the advocates of western expansion in Upper Canada, for it left the question of the validity of the Charter untouched. They had meanwhile been active themselves. The major result of Brown's committee of enquiry was the despatch of an exploring expedition to Red River in July. It was under the command of George Gladman, though it is better remembered by the name of the scientist attached to it, Henry Youle Hind of the University of Toronto. This was the beginning of the Canadian exploration of the Red and Assiniboine valleys, and the lower Saskatchewan; but the expedition's main task was to determine "the best route for opening a communication" between Lake Superior and Red River. Thus Red River, so long isolated, saw the arrival of two exploring expeditions, one British and one Canadian, in the fall of 1857.

It had not been a quiet summer in the settlement. William Kennedy on his arrival had begun an agitation for annexation to Canada. In a public meeting in March, a petition to the Legislature asking for incorporation into Canada had been drafted, and signed by 575 inhabitants of the colony. Further resolutions protesting against the evidence given by Simpson and John Rae before the Select Committee were approved at meetings in May and June, and these with the petition were carried east by Kennedy in June. The agitation in Canada was now matched by one in Red River.

It is improbable that the Red River agitation would have led to serious trouble, unless the Métis had chosen, as they did not, to oppose it. The arrival of the Royal Canadian Rifles by way of York Factory in October removed any possibility of an outbreak, partly by their presence as a force in support of the civil power, partly by the market they, with the exploring parties, provided.

## Problems in the West, 1858

At the beginning of 1858, it was plain, the Imperial Government was faced with three problems requiring solution in the North West. One was that of government of gold rush territory on the Pacific slope; a second was that of the renewal of the Licence over all or a portion of the territory of the Hudson's Bay company; the third was that of the disposition of any territory not brought under a renewed licence. As this territory would be the Red and Saskatchewan valleys, their future disposition raised the questions of the boundaries and the validity of the Charter. Of these three problems, the first two demanded immediate solution and the third was scarcely less urgent.

The first dealt with was the problem of maintaining order and British sovereignty, in a territory suddenly occupied by thousands of miners, most of them Americans, who might, for want of government, set up a provisional government, as in Oregon, and demand union with the United States. Governor James Douglas of Vancouver Island made a Crown Colony in 1857, dealt firmly with the situation on the Fraser by arbitrarily extending his authority to the mainland. In this he was promptly supported by the new Colonial Secretary, Sir Edward Bulwer Lytton. Lytton then introduced a bill to create a Crown Colony of British Columbia in the territory west of the Rockies, which was enacted. Douglas was made Governor of British Columbia as well as Vancouver Island and proceeded to maintain British authority in the mining camps. The Pacific slope was thus made secure for the westward expansion of Canada.

The issues on the west coast were clear and imperative, and the decision, though dealing with great issues, was easy. The solution of the second problem, that of the Licence, was not to be easy. There was a balance of conflicting considerations. On the one hand was the fact that the Hudson's Bay Company had undoubted rights, if only by the prescription of long use, and that only the Company was interested in the trade and government of most of the territories in question. On the other hand were the Canadian agitation for the annexation of the North West and the growing American interest centred in St. Paul. Such a conflict suggested a need to make time for a solution, and Lytton proposed a renewal of the Licence for one year. But the Company, conscious of the disintegration of its authority in Red River and on the Saskatchewan, declined to accept his proposal. With the prospect of the Licence not being renewed, Lytton was left face to face with the question of the validity of the Charter. He determined to have it tested in the courts, as Labouchere had tried to have done. Lytton accordingly proposed to the Canadian Government, now that of Cartier and Macdonald, that it bring an action by a writ of *scire facias*. To his surprise and indignation the Government declined, on the ground that it was for the Imperial, not the Canadian Government, to test the Charter. Before Lytton could take further action, the Government of which he was a member, fell in June 1859. The Company's Licence had by then expired.

The reluctance of the Canadian Government to test the Charter arose from two causes. One was the political difficulty caused by the Reform party's contention that the Charter was invalid and Canada's title clear. For the Government, in face of this contention of a strong opposition, either to imply the validity of the Charter by testing it in the courts, or to consider paying compensation for the surrender of the Charter, would be to play into the hands of its opponents and suffer a loss of support in Upper Canada. The other reason was more obscure, but perhaps more important: it was assumed that if the west were annexed it would be added to Upper Canada. Thus the preponderance of Upper Canada in the United Province, already expressed in the Reformers' demand for representation by population, would be increased manifold. It would have been a matter for wonder if the French of Lower Canada had viewed the prospect without uneasiness.

It is clear in retrospect that the only true solution of the problems posed by westward expansion was a federal one, the creation of new provinces in the west. Yet this solution was not apparent at the time, simply because the Red and Saskatchewan valleys lacked the population to maintain a government or governments. The Imperial Government was reluctant and the Canadian Government unable to contemplate assuming the cost of upkeep of governments in territories so empty. As early as March, 1857, the Governor-General of Canada, Sir Edmund Walker Head, had drafted for the Colonial Office a bill for the creation of a province of "Saskatchewan (or Manitoba)." There was to be talk from time to time of the creation of a Crown Colony like British Columbia in the Red and Saskatchewan valleys. But there was no gold rush on the Saskatchewan big enough to force the reluctant hand of the Imperial Government, and Canada, despite proposals from 1856 on for a federal union of the Canadas or of British North America, failed to realize that only an application of the federal principle would reconcile Lower Canada and the Atlantic Provinces to the annexation of the North West.

**Communications between Canada and the West**

While this deadlock was reached in the political aspects of westward expansion, efforts to initiate commerce between Canada and the North West were proceeding. The physical difficulties were formidable. Whereas on the cart tracks between St. Paul and Fort Garry there were no serious obstacles, no heights, no rocks, there were many obstacles between Canada and Red River. The Great Lakes were not navigable in winter, and there was no winter land route north of Lake Superior. And even in summer travel between Lake Superior and Fort Garry was hard, thanks to the granite ridges and impassable muskegs of the Canadian Shield. The old canoe route of the North West Company was seldom used now; the portage paths were grown over, the corduroy ways rotted.

None the less, the parties who had sent William Kennedy to Red River in 1857 had proceeded to organize the North West Transportation Navigation and Railway Company. It was incorporated in 1858, and the first meeting was held in August of that year. Among the directors were George Gladman and William Kennedy; William McDonnell Dawson was elected president. In October it acquired the steamer *Rescue* and the government contract to carry mail to Fort William and Red River. The Company proposed to revive the old canoe route from Fort William to Red River across the stubborn barrier of the Canadian Shield. And beyond that they had in mind the old overland route to the Pacific.

Thus launched, the Company sought to raise capital in Great Britain. Viscount Bury, then in Toronto, was invited to be a director, in order that his London connections might help with this task. North West experience, Upper Canadian enterprise, and British capital were, it was hoped, to be combined in a new North West Company which would restore the ties of commerce between Canada and the North West.

Similar projects were being pushed in St. Paul, and it was not impossible that the American and Canadian projects might fuse. In St. Paul the Minnesota and Pacific Railway had been chartered. Its projectors planned to build westward by either a southern route in the United States or by a northern route in British territory, or both. They were also looking for a connection eastward with a Canadian railway, either the Grand Trunk at Sarnia or another. The project was, in short, one for an international line. The St. Paul promoters accordingly noted with interest the formation of the North West Transportation Company and Bury's visit, for they would have gladly joined with a Canadian line backed by British capital. And their welcome was inspired not only by need of capital, but also by complete confidence that the "natural" entrance to the North West and the "natural" northern route to the Pacific lay through St. Paul.

This confidence of the Minnesotans, a major factor in the story of Canada's westward expansion, was based not only on the steadily growing trade with Red River, but also on Blodget's theory of the fitness for settlement of the territory north of latitude 43°. A gifted publicist now made this his central theme. James Wickes Taylor had settled in Minnesota and made the opening of the North West to settlement his life's work, a work of devotion which was to win him the nickname of "Saskatchewan" Taylor. He was preaching a message of a North West awaiting the railway and the settler, of an international railway from Canada through Minnesota to the Fraser's mouth, of a British Central America opened to settlement and commerce by the extension of the Reciprocity Treaty to the North West, of a transcontinental flow of commerce from the North West through Minnesota to Canadian canals and railways.

Nothing came of this momentary mutual interest of the expansionist groups in Toronto and St. Paul, and each thereafter proceeded on its separate way to equally unimpressive ends. The truth was that the afflatus of the great enterprises of 1857 was ending, as the depression dragged on, and nothing in fact could be done for another decade to further the annexation of the North West. The North West Transportation Company carried mail to Red River for two years, and then had to give up even that limited undertaking in 1859. The old canoe route from Fort William could not compete even in the carriage of mail, much less in that of goods, with the flat plains route from St. Paul.

The St. Paul Chamber of Commerce had organized the building of the S.S. *Anson Northup,* the first steamboat on the waters of the North West and designed, not to ply Red River, but to ascend the Saskatchewan. It also despatched an expedition under Colonel Nobles in 1859 to explore an overland route, but most of the party, including the leader, turned back at Fort Ellice. The two more famous exploring expeditions completed their work and made their reports about the prospects of western development. The British one, Palliser's, was full of doubts, and dwelt in particular upon the manner in which nature had isolated the North West from Canada; Palliser wrote, "The egress and ingress to the settlement from the east is obviously by the Red River Valley and through the States." The Canadian report, Hind's, was enthusiastic, and the expedition's surveyor, S.J. Dawson, recommended the development of a route between Thunder Bay and Fort Garry similar to the old canoe route but using wagon roads at both ends. One other outcome of the hopes of 1857 was the founding of the newspaper *The Nor'Wester* in Red River in 1859 by William Buckingham and William Coldwell. This was the beginning, with the coming of Henry McKinney in 1859 and his half-brother John Christian Schultz in 1860, of a small "Canadian party" in Red River.

## A Check to Progress

The long pause in westward expansion which followed 1859 was caused by three factors. One was the failure to find a formula which would end a growing deadlock in Canadian politics, a deadlock of which westward expansion was a part. A second was failure to decide how the regime of the Hudson's Bay Company was to be ended. A third was the blocking of enterprise by the commercial depression which had begun in 1857.

To these was to be added in 1861 the outbreak of the Civil War in the United States. The first effect of the war was to end the pressure on the North West which had threatened to absorb that region into the United States. The next was to replace that pressure with the possibility of an Anglo-American war fought in Canada. The result was to turn attention from a merely regional settlement of the future of the North West to a continental one, to westward expansion as part of British North American federation.

The first problem, that of ending the Company's regime, turned in the first instance upon the readiness of the Imperial Government to take action in settling the government of the territory, and, failing that, upon the testing of the validity of the Charter. In 1860 the Colonial Secretary, the Duke of Newcastle, proposed that a Crown Colony be organized in Red River. The proposal was welcomed there, but not in Canada, where opinion tended to see it as a manoeuvre inspired by the Hudson's Bay Company. The Company was in fact only trying to escape from a position of increasing embarrassment. Simpson had died in 1860 and his successors were not as resolute as he in maintaining the Company in its traditional rights and ways. But a colonial government in the North West would have relieved it of some cost and much anxiety. The proposal of 1860 and a similar one in 1863 came to nothing, and the authority of the Company continued to weaken.

Practically nothing was done to check the drift towards anarchy. In 1860 the War Office refused to replace the detachment of Royal Canadian Rifles due for relief, and in 1861 they were withdrawn. No other military force existed, and the only police were local constables in the Red River parishes. In 1862 came the Minnesota massacre and the flight of refugee Sioux over the border in 1863. This brought with it the threat of American pursuit across the border, or an outbreak of fighting with the Ojibwas, the hereditary enemies of the Sioux. And the massacre was only the first of the disturbances which in the next few years threatened to bring the Plains Crees or the Blackfoot raiding to Red River.

At the same time the commercial monopoly of the Company under its Charter was flouted by an ever-growing number of free traders. The Company had in fact become only the greatest and best organized of private traders. Its power and prestige were still overwhelming but it could not employ them to crush its rivals, and a larger and larger portion of the furs and robes of the North West was shipped out by the private traders.

The ending of the Company's commercial monopoly was followed by an attack on its political authority, made by the "Canadian party." This group's first mouthpiece was James Ross, half-breed son of Alexander Ross, the historian of Red River. Ross had been educated in the University of Toronto and after his return to Red River was anxious to bring his native country into the stream of contemporary civilization. In this he was aided by John Schultz, who had become an ardent believer in the future of the North West and a promoter of its opening to settlement. Ross and Schultz came, as did Upper Canadians, to regard the Company as the chief barrier to the opening of the North West. *The Nor'Wester,* which Ross had taken over from Buckingham and Coldwell, became the vehicle of their attacks on the Company. The result was the dismissal of Ross from his office of Sheriff and Postmaster of Assiniboia. Schultz then took over *The Nor'Wester* and continued the controversy. The comment of *The Nor'Wester* was not confined to political polemics, but so inflamed public sentiment as to lead to the jail breakings during the Corbett case in 1864, when the authorities in Assiniboia were shown to be incapable of maintaining order.

## The Federal Idea

While anarchy continued to grow in Red River, in Canada events were moving, if slowly, towards a situation in which westward expansion would become possible. In 1858 Alexander Galt had made acceptance of the principle of colonial federation the condition of his entrance into the Cartier-Macdonald government. The result was the despatch of a delegation to London later that year to press federation upon the Colonial Office. Little, if any, progress was made, because the Colonial Office, under Lytton, was opposed and, perhaps, because Cartier as Lower Canadian leader was still doubtful. The Liberal-Conservative party, however, had taken up the principle which would make the annexation of the North West possible. And in its platform of 1859 the Grit party added the federal principle, confined to the Canadas, to its former demand for the acquisition of the North West. Slowly the necessary elements – another, an inter-colonial railway to bring in the Maritimes, appeared in 1862 – for the union of the North West with Canada and of all British North America in one comprehensive scheme were moving into place – but very slowly.

The delay made time for one more attempt at a piece-meal approach to the problem of westward expansion. It was inspired by the difficulties of the Grand Trunk Railway. That line had been built to draw traffic from the American Middle West to Montreal. The attempt, after much costly construction, had not proved successful. In 1861 the worried directors sent out Edward Watkin to report. His conclusion was that the salvation of the investment lay in westward extension through the Middle West by Minnesota and the Saskatchewan valley to the Pacific. Watkin, like J.W. Taylor, has seen the vision of the great international line by the northwestern route.

His recommendations aroused interest, particularly in the banking houses of Baring Bros. and Glyn, Mills and Co., which had financed the Grand Trunk Railway. Thus when in 1862 the J.S. Macdonald-Sicotte government of Canada considered the subsidization of mail and telegraph communications with the Pacific, Watkin and his supporters seized the opportunity. The Atlantic and Pacific Transit and Telegraph Company was organized. Then, in 1863, the International Financial Society was formed and purchased the stock of the Hudson's Bay Company. In this it received the support of the Colonial Secretary, the Duke of Newcastle. The plan was to build a telegraph line as a preliminary to a railway, and to establish a Crown Colony in the southern territories. Both projects, however, collapsed. The Imperial Government could not bring itself to assume direct responsibility for the government of the North West, and Watkin's efforts to build the telegraph line ended with bundles of wire rusting at Fort Garry and a tramway idle at the Grand Rapids of the Saskatchewan.

At this point the long deadlock in Canadian politics was broken by the formation of the Macdonald-Brown coalition of 1864 which was pledged to carry confederation. At the Quebec Conference of 1864 the North West was unrepresented, but the Resolutions provided for admission of "The North-West Territory." The federal solution had been adopted for the problems of uniting British North America, but only partially with respect to the North West. That region was to come into the new federation as a territory, not as a colony or province.

There still remained the problem of how Canada was to acquire the territory of the Hudson's Bay Company. The various Canadian Governments since 1857 had continued to maintain that the Charter was invalid, at least in the southern regions claimed by the Company, and that it was the responsibility of the Imperial Government to have it set aside. In 1865, however, Macdonald, Cartier, Galt and Brown, still the leading advocates of westward expansion but now in the coalition ministry which was preparing confederation, went to England. They negotiated with the Colonial Office in order to arrive at terms for the transfer. While the task was not completed then, the delegates did accept the principle that Canada should pay the Company compensation for the extinction of its rights. A figure was even suggested, £300,000, an estimate of the cost of the litigation to test the Charter.

There the matter stood while the work of Confederation was carried forward by the drafting and passage of the British North America Act of 1867. Section 146 of the Act provided for admission of "Rupert's Land and the North-Western Territory" to the Union on terms to be arranged.

There was some need to end the dilatory movement of Canadian politics. In 1868 John Schultz once more successfully defied the authorities of Assiniboia in a jail breaking in which he was himself involved. In a trial for murder that same year the accused was defended in the Quarterly Court of Assiniboia by an American citizen and lawyer from Pembina, Enos Stutsman, and no one seemed to think it strange. There were, after all, no lawyers, as there was little law in Red River. In 1866 the Reciprocity Treaty came to an end and Anglo-American relations became strained by the Alabama claims. Anglophobe politicians and Minnesota expansionists, with J.W. Taylor their assiduous "ghost," combined to demand the annexation of Canada, as in the Banks Resolution in Congress, 1866. And in 1867 Russia sold Alaska to the United States, thus recognizing the continental supremacy of the new power created by the Civil War. The North West lay between the new American territory and the old, and only British power remained to offset that of the Republic. What wonder that in 1868 the Legislature of Minnesota demanded that the North West should be annexed to the United States.

### Canada Acquires the North West

But the new Canadian Parliament was acting briskly. It passed Addresses of both Houses in December 1867, praying that Rupert's Land and the North-West Territory be admitted to the Union. Then in the fall of 1868 George Cartier and William McDougall were sent to complete the negotiations for the transfer in London. It was a balanced representation of Lower and Upper Canadian interests, for McDougall was second only to Brown as an advocate of westward expansion and Cartier was the leader of French Canada. He was, however, no longer doubtful of the effects of the acquisition of the North West on French Canada. The federal union had set those doubts at rest and in fact Cartier, because of McDougall's illness and the loss of his wife, actually conducted the negotiations.

These were prolonged and difficult. Cartier did his utmost to minimize the compensation due the Company, and flatly refused to "buy it out." A land grant for compensation and a money payment for the waiving of litigation to settle the validity of the Charter were the most he would accept. The Colonial Secretary, the Duke of Buckingham and Chandos, finally brought the parties to agreement on terms comprising the retention of one-twentieth of the land of "the fertile belt" (the southern territories) with designated blocks of land around its posts and a cash payment of £300,000. The Company was to surrender its government and territories to the Crown, which was to transfer them at once to Canada. The Imperial Government undertook to guarantee a Canadian loan for the amount of £300,000.

All now seemed to be arranged, and all three parties proceeded to carry out the terms agreed upon. The Imperial Parliament passed "The Canada (Rupert's Land) Loan Act, 1869." The Canadian Parliament passed a fresh Address of Both Houses in May 1869, incorporating the terms of the transfer. It also passed "An Act for the Temporary Government of Rupert's Land and the North-Western Territory when United with Canada," which provided for the government of the North West by a lieutenant-governor and a council to be appointed. The Hudson's Bay Company then executed a Deed of Surrender, which was finally completed on November 19, 1869. It only remained to pay over the £300,000 and convey the government and territory of the North West to Canada. But on November 27 the Prime Minister, Sir John Macdonald, cabled that the money must not be paid. The reason was that in Red River armed insurgents had risen to resist the transfer to Canada until terms should be made with the people of the North West.

The story of this resistance and of its aftermath, the Saskatchewan Rebellion, has been told elsewhere.[2] Suffice it to say here that the Red River troubles sprang from the failure of the Imperial Government and Canada to consult the people of Red River about the change, or at the least to advise them of its terms and its date. But they also arose from the fact that the North West had not developed sufficiently to obtain the status of a Crown Colony before the transfer of the territory to Canada. Because of this failure, which is easily to be explained by the circumstances of the North West, annexation to Canada did not mean for Red River and the North West what it had to mean for British Columbia, the coming of full representative and responsible government. Because of this failure, the Canadian Government was not moved to apply the complete federal solution of incorporation of at least Red River as a province of the Dominion. Thus it seemed to the insurgents of Red River to be carrying out the old Upper Canadian policy of outright annexation, and not the new federal policy of union with local rights safeguarded. Canada, in establishing the North West Territories, had adopted an imperial policy, but it had neglected to proclaim that Canadian rule carried with it all the rights of British subjects and all the implications of the federal union of 1867. This oversight it had, after many perils, to put right in the Manitoba Act of 1870 and through the development of self-government in the North West Territories from 1876 to 1905. Lieutenant-Colonel Wolseley's military expedition to Red River in 1870 served to ensure the peaceful inauguration of the new regime established by the Manitoba Act; but the chief importance of this enterprise, carried out in part over the half-constructed "Dawson Route," was that it demonstrated to hostile elements in the United States, and particularly in Minnesota, that the obstacles to communication between Ontario and Red River were not insuperable, and that British and Canadian authority could and would be maintained in the North West.

Even when the province of Manitoba was created, its size was constricted and it was denied control of its public lands. Neither of these things could have been done had Red River become a Crown Colony before 1869. But the federal government needed the land of the west to help subsidize the Pacific Railway which was to complete the work of Confederation, and Manitoba and the North West Territories had to submit to the use of their public lands "for the purposes of the Dominion."

After the Red River passage was secured, Canada could advance unchecked to the Rockies. Beyond lay the great colony of British Columbia. Island and mainland had been united in 1866. The political development of the colony was evident in the lively struggle for responsible government led by Canadian colonists, notably the flamboyant Nova Scotian, Amor de Cosmos. The same people were conducting an active agitation for union with Canada. They prevailed over the inertia of the old colony party and the opposition of the small group of American annexationists. In 1871 British Columbian delegates to Ottawa won most generous terms from the Dominion, including the pledge to begin the Pacific Railway within two years and to complete it within ten of the date of union, July 1, 1871. British Columbia became a full-fledged province on that date, with responsible government and control of its public lands. Union thus brought British Columbia full local self-government, and the generosity of the terms it had won served to underline the fact that the westward expansion of Canada to the North West could take place only on the federal principle.

NOTES

1 W.L. Morton, *The West and Confederation*, Centennial Historical Booklet, 7 (Ottawa: Centennial Commission, 1967), 3–19.
2 Booklet No. 2, G.F.G. Stanley, *Louis Riel: Patriot or Rebel?*

# "A Means to Empire: Canada's Reassessment of the West, 1857–1869"

*Promise of Eden: The Canadian Expansionist Movement and the Idea of the West, 1856–1900*
1980

DOUG OWRAM[1]

In a burst of enthusiasm Canadian expansionists turned their attention to the North West in 1856 and 1857. It had been eastern aspirations, commercial, moral, and national, that had led them to insist that the West should be opened up and claimed as Canada's inheritance. At the same time, even though they realized that the drive to the west obtained its impulse from eastern conditions, the nature of the land itself was important. Although Allan Macdonell might argue that the nature of the land was irrelevant, that "even if the whole country from Lake Superior to the Pacific be a barren country, utterly destitute of any hope of cultivation" Canada should have the right "to participate in the fur trade," he and other expansionists knew that, in fact, the value of the region was crucial.[2] If the North West was really a barren tract, forever destined by its soil and climate to remain a wilderness, then Canada, if it could be roused to action at all, would find its acquisition of limited use. The fur trade was hardly the means on which to build the new power of the British Empire.

Expansionism had raised the question of the ultimate possibilities of the North West as an agricultural frontier. In an attempt to convince themselves, and the rest of Canada, expansionists soon began to make optimistic estimates as to the value of the land and climate. As early as 16 December 1856 the Toronto *Globe* stated hopefully that "there is a stretch of country" between Lake Superior and the Rocky Mountains "containing probably over two hundred million acres of cultivable land." Others, re-reading earlier works on the Hudson's Bay territories, began to find evidence to show, as James Fitzgerald had said years before, that the North West was not a barren land but that its resources had been hidden from the world by the Hudson's Bay Company.[3] Canadian expansionists had to find good land in the West if their visions were to come to anything. In response to their needs, the existing sources began to yield new, optimistic information on the region.

One of the best examples of the changing perspective on the land came in a map drawn up in that centre of expansionism, the Crown Lands Department. The new map of the North West which Thomas Devine created in 1857 was based on the great works of Arrowsmith. Unlike Arrowsmith, however, Devine did not content himself with a delineation of the major physical features of the vast territory. His map was, in fact, as much a product of the expansionist impulse as was any editorial in the *Globe*. Even its title, "Map of the North West Part of Canada," reflected the new possessive attitude of the province to the Hudson's Bay territories. More basic to his purpose, however, was the running commentary, drawn largely from American sources, on the resources and capabilities of the region. The map was covered with such comments as the one placed between the North and South Saskatchewan rivers which described "the scenery of these fertile valleys as magnificent, and the banks of the rivers on either side luxuriant beyond description." Even that area that would soon be described as an extension of the Great American Desert was termed "fine land."[4] Devine's ability to reshape the map of the North West without any new evidence revealed the power which man's perspective has on his conclusions.

All the enthusiastic estimates by the *Globe* and descriptions on Devine's map could not hide the fact that Canadians were largely ignorant of the resources of the North West. Expansionists were all too aware that little was known of the region and that, outside of Red River, agricultural experiments had been spotty and inconclusive. Even Red River had a far from perfect record and 1857, at the very time when the region's agricultural capabilities were being extolled in Canada, brought the destruction of crops by the perennial pest, the grasshopper. Expansionists therefore could use those works that did praise the West with only limited effect. There was not enough evidence to conclude firmly that the West was capable of supporting agriculture.

If anything, all the hard evidence pointed in the opposite direction. When Sir George Simpson testified negatively on the resources of the

West before the British select committee, his comments could be dismissed as coming from a man with an obvious bias. Simpson, however, was not the only man to make a pessimistic assessment of the region. The famous British scientist J.H. Lefroy concluded that "agricultural settlement can make very slender progress in any portion of that region." Sir John Richardson, equally well known and respected for his knowledge of the territory, testified that though "the alluvial points on the Saskatchewan might be productive," the prairie itself, "although fit, probably for sheep pasture, is not a soil that I think would be productive for cereal cultivation." Lefroy and Richardson were joined by Canadian John Ross and even by that original crusader, Alexander Isbister.[5] While few in 1857 would deny Canada the right in principle to open the North West, there were still many who felt that right to be of questionable value.

The Canadian government, although it had laid formal claim to the North West, was especially uncertain as to the actual value of the region. Draper's testimony before the select committee clearly indicated that the position taken by the government in 1857 was essentially a holding action. It was a manifestation of the desire expressed some time earlier by the Montreal *Gazette* to "see that the way is cleared," should Canada decide it wanted to expand.[6] No legal or financial commitments had been made, nor were they likely to be until the government ascertained the nature of the resources and population of the region.

While the Canadian government's position in 1857 annoyed expansionists, it was, in spite of its limitations, a victory for their movement. The Canadian public and the Canadian and British governments had been made aware of the possibilities, and their interest guaranteed that further investigations would be undertaken. Over the next decade dozens of individuals would go west to look at this newly important region and would write of what they saw. Together they would dispel the ignorance of the North West that existed in 1857 and end for all time the negative assessments of the land and climate which had characterized the testimony of people like Lefroy and Richardson.

Those who went west over the next few years ranged from settlers in search of new land to merchants, adventurers, and tourists. Though there were probably as many reasons for going as there were people who went, it is possible to divide them into three general types. The first group to go, in time as well as classification, did so as a direct result of the claim that had been laid by the Canadian government in 1857. Canada had made a commitment and this, no matter how limited or hesitant, resulted, as Draper put it, in "a desire to survey and explore before we do anything."[7] Even as Draper presented the Canadian case in London, preparations were underway to follow up this resolution.

In July 1857 an expedition formed under the auspices of the Canadian government left Toronto for the North West. This group was formally under the charge of George Gladman, a retired fur trader whose primary qualification seems to have been his knowledge of the Hudson's Bay territories. Gladman had testified before the Canadian select committee on the Hudson's Bay Company, and his stated opposition to that organization may have been seen by the government as additional qualification.[8] Gladman, however, proved to be only the nominal head of the party, a fact made clear when he was let go in 1858 as the expedition prepared for the second stage of its investigations.[9] The real charge of the Canadian scientific party rested in the hands of a professor from the University of Toronto, Henry Youle Hind.

Hind had been born in England and educated at Cambridge, emigrating to Canada in 1846. At the time the expedition was formed he was a professor of chemistry and geology at Trinity College. Hind was only thirty-four years old in 1857, but in spite of his relatively youthful age, he was well known in Canadian scientific circles. He was one of the earliest members of the Canadian Institute and had edited that organization's periodical, the *Canadian Journal,* from 1852 to 1855. He was the author of several articles and had firmly established himself as a leading figure in the Toronto scientific community. His work had brought him to the attention of the head of the Canadian Geological Survey, Sir William Logan, and Logan's recommendation had helped secure him a position on the North West party.[10] The expeditions of 1857 and 1858 were to make Hind's name familiar throughout Canada. At the same time, although he lived until 1908, these expeditions also marked the peak of his career. Hind seemed unable to refrain from attacking those who he felt did not recognize his talents, and this inevitably had repercussions.[11] Most of his later years were spent as secretary of a women's school in Nova Scotia where, with one exception, he had little to do with the North West.

Another member of the Canadian expedition was to become almost as well known as Hind. Simon James Dawson was hired by the government to assess the potential of the territory between Lake Superior and the Red River as a line of communication. Dawson, a thirty-seven-year-old native of Scotland and brother of William Dawson, had emigrated to Canada and settled near Richmond in the expansionist Ottawa

Valley. His position with the expedition marked his first senior appointment and began a connection with the region west of Lake Superior that was to last more than twenty years. On Dawson's shoulders fell the immense task of developing an initial transportation link between Canada and Red River.[12]

The Canadian expedition was not the only one to survey the West in 1857. The British government was also interested in the region over which it had ultimate, if remote, control. When a private exploration party was proposed by the prestigious Royal Geographical Society, the government picked up the idea and provided support. Midway through the hearings of the British select committee, authority was given to Captain John Palliser to proceed to the Hudson's Bay territories in order to make a scientific exploration of the country.

John Palliser was a member of the Irish gentry. At the age of forty, the only claim he could make to relevant experience was a hunting expedition he had made to the western United States a few years before.[13] No doubt he had learned something on that trip of the problems of wilderness travel and the necessity for tactful dealings with the Indians. The choice of Palliser as head of the expedition, however, can be most easily explained in terms of the interrelationships of upper-class British society. In his initial support from the Royal Geographical Society and, eventually, from the British government, a string of influential people furthered Palliser's cause. It was influence that raised the Palliser expedition from the status of a private adventure to a major, official exploration under the auspices of the British government. Hudson's Bay magnate Edward Ellice commented caustically of the whole affair that Palliser simply had enough influence to allow him to indulge in his taste for buffalo hunting at government expense.[14] Ellice was too cynical, but only in his assessment of Palliser's motive, not in the degree to which the efforts of others played a role in the formation of the expedition.

Even Ellice could not challenge the credentials of the others who made up the party. A well-known botanist, Eugene Borgeau was added to the group early in the planning stage and provided a high degree of expertise and enthusiasm throughout the exploration. Thomas Wright Blakiston, a British army officer, joined the group on the recommendation of Lefroy to act as magnetic observer; his scientific dedication and rigid personality soon brought him into conflict with Palliser. James Hector, only twenty-three years old and a recent graduate of the medical faculty of the University of Edinburgh, was perhaps the most important addition to the expedition; he worked closely with

Palliser throughout and more than made up for his superior's lack of scientific training.[15]

The two scientific expeditions were perhaps the most important immediate consequence of the expansionist campaign. Others, however, had their interest aroused by expansionist writings and went west for very different reasons. In the years after 1857 the North West became almost fashionable as a destination for the young and adventurous tourist. With increasing frequency between 1857 and 1869, well-to-do young men from Britain headed to the far west in search of new game and new adventures. The purpose and attitudes of these men were in marked contrast to those of the members of the official expeditions. As one of them said, "It was no definite purpose of mine to gather notes, nor closely record the geographical features of the country."[16] Their aim was to experience the excitement of a wilderness before it succumbed to the forces of civilization. Many did not leave any records of their experiences, and only the odd letter or other scrap of information indicates that they went west at all. Nevertheless, those who did write of their travels often provided some of the most acute and sensitive observations of a region in transition.

A third group had motives for going west and an attitude towards the region that distinguished them from both the scientists and the tourists. This group comprised those Canadians whose interest in the North West had been so aroused by expansionism that they emigrated to Red River, perhaps hoping to establish themselves before the rush began. Typical of them was a nineteen-year-old doctor, John Christian Schultz, who set up practice in Red River in 1859. Schultz hoped that the move would enable him to combine an interesting life with a successful career.[17] His hopes were to be abundantly fulfilled. While others were not always as successful as Schultz, they did resemble him in other ways. They were also well-educated, young, and from middle-class Canadian families.[18] Like him they had accepted the promises of expansionism and based their lives on it. Their outlook and their published works reflected this fact.

Members of these three groups were, of course, far from homogeneous in their character or outlook. At the one extreme was the relatively high degree of scientific objectivity which Palliser brought to his examination of the region. Less swept up than others by the rhetoric of expansionism, Palliser refused to minimize those difficulties, particularly in the area of transportation, that would confront a transcontinental Canada.[19] At the other end of the spectrum were people like the young poet from Lanark, Charles Mair. When Mair visited the West in 1868 and 1869, he was already a complete convert to expansionism.[20] As a result he interpreted what he saw within the framework of expansionist ideals. On discovering, for instance, that the "utopia" of Red River was experiencing famine, he tried to dismiss it. "The half-breeds are the only people here who are starving," he wrote, and "it is their own fault – they won't farm."[21] Though Mair's ideas on the famine were later to change, his initial attempt to minimize a major economic crisis indicates the way in which expansionist hopes biased his views of the West.

In spite of their differences, all these people did have one thing in common: they viewed the West in the light of the expansionist campaign. Even those like Palliser who did not completely accept the expansionist image of the West were influenced by it. The events of 1856 and 1857 made it apparent that the region was on the eve of a major change and this alone was sufficient to alter perceptions of the North West. Previously, the West had been viewed in the context of its existent wilderness state; as a result, the land and climate had been judged within the perspective imposed by the fur trade. The expansionist campaign of 1856 and 1857, however, challenged all of the traditional premises and brought a new perspective to bear on the North West.

The difference can be clearly seen in the writings and in the very travels of the men who went to the country after 1857. First, the focus of interest in the Hudson's Bay territories shifted to the south. Until 1857, as Canadians whose interest in the North West had been argued, the majority of scientific expeditions and a large proportion of the writings on the region had been concerned with the Arctic and Subarctic; the region that was to become the agricultural heartland of the West had generally been traversed only in a perfunctory manner on the way to more northerly regions. This changed as questions of settlement and commerce came to the fore. Setting the new pattern were the two official scientific expeditions. Neither Hind nor Palliser went north of the 54th degree of latitude and both spent most of their time within two hundred miles of the American border.[22] As a result, the years after 1857 saw the North West become decreasingly associated with the Arctic.

Second, and even more important in determining the image that was formed of the region, travellers after 1857 began with the assumption not of an economy based on the wilderness but of the potential of an economy based on agriculture. Once again the two official expeditions set the pattern for later observers. Both were instructed to look specifically at those economic questions raised by the idea of expansion.

Hind, for example, was told that the "character of the timber and soil [should be observed] and the general fitness of the latter for agricultural purposes ascertained."[23] The instructions led to an examination of the potential of the region rather than its present state.

The questions asked altered the conclusions that were reached. The West was no longer seen through the eyes of the fur trader or the missionary but through those of the potential farmer. The possibility of agriculture was not only no longer ignored, as it had been in the past, but became the first priority to those who would make observations on the West. Once again man's tendency to find what he expected or wanted to find was revealed. This time, however, all the circumstances oriented the observer towards agriculture rather than the fur trade. None of the travellers after 1857 could really claim to be journeying through unexplored territory. Even the expeditions of Palliser and Hind travelled through regions that had been known to fur traders and buffalo hunters for generations. Nevertheless, their purpose in going over these routes and their perspectives on the country around them made those who went west original observers of the land.

The investigations of the North West that began in 1857 redefined the geographical and climatological structure of the prairie region between Red River and the Rocky Mountains. Newly acquired masses of detail made possible a type of description that had previously existed only for those well-travelled areas adjacent to fur trade posts. This additional information, set out by the Hind and Palliser expeditions, provided the basis for the redefinition of the geography of the North West. The work of Palliser and Hind, to which might be added the writings of the American Lorin Blodgett, reshaped nineteenth-century geographical understanding of the region. Old generalizations concerning the hostile nature of the land were broken down. Such loose definitions and descriptions as had been circulated by fur traders and missionaries were given a new accuracy. The works of Blodgett, Hind, and Palliser became the new standard references for anyone who sought information on the North West.

The first of these men to come before the public was Lorin Blodgett. In 1857 he published his massive book, *The Climatology of the United States and the Temperate Latitudes of the North American Continent.* Blodgett offered little new hard evidence on the resources of the North West; he had only six sets of observations from all of British North America and not one of these was from the Hudson's Bay territories.[24] Nevertheless his work made a significant impact on both the scientific and popular mind. He was one of the first people to look at the West in terms of its agricultural possibilities, and his scientific method, no matter how limited his evidence, contributed to the expansionist campaign.

Blodgett appealed to those who would picture the North West as habitable because he challenged the assumption that latitude determined climate. As long as that belief was widely held, the North West could be viewed as suitable for settlement only with great difficulty. Canadians were aware of the harsh climate north of Lake Superior. The North West was just as far north and, it could be asked, even if the soil improved, was there any indication that climate would not prove an insurmountable barrier to settlement? Blodgett's answer was a resounding affirmative. Basing his work on the concept of the isotherm as developed by Alexander Humboldt, he concluded that such fears were groundless. Climate varies for reasons independent of latitude, and any real understanding of a region has to come from following the isothermic temperature line rather than the degree of latitude. Specifically, in this case, the isothermic lines of the North West indicated "the increase of temperature westward is quite as rapid as it is southward to New Mexico." It was not the climate of Lake Superior which was analogous to the North West but another and much more favourable region in the same latitude: "The west and north of Europe are there reproduced."[25]

Blodgett's work was especially significant because it appeared in time to influence those Canadians who were about to undertake their own investigations of the North West. *Climatology* included in its subscription list the University of Toronto, the Canadian Institute, and the Magnetic and Metropolitan Observatory of Toronto.[26] It was thus well known in Canadian scientific circles in Canada from the beginning and, by 1858 if not before, both Henry Youle Hind and Simon Dawson were aware of Blodgett's conclusions.[27] His optimism and the sense of destiny his style conveyed may have remained with them as they viewed the vast new territory which Canada claimed as its own: "It is demonstrable that an area, not inferior in size to the whole of the United States east of the Mississippi, now almost wholly unoccupied, lies west of the 98th meridian and north of the 43rd parallel, which is perfectly adapted to the fullest occupation by cultivated nations."[28]

For obvious reasons Blodgett's work had a great deal of prestige in expansionist circles and it was to be quoted repeatedly in the future. It was, however, hardly the detailed set of observations which were needed to counter years of skepticism as to the value of the North West. Blodgett's work was inspirational, but it was the evidence accumulated by the expeditions under Palliser, Hind, and Dawson that was to reshape the North West in a new image.

The initial contribution made by Hind and Palliser was their division of the region into identifiable sub-regions.[29] The three "steppes" or levels described by others were confirmed and delineated, and the resources of particular areas such as the valleys of the Swan River, the Assiniboine, and the Saskatchewan were recorded. Even the seemingly homogeneous prairie was found to contain very different conditions of soil and climate from place to place. The work of Palliser and Hind was influenced by the biases of their age, but this does not in any way depreciate the significant contribution to knowledge that resulted from their work in the North West.

What gave the work of Hind and Palliser such impact was the fact that, once they had torn apart old generalizations into more detailed observations, they reassembled the geographical picture of the North West into a clear and dramatic outline. Moreover, as suited their instructions, it was an outline based on the potential of the region rather than its actual state. The two terms which their expeditions made a standard part of geographical description in the West – "the fertile belt" and "Palliser's triangle" – were definitions that made sense only in terms of agriculture and settlement.

"Palliser's triangle" was an area of land "forming a triangle, having as its base the 49th parallel from the longitude 100 degrees to 114 degrees W., with its apex reaching the 52 parallel of latitude." It was a region characterized by the man who gave it its name as one of "arid plains" and "extensive sandy wastes," unfitted in all probability for agriculture.[30] Hind was in full agreement, describing the region as "not, in its present condition, fitted for the permanent habitation of civilized man."[31] Both men thus virtually dismissed over 16,000 square miles of the North West. The lands of the Sioux and the Blackfoot, so long avoided by the Hudson's Bay Company, were now seemingly destined to be avoided by the settler and farmer.

Both Palliser and Hind believed this triangle to be but a sub-region of a much vaster area of poor land and climate. Beginning with the accepted premise that there existed in the United States "a more or less arid desert," Palliser concluded that the area of bad land in the North West was in fact a northerly extension of that phenomenon. Hind, using American sources, came to the same conclusion, stating that "this vast treeless prairie forms in fact the northern limit of the great arid region of the eastern flank of the Rocky Mountains."[32] Whole areas including the upper Qu'Appelle Valley, the South Saskatchewan, and the prairies between them and the border thus became identified with the enormous wasteland which for more than a generation had been accepted as the heritage of the United States.

In such conclusions there was certainly nothing of great inspiration for the ardent expansionist. The identification of the prairie with the Great American Desert had existed long before Palliser and Hind made their trek west. If, however, the triangle did little to encourage the expansionists, the same cannot be said of the fertile belt. It was this term that gave the expansionists what they needed, and ultimately it dominated the image of the sterile triangle in determining the Canadian assessment of the value of the North West. The concept of the fertile belt was essential to those who wanted to annex the North West. Presented most dramatically by Hind in a map in his 1860 *Narrative,* the area of fertility was depicted as a vast band of yellow sweeping in a giant arc from the American border at Red River northwest to the forks of the Saskatchewan and from there along the North Saskatchewan to the Rocky Mountains. As it approached the foothills of the Rockies it turned southward until it reached the border at 114 degrees west.[33] Here was scientific and dramatic support for those who would extend the proven fertility of the Red River valley to the west. The settlement was no longer an oasis in a desert but simply the small, easternmost portion of a vast area of land suitable for settlement.

Interestingly, neither the existence of the triangle nor the fertile belt challenged the older traditional relation between the absence of trees and aridity. The line between the fertile belt and the triangle was the region that Palliser and Hind felt divided the natural prairie from those areas that would support trees. Hind, in fact, began his definition of the area which he thought was an extension of the American desert by describing it as a "vast treeless region."[34] Equally, both parties went out of their way to explain the absence of trees in some portions in the fertile belt. Palliser dismissed the absence of trees in the Battle River area as artificial, pointing to the "debris of large trees" as proof that the area could support vegetation. The lack of trees, both felt, was due to prairie fires, often set by Indians.[35] It was still felt necessary, then, to explain why trees did not exist in a supposedly fertile land.

Given the definition of Palliser's triangle and the caution with which both Hind and Palliser approached the prairie, it is perhaps surprising that they played such an important role in changing the image of the West. Their impact came from the fact that, having accepted an extension of the Great American Desert, they then imposed definite limits on it. Furthermore, they inserted between that area and the other region that had tainted the image of the West, the Arctic, an extensive band of fertile land and appropriate climate. The fertile belt provided the agricultural hinterland and path to the Pacific which the expansionists sought. Hind was acutely aware of this and thought it of sufficient importance to set it down in block letters.

> IT IS A PHYSICAL REALITY OF THE HIGHEST IMPORTANCE TO THE INTERESTS OF BRITISH NORTH AMERICA THAT THIS CONTINUOUS BELT CAN BE SETTLED AND CULTIVATED FROM A FEW MILES WEST OF THE LAKE OF THE WOODS TO THE PASSES OF THE ROCKY MOUNTAINS, AND ANY LINE OF COMMUNICATION, WHETHER BY WAGGON ROAD OR RAILROAD, PASSING THROUGH IT, WILL EVENTUALLY ENJOY THE GREAT ADVANTAGE OF BEING FED BY AN AGRICULTURAL POPULATION FROM ONE EXTREMITY TO ANOTHER.[36]

This fact was what mattered to Canadians. The implications of the fertile belt made all the qualifications of both Hind and Palliser seem largely irrelevant. The point had been made that the North West was not a barrier to the Pacific and that it had resources which would allow it to become a valuable hinterland for Canada.

The importance of the two scientific expeditions was probably best summed up by Hind himself when he commented that "the North-West Territory is no longer a *terra incognita*."[37] The weakest link in the chain of expansionist arguments had been the lack of knowledge concerning the region in which they placed so much faith. Now, with the results of the expeditions, the expansionist could state with certainty that these reports "have established the immediate availability for the purposes of Colonization," of vast portions of the Hudson's Bay territory.[38]

The expansionists had not needed much convincing, of course. They simply found in the efforts of the scientific expeditions confirmation of what they had believed all along. The real importance of the two expeditions lay in the influence they had on those less committed. These people had needed proof, and in the seemingly objective assessments of Palliser and Hind they found strong evidence of the validity of the expansionist position. The work of these two parties provided sufficient material on the potential of the North West to shift the weight of evidence in favour of the expansionist argument. Over the next years it became standard in Canada to accept the conclusion that the North West was suitable for settlement rather than the reverse. By the time the Canadian government, in 1864, talked of the region as being "fertile and capable of sustaining a vast population," the comment was so commonplace as to be almost a cliché.[39]

Scientific reports alone were not responsible for the dramatic change in the image of the North West. While the volumes published on the two expeditions provided an essential basis of evidence, they were hardly the sort of material that could, by themselves, have wrought the transformation that took place in the public mind. Toronto scientist Daniel Wilson summed up their limitations when he commented, "It is an old saying that Parliament can print blue books, but it is beyond its power to make people read them."[40] In order to understand the change that occurred it is necessary to consider all those writings, whether by scientist or layman, that appealed, as one expansionist later put it, to the "mind and emotion of the great agricultural community."[41] The experience of the West after 1857 was as much an emotional process as it was intellectual.

Anyone who went west in the later 1850s or 1860s could not escape the feeling that he was entering a distinct environment. The Hudson's Bay territories were still isolated from the rest of British North America in terms of both trade and transportation. Most who journeyed to Red River had to go by way of the United States to St Paul in Minnesota and then northward. By the time they approached Fort Garry they had left behind such symbols of civilization as the railroad and the telegraph. Those who made the journey saw their own movement from civilization to wilderness as significant. Travellers gloried in their ability to return to a basic, primitive mode of existence and to thrive on it. The travellers of the 1860s, especially those tourists who had come to the West specifically for a wilderness adventure, recreated the sense of romance that had long been apparent in the writings of R.M. Ballantyne. The Earl of Southesk, on leaving Crow Wing, Minnesota, in May 1859, exulted: "At last, I thought, at last the prisoner of civilization is free." British tourist Doctor William Cheadle was in a long-standing tradition when he concluded after his own trip on the prairies that "truly the pleasures of eating are utterly unknown in civilized life."[42]

In spite of the timelessness of such comments, the reaction to the wilderness was changing. In the wake of the expansionist campaign, explorers and travellers approached the wilderness in a manner that differentiated them from both the romantics and those earlier missionaries who had reacted so adversely to a heathen land. Gradually the very idea of the wilderness began to soften and change until it too conformed to the requirements of progress.

The changing approach was typified by the reaction of Henry Youle Hind, one of the first to reconcile the romance of the wilderness with the implications of expansionism. As had many before him, Hind found certain aspects of the wilderness life to be charming. His lengthy description of a camp scene early in the morning, where "the stars are slightly paling," and "the cold yellow light begins to show itself in the east," reveals that his sensitivity was not constricted by his scientific purpose. It was a description, more than anything else, of a peace inherent in nature, where "no sound at this season of the year disturbs the silence of the early dawn."[43] Such scenes and experiences of "boundless prairies, sweet scented breezes, and gorgeous sunsets" made a trip to the North West an emotional as well as an intellectual experience for Hind.[44]

If the beauty and peace of the wilderness were impressive, so was its power. The incredible forces that often shattered the peace of nature were awesome to Hind. "The grandeur of a prairie on fire belongs to itself," he wrote. Only unchecked nature was capable of creating such an impressive sight, since, "like a volcano in full activity, you cannot imitate it, because it is impossible to obtain those gigantic elements from which it derives its awful splendour." Even the tiny grasshoppers, massed in quantities appropriate to the vastness of the West, became an awe-inspiring, if destructive, manifestation of the power of the wilderness: "Lying on my back and looking upwards as near the sun as the light would permit, I saw the sky continually changing colour from blue to silver to white, ash grey and lead colours, according to the numbers in the passing cloud of insects ... the aspect of the heavens during the greatest flight was singularly striking. It produced a feeling of uneasiness, amazement and awe in our minds, as if some terrible, unforeseen calamity were about to happen."[45]

While Hind was awed by the wilderness he felt no temptation to ascribe to it moral attributes superior to civilization. His enthusiasm, for instance, did not extend to the men who lived in the wilderness. His attitude to the Indian, in fact, resembled the disdain and pity of the missionary more than it did the praises of the romantic. The native, he felt, was not in harmony with nature but degraded by it. When Hind visited an Indian village he thought of the comparison "between the humanizing influence of civilization and the degraded, brutal condition of a barbarous heathen race." The power and beauty of the wilderness was indeed impressive, but it was too powerful for man to accept unaltered without becoming dominated by it.

Hind's whole reaction to the wilderness and to the North West rested on his awareness and acceptance of Canadian expansionism. The power and beauty of the wilderness were, for him, inseparable from his hopes for the movement. In fact, it simply demonstrated the importance of expansion: "The vast ocean of level prairie which lies to the West of Red River must be seen in its extraordinary aspects, before it can be rightly valued and understood in reference to its future occupation by an energetic and civilized race, able to improve on its vast capabilities and appreciate its marvellous beauties."[46] Hind felt none of the conflicts of Alexander Ross, because for him the romance of the wilderness was not in its own intrinsic beauty but in its potential.

In the wake of the expansionist crusade the land began to be viewed in terms of agricultural potential not only in the scientific but in the aesthetic sense. Descriptions of present scenes of beauty became prophecies of future development. "I stood upon the summit of the bluff near the Qu'Appelle," wrote James Dickinson, a member of the Hind expedition, "looking down upon the glittering lake 300 feet below, and across the boundless plains, no living thing in view, no sound of life anywhere." It was a romantic scene in itself, but for Dickinson the romance was as much in the mind as in the scene, for he "thought of the time to come when will be seen passing swiftly along the distant horizon the white cloud of the locomotive on its way from Atlantic to Pacific, and when the valley will not resound from the merry voices of those who have come from the busy city on the banks of the Red River to see the beautiful lakes of the Qu'Appelle."[47] Similarly, while traversing a series of hills, the English tourists Milton and Cheadle "remarked to one another what a magnificent site for a house one of the promontories would be, and how happy many a poor farmer who tilled unkindly soil at home would feel in possession of the rich land which lay before us."[48]

In the later 1850s and 1860s man's reaction to the North West began increasingly to be determined by his sense of its potential, in the same way that, in previous years, the missionary's reaction had been conditioned by the fact that it was a heathen wilderness. The prairie took on a new beauty because of the resources it contained. As S.J. Dawson said of Red River, "If the scenic beauty which characterizes the region so near it to the eastward is wanting, this country is incomparably superior in all that can minister to the wants of man."[49] Charles

Mair said almost the same thing a decade later when he enthused that "there is, in truth, a prospective poetry in the soil here – the poetry of comfort and independence."[50] It is not surprising that expansionists paid little heed to the costs that civilization would impose on the North West, for to them the charm of the wilderness lay mainly in its potential for development.

The expansionists' belief that civilization was, unquestionably, preferable to wilderness placed them closer to the missionary than to the romantic. Even the rhetoric of expansionism often resembled the earlier missionary tracts. Both groups looked forward continually to a time when "the deserts of the North-West shall blossom as a rose where now a few thousand savages drag out a miserable existence."[51] The views of the two groups were, however, far from identical. The missionary had found little beauty or romance in the wilderness. Landscape had, for him, been viewed against the heathen and miserable condition of the Indian. The expansionists, on the other hand, enthused over the land and scenery, even as they looked to the time when it would be transformed. Whereas the missionary had found the wilderness a reproof to the moral sensibilities of man, the expansionist saw as positive the very fact that the land was still a wilderness.

The fact that vast areas of good and habitable land still existed was in fact providential. The region had been kept isolated from the rest of the world until Canada had been prepared to occupy it.[52] Now, however, its potential was becoming known. As George Brown pointed out, it involved an area "greater in extent than the whole soil of Russia," and that vast resource would be "opened up to civilization under the auspices of the British American Confederation."[53] The millions of acres available for the farmer were valuable precisely because even after centuries of expansion and settlement they lay "free and unoccupied."[54] The missionary had felt blocked and frustrated by the isolation, emptiness, and seeming permanence of the wilderness in which he worked. In contrast the wilderness state added to the expansionist's estimate of the region. "Man is a grasshopper here," wrote Charles Mair, "making his way between the enormous discs of heaven and earth. And yet man is master of all this."[55]

This reaction to the wilderness was reinforced by the fact that the North West was in a state of flux. The wilderness, as if preparing for things to come, already seemed to be receding. "The days when it was possible to live in plenty by the gun and the net alone, have already gone by on the North Saskatchewan," wrote Milton and Cheadle. While the disappearance of game signalled the end of the wilderness, other developments predicted the coming of civilization. "The river communication has been opened up," Bishop Anderson noted in 1860; "the road over the prairie has been traversed; and the appliances of modern science have rendered more easy the production of some necessities of modern life."[56]

Observations such as these, and the continued orientation towards the potential of the region, began to diminish the image of the wilderness in the minds of those who observed the North West. Wilderness, by definition, implied a region where the natural dominated the works of man, whether those works be put in technological, legal, or spiritual terms. This view was common to Hind, Ross, and the early missionaries. Where earlier observers differed from the expansionists, however, was in the implication they drew from this fact. In various ways both the missionaries and Ross had tended to see the wilderness as irreconcilable with civilization; there was, in a sense, an adversary relationship between the two states. To Hind and the expansionists no such implication was thought to be necessary; rather civilization, the works of man, were a superstructure to be imposed on nature. The only necessary question, therefore, was whether the natural environment was suitable as a base for European society. The re-evaluation of the climate of the North West had, seemingly, answered that question, and thus in a very real sense the distinction between wilderness and civilization was reduced to a matter of time. The only difference between the resident of the North West and that of Europe was "if the greatness of his country is past or passing, ours is yet to come."[57]

The more that men viewed the North West in terms of its potential, the more they began to concentrate, either inadvertently or deliberately, on those attributes of the region that reinforced the new image. Those facets of the North West which had previously been used to emphasize its wilderness state – isolation, savagery, harshness – were downplayed and replaced with quite different attributes. Ruggedness of land and climate was scarcely mentioned; instead, the North West began to be described in terms more appropriate to the estate of a well-to-do landowner than to a vast unpeopled land: "There are many delightful spots in the belts, the herbage is clean as well shaven lawn, the clumps of aspen are neatly rounded as if by art, and where little lakes alive with waterfowl abound, the scenery is very charming, and appears to be artificial, the result of taste and skill, rather than the natural features of a wild, almost uninhabited country."[58] While the harsh and wild aspects of the North West were not ignored, there was an increased tendency, from the time of Hind on, to look on the North West as a rather tame wilderness.

Man's work in this vast land was not overlooked in the process. The expansionists turned to Red River as proof that men could live in the North West; even in the midst of an empty land it was possible to develop a comfortable and civilized way of life. By its very nature the expansionist approach challenged Ross's argument that this isolated settlement was in danger of being overwhelmed by the wilderness that surrounded it. Rather, Red River was viewed as a somewhat quiet place with all the basic attributes of a civilized community: the people were "hardy, industrious, and thrifty," living in a settlement with "churches many; and educational advantages which will endure comparison with those of more pretentious communities."[59] In going to Red River the Canadian was not entering the howling waste that had been imagined. Comfort was not just a thing of the East for, as Charles Mair wrote of Red River, "they live like Princes here." Houses were "all snug and respectable" and there was even "a hotel with two billiard tables."[60]

Canadians wished to see Red River as a civilized community, and every opportunity that allowed them to do so was given great play. Typical of this was the attention given to the formation of the "Institute of Rupert's Land," a western version of the Canadian Institute. The *Nor'Wester,* that western voice of Canadian expansion, devoted columns to the event while the meeting itself attracted most of the leading members of the community. In Toronto the *Canadian Journal* noted the event, and well-respected Daniel Wilson wrote a long and laudatory article on its importance.[61]

The significance attached to the formation of the institute was very much a by-product of the Canadian expansionist outlook. The expansionist perspective had altered the social image of the region; in the most basic sense it can be said that those interested in or affected by expansionism had ceased to see the region as a true wilderness at all and were, instead, judging it as the outpost of an expanding and powerful civilization. Events that reinforced this image became, in themselves, further proof of the expansionist argument. As Daniel Wilson pointed out, the importance of the formation of the institute lay as much in the principle as in any contribution which might actually be made in the field of science. Its very existence was proof "of the changes which are slowly but surely revolutionizing this vast continent; and giving evidence of an intellectual dawn which heralds the period when states and empires of the great northwest are to claim their place in the world's commonwealth of nations." Given the historical significance of the occasion, it was somewhat unfortunate that the *Nor'Wester* referred to a number of stuffed animal specimens presented to the institute as "tastily arranged."[62]

If civilization triumphed over savagery in Red River it was in part because that settlement was no longer an oasis in a dangerous and hostile wilderness. If one accepted the existence of the fertile belt, it was simply the eastern point of a vast region suited for the settlement of man. In social and political terms it was no longer viewed as an island of civilization in the midst of barbarism, but simply the first of many centres of civilization. In fact, it came to be seen as the natural staging ground for other communities in the North West. As the *Globe* suggested as early as 13 December 1856, it could be made "the *point d'appui* for the Canadian government's operations in opening up the Hudson's Bay Territories for settlement." The more evidence that accumulated on the resources of the West, the more common this idea became. Expansionists began to realize that the presence of the settlement would make their task all that much easier. As S.J. Dawson argued in 1859, "There is already a nucleus where the wants of settlers may be supplied in the first instance, and the population of ten thousand ready to welcome them and give them the advantage of their experience."[63]

The new role which expansionists envisaged for Red River also meant that that community ceased to be seen in terms of its own history or society. Instead it came to be viewed, in the same manner as the wilderness, in terms of its future potential and in relation to Canadian expansion. "This settlement," wrote one George Le Vaux in 1869, "now surrounded by a vast wilderness, and far removed from the civilized world, is nevertheless destined to become the nucleus of a new empire."[64] That empire was to be the product of Canadian expansion, and, from, at least 1860 on, Red River was viewed as the outpost of Canadian-Britannic civilization. Such an image not only had no place in it for the concept of an oasis but equally made impossible Alexander Ross's hope that it might serve as a link between the wilderness and civilization. Red River was to represent the force of civilization, and the wilderness was to be subjugated.

Cumulatively, the writings on the West in this period shifted the tone of the expansionist campaign. Previously, the expansionist image of the settlement frontier had always been left ill-defined. In the wake of the exploring expeditions and the increasingly optimistic reports on the region, however, more attention began to be paid to the potential benefits of agricultural settlement. The populating of the prairies, rather than a hazy by-product of expansion, became an immediate and major reason for it. As early as 1865 George Brown talked ambitiously of the North West as the key factor in a scheme to establish "a government that will seek to turn the tide of European emigration into this northern half of the continent."[65] Such statements revealed that by the mid-1860s the idea of the West as an agricultural empire was becoming an important part of expansionism. Minerals, furs, and even the route to Asia began to be subordinated to the hope that the North West would become the seat of an industrious, prosperous, and powerful people.[66]

As agriculture assumed greater importance, expansionists began to appeal not only to those in the East who would benefit from annexation but to those who would go west to take up farms. The land began to be talked of as a place where "millions yet unborn may dwell in peace and prosperity."[67] Once it was ascertained that the North West did have resources to offer "temptation to the emigrant nowhere excelled," that fact became central to the expansionist campaign.[68] At the same time, this emphasis on the farmer did not alter the commercial orientation of the movement. The farm, rather than the fur trade or Asia, was now seen as the primary source of trade, but it was still trade that was discussed. There would be a "joint extension of settlement and commerce."[69] The future farmer of the North West was to be a man who bought and sold goods, not one leading a self-sufficient existence.

The idea of an agricultural empire significantly reinforced and extended the importance of the North West in the Canadian mind. More and more, in a time of uncertainty, it was looked to as the most important single guarantee of Canada's future existence. In terms of external relations it would permit the development of a British North American nation with enough power to withstand any hostile pressures from the south. As one anonymous writer put it, the possession of the North West would make Canada "an almost impregnable military post in an enemy's country" and would be the best possible barrier against aggression.[70] Charles Mair's friend, the formidable George Denison of Toronto, agreed. "I am very glad to hear such good accounts of the resources and fertility of the great North West," he wrote Mair in 1869, for "I have every confidence in time it will prove a great source of strength to the Dominion and together we men of the North (as Haliburton says) will be able to teach the Yankees that we will be as our ancestors have always been[,] a dominant race."[71]

Denison's interest in the whole question reveals the broadening appeal of the expansionist movement by the later 1860s. As estimates of the importance of the North West increased, the idea of expansion became a sort of umbrella solution for all of Canada's problems. As such, it appealed increasingly to all those Canadians who considered themselves ardent nationalists. Denison saw the region as the means by which his particular phobia, American annexation, could be avoided, but others, with different concerns, also looked to expansion as a solution. The response of the Canada First group, formed in Ottawa in 1868, was typical. Its members included, initially, Denison, Mair, R.G. Haliburton, W.A. Foster, and H.J. Morgan.[72] Of all these men only Mair could be considered an expansionist; the others had different causes to keep them occupied. Yet all of them seem to have felt that the annexation of the North West was a necessary corollary to the preservation of the Canadian nation.

By the later 1860s expansionism had become intertwined with nationalism. The very definition of the young Dominion of Canada and its hopes for the future were increasingly thought to be inseparable from the opening of the West. An editorial entitled "Patriotism" in the Toronto *Globe,* on 16 February 1869, summed up the relationship. In order to build a great country, Canadians had first to understand that their nation, while just emerging, was inferior to none, and, the *Globe* argued, there was no reason to feel ashamed: "There are few countries, indeed, on the face of the earth of which the inhabitants have more reason to be proud." The source of that pride was the "mighty resources of the North West." Thomas D'Arcy McGee, Canada's most eloquent nationalist, put it even more succinctly when he concluded in 1868 that "the future of the Dominion depends on our early occupation of the rich prairie land."[73]

In the 1850s Canadians had sensed, or hoped, that they were on the threshold of some new stage in their evolution as a people. In their efforts to assure that this new stage would be attained, a number of them turned to the North West. By 1869 these expansionists had determined that future development to their own satisfaction. For them, the years between 1857 and 1869 simply brought confirmation of the belief that Canada's route to greatness was through the opening and settlement of the North West. The next stage had been defined, and in that definition the expansionist saw, as Mair put it, "the significance and inevitable grandeur of his country": "Far behind him are his glorious and old native province, the unsullied freedom of the North, the generous and untiring breed of men. Before him stretches through immeasurable distance the large and lovelier Canada." Mair's description of man's movement onto the prairies contained within it the expansionist vision of Canadian development. It was an image of history and destiny, for by imposing the traditions and energy of Canada's past to the potential for the future that existed in the North West lay "the path of empire and the garden of the world."[74]

NOTES

1 Doug Owram, "A Means to Empire: Canada's Reassessment of the West, 1857–69," in *Promise of Eden: The Canadian Expansionist Movement and the Idea of the West, 1856–1900* (Toronto: University of Toronto Press, 1980), 59–78.
2 Great Britain, House of Commons, *Report from the Select Committee on the Hudson's Bay Company*, app. 8, pp. 399–400.
3 See comments by William Kennedy in the *Globe*, Toronto, 21 Aug. 1857; and report of meeting in Hamilton, *ibid.*, 25 Sept. 1857. See also Province of Canada, *Journals of the Legislative Assembly*, 1857, app. 17.
4 Public Archives of Canada (PAC), Devine, "North West Part of Canada," VI-1100-57, Toronto, March 1857.
5 *Select Committee*, "Minutes of Evidence," 13, 152, 124–5.
6 *Gazette*, 8 Jan. 1856.
7 *Select Committee*, "Minutes of Evidence," 212.
8 *Ibid.*, app. 8, contains Gladman's testimony.
9 Henry Youle Hind, *Narrative of the Canadian Red River Exploring Expedition of 1857 and of the Assiniboine and Saskatchewan Exploring Expedition of 1858* (London 1860), I, 267.
10 Morris Zaslow, *Reading the Rocks* (Toronto 1975), 78, and as yet unpublished biography of Hind by W.L. Morton.
11 *Ibid.*, 96.
12 J.K. Johnson, ed., *The Canadian Directory of Parliament* (Ottawa 1968), 155–6.
13 Palliser, *Solitary Rambles and Adventures of a Hunter in the Prairies* (London 1853).
14 Irene Spry, ed., *The Papers of the Palliser Expedition, 1857–1860* (Toronto 1968), "Introductions," xxiii, xxi.
15 *Ibid.*, xxi.

16 Earl of Southesk, *Saskatchewan and the Rocky Mountains* (London 1875), xxxii.
17 Public Archives of Manitoba, Winnipeg, Schultz Papers, vol. 16, Henry McKenney to Schultz, 22 March 1859.
18 The relative youthfulness of this group is easy to demonstrate: William Buckingham was twenty-six when he moved to Red River; William Coldwell, twenty-four; Alexander Begg, thirty; Thomas Spence, thirty-four; Charles Mair, thirty-one.
19 United Kingdom, *Further Papers Relative to the Exploration of British North America* (London 1860), 5.
20 See Schultz Papers, vol. 16, Mair to Schultz, 14 May 1866, for an indication of his earlier interest in the West.
21 *Globe*, 4 Jan. 1869; letter from Mair.
22 Hind, *Narrative*, contains the route map; PAC, "Route of the Exploring Expedition under Command of Captain Palliser," VI/701, 1857–58, shows the route taken by that expedition.
23 T.J.J. Loranger to Hind, 27 April 1858; cited in Henry Youle Hind, *North-West Territory: Report on the Assiniboine and Saskatchewan Exploring Expedition* (Toronto 1859), 2.
24 G.S. Dunbar, "Isotherms and Politics," in A.W. Rasporich and H.C. Klassen, eds., *Prairie Perspectives* 2 (Toronto 1973), 89.
25 Blodgett, *Climatology* (Philadelphia 1857), 533, 529.
26 *Ibid.*, "Introduction."
27 Dawson cites Blodgett in his 1859 report; *Journals of the Legislative Assembly*, 1859, app. 36. "The Great North-West," *The Canadian Almanac and Repository of Useful Knowledge*, 1858, also cites Blodgett and is attributed to Hind in John Warkentin, "Steppe, Desert and Empire," Rasporich and Klassen, *Prairie Perspectives* 2, 132–3, n 40.
28 Blodgett, *Climatology*, 529.
29 Warkentin, "Steppe, Desert and Empire," 116–21.
30 United Kingdom, *The Journals, Detailed Reports and Observations Relative to the Exploration by Captain Palliser*, 1859, "The General Report," 7, 10–11.
31 Hind, *North-West Territory*, 31.
32 *Journals … by Captain Palliser*, "General Report," 7; Hind, *ibid.*, 123.
33 Hind, *Narrative*, I, "Map of the Country from Lake Superior to the Pacific Ocean."
34 Hind, *North-West Territory*, 124.
35 *Journals … by Captain Palliser*, 86; Palliser, *Papers Relative to the Exploration of British North America* (London 1859), 30; Hind, *ibid.*, 53.

36 Hind, *Narrative,* 11, 234.
37 [Hind], "North-West British America," *British American Magazine,* May 1863, p. 3.
38 *Nor'Wester,* "Prospectus," 1859.
39 "Report of the Committee of the Executive Council," approved 11 Nov. 1864; *Documents Relating to the Opening Up of the North West Territories to Settlement and Colonisation* (np 1865), 4.
40 *Canadian Journal,* March 1861, p. 175.
41 Charles Mair, "The New Canada: Its Natural Features and Climate [Part 1]," *Canadian Monthly and National Review,* VIII (July 1875), 1.
42 Southesk, *Saskatchewan and the Rocky Mountains,* 13; Viscount Milton and W.B. Cheadle, *The North-West Passage by Land* (London 1865), 98.
43 Hind, *Narrative,* I, 70–2.
44 Hind, T.C. Keefer, J.G. Hodgins, Charles Robb, M.H. Perley, Rev. W. Murray, *Eighty Years' Progress of British North America* (Toronto 1863), 88.
45 Hind, *North-West Territory,* 52, 44.
46 Hind, *Narrative,* I, 124, 134.
47 *Ibid.,* 373.
48 Milton and Cheadle, *North-West Passage by Land,* 72.
49 *Journals of the Legislative Assembly,* 1859, app. 36.
50 *Globe,* 20 Jan. 1869; letter from Mair.
51 George V. Le Vaux, "The Great North West – No. II," *New Dominion Monthly,* Jan. 1869, p. 226.
52 Alexander Morris, *The Hudson's Bay and Pacific Territories* (Montreal 1859), 7–10.
53 Province of Canada, *Parliamentary Debates on the Subject of the Confederation of the British North American Provinces* (Quebec 1865), 86.
54 Hind, *Narrative,* I, 191.
55 *Globe,* 28 May 1869; letter from Mair.
56 Milton and Cheadle, *North-West Passage by Land,* 160; David Anderson, *A Charge Delivered to the Clergy of the Diocese of Rupert's land at His Triennial Visitation, January 6, 1860* (London 1860), 8.
57 *Nor'Wester,* 14 Feb. 1860.
58 Hind, *North-West Territory,* 68.
59 *Nor'Wester,* "Prospectus."
60 *Globe,* 14 and 27 Dec. 1868; letters from Mair.
61 *Nor'Wester,* 5 Mar., 16 Apr. 1862; Wilson, "Science in Rupert's Land," *Canadian Journal,* July 1862, pp. 336–47.
62 Wilson, *ibid.,* 336; *Nor'Wester,* 16 Apr. 1862.
63 *Journals of the Legislative Assembly,* 1859, app. 62 36.

64 Le Vaux, "The Great North West No. II," 222.
65 *Confederation Debates*, 86.
66 Hind *et al.*, *Eighty Years' Progress*, 80.
67 "W.H.W.," "The Red River Settlement," *New Dominion Monthly*, May 1868, p. 101.
68 *Nor'Wester*, "Prospectus."
69 Alexander Russell, *The Red River Country, Hudson's Bay and the North-West Territories Considered in Relation to Canada* (Ottawa 1869), 5.
70 *The Interests of the British Empire in North America* (Ottawa 1868), 5.
71 Queen's University Library, Kingston, Mair Papers, vol. 1, Denison to Mair, 10 Mar. 1869.
72 Carl Berger, *The Sense of Power: Studies in the Ideas of Canadian Imperialism, 1867–1914* (Toronto 1970), 49–51.
73 Speech read before the Montreal Mechanics' Institute; cited in *Nor'Wester*, 15 Apr. 1868.
74 *Globe*, 28 May 1869; letter from Mair.

# VII

# The Geopolitics of Confederation

Thus far, the anthology has focused on perspectives that emphasize fault lines internal to the Canadian experience – English and French, central and peripheral, unitary and federal. But the lead up to Confederation was profoundly influenced by external factors as well. These exogenous conditions and causes are the focus of this section.

There were, of course, two countries with a particular interest in Canada and its future beyond all others and neither could be ignored – the United Kingdom and the United States. The politics and objectives of each country were a source of wind for the sails of Confederation, with both blowing the colonies towards a more united and independent path by the late 1860s. In 1867 Canada was, of course, a collection of colonies at the height of colonialism – the fluctuations of imperial sentiment were a very immediate concern to the local elites. That sentiment was not settled on the value of empire – something the Canadians understood very well. But the British were not the only power at play; the United States, as the successor power to the United Kingdom, was not as remote a presence in Canadian politics as it might have been in other British colonies such as Australia, New Zealand, or South Africa. It was next door, and it had a menacing history of conquest and expansion that was only beginning to fade from living memory. The Canadian need to take stock of the thinking in Washington did not begin with Confederation of course; it is an imperative that began with that country, not ours. And the sense was that a wounded, post–Civil War America might not pass up another chance at ousting the common colonial ancestor. Together, Canada was physically, intellectually, and constitutionally bound up in the greater global context of the time, and, while there may have been little it could do to change the bigger picture, there were things that could be done locally to help secure itself from the dangers it presented.

Interestingly, much of the most important, influential, and provocative scholarship that surveys the external environment in which Confederation was formed is also the oldest scholarship. We begin with what may be the first full treatment of Confederation, John Hamilton Gray's account, published in 1872, of the road to Confederation. In it, Gray (who participated, as a New Brunswicker, in the Confederation negotiations) argues that the union of British North America suited Britain's desire to protect its imperial interests from American expansion without having to contribute massively to that protection. Chester Martin, one of the dominant Canadian historians in the early decades of the twentieth century, argues in the same vein, though with a slightly different focus. In Martin's view, the American Civil War and the threat of American expansion thereafter concentrated British attention on the importance of a united British North America. That is why British officials, who had originally been indifferent to federal union, rather suddenly became enthusiastic supporters. C.P. Stacey, one of Canada's great military historians, argues provocatively that in the 1860s Britain found itself threatened both in the East (from a militarized Prussia) and the West (from the United States). The union of British North America, in his view, needs to be understood as a measured and calculated response to the problem of being squeezed simultaneously on two fronts.

Writing in 1967, Yves Roby is far more single-minded in his focus on the ways in which the fear of American expansionism – symbolized at the time by the Fenian raids of 1866 – built support for Confederation and for nascent Canadian nationalism. Roby's field of expertise is American history, and he will be known later on for his work on Franco-Americans. The Fenian threat, he argues, "reinforced Canadian nationalism, based for a large part on anti-Americanism, and put the adversaries of Confederation at a disadvantage." The final selection in this section, David Shi's account of Secretary of State William Seward's attempt to annex British Columbia, continues the American theme. Shi concludes that the attempt to annex British Columbia ultimately collapsed because Seward and his agents "consistently misunderstood and underestimated" the "strength and vitality of Canadian nationalism." Here is the lesson to be drawn from these various and historically separated works: in attempting to understand Canada, it is important to look outside the country as well as in.

# *Confederation; or, The Political and Parliamentary History of Canada from the Conference at Quebec, in October 1864, to the Admission of British Columbia, in July 1871*

1872

JOHN HAMILTON GRAY[1]

The policy of the Imperial Government towards its possessions in British North America for many years after the American Revolution was one of disintegration, rather than consolidation. "Ships, Colonies and Commerce" remained the chosen motto of the Empire. The strength acquired by the union of the thirteen United States indicated, as it was conceived, future dismemberment and severance of the remaining Colonies, should they be allowed to coalesce too much.

Convenience for the administration of local affairs in countries so widely extended and so sparsely settled, also in some degree tended to keep the remaining Provinces apart. New Brunswick was separated from Nova Scotia; the two Canadas were divided; Cape Breton was constituted a distinct government; Prince Edward Island, with its scant population and limited area, retained its old isolation; and Newfoundland was made a post captain's appointment. Separate governments, separate parliaments, different laws, and hostile tariffs fostered local prejudices and created divergent interests.

Thirty-five years ago the voice of Free Trade was heard in England. Protection was assailed. The change was rapid. In a few years the preferential duties in favour of colonial timber were abolished. The old idea of restricting the trade of the Colonies to the mother country was abandoned. The Cromwell code of the navigation laws lost its hold upon the country; the corn laws were swept away. "Buy in the cheapest market, sell in the dearest" was heard from Manchester and Birmingham, echoed in Liverpool and London, and rolled back from the Solway and the Clyde. The policy of the Empire was changed. The United States were better customers than the British North American Provinces. Why, then, it was asked, retain the latter at the expense of the over-taxed citizens of England? British interests, it was said, required that they should be severed from the parent state. British honor forbade that they should be abandoned, until able to take care of themselves. They must be taught self-reliance; to share largely, nay, to bear almost entirely, the burden of their own defence. Having the entire and absolute control of all local sources of wealth, with unrestricted powers of legislation in all matters save those affecting Imperial interests, they had been for fifteen years past, in all but the tie of a willing allegiance, independent countries. But they must not be allowed to fall into the United States, and add to the aggressive power of that already great Republic. The loyal sentiment of the people must be nurtured; the attachment of a free people to the mother country must not be rudely sent asunder. Sustained and strengthened by the Imperial connection, they must be guided on to a development of power, of nationality, that would enable them at a future day to take their place amid the nations of the earth, the friend, and not the foe of England. Opinion changed. Union is strength; and Consolidation becomes the policy of the Empire.

Such was the working of the public mind in England. But during these same thirty-five years, the public mind in British North America had not been stationary. Equally progressive, it had passed from the weakness of infancy and pupilage to the strength of maturity and manhood. Thirty-five years ago, these Provinces were governed from England; load appointments of honor and emolument were made from England. A few favored families held the patronage of the country. The debates of the legislative councils were held with closed doors. Irresponsible office-holders, bishops and judges were members. They admitted no right in the people to question the sacred character of their proceedings. The public lands and public revenues, the mines and minerals, were Imperial property, and disposed of by Imperial direction; sometimes to pay the debts of a spendthrift duke, sometimes to provide for a needy baronet, and sometimes for the colony. Treaties were made by which Provinces were dismembered without consulting the Colonial authorities or considering the Colonial interests; engendering future complications with foreign countries, and leaving to the Colonies the seeds of future permanent injury, though giving to the mother country a temporary relief from anxiety. Measures of internal vital importance, passed by the local legislatures, were ignored. Complaints against public officers were studiously disregarded, or, if acceded to, neutralized by the action of irresponsible ministers, holding their appointments from abroad, irrespective of the wishes of the people whose interests they were to serve. Sustained, though condemned, the official retained his place. *"Hic est damnatus inani judicio at tu victrix Provincia ploras."*

This could not last. Howe in Nova Scotia, Wilmot in New Brunswick, Papineau in Lower, and Baldwin in Upper Canada struggled for reform. They demanded for the people the control of the local revenues, the appointment of Provincial officers, and the constitutional selection of ministers responsible to the people of the country for the administration of local affairs. Theirs was no pigmy contest in those days; every vested interest arrayed its hydra head against them. Persons whose families had held office until they deemed the succession should be hereditary, denounced them as rebels – as disloyal. Misrepresentation and calumny followed them abroad, social ostracism at home. The Lieutenant-Governors, regardless of their duty, became partizans in the contest, and put themselves in personal antagonism to the friends of progress. To such an extent did this go that Sir Archibald Campbell, the sturdy old conqueror of Burmah, the then Lieutenant-Governor of New Brunswick, coolly informed the Legislature of that Province, in answer to an overwhelming address from that body for his removal, "that he had served his Sovereign so long abroad, that he did not care for their opinion." Between Mr. Howe and Lord Falkland, the Lieutenant-Governor, the altercation went so far that the indignant Nova Scotian threatened to hire a black man to horsewhip the representative of the Sovereign. Papineau did not stop on the verge of rebellion, and the language of Rolph and Baldwin had the ring of Massachusetts Bay in 1776.

American experience was not thrown away on England. The broad intellect of Lord Durham and the constitutional knowledge of Charles Buller quieted the storm. The practical concession of their rights having been established, the people of British North America set themselves to work, each Province in its own way, to develope the resources of its own locality. A healthy climate and great natural advantages bore them onward, but no one common direction governed the general movement. Each did what was best for itself, regulated its tariff by its own immediate wants, built its little Chinese wall round its own frontier, and taxed the manufactures of a sister Province as readily as those of Russia or the United States. Resting on its mother's leading hand, each toddled along in its own harmless way. But science, steam, telegraphs, and railways had taught a new education. The stupendous progress of the United States, with an unrestricted commerce from Florida to Maine, stood out in bold contrast to the narrow policy of Provincial isolation; and thinking minds, in advance of their time, conceived that if all the Provinces of British North America were united, with a common tariff and an unrestricted internal trade, a similar result, to a certain extent, might be obtained.

The dream of the political economist was brought about by causes, the effect of which, at their inception, was not foreseen. Many years previous to the Ashburton treaty – as far back as 1834 or 1835 – John Wilson, an enterprising merchant of St. Andrews, in the Province of New Brunswick, had originated a company for the construction of a railway from St. Andrews to Quebec; and a survey of the same had been made, under the direction of Major Yule, an officer of the Royal Engineers. This line, though countenanced by the British Government, owed its contemplation more to its commercial than to its military importance. Its course was comparatively straight and short. But, pending this survey, the United States Government claimed the territory through which it passed. The border difficulties of 1839 and 1840 – during which war was only averted by the prudence of Sir John Harvey and General Scott – terminated in disgraceful concession. The "Ashburton capitulation," as Lord Palmerston called it, was signed in 1842. A wedge of foreign territory was thrust up between Canada and New Brunswick, without consulting those Provinces; and the opportunity of constructing, on British soil, speedy and direct land communication between the two, was lost forever.

Resulting from the disturbances in Canada previous to and during the years 1837 and 1838, the circumstances attending the claim of the United States to the frontier boundary, and other occurrences about the same time, the attention of the British Government, which had before been turned to the construction of a military road from Halifax to Quebec, sufficiently far removed from the American frontier to be always available, was materially strengthened. The proposition to substitute a railroad in lieu of such military road had been thrown out by Lord Durham, but in no way acted upon. In 1845, the Governor of Nova Scotia applied to Her Majesty's Government to conduct a survey under the direction of competent military engineers, either at the expense of the British or Colonial Governments; suggesting at the same time that the importance of the ultimate object was so great, that he hoped this preparatory step might be deemed worthy of Imperial assistance. Her Majesty's Government assented to the application, but declined granting Imperial aid; and a survey and exploration of a line from Halifax to Quebec, through the northern part of New Brunswick, made at the joint expense of the three Provinces of Nova Scotia, New Brunswick and Canada, under the direction of Major Robinson, an officer of the Royal Engineers, was commenced in 1846, and completed in 1848. No immediate action was taken on this survey; but, after several years of negotiations, principally through the exertions of Mr. Howe, the Imperial Government, in 1851, by the Colonial Secretary, Lord Grey, made a specific offer to aid with an Imperial guarantee the construction of a railway on the route surveyed by Major Robinson, if the Provinces of Canada, New Brunswick and Nova Scotia would undertake to build one, subject to the approval of Her Majesty's Government. A re-formation of the Government of New Brunswick, in 1851, based upon a demand for a similar extension of the Imperial guarantee to the construction through Now Brunswick of the European and North American Railway, then lately originated at a railway convention held at Portland, in the State of Maine, and legislated upon by the Provinces of New Brunswick and Nova Scotia and the State of Maine; and the refusal of the British Government to extend that guarantee – upon the ground that the newly proposed road could not be regarded as of the same Imperial character or importance as the Intercolonial, and that the language of the despatch, upon which such demand had been made, was misunderstood – prevented at the time any action upon the offer. In the subsequent year, 1852, Canada (through the instrumentality of Messrs. Hincks, Young and Taché, members of the Government) and New Brunswick agreed upon a line to be built by their Governments, through the valley of the St. John; but to this Nova Scotia objected; and the Colonial Minister having refused the guarantee to the new route, upon the ground that the negotiations had been based upon the Major Robinson line, or an approximation to it, efforts for its construction ultimately died out. The three Provinces, therefore, if they desired to act conjointly and obtain the Imperial guarantee, were compelled to adopt a line sufficiently removed from the American frontier to comply with the military character of the work for which the guarantee was originally offered.

Though, owing to these different complications in the Provinces, the work was thus retarded, the idea was never abandoned, and at various times between that period and 1860, numerous negotiations were had between the Provinces touching its construction. In 1862–3, these had proceeded so far, that an apportionment of the relative expense to be borne by the Provinces separately had been agreed upon, and laws passed in the Legislatures of New Brunswick and Nova Scotia to confirm the arrangement. From some cause, which to the maritime Provinces was never satisfactorily accounted for, the arrangement was not adhered to by Canada. During the same period efforts had also been repeatedly made by the several Governments to bring about a union of postal and fiscal regulations, and a similarity of tariffs, but the local necessities of each, and the supposed divergence of interests, had rendered those efforts ineffectual.

No serious attempt, however, at a political union had been made; but the public mind was rapidly expanding both to its importance and necessity. In 1854 the question had been brought up in the Nova Scotia House of Assembly, and the great leaders of the Conservative and Liberal parties, Messrs. Johnston and Howe, throwing aside the rivalry of party, had delineated with equal power, the advantages that would result from combining the scattered elements of prosperity and strength separately possessed by the several Provinces.

In 1858, in the Canadian Parliament, the movement assumed a more tangible shape, and union was made a part of the policy of the Government. Mr. Galt, on his becoming a member of the administration, insisted on its being made a cabinet question; and Sir Edmund Head, in his speech at the close of the session, intimated that his government, during the recess, would take action in the matter. Those tendencies, however, were all abortive; they produced nothing. On this subject, at that time, the Imperial Government itself had no definite policy. In 1857, when, in furtherance of the movement in the Nova Scotia Parliament, the Hon. Messrs. Johnston and Adams G. Archibald had gone to England to confer with Her Majesty's Government on that as well as on other matters, Mr. Labouchere, the Secretary of State for the Colonies, intimated to them that it was a question entirely for the Colonies themselves, and that no obstacle to its accomplishment would be thrown in their way. In 1858, when, in furtherance of the then adopted policy of the Canadian Government, Messrs. Cartier, Galt and Ross specially waited upon the Imperial Government, requesting authority for a meeting of delegates from each of the Colonies, to take the question into consideration, Sir Edward Bulwer Lytton, the then Secretary, replied that the question "was necessarily one of an Imperial character," and declined to authorize the meeting because, with the exception of one, he had received no expression of sentiment from the Lower

Provinces on the subject. In 1862, the Duke of Newcastle, the then Colonial Secretary, in a dispatch to the Governor-General, after stating in explicit terms that Her Majesty's Government was not prepared to announce any definite policy on this question for a similar reason, added that "if a union, either partial or complete, should hereafter be proposed, with the concurrence of all the Provinces to be united, I am sure that the matter would be weighed in this country, both by the public, by Parliament, and by Her Majesty's Government, with no other feeling than an anxiety to discern and promote any course which might be the most conducive to the prosperity, the strength and harmony of all the British communities in North America."

The war in the United States, however, and the Trent affair of 1861–2, put an end to all vacillation on the part of the Imperial Government; and from the Prime Minister to the peasant, whether Liberal of Conservative, whether Tory or Radical, but one policy for the future was to prevail. British America was to be consolidated; British America was to be made self-reliant; British America was to be put in a position to require as little from the British Government as was possible, with an allegiance that was voluntary, and a connection that was almost nominal. The integrity of the Empire was to be preserved, but the outlying frontier was to be mainly instrumental in preserving it. Union received an astounding impulse. It perhaps never before occurred that two independent bodies, moving in their own orbits, so suddenly and so simultaneously received an influence from different causes, impelling them in the same direction, and that direction to result in their mutual good. The force was irresistible; it was to the same end, but neither body was to be coercive of the other. The outward pressure of mutual necessity and mutual advantage broke like light upon the public mind. Both parties were to be strengthened, but the result was to be obtained by the voluntary action of a free people, the exercise of their constitutional rights, the assent of the national judgment. Events moved on with startling rapidity. What, up to 1861, had been the shadowy outline of a patriot's broad conceptions, or the enthusiast's dream, suddenly sprang into a tangible creation, "*rudis indigestaque moles*" at first, but soon to be moulded into shape, each fragment taking its proper place, each individual part fitting to its proper sphere, and standing forth a compact and substantial fabric.

In the winter of 1864, though the public mind was thus agitated, all reasonable hopes of effecting any arrangement with Canada, either of a fiscal nature or for the construction of the intercolonial road at an early day, seemed to have been abandoned in the Lower Provinces; and the Legislatures of New Brunswick, Nova Scotia and Prince Edward Island had, at their sessions in that year, severally passed resolutions authorising their respective Governments to enter into negotiations, and hold a Convention for the purpose of effecting a union of the Maritime Provinces, political, legislative and fiscal. That Convention was appointed to meet at Charlottetown, in Prince Edward Island, in the month of September following.

It is necessary here to retrace our steps for a moment, and take a rapid glance at the position of Canada. During the previous ten or fifteen years, though politically united, the conflicting interests of Upper and Lower Canada had become more divergent. At the union of the two Provinces, under Lord Sydenham, in 1841, the Parliamentary representation was rather in favour of Lower Canada; and the rule of equal territorial representation, which, in the interests of Upper Canada, was at that time adopted, in order to neutralize the supposed inequality, was, owing to the more rapid increase in wealth and population of that Province, found soon to operate to its disadvantage. In a short time Upper exceeded Lower Canada in its population by many hundred thousands (nearly half a million), without having received any corresponding increase in representation, or influence in the raising or disbursement of the revenues obtained from the taxation of both. Thus, prominent among the political questions of the day became Representation by Population.

But the governing of double majorities was equally a source of difficulty. It was necessary that the portion of the cabinet formed from each Province should carry with it the support of the majority of the representatives of the Province from which it came. A more absurd mode of government could hardly be conceived; for while the leading ministers and statesmen of both Provinces might be thoroughly united on a question of general importance to the whole, the local jealousy of a part of either one particularly affected might deprive the portion of the cabinet belonging to that Province of its support, and thus defeat a ministry commanding the confidence of the whole country, and a majority of the Parliament, but unable, from some local cause, to carry a particular section. Under such a system, local jealousies are fostered, broad and liberal views are abandoned, sections become powers, principles degenerate into personalities, consistency is sacrificed for place, and the parliamentary debates become remarkable for the acerbity they display, rather than for the talent they evolve.

The jealousies between the Upper and Lower Canadas increased; party lines became more clearly defined (if adherence to persons and sections more than to principle can be called party); and government, in a parliamentary sense, became practically impossible. In the session of 1863, on all questions affecting the then existing ministry, under the leadership of the Hon. John Sandfield Macdonald, the divisions were so nearly equal that the Government ceased to command its proper influence. At the re-assembling of Parliament in February, 1864, finding that no additional strength had been acquired during the recess, though a dissolution had taken place and a general election had been held for the purpose of testing public opinion, the Government resigned; and in March, 1864, a new administration under Sir E.P. Taché, was formed. Up to June the divisions showed a similar position for the new Government. On the 14th of June the Journals of the Legislative Assembly have the following entry: –

> The Hon. Mr. Brown from the select Committee appointed to enquire into the important subjects embraced in a dispatch to the Colonial Minister, addressed to him on the 2nd Feb., 1864, by the Hon. Geo. E. Cartier – the Hon. A.T. Galt and the Hon. John Ross, then members of the Executive Council of the Province, while in London, acting on behalf of the Government of which they were members, in which they declared that "very grave difficulties now present themselves in conducting the Government of Canada in such a manner as to show due regard to the wishes of its numerous populations." That "differences exist to an extent which prevents any perfect and complete assimilation of the views of the two sections." That "the progress of population has even more rapid in the western section, and claims are now being made on behalf of its inhabitants for giving them representation in the Legislature in proportion to their numbers." That "the result is shewn by an agitation fraught with great danger to the peaceful and harmonious working of our constitutional system, and consequently detrimental to the progress of the Province," – and that "necessity of providing a remedy for a state of things that is yearly becoming worse, and of allaying feelings that are daily being aggravated by the contention of political parties, has impressed the advisers of Her Majesty's Representative in Canada with the importance of seeking such a mode of dealing with the difficulties as may forever remove them," – and the best means of remedying the evils therein set forth, presented to the House the Report of the said Committee, which was read as followeth: "That the Committee have held eight meetings, and have endeavoured to find

some solution for existing difficulties likely to receive the assent of both sections of the Province." – A strong feeling was found to exist among the members of the Committee in favour of changes in the direction of a Federative system, applied either to Canada alone, or to the whole British North American Provinces, and such progress has been made as to warrant the Committee in recommending that the subject be again referred to a Committee at the next Session of Parliament.

The whole respectfully submitted.
George Brown,
Chairman.

On the same day the Government was defeated by 60 to 58, on a vote of censure relative to some transactions connected with bonds of the City of Montreal, and to the Grand Trunk Railway in 1859, five years before, under a previous administration. The contest was personal, – the Dead Lock had come. Between that day and the 30th June the supplies were hurried through, and the House was prorogued. On the 23rd of June, previous to the prorogation, when the Orders of the Day were called, the Hon. Attorney-General Macdonald rose to make ministerial explanations in regard to the recent negotiations for strengthening the Government. He read the following statement of what had passed between the Government and Mr. Brown from the commencement to the close of the negotiations.

Immediately after the defeat of the Government on Tuesday night (the 14th), and on the following morning, Mr. Brown spoke to several supporters of the Administration, strongly urging that the present crisis should be utilized in settling forever the constitutional difficulties between Upper and Lower Canada, and assuring them that he was prepared to co-operate with the existing, or any other Administration that would deal with the question promptly and firmly, with a view to its final settlement.
[...]
After much discussion on both sides, it was found that a compromise might probably be had in the adoption either of the Federal principle for all of the British North American Provinces, as the larger question, or for Canada alone, with the provision for the admission of the Maritime Provinces and the North Western Territory, when they should express the desire. Mr. Brown contended that the Canadian Confederation should be constituted first, in order that such securities might be taken, in regard to

the position of Upper Canada, as would satisfy that section of the country; that in the negotiations with the Lower Provinces, the interests of Upper Canada would in no case be overlooked.

[...]

MEMORANDUM – CONFIDENTIAL

The Government are prepared to state that immediately after the prorogation they will address themselves, in the most earnest manner, to the negotiations for a confederation of all the British North American Provinces.

That failing a successful issue to such negotiations, they are prepared to pledge themselves to legislation during the next Session of Parliament, for the purpose of remedying existing difficulties by introducing the Federal principle for Canada alone, coupled with such provisions as will permit the Maritime Provinces and the North-Western Territory to be hereafter incorporated into the Canadian system.

That for the purpose of carrying on the negotiations, and settling the details of the promised legislation, a Royal Commission shall be issued, composed of three members of the Government and three members of the Opposition, of whom Mr. Brown shall be one; and the Government pledge themselves to give all the influence of the Administration to secure to the said Commission the means of advancing the great object in view.

That subject to the House permitting the Government to carry through the public business, no dissolution of Parliament shall take place, but the Administration will meet the present House.

[...]

On the 30th of June, simultaneously with the prorogation, a new Government was announced. The Hon. George Brown, with Messrs. Mowat and Macdougall, two other prominent Reformers, had taken the place of Messrs. Foley, Buchanan, and Simpson, in the existing Administration. A coalition had been formed between the leaders of the Reform and Conservative parties, with the general assent of their supporters. They agreed to unite to bring about a measure, which they hoped and believed would remove the difficulties then obstructing the successful administration of Constitutional Government of Canada. That measure was the Confederation of the Provinces of British North America, on the Atlantic side, with the prospect at some ultimate day of bringing in the North West and Hudson Bay Territories, and British Columbia.

We now resume the current of events in the Maritime Provinces. The action of Canada had not been unnoticed, but the Governments of New Brunswick, Nova Scotia and Prince Edward Island proceeded with their original design. In order that the question of their Union might, as much as possible, be removed beyond the pale of party conflict, the delegates to attend the Convention at Charlottetown were selected from the Liberal and Conservative ranks alike. Dr. Tupper, the leader of the Government of Nova Scotia, with his own colleague Attorney-General Henry, and Mr. Dickey, a Conservative supporter, had included the Hons. Adams G. Archibald and Jonathan McCully, long and well-known leaders of the Liberal party. Mr. Tilley, the leader of the Government in New Brunswick, with his own colleagues, Messrs. Johnston and Steves, had included the Hons. Edward Barron Chandler and John Hamilton Gray, prominent and well-known leaders of the Conservative party there; whilst in Prince Edward Island the Premier had, with equal consideration, selected the Island delegates from both sides of the House. The recommendations for the respective Governments were approved by the Lieutenant-Governors, and the Convention was opened in due form at Charlottetown, September 8th, in the Chamber of the House of Assembly.

The Premier of Prince Edward Island, the Hon. John Hamilton Gray, was unanimously chosen Chairman, and the Convention as organized, stood thus:

Nova Scotia – The Hon. Messrs. Tupper, Henry, Dickey, Archibald, and McCully

New Brunswick – The Hon. Messrs. Tilley, Steves, Johnston, Chandler, and Gray

Prince Edward Island – The Hon. Messrs. Gray, Coles, Pope, Palmer, and Macdonald

The first question submitted was, whether the sittings of the Convention and its deliberations should be with closed doors, or open to the public? After consideration it was determined that the proceedings should be with closed doors, to avoid as much as possible, any undue pressure upon the Island delegates from their constituencies, which surrounded them – to ensure an unrestrained freedom of discussion – and a clear, candid, and business-like consideration of the important questions involved – in a word, to remove all inducements to "buncombe." There being no occasion for display, the speeches were practical and to the point. It is to be borne in mind that this Convention was not a public representative body having power to legislate, determine, or finally affect the public interests, but rather a committee of public men, deputed by their several Governments to enquire and report upon a proposition which might or might not ultimately be adopted, but which before either its adoption or rejection, would be subject to a searching and exhaustive public discussion in the several Legislatures of the Provinces.

The departure from Quebec of certain members of the Canadian Government who had been deputed by the Governor-General to attend the Convention, having been announced by telegram, and it having been determined to receive the deputation, and to consider any propositions they might make with all fairness, it was agreed to postpone the consideration of the union of the Maritime Provinces, until after the Canadian deputation had been heard. The following morning the Canadian Government steamer arrived, the deputation was received with a cordial welcome, and in due time introduced to the Convention. The Hons. John A. Macdonald, Geo. Brown, Geo. E. Cartier, Alex T. Galt, Thos. D'Arcy McGee, Hector L. Langevin, Wm. McDougall, and Alex. Campbell were men who had made their mark in their own country, and had been wisely selected to put the case of the broader union of British North America as contra-distinguished to the more limited one of the Maritime Provinces before the Convention in a clear and comprehensive manner.

NOTES

1 John Hamilton Gray, "Chapter I," *Confederation; or, The Political and Parliamentary History of Canada from the Conference at Quebec, in October, 1864, to the Admission of British Columbia, in July, 1871*, 1 (Toronto: Copp, Clark, 1872), 2–20, 23–24, 28–31.

# "British Policy in Canadian Confederation"

*Canadian Historical Review*
1932

CHESTER MARTIN[1]

The conventional approach to Canadian history through the history of New France has left many of the early traditions of British North America curiously distorted and unconvincing. The same tendencies have survived in the conventional approach to Confederation through the old province of Canada – with a similar effect upon historical perspective. Beyond a doubt the tendencies in this instance have a warrant in history as well as in tradition, since the political deadlock which was discernible to Galt and Sir Edmund Head in the old province of Canada as early as 1858 was at that time the only driving force of federalism as a solution for the problem of British American union. For the other provinces and for British policy, however, there was another approach with another alternative, and both have been almost grotesquely foreshortened by the prevailing traditions of Confederation.

Three years before the federation of the British provinces in 1867, British policy with regard to them underwent a violent and far-reaching change. Until 1864 the project for the legislative union of the Maritime Provinces as distinct from the federal union with Canada had received every encouragement from the Colonial Office. The union of Nova Scotia and New Brunswick at least seemed assured until delegates from the old province of Canada appeared at the Charlottetown conference in September 1864 to urge a broader federal union of all the British provinces.

Within three months British policy was reversed and the whole groundwork was laid for the Canadian federation. Two of the three constituent parties to the project, however, remained hostile to the federal union with Canada. New Brunswick defeated the project overwhelmingly at the polls. In Nova Scotia the same result was avoided only by evading an election altogether. In the end, both provinces were carried into Confederation by the use of desperate and uncompromising "means" from Canada and the direct influence of the Colonial Office exercised without restraint through the lieutenant-governors of both provinces.

How is this violent reversal of policy by the Colonial Office in 1864 to be explained, and how far was it, in the last analysis, the cardinal factor in the actual achievement of Confederation? For the second of these problems conclusive evidence, it would seem, is already available. For the first it may be possible to attempt at least a forecast. The conventional story of Confederation in this respect is singularly unconvincing. Is the key to British policy to be found in the relations with the United States during the Civil War?

## I

It will not be necessary to trace in detail from 1850 to 1862 the preliminary stages of the movement for Maritime union. The weightiest opinion, it would seem, in the esteem of the Colonial Office, was that of Sir Edmund Head.

It is true that Head, then lieutenant-governor of New Brunswick, had drafted a secret memorandum for a federal union of all the British provinces in 1851 – the first practical project of federation based squarely upon the dynamics of responsible government. His forecast was "a powerful and independent State" under the British crown, with a uniform currency, "a mint of their own," a distinctive flag and "a national destiny."[2] It is true also that Head was the first to launch the project of federal union into practical politics as governor-general of Canada in 1858, thus sharing with Galt, as I have tried to suggest elsewhere, the credit of gauging for the first time the forces that were to prove so powerful in 1864.[3] But both during the interval between 1851 and 1858, and afterwards, Head reverted to the more feasible project of Maritime union. In 1856 he wrote to Labouchere,

> I do not now believe in the practicability of the federal or legislative Union of Canada with the three "Lower Colonies" – I once thought differently

> but further knowledge and experience have changed my views – I believe however that it would be possible, with great advantage to all parties concerned to unite under one Government Nova Scotia, Prince Edward's Island, and New Brunswick.[4]

With this project for Maritime union was combined another for the annexation of the Red and Saskatchewan River valleys to Canada and for the union of Vancouver Island and New Caledonia west of the Rocky Mountains.[5]

There were thus to be three great preliminary regional unions across the continent. Again in 1859, after the crisis of 1858 had passed in Canada, Head reverted to the project of Maritime union.[6] A confidential memorandum which he had drafted "when in England in 1857" for Labouchere was now sent to the Colonial Office at Newcastle's own request. This copy is now nowhere to be found, but one of Merivale's confidential minutes at the Colonial Office is no doubt a correct interpretation:

> It was Sir E. Head's opinion (founded on his knowledge both of N. Brunswick & Canada) that the best prospect for the so called Lower Provinces was an Union between them (legislative, as I think, and not federative) to the *exclusion* of Canada with which a subsequent *federal* union might or might not be formed.[7]

By far the most exhaustive analysis, however, had come from the Earl of Mulgrave, lieutenant-governor of Nova Scotia. In a confidential despatch of December 30, 1858, which Herman Merivale, Lord Carnarvon, then under-secretary, and Lytton himself alike commended ("perhaps the cleverest despatch we have had on the subject") Mulgrave estimated "the advantages to be derived by the Lower Provinces" by a federal union with Canada as "very problematical." A few months later he could see "no reason to change" his views on federal union with Canada; but avowing a "very different feeling" with regard to the legislative union of the Maritime Provinces, he drafted a case for Maritime union which remained a classic until it was discarded by the reversal of British policy in 1864.[8] One reflection of Mulgrave's has now, in retrospect, a curious poignancy: in case of federation with Canada,[9] he maintained, it was essential for the Maritime Provinces to come in "on something like equal terms" and after being "thoroughly amalgamated" by a previous union among themselves. Upon the margin of Mulgrave's despatch is a memorandum by Fortescue of the Colonial Office: "This agrees with Sir E. Head's opinion." The papers on the union of the British provinces were printed by the Foreign Office for confidential use in London. The cause of Maritime union was clearly in the ascendant.

## II

The developments of the next four years are traceable from a variety of sources. In 1861 (September 27) Lieutenant-Governor Manners Sutton of New Brunswick, in compliance with "a strong and growing opinion here in favor of the Union, Legislative, of the three Lower Provinces," reported a project for free interprovincial trade in colonial produce and manufactures.[10] Newcastle, who had just had a round with a "host of pedantic objections" raised by the Board of Trade (the phrase is that of the Colonial Office itself), cut the Gordian knot by conceding the right to "free Commercial intercourse between the different Provinces" and thus confronting the Board of Trade with a *fait accompli.*[11] Even Galt discovered that he had a secret ally in Newcastle against the Board of Trade in the famous tariff controversy of 1859.[12]

British policy was further crystallized by Newcastle's visit to the British provinces with the Prince of Wales in 1860 and by Howe's resolutions of 1861 in Nova Scotia for "mutual consultation" with regard to union. Mulgrave's correspondence again provides the clue to British policy. Elliott of the Colonial Office has a confidential minute upon the despatch of May 21, 1862:

> It appears to me that there are strong reasons for encouraging a Union, both Commercial and Legislative, of all the Lower Provinces, but that whether it would be advisable to promote, – or to foster the discussion of, – their Incorporation into Canada is far more doubtful.[13]

A minute by Newcastle himself would seem to be conclusive:

> I have always been of opinion that the necessary preliminary to a Legislative Union of the Lower Provinces is an Intercolonial Railway, and that the completion of *both* these schemes must precede a Union with Canada. The latter event may be hastened by the present condition of the neighbouring Country,[14] but I do not expect success to any project which attempts it

> without first *settling* (if not *accomplishing*) both the smaller Union and the Railway ... I am well inclined to enter heartily into any well-considered plan which has the concurrence of all Parties concerned.[15]

It is significant that the interprovincial conference which met at Quebec in September 1862 waived, for the time, the discussion of union and addressed itself to the building of the intercolonial railway. Newcastle himself renewed with alacrity the imperial guarantee which had gone by the board during the embroglio between Grey and Howe in 1852; while a virtual contract between Canada, Nova Scotia, and New Brunswick divided the prospective cost of the railway in the ratio of 10, 7, and 7. The necessary legislation was passed by both Nova Scotia and New Brunswick, but when one of the kaleidoscopic administrations in Canada during this period abrogated the contract altogether, there was a bitter exchange in which charges of selfishness and bad faith were freely made.[16] This too – the "Canadian fiasco" as it was called – confirmed the drift towards Maritime union, and a definite project was soon under way with every prospect of success.

After the retirement of Mulgrave from Nova Scotia, Sir Arthur Gordon, lieutenant-governor of New Brunswick, became the chief exponent of Maritime union, with the full imprimatur of the Colonial Office. "I shall be glad," Newcastle wrote confidentially on July 31, 1863, "to learn that you have taken all prudent means, without committing the home Government beforehand, to bring about a proposal from the Lower Provinces for a Legislative Union."[17] By August, Gordon reported "every reason to hope that ... the Legislatures of New Brunswick, Nova Scotia and Prince Edward Island will concur during the next Session in an Address ... for the immediate union of the Lower Provinces."[18] In September, Tupper of Nova Scotia foreshadowed a "resolution in its favour ... by the Legislature of Nova Scotia without a single dissentient vote,"[19] and again Newcastle in reply expressed his "satisfaction at the concurrence of sentiment."[20] By December the project had been "favourably received" by the executive council of New Brunswick, and "no punctilio" was to interfere with "the end in view."[21] Concurrent resolutions were drafted for the three legislatures. When Gordon returned to England on leave of absence in April 1864, there were gathering difficulties in Prince Edward Island[22] but excellent prospects for the union of Nova Scotia and New Brunswick. Gordon returned in August in time to appoint the delegates to the Charlottetown conference, September 1, and to attend for several days in person. He afterwards reported that "the Delegates from Nova Scotia [representing both parties] were unanimous in favour of the immediate Legislative and administrative union of the Lower Provinces." Those from New Brunswick, though divided in opinion, expressed no dissent from the avowed policy of Tilley and the majority. Prince Edward Island was to prove hostile to both forms of union pending a settlement of the land question, but the union of the other two seemed "certain of adoption."[23] "But for the proposals from Canada," added Gordon, "I have no hesitation in saying that the union of the Maritime Provinces would have been effected, for the Delegates both of Nova Scotia and New Brunswick were fully agreed on the determination not to permit the reluctance of Prince Edward Island to affect their determination."[24]

It may not unfairly be assumed that the relations with the United States during the Civil War – no small factor, as we shall see, in the federal union with Canada – would have subserved with equal effect the original project of Maritime union had the Colonial Office continued on that side of the balance the decisive influence which they now cast into the other. Such were the prospects of success for Mulgrave's scheme of Maritime union as a prelude to federal union with Canada "on something like equal terms."

## III

The reversal of British policy has been obscured in Canadian history by the familiar theme of the Canadian coalition of June 1864, and the "Ride of the Valkyries" to Charlottetown. The preoccupation of the Canadian statesmen with their own desperate *impasse* in Canada was well known to the Maritime Provinces. Brown had entered the coalition upon the specific pledge that if a general federation were to prove impracticable, the existing Canadian union was to be broken up and replaced by a dual federation. The sardonic comment of the executive council in New Brunswick that the chief concern in Canada for union was to break up the only effectual union which already existed, that of the two Canadas, may not have remained true, but it was very nearly true at the beginning. In the despatch in which Monck announced the coalition of June 1864, the federation of the British provinces is never once mentioned. "The only question," he wrote, "about which there has been for a long time any serious difference of opinion in the Province is ... the equal division of representation between Upper and Lower Canada ... I trust a compromise satisfactory to both sides may be devised."[25] When the

Canadian delegates asked permission to attend the Charlottetown conference, they were informed that "as the Delegates were appointed solely for the purpose of considering the proposed Legislative union of the Lower Provinces, it would not be competent for them officially to discuss the larger and more novel proposal now made by Canada";[26] and, when the Colonial Office heard by way of Nova Scotia of the proposed Canadian delegation, Cardwell addressed to Monck, the governor-general, a curt request for an explanation. Monck's reply is a laboured apology for the intrusion into what he conceded to be "the primary object of the conference."[27] As late as August 1864, Cardwell himself wrote that "the official Mission of the Delegates should be limited to the Union of the Lower Provinces," and that he was "not yet prepared to enter" upon the wider question of a federal union with Canada.[28] It seems clear that the reversal of British policy was not due to the change of personnel at the Colonial Office.

This was in August 1864. The Charlottetown conference assembled on September 1, and the Quebec conference adjourned at Montreal on October 29. A little more than two months, therefore, saw the complete reversal of the policy of Maritime union and the completion of the Quebec resolutions for ratification by the respective legislatures. The reversal of British policy is equally forthright and decisive. Monck's first despatch with details of the Quebec resolutions is dated November 7. On December 3 the full imprimatur of the Colonial Office was given to the cause of federal union. Prince Edward Island resolutely refused to enter Confederation until 1873 and Newfoundland still remains outside the Dominion. In New Brunswick, however, Sir Arthur Gordon, whose voluminous despatches up to January 2, 1865, were a frantic attempt to salvage his original project of Maritime union, was forced to reverse the engines and to carry the Canadian scheme through the legislature and at the hustings by means that are not pleasant to reflect upon. The official instructions and above all the private letters from Cardwell were in truth mandatory: "I shall act," Gordon replied, "in conformity with ... commands therein signified to me."[29] Under instructions from the Colonial Office to complete the ratification of the Quebec resolutions if possible in time for an act of the British parliament during the session of 1865, Gordon and Tilley decided upon an immediate dissolution. There was "no doubt [thought Gordon] of the triumph of the Government," since with the exception of three constituencies where "the question of Confederation will in some degree affect the result," the elections would probably be determined by "local interests and local partialities."[30] Whatever reason there may be in this to credit Gordon's good faith, his judgement was less defensible. In the elections of March 1865, the cause of Confederation was overwhelmingly defeated. Tilley, Gray, and Fisher themselves were among the vanquished in the three most influential constituencies in the province. Nova Scotia, by Tupper's own admission, avoided the same fate only by evading an election altogether.

## IV

Some of the desperate methods used to reverse this verdict are now but too clearly traceable and must be set down without extenuation.[31] There is evidence of an understanding at Quebec that Canadian resources would be forthcoming for the contest in Nova Scotia and New Brunswick. The by-election in York County in October 1865, which was interpreted as the turning of the tide, is the subject of some interesting correspondence in the *Macdonald Papers.* "I am quite certain," wrote Tilley, "Fisher can be returned under any circumstances with an expenditure of 8 or ten thousand Dollars ... Is there any chance of the friends in Canada providing half the expenditure?" Upon the back of this letter is a memorandum in Macdonald's handwriting: "My dear Galt Read this. What about the monies?"[32] "Do not allow us to want now," added Fisher, "[or] we are all gone together."[33] The governor-general himself, then in Britain, regarded the York by-election as "the most important thing that has happened since the Quebec Conference, and if followed up judiciously affords a good omen of success in our spring campaign."

Less than a month after the defeat of Tilley and Confederation in New Brunswick, the strongest delegation which had ever left Canada – Macdonald, Galt, Brown, and Cartier – was on its way to Downing Street, charged among other things with the necessity of reversing the fatal verdict. "The British Government," wrote Macdonald,[34] "will carry their point if they only adopt vigorous measures to that end, and we shall spare no pains to impress the necessity of such a course upon them." As it happened, the incitation of Macdonald and his colleagues was unnecessary. The "vigorous measures" of the British government are attested alike by Galt's own memoranda in the *Macdonald Papers* and by the emphatic despatches which bore down all before them, as we shall see, in New Brunswick and Nova Scotia. The first of these was already on its way a fortnight before the Canadian delegates reached Downing Street. By Gordon's own admission he was in constant collusion with Tilley against his own constitutional advisers, and the act by which he finally precipitated another election in 1866 was an outrage against the principles of responsible government. "This transaction," he confessed ruefully at that time, "has throughout caused me the deepest mortification. It is mortifying to know that efforts to effect in a tranquil manner ... a great object desired by the Imperial Govt. have proved wholly abortive."[35]

Meanwhile there can be no doubt that "the needful," as Tilley called it, was forthcoming from Canada. He wrote to Macdonald:

> We must have the arrangement carried out and without delay that was talked of when I met you at Quebec ... telegraph me in cypher saying what we can rely upon ... The elections must be carried at all Hazards....
>
> We can send a respectable man ... to Portland where he might [meet] Brydges or some other person to arrange Finances. It will require some $40,000 or $50,000 to do the work.[36]

A few days later he added:

> To be frank with you the election in this Province can be made certain if the means are used ... If you give us aid as indeed you must to ensure success, you can arrange details as you think best.

The governor-general added his own appeal and Gordon's for prompt measures. He telegraphed to Macdonald,

> I have seen Galt and I think it very desirable that he should undertake the journey to Portland.

The counterpart to this is a note from Galt himself in the *Macdonald Papers*:

> I saw Lord Monck today (Sunday) ... He agrees ... that means had better be used – I think we must put it through coûte que coûte – and that I had better discuss it in this sense with Tilley – I should like to take Brydges to Portland with me.

The elections of June 1866, which reversed the verdict of the previous year, are still a tradition in New Brunswick. It is but fair to add that no small amount of "the needful" was in evidence against Confederation, and that the source of much of it still remains a mystery.

In Nova Scotia Tupper's course was the direct result of the hostile verdict in New Brunswick. Even in the legislature, he found, "all ... ingenuity would be required to avert the passage of a hostile resolution."[37] "There can be no doubt," Tupper afterwards conceded in reviewing his policy in Nova Scotia, "that an appeal to the people here ... would have resulted as it has in that Province in placing the opponents of Confederation in power and affording them the means of obstructing that great measure." In desperation he fell back upon a resolution for Maritime union as a preliminary step to Confederation, but the Colonial Office was now no longer prepared to countenance "any proposals which would tend to delay the Confederation of all the Provinces." Maritime union was no longer acceptable unless it "formed part of the scheme for general union."[38] At the same time Tupper, sensitive, as usual, to the temper of his countrymen, deprecated any appearance of "coercive measures on the part of the Imperial authorities" as likely to be "prejudicial to the cause."[39] In the end Nova Scotia was voted into Confederation by a legislature elected months before on vastly different issues, and the first federal election sent eighteen out of nineteen members to Ottawa pledged to abrogate the union. The provincial elections, held at the same time, returned but two out of forty members in favour of Confederation, and one of these was almost immediately unseated and replaced by an anti-federalist.

## V

The worst, I think, in this desperate programme has been set down without extenuation, but it would be a monstrous perversion of the truth, I am sure, to attribute the success of Confederation primarily to these "means." None could read the debates and correspondence of that period without the conviction that the national destiny of the British provinces had grown in public estimation from the size of a man's hand until it filled the whole sky. Those who saw what had to be done did it without squeamishness and without apology. "Small thanks," exclaimed Carlyle, "to the man who will keep his hands clean but with gloves on." Many other factors are obvious. The desperate *impasse* in Canada in itself was enough to force the Colonial Office to acquiescence, though not perhaps to the inflexible policy of 1866. The ardour of the Canadian federalists can scarcely be overestimated. No other such exploit of high-pressure, political salesmanship is to be found in the history of Canada as the advocacy of the Canadian delegates at the Charlottetown and Quebec conferences. The pervasive influence of Watkin and Brydges of the Grand Trunk and of other British financial interests in Canada and at Downing Street is a whole chapter in itself. But it will be conceded that all these, with Tilley's "fair share of the needful" thrown in, would have been powerless to carry New Brunswick and Nova Scotia into Confederation had the Colonial Office been hostile or neutral and allowed Gordon, an avowed enemy of federation, a free hand to support his constitutional advisers after the election of 1865. Here, it would seem, is the central problem of Confederation. How is one to account for the violent reversal of British policy during those critical weeks of November 1864?

My thesis is that the relations with the United States loom larger and larger with every chapter of research into these eventful months. There has been no attempt to trace these relations here; and, indeed, they form no pleasant theme for this generation. The *Trent* affair, the exploits of the *Alabama*, the *Chesapeake* affair, the St. Alban's raid, Seward's passport system, the projected abrogation of the Reciprocity Treaty and of the Rush-Bagot convention, the strained diplomatic relations intensified by the impending triumph of the North, and finally the Fenian raids upon the New Brunswick and Canadian borders, all suffused the issue with new and portentous possibilities. Macdonald surmises that had it not been for the problem of the defence of Canada, Great Britain, like France, would have recognized the Southern Confederacy. The deluge of despatches, commissions, and reports on the problem of defence dwarfs almost every other issue in the *G Series*. Military missions to the Maritime Provinces and to Canada magnified the menace without removing it. Men like Brown and Galt and Lord Lyons and Earl Russell himself never doubted the solid goodwill and magnanimity of Abraham Lincoln, but once the Canadian coalition had committed itself to Confederation, the drumbeat of American relations was never allowed to pass into silence. The speeches of Whelan and McGee ring the changes upon this theme. The Fenian raids synchronize with the most critical stages of the movement. During the decisive election of June 1866 in New Brunswick, Gordon, who conceded that the reports were "very much got up for election purposes," replaced the militia at the border by regulars in order that the "Volunteer Battalion should be at St. John during election. Nearly all are voters and a majority favourable."[40] In Canada the departure of the Canadian delegates and of the governor-general himself for the final conference in London was delayed by local panics with regard to the Fenians.[41]

## VI

It is well to remember that subtler motives and broader issues were involved than the defence of the international boundary. How far was it possible to carry through the policy of "calling home the legions," of devolving upon a British American federation the responsibility not only for defence but for internal development and for expansion westward to the Pacific?

Throughout the discussion of federation, however, the problem of defence in a more concrete and practical form is traceable like a red thread in British policy. From the defeat of the Militia Bill in 1862 to the summer of 1864, the issue is marked by mutual concern and, it may be added, by mutual misunderstanding. The relations with Great Britain during those critical years – the scathing comments of the British press and the repercussion of bitterness and resentment in Canada – can scarcely now be reconstructed even in imagination. A month before the Charlottetown conference a confidential report by Colonel Jervois reached Canada with the stringent comment from the Colonial Office that "her defence must ever principally depend upon the spirit, the energy and courage of her own People."[42] Unknown as yet to Cardwell, the Canadian coalition had put its hand to the plough, and the official Canadian attitude towards defence changed almost overnight. The British attitude towards Canada changed with it. A week after Monck's first despatch on the Quebec resolutions he reviewed the altered prospects for defence. "Should the Union take place," he wrote to Cardwell, "those who are likely to compose its Executive will be animated by the strongest desire to meet the views of Her Majesty's Ministers." As proof of good faith, the Canadian government was already prepared to spend a million dollars on militia and to fortify Montreal. "This is the first instance," he added, "in which a colony has offered at its own expense to erect permanent defensive works."[43]

There can be no doubt that Monck's despatches and particularly his private letters had a profound influence at the Colonial Office. From August 1864, when Cardwell first discovered the existence of the Canadian project, to December 3, when he gave it his official support, this correspondence was the chief, if not the only, official avenue of approach to British policy. Late in November the despatches were printed confidentially for use in London. With Monck was now associated also the apostolic ardour of George Brown. It is clear from the correspondence of both men that no direct personal influence had outweighed the governor-general's in bringing Brown into the coalition of 1864. No name in Canada was now more admirably calculated to repair the unfortunate impression left in Great Britain by the Sandfield Macdonald-Sicotte policy of defence. Brown's lone mission to London late in November 1864 was a tactical move of the first importance. Brown himself afterwards reported that the scheme gave "prodigious satisfaction." "The Ministry, the Conservatives and the Manchester men are all delighted with it and everything Canadian has gone up in public estimation immensely." Both Lord Monck and George Brown, it is safe to say, have yet to be accorded the place to which they are entitled in the creation of the new Dominion.

Among the motives of the Colonial Office in approving the result of the Quebec conference, Cardwell himself gives first place to the fact that "it was eminently calculated to render easier and more effectual the provisions for the defence of the several Provinces."[44] The resourcefulness of the Canadian delegates to London after the adverse election of March 1865 in New Brunswick thus met with an immediate response. Defence was now perhaps the burden of their mission. The arguments plied at the Colonial Office are to be found in Galt's memoranda in the *Macdonald Papers*. "Believing that the Defence of the Country was most intimately connected with the Union," Cartier suggested that "the Imperial Government who were charged with the responsibility ... might properly exercise a very great influence thro' a decided expression of their views." In reply Cardwell pledged the British government anew "to use every proper means of influence to carry into effect without delay the proposed Confederation."[45] In truth British policy, as I have already suggested, required no such stimulus. In a despatch to Gordon a fortnight before the arrival of the Canadian delegates, we have Cardwell's first impressions of the New Brunswick elections. For the benefit of Gordon's "new Advisers" he pointed out "the intimate connection ... between the numbers of the population and the measures proper to be taken for the defence of the Province." "It will only be right," he added, "for New Brunswick to bear in mind" that as a separate province it could "make no adequate provision for its own defence" and would therefore "rest in a very great degree upon the defence which may be provided for it by this Country. It will, consequently, be likely to appear to your Advisers reasonable and wise that, in examining the question of the proposed Union, they should attach great weight to the views and wishes of this Country ... and to the reasons on which those views have been based."[46]

A few days after the departure of the Canadian delegates Cardwell repeated in its final form the "strong and deliberate opinion" of the British government. He wrote to Gordon:

> There is one consideration which Her Majesty's Government feel it more especially their duty to press upon the Legislature of New Brunswick. Looking to the determination which this Country has ever exhibited to regard the defence of the Colonies as a matter of Imperial concern, – the Colonies must recognize a right and even acknowledge an obligation incumbent on the Home Government to urge with earnestness and just authority the measures which they consider to be most expedient on the part of the Colonies with a view to their own defence.[47]

The reply of the New Brunswick cabinet to this exhortation was perhaps the most spirited and incisive rejoinder of the entire controversy.[48] But the patient insistence of the Colonial Office was not to be denied. The reception which awaited Smith, the new prime minister of New Brunswick, and J.C. Allen, the attorney-general, in their anti-confederate mission to the Colonial Office a few weeks later can easily be surmised, and it is fair to conclude from Gordon's confidential despatches that both were fairly committed to the cause of union. Upon Gordon himself and Lieutenant-Governor MacDonnell of Nova Scotia the pressure was less complaisant. The Canadian delegates in April 1865 (charged, we now know, by Tilley and Tupper) had suggested bluntly to Cardwell that "the action of the Lieut.-Governors both of Nova Scotia and New Brunswick had been calculated to defeat the measure." Both Gordon and MacDonnell found themselves on leave of absence in London in the autumn of 1865. It would seem to be unnecessary to trace the influence of the Colonial Office through to the final conference in London. Galt's forecast in 1865 was warranted by the facts. "A decided expression" of British policy would have "a most marked effect on the loyal and high-spirited people of the Maritime Provinces" in favour of "a plan which will assure to them the continuance of the British connection."

## VII

The elements of fortune in the Canadian Confederation were so numerous that it would be impossible here to appraise them in detail; but two or three major factors may be distinguished (in the words of Galt and Cartier in 1865) as "an extraordinary and happy combination of circumstances."

From the *Confederation Debates* it would appear that Macdonald regarded the Charlottetown conference as the turn of fortune. "If it had not been for this fortunate coincidence of events, never, perhaps, for a long series of years would we have been able to bring this scheme to a practical conclusion."

To others, more familiar with the cause of Maritime union, a more dynamic element of chance was the local deadlock in Canada which the coalition of 1864 was pledged by solemn resolution to dissolve: "For the final settlement of sectional difficulties," they agreed, "the remedy must be sought in the federal principle." The view that federation was thus the by-product of "local exigencies" in Canada was explored unsparingly by the opponents of the measure in New Brunswick. Here, they said, was "the motive and groundwork of the scheme." "Federal Union was only sought as a means of separating the Canadas," and "the eagerness with which they seek to force its immediate adoption upon unwilling communities" was due to the fact that the alternative could not be represented "even speciously ... to the Imperial Government as in any manner a scheme of Union."[49] Without subscribing to these sardonic comments, it may be assumed, I think, that the deadlock in Canada was the mainspring of the federal movement. Without it the clock would almost certainly have run down. Without it, assuredly, the clock, for that decade at least, would never have been wound up.

But next to the *impasse* in Canada, the American Civil War, I am inclined to think, was the greatest fortuitous agency for the federation of the British provinces. There were other factors innumerable. The rescue of the West from annexation to the United States was never far removed from Brown's resolute mind. Beyond a doubt the sudden alacrity of the Canadian coalition for an intercolonial railway had a far-reaching effect upon Maritime opinion, while Watkin, Brydges, and "big business" had their share of influence, both there and in London. The decisive factors, however, belong to another order. The abandonment of Maritime union, the inordinate haste towards a general federation, the domination of

Gordon and MacDonnell by the Colonial Office, the concerted plan for the use of "every proper means," as pledged by Cardwell, "to carry into effect without delay the proposed Confederation," the ominous omission of the adjective by Galt and Monck himself when the time came to use "means" in New Brunswick, all reflect a more sudden and urgent motive. Relations with the United States supplied the temperature and the pressure which enabled the experts who presided over the process to bring the most sluggish reagents at last into reaction.

Once that reaction had taken place, the removal of pressure and temperature left a stable political compound, perhaps the strongest government, from the federal point of view, in the modern world. The federal powers in the Canadian constitution, by comparison with the provincial or state powers, are stronger than in the United States, or Brazil, or Australia – a virtue which was due in no small measure to the discerning policy of Canadian statesmen at a time when the issues of state sovereignty were being decided by two millions of men in arms across the border. The bearing of this phase of United States precedent upon the Canadian federation, however, is a theme in itself. One is justified, at any rate, in regarding the American Civil War as one of the profoundest influences in Canadian history, and there may be an element of ironic truth in the reflection that even the Fenian brotherhood is entitled to unsuspected credit in the federation of British North America.

NOTES

1 Chester Martin, "British Policy in Canadian Confederation," *Canadian Historical Review,* 13, 1 (1932), 3–19.
2 Chester Martin, "Sir Edmund Head's First Project of Federation, 1851" (Canadian Historical Association, *Report,* 1928, 14–26).
3 Chester Martin, "Sir Edmund Head and Canadian Confederation, 1851–1858" (Canadian Historical Association, *Report,* 1929, 5–14).
4 Public Archives of Canada, *Series G,* vol. 206, "Private and confidential," September 3, 1856.
5 *Confidential Drafts,* 1856–1866, March 2, 1856.
6 Public Archives of Canada, *Series G,* vol. 180B, no. 45, Head to Newcastle, "Confidential," December 1, 1859.
7 Public Archives of Canada, *C.O. 188,* vol. 132, Minute on Manners Sutton's despatch to Newcastle, "Private and confidential," September 29, 1859.

For the loss of Head's memorandum see the minutes on Head's despatch of February 9, 1860, Public Record Office, London, *C.O. 42*, vol. 622.

8 Public Archives of Canada, *C.O. 217*, vol. 226, Mulgrave to Newcastle, "Confidential," March 1, 1860. The chief arguments may be summarized as follows: the numbers in the legislatures were so small that "the weight of each individual vote, obtains an undue influence" (p. 37); there were not in each party "a sufficient number of men of talent and position" to form a strong and homogeneous government, while "party spirit and animosity ran to a height utterly unknown in England"; the chief justice of Nova Scotia, Sir Brenton Halliburton, was eighty-six years of age and "it is a fact beyond dispute" that the feud between the parties led by Mr. Young and Mr. Johnston was due chiefly to "the anxiety of these two gentlemen to succeed to the Chief Justiceship," and the "fear that this prize might be gained or lost by a few weeks delay" in retaining or regaining office; corrupt practices were in the ascendant and men were frequently "forced on by pecuniary necessity"; union would provide better rewards for legitimate ambition, a broader field and a higher level for public life, marked economies in administration, a "stimulus to industry and trade" and a prospect of public enterprise quite beyond the resources of the divided provinces.

9 "I cannot help feeling," he added, "especially if things are left in their present state, that the question of a Union with Canada will be pressed, and perhaps ultimately carried."

10 *C.O. 188*, vol. 134.

11 *Ibid.*, vol. 41, November 5, 1861.

12 Public Archives of Canada, *Macdonald Papers*, Galt to Macdonald, December 14, 1859.

13 *C.O. 217*, vol. 230.

14 A shrewd commentary, as we shall see.

15 In the reply to Musgrave was outlined for the first time the official procedure by which union was to be, and was in fact eventually, effected – by resolution or address from the several provinces and by consultation with the Colonial Office.

16 Public Archives of Canada, *C.O. 189*, 8, vol. 1, p. 358, Gordon to Monck, October 7, 1863.

17 *C.O. 188*, vol. 43.

18 *C.O. 189*, 8, vol. 1, p. 342, "Most confidential," August 29, 1863.

19 *Ibid.*, p. 354, Gordon to Newcastle, "Most confidential," September 25, 1863.

20 *C.O. 188*, vol. 43, "Confidential," October 23, 1863.

21 *C.O. 189,* 8, vol. 1, p. 413, Gordon to Newcastle, December 7, 1863.
22 Chiefly over the "land question" which was not solved until Prince Edward Island entered Confederation in 1873.
23 *C.O. 189,* 9, vol. 2, p. 1, Gordon to Cardwell, September 12, 1864.
24 *Ibid.*: "The ultimate concurrence of that Island was a matter of certainty and in the meantime a temporary delay on its part would have inflicted no real inconvenience on the two chief Maritime Provinces in the event of their Union."
25 *Series G,* vol. 465, p. 125, Monck to Cardwell, June 30, 1864.
26 *C.O. 189,* 9, vol. 2, p. 1, Gordon to Cardwell, September 12, 1864.
27 *C.O. 189,* 9, vol. 2, p. 1; *Series G,* vol. 172, August 13, 1864; *ibid.,* vol. 465, p. 145.
28 Public Record Office, London, *C.O. 217,* vol. 234, Cardwell to MacDonnell, August 9, 1864.
29 *Macdonald Papers,* VI, 83, Tilley to Galt, n.d; *C.O. 189,* 9, vol. 2, p. 71.
30 *Ibid.,* p. 107.
31 The first attempt in print to examine this evidence is Professor George E. Wilson's stimulating article, "New Brunswick's Entrance into Confederation" (*Canadian Historical Review,* March, 1928, 4).
32 *Macdonald Papers,* VI, 133, September 13, 1865.
33 *Ibid.,* 162.
34 *Ibid.,* to Gray of P.E.I., March 24, 1865, "Private."
35 *C.O. 189,* 9, vol. 2, p. 292, "Confidential," April 23, 1866.
36 April 17, 1866.
37 *Macdonald Papers,* VI, Tupper to Macdonald, April 9, 1865.
38 *Series G,* vol. 174, Cardwell to Monck, July 29, 1865, enclosures.
39 Though he was quite prepared to welcome the coercion of Howe: "I wish Lord Monck would write to Earl Russell to choke him off." Howe was then commissioner of fisheries under the Foreign Office.
40 Public Archives of Canada, *Series C,* vol. 1672, Gordon to Doyle, in cypher, May 25, 1866.
41 See C.P. Stacey, "Fenianism and the Rise of National Feeling in Canada at the Time of Confederation" (*Canadian Historical Review,* September 1931, 238).
42 *Series G,* vol. 172, p. 205, Cardwell to Monck, "Confidential," August 6, 1864.
43 *Ibid.,* 180B, no. 61.
44 *C.O. 188,* vol. 45, Cardwell to Gordon, April 12, 1865.
45 *Series G,* vol. 174, p. 54, Official memorandum of conference in Cardwell to Monck, June 17, 1865.

46 *C.O. 188*, vol. 45, Cardwell to Gordon, April 12, 1865.

47 *Ibid.*, June 24, 1865.

48 Not even excepting the philippics of Howe in Nova Scotia. Public Archives of Canada, *C.O. 189*, 9, vol. 2, p. 183, Minute of executive council enclosed in Gordon to Cardwell, July 15, 1865.

49 *Ibid.*, p. 185, Minute of executive council, July 12, 1865.

# "Britain's Withdrawal from North America, 1864–1871"

*Canadian Historical Review*
1955

C.P. STACEY[1]

One of the most familiar vices of historians is their inveterate tendency to compart history. We partition it off chronologically, chopping it into neat periods. Thus the student who is being taught about the fifteenth century is only too likely to get the impression that at some date during that century a new heaven and a new earth suddenly came into being. The date varies according to the particular course to which the student is being subjected at the moment: it may be 1453, or 1485, or 1492, or 1494. That sort of thing is probably in some degree inevitable. More serious is our tendency to compart by topics. A person who writes a textbook – or even a book – on a period of modern British history is almost certain to divide it into topical chapters or groups of chapters. Thus a long chapter, "Domestic Problems," is usually followed by a rather shorter one, "The Ebb and Flow of Foreign Policy." Next comes a still shorter chapter, "Colonial Policies and Problems." Finally, the book almost invariably ends with a chapter called "Intellectual Currents."

The weakness of this kind of approach is most evident in cooperative works where the chapters are written by different hands, but even where the book is the work of one author there is a tendency for the division between the chapters to become absolute. The reader forgets that the men sitting around the table in Downing Street and controlling events (or trying to) were dealing simultaneously with all departments of policy, domestic, colonial and foreign, to say nothing of the fact that they were doubtless swayed by intellectual currents.

The same tendency to compart appears in more specialized fields, and here I come to my theme. Students of British foreign policy in the mid-Victorian era are familiar with the difficulties which resulted from Bismarck's wars; they are also acquainted with the fact that the same period witnessed a prolonged and severe crisis in Anglo-American relations (though it must be said that scholars in the United Kingdom have usually been less interested in this than in the continental developments). It is rather extraordinary, however, that so few students on either side of the Atlantic should have noted the extent to which these two aspects of British policy were practically interconnected. The same statesmen who dealt with Prince Bismarck and Napoleon III had to deal with President Lincoln and President Grant; and it was this fact that was basically responsible for the ineffectiveness of British policy in both hemispheres. Historians have rightly recognized that it was military weakness that paralysed the action of the United Kingdom in Europe;[2] they have failed to point out that that weakness was the more serious in that British statesmen had to face the fact that if compelled to fight in Europe they would quite probably find themselves fighting the United States in North America at the same time. The British Army in the years dealt with in this paper was an inadequate instrument to deal with either of these emergencies singly; it was monstrously inadequate to deal with a war on two fronts, one on each side of the Atlantic. British policy has rarely if ever been faced with a more unpleasant dilemma. It was painfully evident to contemporaries, and it is really surprising how completely it has escaped the authors of such valuable and scholarly works as the *Cambridge History of British Foreign Policy.* Comparing that history published soon after the First World War with earlier British writings in the same field, one applauds the increased (though still inadequate) attention given to relations with the United States; but one remains impressed by the failure to observe the effects in Whitehall of the interaction of events in America and events in Europe.[3]

Such interaction was not, of course, entirely a new thing in the 1860's. It had appeared half a century before, during the Congress of Vienna, when British statesmen confronting Prussia and Russia found it embarrassing that their best troops should be fighting in America, and hastened to make peace with the United States so Britain's hands might be freed for more important matters.[4] In those days the United States was weak. Britain had in fact fought the French and the Americans simultaneously for three years without incurring fatal results. But half a century worked great changes. It is true that as late as 1861, when the *Trent* affair brought war between Britain and the United States very close, some Englishmen were still able to view the prospect with comparative equanimity. Lord Palmerston's Secretary of State for War, in the midst of hurrying off reinforcements to Canada, observed, "We shall soon *iron the smile* out of their face."[5] The United States had just been disrupted by civil war; the breathless withdrawal of the Northern army from the field of Bull Run was fresh in the public mind; and for the moment Europe was comparatively quiet.

During the next three years the whole scene was transformed. The Southern Confederacy's early hopes of victory and independence were not realized. The Northern States became the greatest military power on earth, and their hostility to Britain was as evident as their strength. At the same time new and terrible forces were on the march in Europe. Bismarck had become Minister-President of Prussia in 1862 and had set about strengthening the army, in defiance of Parliament, and preparing for those trials of strength with Austria and France that were necessary preliminaries to unifying Germany under Prussian leadership. Britain's first real embarrassment came early in 1864, when Prussia and Austria attacked Denmark over Schleswig-Holstein. Palmerston had made the mistake of saying loudly that aggressors would find that "it will not be Denmark alone with whom they will have to contend." But the German monarchies were quite unmoved by such threats.[6]

At the same time the British Government discovered that nearly 15,000 of its regular troops were in British North America and that this would add greatly to the difficulty of collecting any kind of expeditionary force for Denmark. Orders were accordingly issued to reduce the force in Canada. What alarmed Canadians most was a proposal that the troops remaining in their country should be concentrated entirely at Quebec and Montreal, leaving Upper Canada without a British soldier.[7] This clearly reflected the British Government's new and solid respect for American military power; and in the course of the next few months editorials in *The Times* and debates in Parliament testified to the extent to which the scorn and bluster with which so many Englishmen had regarded the Northern forces and the Northern cause had now changed to apprehension and dismay.[8] The British governing class never appeared to worse advantage than in its attitude to the Civil War in the

United States; and there is a certain poetic justice in the fact that that war did so much to advance the cause of political democracy in Britain and the transfer of power to other hands.

The Cabinet's position with respect to North America at this period was extremely difficult. No administration headed by Palmerston was likely to adopt a policy of scuttle, even when so many voices were raised in favour of it. The Government in fact steered a middle course. It refused to have anything to do with the ideas of Little Englanders like Robert Lowe, who urged that every Imperial soldier should be withdrawn from Canada at once; and on the other hand it argued that Canada's defence must rest "mainly and principally upon Canada herself."[9] The determination to maintain the Imperial military connection with Canada was strikingly symbolized by the decision taken at the beginning of 1865 to set about strengthening the fortress of Quebec at British expense. It was significant, however, that this decision was fiercely contested at the Cabinet table by the Chancellor of the Exchequer, W.E. Gladstone.[10]

The other aspect of the Government's policy was expressed mainly by the Colonial Secretary, Edward Cardwell. It appears very strikingly in the ministry's attitude towards the Canadian political developments of 1864. Back in 1858 the Colonial Office had been more hostile than friendly when dispatches arrived from Canada suggesting the possible desirability of a federal union of British North America.[11] Things were different now. When the Quebec Conference's resolutions reached London, Cardwell was almost comically eager to embrace the scheme. On November 26, 1864, he wrote the Lieutenant-Governor of New Brunswick that the resolutions had been circulated to the Cabinet only the night before, and it "would, of course, be premature for me to anticipate their decision." Then he proceeded:

> But I think I may safely assure you that they are one and all most anxious to promote the end in view, that they will allow no obstacles to prevent it, if those obstacles can be surmounted: and that if there are provisions which they do not entirely approve, they will be very slow to consider those provisions as rising to the magnitude of insurmountable obstacles.
>
> I fully expect that I shall soon have to instruct you in their name to promote the scheme of the Delegates to the utmost of your power.[12]

This forecast proved accurate. One week later Cardwell wrote officially, warmly approving the Quebec scheme.[13]

From this moment the Imperial Government steadily supported the federation plan. And there is little doubt that the chief reason for this was the scheme's obvious military importance. In the spring of 1865 a Canadian delegation went to London to discuss the defence of the country with the British Government. One result was a formal exchange of assurances of the two governments' determination to devote all their resources, if need be, to maintain the connection between Britain and Canada. Another was the mobilization of the fullest degree of Imperial influence to ensure the victory of the confederate cause in the Maritime Provinces. In a dispatch sent to the Maritime governors in June, 1865, Cardwell instructed them to inform their legislatures that it was "the strong and deliberate opinion of Her Majesty's Government" that it was desirable that all the British North American colonies should "unite in one Government." The paramount argument employed was that of defence. Cardwell wrote,

> Looking to the determination which this country has ever exhibited to regard the defence of the Colonies as a matter of Imperial concern, the Colonies must recognize a right and even acknowledge an obligation incumbent upon the Home Government to urge with earnestness and just authority the measures which they consider to be most expedient on the part of the Colonies with a view to their own defence. Nor can it be doubtful that the Provinces of British North America are incapable, when separated and divided from each other, of making those just and sufficient preparations for national defence, which would be easily undertaken by a Province uniting in itself all the population and all the resources of the whole.[14]

In October 1865, Palmerston died. Lord Russell carried on the government until the following summer, when a Conservative ministry headed by Lord Derby came into office. During these months the British ministers watched with alarm as Bismarck manipulated the Schleswig-Holstein question to produce the war he wanted with Austria. But they had learned their humiliating lesson, and there was no more loose talk of intervention. Russell's Foreign Secretary, Lord Clarendon, wrote to the Queen, "We have spoken in defence of right; we cannot actively interfere with those who are quarrelling over the spoils; and in the present state of Ireland, and the menacing aspect of our relations with the United States, the military and pecuniary resources of England must be husbanded with the utmost care."[15] Three days after the formation of

Derby's Government the Prussian Army humbled Austria at Sadowa, displaying in the process an efficiency which Englishmen found both unfamiliar and alarming. As a result, Army reform suddenly became an important political issue.

The Government could draw some comfort, it is true, from the fact that in America the Civil War had ended, the Union Army had been largely disbanded, and the wanton attack on Canada which had been feared when fighting ended in the South had not eventuated. But on the other hand the Fenians were enjoying their heyday; they mounted a large-scale operation in 1866. The Canadian Government begged for help from England, and England sent a very considerable regular reinforcement. It was the last time such a thing was to happen. The action taken was not popular with Derby's chief lieutenant, Disraeli; it was at this moment that he wrote to the Prime Minister, "What is the use of these colonial deadweights which *we do not govern*?"[16]

In 1867 the Dominion of Canada duly came into being. The London *Times'* comment on the event was severely practical: "We look to Confederation as the means of relieving this country from much expense and much embarrassment.... We appreciate the goodwill of the Canadians and their desire to maintain their relations with the British Crown. But a people of four millions ought to be able to keep up their own defences."[17] Nevertheless, in the first instance Confederation brought no relief to Britain's strained "military and pecuniary resources." In all the circumstances of the time, it is perhaps not surprising that some Englishmen found themselves regretting that the British Empire had a North American frontier. Early in 1867 Derby's son and Foreign Secretary, Lord Stanley, wrote to the British Minister in Washington, who had suggested the possibility of giving British North America representation in the House of Commons at Westminster, that he had once held the idea himself: "But I have never found it take in this Country. Many people would dislike the long boundary line with the United States (they look now to an early separation of Canada)...."[18] A few weeks later Stanley, fresh from putting a stop to the dangerous idea of calling the new political entity the Kingdom of Canada, wrote to Sir Frederick Bruce again: "There is no idea of a new monarchy, and that may as well be explained. The Colonies will remain Colonies, only confederated for the sake of convenience. If they choose to separate, we on this side shall not object: it is they who protest against the idea. In England separation would be generally popular."[19]

Late in 1868, a general election put the Conservatives out and brought in a Liberal ministry, headed by Gladstone, with a large majority behind it. The Continental situation remained uncertain. The Army remained unreformed; a proper Reserve could not be organized without an increased supply of recruits, and recruiting would not improve as long as British soldiers spent most of their lives abroad. For some twenty years successive British governments had been striving to reduce the colonial garrisons; but not much had been accomplished. Above all, the *Alabama* question remained unsettled, the Fenians were still active, and therefore Anglo-American relations were in a constant state of crisis.

Almost the first act of the new ministry was an attempt at settlement with the United States. Following a line already charted by the Conservatives, they signed the Johnson-Clarendon Convention in January, 1869. It was a disastrous failure. The Convention was thrown out by the United States Senate by a vote of 54 to 1 after a speech by Charles Sumner which seemed to estimate the amount of the *Alabama* claims at half the total cost of the Civil War. When this news reached London, Lord Clarendon wrote grimly, "I believe that Grant and Sumner mean war; or rather that amount of insult and humiliation that must lead to it."[20]

For the Gladstone Cabinet's appreciation of the situation that now confronted it there is considerable evidence. The essence of it was the fact that as long as things in North America did not improve, British policy in Europe would be hamstrung. In the spring of 1869 the Foreign Secretary was writing to the Queen of the dangers latent in the treaties concerning Belgium and Portugal to which Britain was a party. "It seems to be the duty of your Majesty's Government to bear in mind how widely different are the circumstances of this country now to when those Treaties were concluded, and that, if their execution were to lead us into war in Europe, we should find ourselves immediately called upon to defend Canada from American invasion and our commerce from American privateers."[21] This was before the news of Sumner's speech arrived. When it came, Clarendon wrote to the Queen again: "It is the unfriendly state of our relations with America that to a great extent paralyses our action in Europe. There is not the smallest doubt that if we were engaged in a Continental quarrel we should immediately find ourselves at war with the United States."[22] These views were not confined to Clarendon. His successor at the Foreign Office, Lord Granville, wrote to John Bright when Bright resigned from the government:

> Your guidance would have been invaluable as regards the United States. I can conceive no greater object than to put our relations on a satisfactory footing with them. Our present position cripples us in every way. Not only would it do so if we wished for war, but it impedes our pacific efforts, making people attribute to fear that which is prompted by a sense of duty.[23]

The First Lord of the Admiralty had already suggested to Granville, when there seemed to be danger of a war with Russia over the Black Sea, that it was "very important" to get the differences with the United States out of the way: "Otherwise there can be little doubt that, however unprepared they may be just now, sooner or later we shall have them on our hands."[24]

What remedy could the Government provide? One obvious procedure was to liquidate the quarrel with the States at any cost which the British taxpayer could be made to swallow. In point of fact this was ultimately done, and historians would be well advised not to forget the European situation in interpreting British policy in connection with the Treaty of Washington and the Geneva Arbitration. But in 1869 the Americans had struck aside the hand that Britain offered, and it would be two years before real negotiation would again be practicable.

There was however another possibility. That was to get out of North America. At the beginning of 1869 Great Britain was still deeply involved in this continent, and the symbol of this investment was the 12,000 British regular troops stationed in Canada and Newfoundland.[25] There is ample evidence that many influential Englishmen considered these troops "hostages … for British good behavior"[26] and an incitement to the Americans to make war. It was obvious that merely to get them home would be an advantage to the security of the United Kingdom; it would be doubly so if their removal from Canada made conflict with the United States less likely. And the fact that, with the mother country's encouragement, a new political unit capable of assuming national responsibilities had now been created in British North America, gave such a policy more than a colour of justification.

There is no doubt that some members of Gladstone's Government would have welcomed a complete severance of the ties with Canada. However, they found themselves faced with an obstacle – that rather inconvenient Canadian loyalty which Lord Stanley had noted. In a crisis, this loyalty would probably have found considerable support in the British House of Commons. But the separatists were influential, and the high point of their activity was reached in the gloomy days after the rejection of the Johnson-Clarendon Convention. For many years British public men had been in the habit of referring to the relation between Britain and the colonies in terms which suggested that it was a temporary arrangement. Now this idea appeared in an official Colonial Office dispatch. On June 16, 1869, Lord Granville wrote confidentially to the Governor General of Canada, saying that the Imperial Government had no desire to maintain the connection "a single year" after it became "injurious or distasteful" to Canada, and concluding with an order: "You will ... be good enough to bring to my notice any line of policy or any measures which without implying on the part of Her Majesty's Government any wish to change abruptly our relations, would gradually prepare both Countries for a friendly relaxation of them."[27]

On their own side Granville and his colleagues were slackening off the painter. Cardwell, now Secretary of State for War, was actively setting about the reform of the Army; and he had explained to Gladstone on undertaking the task, "The with-drawal of Troops from distant Stations is at the bottom of the whole question of Army Reform...."[28] In the spring of 1869 Canada was told that her garrison, apart from the troops at Halifax, was to be reduced to about 4,000 men, and it was indicated that even this force was not to remain long.[29]

At this moment the British Cabinet was faced with a fundamental decision, summed up by Granville in a private letter to Cardwell thus: "... the practical question is whether Quebec is to be considered an Imperial or a Colonial Fortress."[30] Although the British Government had been striving for years to reduce its force in Canada, it had never before been seriously suggested that Imperial troops would cease to garrison Quebec. In 1863 the Defence Committee had reported on the strategic importance of the fortress in these terms: "Since Quebec is the place through which all succours from Great Britain to Canada must pass, it is obviously necessary that this fortress should be maintained in the most efficient and secure condition. If it fell into the hands of an enemy, the military communication between the province and the mother country would be cut off. The Committee are therefore of opinion that Quebec should be kept up as a first class fortress...."[31] This was the thinking that led Palmerston and his Cabinet to override their colleague Gladstone and undertake improvements in the fortress in 1865. By 1869 a great new fortified bridgehead had appeared on the south shore of the St. Lawrence opposite Quebec; but now Gladstone was Prime Minister and a different spirit ruled in Whitehall. It is evident that in April 1869,

Granville and Cardwell brought the question of the status of Quebec before the Cabinet.[32] I have been unable to find any definite record of the discussion or the decision; but it seems likely that the Cabinet decided at this time that Quebec was no longer to be an Imperial fortress, though it would appear that no final moment for withdrawal was fixed.

The Government's determination not to be turned from its course was demonstrated after the news of Sumner's speech arrived. Although, as we have seen, members of the Cabinet felt that it might be a sign of coming war, it caused no change in the plans for withdrawing troops from Canada. In the Cardwell papers there is what is evidently a note passed by Cardwell to Gladstone in the House of Commons in connection with a question on this point. It remarks that he proposes to reply simply that the orders were being executed, and it was not intended to countermand them. Gladstone's minute on the paper reads, "By all means."[33] However, events in North America did complicate the later stages of the withdrawal. There was a Fenian raid in the spring of 1870, and at the same time the need arose for sending an expedition to Red River. The Imperial Government consented to allow its troops to take part in the Red River operation; but it did so only on very strict conditions, and particularly emphasized that the regulars should be absolutely certain of getting back to the East before the winter. It is worth recalling that the London *Times,* in commenting on the Imperial share in the Red River expedition, remarked, "The British Parliament is now called upon to intervene for the last time in the affairs of the American Continent."[34]

These events in Canada were overshadowed by contemporary happenings in Europe. In July 1870, war broke out between France and Prussia. In London there was great anxiety over an apparent threat to Belgium, and at the very outset of the struggle Gladstone asked Cardwell "to study the means of sending 20,000 men to Antwerp with as much promptitude as at the Trent affair we sent 10,000 to Canada."[35] The withdrawals from the colonies had allowed the Government to cut the cost of the British Army and reduce its over-all size while at the same time increasing the force in the United Kingdom. This happy situation now ended; 20,000 additional men were hastily voted for the Army, and the estimates leaped up in proportion.[36] In the minds of Englishmen the mistrust of France, which was so marked at the beginning of the war, changed, as the war progressed, to fear of Prussia. Lord Kimberley, the new Colonial Secretary, wrote to one of his colleagues in September 1870, "We are only at the end of the first act of the tragedy,

& we shall be fortunate if the next acts are not more gloomy & horrible still."[37] With the safety of Britain herself apparently in question, the urge to liquidate the country's responsibilities in North America was even stronger than before.

The day before the Battle of Sedan, Cardwell asked Kimberley whether the time had come to offer officially the transfer to Canada of the Citadel of Quebec. Although the Dominion had already been given an indication that the Imperial force would be withdrawn in 1871, Kimberley preferred not to pursue the question at that moment and it was shelved for a few months.[38] But it came up again in December 1870, by which time the British force in central Canada was down to a small remnant. Kimberley inclined to the view that it would do no harm to leave this force at Quebec, for the moment, as a concession to Canadian feeling; but Cardwell remarked, "A single Regiment & two Batteries at Quebec may be considered by the Cabinet a very awkward committal for the British Flag in case of rupture with the U. States."[39] It was agreed that the matter should go to the Cabinet for decision. Kimberley laid it before the Prime Minister in a letter and said he would "bring the matter forward at the next Cabinet."[40] No doubt he did, and it is evident that the decision was in favour of withdrawal. The Canadian Government tried hard to get the men in Whitehall to change their minds, but it was no use. In the autumn of 1871 the last British troops left Quebec, and thereafter the only British garrison in Canada was that of Halifax.[41] By this time the Treaty of Washington had made provision for settlement of the various issues between Britain and the United States. There was another period of serious anxiety early in 1872, and then the award of the Geneva Tribunal finally laid the *Alabama* claims to rest.

The departure of the 60th Rifles from the Citadel of Quebec on November 11, 1871, was a landmark in the foreign as well as the colonial policy of Britain. Eight years before, the highest military authorities in the Empire had declared that it was essential to maintain Quebec as an Imperial fortress. Six years before, the British Government had decided to renovate the defences at great expense. Now about a quarter of a million British pounds had been spent, the new forts were still not quite complete, and yet the Imperial troops departed. This somewhat peculiar train of events reflects the course of British policy in this troubled era.

Confronted simultaneously with menaces in both Europe and North America, a situation whose potentialities their military resources were quite unequal to coping with, Gladstone and his colleagues came, in effect if not in form, to a decision to abandon Britain's political and military responsibilities in America, to withdraw from this continent to the utmost possible extent, and to concentrate their country's power at home, where it would be available to deal with European foes. The adoption of this policy was facilitated by the fact that earlier British administrations had encouraged the federation of British North America. Palmerston seems to have thought in terms of the new Dominion sharing Britain's North American responsibilities. Gladstone's Cabinet thought in terms of *transferring* those responsibilities to Canada, so far as she was able and willing to assume them – but, whether Canada assumed them or not, Britain clearly intended to get rid of them.

It seems evident that there was never a specific or formal decision in favour of this policy of abdication and withdrawal. It was never quite fully avowed by those who seem to have been most devoted to it. In 1869 Granville wrote to Cardwell on the necessity of making an early decision on what to do about the troops remaining in Canada. "I do not think this will be difficult," he wrote. "What will be more so is the language to be held in debate about our future relations with the Dominion. I do not think it would be wise to be abrupt on the subject."[42] There was always some opposition, in Parliament and in the country, to Gladstonian colonial policies, and it is even possible that too forthright a declaration of the view which Granville represented might have produced opposition within the Cabinet.

Finally, it must be added that the policy of withdrawal was never complete. In 1870–71 Britain got out of the interior of North America, but she did not get out of Nova Scotia. The Halifax base was evidently considered on balance a military asset rather than a liability, and there the British troops remained until well into the twentieth century. Also the British Government never went so far as to declare that it would not defend Canada in case of war. On the contrary, the dispatch which early in 1870 announced the impending withdrawal of the troops took care to specify that the proposed arrangements "are contingent upon a time of peace, and are in no way intended to alter or diminish the obligations which exist on both sides in case of foreign war."[43] Those obligations could scarcely have been escaped without a formal separation; and however much some people might have welcomed this, Britain never got to the point of declaring herself independent of Canada. She did, however, effect, in the course of a few years, a complete revolution in her relations with North America. On one side, she settled, at heavy cost to herself and also to Canada, the issues outstanding between her and the United States, and thereby put an end to any immediate threat of an Anglo-American war. On the other, she suddenly withdrew from her traditional military responsibilities in the interior of this continent, thereby saving roughly a million pounds a year, facilitating the reform of her army, and materially strengthening her military position with respect to Europe. By 1872 it could almost be said that Great Britain had ceased to be a North American power; and it would seem that there were comparatively few Englishmen who regarded the change with any feeling except the deepest satisfaction.

NOTES

1 C.P. Stacey, "Britain's Withdrawal from North America, 1864–1871," *Canadian Historical Review*, 36, 3 (1955), 185–98. This paper was read before Section II of the Royal Society of Canada at the June meeting of 1955. In a book called *Canada and the British Army, 1846–1871*, published in 1936, the present writer ventured the remark, with respect to the Danish War, "The fashion in which, at this period, the uncertainty of the situation in America hampered Britain's action in Europe, and *vice versa*, has been too little studied" (p. 154, n. 5). In this paper he attempts to expand that suggestion.

2 See, e.g., Arthur Hassall, *The History of British Foreign Policy, from the Earliest Times to 1912* (Edinburgh and London, 1912), 281.

3 A.J.P. Taylor shows some awareness of the matter in *The Struggle for Mastery in Europe, 1848–1918* (Oxford, 1954); see pages 129 and 199. But he does not mention the *Alabama* question, indicate how serious was the problem confronting Gladstone's ministry in 1868–71, or describe the means adopted to deal with it.

4 A.T. Mahan, *Sea Power in Its Relations to the War of 1812* (2 vols., London, 1905), II, 423–34.

5 Lewis to Twisleton, Dec. 5, 1861: Sir G.F. Lewis, ed., *Letters of the Right Hon. Sir George Cornewall Lewis* (London, 1870), 406.

6 *Cambridge History of British Foreign Policy*, II, chap. XIII. *Schleswig-Holstein* ("Handbooks prepared under the Direction of the Historical Section of the Foreign Office," no. 35, London, 1920), 75 ff. Palmerston and Russell, in spite of the country's weakness, showed a tendency to persist in a warlike policy, but were restrained by their colleagues and by the Queen. It was at this time that the Queen described her two senior ministers as "those two dreadful old men" (to King Leopold, Feb. 25, 1864, G.E. Buckle, ed., *The Letters of Queen Victoria, Second Series*, I, 168).

7 *Canada and the British Army*, 154–60.
8 *Ibid.*, 171–3.
9 *Ibid.*, 173. The words quoted are Cardwell's. See Palmerston's report to the Queen, March 13, 1865, *Letters of Queen Victoria, Second Series*, I, 262–3.
10 *Canada and the British Army*, 171–2.
11 D.G.G. Kerr, *Sir Edmund Head: A Scholarly Governor* (Toronto, 1954), 194–200.
12 Public Record Office, London, 30/48, Cardwell Papers, Box 6/39 (Microfilms in Public Archives of Canada), Cardwell to Gordon, Nov. 26, 1864. The recent acquisition of these microfilms is due to the laudable initiative of the Dominion Archivist, Dr. W. Kaye Lamb.
13 Cardwell to Monck, Dec. 3, 1864, P.A.C., G 21, vol. 26.
14 *Papers Relating to the Conferences Which Have Taken Place between Her Majesty's Government and a Deputation from the Executive Council of Canada…* (Quebec, 1865), Cardwell to Lieut.-Governor of New Brunswick, June 24, 1865.
15 March 31, 1866, *Letters of Queen Victoria, Second Series*, I, 314–15.
16 *Canada and the British* Army, 191–4.
17 March 1, 1867.
18 P.A.C., Transcripts of Derby Papers from Knowsley Hall, Stanley to Bruce, Jan. 25, 1867.
19 *Ibid.*, Mar. 23, 1867.
20 Allan Nevins, *Hamilton Fish: The Inner History of the Grant Administration* (New York, 1936), 147–52. Sir Herbert Maxwell, *The Life and Letters of George William Frederick, Fourth Earl of Clarendon* (2 vols., London, 1913), II, 358, Clarendon to Lady Salisbury, May 9, 1869.
21 April 16, 1869, *Letters of Queen Victoria, Second Series*, I, 589–91.
22 May 1, 1869, *ibid.*, 594–5.
23 Nov. 21, 1870, Lord Edmond Fitzmaurice, *The Life of Granville George Leveson Gower, Second Earl Granville…* (2 vols., London, 1906), II, 28–9.
24 Spencer Childers, *The Life and Correspondence of the Right Hon. Hugh C.E. Childers, 1827–1896* (2 vols., London, 1901), I, 173–4, Childers to Granville, Nov. 19, 1870.
25 Parliamentary Papers, House of Commons, United Kingdom, 1870, no. 254, vol. XLII (12,014 all ranks on March 31, 1869).
26 *The Times*, March 29, 1867.
27 *Canada and the British* Army, 216.
28 Jan. 9, 1869, Cardwell Papers, Box 2/6.
29 *Canada and the British* Army, 214.
30 April 14, 1869, Cardwell Papers, Box 5/28.
31 Report of Jan. 8, 1863, *ibid.*, Box 6/40 (confidential print).
32 Correspondence in *ibid.*, Box 5/28.

33 March 13, 1869, Cardwell Papers, Box 2/6. Cf. *Canada and the British* Army, 213.

34 *Canada and the British Army*, 243.

35 Morley, *Life of Gladstone*, II, 339.

36 *Canada and the British* Army, 247–8. See Cardwell's speech in the House of Commons in introducing the Army Estimates, Feb. 16, 1871.

37 Kimberley to Cardwell, Sept. 7, 1870, Cardwell Papers, Box 5/31.

38 Cardwell to Kimberley, Aug. 31, 1870, Kimberley to Cardwell, Sept. 1, 1870, *ibid.*, *Canada and the British Army*, 226–7.

39 Cardwell to Kimberley, Dec. 6, 1870, Cardwell Papers, Box 5/31, and other letters in same box.

40 Kimberley to Gladstone, Dec. 9, 1870, *ibid.*

41 *Canada and the British Army*, 252–3.

42 Granville to Cardwell, Sept. 9, 1869, Cardwell Papers, Box 5/28.

43 *Canada and the British* Army, 226–7. Britain also retained the small naval station at Esquimalt in British Columbia, but there was no army garrison there at this period.

# The United States and Confederation

## Centennial Historical Booklet 1967

YVES ROBY[1]

"The situation which arose out of the Civil War in the United States neither created nor carried Confederation, but it resulted, through a sense of common danger, in bringing the British provinces together and in giving full play to all the forces that were making for their union."

In this paragraph the historian, Colquhoun, summarized the fundamental yet complex influence which the American Civil War exercised on the union of the colonies of British North America. The cumulative weight of not only the war itself but also its side-effects, the "Trent" affair, the frontier incidents, and the Fenian threat should not be underestimated. Without doubt these events stimulated colonial and imperial statesmen to search for a joint solution which would both correct the ills from which the colonies suffered and allow the Mother Country to pursue its policy of retrenchment.

### Failure of a Plan of Union

On August 16, 1858, Sir Edmund Head, Governor of Canada announced the intention of his government to discuss with the imperial authorities and those of the neighbouring colonies the possibility of a federal union. This project, however, met with failure.

In 1868 New Brunswick and Nova Scotia were hardly disposed to sacrifice their political independence. It is true that certain Maritime politicians wished to join Canada; others, notably the Governors Manners-Sutton and the Earl of Mulgrave, preferred a more restricted union of the colonies of the Atlantic. But both schemes were in conflict with local loyalties. Furthermore, many in the Maritimes felt that sufficient political links existed between the colonies by virtue of being part of the Empire. Consequently, the delegations which New Brunswick and Nova Scotia sent to London in 1858 to join the Canadian representatives were not at all interested in union. What concerned them was the construction of an intercolonial railway. They argued that such a railway would have to precede any kind of union with Canada.

London, too, was hardly enthusiastic about the project. It was not then concerned with the problems of defence. It knew that the Maritimes were against such a union. Thus in replying to the Canadian proposal the Colonial Secretary Newcastle stated that the imperial government would consider sympathetically all projects of union elaborated by the colonies, but that it refused to undertake any initiative. Newcastle also reserved the right to approve of a convention called together to discuss such schemes.

As a result of these unenthusiastic and negative responses, Canada abandoned its plan in 1860. Yet the tragic events which, from 1861 on, were to shake the American republic were to compel the colonies and the Mother Country to reconsider the future of British North America.

## The American Civil War and the "Trent" Incident

In 1860 Canadian-American relations, without being excellent, were at least cordial; the Reciprocity Treaty of 1854 had inaugurated a period of harmony between the United States and its neighbour to the north. Still, there were some discordant notes. The problem of San Juan Island was still not solved. American manufacturers of the north east were greatly dissatisfied with Galt's tariff, which they considered a violation of the spirit, if not the letter of the Reciprocity Treaty. On its side, Canada was alarmed at the widely held opinion in Washington that a foreign war would be useful in dampening the rivalry between North and South.

The beginning of hostilities at Fort Sumpter at 1861 opened an era of serious crises in Anglo-Northern relations. When Great Britain in 1861 proclaimed its neutrality in the conflict, it recognized in practice the belligerency of the Confederate states. The North, which was then undergoing grave internal difficulties and serious reversals on the fields of battle, became inflamed still more over the refusal of the imperial government and the colonies to see in its struggle a crusade for human liberty as well as a defence of the republican experiment. It regarded the proclamation of neutrality as a sign that the British intended to support the South. Until 1863, English diplomacy did much to feed this conviction. The result was a hardening posture of the North towards Great Britain and her colonies in America. The virulent tone and the annexionist aims of the press in New York and Boston reflected these hostile attitudes. This climate of opinion explains the orders of American Secretary of State Seward to the border states to fortify themselves against the eventuality of a foreign attack.

At the beginning of the conflict the Canadians, who were antislavery and anti-secessionist, were friendly towards the North. The honeymoon did not last long. The economic difficulties brought about by the Civil War, the fear of an American attack, kept alive by annexationist writings, the realization that the conflict had the aim of not abolishing slavery but only crushing the South and forcing it back into the union, rapidly undermined the pro-Northern sympathies of Canadians. Greater and greater numbers of those north of the frontier came to hope for a victory for the South. The successful resistance of the Confederate states appeared to them to be their strongest defence and the best guarantee of their independence. By autumn of 1861 public opinion on both sides of the frontier was so exacerbated that a serious incident could easily have resulted in a war.

On November 8, 1861, Captain Charles Wilkes of the S.S. "Jacinto" stopped the British mail packet, "Trent," and forcibly removed as contraband of war two Confederate agents, Murray Mason and James Slidell and their two secretaries, who were proceeding to London on a diplomatic mission.

Angered by this flouting of international laws, the imperial government demanded an apology and the immediate release of the four Confederates. Lincoln, however, did not release the prisoners until the 25th of December. During this interval of more than a month, Canada and the Maritimes realized with horror that they could certainly become the battlefield of any Anglo-Northern war and called up their militia. London too, in view of the crisis, announced its intention of defending its colonies with all the power of the Empire and dispatched fourteen thousand officers and men as reinforcements. On Christmas Day Lincoln, without making any apologies, freed the prisoners. The danger of war had been averted for the moment.

The crisis had not lasted long. But because of its intensity it had, in the long run, a considerable influence on the union of the British colonies. Confronted with the possibility of a war with the United States, British North America had demonstrated its attachment to the Empire and its willingness to fight for its independence.

Beyond doubt this desire to remain British was a necessary condition for union. Moreover, the "Trent" incident had revealed the precariousness of the system of communications between Canada and the Maritimes. It had become necessary to transport a part of British reinforcements by sleigh from St. John to Rivière-du-Loup. The Madawaska route, only practicable in the winter, ran along the American frontier and could be cut easily in case of conflict. The crisis had demonstrated the urgency of an intercolonial railway.

Although it had shown its firm intention of defending its colonies, the imperial government did not give up its policy of retrenchment. It wished the colonies, which had won responsible government, to assume as much of the heavy burden of their defence as possible.

Furthermore, the "Trent" incident induced London to look for means which would permit it to avoid the risk of a conflict in America in the future.

"The effect of the 'Trent' affair," wrote the historian Morton, "was to make British opinion determined, once it could be done without loss of prestige before the United States and on an honourable and decent basis with the colonies, to withdraw their garrisons from British America, always excepting the Naval base of Halifax. That honourable and decent basis, it was to become apparent in the next two years, was to be found in the federation of British America."

These preoccupations explained the interest which London now showed in the problems of colonial defence and the construction of the Intercolonial.

In April 1862, Newcastle sent a dispatch to the governors of the colonies suggesting a common system of defence, but Canada turned a deaf ear. As a matter of fact, a month later its legislature rejected a bill recommending an increase of expenditures on the militia. Many Canadians believed that the security of Canada lay in the victorious resistance of the Confederate states and not in a costly and elaborate program of defence. Others insisted that London assume a large part of the burden of colonial defence. To justify their point of view, they claimed that a war with United States would take place only within the framework of an Anglo-American war.

In July at a banquet in Montreal, Lord Monck categorically denounced the Canadian attitude. His criticism as well as that of the "Times" of London, reflected exactly the outlook of the imperial government on the question.

"The question," wrote the "Times," "is much simpler than Canadians think. If they are to be defended at all, they must make up their minds to bear the greater part of the burden of their own defence."

The "Trent" incident explained the renewal of interest which the imperial government showed in the construction of the Intercolonial. Until now, despite the repeated demands of the colonies, London had refused an imperial guarantee for a loan necessary for the construction of the railroad. Now in 1862, Newcastle, interested in the strategic value of the Intercolonial, was prepared to make a new offer. It was true that in this case as in that of colonial defence, the actions of London showed that it was not ready to take the initiative in favour of a political union of the colonies. All the same, under the influence of the "Trent" incident, the attitude of the imperial government towards such a development had become considerably more positive since the first evasive response to the Canadian proposal of 1858.

Still, the colonies, in 1862–1863, were not ready for union. Furthermore, the new government of Macdonald-Sicotte, in Canada, was reluctant to co-operate with the Maritime colonies, even in construction of an intercolonial railway, let alone changing the political framework. Domestic problems kept their attention. The fear of the United States, so vividly felt at the time of the "Trent" incident, faded away. In June 1862, the victorious defence of Lee against the army of the Potomac in the battle of Seven Days confirmed Canadians in their belief that the South could not be conquered by arms. In the absence of external pressures, would not a firm undertaking by the Canadian government to assume a large part of the financial burden of the Intercolonial risk the aggravation of internal dissensions in Canada and the loss of some of their support? Furthermore, their followers in Upper Canada believed that the American lines would remain open while those of Lower Canada did not have the same interest in winter ports.

The pre-occupation with domestic political problems as well as the lessening of this fear of the North explained the decision of the Canadian government not to undertake five-twelfths of the cost of Intercolonial as it had promised to do in 1862. Thus even intercolonial cooperation, desired by Newcastle as a preliminary for a union in 1862–1863, met with failure.

## Gettysburg, Vicksburg, and the "Chesapeake" Incident

In July 1863, Lee, the conquerer of the army of the Potomac at Fredericksburg, continued his offensive against the North. On the sixth, his army and that of General George E. Meade became locked in a furious and tragic battle at Gettysburg. At the end of the engagement, Lee was compelled to retreat to the south of the river Potomac. The emotion which the news of this event provoked in Canada and in the Maritimes illustrated clearly the importance that it took on in the eyes of the colonials. In the beginning, they refused to believe it or attempted to minimize the importance of it.

"The Yankee Press," wrote the Halifax *British Colonist,* "had such a monstrous talent for lying, that it would be gross folly to believe, in all its minutiae, anything which it publishes."

Nevertheless, the fear of a victory of the Union seized all those who up to now had believed in that the Confederate states were invincible. A few days later, the victory of General Ulysses S. Grant at Vicksburg, which split the South and opened the Mississippi to the armies of the North, added to their apprehension.

At first the colonial governments reacted only feebly to this new situation. Still, New Brunswick tripled the sum allotted to defence. And under the pressure of Governor Monck, Canada came around to believe that something should be done for the efficient defence of the country. Parliament voted measures reorganizing the militia, establishing military schools and raising the number of volunteers to 30,000. In the long run, the events in the United States had a notable influence on the project of the union of colonies.

As W.L. Morton, an authority on Confederation, writes, "From July 1863, defence, and federation as a means to defence, came more and more to be viewed by the great majority of British North Americans in terms of a Southern defeat. And defence, hitherto an isolated issue, began to become more and more part of the thoughts of federation."

As the year drew to its close, the "Chesapeake" incident revealed to the British colonies the presence of another danger, which the turn in military events in the United States had brought about. On December 7, 1863, a group of Confederates seized the ship "Chesapeake," which was making its run between New York and Portland. Quickly, they reached the British territorial waters close to the coasts of New Brunswick and Nova Scotia. Their aim was to sell the ship's cargo in the Maritimes, buy arms, and convert the "Chesapeake" into a privateer to attack the merchant ships of the Northern states. On the 16th, the ship was captured by two northern war vessels, the U.S.S. "Ella and Annie" and the U.S.S. "Dacota," before it could come out of St. Margaret's Bay in Nova Scotia. In the course of the operation the Americans, on the look-out for fugitives, searched a little boat from Nova Scotia, the "Investigator," while still in British territorial waters. The next day the Americans brought the "Chesapeake" and the prisoners to the authorities of Halifax so that they might be tried. There had been a violation of British neutrality by both the Confederates and the Northerners. Although there were no immediately serious consequences, the event acted as a warning to the British colonies. It showed that the South, experiencing more and more difficulties in the war, would attempt to use Canada and the Maritimes in the future as bases for territorial and naval attacks against the North. Colonial authorities would likely encounter many difficulties in maintaining strict neutrality, the more so because they would be dealing with a population overtly pro-South or at least anti-North.

## The Conferences in Charlottetown and in Quebec

In the summer of 1864 the population of the British colonies which, in the previous autumn, had seen Northern triumphs and been excited by the "Chesapeake" affair, took on new hope. The prospect of a victory for the forces of the Union, which had seemed so close at the time of Vicksburg, was vanishing. If Sherman was advancing rapidly towards Atlanta, Grant was marking time before Petersburg. The morale of the North, discouraged by the slowness of the operations at a time when the end had seemed so near, was at its lowest. Inversely, the Canadian population revived its optimism in the successes of the South. The "Leader" of Toronto, wrote, "The independence of the South is as good as achieved." The belief of the British colonials that imperial aid on the one hand and the victorious resistance of the South on the other constituted the best guarantees of their independence seemed to have been thus confirmed. Nevertheless, the fear of a reversal of the situation remained in the minds of all. It was in this atmosphere that the conferences of Charlottetown and Quebec took place.

From 1861 to 1864, the history of Canadian-American relations, with its alternate periods of tension and calm, of fear and confidence, obliges the historian who asks himself about the influence which the United

States exercised on the union of British colonies to be very prudent. Without doubt the fratricidal battle, to which the supporters and adversaries of the Union surrendered themselves, modified the imperial outlook on defence and intercolonial cooperation. Under the pressure of these events, London, in 1865–1866, did not hesitate to throw its weight in the favour of union. Moreover, despite the victorious resistance of the South from 1862 to 1863, the problems of defence and communications acquired a new urgency for the colonial government as well. Although it is difficult to determine their direct influence, these preoccupations certainly held the attention of those in conference at Charlottetown and Quebec. Yet these historic conferences had a much more positive objective, that of creating a new country, fragmented until now into regions. It is in this sense that it is necessary to interpret the opinion of historian D.G. Creighton: "Both Maritime Union and Confederation were to be planned and considered by themselves, largely apart from the dangerous turmoil to the South." Nevertheless, this statement, which refers to the military situation in the summer of 1864, does not deny at all the long-term and indirect influence which the American threat played.

It was the republican experience of their neighbours to the south rather than the military threat to British North America which they represented that preoccupied the Fathers at Charlottetown and Quebec. They feared the destructive force of federalism, as illustrated by the horrors of the American Civil War. But French Canada, anxious to protect its nationality, not only opposed a legislative union but also deserved as much autonomy as possible. The wishes of the delegation of Prince Edward Island as well as those of certain representatives from New Brunswick to preserve partially their local sovereignty, reinforced the opposition to legislative union. Against their own wishes the majority of the Fathers accepted the federal principle, on the express condition that this federation would be based on a strong central power, thus creating a situation radically different from that which, in their view, had led to the Civil War. "States' rights" – the reservation by each state of all sovereign powers, "save the small portion delegated" to the general government – was, declared Macdonald in his speech on October 11, 1864, the "primary error" of the American constitution.

"We must reverse this process," he continued, "by strengthening the general government and conferring on the provincial bodies only such powers as may be required for local purposes."

## The Saint-Albans Raid

On October 19, 1864, while the discussion on the constitution of local governments was drawing to a close in Quebec, the attention of the delegates was caught by the raid at Saint-Albans. This ominous incident did not have a direct influence on the outcome of the conference of Quebec, but it inflamed public opinion on both sides of the frontier. In 1864, despite what Canadians may have thought, the military position of the South was deteriorating gradually. It was now or never, if the Confederate forces were to use British North America as a base for some desperate operation against the North. On September 18 and 19, 1864, Southern agents attempted to seize the steam boat "Philo Parsons" at Amherstburg and to use it to capture the U.S.S. "Michigan," an American gunboat. Their ultimate objective was to free Southerners, prisoners on Johnson Island in Lake Erie. This scheme was checkmated.

The raid of Saint-Albans followed a little while later. In the afternoon of October 19, 1864, a group of Confederate agents, dressed in civilian clothes, robbed three banks in the little village of Saint-Albans in Vermont, situated fifteen miles south of the Canadian frontier. Taking with them some two hundred thousand dollars, they took flight on stolen horses, crossed the Canadian frontier, and finally reached Montreal. Although the incident resulted only in one death among the pursuers from Vermont, it threatened to plunge British America into an armed conflict with the United States. The Canadian government arrested the raiders and recovered the money. These measures, however, proved insufficient to calm the fears and appease the anger of the Northern states, who saw in this incident the consequences of the policy of neutrality of Canada and its hostility to the Union cause. As soon as he had word of the incident, General John A. Dix, Commander of the Military District of the east, ordered American troops to pursue the raiders into Canadian territory, if necessary, and wipe them out. This order, if it had been carried out, would have violated Canadian neutrality and could have resulted in war. After two months' delay, Lincoln and Seward, realizing that a Canadian-American conflict would only help the South, revoked Dix's order. Nevertheless, to show the North's anger, Seward ordered the American ambassador in London to give six months' notice for the abrogation of the Rush-Bagot Convention of 1817 which had limited naval armament on the Great Lakes. Finally, it was rumored that the Reciprocity Treaty would be abrogated.

The crisis was serious, but it did not unduly worry public opinion in the British colonies, especially those of the Maritimes. At least they gave that impression by the way they received the project of Confederation as drawn up by the Fathers at Quebec.

The plan easily won support in Upper Canada, where it had only to submit to the attacks of some Conservatives, Grits, and Liberals. In Lower Canada, however, it aroused the lively opposition of the Rouge minority led by Antoine-Aimé Dorion. The Rouges were against too great a centralization of powers. "It is not then a Confederation which is proposed to us," declared Dorion on November 7, "but simply a Legislative Union disguised in the name of Confederation." Naturally, the moderates and the Bleus, who had the support of the hierarchy of the Catholic clergy, claimed on the contrary that the proposed union would be a true federation, protecting the rights of the French-Canadians as an ethnic and cultural group. They posed the question of whether the annexation to the United States, "the most immoral of modern nations," in which French Canadians would certainly lose their autonomy and faith, was not to be feared more than Confederation.

The reception which the Maritimes reserved for the project was cooler. In New Brunswick, the advantages of the construction of the Intercolonial and the access to the markets of Canada induced the pro-Confederation forces to expect a favourable reception. Nothing of the kind took place. The opposition was so strong that Tilley, a supporter of Confederation, refused to submit the question to the legislature before the coming elections of February 1865. The adversaries of the scheme were just as active and powerful in the other Maritime colonies. In Nova Scotia, the governor thought the opposition so forceful that he doubted whether the plan could be approved. In Prince Edward Island, it seemed that the great majority of the population was hostile to the Quebec Resolutions. As to Newfoundland, few expected its entry into the union.

In contrast, the reception which the scheme received from British public opinion and the imperial government could not have been more favourable. Seeing in the union of the colonies a considerable aid to defending British North America against an American attack, they praised the wisdom of the Fathers of Confederation. On December 3, 1864, Cardwell, the new Colonial Secretary, assured the governments of Canada and the Maritimes that London would give all assistance possible to the adoption of Confederation.

At the beginning of the year 1865, the Quebec Resolutions had been received with warmth in London and in Upper Canada. In Lower Canada, however, they were confronted by the well-organized opposition of the Rouge minority. In the Maritimes, their future looked dark. In any case, the dangers resulting from the American Civil War as in the flouting of Canadian neutrality by the raiders of Saint-Albans, did not seem to have directly influenced the acceptance or rejection of the project.

### The Decision of Judge Coursol and the Southern Defeats

Although the raid on Saint-Albans had only a secondary influence on the Quebec Resolutions in the autumn of 1864, it obliged the Canadian authorities to adopt measures to reinforce the system of defence to protect the neutrality of the country. Among other things, Monck appealed for two thousand volunteers to guard the frontier permanently. Canada still considered that the responsibility for defence belonged to the Empire, but under the pressures of external events it was prepared to accept heavier sacrifices. It offered to fortify Montreal on condition that Great Britain would do the same for Quebec City. Moreover, it undertook to propose a sum of $1,000,000 (as against $394,745 in 1864) for the militia to the Assembly.

These measures were not superfluous in December 1864. The consequences of the trial of the raiders of Saint-Albans proved how vulnerable the security of Canada could be, and how necessary was a vast program of defence. On December 13, as the result of the preliminary inquiry of the Southern prisoners, Judge C.J. Coursol released the prisoners, declaring that, as a result of a technicality in the Canadian law of extradition, the court had no jurisdiction in this affair. So great was the judge's generosity that he ordered the stolen money returned to the Southern agents.

The reaction of the United States was even more violent than that which had been provoked by the raid itself. American newspapers spoke of raids of reprisals, of total war. "We were never in a better condition for a war with England," wrote the *New York Times*, on December 16, 1864. Once more, General Dix ordered his troops to pursue all Southerners to Canada, if necessary, and bring them back to the United States, transfer them to a court-martial, but in no case to hand them over to the Canadian authorities. Lincoln, on December 17, disavowed his general for the second time, but the same day an order of the Secretary of State required a passport from anyone desiring to enter the United States. On the very day that Coursol freed the prisoners, the Chamber of Representatives voted in favour of the abrogation of the Treaty of Reciprocity. It should be noted, however, that the Chamber took no notice of the news of the release and that the adversaries of the Reciprocity Treaty were already numerous in the Congress. In contrast, the vote of the Senate on January 12, in favour of the abrogation of the treaty was, from all evidence, strongly influenced by the events north of the frontier.

In Canada the concern was great. The government acted promptly. The patrols along the frontier were reinforced, a service of counter-espionage was created, a certain number of prisoners were re-arrested, and Cartier was sent to Washington to mollify Lincoln's government. Washington, realizing that an Anglo-Northern war would aid the Confederates to win their independence, accepted the Canadian declaration that they intended to remain neutral. All the same, American public opinion was so inflamed that the danger remained real. In Canada the whole defence problem was seen in a new light. The debates on Confederation in the Assembly showed that this Northern threat strengthened the cause of union.

Although the result of the decision of Judge Coursol provoked a lively anxiety in Canada and there reinforced the cause of union, the American threat by itself was incapable of ensuring the adoption of Confederation by the Maritimes. At the beginning of the year 1865 the electoral campaign was in full swing in New Brunswick. Since November, the adversaries of the Quebec Resolutions had warned the electors about the danger of Canadian domination, while Tilley and his supporters had insisted on the advantages which the colony would draw from the union. The crisis which followed the judgment of Coursol in the Saint-Albans affair influenced the tactics of Tilley, who warned the electorate that the rejection of Confederation would be an invitation to American aggression. This claim had no effect on the results of the election. The supporters of Confederation were beaten; even Tilley lost his seat.

Tupper, the Premier of Nova Scotia, faced with an opposition greatly encouraged by the news of the defeat of Confederation in the neighbouring province, did not dare to submit the project to his Assembly. On March 6, the Assembly of Newfoundland decided to wait until after the general elections before discussing the question and at the end of March Prince Edward Island rejected the Quebec project.

By February the Canadian government had become worried about conflicting reports from the province of New Brunswick. But equally, it had other concerns. The previous Christmas Eve, Sherman, after his destructive march across Georgia, announced the capture of Savannah. Quickly he continued his drive towards Richmond to complete the encirclement of the Southern forces. In February the situation of the South was desperate, the victory of the North quite near. The fear of a war with the victorious forces of the Union preoccupied Canadians. Moreover, the news about imperial defence policy which came from London did not contribute to easing this tension. At the beginning of February the Canadian Government had learned that Great Britain agreed to fortify Quebec, but the dispatch had not mentioned any concrete figure. It was in this climate of uncertainty that on March 4, Canada learned of the defeat of Tilley and Confederation in New Brunswick. The Assembly was asked to adopt the Quebec Resolutions to encourage the other Maritime colonies and to prove to London that the Confederation was a source of strength. Macdonald's determination became even stronger when he learned that the House of Commons in the United Kingdom had limited the expenditure on the fortifications of Quebec to 50,000 pounds in 1865. On March 11, 1865, the Assembly approved of Confederation, without amendment, by a majority of 91 to 33. It was decided to send a mission to London to save the scheme which now seemed threatened by the response of New Brunswick.

It is certain that the Canadian members during these trying days discussed the project of union for its intrinsic merits. All the same, the American threat, which seemed to be coming more and more definite, haunted their minds. The insistence with which many speakers invoked it suffice amply to prove this. Few attached more importance to this matter than the French-Canadian speakers.

"To be thrown violently into the American union, if this project of Confederation does not pass," declared Taché, "seems to me as the probable result."

Georges-Étienne Cartier took up the same theme: "Those who claim that the provinces of British North America are not more exposed while thus separated than they would be united in Confederation, make a great mistake. The time has come for us to form a great nation, and I maintain that Confederation is necessary for our own commercial interest, our own prosperity and our own defence."

George Brown was certainly one of those who had best grasped the different facets of the American threat. "The civil war ... in the neighbouring republic, the threatened repeal of the Reciprocity Treaty; the threatened abolition of the American bonding system for goods in transition to and from these provinces; the unsettled position of the Hudson's Bay Company; and the changed feeling of England as to the relations of Great colonies to the present states; – all combine at this moment to arrest earnest attention to the gravity of the situation, and unite us all in one vigorous effort to meet the emergency like men."

Others saw in Confederation a means of dealing with the American threat to abrogate the Reciprocity Treaty and to withdraw privileges granted in 1845, which allowed Canada to export and import goods in transit through the United States without the payment of duty on them. Faced with the loss of a vast and profitable market, the supporters of federal union suggested that the only solution or compensation was the creation of a national market. "I confess to you," declared George Brown, "that in my mind, this one view of the union – this addition of nearly a million people to our home consumers – sweeps aside all the petty objections that are averred against the scheme."

But, even when the project was accepted by the Legislature, the troubles of the government were far from over. The whole scheme had been put in jeopardy by the hostility of the Maritimes. Moreover, the imminent defeat of the South might allow the North to unleash its forces against Canada. Thus, to ensure both its scheme of Confederation and its defence, Canada needed the co-operation of London.

**The End of the War and the Fenian Threat**

In April the fall of Richmond, capital of the Confederate states, and the surrender of Lee and his army at Appomattox established the defeat of the South. What did the future hold? Peace or war? More than ever an Anglo-Canadian agreement on the defence of the British colonies in North America was necessary.

The news from a Canadian mission sent over to discuss this question with the imperial authorities was hardly encouraging. English public opinion, liberals and radicals in Parliament, were hostile to any addition to the military imperial burden. In the end, however, with much reluctance, Great Britain agreed to guarantee the necessary loans for the fortifications of Montreal. It was little enough. Still, the threat which the end of the American Civil War represented had strengthened the British conviction that the union of her colonies in America was essential to the maintenance of their independence. For this reason London promised to press for the acceptance of the Quebec Resolutions by the Maritimes. The Colonial Secretary called upon the Governors of New Brunswick and Nova Scotia to use their influence to achieve this goal.

On their return, at the end of the summer of 1865, the Canadian delegates were optimistic. Thanks to the promise of imperial aid, the cause of Confederation was not definitely lost in the Maritimes. They also found the Cabinet more and more confident that the American attack would not materialize.

In the previous spring, the United States had revoked the executive order establishing the system of passports. At the same time, the Secretary of State had renounced the abrogation of the Rush-Bagot Agreement. In August while on a visit to Quebec, Ulysses S. Grant, the conqueror of Lee, assured Monck that his country would not attack Canada as long as Great Britain did not support France in its Mexican adventure. These were, without doubt, promising signs.

The easing of the threat of invasion did not settle all the elements of Canadian-Anglo-American contention. It was a widespread belief in the United States that the policy of neutrality of Great Britain and, above all, the damages caused by the Alabama and other Southern cruisers constructed and armed in English ports, had prolonged the Civil War. The Canadians feared that these grievances might be used for political ends. The future of the Reciprocity Treaty was also quite uncertain. On March 17, 1865, the United States gave the required year's notice for its abrogation. Canadians believed that their pressure, along with that of the farmers and businessmen of the north-west and the fishermen of the north-east, would be sufficient to obtain its renewal. This hope was in vain. The opposition was too great. The anger provoked by the conduct of the Canadians and the British in the conflict, the popular belief that reciprocity, especially after the tariff of Galt, was more favourable to Canada than to the United States, and the need to increase the revenues militated in favour of the abrogation of the Treaty. Moreover, many Canadians believed that this act of Congress aimed at forcing them to join the American Republic. Consequently, despite many promising signs, not all tension had passed. A spark would be sufficient to re-light the animosity and once again bring the relations between the two countries to a breaking point. This was to be the danger which the Fenian movement presented.

The origins of the Fenian brotherhood go back to 1858. The aim of the Fenians was to liberate Ireland from the British yoke by fermenting a rebellion in the mother country. The end of the American Civil

War gave the movement a new direction and a vigorous impetus. In the months which followed the surrender of Lee at Appomattox, the most militant branch of the Fenian brotherhood declared that the best way to liberate Ireland was to conquer British North America. This plan was realistic enough to worry colonial governments. The Fenians, they thought, could count on thousands of Irish veterans of the armies of the Union. Would not the anti-British sentiment of the United States find in the uproar created by the Irish American patriots a means of expressing itself concretely? On the eve of the Congressional elections of November 1866, the Canadians could hardly expect a firm attitude from the American authorities. On the contrary, it was to be feared that the Republican administration, wishing to maintain itself in power, would adopt a policy of expediency and non-intervention so as not to offend the Irish voters. Furthermore, the reactions of numerous Irishmen living in Canada was, as yet, unforeseeable. Finally, the defence of the frontiers against numerous raids was going to be difficult. All these fears occupied the thoughts of Canadians at the end of 1865 and at the beginning of 1866. In fact, the Fenian threat was to prove much weaker than expected, yet it did exercise a considerable influence on the movement for Confederation. This was particularly true in the Maritimes.

At the beginning of 1866, New Brunswick, warned that the Fenians were collecting arms in Maine, became concerned. In April the rumor that the Fenians would mount an attack against the colony became more definite. Since the beginning of the month hundreds of Fenians had been gathering in little localities on the northeast coast of Maine, possibly with a view to a raid against St. Andrews, the isle of Campobello, and other little isles at the entrance of Passamaquoddy Bay. Late in the night of April 14 the Fenians invaded Indian Island, a little island close to Campobello. Without delay, the governor mobilized the militia and appealed to the British command at Halifax. The latter immediately dispatched war ships and regular soldiers. Frightened, the Fenians, whose movements were henceforth to be watched by a detachment of the American army, fled from the little frontier localities. This was the end of the Fenian offensive operation in this region. Nevertheless, the rumors that thousands of Fenians, armed to the teeth, prepared to invade New Brunswick, had a profound influence on the electoral campaign in the colony which took place in May and June of 1866.

In May 1866, Tilley was in a much better position than in 1865 to win the election. The unqualified support of the imperial government for Confederation was known to all. The financial aid of the Canadian government constituted another asset for Tilley's party. When the abrogation of the Reciprocity Treaty, March 17, 1866, put an end to the hopes of maintaining close commercial relations with the United States, many saw no other alternative than Confederation. The Fenian threat delivered the final blow to the adversaries of the project.

To begin with, it constituted a formidable argument for those who presented Confederation as a measure of urgent and necessary defence. "If there is one argument in favour of Union stronger than another," wrote the *Saint Croix Courier*, on May 19, 1866, "it is the necessity that exists for a good and efficient system of mutual defence. We have sometimes regarded this as one of the weaker points in favour of Union. Invasion or trouble seemed to be at so great a distance, but now when we see how soon sudden danger can threaten us, and how our enemies may concentrate within a gunshot of our very doors, the man must be blind, infatuated, or prejudiced who can fail to recognize its force."

Moreover, the Fenian menace compelled the Catholic hierarchy of Irish origin to define its position clearly. Bishop Rogers of Chatham publicly supported Confederation and explained why he preferred it to annexation to the United States. The result of his stand as well as that of Archbishop Connolly of Halifax was to rally a large part of the New Brunswick Irish to the cause of Confederation.

All these reasons explain the easy victory of Tilley in June. Without claiming that the Fenian threat was the only or even the main cause of the victory of Tilley in 1866, it ought to be recognized as a factor of great importance. Tilley himself felt this. Another proof of its importance is to be found in the rumor which held that the supporters of Confederation had incited the Fenians to action with the aim of frightening the people and leading them to support the federal union. "The Fenian excitement continues on our border," wrote Tilley to Macdonald, on April 21, 1866, "and you will laugh when you see the Antis are endeavoring to make people believe that you Canadians have sent them to aid Confederation."

Consequently, by mid-June the province of New Brunswick, which constituted an essential tie between Canada and the other Maritime provinces, was ready to take part in Confederation and to send its delegates to London to prepare the concrete terms of union.

In April Nova Scotia, despite the very strong opposition of Joseph Howe and his supporters, had already agreed to the sending of a delegation to the conference in London. There also, as in the neighbouring province, the problems resulting from the Civil War, the abrogation of the Reciprocity Treaty, and the Fenian movement had a considerable influence on the march of events.

At the end of June, Tilley and Tupper wished to take advantage of the events to complete the project before the ending of the session of the British Parliament in August. Nevertheless, it was not until the beginning of November that the Canadian delegation was able to leave for England. In Canada, that summer the problem of defence was of more concern than the question of Confederation. Since the beginning of the year rumors reported by the police and the British consuls predicted an attack against Canada by the Fenians. It was expected on St. Patrick's Day, March 17. A week before, 10,000 militia men were called out, but the day passed without incident. In the same way, April and May were quiet.

Suddenly, at the end of May, the threat became more definite. On the night of May 31 Colonel John O'Neil and about 1,000 supporters crossed the Niagara River; two days later they took a position not far from the little village of Ridgeway. Monck appealed to 20,000 militia men and ordered an immediate attack against the invaders. The Canadians gave a good account of themselves and compelled the enemy to retreat, but a countermanded order of their commander left them exposed to the heavy fire of Fenians. Nine Canadians were killed and thirty wounded. Since the arrival of reinforcements was imminent, Colonel John O'Neil ordered his men to recross the frontier. Another attempt on June 7, at Pigeon Hill some miles north of the Canadian frontier in the region of Lake Champlain, ended in total failure. This last episode marked the end of the Fenian "invasion" of Canada in 1866.

On June 6, Washington issued a proclamation of neutrality which satisfied Monck. The fear and anger of the population persisted. The invasion of their country, the weakness of efforts of the American authorities to prevent it, the hostility of certain American newspapers, the annexionist aims of some politicians reinforced the anti-American sentiments of Canadians. Canadian-American relations had not been so bad since the "Trent" incident. The Fenian threat did not have the same influence on Canada that it had on the Maritimes; they had already approved of Confederation well before the events of March and June 1866. Still, it reinforced Canadian nationalism, based for a large part on anti-Americanism, and put the adversaries of Confederation at a disadvantage. It was in this climate that the Canadian delegates reached England for the conference in London at Westminster. The conference accepted the Quebec Resolutions with only minor changes. In 1867, the union of the British provinces of North America was ratified by the two houses of the English Parliament and came into force on July 1.

Confederation was the response of politicians towards a whole range of problems. It is not easy to determine in an exact fashion the direct influence which the events resulting from the Civil War exercised. But the "Trent" affair, the frontier incidents which reached their culmination in the raid of Saint-Albans, the plans to abolish the Rush-Bagot Agreement and the Reciprocity Treaty, without doubt weighed heavily in the balance and induced the British provinces to more speed. The pressures of London, notably in the case of the Maritimes, can be explained only with difficulty without the American influence. The United States, then, contributed to the creation of Confederation, and by its presence alone has continued to influence the development of Canadian history.

## NOTES

1 Yves Roby, *The United States and Confederation*, Centennial Historical Booklet, 4 (Ottawa: Centennial Commission, 1967), 3–20.

## BIBLIOGRAPHY

Bonenfant, J.-C. *Les Canadiens-Français et la naissance de la Confédération*. CHAR (1952): 39–45.

Creighton, Donald G. *The Road to Confederation: Tthe Emergence of Canada: 1863–1867*. Toronto, Macmillan, 1964.

Creighton, Donald G. *The United States and Canadian Confederation*. CHR, 39 (1958): 209–222.

Davis, Harold A. *The Fenian Raid on New Brunswick*. CHR, 36 (1955): 316–334.

Landon, F. *The American Civil War and Canadian Confederation*. TRSC, 1927, section II.

Martin, Chester. *The United States and Canadian Nationality*. CHR, 18 (1937): 1–11.

Morton, W.L. *The Critical Years:. The Union of British North American, 1857–1873*. Toronto, McClelland and Stewart, 1964.

Stacey, C.P. *British Military Policy in Canada in the Era of Federation*. CHAR, (1935): 20–30.

Stacey, C.P. *Fenianism and the Rise of National Feeling in Canada at the Time of Confederation*. CHR, 12 (1931): 238–262.

Stewart, Alice R. *The State of Maine and Canadian Confederation*. CHR, 33 (1952): 148–164.

Trotter, R.G. *Some American Influences upon the Canadian Federation Movement*. CHR, 5 (1924): 213–227.

Waite, Peter B. *The Life and Times of Confederation, 1864–1867*. Toronto, University of Toronto Press, 1962.

Winks, Robin W. *Canada and the United States: The Civil War Years*. Baltimore, 1960.

# "Seward's Attempt to Annex British Columbia, 1865–1869"

*Pacific Historical Review*
1978

DAVID E. SHI[1]

Secretary of State William H. Seward's attempt to annex the Crown Colony of British Columbia has been touched upon by historians, but it has never received careful analytical treatment. Canadian scholars, while examining annexation sentiment within the colony, have devoted little attention to Seward's efforts to acquire the area.[2] American diplomatic historians, on the other hand, have either casually dismissed the episode or ignored it altogether.[3] Thus, information concerning Seward and British Columbia remains scattered and superficial. This essay offers a comprehensive account of this neglected aspect of Seward's expansionist program. Seward's actions towards British Columbia not only confirm his commercial orientation, but they also provide fresh perspectives on the Alaska purchase and the *Alabama* claims negotiations.

Early in his political career, Seward postulated that to facilitate economic development, the United States should extend its sovereignty "to the Pacific and grasp the great commerce of the east."[4] He envisioned an American commercial empire based upon control of the entire Pacific Coast. Although opposed in 1846 to the bellicose demands of the "All Oregon" movement, he expected the United States eventually to absorb the disputed area:

> Let the Oregon question be settled when it may, it will, nevertheless, come back again. Our population is destined to roll its restless waves to the icy

> barriers of the north, and to encounter oriental civilization on the shores of the Pacific.[5]

In the autumn of 1860, Seward again articulated his vision of America's destiny. He told a St. Paul, Minnesota, audience that the British territory in the Canadian West from St. Boniface (Manitoba) to Victoria (British Columbia) would inevitably gravitate to the United States. The Canadians, he boasted, "are building excellent states to be hereafter admitted to the American Union." Seward also recognized the Russian presence in the Pacific Northwest and likewise predicted that those settlements would "yet become the outposts of the United States."[6] He believed that Russian America and the Canadian West would one day join the United States of their own accord.[7] His was a naive assumption, however, for it betrayed an utter lack of understanding of the forces that were even then driving the Canadians toward confederation and self-government in 1867.

Seward's idealistic faith in the "manifest destiny" of the United States to incorporate contiguous areas was not an isolated phenomenon. Following the Civil War, many Americans called for a new era of territorial expansion, and politicians from the northern tier of states demanded the immediate annexation of Canada.[8] Seward led the chorus of those who believed that Great Britain would peacefully accede to this demand. The Oxford professor Goldwin Smith, who later emigrated to Canada, advised Seward that Canada "seems likely (unless our statesmen adopt a different policy) to fall into your hands of itself, perhaps before you want it."[9] The London *Times* echoed Smith's assessment, reporting that Britain would not object if Canadians wished to join the United States, but if a union was promulgated by force, Her Majesty's government would protest.[10] This was a common view of British scholars and politicians, who had little faith in Canada's future and even less regard for her aspirations for dominion status.

Responding to what appeared a favorable climate for expansion, Seward initiated a series of negotiations designed to acquire territories he considered valuable to American commerce. While decrying the use of force or schemes of military conquest, he emphasized in 1866 that "wisdom, justice, and moderation in the conduct of our foreign relations make it easy to acquire by peaceful negotiations, all the more than could be obtained by unlawful aggression."[11] Eager for the United States to capture Asian markets, Seward believed America first had to remove all foreign interests from the northern Pacific Coast and gain access to the region's valuable ports. Furthermore, events during the Civil War had convinced him of the need to obtain naval bases in the northern Pacific. Near the end of the war, the Confederate privateer *Shenandoah* had captured thirty-eight Union vessels in the Pacific without any resistance. According to his son Frederick, Seward had discovered the government "laboring under great disadvantages for the lack of naval outposts in the … North Pacific. So, at the close of hostilities he commenced his endeavors to obtain a foothold in each quarter."[12]

Between Russian America and Washington Territory lay the British colony of British Columbia. Until 1858 the area had been an underdeveloped and sparsely populated region, serving primarily as an outpost for the Hudson's Bay Company. In that year, however, the discovery of gold brought an influx of American miners. This rapid growth led to the formation of the Crown Colony of British Columbia. Its boundaries extended from the summit of the Rocky Mountains on the east to the Pacific Ocean and the Gulf of Georgia on the west, and from the Finlay branch of the Peace River and the Nass River on the north to the 49th parallel on the south. Vancouver Island remained a separate colony until 1866.[13]

British Columbia's rapid growth and prosperity, however, quickly subsided. By 1865 the colony was in a state of decay, a "poor, struggling, bankrupt colony on the edge of things."[14] As the gold deposits were depleted, the populace began to drift away, leaving less than 10,000 inhabitants in 1866, three-quarters of whom were of British or Canadian origin. Moreover, since the Hudson's Bay Company owned the territory from the head of the Great Lakes to the Rocky Mountains, the colony remained isolated from the rest of Canada East and West.[15] Consequently, the British Columbians, especially those on Vancouver Island, maintained closer economic and social relations with the western American territories and states than with either Canada or Great Britain.[16]

The belief among many colonists that the Home Office had abandoned them further contributed to their sense of isolation and frustration. During the Civil War, British Columbia alone of the British North American colonies was left undefended. Rear Admiral Joseph Denman informed the Admiralty that the colony did not warrant protection: "I would consider it would be greatly for the interest of England to divest herself of these possessions by any means consistent with honor and with justice to the English settlers."[17] Denman's comments were symptomatic of a general spirit of Little Englandism emerging in Great

Britain during the 1860s, a spirit that caused great concern among the colonists in British Columbia.

In such an unstable situation, growing support among the colonists for annexation to the United States represented a logical development. Many were painfully aware of the prosperity and lower taxes prevalent in the neighboring American states. Agitation for annexation began in 1866 and remained a prominent issue for several years. Vancouver Island emerged as the center of support for the movement, particularly the port town of Victoria.[18]

Seward learned of the support in British Columbia for annexation from several sources. In January 1866, he received an extensive report from E.H. Derby, a congressional investigator. Citing the rising discontent among the colonists in British Columbia, Derby suggested that Great Britain cede its Pacific territory to the United States as payment of the *Alabama* claims:

> If Great Britain desires to propitiate this country after all that has occurred, would it not be her true policy to cede to us a portion of her remote territories, valuable to us, but of little value to her? Were she to cede us Vancouver's Island and British Columbia ... might she not easily bring our claims to a peaceful solution...[?][19]

Seward responded favorably to Derby's suggestion. After sending the report to the Senate for consideration, he began negotiations with Great Britain on the subject.[20]

Discussions concerning the *Alabama* claims had begun immediately after the Civil War. The main issues were Great Britain's recognition of the Confederacy and her building of Confederate privateers. By 1866 the negotiations had reached an impasse. Seward wanted Britain's policies judged before a neutral arbitration court. Lord Russell refused, arguing that his country's actions were beyond the jurisdiction of any foreign court.[21]

In June 1866, Russell's government fell. As the Conservatives assumed power, conditions appeared favorable for reopening the negotiations. In a lengthy dispatch to the new government, Seward listed the American claims against Great Britain for her part in building the privateers.[22] Lord Stanley, the new Secretary of State for Foreign Affairs, finally replied in November, professing his willingness to accept arbitration of the American claims, apart from those involving the right of the British government to recognize a state of belligerency.[23] Seward countered in January 1867, stressing that the individual claims represented only a small part of the much greater losses caused by British actions which had prolonged the war. He implied that he was holding Great Britain responsible for indirect damages that could produce enormous claims.[24] Apparently following the plan outlined earlier in Derby's report, Seward hoped to raise the claims high enough to convince British officials to agree to a *quid pro quo* settlement, ceding British Columbia in exchange for the claims.

For several months prior to this last dispatch, Seward had been receiving additional evidence from British Columbia indicating substantial support in the colony for annexation. Allen Francis, the American consul in Victoria, reported in September 1866 that "the people of Vancouver Island, and of British Columbia, are almost unanimous in their desire for annexation to the United States." He included an article excerpted from the *Victoria Evening Telegraph* of September 5, 1866, which characterized British Columbia's relations with the United States as being closer "than our relations with any of the colonies." Two weeks later a public meeting in Victoria voted to request Great Britain to permit annexation to the United States.[25]

Such promising information influenced Seward to approach British officials in Washington directly on the subject of annexation, but he received no encouragement.[26] He needed considerably more diplomatic leverage to convince Great Britain to transfer such a strategic possession, especially since public opinion within the colony was still divided on the issue. Fortunately for Seward's aspirations, the Alaska purchase soon provided an opportunity for him to achieve his objective – American control of the Pacific Northwest.

Late in 1866 the Russian government decided that Alaska (Russian America), which had long been an unprofitable colonial possession, was expendable. In early February 1867, Edouard de Stoeckl, the Russian minister in Washington, indirectly informed Seward that Alaska was available for purchase. Seward jumped at the opportunity, for he knew that by obtaining Alaska, he could also facilitate the acquisition of British Columbia. A few days after learning of the Russian offer, he informed President Andrew Johnson that parts of the Canadian West might soon become "coordinate members of the United States of America."[27]

The story of the Alaska purchase is a familiar one.[28] What is not so well known is that Seward considered the purchase as only a first step in a comprehensive plan to gain control of the entire northwest Pacific

Coast.[29] On the day the treaty was signed, he met with John Bigelow, a close friend and former minister to France. Bigelow urged him to obtain British Columbia in exchange for the *Alabama* claims. Seward told him he had already "sounded the Government in that direction, but that they – the British ministers – dared not." The Secretary then "intimated that this Alaska purchase was part of a system of negotiations which he was conducting, he thought to a successful issue."[30]

Seward thought that British Columbia, bordered on three sides by American territory, would probably ask for annexation and that Great Britain, recognizing this fact and eager to settle the *Alabama* claims, would consent. Soon after the Alaska purchase, he told reporters his object in acquiring the territory was to prevent its purchase by Great Britain, thereby precluding the extension of the British coastline on the Pacific. The acquisition, he also noted, would strengthen annexation sentiment in British Columbia.[31] A few days before the Senate ratified the Alaska treaty, Charles Francis Adams, Jr., found Seward "all agog" over Alaska. The Secretary of State told him the *Alabama* claims "would soon be settled, but *now* they could be settled in one way, by such acquisition from England as would enable us to round off our North-Western territory."[32] Baron de Stoeckl expressed a similar view of the purchase's significance. Three weeks after the treaty was signed, he predicted the transfer of Alaska would be "followed sooner or later by the annexation to the country of the immediate coast of the Pacific Ocean now forming a part of the British possessions."[33]

Public opinion in British Columbia reacted sharply to the news of the Alaska purchase. Many colonists were shocked to learn from a New York dispatch that "negotiations were pending between the United States and Great Britain for the cession of British Columbia, or at least a portion of the colony, to the American Republic as settlement of the *Alabama* claims."[34] Responding to such information, John Robson, editor of the *British Columbian* and an opponent of annexation, asserted, "The American doctrine … of general absorption is well known, but these things … will all tend to rouse the old sleepy British Lion, and open its eyes to the values of the Pacific territory."[35] Other colonists, however, expressed a different reaction to the purchase and its repercussions. Allen Francis forwarded to Seward a petition submitted by residents of Victoria which expressed "very succinctly their estimation of the value of the newly acquired Russian territory." Francis noted a marked increase in annexation sentiment among the colonists.[36] The *British Colonist*, another newspaper in the colony, offered several reasons for supporting annexation to the United States. One was that annexation would offset the continuing *Alabama* claims controversy. The "transfer of the Colony to the United States," the editor concluded, "would be hailed with satisfaction by many of our people."[37]

British officials immediately recognized the impact of the Alaska purchase upon British Columbia. The *New York Times* reported, "The British diplomats are highly excited, and object to this hemming in of the British American Territory by the United States."[38] On the same day, April 1, 1867, the London *Times* warned that the primary effect of the purchase would be to "exclude British Columbia almost entirely from the Pacific."[39] Sir Frederick Bruce, the British minister in Washington, reflected the concern of British officials when he predicted to Lord Stanley that the United States would soon attempt to acquire their Pacific colony. "Unless a great change takes place in public opinion," Bruce concluded, "this policy will meet with general support in the United States."[40]

Indeed, American expansionists strongly endorsed Seward's aspirations in the Pacific Northwest. One correspondent urged him to secure the British Pacific territory next: "We must own the Pacific coast from the isthmus up."[41] D.A. Mahoney, publisher of the St. Louis *Times*, sent Seward an editorial calling for the "acquisition, by one means or another, of that portion of North America lying on the Pacific Ocean.... If Mr. Seward has not already made the proposition to Great Britain for the acquisition ... we suggest that he do so at once."[42] Likewise, the *St. Paul Press* described the Alaska purchase as providing "a new anchorage for that policy of northward expansion by which Mr. Seward hopes, before long, to absorb the immediate British possessions."[43] Other newspapers offered further support for the annexation of British Columbia.[44]

Thus, Seward's efforts to obtain British Columbia appeared to be gaining momentum. It looked as if Great Britain would relent under the combined pressure of the Alaska purchase and the desires of the colonists, and agree to exchange the territory as payment of the *Alabama* claims.[45] Unfortunately for Seward's plans, however, another event intervened which was to have a significant impact upon British-American relations. On the day before the Alaska treaty was signed, the Queen of England assented to the *British North America Act*, which created a confederation of four provinces – Ontario, Quebec, New Brunswick, and Nova Scotia. As news of the Dominion of Canada spread, a wave of nationalism swept over the provinces. The supporters of Confederation wanted a united Canada, and British Columbia remained outside the Dominion. Proponents of a united Canada realized that British Columbia, with its Pacific ports and valuable resources, constituted a vital element in their plans. The new Dominion officials feared that the colony, bordered by American territory and separated from the nation, would now choose to join the United States. Alexander Galt, a key figure in the Canadian confederation movement, warned, "If the United States desires to outflank us on the west, we must ... lay our hands on British Columbia and the Pacific Ocean. The country cannot be surrounded by the United States."[46]

British Columbia's destiny thus had developed into a complicated international issue. Not only did Seward have to assess American opinion, but he had to gauge annexation support in the colony as well. He also was forced to consider changes in Great Britain's official position on the subject. To complicate matters further, the new Dominion of Canada actively began to solicit the entry of British Columbia into the Confederation. Seward then decided to concentrate his efforts on the *Alabama* claims negotiations, since he believed annexation depended upon a *quid pro quo* territorial settlement of the claims dispute.

Charles Francis Adams, as American minister to Great Britain, subsequently played a key role in Seward's plans. Wary of the Secretary's expansionist proclivities, Adams advised Seward on April 25, 1867, to modify his stand on the claims question. He recorded in his diary that Seward had assumed an obdurate position in the claims negotiations in order to convince Great Britain to transfer Canada to the United States. Great Britain, however, "would not confess a wrong and sell Canada as the release from punishment."[47]

Seward demonstrated his attitude on the subject during the spring of 1867. On May 2, Adams reported "the line of difference between the two countries was becoming thinner and thinner.... Assuming any tolerable share of good will I saw no reason why earnest efforts might not eliminate it altogether."[48] Seward, however, perceived "no prospect of coming to an agreement ... upon the so-called *Alabama* claims, and thus the whole controversy between the two states must remain open indefinitely."[49] The London *Times,* in analyzing Seward's obstinate stand, correctly identified the reason for the impasse:

> This leaves the *Alabama* dispute about where it started.... Secretary Seward has his eye on British Columbia and desires to obtain it.... As the *Alabama claims* must at an early date come up for settlement ... it is probable that

> the Secretary will then present the subject of the purchase of the British possessions on the Pacific coast to the British minister, and it will be considered in connection with the *Alabama* controversy.[50]

According to Adams, Seward favored "the continuation of the differences between Great Britain and the United States."[51] Seward hoped to delay the claims negotiations, thus allowing annexation support in British Columbia to increase to a point where the British government would have no alternative but to consent to the union. Most indications were that such would be the case.

In May 1867, C.B. Adderly, parliamentary undersecretary for the colonies, predicted in a speech, "It seems to me impossible that we should long hold British Columbia from its natural annexation."[52] A few weeks later, the *New York Times* characterized the "entire press of Vancouver's Island" as "unanimous in representing that annexation is now the only possible remedy for the political grievances of the colony."[53] Seward, the *Montreal Gazette* reported, "has his eye on British Columbia and he wishes to make a settlement with England for the *Alabama* claims by the annexation of that territory."[54]

In Adam's view, Seward intended "to extend our jurisdiction not simply by purchase and directly, but by indirection through keeping open all unsettled questions with this country."[55] In August 1867, after concluding that Seward's goal was indeed British Columbia, he decided the Secretary was going too far. In a dispatch labelled "Confidential," the minister described the prevailing view in London as not at all sympathetic to the introduction of new elements into the claims negotiations. But Whitehall was prepared to reverse the policy of its predecessors and renew negotiations on the *Alabama* claims.[56]

Adams then presented a significant analysis of the British attitude concerning Canada. Alarmed at Seward's territorial ambitions, he warned,

> Least of all is the policy towards British America likely to be altered so long as the people of the region manifest an inclination to maintain the connection.... In my belief, the maintenance of the connection with Canada is a matter of pride with the British nation which will be only made the more stubborn in resistance to change by the smallest indication on our part of a disposition to impair it. The solution of all questions of that sort must be found in the voluntary sentiment of the population inhabiting that wide region, when generally and clearly declared in favor of separation. I have

> no idea that it could be brought about ... by any diplomatic intervention whatever.[57]

Seward knew he was in no position to make aggressive demands over British Columbia. Unlike his anti-expansionist minister, however, he viewed the *Alabama* claims negotiations as a means of influencing British policy towards the Pacific colony. If the British would not agree to a territorial exchange for the claims, Seward hoped at least to persuade them to stay out of the competition between the United States and the Dominion for British Columbia.

Developments by mid-1867 introduced new problems for Seward's plans. Colonial leaders in British Columbia decided that primarily one factor would determine their future political status. To overcome its isolation both from the new Dominion and the American Midwest, the colony required a connecting railroad system. The ever-interested *New York Times* recognized this reality in a column published on July 17, 1867. After noting that opinion in British Columbia favored admission to the United States, the editorial warned,

> The tide of opinion might be partially turned, were there a way opened for the Pacific colonies to come into the Canadian Union. But without the opening of a railroad connection by way of the Red River, British Columbia finds no more natural attraction in Canada than in Denmark.[58]

At approximately the same time, Bruce advised the Foreign Office that unless Canada met the demands of British Columbia for a connecting railroad, the American effort to obtain the colony "will be powerfully reinforced by the material interests of the Northwest which will be enlisted in favor of ... annexation."[59]

The international competition for the colony thus developed into a contest to build a transcontinental railroad to British Columbia. Aware of the importance of constructing such a link, Seward encouraged American entrepreneurs to undertake the venture. But they first had to gain access to the intervening Canadian territory between the Great Lakes and British Columbia owned by the Hudson's Bay Company and popularly known as Rupert's Land. In April 1867, Seward had Adams protest to the British that Indians had repeatedly "committed outrages" in American territory and returned to safety inside Rupert's Land. The American minister requested permission for American troops to pursue the Indians across the border. As John S. Galbraith has demonstrated, this incident revealed the state of chaos then existing in the Hudson's Bay Company lands. The company had lost effective control, and Great Britain looked to the Dominion to assume authority for the region.[60]

Seward sought to take advantage of the unsettled situation in Rupert's Land. In August 1867 Bruce reported a recent meeting at which Seward had urged an American capitalist "to organize a company for the purpose of buying up the rights of the Hudson's Bay Company, and of thus obtaining command of what he considers would be the best line for a northern communication between the Atlantic and Pacific Oceans." Bruce perceptively concluded, "It is certain that he does not contemplate in such a contingency that the line between the Lakes and Vancouver's Island will remain in any hands but the United States."[61] Seward's interest in a northern transcontinental route gained welcome support from the Northern Pacific Railroad Company. Then under new management, it began an intensive lobbying campaign in the summer of 1867 to gain congressional appropriations for construction of a line through western Canada to British Columbia.[62]

Meanwhile, a territorial settlement with Great Britain of the *Alabama* claims remained a possibility. In an article entitled "A Colony in Trouble," the *Pacific Tribune* predicted that soon the *Alabama* claims and "the transfer of British Columbia will all be settled at once and altogether."[63] In pursuit of this goal, Seward told Adams in December to combine all the claims into a general negotiation. Adams, reacting to this new initiative, surmised,

> I saw very clearly the drift of this to be a bargain for the British territory in the northwest ... more or less in lieu of all demands. Mr. Seward's thirst for more land seems insatiable. I did not however hint at any such thing in my answer to his Lordship for I knew how entirely it would block up any avenue.[64]

Yet contrary to Adams's forebodings, Seward's plans seemed to be gaining support both at home and in the colony. According to the *New York Evening Post,* dispatches "from British Columbia, through an authentic source, represent public sentiment in that region as almost universally in favor of annexation to the United States."[65] Then, on December 17, 1867, Senator Alexander Ramsey of Minnesota presented a memorial to the Senate calling for the construction of a northern transcontinental railroad to the Pacific. The document emphasized "the influence which the construction of this road will have upon our northern neighbors."[66] Shortly thereafter the Northern Pacific Railroad Company issued a promotional pamphlet stressing the danger of a Canadian company building a railroad to British Columbia first: "The construction of such a road would preclude the idea of political relations between that people and our own."[67]

Observers in Great Britain recognized the possibility of the colony joining the American Union. The United States, predicted the *London Daily News,* "unless swayed from its course by the exigencies of domestic politics, will probably do nothing precipitately, especially if it perceives that it may equally gain its object without war." After warning that Great Britain would defend the Canadian territories from attack, the article concluded, "It is equally well understood that it is only while the Canadians desire to remain a part of our Empire that our obligation will exist."[68] In British Columbia, however, popular support for joining the Dominion was growing. At a public meeting in Victoria in January 1868, the colonists declared their preference for union with Canada if certain preliminary demands were met. Included among the conditions was a guarantee to construct a railroad connecting the colony to the Dominion.[69]

Seward, perhaps because he knew little of the true situation in British Columbia, remained optimistic. In late January, Orville Browning, a Republican senator, visited the Secretary and recorded in his diary,

> In conversation about Alaska and British Columbia Mr. Seward expressed his views of the value of the latter to us from the islands to the mountains, and thought that we would ere long get it.... All grievances on both sides would be taken out to balance another until all were disposed of. In this way we would pay for British Columbia with the *Alabama* claims.[70]

Seward's optimism may have been based upon reports from James W. Taylor, a former Treasury agent and ardent expansionist, whom the Secretary had appointed as special agent for Red River affairs. Taylor forwarded dispatches which outlined plans for Great Britain to transfer its western Canadian territories in settlement of the *Alabama* claims. In a personal note to Seward, he wrote, "I enclose another contribution towards the consummation of your program northwest of the Capitol steps at St. Paul."[71]

Then, late in March 1868, Seward suddenly altered his policies. He instructed Adams to propose a conference to settle all outstanding questions between the two countries. Responding to Seward's *volte-face,* Adams observed that it "is plain that Mr. Seward has opened his eyes to the proximity of his term."[72] Seward's tenure as Secretary of State was to end in one year, and Adams believed he desired to retire with a settlement of the claims dispute, with or without a territorial exchange.

Time was indeed a factor in Seward's policy reversal. The contest for British Columbia had developed into a complex diplomatic tangle. Despite enthusiastic reports from the American consul in Victoria, support in the colony was not as strong as Seward had expected, largely because Dominion officials had launched a spirited and effective campaign to win support for Confederation. On March 25, 1868, the Canadian government officially informed British Columbia that it desired union and had approached Great Britain on the subject.[73] At the same time, American attempts to construct a northern transcontinental railroad were meeting stiff resistance from congressional interest groups.[74] Consequently, Seward, while not abandoning the idea that British Columbia might one day join the Union, decided to salvage what he could from the claims negotiations.

Meanwhile, conditions worsened for any chance of a territorial settlement. Until the spring of 1868, Whitehall had taken the position of a passive observer of events in British Columbia.[75] On June 9, 1868, however, Sir Harry Verney challenged this attitude in a speech in Parliament. He moved a bill to facilitate settlement of the area between Lake Superior and the Pacific, including the construction of a transcontinental railroad. As he described it, his motion was designed to put a stop to any "depredatory measures on the part of our neighbors who might cast a wistful eye on countries whose value England seemed to ignore."[76] Although Verney's successful motion by no means assured the union of British Columbia with the Dominion, it did help thwart Seward's attempted territorial settlement of the *Alabama* claims. Great Britain would not permit such a vital region to be annexed by a trading rival when its own Dominion could secure it.

Still, some Americans continued to advocate annexation of British Columbia. In early summer 1868, during the House debate on the appropriation of the Alaska purchase, congressmen expressed their desire to acquire the British colony. Ignatius Donnelly, representative from Minnesota, viewed the Alaska purchase as leading "the way to the acquisition by the United States of that great and valuable region, Western British America."[77] Illinois congressman Green B. Raum agreed and predicted that British Columbia would "drop into our hands like a ripe pear."[78] Other representatives expressed similar sentiments.

While the congressional debate continued, Seward tried to negotiate a settlement of the *Alabama* claims without reference to British Columbia. On July 5, 1868, he begrudgingly admitted that

> public attention sensibly continues to be fastened upon the domestic questions which have grown out of the late civil war. The public mind refuses to dismiss these questions even so far as to entertain the higher but more remote questions of national extension and aggrandizement.[79]

Seward finally had realized that most Americans were too preoccupied with the problems of Reconstruction to consider such questions as territorial expansion. Moreover, he had come to view the continuing *Alabama* claims controversy with Great Britain as a detriment to commercial relations between the two countries. In a dispatch to Reverdy Johnson, Adams's successor in London, Seward emphasized the "urgent necessity" for a settlement of the dispute. "It is a truism," he explained, "that commercial and industrial interests continually exert a powerful influence in favor of peace and friendship between the government and people of the United States and Great Britain."[80] He had finally decided, although reluctantly, that the cession of British Columbia was not then a negotiable issue.

Seward's policy reversal resulted in the signing of the Johnson-Clarendon Convention on January 14, 1869. It contained provisions for the arbitration of claims between the two countries dating back to 1853. There was no British apology or expression of regret over the building of Confederate privateers; nor was there any reference to the indirect or general damages Seward had earlier attributed to British recognition of Confederate belligerency.

Seward left office on March 3, 1869. On April 13, during congressional debate on the Johnson-Clarendon Convention, Charles Sumner, then the powerful chairman of the Senate Committee on Foreign Relations, delivered a lengthy denunciation of the treaty. Although Sumner did not explicitly say so, most historians agree that what he wanted from Great Britain was all or part of Canada as payment of the *Alabama* claims.[81] Largely because of Sumner's effective speech and congressional hostility to Seward for his support of Andrew Johnson, the Senate overwhelmingly rejected the Johnson-Clarendon Convention. The British government reacted angrily and initiated preparations for a possible war.[82]

Seward, unlike Sumner and other expansionists, had decided Great Britain would never cede British Columbia until opinion in the colony definitely supported annexation. Yet he still retained a persistent belief in the "manifest destiny" of the United States to gain control eventually of the entire Pacific Coast, if not all of North America. In August 1869, he visited the area of his famous purchase, and, in the course of his trip, made several speeches. At Victoria, British Columbia, Seward boasted of never hearing "any person, on either side of the United States border, assert that British Columbia is not part of the American continent."[83] In a later address at Salem, Oregon, he left no doubt as to his vision of British Columbia's future:

> Although British Columbia remains, as Oregon not long ago was…, subject to a European power, I[,] nevertheless, found existing there commercial and political forces which render a permanent political separation of British Columbia and Washington Territory impossible.[84]

Like Seward, many Americans still stubbornly supported the eventual absorption of British Columbia and Canada. They tried, both in the government and out, to persuade British Columbians that their welfare could best be served by joining the United States and not Canada.[85] Notwithstanding these efforts, the Legislative Council of the colony voted overwhelmingly for Confederation in November 1870, and three months later, it approved the terms of entry into the Dominion. The deciding factor had been the Prime Minister's promise to start construction of a connecting railroad within two years.[86]

British Columbia joined the Dominion instead of the United States because Canada could better satisfy the demands of the colonists. In the process Seward's negotiating strength had withered. Unlike American diplomats in the 1840s, he could not rely on strong public support for his expansionist program. Exhausted by the Civil War and fraught with problems resulting from it, Americans in the Reconstruction era concentrated on developing existing territories.[87] Consequently the informed public as well as a large bloc of congressional leaders eschewed Seward's policies for domestic reasons. On reflection, Seward observed that "the fact that they [his treaties] were made by President

Johnson's Secretary of State and Minister was reason enough for refusing to accept them."[88]

Of course, British policy decisions involving Canada deeply influenced the outcome of the issue. Whitehall initially adopted a "wait and see" attitude, but reversed its indifferent position because of the success of Canadian confederation after 1867 and the pressure of British capitalists who had invested heavily in the colony.[89] One such investor, A.R. Roche, disturbed at the "grasping propensities" of the United States, convinced the Royal Colonial Institute to launch a lobbying campaign to counteract the spirit of anti-colonialism in England.[90] Britain's resulting political support for the transfer of the Hudson's Bay Company lands to the Dominion and financial aid for the construction of a transcontinental railroad through the Canadian West helped persuade British Columbians that union with Canada was altogether feasible.[91]

The strength and vitality of Canadian nationalism, which Seward and his agents consistently misunderstood and underestimated, proved most important in the collapse of the American effort to annex the colony. If Seward overreacted to exaggerated reports from American officials in Canada, he himself was partly to blame for misreading the attachment felt by British Columbians to the British Empire and the effectiveness of Dominion efforts in retaining the colony for Canada.

NOTES

1 David E. Shi, "Seward's Attempt to Annex British Columbia, 1865–1869," *Pacific Historical Review*, 47, 2 (1978), 217–238. Reprinted with permission from the University of California Press.

2 See F.W. Howay, "British Columbia's Entrance into Confederation," *Canadian Historical Association Annual Report* (1927), 68–69; Hugh Keenleyside, "How British Columbia Was Almost Annexed by the U.S.A.," *Canadian Dimension*, VIII (1971), 27.

3 In the latest study of Seward's diplomacy, Ernest Paolino asserted that "on the mainland of the western hemisphere Seward tried only to acquire Alaska and the Isthmus of Panama." *The Foundations of the American Empire* (Ithaca, N.Y., 1973), 23. Other studies only briefly mention the Secretary's desire to obtain British Columbia. Glyndon Van Deusen, *William Henry Seward* (New York, 1967), 548–549; Adrian Cook, *The Alabama Claims: American Politics and Anglo-American Relations, 1865–1872* (Ithaca, N.Y., 1975), 38–39,

48–49; Howard I. Kushner, *Conflict on the Northwest Coast: American-Russian Rivalry in the Pacific Northwest, 1790–1867* (Westport, Conn., 1975), 153–154.

4 George E. Baker, ed., *The Works of William H. Seward* (5 vols., Boston, 1884), V, 320 (hereafter cited as Seward, *Works*).

5 Speech at Chautauqua, March 31, 1846, *ibid.*, III, 409.

6 *Ibid.*, IV, 333.

7 Paolino, *The Foundations of the American Empire*, 12–13; Albert K. Weinberg, *Manifest Destiny: A Study of Nationalist Expansionism in American History* (Chicago, 1963), 224–251.

8 There are two excellent studies of congressional support for expansion. Joe Smith, "The Republican Expansionists of the Early Reconstruction Era" (Ph.D. dissertation, University of Chicago, 1930), concludes that enthusiasm for Canada was merely a political move to gain votes; Alvin C. Glueck, Jr., *Minnesota and the Manifest Destiny of the Canadian Northwest* (Toronto, 1965), disagrees, maintaining that the proponents of expansion were sincere.

9 Goldwin Smith to Seward, April 16, 1865, William H. Seward Papers, University of Rochester.

10 *The Times* (London), Dec. 5, 1865.

11 Paolino, *The Foundations of the American Empire*, 11–12.

12 Frederick W. Seward, *Reminiscences of a War Time Statesman and Diplomat, 1830–1915* (New York, 1916), 360.

13 The standard history of British Columbia is Margaret A. Ormsby, *British Columbia: A History* (Vancouver, 1958).

14 F.W. Howay, W.W. Sage, H.F. Angus, *British Columbia and the United States: The Northern Pacific Slope from Fur Trade to Aviation* (Toronto, 1942), 183.

15 The proper names for Quebec and Ontario between 1846 and 1867.

16 *H. Ex. Doc. 128*, 39 Cong., 1 sess. (1866), 4.

17 Quoted in Ormsby, *British Columbia*, 218.

18 Donald F. Warner, *The Idea of Continental Union: Agitation for the Annexation of Canada to the United States, 1849–1893* (Lexington, Ky., 1960), 129.

19 *Sen. Ex. Doc. 30*, 39 Cong., 2 sess. (1866), 64.

20 Van Deusen, *William H. Seward*, 548–549.

21 Russell to Adams, Aug. 30, Oct. 14, 1865, enclosed in Adams to Seward, Sept. 7, Oct. 19, 1865, Diplomatic Dispatches to the Department of State (Great Britain), 1865, National Archives.

22 Seward to Adams, Aug. 27, 1866, Diplomatic Instructions, Great Britain, Department of State, National Archives.

23 Lord Stanley to Frederick Bruce, Nov. 30, 1866, FO 5/1326, Public Record Office, London.

24 Seward to Adams, Jan. 12, 1867, Diplomatic Instructions.
25 Allen Francis to Seward, Sept. 15 and 23, 1866, Consular Dispatches (Victoria), Department of State, 1866, National Archives.
26 John Bigelow, *Retrospection on an Active Life* (5 vols., New York, 1913), V, 58.
27 Seward to Andrew Johnson, Feb. 26, 1867, Andrew Johnson Papers, Library of Congress.
28 See Thomas A. Bailey, "Why the United States Purchased Alaska," *Pacific Historical Review,* III (1934), 39–49; Victor Farrar, *The Annexation of Russian America to the United States* (New York, 1967); Frank Golder, "The Purchase of Alaska," *American Historical Review,* XXV (1920), 411–425.
29 This was not an original idea. In January 1860, Senator William Gwin of California supported the purchase of Russian America in order to "displease to the last degree Great Britain and to weaken that power upon the Pacific by the sale of Alaska to the United States. Thereby, British Oregon would be isolated by the American barriers both on the northern and southern sides." H.M. McPherson, "The Interest of William McKendree Gwin in the Purchase of Alaska," *Pacific Historical Review,* III (1934), 37.
30 Bigelow, *Retrospections on an Active Life,* V, 58.
31 John Foster, *A Century of American Diplomacy* (Boston, 1900), 409; see also Donald M. Dozer, "Anti-Expansionism during the Johnson Administration," *Pacific Historical Review,* XII (1943), 258; Warner, *The Idea of Continental Union,* 134.
32 C.F. Adams, Jr., to C.F. Adams, June 29, 1867, Adams Papers, Library of Congress.
33 Edouard de Stoeckl to Alexander Gorchakov, April 19, 1867, Alaska Cession Correspondence, Dept. of State Records, National Archives.
34 Walter N. Sage, "The Annexation Movement in British Columbia," *Royal Society of Canada Proceedings,* XXI (1927), 102.
35 *British Columbian,* Apr. 27, 1867.
36 Francis to Seward, Apr. 23, 1867, Consular Dispatches (Victoria).
37 *British Colonist,* Apr. 25, 1867.
38 *New York Times,* Apr. 1, 1867.
39 *The Times* (London), Apr. 1, 1867. This comment reflects an ignorance of geography, since the Alaska coastline extended only partially down the colony's border.
40 Bruce to Stanley, Apr. 2, 1867, FO 115/465.
41 W.W. Dennison to F.W. Seward, May 1, 1867, in *H. Ex. Doc. 177,* 40 Cong., 2 sess. (1867), 234.

42 D.A. Mahoney to Seward, Apr. 10, 1867, Miscellaneous Letters of the Department of State, 1867, April, I, National Archives.
43 *St. Paul Press,* Apr. 10, 1867.
44 *Philadelphia North American and Gazette,* Apr. 12, 1867; *New York World,* Apr. 12, 1867.
45 Reginald Trotter, "Canada as a Factor in Anglo-American Relations in the 1860's," *Canadian Historical Review,* XVI (1935), 354.
46 *Montreal Gazette,* May 24, 1867.
47 Charles Francis Adams, Diary, Apr. 25, 1867, Adams Papers.
48 Adams to Seward, May 2, 1867, Diplomatic Dispatches.
49 Seward to Adams, May 2, 1867, Diplomatic Instructions.
50 *The Times* (London), May 11, 1867.
51 Adams, Diary, May 22, 1867, Adams Papers.
52 Quoted in P.B. Waite, *The Life and Times of Confederation: Politics, Newspapers and the Union of British North America* (Toronto, 1962), 317.
53 *New York Times,* June 26, 1867.
54 *Montreal Gazette,* June 27, 1867.
55 Adams, Diary, July 3, 1867.
56 Adams to Seward, Aug. 2, 1867, Diplomatic Dispatches.
57 *Ibid.*
58 *New York Times,* July 17, 1867.
59 Cited in Harold Schoenberger, *Transportation to the Seaboard: The "Communication Revolution" and American Foreign Policy, 1860–1900* (Westport, Conn., 1971), 24.
60 John S. Galbraith, *The Hudson's Bay Company as an Imperial Factor, 1821–1869* (Berkeley, 1957), 410–412.
61 Bruce to Stanley, Aug. 30, 1867, FO 115/466.
62 *American Railway Times,* June 15, 1867; see also Leonard B. Irwin, *Pacific Railways and Nationalism in the Canadian-American Northwest, 1845–1873* (Philadelphia, 1939), 106; E.V. Smalley, *History of the Northern Pacific Railroad* (New York, 1883), 146.
63 *Pacific Tribune,* Aug. 31, 1867.
64 Adams, Diary, Dec. 24, 1867.
65 *New York Evening Post,* Nov. 5, 1867.
66 "Memorial for Northern Pacific Railroad," *Sen. Misc. Doc. 9,* 40 Cong., 2 sess. (1867), 3.
67 Northern Pacific Railroad Company, *Statement of Its Resources and Merits as Presented to the Pacific Railroad Committee of Congress, House of Representatives* (n.p., 1868), 14.
68 London *Daily News,* Jan. 2, 1868.

69 Howay, "British Columbia's Entrance into Confederation," 68–69.
70 Calvin Pease and James G. Randall, eds., *The Diary of Orville Hickman Browning* (Springfield, Ill., 1933), 213.
71 James W. Taylor to Seward, Feb. 26, 1868, Seward Papers. Taylor asked Seward, "Will not Great Britain join in the cession of British Columbia if the United States will assume the indemnity of our citizens on account of the Alabama depredations?" Taylor to Seward, Nov. 18, 1868, Consular Dispatches (Winnipeg).
72 Adams, Diary, Mar. 26, 1868.
73 Keenleyside, "How British Columbia Was Almost Annexed by the U.S.A.," 27.
74 Irwin, *Pacific Railways,* 106. Besides a trend toward financial retrenchment in Congress at the time, the Northern Pacific's attempt to gain appropriations was hindered by the more effective lobbying of Tom Scott, who sought a southern transcontinental route.
75 Howay, *et al., British Columbia and the United States,* 184.
76 *Hansard Parliamentary Debates,* CXCII, 3rd series (London, 1803–1908), June 9, 1868, p. 1340.
77 *Cong. Globe,* 40 Cong., 2 sess. (July 1, 1868), 3660.
78 *Ibid.* (July 7, 1868), 3813.
79 Cited in William Stull Holt, *Treaties Defeated by the Senate: A Study of the Struggle between the President and Senate over the Conduct of Foreign Affairs* (Baltimore, 1933), 108.
80 Seward to Reverdy Johnson, July 20, 1868, Diplomatic Instructions.
81 See Henry Temple, "William H. Seward," in *The American Secretaries of State and Their Diplomacy,* ed. by Samuel F. Bemis (New York, 1928), VII, 133; Maureen Robson, "The *Alabama* Claims and the Anglo-American Reconciliation, 1865–1874," *Canadian Historical Review,* XLII (1961), 3; Joe Smith, "A United States of North America: Shadow or Substance?" *Canadian Historical Review,* XXVI (1945), 117; David Donald, *Charles Sumner and the Rights of Man* (New York, 1970), 392.
82 C.P. Stacey, "Britain's Withdrawal from North America," *Canadian Historical Review,* XXXVI (1955), 185–198.
83 Seward, *Works,* V, 569–570.
84 *Ibid.,* 574.
85 Hamilton Fish, Seward's successor, continued an active interest in the future of British Columbia. See Hamilton Fish to James W. Taylor, Dec. 20, 1869, Diplomatic Instructions, Special Missions File, 1852–1886; see also *Cong. Globe,* 41 Cong., 2 sess. (1870), 324; Alvin G. Glueck, Jr., "The Riel Rebellion and Canadian-American Relations," *Canadian Historical Review,* XXXVI (1955), 209.

86 Howay, "British Columbia's Entry into Confederation," 72–73.
87 Theodore C. Smith, "Expansion after the Civil War," *Political Science Quarterly*, XVI (1901), 412.
88 Frederick W. Seward, *William H. Seward: An Autobiography with a Memoir of His Life and Selections from His Letters* (3 vols. New York, 1877), III, 395.
89 Howay, *et al.*, *British Columbia and the United States*, 184.
90 Ormsby, *British Columbia*, 236.
91 G.P. de T. Glazebrook, *A History of Transportation in Canada* (Toronto, 1938), 196, 238.

# VIII

## 1867: A Formative Event?

What if Confederation was not, when appreciated in a wider historical context, really all that important after all? The selections here remind us that there are other forces at play that, when taken into account, might well overshadow Confederation when examining Canadian political development.

The first selections suggest that Canada is best seen through ideological lenses, and that when done so 1867 can really be seen only as the logical, and perhaps even inevitable extension of the society and the interests the colonies were already serving. The selection by Stanley Ryerson takes this approach from the left, offering one of Canada's few Marxist examinations of the event. The event was based on the need to enhance the environment for capital accumulation. Ian McKay agrees with Ryerson that Confederation was fundamentally in the interests of the business class, but that it is better explained from a liberal perspective. In a magisterial article published in 2000, McKay enunciated a new framework for understanding the nation-building process since 1850. McKay did not define 1867 as a turning point for Canadians. On the contrary, what McKay has called the "liberal order framework" had started with the failure of the 1837–38 Rebellions. This system of governance centred on the preservation of property rights and capital went through a process of consolidation throughout the second half of the nineteenth century, and Confederation was part of this process.

Adele Perry's research reminds us that understanding the making of Canada doesn't encompass just constitutional provisions, trade arrangements, and railway lines, but that at its heart, it is a larger and more encompassing story about colonial history. Perry argues that history needs to be written in a way that recognizes the centrality of Indigenous peoples and the many ways in which they challenged imperial ideals and transgressed colonial norms. Using British Columbia as her case study, she underscores the importance of race and gender to analyse colonialism.

In his seminal book on the foundation of Quebec society, sociologist Fernand Dumont analysed the political, social, and economic conditions that confined Quebeckers to survive as a people from 1838 to 1960. Dumont identified this time period as *le long hiver de la survivance* (the long winter of survival). According to him, Confederation was not a turning point. On the contrary, Confederation consolidated and expanded the system of governance that confined Quebec to a state of subordination and led its political and religious elites to develop myths such as "the chosen people that had to survive." This state of subordination was a legacy of the failure of the 1837–38 Rebellions that led to the amalgamation of Lower Canada and Upper Canada into the Province of Canada. This new political order was the basis of the 1867 constitutional framework. Furthermore, the real meaning of the constitution might not have been particularly well understood in French Canada – for all the struggles that French Canada has had with federalism, did the founders really understand the concepts as we have come to know them today?

Finally, Confederation might not have been that important at all, simply representing yet another technical shift in the governance of the colonies but meaning very little in terms of power relations on the continent. This point is made by James Daschuck in his selection, noting that for many Indigenous Canadians in the West, the formative events of privation, disease, and genocide were happening in parallel to (and with little regard for) the Confederation events in the East. While the Fathers of Confederation were dreaming of taking ownership of the Prairies, they had little concern for those living there. It mattered little once the region was more fully integrated into the Canadian political space in the decades afterwards; the damage had been done.

Other perspectives and views might have been included. But it is worth recognizing how little changed, in some ways, in 1867. Many of the basic ideas of constitutional government, including responsible government, had already been achieved by the 1840s. Canada would not truly become independent, a *sine qua non* of nationhood, until the Statute of Westminster in 1931; it did not have a final say over the judicial branch until 1949; and it did not gain formal control of the constitution until 1982. Indigenous peoples were displaced from their lands both before and after Confederation. While 1867 serves as a clear benchmark for when the British colonies united, it would be wrong to mark that date for when Canada became complete – that is still in progress.

# "Engineering a Federal Union"

## *Unequal Union: Roots of Crisis in the Canadas, 1815–1873* 1973

STANLEY B. RYERSON[1]

What broke the log-jam in the summer of 1864 was the formation of a Canadian coalition government dedicated to finding a solution to the constitutional question in the direction of federation. In June, a parliamentary committee formed on Brown's initiative had reported "a strong feeling ... in favor of changes in the direction of a federative system, applied either to Canada alone, or to the whole British North American provinces...."[2] The following day the Taché-Macdonald government – the tenth in a decade – lost its precarious majority; and, through the intermediary of Alexander Morris (the lecturer on "Nova Britannia") and James Ferrier (of the Grand Trunk), negotiations between Brown and Macdonald, Galt and Cartier were started, leading to formation of the historic coalition.

It was George Brown's decision to offer to join forces with his ancient adversaries Macdonald and Cartier in an attempt to reach a solution in federation that made the new arrangement possible. It was Macdonald's canny management of the very mixed forces in the new coalition, and his leadership in the conferences with the Maritime delegates, that finally brought the Confederation project to fruition.

In the "Great Coalition" Macdonald, with Galt, represented the general interest of the leading English-Canadian business community, closely tied in with London and the Grand Trunk, and having Montreal as its main headquarters.

Brown spoke for the industrial and commercial leaders of Toronto, rivals of Montreal, and a large area of rural as well as urban Reform opinion in Canada West.

Cartier was the spokesman of the conservative wing of the French-Canadian bourgeoisie and of the Church, allied with Anglo-Canadian capital. Their adherence to the federation scheme had been secured since 1858, with Cartier's acceptance of it as the basis for his joining an administration led by Galt and Macdonald. The interests for whom Cartier spoke were secured by a twofold bond: association with the Grand Trunk and the Bank of Montreal; and a common abhorrence of the radical democracy of the *Parti rouge,* whose exclusion from the coalition was not the least of its attractions for them.

The radical democrats of Canada East combatted the Macdonald-Cartier proposals as being undemocratic on two main counts: their inadequate recognition of the rights of the French-Canadian nationality,[3] and an undue recognition of the rights of property. "The Grand Trunk people are at the bottom of it," Dorion charged, citing Edward Watkin's glowing assurances to the investors on "the enhanced value which will be given to their shares and bonds, by the adoption of the Confederation scheme and the construction of the Intercolonial...."[4]

The new state structure was indeed designed to meet the economic and political requirements of the "dominant social groups" in the colonies and in the imperial metropolis. As Professor Alfred Dubuc points out,

> In economic terms Confederation was essentially an instrument of public finance whose object it was to make available to those responsible for effecting investment, the resources necessary for the unified economic development of the British colonies in North America.[5]

Geared to an overall project of growth within the Empire, embracing farming and forest industries, protected manufactures and mass immigration, the approach "assumed that one economic sector could be nurtured for the benefit of all...."

> The privileged sector was to be that of the railroads. It was precisely the interest of groups associated with the railroads which inspired Confederation.

On these economic foundations was to arise a state structure that would best serve the needs of the "rising capitalist class" whose new ascendancy is now being recognized as the crucial development of the mid-19th century. Alfred Dubuc continues,

> The Canadian state was to be a bourgeois and capitalist state; through their lobbies the great financial institutions and the great industrial enterprises would dominate the political parties as much as the various ministries ... Confederation, in the form it took, was made possible through the domination of the financial and commercial upper middle class over the lower middle class.

The "upper middle class" in question was actually the colonial ruling class: the financial-industrial bourgeoisie, than whom no other group stood higher in the social pyramid. Galt, Cartier, John Ross, at once Conservative cabinet members and Grand Trunk administrators, were the political protagonists of its Montreal wing.

While Canada West furnished the Conservatives with such prominent businessmen as John Ross and a number of railway promoters, an important grouping of Toronto capitalists supported the Liberals under George Brown's leadership. Toronto in 1863 was represented in the Canadian Assembly by "two wealthy Liberal business men," J. Macdonald and A.M. Smith; W.P. Howland and Adam Wilson were among the leaders of "Toronto's Liberal commercial group."[6]

By the time Confederation became a reality, the leading Toronto Liberals were men "well established in the city's business community ... owners of leading city firms."[7] John McMurrich, William McMaster, and the Howlands are among the names; the same ones largely recur in the list of directors of the newly formed Bank of Commerce, "Toronto's latest answer to the Bank of Montreal," as Professor Careless calls it. George Brown was a substantial shareholder, and McMaster the bank's first president. Not only were these men leading spokesmen of capitalist interests in the Province of Canada; they at the same time "were concerned with both political and economic control over the West. It was quite natural that the same men should be at the core of both the western Reform party and the big new western banking institution, each of which was dedicated to gaining power in the Dominion that was so soon to be established."[8]

Herein lies the real significance of the alliance that Brown negotiated with Macdonald in the meetings at the Hotel St. Louis, Quebec, in June 1864. The resulting "great coalition" was a coalition of the two key sections of Anglo-Canadian business. Traditionally, historians in English Canada have hailed as decisive the Macdonald-Brown agreement to join forces in order to break the political deadlock and together solve the constitutional problem. Tribute to their statesmanship, however, has seemed to require a certain reticence about the class forces and class interests to which the Confederate leaders gave expression. Yet historically, it was just these forces that lent the alliance its decisive character.

Another related facet of the "great coalition" that is generally obscured should be mentioned.... It is the relatively minor importance usually attached to Cartier's adherence to the coalition, as compared with Brown's decisive role in its formation. It is not only that Cartier had been committed to the scheme since 1858; it is the fact that the adherence of the clerical and French-Canadian business interests, while indispensable for British-American union, quite definitely stood second in importance to the political consolidation of the English-speaking capitalist groupings for whom Brown and Macdonald spoke. The Canadian bourgeois state was to embody the political and economic hegemony of Anglo-Canadian business,[9] the ruling interest in British North America.

If the formation of the Brown-Macdonald coalition government marked one decisive stage in the union process, negotiations with the Atlantic colonial provinces were another.

The new government, aware of the impending conference on Maritime Union, took advantage of the opportunity it offered. A communication went to the three provinces asking if they would agree to a delegation from Canada participating, "to ascertain whether the proposed Union may not be made to embrace the whole of the British North American Provinces." The response was favorable, but with the proviso that it be an informal participation.

Accordingly, at the end of August, eight Canadians embarked for Charlottetown: John A. Macdonald, George Brown, G.E. Cartier, A.T. Galt, T. D'Arcy McGee, H. Langevin, William McDougall, and Alex Campbell. On the morning of September 1 the Maritime delegates, gathered in the Colonial Building, decided to postpone discussion of a Maritime Union until the Canadians (whose ship was just then entering the harbor) had presented their point of view. Representing the Maritimes were, from Nova Scotia: Charles Tupper, W.A. Henry, R.B. Dickey, A.G. Archibald, and J. McCully; New Brunswick: S.L. Tilley, W.H. Steeves, J.M. Johnson, E.D. Chandler, J.H. Gray; and Prince

Edward Island: John Hamilton Gray, G. Coles, W.H. Pope, E. Palmer, and A.A. Macdonald.[10]

The Conference, under the chairmanship of Col. J.H. Gray, Premier of P.E.I., was largely taken up with addresses by the leading Canadian delegates on various phases of the confederation scheme. On Friday, September 2, Cartier and Brown each gave a general introduction, dealing with both the broad perspective and the specific question of provincial rights, about which their hearers were particularly concerned; Brown introducing the idea of combining representation based on population in the future federal lower house with equality of representation in the upper house for each of the three sections (the two Canadas and the combined Maritimes). Macdonald, while not actually rejecting the federal principle, to which the Canadians were already committed, put great emphasis on the need for a strong central power. The argument is conveyed in a speech he made a few days later in Halifax (by agreement, no record was kept of the speeches in conference; this was also the procedure at Quebec). Pointing to the U.S. experience, where all power not specifically ceded to the central government had remained vested in the separate states, he observed,

> The dangers that have arisen from this system we will avoid, if we can agree upon forming a strong central government, a great central legislature, a constitution for union which will have all the rights of sovereignty except those that are given to the local governments.... I hope that we will be enabled to work out a constitution that will have a strong central government, able to offer a powerful resistance to any foe whatever, and at the same time will preserve for each Province its own identity, and will protect every local ambition: and if we cannot do this, we shall not be able to carry out the end we have in view.[11]

This was indeed the problem; its solution required agreement on complicated financial as well as political questions, a basis for which was offered in Galt's speech on the Monday. But first, and above all, there had to be general agreement in principle with the idea as a whole. On each of the addresses there had been questions and discussion; there was one more day of general deliberation, concluding with an invitation by the Canadians to an official conference, to be held a month later at Quebec; and the day following, the Maritime representatives met separately. It then became apparent that the project of a Maritime legislative union was unworkable, since Prince Edward Island would not give up its separate legislature and insisted on Charlottetown as the capital of the union. The conference as a whole then adjourned to Halifax (D'Arcy McGee having meanwhile delivered a lecture in Charlottetown on Robert Burns), where agreement was reached on the Canadian proposal for a formal conference in Quebec, to open on October 10.

The idea of a larger federal union had won acceptance – in principle. At Quebec, the federal compact was embodied in seventy-two resolutions, which became the basis of the British North America Act of 1867. The first three resolutions read as follows:

1. The best interests and present and future prosperity of British North America will be promoted by a Federal Union under the Crown of Great Britain, provided such a Union can be effected on principles just to the several provinces.
2. In the Federation of the British North American Provinces the system of government best adapted under existing circumstances to protect the diversified interests of the several Provinces, and secure efficiency, harmony and permanency in the working of the Union, would be a General Government charged with matters of common interest to the whole country, and Local Governments for each of the Canadas, and for the Provinces of Nova Scotia, New Brunswick and Prince Edward Island, charged with the control of local matters in their respective sections; provision being made for the admission into the Union, on equitable terms, of Newfoundland, the North-West Territory, British Columbia and Vancouver.
3. In framing a Constitution for the General Government, the Conference, with a view to the perpetuation of our connections with the Mother country, and to the promotion of the best interests of the people of these Provinces, desire to follow the model of the British Constitution, so far as our circumstances will permit.[12]

Thus was fashioned, in 1864, the cornerstone of the unified Canadian federal state.

The year and a half that intervened between the Quebec Conference and the proclamation of the British North America Act were marked by controversy, frustration, and uncertainty. Debate waxed and waned in the Maritimes and Canada East: two of the three areas whose incorporation into the new Dominion presented thorny problems. The third – the Northwest – erupted later.

While the Legislative Assembly of the Province of Canada was debating the Quebec resolutions, a swelling surge of anti-Confederation sentiment in the Maritimes threatened rejection of the scheme of union. This challenge called forth strenuous efforts by both railway-promoter-politicians and the Colonial Office to put through the project, which the needs of economic development and military security alike made imperative. As a strong reason for union with Canada, Tilley of New Brunswick pointed to the prospect of abrogation of Reciprocity. For his part, Tupper of Nova Scotia had warned the Charlottetown Conference that the end of the Civil War might see the armies of the U.S. moving against the British provinces. Gray of P.E.I. "saw the issue squarely as a choice between federation and absorption by the United States."[13]

Yet no sooner had the Canadian Assembly endorsed the Quebec Resolutions than the New Brunswick electors resoundingly repudiated them. Tilley's pro-confederation government was voted out of office at the end of March 1865. In Nova Scotia a storm of opposition was brewing and Tupper, to avoid an upset, tacked hastily: he revived consideration of Maritime union, rather than steer head-on into the squall over Confederation. The governors of both provinces had intrigued and lobbied to defeat the project of a larger union. Both were firmly told by the Colonial Office that they were off course: the new imperial policy favored confederation. Prince Edward Island's legislature voted down the federation proposals. The Newfoundland government, after keeping the question in suspense for several years, moved toward agreement, then was repudiated at the polls.

Opposition to the confederation proposals in the Atlantic provinces in part reflected the concern of local commercial capitalist interests for their competitive position, in part the strong attachment of the people to their regional identity and autonomy. Some merchants in Saint John and Halifax were more interested in strengthening their ties with New England than with the Canadas. According to J.H. Gray of New Brunswick, the bankers of Saint John "dreaded the competition of Canadian banks coming here and the consequent destruction of (their) monopoly."[14] Railway promoters in the same city wanted to put through an extension to Maine of their European & North American Railroad, so that "people ... who had an eye to our resources" would be induced "to come in and develop them." Small manufacturers feared that larger Canadian producers would swamp their local market. There was anxiety lest Canada's burdens of debt be thrust on to Maritime taxpayers. Newfoundlanders feared that their interest in the fisheries would not be safeguarded in Canadian trade agreements with the United States; moreover they looked to London for support in resisting the encroachments of the French fishery. All four Atlantic colonies considered the financial arrangements worked out at Quebec to be unsatisfactory. As Joseph Howe put it, "All our revenues are to be taken by the general government, and we get back 80 cents per head, the price of a sheepskin."

The feeling of a regional – almost national – identity that had grown up among the inhabitants of the Maritimes found vehement expression.[15] The method by which the federation scheme was being pursued – behind closed doors and without popular consultation – strengthened the fear that democratic gains won in the 1830s and 1840s might be sacrificed. Howe, while stating his readiness to agree to union on terms fair to the Maritimes, declared,

> The people of Nova Scotia for 108 years had their own Parliament, and responsible government for 25. I hold that to deprive them of these rights by an arbitrary act of Parliament, passed at the instigation of the Canadians, who have never invested a pound of capital in our country, would be an atrocious proceeding, out of which would grow undying hatreds and ultimate annexation.[16]

To him, as to many, Nova Scotia was "our country." Howe's lieutenant, Annand, wrote, "We will not willingly allow ourselves to be brought into subjection to Canada or any other country."[17] He demanded "exact equality" and not "the detestable confederation that has been attempted to be forced upon us … a union brought about by corrupt and arbitrary means." Another journalist warned, "Our nationality would be merged into that of Canada …"

In New Brunswick the anti-confederation forces charged that the delegates to Charlottetown had "arrogated to themselves powers that did not legitimately belong to them, and undertook to alter the institutions of the country and surrender the independence we have so long enjoyed." Canada, a Fredericton editor declared, had "a pressing internal difficulty to overcome," and through union would gain "considerable material advantages." New Brunswickers surely would regret "to see their roads, by-roads, bridges and schools going down, down, while they see Canada growing greatly partly by their money."

The rejection of the confederation proposal by the New Brunswick electors in March 1865 necessitated a combined operation to reverse the verdict. As a result of the exertions of the Colonial Office, the Governor General, the Lieutenant-Governor of New Brunswick, the Canadian Government, and the Grand Trunk, by the spring of 1866 the Smith government found itself obliged to appeal to the electorate. Tilley thereupon wired John A. (in code), "Will need $40 or $50 thousand."[18] A few days later he followed up with a letter: "The election can be made certain if *the means* are used ... It must be done with great caution and in such a way as not to awaken suspicion." The arrangements were to be worked through the intermediary of a wealthy Saint John ship-owner ("worth at least $100,000") who was to meet Brydges, the Grand Trunk manager, in Portland, Maine. Nor were the anti-Confederationists without cash backing. Together with assistance from U.S.-linked trading houses and railway speculators, they could count on "a certain enterprising lumber operator" who bolstered their campaign fund in exchange for 15,000 acres of the public domain.

For their part, the Colonial Office and Governor-General Monck exerted themselves as vigorously as the Canadian politicians and railway magnates in the cause of union. The Colonial Secretary penned a dispatch to the Maritimes stating as "the strong and deliberate opinion of Her Majesty's Government" that it was "an object much to be desired and that all the British North American colonies should agree to unite in one Government."[19]

The "loyalty" cry was worked to the limit, with the Montreal *Gazette* admonishing the reluctant New Brunswick neighbors, "It is idle for them to conceal the fact from themselves – confederation or union of some sort is a condition of the continuance of the British connection"; it was up to them to show whether theirs was "mere lip loyalty." The alarms attendant on the Fenian raids of 1866 contributed a further element of leverage: a "war scare" hysteria was calculatingly kept up with the help of troop movements and parades, in Saint John especially. Tilley and the pro-confederation forces carried the election handily.

Tupper in Nova Scotia meanwhile managed to get around the difficulty of popular opposition to the confederation terms by having the Assembly pass a resolution in favor of "union" in general, to be negotiated with Britain and the provincial governments. In the fall of 1866 delegations from Nova Scotia and New Brunswick proceeded to London, to meet with representatives from Canada and the imperial authorities.

The Maritimers' concern for regional and local autonomy was reinforced by concern for democratic rights. In both respects their sentiments paralleled the attitude of the Canada East opposition. The leaders of the confederation movement did in fact betray a notable aversion to popular consultation. Union was to be effected "from above," in close and confidential association with key figures in the world of business and with the imperial authorities. Macdonald was quite explicit: "As it would be obviously absurd to submit the complicated details of such a measure to the people, it is not proposed to seek their sanction before asking the Imperial Government to introduce a Bill in the British Parliament." When the measure was in the early stages of preparation in London, in October 1866, Macdonald wrote to Tilley, who was already in England,

> It appears to us to be important that the Bill should not be finally settled until just before the meeting of the British Parliament. The measure must be carried *per saltum* [in one leap], and no echo of it must reverberate through the British provinces till it becomes law.... The Act once passed and beyond remedy the people would soon learn to be reconciled to it.[20]

The character of the state that was in the making would be democratic only to a partial and limited degree. The popular liberties won in past struggles could not, assuredly, be effaced or altogether denied: yet they must be kept firmly within bounds! The bounds were set by property and class interest. After all, the men who shaped Confederation, the political spokesmen of the banking, trading, and railway interests – the rising Canadian capitalist class – were themselves men of property, concerned with property. A spokesman for the seigneurs warned the Legislative Council against the possibility of local legislatures repudiating payment of the seigneurial debt (payment to the seigneurs guaranteed by the 1854 Act abolishing the tenure). "On this question," he said, "it will be easy to excite the passion of the people, prejudiced as they already are against the seigneurs. *Chiefly, and above all, we are bound to respect vested rights.*"[21]

As his biographer Joseph Pope relates, Macdonald, until the last day of his life viewed universal suffrage "as one of the greatest evils that could befall a state.... The idea that a man should vote simply because he breathed was ever repellant to Sir John Macdonald's conception of government."[22] In 1861 he had argued that "unless property were protected, and made one of the principles upon which representation was based, we might perhaps have a people altogether equal, but we should cease to be a people altogether free."[23] In the Confederation debate he reported that at Quebec "not a single one of the representatives of the Government or of the Opposition of any one of the Lower Provinces was in favor of universal suffrage. Everyone felt that in this respect the principle of the British constitution should be carried out, and that classes and property should be represented as well as numbers."[24]

The radical democrats in both the Canadas, who saw in the bankers and railway financiers the principal opponents of a broader democracy, fought unsuccessfully for universal suffrage and the elective principal at all levels of government.

Despite the fact that in the Province of Canada popular pressure had secured an elective Legislative Council in 1856, the delegates at Quebec agreed readily to a non-elective upper chamber. A.A. Dorion denounced "the proposal to restrict the influence and control of the people over the Legislature of the country by substituting a Chamber nominated by the Crown for an Elective Legislative Council."[25] The non-elective Senate was simply a rather more glaring instance of the manifold ways in which a business democracy saw to the safeguarding of the rights and privileges of those – the men of property – who comprise its permanent minority government. The prerogatives of the Crown were seen as a further reassurance.

The Act that enshrined at Westminster at once the interests of property and the deeper aspirations of those who sought "a new political nationality" was the joint product of colonial initiative and pressure and imperial strategy. The birth certificate of the new transcontinental colonial state bore the imprint of this mixed parentage; the opening words of the British North America Act (1867) proclaim:

> Whereas the Provinces of Canada, Nova Scotia, and New Brunswick have expressed their desire to be federally united into one Dominion under the Crown of the United Kingdom of Great Britain and Ireland, with a constitution similar in principle to that of the United Kingdom: Be it therefore enacted and declared by the Queen's most Excellent Majesty … (that) the Provinces of Canada, Nova Scotia and New Brunswick shall form and be one Dominion under the name of Canada….

"Canada cannot remain as she is at present," John A. Macdonald had asserted at Quebec three years before. The imperatives of change were working their way toward a new political state, a semi-autonomous federation of colonial provinces, a "Dominion" under the aegis of an Empire which still retained the powers of decision in foreign relations and peace and war. The "dominion from sea to sea," in the text from which the term derived (72 Psalms, v. 8) referred to a fiefdom of the Deity. In practical terms, however, most British Americans took it to mean the domain of Empire that it was in fact. For some, in French Canada particularly, the dominion was exercised by the "other nation" – that of the heirs to the Conquest. First in Lower Canada, then among the Métis of the Northwest, that dominance was questioned.

NOTES

1 Stanley B. Ryerson, "Engineering a Federal Union," in *Unequal Union: Roots of Crisis in the Canadas, 1815–1873* (Toronto: Progress Books, 1973), 342–357.

2 *Journals of the Legislative Assembly* (1864) 384; R.G. Trotter: *Canadian Federation* (1924), 64.

3 Cf. below: "French Canada and the Terms of Union." On this as on the role of the railway question, the criticism of the *Rouges* of a century ago is finding confirmation in the judgments of not a few of today's political scientists.

4 *Confederation Debates*, 251.

5 A. Dubuc, "The Decline of Confederation and the New Nationalism," in Peter Russell, ed. *Nationalism in Canada* (1966), 114, 119.

6 J.S. Careless, *Brown of the Globe* (1963), ii, 96.

7 P.G. Cornell, *Alignment of Political Groups in Canada 1841–1867* (1962), 50.

8 Careless, op. cit., ii, 244.

9 Trotter, 88.

10 The foregoing, together with ten others who took part in the Quebec Conference a month later, comprise the "Fathers of Confederation." All thirty-three were at Quebec; the ten who were at Quebec and not at Charlottetown were, from Canada: E.P. Taché, Oliver Mowat, J.C. Chapais, J. Cockburn; New Brunswick: Peter Mitchell, C. Fisher; P.E.I.: T.H. Haviland, E. Whelan; and Newfoundland: F.B.T. Carter and Ambrose Shea. At the Conference in London, in December 1866, P.E.I. and Newfoundland were not represented, having withdrawn from the

negotiations; and the Canadian delegation included one member who had not been at either Charlottetown or Quebec – W.H. Howland, a leading Toronto businessman.

11 Gray, *Confederation*, 44–5.
12 Ibid., 66.
13 Glazebrook, *Short History of Canada* (1950), 97.
14 Gray, 382.
15 M.O. Hammond, *Confederation and Its Leaders* (1917), 277.
16 Chisholm, *Letters & Speeches*, ii, 46344.
17 Hammond, 68, 290, 292.
18 Tilley to Macdonald, April 14, 17, 20; cf. Creighton, *Road to Confederation*, 373.
19 Trotter, 130, 139.
20 Pope, *Memoirs…*, 326–7.
21 J.O. Bureau; in *Confederation Debates*, 191.
22 Pope, 242, 616.
23 *Ibid.*, 242.
24 *Ibid.*, 294.
25 *Confederation Debates*, 245.

# "Gender, Race, and Our Years on the Edge of Empire"

## *On the Edge of Empire: Gender, Race and the Making of British Columbia, 1849–1871*
## 2001

ADELE PERRY[1]

Our years on the edge of empire were dominated by a protracted and many-pronged effort to reconstruct British Columbia as a white society. This effort was premised on powerful and overlapping critiques of both First Nations and settler society. Dispossession and settlement were not discrete processes: they were mutually dependent and deeply intertwined. Marginalizing First Nations and fostering white society were two sides of one colonial coin, and it is gender that makes their entwined character most clear. Examining the place of gender in British Columbia's colonial project has implications for how we understand British Columbia's past and its present. For historians, these years on the edge of empire suggest the significance of imperialism to British Columbia history and the importance of gender to this and other colonial projects. For British Columbians, especially white ones, the connections between gender, race, and colonial society raised between 1849 and 1871 suggest the necessity of rethinking our fraught relationship to race and place.

British Columbia's problems were the empire's problems. The social history of mid-nineteenth-century British Columbia cannot be adequately understood unless we approach it as a chapter in the international history of imperialism. Mid-nineteenth-century settlers spoke of themselves, their neighbours, and their place using the language of imperialism: they were a civilized and white people surrounded by savage

Indians in an empty and undeveloped place that could be transformed into an exemplary British colony. As a diverse body of work usually lumped together under the awkward rubric of "post-structural" or "post-modern" theory reminds us, language counts. The language of colonial British Columbia suggests the centrality of imperialism to that society. There was nothing natural or destined about a patch of northwestern North America becoming an outpost of British empire: to the extent it became one demands and deserves our self-conscious explication. This task is eased considerably by the development of a rich literature on colonial and postcolonial societies that suggests the important connections between local colonial projects and empire writ large.

While British Columbia is imperial history, it is hardly an example of imperialism's unmitigated success. The many and varied efforts to transform British Columbia from a First Nations territory to a white settler colony do not suggest imperial triumph as much as they hint at imperial vulnerability. Much of this vulnerability stemmed from the active resistance of British Columbia's large First Nations population. Colonial weakness also was generated by the conflicts encoded in imperialism's very structure. Empires were designed and promulgated in the name of high-minded ideals and responsibilities and in the interests of power and money. Yet they were practically enforced by large bodies of men whose commitment to colonialism's putative aims was always different and sometimes weak. Throughout the imperial world, officials debated how unruly lots of unattached soldiers, miners, and other working-class men could be transformed into suitable representatives of their race, fit to rule over their racial inferiors. In French Indochina and the Dutch Indies, as Ann Laura Stoler has demonstrated, poor white migration was restricted and *petit blancs* regulated,[2] while in British India, an elaborate system of regulated prostitution was inaugurated around military cantonments.[3] Reformers proffered different solutions in British Columbia. There, they tackled the sharpest symbols of colonial difference by working to regulate the rough homosocial culture that flourished in the colony's backwoods, transforming the many conjugal relationships forged between First Nations women and settler men, tinkering with land and immigration policies, and, ultimately, importing white women.

However various and constant, these efforts did not succeed in transforming British Columbia into the orderly white-settler colony that so dominated settler dreams. As Tina Loo has wisely commented, historians of Aboriginal-white relations have "been forced to grapple with two countervailing pressures: the need, on the one hand, to acknowledge Aboriginal resistance and agency, and the need, on the other, to recognize their subjugation."[4] Colonialism was both fragile and formidable in mid-nineteenth-century British Columbia. To be sure, imperialism was triumphant insofar as the years between 1849 and 1871 marked the onset of sustained European occupation, a political, economic, and cultural arrangement that has subsequently been persistently challenged but never defeated. However successful the colonial state was in conclusively asserting its authority, it fundamentally failed to recast the society it governed in its own image. First Nations resistance and persistence thwarted visions of a European-dominated agricultural society, as did the unwillingness of settlers to live up to the narrow roles accorded them in colonial discourse. Aboriginal people remained the majority of the population until the final years of the nineteenth century, and the small colonial settlements continued to depart from the norms and values of mainstream Anglo-American society.

Recognizing the significance of colonialism to British Columbia history necessitates rethinking First Nations history and its relation to Canadian history as a whole. Canadian history as it has generally been articulated in the late twentieth century tends to neutralize colonialism by describing it as "settlement" and subtly but pervasively implying that Aboriginal people ceased to be significant historical players sometime around 1812 in central Canada and 1886 in Western Canada. It is as if the ultimate success of the colonial project in Canada blinds us to its own history. First Nations stories are instead relegated to what we might call "genre-Aboriginal history." At best this scholarship offers sensitive cultural studies, while at worst it suspends the First Nations in an anthropological moment that, as Anne McClintock argues, situates non-Western people irrevocably outside of history.[5] A perhaps uniquely North American variation that persists in Canadian history textbooks is to associate First Nations people with the land, to insert them in discussions of landscape and geography, and in doing so, substitute the archeological moment for the anthropological one.

The frameworks through which historians have analysed First Nations people and their relationship to Canadian society need to be revised if we are to adequately comprehend societies like mid-nineteenth-century British Columbia. Its social history cannot be adequately accessed unless First Nations demographic dominance, social centrality, and political agency are recognized. To suggest that Aboriginal history is social history is not to deny either the cultural specificity of First Nations experience or Western historical methodology. There are profound limits on the extent to which a methodology premised on written records can capture the history of oral cultures. Work produced, in Himani Bannerji's words, "solely within the parameter of neglect of the question of location and the colonized's history, language, and culture" is necessarily partial and profoundly flawed.[6] Non-Aboriginal historians like myself need not only to borrow the ethnohistorical methodologies being developed by scholars like Georges Sioui, but to recognize the limits as well as the benefits of research that is simultaneously cross-cultural and historical.[7] Doing so does not invalidate historical scholarship on First Nations society as much as it complicates it.

It is not First Nations history alone that deserves our critical rethinking. Analysing British Columbia history as colonial history also prompts a recognition and exploration of the history of whiteness. White people, like peoples of colour, were racialized, and the historical processes by which whiteness was constituted and empowered can and must be excavated. Yet, as Catherine Hall notes, because whiteness is a signifier of dominance and "the dominant rarely reflect on their dominance in the ways that the subjected reflect on their subjection,"[8] it has rarely been the subject of serious investigation. The history of colonial British Columbia stands as a sharp example of how whiteness was far from given or salient. Whiteness was constructed, problematic, and fragile, an identity that was simultaneously created and destabilized by the backwoods experience. In First Nations territories and among a plural settler community, people both learned to be white and had their whiteness threatened. Whiteness was at once powerful and precarious. Exploring its dual character puts a signifier of dominance under the analytic lens usually reserved for subjection.

Colonialism was never about race alone. Gender was key to colonialism in British Columbia just as it was to the imperial world. It figured prominently both in the critique of British Columbia society and in that society's attempted remaking. The very processes of cultural contact were themselves literally and highly gendered. First Nations and settler usually met not as ungendered subjects but as men and women. The colonial society they built fostered gendered identities and relations that departed meaningfully from the norms and mores of dominant Anglo-American culture. White male homosocial culture and heterosexual relationships forged between First Nations women and settler men stand as special examples of the novelty of gender on this edge of empire. Gender was similarly prominent in the attempts to reconstruct

British Columbia as an orderly white society. For many critics and reformers, homosocial culture and mixed-race relationships – and the notions of manliness and womanliness they contained – seemed special affronts to visions of imperial respectability. For them, the colony was not simply a poor fit with models of appropriate racial subjectivity and behaviour, but a place that fostered alternative and perhaps dangerous ways of being male, female, and sexual. Campaigns to bring metropolitan manliness to the backwoods, to reformulate or eradicate mixed-race relationships, and to create activist land and immigration policies were all attempts to alter gender. That these campaigns culminated in the importation of working-class women from Britain indicates the significance of white womanhood to the gendered history of colonial British Columbia.

But exploring the place of gender in British Columbia's colonial project means more than noting the existence or significance of women. It means, as historians of gender have now long attested, interrogating the significance of manhood as well as womanhood. Had masculinity been neither historical nor variable, the rich homosocial culture would never have developed in British Columbia's backwoods, nor would it have become the object of a spate of regulatory schemes. Nor, for that matter, would the fates of settler men connected to First Nations women have become the objects of such anxiety. Examining masculinity does not, however, necessarily mean a weakening of our commitment to critically analysing gendered power relations or relinquishing serious feminist scholarship for a hazy "I've got gender, you've got gender" approach. Undertaking critical scholarship on masculinity, like whiteness, instead means exposing the deep connections between gender and race and power in a way that recognizes their historicity and interconnectedness.

In colonial British Columbia, gender derived its particular shape and significance not from its separateness but from its deep connections to race. As the growing international literature probing the entangled nature of gender, race, and imperialism suggests, it is as futile to speak of women or men as undifferentiated masses as it is to read contact and colonialism outside of the lens of gender. Colonial social organization and discourse ensured that what it meant to be a white woman or a First Nations woman was profoundly different. Gender was deeply racialized and indeed cannot be comprehended otherwise. In British Columbia, it was racialized in a way that often explicitly benefited white women, who were accorded a prestige and authority by virtue of their unique position within the colonial project. Recognizing the specificity of white womanhood, in British Columbia or elsewhere, is a small step in the larger effort to interrogate the salient limits on universalizing analyses of gender and patriarchy. False and ultimately dangerous notions of universal womanhood have informed Canadian gender history as much as they have underpinned other literatures. In response, we need what Ruth Frankenberg calls "the reciprocal specification of *white* womanhood" as demanded by the rigorous examination by women of colour of the refraction of gender through race.[9]

To suggest that white women held a special if contested place in the construction of the local colonial project is not to blame the brutal enterprise of imperialism on a handful of relatively powerless settler women. A series of works have persuasively argued that, contrary to reputation, white women were not the "ruin of empire," destructive and petty agents bent on wrecking harmonious race relations in colonial contexts.[10] To suggest otherwise is to romanticize colonial experience before white women's arrival and to exaggerate white women's racism in the interest of absolving white men of their fundamental responsibility for imperialism. While these studies have been crucial in restoring women's place in colonial history, they have also, as both Margaret Jolly and Jane Haggis point out, minimized or indeed rendered invisible the politics of race and empire. "In the ways in which white women have been brought to the fore of the historical and analytical stage," writes Haggis, "colonialism is no longer a problem of power, exploitation, and oppression, but rather of the gender identity of the rulers."[11] Haggis's trenchant critique serves as an important caution for historians of white women and colonialism. While examining white women can problematize their privilege, it can also unwittingly reaffirm it by ignoring or minimizing white women's embeddedness in structures and practices of racial domination. Studies of white women in colonial contexts, indeed, can repeat some of the hoariest tropes of Western gendered wisdom by portraying white women as sensitive, kindly, benevolent, and suffering.

Without denying that white people's experience was profoundly gendered, historians need to recognize that white women were also racialized, and critically examine their relationships with people of colour and to the colonial projects. White women were not the "ruin of empire," but neither were they hapless, misunderstood, latent antiracists. Rather, much like Marx's proverbial men, they made their own history, but not in circumstances of their own making. White women in colonial British Columbia were ordinary women imbued by others with a specific racial and social mission. Few explicitly challenged this mission, but few dutifully fulfilled it. Much like their male counterparts in the backwoods who tormented reformers by living a vision of white manhood that departed significantly from that promoted in mainstream nineteenth-century Anglo-American culture, white women in mid-nineteenth-century British Columbia frequently failed to live up to the roles colonial discourse assigned them. Their lives were dominated by work and dependence on men, and by a sometimes empowering and sometimes restricting place within colonial discourse that some embraced and others challenged. Acknowledging the combination of power and powerlessness that characterized their lives suggests some of the limits of the concept of "agency" to describe the simultaneity of choices and constraints that characterizes so much of human history.

The issues of colonialism and the significance of gender to it did not conveniently disappear when British Columbia became a Canadian province in the summer of 1871. As much as British Columbia has persistently thwarted efforts to remake it in the name of Britannic order, settler British Columbia has persisted in asserting its own whiteness. In the mid-nineteenth century, claims to whiteness were articulated primarily against the First Nations majority. In the late-nineteenth and twentieth century, these claims to whiteness were increasingly voiced in response to the presence of East Asians and, to a lesser extent, South Asians. If Aboriginal presence suggested the frailty of British Columbia's colonial society, the plurality of the settler society seemed to imperil the effort to recast it in the name of Britishness and whiteness. British Columbia has struggled constantly against these perceived threats to prove to itself and others that it was, to borrow Patricia Roy's apt phrase, "a white man's province."[12]

The power, danger, and irony of these constant claims to whiteness lie in the fact that British Columbia was never "a white man's province." Its roots as a First Nations territory have never been successfully erased. From the plural colonial settlements of the 1860s to the land claims struggles of the 1990s, Aboriginal people have asserted their presence and territorial claims to the place we call British Columbia. The settler population has similarly belied aspirations to whiteness and, more especially, Britishness. British Columbian colonial settlements were never "little Englands." They were diverse, hybrid collections of humans drawn, in varying degrees, from East Asia, Europe, Australasia, South Asia, the Americas, and the African diaspora.

The extent to which British Columbia was ever a "white man's province" was achieved only with the help of massive Aboriginal depopulation and the draconian immigration policies of the last decades of the nineteenth and the first half of the twentieth centuries. British Columbia made the transition from a struggling colony to a secure province in the fin de siècle, the same years that saw disease and dispossession bring First Nations population to an all-time low. The two phenomena are not unrelated. Nor is the fact that the heyday of British Columbia's whiteness between 1911 and 1961 tidily coincided with the zenith of anti-Asian legislation. As Veronica Strong-Boag points out, the years when British Columbia most closely resembled a "white man's province" were the same ones when the so-called Gentleman's Agreement of 1908 limited Japanese immigration, the "continuous journey" regulation excluded immigrants from the Indian subcontinent, the Chinese Exclusion Act of 1923 severely restricted Chinese immigration, and Japanese Canadians were interred and later dispersed in the name of the Second World War.[13] British Columbia's whiteness, to the extent that it was ever achieved, was accomplished through human action and history rather than destiny.

In contemporary newspapers and conversations, white British Columbians often long for the days when our society was unquestionably British, when our tea and crumpets were not disrupted by Asian neighbours or First Nations demands for land and recognition. When we do so, we long for a fiction of our own invention. When we argue that special immigration laws, language policies, or building codes are required to protect the "Canadian" character of our communities, we both construct Canada in overtly racialized terms and misunderstand our own history. From the *Komagata Maru* of 1914 to the "illegal" Chinese migrants of 1999, it has been ordinary people who have borne the painful brunt of our failure to understand our own society. When we fear the renegotiation – however imperfect – of British Columbia's relationship with First Nations people contained in the process that has produced the recent Nisga'a treaty, we deny the devastation of colonialism and our own complicity in it.[14] The fiction of a white British Columbia persists not because it accurately describes our history, but because it implicitly serves white interests and salves white consciousness.

White British Columbians need to rethink our relationship to the society we call home. Doing so involves critically re-accessing our history. If we look seriously at that history, we will not find a "white man's province," but a society where colonialism was constantly challenged both by First Nations presence and settlers' divergence with imperial ideals. As much as reformers consistently argued that British Columbia's future was as a respectable white settler colony anchored in orderly gendered and racial identities, British Columbia asserted its own distinct social organization. Evaluating and valuing the history of gender and race on this edge of empire helps us rethink not only our past, but the vision of the future it silently but so surely props up.

NOTES

1 Adele Perry, "Gender, Race, and Our Years on the Edge of Empire," *On the Edge of Empire: Gender, Race and the Making of British Columbia, 1849–1871* (Toronto: University of Toronto Press, 2001), 194–201.

2 Ann Laura Stoler, "Rethinking Colonial Categories: European Communities and the Boundaries of Rule," *Comparative Studies in Society and History* 31 (Jan. 1989): 135–61; and Stoler, "Sexual Affronts and Racial Frontiers: European Identities and Cultural Politics of Exclusion in Colonial Southeast Asia," *Comparative Studies in Society and History* 34 (July 1992): 514–51.

3 Mrinalini Sinha, "Gender and Imperialism: Colonial Policy and the Ideology of Moral Imperialism in Late-Nineteenth-Century Bengal," in Michael S. Kimmel, ed., *Changing Men: New Directions in Research on Men and Masculinity* (New York: Sage, 1987); Kenneth Ballhatchet, *Race, Sex, and Class under the Raj: Imperial Attitudes and Policies and Their Critics, 1783–1905* (London: Weidenfeld and Nicholson, 1980).

4 Tina Loo, Review of Cole Harris, *The Resettlement of British Columbia: Essays on Colonialism and Geographic Change, BC Studies* 117 (Spring 1998): 66.

5 Anne McClintock, *Imperial Leather: Race, Gender, and Sexuality in the Colonial Conquest* (New York: Routledge, 1995), 36–9.

6 Himani Bannerji, "Politics and the Writing of History," in Ruth Roach Pierson and Nupur Chaudhuri, eds., *Nation, Empire, Colony: Historicizing Gender and Race* (Indianapolis: University of Indiana Press, 1998), 290.

7 Georges E. Sioui, *For an Amerindian Auto-History: An Essay on the Foundations of a Social Ethic*, Sheila Fischman, trans. (Montreal and Kingston: McGill-Queen's University Press, 1992).

8 Catherine Hall, *White, Male, and Middle Class: Explorations in Feminism and History* (London: Routledge, 1992), 21.

9 Ruth Frankenberg, *White Women, Race Matters: The Social Construction of Whiteness* (Minneapolis: University of Minnesota Press, 1993), 10.

10 Claudia Knapman, *White Women in Fiji, 1835–1930: The Ruin of Empire?* (Sydney: Allen and Unwin, 1986); Helen Callaway, *Gender, Culture, and Empire: European Women in Colonial Nigeria* (Urbana: University of Illinois Press, 1987); Beverly Gartrell, "Colonial Wives: Villains or Victims?" in Hilary Callan and Shirley Ardner, eds., *The Incorporated Wife* (London: Croom Helm, 1984); Margaret Strobel, *European Women and the Second British Empire* (Bloomington: Indiana University Press, 1991). In Canada, see Barbara Eileen Kelcey, "Jingo Bells, Jingo Belles, Dashing through the Snow: White Women and Empire on Canada's Arctic Frontier," PhD dissertation, University of Manitoba, 1994.

11 Jane Haggis, "Gendering Colonialism or Colonising Gender? Recent Women's Studies Approaches to White Women and the History of British Colonialism," *Women's Studies International Forum* 13, 1/2 (1990): 105–15. Also see Margaret Jolly, "Colonizing Women: The Maternal Body and Empire," in Sneja Gunew and Anna Yeatman, eds., *Feminism and the Politics of Difference* (Halifax: Fernwood Press, 1993).

12 Patricia E. Roy, *A White Man's Province: British Columbia Politicians and Chinese and Japanese Immigrants, 1858–1924* (Vancouver: UBC Press, 1989).

13 Veronica Strong-Boag, "Society in the Twentieth Century," in Hugh Johnson, ed., *The Pacific Province: A History of British Columbia* (Vancouver: Douglas and McIntyre, 1996) 277.

14 See articles in "The Nisga'a Treaty," a special issue of *BC Studies* 120 (Winter 1998–9).

# "Development and Survival"

*Genèse de la société québécoise*
(Translated by Lin Burman)
*The Origins of Quebec Society*
1993

FERNAND DUMONT[1]

[...]

## Politics and Nationhood

Union of the two Canadas brought about radical political change, of which Confederation in 1867 was, in actual fact, the continuation. The new province of Canada was under the authority of a governor, an executive council, and a legislative council. The Legislative Assembly had forty-two representatives for each of the two sections, whereas, let us not forget, the population of Canada East was much larger than that of Canada West (650,000 compared to 450,000).

In the Assembly so formed, the leaders of both groups were able, with some difficulty, to muster the majorities they needed; for a time, by allying the Reformists of both sections, La Fontaine and Baldwin succeeded in doing so. Coalitions were precarious and were possible only in the case of a double majority,[2] which presumed similar allegiances on both sides. What happens when a coalition finds itself in the majority in one section and in the minority in the other? The result was crisis, one that deepened when more radical groups, the Clear Grits in Upper Canada and the Reds of Lower Canada, were formed. Compromises were fragile; there followed a succession of some ten ministries from 1854 to 1864.

How were such chronic problems to be overcome? The solution lay in recourse to federation. Durham himself had considered it. Besides, did Union not function as a type of federation? In many respects, the two Canadas retained their own entities: equality of representation in the Assembly, the interplay of double majority and partial duality of the administrative system. Bills sometimes had to do with the whole entity and at others with only one of the two sections. Furthermore, fear of the American neighbour, as well as economic imperatives, encouraged strengthening of the colonies. When the Reciprocity Treaty with the United States (1854) expired, a new market had to be created. Resources had to be collected to build railways and mobilise the cooperation of businessmen and politicians. Without any consultation of their populations, the federation of Quebec, Ontario, New Brunswick, and Nova Scotia was created in 1867. Subsequent expansion took place gradually: the West was bought in 1868; one after the other, Manitoba (1870), British Columbia (1871), Prince Edward Island (1873), Saskatchewan, and Alberta (1905) were integrated. These constitute a few surface markers to keep in mind, but what is of real interest here are the repercussions of Union and Confederation on the identity and configuration of the social group they claimed to be fashioning.

Union in 1841 was supposed to merge the two communities. The will of the home country was steadfast, and the governor responsible for carrying it out was the man for the job; Poulett-Thompson (who was soon to be Lord Sydenham) was a first-class politician and an experienced businessman who intended to impose the new regime vigorously and who had strong opinions on French Canadians. Hardly had he set foot in the country when he wrote, "From the French, I expect nothing but trouble. The fact is that they are incapable of any representative government." His opinion of the inhabitants of Upper Canada was more favourable: "Any one of its districts (of Upper Canada) contains more real wealth and intelligence than the whole of Lower Canada, with the exception of the Townships" (where the English were in the majority). This gentleman was not exactly partial to democracy, at least when there was a risk of it being practised by French Canadians: "If the thing were possible, the best solution for Lower Canada would be some ten years of despotism, for in truth the people are not sufficiently mature for the higher form of government represented by autonomy." Confronted with this obvious difference in political intelligence and ability between Upper and Lower Canada, the representative of Great Britain was obliged to resort to expedients. The Executive Council would not include any French Canadians; the governor moved the capital to Kingston in order to remove the francophone representatives from the bad influence of their constituents; in Montreal and Quebec City, he divided up the electoral ridings in such a way as to increase British participation in the vote; in some regions, he located the polling stations as far away as possible from French voters; and he had no qualms about resorting to bullies to ensure victory for the right cause. No means were spared to create a new political community....

Were there resources for some sort of community spirit to be found in the groups themselves?

The governor consulted the people of Upper Canada, starting with the Chambers. Étienne Parent provides the following account: "We were expecting to find in the British population of Upper Canada, in the person of their representatives, the same spirit of justice, tolerance, brotherhood, and goodwill with which we ourselves were prepared to enter the Union, but what did the Debates, Resolutions, and speeches in the Chambers reveal? – Precisely those same arrogant attitudes, the same pretentions of superiority and ancestry that have dominated the so-called British party in Lower Canada." The councillors of Toronto asked the governor that the privileges granted to anglophones not be granted to "that part of the population which, by reason of education, habits and prejudices, is foreign to our nation." In Lower Canada, anglophone newspapers added their voices. The *Montreal Herald* proposed dividing up members of the future Parliament as follows: 103 English, 25 francophones. The *Montreal Gazette* went into more detail: voters must be able to sign their name and candidates would have to speak English, since French would be eliminated from debates in the Assembly. In 1849, when remedial legislation was passed to compensate those who had suffered losses in the rebellions, hatred erupted in the English newspapers; this was followed by the riot and the fire in Parliament. In a debate in the Assembly, Sir Allan McNab exclaimed, "Union has completely missed the mark. It was created for the sole purpose of subjecting French Canadians to English domination. It has resulted in the opposite. The ones who should have been crushed are dominant! Those for whose sake the Union was created are serfs of the others!" Sir Allan issued a solemn warning: the people of Upper Canada will not agree to being "governed by foreigners."

The threat soon took effect. Disappointed by the new British policy that no longer protected Canadian business, anglophone businessmen in United Canada started a movement in favour of annexation to the

United States. They had the backing of the English newspapers: the *Herald*, the *Courrier*, the *Montreal Gazette*, and others; Galt, a future Father of Confederation, became their spokesman. The *Gazette* wrote, "Should you no longer be British, you will be English." Created for the occasion, the British American League tried to rally French Canadians, but it scarcely concealed what the *Courrier* stated openly: annexation would be an excellent way to assimilate the francophones. As far as the *Hamilton Spectator* was concerned, "rather than be dominated by the French in decline, let us at least try to ally ourselves with a race of the same family."

For anglophones, Union was therefore far from portending the creation of a common frame of reference. What did the French of Lower Canada think about this? For them, the situation was altogether different, and the choices far more difficult. Union looked like the Conquest of 1760 all over again; it brought back the old threats of radical assimilation. Political leaders were divided into two camps. Some categorically denounced the regime, demanding that it be repealed; others even advocated abstaining from any participation in the government. The others, while protesting against the injustice of Union, argued for a steadfast commitment to compromise.

For a long time, French Canadians had voted as one in elections; Papineau's group was a type of national party. Governor Metcalfe lamented the fact. His successor, Lord Elgin, saw the situation clearly: "I think for my part," he wrote to Lord Grey in 1847, "that the difficulties posed by the government of united Canada would disappear if the French were divided between a Liberal party and a Conservative party and they rallied to the parties thus named in Canada.... The national factor must therefore merge with the political factor if we want to achieve the division to which I refer." The man was a good prophet. The reshuffling of the parties, which took place little by little, was indeed to produce a crossover of national and political consciousness, which was to have a profound effect on ideologies in the next century.

When Union was proclaimed, the same issue of nationhood arose in a climate of anxiety. This was 1839; Parent had just read the Durham Report. Stunned, in *Le Canadien* of 13 May, he invited his compatriots to accept the inevitable "in the hope that the neighbouring peoples will not make the sacrifices we shall have to make too hard or too hasty." Parent pointed out that in 1791, with the constitutional regime, French Canadians had believed in their survival, trusting in the support of the mother country; they now had to put their trust in the neighbouring English populations and "place their hopes in them and join their social interests and national affections with their own." As for assimilation, Parent had no hesitation in saying that it "will occur gradually and without upheaval, and will be all the quicker for being allowed to take its natural course, and Canadians will come round to it in their own interest, without their self-esteem being too much affected."[3]

Reading such remarks, we must take into account the circumstances, and the discouragement of a man who had long defended the opposing view and had bowed to the inevitable. Nevertheless, Parent did not gainsay his previous efforts entirely; he retreated into survival instincts dating back to the aftermath of the Conquest. What we "intend to abandon," he submitted, "is the hope of seeing a purely French nation," but not "our institutions, language and laws inasmuch as they may be coordinated with the proposed new political state of existence which is to be imposed on us." Until when? It was like a replay of what had been said in the first session of Parliament in 1792: yes, preserve the French language, but until such time as the population had become familiar with the English language. In reality, what other outcome was there? With the "populations which are all round us," wrote Parent, "we shall create a homogeneous mass of people, with a community of interests, opinions, and affections, from which a great Canadian nation will emerge."[4] What kind of nation would it be? If I understand the idea that was laboriously taking shape, that nation would be an essentially political one. It was an extremely backward step, and one that gave rise to a dichotomy: on the one hand, a *political* nation, and on the other, a *cultural* one. Confederation was to establish that duality, around which ideologies would be poised, until the present day.

Was there in fact any rekindling, beyond the ferment of the 1830s, of the ideology that developed after the advent of the Constitution of 1791? It will be recalled that the definition of community defended by the francophone elites at the time was above all a political one and that the idea of nationhood was subordinate. Was not the main aim of the constitutional battles that took place before 1837 to put an end to the arbitrary power of the governor and take executive power away from him and return it to the Assembly elected by the people? Was it not considered a condition of political equality between populations divided into different ethnicities? The Durham Report challenged the "prejudices of race" but declared itself in favour of responsible government. Would the focus not be placed once more on the former objective? Parent invited people to put aside national "prejudice" in order to ally themselves with those who were pursuing the same end. He therefore addressed himself to the Reformists of Upper Canada.

The situation was moving towards a coalition based on that foundation. Hincks, one of the leaders of Upper Canada, wrote to La Fontaine in April 1839 to test the waters. Hincks, like many of his peers, was very much in favour of Union; the vague "national" desires of French Canadians did not bother him one bit: "Lord Durham imputes national designs to you; if he is right, Union means your ruination; but if he is wrong and you really want liberal institutions and economic government, Union would, in my opinion, bring you what you may wish for, as a united Parliament would have a huge Reformist majority." To both sides, Hincks proposed uniting "as Canadian citizens," by eliminating "the excuse of national hatred."[5] Language, he stated, would pose no difficulty as the French-Canadian leaders all spoke English....

The aim was to mobilise French Canadians in order to achieve responsible government, which the Upper Canada Reformists could not obtain on their own. The contribution of the French of Lower Canada was all the more important, as they were in the habit of voting as one. That vote, however, was unanimous because it was based on national solidarity. La Fontaine, while officially putting ethnic motives on the back burner, used them as a major theme in his campaign on the ground. Such duplicity would subsequently be cultivated by a large number of politicians, as we know. Discretion was in order, as La Fontaine informed one of his faithful followers, Joseph Cauchon. Cauchon politely retorted, "I remember what you told me with regard to the national question, but I replied that it was the only sensitive chord that could be struck successfully."[6]

That national sentiment was a useful tool, and one to be handled with care, as it threatened to deny the increasingly widespread idea of a political community. In the spirit of the promoters of Confederation, the idea was to create a "new nation." The expression was Tupper's, who added, "Instead of Newfoundlanders, Nova Scotians, island dwellers of Prince Edward Island, New Brunswickers, and Canadians, we shall be universally known as *British Americans*." Macdonald did not think otherwise: Confederation would bring together "British Americans under the authority of the British sovereign." For George-Étienne Cartier, his compatriots were "English citizens who spoke French." French-Canadian leaders did not usually venture so far. Hector Langevin intervened in the debates of 1865: "We are told: you wish to create a new nation. We must agree on this word, Mr. Speaker. What we desire and what we want, is to defend the interests of a large country and a powerful nation, by means of strong central power. On the other hand, we do not wish to get rid of our different laws and customs: on the contrary, those things are precisely what we want most to protect by Confederation."[7] Here again we see the fluctuation between the "new nation," the *political* one, and the other one, which was a collection of laws and customs to be preserved.... Cartier, for his part, in the same debate, supported multiculturalism within "political nationhood independent of national origin or any individual's religion."

From the perspective of the province of Quebec, the words do not have quite the same meaning. In its issue of 1 July 1867, *La Minerve,* which was the mouthpiece of the Fathers of Confederation, saw in the new Constitution "the recognition of French-Canadian nationhood as a distinct and separate nationality; we are a state within a state, in full enjoyment of our rights, with formal recognition of our national independence." This was a singular contradiction of the idea of "new nation." On 6 April, *La Minerve* provided an explanation: "If the horizons of the Province of Quebec are not as wide as those of Power, they nevertheless contain more ideas and aims that can be applied to everyday needs; human life is played out there." Presenting his first budget to the provincial Assembly, Christopher Dunkin took up the idea: "There are, among the issues within our jurisdiction, interests which are closer to the heart and feelings of most of the people and have a more direct bearing on their interests. The pulse of social life will be more seriously affected by what we do here than by acts of the Parliament in Ottawa." Siméon Lesage wrote to Hector Langevin in July 1867 that it was in Quebec "that the damned French Canadians will at last feel they are living their own lives."[8] The idea of a "distinct society" goes back a long way....

Conceptions of Confederation were therefore not based solely on legal texts. They fluctuated between the "new nation" that Canada was supposed to embody, and the refuge of the (French) Canadian nation in the province of Quebec. It was, in fact, the realization of an old idea that ... had been entertained since the Conquest, first with the conqueror and also with Canadians: that of the French *réserve*.

The responsibilities granted to the Quebec government were apparently many. Education, civil law, justice, roads, and municipal affairs: this is what *La Minerve* termed "everyday life." Agriculture, settlement, and use of natural resources came under control of the province. The federal government, however, kept the lion's share for itself. Macdonald, who would have liked a legislative union, stated that the provinces were subject to the federal government in the same way that the latter was subordinated to the empire; this meant that the provinces were colonies of Confederation. Moreover, the Quebec budget confirmed the fact: from 1 July 1867 to 31 December 1868, it added up to $1,076,677, of which $600,175 came from the central government subsidy; in 1870–1, revenues totalled $1,651,287, of which $790,000 was federal subsidy. The lieutenant governor was appointed by the federal government, and the Constitution stipulated that he exercised the right of reserve over provincial legislations; from 1867 to 1896, sixty-six Quebec laws would be overturned. The first Quebec ministerial cabinet was formed with the approval of the federal leader, George-Étienne Cartier; the cabinet of 1873 was the result of a decision by Langevin, another federal leader. The double mandate, which until 1874 allowed candidates to be elected to both Parliaments, ensured the presence of federal leaders within the provincial legislature. On both sides, there was consultation on strategies and patronage. The party was the strongest link between the two governments; the strings were pulled in Ottawa.

Confederation sanctioned the organisation of two parallel societies and was an ancient tradition. It reproduced that organisation within the province of Quebec. The anglophones of Quebec had newspapers, institutions, and associations of their own at their disposal; the wealthiest dominated the economy. The treasurer of the province was an anglophone, which guaranteed connections with the business world. Cartier intervened to that end, at the instigation of Montreal financial circles. The budget speech was written in English until 1878. Bilingualism was *de rigueur* in the Quebec Assembly, where almost a third of the speeches were delivered in English. Anglophones had their acknowledged leaders: Dunkin, Robertson, Church.... Anglophone representatives stood together over and above their partisan allegiance. Electoral ridings were protected to their advantage: any change required the unanimous consent of their representatives. Macdonald rejected a legislative council for Ontario, but Cartier requested one for Quebec: officially, it was to enhance the prestige of the legislative authorities; in actual fact, it was to defend the English minority against the French majority in the Quebec Assembly. Duality did not end with political institutions; from 1869 onwards, two school systems coexisted in Quebec. The Ministry of Education having been abolished in 1875, the Council of Public Instruction consisted of two separate committees, Catholic and Protestant; the council met seldom after that, and never again after 1908.... The children of both

Quebec societies would be schooled separately: it was the ultimate confirmation of a split between the two societies that had been completed a long time before.

Is there a comparison to be drawn with the other provinces? At the start of Confederation, 75,000 French Canadians lived in Upper Canada. It seems that the francophone Fathers of Confederation forgot them; the two societies apparently existed only in the province of Quebec. In 1865, Hector Langevin declared, "Upper Canada has a homogeneous population professing various religions." George-Étienne Cartier thought similarly in 1866: "Upper Canada is inhabited by one single race, the situation is otherwise in Lower Canada." During the debates preliminary to Confederation, Acadians were treated to emotional reminders of deportation; as Catholics, they were promised some degree of protection, of which there would no longer be any question once Confederation was concluded. For the rest, according to Cartier, the principle was assured: "Under the system of federation, which leaves the central government control of the main questions of general interest, in which differences of race will have nothing to contribute, it will not be possible to disregard the rights of race or religion." The anglophones of Quebec did not share that optimism and demanded precautions accordingly. The francophones of the other provinces were to learn, over the course of the next century, that the few francophone Fathers of Confederation had not clearly charted the paths of survival.

[...]

## Surviving

Those who were formerly referred to as Canadians became French Canadians destined henceforth to survival.

They pursued that vocation under the aegis of the British Empire, which had either wanted to assimilate them or had used them as a bulwark against the United States. They had sometimes come to the defence of their guardian; they had never agreed to submit to it entirely. They had not always approved the professions of loyalty made on their behalf. In the crisis of 1837–8, many of them had attempted emancipation but had had to resume the yoke of colonisation. Resigned to their fate, they were nevertheless not impervious henceforth to the periodic call by leaders wanting to stir up revolt against the imperialism, whose appetite for conquest would not be satisfied for a long time. As with Union of the Canadas, Confederation had its origins in economic calculations that did not in any way meet the demands for growth of the Quebec economy, which lacked its own base for development. Empire, Confederation, and Quebec: the politicians' treatment of each varied according to circumstance.

All things considered, French-Canadian elites did not possess the vast powers they were said to have. Politicians and clergymen brandished declarations of authority; for the most part, they were merely intermediaries. Their influence came, not so much from the top where important decisions were taken, as from their involvement in people's daily life through patronage, control of public opinion, pastoral work, education, and help for the poor.

Party political games diverted attention from the big challenges: economic dependence, the failure of agriculture in many areas, proletarianization and unemployment, the obstacles encountered by colonisation, and loss of population through emigration. The population became used to narrow horizons, unless they ventured to the margins or travelled further afield. Popular culture, in which basic solidarity was combined with religion, represented a set of basic models and a source of identity that people could take with them to towns in colonised territory or the United States. Occasionally rising up in futile resentment against the timber barons or the English entrepreneurs, the people was generally kept on the straight and narrow by the elites, comforted by religion, and resigned to a state of what seemed to them congenital inferiority. Such was the cost of survival.

Nevertheless, survival was more than the monotonous flow of existence. It was inevitably driven by the need to go beyond that, even if this was a diversion. How to survive without today's inertia spilling over into the future, without resorting to Utopia? How to survive without summoning up the past, since a nation which was above all a culture, was reduced to no more than its heritage? The dual recourse to hope and memory was its justification. It was also a long-term guarantee. What was to emerge, through the power of writing, was the construction of a frame of reference that would make a people aware of its history.

NOTES

1 Fernand Dumont, "Development and Survival," in *The Origins of Quebec Society*, a translation of material from chapter 6, *Genèse de la société québécoise* (Montreal: Boréal, 1993), 202–11, 235–6, 375.

2 In 1845 René-Édouard Caron provided the formula for double majority: "It has been posed in principle … that any administration should last only as long as it is sustained by a respective majority in every section of the province."

3 He even added a few months later that assimilation was "a desirable aim towards the achievement of which everyone must work together" (*Le Canadien*, 4 November 1839).

4 *Le Canadien*, 6 July 1840.

5 Quoted by Jacques Monet, *La première révolution tranquille. Le nationalisme canadien-français (1837–1850)*, translated from the English (Montreal: Fides, 1981), 65, 67. Classic work on the period, which stresses the political aspect.

6 Quoted by Jacques Monet, "La Fontaine," in *Dictionnaire biographique du Canada* (Quebec: Les Presses de l'Université Laval, 1977), 9:493.

7 Quoted by Lionel Groulx, *La Confédération canadienne* (Montreal: Imprimerie du Devoir, 1918), 233. Twenty years previously, as a young editor at the *Mélanges religieux*, Langevin wanted the advent of a federation, which "must eliminate differences of origin, languages, customs and religions."

8 Essays in Marcel Hamelin, *Les premières années du parlementarisme québécois (1867–1878)*, op. cit., 8. Letter of Lesage quoted by Andrée Désilets, *Hector-Louis Langevin, un père de la confédération canadienne* (Quebec: Presses de l'Université Laval, 1969), 194–5.

# "The Liberal Order Framework: A Prospectus for a Reconnaissance of Canadian History"

*Canadian Historical Review*
2000

IAN MCKAY[1]

The present world of Canadian historians is at once proliferous and exhilarating, deprived and crisis-ridden. Proliferous: few humans could possibly absorb the yearly output of monographs, articles, theses, papers, and books through which hundreds of scholars pay homage to the ideals of detailed archival research, monographic thoroughness, and analytical objectivity. An ever-expanding literature, increasingly based on the specialized languages of social science and cultural studies, much of it written in the other official language, often hidden away in unpublished studies, and now ranging across many "disciplines" and practices other than academic history, defies the most disciplined of readers. Exhilarating: one is over and over again reminded of the politico-ethical centrality of historical exploration, of the new knowledges, truths, and critiques that only detailed empirical research can generate. Deprived: most of all, of strategies of integration, whose feasibility seems to recede with each new addition to the sum of historical research. And crisis-ridden: there is a "pre-millennial" atmosphere among Canadian historians, a sense that the field, like the country it seeks to understand, is in crisis.

In this charged environment, calls for a return to centrally managed and well-disciplined nation-building political narratives have the paradoxical effect of inducing further fragmentation. Such "traditionalist" interventions often miss the point that fears of irrelevance, incoherence, and balkanization are widely shared. Many historians in a variety of "camps" are asking disturbing questions – if sometimes only in private conversations and correspondence. Why even have a field called history if it lacks internal coherence, if its distracted practitioners are too busy to attend seriously to each other's work, if many of their primary loyalties lie with other (sometimes ahistorical) theoretical and methodological traditions? Should we keep on producing historical monograph after monograph if neither we historians nor "our audience" – a nebulous entity under conditions of postmodernity – will ever read more than a fraction of them? And why have a field of Canadian history if even the most powerful and far-reaching methodologies often treat Canada as a "stage" on which relatively universal processes and formations interact? If Canada is more or less just a "vacant lot," one more (relatively minor) place where class, gender, race, ethnicity, sexual orientation, and so on, interact – as they do everywhere else on the planet – why not go to where the action really is, to the United States, to Europe, or "global" analyses? What, besides narrow horizons, arbitrary and dated disciplinary boundaries, or sheer timidity, would hold us to this "vacant lot"?

In our own thinly Canadianized "History Wars North,"[2] we have dutifully followed our international mentors in demonizing the Other within our gates, all the better (perhaps) to keep our own more disabling fears of nihilism at bay. It is always the Other who threatens to destroy the Muse of History, by suffocating her in the airless corridors of the state or by dismembering him[3] in a postmodern orgy of self-indulgence, subjectivism, and cultural disorder. Such dualisms allow one both to describe a crisis and to exempt oneself from it. A panic-stricken polemical extravagance – the end is nigh! there is a corpse on the floor! – is paradoxically combined with the most complacent and removed sense of self-satisfaction.

The emergence of a substantial new Canadian political history in the past decade, centred on the themes of "ideology," "state formation," and "law and order," suggests a way out of this impasse. Drawing innovatively on international theory and historiography, these three streams have made a particularly strong contribution to the study of mid-nineteenth-century Canada. The new history of political thought, much of it written outside the discipline of history, has rediscovered Canada's nineteenth-century civic humanists, situated them imaginatively in a transatlantic debate centred on liberalism and communitarianism, and attempted to re-periodize Canadian history with respect to certain broad ideological patterns. The new history of state formation, influenced to a greater extent by Marxist political economy and theories of the state, and also by such theorists as Gramsci and Foucault, has tracked the rise and consolidation of "colonial leviathan" and focused on the fine grain of "governmentality" as well as on the broader patterns of ideology. The new history of Canadian law and order has probed not just the empirical history of jurisprudence, but reconstructed the form of law as a determinate abstraction, necessarily of a certain type and yet, at the same time, specific to its time and place. If one were to pass from praising the innovative and imaginative work associated with all three streams to a more critical observation, one might say that scholars in all three clusters have been unselfconsciously regional in range, monographic in strategy, and cautious about generalizing beyond tightly defined localities and "cases" many of them have proved remarkably resistant even to referring to the work of differently situated scholars on topics very close to their own. This review article would like to take the risk of predicting that these themes, brought together in a new strategy of reconnaissance, could provide us with a "third paradigm" beyond the traditional nationalist and socio-cultural history narratives – a way of "going beyond the fragments" in Canadian history writing. This prospectus is an early and inevitably flawed and partial reading of what this potential paradigm might hold for the writing of Canadian history in the twenty-first century.

The core argument is succinct: the category "Canada" should henceforth denote a historically specific project of rule, rather than either an essence we must defend or an empty homogeneous space we must possess. Canada-as-project can be analyzed through the study of the implantation and expansion over a heterogeneous terrain of a certain politico-economic logic – to wit, liberalism. A strategy of "reconnaissance" will study those at the core of this project who articulated its values, and those "insiders" or "outsiders" who resisted and, to some extent at least, reshaped it.

Rather than beginning with the ambition of "rethinking Canada" in one great social or political synthesis – a procedure that often takes for granted the very boundaries of the "Canada" to be rethought – we could begin with the more modest goal of combining the new tools of social and cultural theory with more traditional political narratives and economic analyses. In this more problem-centred approach, to "rethink" Canada does not mean to synthesize and integrate all Canadian experience into an account that, in the best of worlds, would be acceptable to everyone. It would entail, rather, probing the Canadian state's logical and historical conditions of possibility as a specific project in a particular time and place. Although this approach obviously shares a great deal with both the traditional nation-building and the newer socio-cultural schools, its development would require the elaboration of a new general paradigm distinct from either. Once we have abandoned synthesis as an unattainable goal, we can "think Canada" in a different way.

We are missing a large library of big books that would help us do so. Where is our late-twentieth-century general interpretation, deeply informed by critical theory and enriched by a nuanced reading of a vast range of the primary and secondary sources, of "French/English relations"? Or the substantial and sophisticated book, written with the historian's distinctive concern for the specific as well as the general, of the Quiet Revolution?[4] Or its counterpart, an equally "big book" offering a general historical interpretation of Canadian regionalism, east and west? This questioning is not in any sense to minimize the political historians' achievements – in the writing of biographies and studies of specific trends, in the interpretation of federalism, and in writing subtle and interesting colony-to-nation and regional narratives – that many social and cultural historians have too easily cast aside; rather, it is to imagine a dialogue in which both camps add their insights to understanding Canada as a political and socially specific solution to a series of historical problems. Nor does it mean jettisoning the outlook and achievements of social and economic history, particularly as it has indispensably reflected the insights of Marx into the complex logic of capitalism;[5] it is, rather, to imagine what would happen if the workaday adjective "Canadian" – Canadian working-class history, Canadian women's history, Canadian gay and lesbian history – exerted the "force of qualification" over that which it modifies. It is to imagine a way of doing history that locates the "problem of Canada" within the history of power relations: to map, across northern North America, both the grids of power (penitentiaries and criminal codes, schools and legislatures) through which a given hegemonic "social" was constructed and centred, and the forces of resistance capable, at certain times, of effecting far-reaching changes of the project itself. It is to imagine a Canada that, however "solidly" if deceptively reified as a sovereign nation-state among nation-states, is nonetheless "unsolidly" haunted by the insubstantiality of much of its "sovereignty" – a Canada non-identical, in crucial respects, with itself, and non-reducible to some natural or supernatural agency or essence (such as the St Lawrence River, the Canadian

Shield, or the workings of "inevitability," "Fate," and "Providence"). On this new reading, Canada becomes less a self-evident and obvious unit, and more an arrestingly contradictory, complicated, and yet coherent process of liberal rule. It is to imagine a "Canada" simultaneously as an *extensive* projection of liberal rule across a large territory and an *intensive* process of subjectification, whereby liberal assumptions are internalized and normalized within the dominion's subjects.

A liberal order is one that encourages and seeks to extend across time and space a belief in the epistemological and ontological primacy of the category of the "individual." It is important to make the analytical distinction between the liberal order as a principle of rule, and the often partisan historical forms this principle has taken through 150 years of Canadian history. Canada as a project can be defined as an attempt to plant and nurture, in somewhat unlikely soil, the philosophical assumptions, and the related political and economic practices, of a liberal order. As Fernande Roy has remarked in her pathbreaking monograph on turn-of-the-twentieth-century Quebec, the term "liberalism" simultaneously suffers from semantic overabundance and poverty; it is all too easily confounded with capitalism on the one hand and democracy on the other.[6] Liberalism begins when one accords a prior ontological and epistemological status to "the individual" – the human being who is the "proprietor" of him- or herself, and whose freedom should be limited only by voluntary obligations to others or to God, and by the rules necessary to obtain the equal freedom of other individuals.[7] In the sense brought to life by Margaret Thatcher and theorized by many contemporary neo-liberals, it is the individual who truly exists, in a way "society," "community," and "the cosmo" do not. The state in particular lacks any finality of its own; it is the individual, whose rights are predicated on self-possession and property, whose purposes, knowledges, and practices truly exist, and whose "interests" are "obvious." Roy suggests that "liberalism" is best grasped as an ideology performing both a cognitive and a mobilizing function, which resolves antinomies by ranking three core elements: first "Liberty," which gives its name to the entire ideology (and from a basic affirmation of an individual's "natural right" to liberty, we can move quickly to the claim that there exists a subset of liberties, encompassing "free labour," "free trade," a "free press," and so on); second, "Equality," which is always subordinated to the first principle of individualism, and interpreted in ways that render "commonsensical" the particular inequalities stemming from the exercise of the individual's liberty; and third "Property" – more exactly, the individual's right to hold property – which is in a sense even more "fundamental" than "liberty," for if one's property in oneself is the precondition of one's liberty in the first place, the pursuit of property requires the further development of those characteristics that define one as a free-standing individual. In its classical, nineteenth-century form, liberalism entailed a hierarchy of principles, with formal equality at the bottom and property at the top. Conceptualized in this way, liberalism as a hierarchical ensemble of ideological principles can be distinguished from the historical forms it has assumed, and it can also be distinguished from the competing ideological formations alongside which it evolved and which it worked to envelope and "include" – or to silence or even eliminate.

The liberalism that a liberal order sought to install as the structured and structuring principle of both public and private life is, in this reconnaissance of Canadian history, something more akin to a secular religion or a totalizing philosophy than to an easily manipulated set of political ideas; and, in this context, it is something more than one bounded ideology among other ideologies. The "individuals" at its conceptual nucleus are not to be confused with actual living beings. Rather, "the individual" is an abstract principle of the entity each one of them might, if purified and rationalized, aspire to become. In the classical liberal model, hegemonic in Canada from the mid-nineteenth century to the 1940s, a true individual was he who was self-possessed – whose body and soul was his alone; only those human beings who met the criteria of true self-possession were "true individuals." It appears to be a paradox that mid-Victorian liberals in Canada sought to limit the right to vote for both women (on the grounds of gender) and adult men (on the grounds of property) that they imposed high property qualifications for such institutions as the Senate, and that they felt obliged to exclude from the franchise those from other races (notably the Chinese and Japanese, as well as unassimilated Amerindians) who, as deficient individuals, were not to be trusted with it. Catholics, the largest denomination of Christians in northern North America, could not realistically be so excluded, but there remained a perceived tension between the demands of their faith and the claims of liberal individualism: they were, at least until the 1890s, in a sense probationary liberals.[8] Mid-nineteenth-century liberal discourse is also strikingly characterized by a hesitation to enfranchise even male adult workers and to extend to them the right to free association: uneducated, prisoners of their passions, prone to disrupt with their conspiracies and strikes the calculus of individual interest, and hence tendentially aliberal in their collectivism, workers were often conceptualized as doubtful prospects for liberal individualism. Women, tied as mothers or mothers-to-be by nature and society both to their bodies and to wider networks of family and kin, were also often excluded from individualism in this order.[9] And the same definitional rigour excluded Amerindians, many of them imprisoned in "communism" and standing in the way of free-market "development."[10] Women, workers, ethnic minorities, and Amerindians all obviously have their own histories, which should not be lumped together into one homogeneous "Canadian" synthesis; but their stories can all be related to each other by noting the consistency of a liberal model, which tended to mark them all out as "Other," and which, in the nineteenth century, excluded them from the burdens and responsibilities of full individuality. There is a liberal-order "bridge" connecting these autonomous subaltern histories of experience and struggle.

To rescue the rational kernel from the mystical "Lockean" shell of Louis Hartz, famously associated with the thesis that American society was liberal from its inception,[11] one would say that, far from being already a "consensus" viewpoint in northern North America, liberalism was, as late as the 1840s in the eastern British North American colonies, and the 1880s in the Prairies and Pacific West, a highly contentious and endangered program. Its adherents, who from the 1840s to the 1870s had won and consolidated hegemony within the Canadian and Maritime colonies, and in the federal state, nonetheless had to scramble to understand, control, and project into the future a liberal concept of their dominion. Liberal Canada was surrounded by "exceptions" that defined the "rule": and sovereign was he who decided on the exception – whose defence of the sovereignty of the core of liberal order required decisions to use force, cultural coercion, and other extraordinary but necessary measures against those spatially or conceptually on its periphery.[12] And one would also say that in contrast to the tendency of both Hartz and his "civic humanist" critics to personify ideologies as agents in history, the Gramscian liberal-order research program would prefer to interpret ideological formations as being only relatively autonomous within social and economic formations. A distinguishing mark of the liberal-order framework would be the importance it attaches to the function of property, the *primum inter pares* in the trinity of liberal values, as the precondition of a liberal's identity. And one would also underline a difference in methodology. Arguments from the political-thought stream often seem both abstract and non-falsifiable because of their essentialism: more specifically, we are often launched on quixotic and somewhat ahistorical quests for the "origins" of Canadian politics, on the assumption that they might prove to consist of a single idea set. The liberal-order strategy prescribes a more modest tactic of reconnaissance. It is conceded at the outset that, within the overall framework of the Canadian project of liberal order, a multitude of liberalisms share a definitional family resemblance, but not an essential identity. The realities of class, ethnicity, nation, regionality, gender, religion, and sexual orientation, which both Hartzians and their civic-humanist critics might treat as inessential, would be redescribed in this strategy as distinct but also related categories of analysis. Such categories are distinct in that they emerge from their own levels of generality and are pertinent at their own levels of magnification, and can and should "stand alone" in appropriate historical discussions. Yet they can also be illuminatingly related to each other. At a different level of magnification, a re/connaissance (a knowing again) of their interaction, and above all their general articulation with the project of Canada as a project of liberal rule, will lead us to a newly contextualized appreciation of (and eminently empirical propositions concerning) the many political and social realities a liberal order simultaneously preserved, cancelled, and transformed.

Placed beside mode-of-production Marxism, ready to "expose" liberalism as an apology for emergent capitalist social relations, a liberal-order approach, although it comes from the same universe of interpretation and shares much the same drive to ideological critique, nonetheless suggests an alternative line of inquiry. Classical Marxist political economy and class analyses are fundamental to the understanding of the Canadian past, yet they have falteringly interpreted the rise of Canada itself. Their power has been greatest at the monographic, not the general, level where "Canada" is often dissolved into "the capitalist mode of production" or "North America." It has been empirically difficult, if not impossible, for Marxists to fortify a base-and-superstructure model with the argument that capital as such required a separate state in northern North America. Such a classical Marxist position is problematical in a colonial framework such as pertained through much of British North American and Canadian history, crowded as it is with liberal activists who, rather like communists in twentieth-century Third World countries, were the active "superstructures" of a future base they earnestly struggled to build. They were determined to create in Canada, through tariffs, railway construction, a homegrown industrial transformation, and an expansive immigration policy, the material preconditions of a liberal society. And classical Marxist exposures often have "read off" class interest simply from class position. If Antonio Gramsci's theory of hegemony has taught us anything, it is to appreciate the extent to which a given social group can exercise leadership over others only by going beyond its immediate corporate interests to take into account the interests of other groups and classes. This group – in general, but not always, a social class – must secure its position of cultural leadership through a combination of coercion and consent, in a day-by-day process that is never finally completed, "total," or secure; it must also defend its claim to sovereignty against rival state projects. The "historic bloc" that emerges from the transcendence of immediate corporate interests must engage in far-ranging compromises, both economic and cultural, with those subaltern groups necessary for its material survival; it must transcend, in a sense, its own temporality, by actively imagining as part of its project of rule the economic base most suited to its vision. (It is never denied, of course, that past economic structures set the material limits within which such strategies could be articulated and realized.) A liberal-order framework constructed on Gramscian lines would treat liberal politics not as something to be "exposed," and whose secret already lies in an underlying economic reality. Rather, politics is something to be "explored," a terrain in which people became aware of their interests and struggled, politically, to fight for them. In the case of the liberal order, the new framework had to be constructed against or alongside radically different ways of conceptualizing human beings and societies. In contrast with classical Marxism, this neo-Marxist liberal-order framework would not necessarily privilege economic and class relations as the site, but rather as a crucial site, of liberal rule. At a certain level of magnification, it is as crucial to look at the power exerted by men over women, or by heterosexuals over homosexuals, as it is to attempt to trace all things back to class. Finally, it is an awkward fact that the nineteenth-century consolidation of the Canadian project required a massive extension of a relatively autonomous state, whose newly institutionalized capacities – in the census and in hospitals, in penitentiaries and insane asylums, the Criminal Code and the police, the tariff and the poorhouse – all bore witness to a dramatic new unleashing of institution building, a newly intense drive to master the chaos of life and liberalize social relations, often before the development of the "fundamental classes" classical Marxists view as pivotal to capitalism.

For many working in political theory, "liberal" values are self-evidently good; the organizing binary is "liberalism/illiberalism."

At the close of the twentieth century, liberal assumptions have been so successfully and massively diffused through the population that it is difficult to see, let alone treat accurately and with scholarly empathy, the aliberal positions they have replaced. A liberal-order strategy of reconnaissance would attempt to do so, by treating "liberty" and "freedom" and (above all) "the individual" as the contestable and historically relative terms of a particular and probably transient political program. A liberal-order reconnaissance would aim to see our present-day politics afresh, to make the familiar unfamiliar, to destabilize the conventional first-order apprehension of our own world. The presentist and hubristic catalogues of abnormalities, crimes, and mistakes that revisionist Canadian history has produced in such quantities – "they were so misguided in the old days," we say to ourselves, as we read of past racism and sexism – would give way to a more dispassionate and realistic analysis of the developmental logic, the socio-cultural structures, the non-accidental and general reasons for such phenomena. The paradoxical result might well be an appreciation of the enormity of what the Canadian liberal order undertook – the replacement, often with a kind of revolutionary symbolic or actual violence, of antithetical traditions and forms that had functioned for centuries and even millennia with new conceptions of the human being and society. It was no small matter to divorce "man" from his surroundings, to make his economic and symbolic interests the centrepiece of political and social endeavour, to assert, with all the certainty of scientific political economy, that one could read the signs of his spiritual and material well-being from the data of the market. The construction of this "individual" was a momentous and complex enterprise. It was not merely a weekend's work to wrench "values" from the fabric of the cosmos, where, *inter alia*, Aristotle and the church fathers had found them, and to assert the "individual's" right and duty to justify his own norms. It was not the work of an idle week to "normalize" the laws of liberal political economy and society, with all their wrenching impact on the lives of settled communities and traditions, and to so consolidate the intellectual authority and prestige of those "professionals" who commanded this language that their elevation within the state apparatus in the first quarter of the twentieth century would seem more the working out of an inevitability than the consequence of a political choice.[13] These successive revolutions required a degree of inner certainty and ruthlessness; they required, one might even say, a liberal vanguard of "free" and "cultured" men willing to restrict "democracy" (which many of them distrusted well into the twentieth century) in the interests of safeguarding the true interests of "individuals." It would be easy for a contemporary mind, inescapably shaped by the liberal order, to miss what was startling, revolutionary, and endangered about the nucleus of liberalism when it first assumed its pedagogical role in northern North America, before its mid-century transition to a hegemonic ideology in the centre and its late-century transition to state hegemony from coast to coast. Judged in the light of a condescending posterity, these Canadian liberals can be defined by their limitations and timidity; but evaluated according to a different standard, one that pays attention to the demographic and cultural influence of forces arrayed against them and the totalizing force of their implicit vision, they can be realistically "re-viewed" as something more like revolutionaries. Compared to *ancien régime* societies, both in New France and in early mercantile British North America, in which honour was profoundly connected to rank – a principle of order connecting human beings to a vast, complicated, and dense social fabric – a liberal order was a kind of revolutionary simplification. Compared with Amerindian societies, which saw humanity as positioned on a continuum in which animate and inanimate, human and animal, natural and supernatural were all interconnected – to the point that such contemporary categories themselves can only simplify the profoundly holistic Amerindian vision of the universe – the liberal vision saw individuals as separate from, and acting upon, the natural world.[14] Out of a colonial population divided among a dozen-odd political entities, and substantially influenced by aliberal *ancien régime* cultures, emerged a small vanguard of true believers, fired by a utopian vision of progress, rationality, and individualism, who brilliantly adapted ideas and practices drawn from a North Atlantic triangle of liberal discourse to a highly heterogeneous and even unpromising early-nineteenth-century northern North American reality.

The book(s) we are missing on this theme of "The Canadian Liberal Revolution" would necessarily dwell on seven arresting moments. First, the Rebellions of 1837, Lord Durham's Report, and the Act of Union of 1841 taken together as one moment could be interpreted as the high point and defeat of liberalism's civic humanist adversary;[15] and Lord Sydenham could be taken to be a liberal revolutionary, whose campaign of state violence and coercive institutional innovation was empowered not just by the British state but also by his Benthamite certainties.[16] Second, the "historic compromise" of reconstructed Tories and "reformed" radicals that British power did so much to effect was the necessary precondition of "responsible government," the formula for political compromise first tried out in Nova Scotia, which was so successfully generalized across colonies of markedly different economic and political circumstances. Third, Confederation – interpreted more broadly and comprehensively than the political reorganization of 1864–7 to include the subsequent elaboration and stabilization of a federal system down to 1896 – could be seen not so much as the "birth of a nation" as the "consolidation of a general liberal state program"; here one would take on board Paul Romney's profoundly important questioning of the centralist "myth of Confederation" and see this extended moment as one that was more profoundly shaped by liberalism than is suggested in many conventional accounts. Fourth, the "liberalization" of the West, first by the replacement of the paternalist Hudson's Bay Company with such new British colonies as Vancouver Island, and then by the Canadian state, and also through a massive extension of private property on the basis of the homestead acts and freehold tenure, would constitute an obvious theme of significance.[17] Fifth, the great historic compromise in the 1870s through which a National Policy of tariff protection designed to secure liberal objectives through the protection of industry was made palatable, first to a restive population largely dependent on primary production, and then to the Liberal Party, which after 1896, by inheriting and strengthening a policy it had once maligned, marginalized a once-powerful and pervasive radical critique of liberal political economy. Sixth, the "liberalization" of Quebec, through patronage and, more crucially, strategic political compromises, which combined to neutralize and contain the civic humanist critique of liberalism and capitalism, given solidity – particularly in Quebec, but to a lesser degree in other provinces – by the Catholic Church. And seventh, codification of a framework of civil and criminal law, culminating in the world novelty of the Criminal Code of Canada (1893), which solidified the liberal ideal of "equality before the law" in a way that potentially made an abstract principle into a tangible reality for every adult Canadian. This ability to bring a liberal discourse on property and conduct into direct contact with every subject – there were legally, revealingly, and crucially, as yet no Canadian "citizens"[18] – is as good an indication as any of a liberal project of Canada that, over sixty years, had achieved dominion-wide hegemony.

Another approach would be the systematic study of the obstacles to liberalism in northern North America, a method which, in itself, would serve to defamiliarize the ruling ideology. One can think of three sorts of major impediments, categorized according to how closely they were situated (both conceptually and, often, geographically) to the individualist nucleus of the project. First, there were those who were "internal" to the project: not just "republicans" and "Tories" who had been "persuaded" into liberalism in the 1840s, but also those who persistently confronted and were often influenced by different imperatives of liberalism in the United States.[19] Civic humanism was not so much a memory of the past as it was a cultural resource in the present: it did not die with William Lyon Mackenzie and A.A. Dorion, but persisted into the twentieth century, especially on the socialist left. It would modify the strict reading of liberal order among subalterns. Labour historians have been hesitant to acknowledge the impact of liberalism on Canadian workers, who have given the Liberal Party far more support over time than the parties claiming to speak on their behalf. The first women's movement in Canada suggests parallels. The elevation of women, even if in a separate sphere, was implicitly a collective goal requiring a collective subject; and the first-wave feminists placed great strain on liberal definitions (implicit or explicit) of the "individual," whose family contexts and responsibilities they underlined, and whose sexual identity many of them came to question – a point not missed by the many ideologically consistent liberals who spoke against the enfranchisement of women from the 1880s on.[20] The social reforms with which feminism was closely allied, such as temperance, also caused many liberals great concern because these reforms tendentially interfered with the rights of free individuals and free enterprise. It was characteristic of the workers' and women's movements that their political language was deeply marked by the liberalism they both implicitly and explicitly questioned.

Second, another category of opposition was that associated with francophone and Catholic Quebec, ambiguously situated "within" the project (indeed, at its very geographical centre), yet culturally distanced from it by reasons of nationality and religion.[21] That the making of the liberal order in Quebec necessitated far-ranging compromises of liberal ideological principles can illuminate the more general issue of how the order was articulated to (and sought to incorporate) pre- and aliberal sociopolitical forms. That the British North America Act says so little about issues now taken to be fundamental, such as language rights, testifies to its profoundly liberal character; but that it says something about language at all, in section 133, later confirmed in the Manitoba Act, and something more about religious education, brings out the historic price liberals were willing to pay to achieve their dominion. In order to achieve a historic bloc that would allow them to convey liberal rule to as wide a population as possible, liberals were willing to compromise on the question of the separation of church and state and, to a point, on other sociocultural issues – but on the crucial condition that Catholic communitarianism be restricted as much as possible to Quebec (and even there subordinated in the hierarchy to a state liberalism that would remain, down to the 1950s, eminently "classical").[22] The hegemonic incorporation of Quebec was indispensable to the achievement of liberal order and could be achieved only through a carefully articulated politics of elite accommodation and cultural compromise, which has gone on to become misleadingly mythologized as a defining feature of Canada itself. What is misleading about this myth is that it overlooks the uncompromisingly liberal context within which such "accommodations" and "compromises" were made and which they were designed to preserve: these were less "compromises" than "bargains with liberal hegemony."

Finally, there were, on the edges of a liberal dominion, other aliberal entities more completely external to its project of rule. Long-established and once militarily powerful, Aboriginals, the demographic majority in most of the territory eventually to be claimed by the liberal dominion, were people whose conceptions of property, politics, and the individual were scandalously not derived from the universe of Locke, Smith, Bentham, or Lord Durham. The containment of these alternative logics was an ideological imperative of the liberal order, without which it could not exist as a transcontinental project. A reconnaissance of this "Other" would mean relativizing the Canadian/liberal claim to represent the rule of law; the Canadian project would be seen instead as a historically contingent formula for liberal order, in competition with older and long-established Aboriginal practices. It would mean revisiting the history of prairie reservations and Native agricultural policy, which has already been well explored and theorized, to ask what it tells us about the process of the Canadian liberal revolution in general. It would mean a revaluation of Ottawa's handling of the "Indian Question" as not just a series of misunderstandings, premised on a distanced misreading of Native societies, but rather as a fulfillment of liberal norms, which required the subordination of alternatives. Canadian imperialism in the High Arctic and in the West was not incidentally related to the Canadian values articulated by the "Ottawa men" of the nineteenth and early twentieth centuries. From Joseph Howe and John

A. Macdonald down to the 1940s, there was a consistency of approach to Amerindian issues which invites theorization within a liberal-order research program.[23] It was perhaps in the residential schools that the full utopianism of a vanguard liberalism came to the fore, for within these Christian/liberal manufactories of individuals, pre-eminent laboratories of liberalism, First Nations children were "forced to be free," in the very particular liberal sense of "free," even at the cost of their lives.[24]

A liberal-order reconnaissance of Canadian history, which can be conveyed only partially and telegraphically here, entails seeing how far and how complexly this principle of liberal order functioned across the wide array of social formations and territories that ultimately cohered, from the 1860s to the 1890s, into the Dominion of Canada. It cannot, will never, and is in fact not designed to stand in for "other" subaltern histories – the record of working-class struggle, the formation of the Quebec nation, emergence of first-wave feminism among women, and so on. A reconnaissance is not a synthesis. It is a contingent, partial, and (perhaps) somewhat risky attempt to derive a sense of general patterns from particular discrete sightings; its preferred tactic is to relate some of these autonomous histories to each other via bridging concepts and plausible correlations. A liberal-order framework, by beginning with the fact of the Canadian state project, might well be falsely accused of returning to a top-down, state-centric line of interpretation. The more accurate charge would be that this approach radically calls into question the "top/bottom" binarism that has condemned so much historiographical debate in Canada to a wearisome and fractious sterility. From this perspective, there is no "top" and no "bottom": there is a centre and a periphery, a liberal project and its "resistors."[25] One can read as much "liberal ordering" into inheritance patterns, or the conception of the household as a "private sphere" ruled by an authorized free-standing individual patriarch, or even in the location of a particular fence post, as one can into the National Policy. What connects the farmer's fence with Macdonald's tariff is a common respect for private property and the propertied individual as the foundation of a sociopolitical order ultimately defended by the state's legitimate violence. What it meant to succeed, to own things, to shine as a success in the eyes of one's parents,[26] to be a real man, to construct lines on maps and barriers around whole countries, to separate what's "mine" from "yours," "ours" from "theirs": with regard to these fundamental questions of property, the farmer's fence post and the prime minister's tariff policy share a common universe of assumptions and values.

A central, and difficult, issue will be that of saying when the liberal order had attained hegemony – which, we remember from reading Gramsci, is never a once-and-for-all achievement of some (unverifiable) majority consensus, but a consistent (and verifiable) logic of rule. An equally challenging and interesting question for this project will be that of "where." Often imprisoned by the present-day Canadian nationalist myth-symbol complex, historians are inclined to write "continuous national histories," a strategy that tends to eternalize the present-day map of Canada and to attribute to the entire dominion patterns characteristic only of one of its parts. It would be more interesting to devise ways of mapping the spread of liberalism across both space and time, as it extended its grasp from a few nineteenth-century southern outposts to encompass, by the early twentieth century, a subcontinent. If the urban Maritimes and the St Lawrence Valley functioned as a sort of "Piedmont" of liberal ordering, where the Canadian liberal formulae were first fully worked out, documenting and explaining the extension of these formulae from coast to coast to coast, in social and political conditions often bearing little resemblance to those of the "liberal nucleus," is the obvious and necessary following step. Even so, even reading backwards from the "end" of this process, one would want to avoid colouring the Canadian map a homogeneous liberal red: there would remain many places, and are to this day, where *de jure* liberal rule coexists with the *de facto* power of very different conceptions of the political and social world.

A further challenge to confront a liberal-order framework as a new reconnaissance of Canadian history would be the related one of articulating the distinctiveness of the liberal order in Canada: that is, in trying to explain the country's existence in terms distinct from the essentialist generalizations of Laurentianism, frontierism, or the (now widely disputed) neo-Hartzian "Tory touch" thesis.[27] Canada's "origins" are typically sought in a river system, a rock formation, a mode of production, or the (highly debatable) ideological "core" of its supposedly pivotal (Ontario Loyalist) settlers. Liberal-order arguments are admittedly not all that well suited to the Quest for Canadian Exceptionalism. Nonetheless, one anticipates they will develop a different, more modest explanation of Canada's separate North American existence, placing greater emphasis on the cumulative impact within a transatlantic liberal universe of marginal differences – "adaptations," to invoke social evolutionism for a moment – through which a universal ideology and general project of rule confronted, changed, and was changed over time by the particularities of its surroundings, most notably the strength of its opponents.

We know that principles of liberal governmentality and liberal political economy were directly imported from the colonial metropole. They also reflected, to an extent present-day historiography is only starting to recover, a dialogue with the republican founding principles and subsequent hegemonic liberalism of the United States. Against the environmentalism and naive nationalism of older interpretations of Canada's existence, against the "Toronto School Syndrome," the liberal-order reconnaissance would not look for a providential or natural something "outside history" on which to secure the possibility of the "Canadian" state project. It would rather explore the contingent and pragmatic reasons why one type of liberal state experiment might have been considered more efficient and less risky than another – why, for example, some quite astute liberal minds in Canada thought that "(Liberal) Freedom (Necessarily) Wore a Crown."[28]

In this sense, derivative as most liberal ideas were in Canadian history, they became cumulatively less so as they were adapted to the heterogeneous social and cultural terrain of northern North America. Thus the Canadian liberal order, inspired in many ways by its British prototype, and secondarily by its American competitor, was shaped and reshaped by the complexity of the pre-liberal and aliberal British North American worlds it had simultaneously to preserve, cancel, and transcend. Here, and not in any "foundation" or "essence," is the complex logic of Canadian distinctiveness. It lies in the liberal imperative to harmonize older ways with its new, underlying conception of the world. As it expanded from its core in a few eastern centres to take ownership of a dominion encompassing a subcontinent, Canada as a liberal project of rule was shaped not only by its founding values but by the necessary and often difficult compromises that were required if such values were to become hegemonic – that is, durably install themselves in law, daily experience, personal conduct, and intellectual life.

From the beginning, this was an inescapably hybrid political project. In the mid-century making of Canada, the signs of "bargaining with hegemony" were everywhere: a language of politics in which civic humanism, contractualism, and utilitarianism were woven together, often in the speeches of one and the same liberal activist; a "mixed constitution" allowing for both monarchy and a measure of carefully controlled popular participation, a "partial separation" between church and state that nonetheless left the Christian churches with a pivotal role in educating the young and "civilizing" Amerindians, and a constitutional framework that left room, in a system of checks and balances, for local substates to flourish within a liberal dominion and under the sovereignty of the Crown. Such characteristics were not awkward compromises incidental to the liberal project of Canada, but indications of concessions that, in seemingly qualifying the liberal vision, also brought it down to Canadian earth – a specifically Canadian answer to such liberal challenges as political obligation, social cohesion, and economic development. Their cumulative impact was to give the Canadian liberal order its peculiar traditions and, one might say, its uncanny persistence.

Turn-of-the-century Canada represented, in many respects, the apex of the liberal project. With Laurier in power after 1896, the Catholic ultramontanes' communitarian critique of liberal order seemed to have been contained, if not silenced; with the Liberal Party's acceptance of the National Policy tariffs, a *modus vivendi* had been reached on the subject of the most corrosive single economic issue in Canadian politics. Across a wide political spectrum, Canadian political thinkers, even a French-Canadian nationalist like Henri Bourassa, saluted the brilliance of a classical liberalism inherited from Britain and developed afresh in northern North America. After years of disappointment, the West was being settled under the decisive policies of Clifford Sifton: as one would expect, the state left the key problems of accommodation to a strange and difficult terrain to the immigrant families themselves on their independent homesteads. Perhaps the *pièce de résistance* of the Canadian liberal order was to carve upon the map, in lines that majestically remind us of Euclidean geometry and panoptical state power, the perfect geometry of the Province of Saskatchewan: perhaps even more impressive, however, than this quadrilateral demonstration of panopticism was the molecular checkerboard of quarter-sections and individual properties contained within the new province's boundaries – a social ideology set down on the land and hence made part of everyday western experience.

Even the new immigrants in their "sheepskin coats," drawn to Canada through the free workings of an international labour market that operated just as liberal political economy said it would, could be "Canadianized" (liberalized) in a generation. And when critics pointed out the anomalies in the pattern – a state-subsidized Canadian Pacific Railway enjoying monopoly privileges and enormous corporate and political power, or Ottawa's colonial policy of retaining control over

Crown land and mineral resources – they would be answered by other voices: such anomalies, often described as "emergency measures," indicated merely that Canada needed to return to its founding liberal principles.

In Winnipeg and in Saskatoon, one burned a lamp, in the early twentieth century, for the eternal truths of liberalism: no sense of the "nucleus" of the twentieth-century liberal project could exclude one of its most powerful and prescient organic intellectuals, J.W. Dafoe of the *Manitoba Free Press*. In the twentieth century that "belonged to Canada," racial minorities would long be excluded from the franchise, only a minority of adults could vote in federal and provincial elections (in Quebec, this restriction would persist until 1940), and there were, until the 1940s, subjects but not citizens. The magic of nationalism has converted this "Canada" into a country like the one we now inhabit – but it was essentially a liberal empire, not a nation, and not a democratic state.

There is a textbook answer to explain a supposed transition from the nineteenth-century dominion to the multicultural liberal democratic nation state: Canada simply glided, slowly and surely, down Arthur Lower's *Most Famous Stream* of liberal democracy. More and more people were brought aboard the good ship, and the unsightly detritus of the past vanished into the distance. The liberal-order approach, centred on the Gramscian concept of "passive revolution," would undoubtedly offer a much bumpier and less pleasant ride.[29]

Liberal ideas and practices were undeniably rethought in the early twentieth century, by intellectuals such as John Watson and Mackenzie King, by Social Gospellers and Progressives – by a host of "New Liberals" whose key insight was that the rights of the classically defined individual could no longer be the foundation of politics and social life. The requirements of society, that "evolving social organism," could be safeguarded only through a greatly expanded and much more activist state responsible for the general welfare of its citizens.[30] In much historical writing, the nineteenth-century liberal order is retrospectively abolished by such turn-of-the-century reformers; or else it is subdued in the second quarter of the twentieth century by the liberal order's first powerful "opposition" outside itself, the socialist movement, which in Canada articulated a civic humanist argument for a post-liberal democracy. Just as the first four decades of the nineteenth century can be mapped as ones in which, from a multitude of interests and identities, a new project of liberal state formation eventually emerged to effect a historic compromise, so too might the first four decades of the twentieth century be mapped as ones in which a new democratic state formation slowly emerged which sought to redefine the meaning of the word "Canada."

It is an often-related narrative, and much of it captures a truth. Yet in many respects this "new democracy" was contained: classical liberal assumptions did not disappear, and there was no "institutional rupture" marginalizing either the Liberal Conservatives or the Liberals as continuing political formations. Another big book is waiting to be written on the ways the left program of new democracy was contained in the middle years of the twentieth century through a seemingly conciliatory, ultimately profoundly disintegrating, process of "passive revolution" in which, unusually in world terms, Canadian liberalism vanquished its enemies within and without. The thesis of "passive revolution" maintains that, confronted with a serious quasi-revolutionary challenge to its hegemony, the liberal state executed far-ranging changes in its social and political project to "include" some of those previously excluded, with the *quid pro quo* that they divest themselves of the most radical aspects of their oppositional programs (such as demands for a comprehensive change in property relations or in the nature and function of political "representation"). The crucial cases for examination in Canada would be that of the Co-operative Commonwealth Federation, the Communist (subsequently Labor-Progressive) Party, and the left-led industrial unions. Substantial institutional concessions were made to this multi-voiced left, but only at the cost of "editing" out their unacceptably aliberal elements. The "passive revolution" imprisoned the left advocates of "new democracy" in an ever-constricting iron cage of liberal pragmatism. The Canadian "Keynes" revealingly lost, somewhere in his transatlantic passage, his quirky interest in the comprehensive socialization of investment along with his far-ranging schemes for regional development. What had once seemed a new democratic transformation of the locus of sovereignty in the 1940s – an event duly eternalized within the intertwined memories of social democracy and Canadian nationalism – proved deceptive. Since the 1950s the "collective prince" has been not the people, but the market and the managerial state. Fiscal exuberance and a ballooning public debt did not change, but, in many respects, underwrote this reality.[31] It might be said that, if the collapse of the British Empire made the new Canadian democracy possible, the rise of the American Empire made it unlikely: postwar Americanization of popular culture and the economy was the ironic counterpart to the emergence of the "new democratic nationality."

An even more profound contradiction was that the new democracy never effected a political separation from the undemocratic liberal formulae from which it had descended. The new ideologues invested themselves completely in imperial state forms that, by design, had never explicitly articulated a doctrine of popular sovereignty. If the nineteenth-century dominion had never been the free state of a sovereign people, but was rather a locally managed dominion within a liberal empire, whose territorial claim rested fundamentally on the legacy of Britain's commercial might and armed violence in North America, the twentieth-century dominion, however much influenced by the Social Gospel, the "new democracy," the socialist ideals of the CCF and the Communist Party, and so on, nonetheless never decisively distanced itself from this imperial legacy. This was still, in many critical eyes, perhaps most decisively those of Québécois, the same old empire, with the same kinds of men in charge, revering the same distant queen, jockeying for the same threadbare colonial honours, flocking in their sunset years to the same anti-democratic Senate.

To abbreviate and anticipate what should some day be a long and more subtle discussion: the reconceived centre could not hold. It could not, without the old ideological resources of empire, or a new and more rigorous sense of its vocation, even become much of a hegemonic centre. An immensely powerful complex of liberal myths and symbols, amply sustained in a corporate guise by American multinationals and foundations, never went away in the days of the "new democracy." Since 1975, as the idea of new democracy and the "Canada" it articulated has progressively faded from view, the country has rung, again and again, to manifestos of the "true believers" of the doctrines of classical liberalism. After their brilliantly executed struggle for cultural hegemony, classical liberal individualism rides high again, and what had once appeared a decisive "transcendence of the classical liberal order of the nineteenth century" stands revealed as something more like an interregnum, a temporary moment of emergency social legislation.

Can Canada be reprogrammed a third time, along the lines of this undoubtedly massive shift away from the values of the new democracy, towards a restoration of the nineteenth-century paradigm? Notwithstanding the depth and tenacity of the liberal order in Canadian history, this refocus seems unlikely. Had we asked a Victorian liberal why one should support the project of Canada, the answer might well have entailed some version of "Peace, Order, and good Government" – the benefits to all free-standing individuals of living in a stable British country, governed sensibly by a parliamentary monarchy, and anchored in a deep sense of the British Constitution and the Queen's law. If we asked a mid-twentieth-century Canadian the same question, we might well have heard a new democratic defence of national distinctiveness in terms of universal social programs, democratic inclusiveness and tolerance, east-west economic linkages, and international peacekeeping. How (or if) neoliberals will attempt to "Canadianize" themselves is an intriguing mystery. True believers in unfettered individualism and global markets, these exponents of the hegemonic ideology presently, lack any persuasive justification for Canada in the reductionist market terms in which they seek to cast social and political questions. Most of the neo-liberals' grand economic objectives would, in fact, be better realized without a separate Canadian state in northern North America – and they know it.[32] Theirs is a brilliant definitional challenge that should arouse Canadian historians from their dogmatic slumbers, petty debates, and narrow horizons.

NOTES

1 Ian McKay, "The Liberal Order Framework: A Prospectus for a Reconnaissance of Canadian History," *Canadian Historical Review*, 81, 4 (2000), 617–651. Notes have been condensed.

2 For the American prototype, see Edward T. Linenthal and Tom Engelhardt, *History Wars: The* Enola Gay *and Other Battles for the American Past* (New York: Metropolitan Books 1996).

3 After all, in a twenty-first-century context, there is no reason why Clio should be assigned a fixed gender identity.

4 This is not to detract from Kenneth McRoberts's classic *Quebec: Social Change and Political Crisis* (Toronto: McClelland & Stewart 1988), and similar titles from political science.

5 On Marxist attempts to write the "general history of Canada," see especially the often rich and suggestive work of Stanley Ryerson, *The Founding of Canada: Beginnings to 1815* (Toronto: Progress, 1972); and Ryerson, *Unequal Union: Confederation and the Roots of Conflict in the Canadas, 1815–1873* (New York: International Publishers, 1968).

6 Fernande Roy, *Progrès, harmonie, liberté: Le libéralisme des milieux d'affaires francophones de Montréal au tournant du siècle* (Montreal: Boréal, 1988), 45–58. The discussion of the next two paragraphs is in all respects heavily dependent on Roy's discussion.

7 C.B. Macpherson, *The Political Theory of Possessive Individualism: Hobbes to Locke* (London: Oxford University Press, 1962), 264.

8 See Rainer Knopff, "The Triumph of Liberalism in Canada: Laurier on Representation and Party Government," in Ajzenstat and Smith, eds., *Canada's Origins*, chap. 7.

9 For an interesting distillation of the large literature on liberalism and patriarchy, see Mary Dietz, "Context Is All: Feminism and Theories of Citizenship," in Chantal Mouffe, ed., *Dimensions of Radical Democracy: Pluralism, Citizenship, Community* (London: Verso, 1995), 63–85.

10 Perhaps the most suggestive account from a liberal-order perspective is that of Sarah Carter, *Lost Harvests: Prairie Indian Reserve Farmers and Government Policy* (Montreal and Kingston: McGill-Queen's University Press, 1990).

11 See Louis Hartz, *The Liberal Tradition in America: An Interpretation of American Political Thought since the Revolution* (New York: Harcourt, Brace & World 1955), chap. 1.

12 For an important discussion, see John P. McCormick, *Carl Schmitt's Critique of Liberalism: Against Politics as Technology* (Cambridge: Cambridge University Press, 1997), chap. 3.

13 See J.L. Granatstein, *The Ottawa Men: The Civil Service Mandarins 1935–1957* (Toronto: Oxford University Press, 1982); Doug Owram, *The Government Generation: Canadian Intellectuals and the State, 1900–1945* (Toronto: University of Toronto Press, 1986); and Barry Ferguson, *Remaking Liberalism: The Intellectual Legacy of Adam Shortt, O.D. Skelton, W.C. Clark, and W.A. Mackintosh 1890–1925* (Montreal and Kingston: McGill-Queen's University Press, 1993).

14 I am drawing upon Georges E. Sioui, *For an Amerindian Autohistory* (Montreal and Kingston: McGill-Queen's University Press, 1992); and Olive Patricia Dickason, *Canada's First Nations: A History of Founding Peoples from Earliest Times* (Toronto: McClelland & Stewart, 1992), 79–83.

15 For the "civic humanist" credentials of the Patriotes, see Louis-Georges Harvey, "The First Distinct Society: French Canada, America, and the Constitution of 1791," in Ajzenstat and Smith, eds., *Canada's Origins*, chap. 4.

16 See Ian Radforth, "Sydenham and Utilitarian Reform," in Greer and Radforth, *Colonial Leviathan*, 64–102; Janet Ajzenstat, *The Political Thought of Lord Durham* (Montreal and Kingston: McGill-Queen's University Press, 1988); Phillip Buckner, *The Transition to Responsible Government: British Policy in British North America 1815–1850* (Westport, Conn.: Greenwood Press, 1985).

17 Tina Loo, *Making Law, Order, and Authority in British Columbia 1821–1871* (Toronto: University of Toronto Press, 1994), which stands as one of

the most exciting and provocative studies of the emergence of "liberal legality."

18 See William Kaplan, ed., *Belonging: The Meaning and Future of Canadian Citizenship* (Montreal and Kingston: McGill-Queen's University Press, 1993), although this volume does not succeed in placing the concept of citizenship in an international or long-term perspective.

19 Vipond, *Liberty and Community*, brings David Mills, MP for Bothwell, and subsequently minister of justice under Laurier from 1897 to 1902, to life as a significant "decentralizer" in Canada's constitutional history; Mills's liberalism, voiced eloquently in the London *Advertiser*, was very much influenced by the teachings of Thomas Cooley at the University of Michigan, one of the most important legal minds in the United States.

20 Note in particular Stephen Leacock, "The Woman Question," in *Social Criticism: The Unsolved Riddle of Social Justice and Other Essays* (Toronto: University of Toronto Press, 1996), 51–60, which turned to the "law of supply and demand" for support for its argument against women's rights.

21 See Ronald Rudin, *Making History in Twentieth-Century Quebec* (Toronto: University of Toronto Press, 1997), for an exploration of the ways in which Quebec historians have sought to "normalize" their society's distinctiveness.

22 For a sophisticated and convincing elaboration of this point, see Gilles Bourque, Jules Duchastel, and Jacques Beauchemin, *La société libérale duplessiste 1944–1960* (Montréal: Les Presses de l'Université de Montréal, 1994).

23 See E. Brian Titley, *A Narrow Vision: Duncan Campbell Scott and the Administration of Indian Affairs in Canada* (Vancouver: UBC Press 1986); Frank James Tester and Peter Kulchyski, *Tammarniit (Mistakes): Inuit Relocation in the Eastern Arctic, 1939–63* (Vancouver: UBC Press, 1994).

24 On the residential schools, see J.R. Miller, *Shingwauk's Vision: A History of Native Residential Schools* (Toronto: University of Toronto Press, 1996); and John S. Milloy, *A National Crime: The Canadian Government and the Residential School System 1879 to 1986* (Winnipeg: University of Manitoba Press, 1999).

25 See Dante Germino, *Antonio Gramsci: Architect of a New Politics* (Baton Rouge: Louisiana State University Press, 1990), 57–8, for a discussion of this Gramscian innovation in the language of Marxist politics.

26 For "vulgar liberalism," see Allan Smith, "The Myth of the Self-Made Man in English Canada 1850–1914," in *Canada: An American Nation? Essays on Continentalism, Identity, and the Canadian Frame of Mind* (Montreal and Kingston: McGill-Queen's University Press, 1994), 324–58.

27 See Gad Horowitz, "Conservatism, Liberalism, and Socialism in Canada: An Interpretation," in Ajzenstat and Smith, eds., *Canada's Origins*, chap. 2.

28 See John Farthing, *Freedom Wears a Crown* (Toronto: Kingswood House, 1957).

29 For the concept of passive revolution, see Antonio Gramsci, *Selections from the Prison Notebooks*, ed. and trans. Quintin Hoare and Geoffrey Nowell Smith (London: Lawrence & Wishart, 1971), 207.

30 See Ramsay Cook, *The Regenerators: Social Criticism in Late Victorian Canada* (Toronto: University of Toronto Press, 1985). For an interesting account of changing political ideals, see John English, *The Decline of Politics: The Conservatives and the Party System 1901–20* (1977; Toronto: University of Toronto Press 1993). The pioneering exploration of the concept of the "new democracy" is James Naylor, *The New Democracy: Challenging the Social Order in Industrial Ontario 1914–25* (Toronto: University of Toronto Press, 1991).

31 See James Struthers, *The Limits of Affluence: Welfare in Ontario 1920–1970* (Toronto: University of Toronto Press for the Government of Ontario 1994), for a careful deromanticization of the partial transition to "social citizenship."

32 See Thomas J. Courchene with Colin R. Telmer, *From Heartland to North American Region State: The Social, Fiscal and Federal Evolution of Ontario. An Interpretive Essay*. Monograph Series on Public Policy (Toronto: University of Toronto, Faculty of Management, 1998).

# "Expansion of Settlement and Erosion of Health during the HBC Monopoly, 1821–1869"

## *Clearing the Plains: Disease, Politics of Starvation and the Loss of Aboriginal Life* 2013

JAMES W. DASCHUK[1]

The end of the fur trade wars in 1821 ushered in a new era for the people of the Canadian northwest. For half a century, the Hudson's Bay Company was the de facto government of Rupert's Land and tried, with varying degrees of success, to control the people and economy of the region. George Simpson, the London clerk who came to be known as the "Little Emperor," was governor of the HBC through most of the monopoly period. The guiding principle of his tenure was maximum returns with minimum investments.[2] Simpson closed many of the competing posts that had littered the landscape during the decades of desperate harvesting.[3] The combined total of sixty-eight HBC posts and fifty-seven Canadian posts prior to the union was slashed to slightly over fifty after the merger.[4] The result of the downsizing was a region-wide labour crisis as the majority of fur trade workers found themselves without employment.[5] The company curtailed, and eventually prohibited, the flow of alcohol to large portions of the interior.[6] The HBC also worked to prevent contagious diseases, especially smallpox, with the widespread distribution of vaccine. For the first time, the people and environment of the northwest came under the management of a single corporate entity. Company policies met with different levels of success but had profound impacts on the development of First Nations in the northwest.

During the monopoly period, the growth of the agricultural community at Red River, part of the wider phenomenon of westward expansion of European settlement, led to fundamental changes in the demography and economy of the northwest. The burgeoning demand from the colony for meat eventually strained the viability of bison herds, a resource once thought to be almost limitless. With diminished supply and increased demand, conflict grew. The growing human population served as an ever-increasing repository of infection that threatened the indigenous communities of the west. Improved transportation networks delivered pathogens to the susceptible with greater speed. By the mid-nineteenth century, the heightened disease load signalled "a change in status in which the region moved from the periphery of several urban disease pools to being within the immediate hinterland of the eastern pool."[7] Relentless microbial attacks brought some indigenous communities to the brink of collapse. Others were spared by medical intervention that came with their commercial relationships with British traders, equipped with medicines that made the difference between life and death. During the HBC monopoly, differential demographic outcomes of disease episodes among plains groups shaped the pattern of territorial occupancy that largely remains to this day. The unstoppable movement of the settlement frontier, particularly in the United States, also increased pressures on game populations to unsustainable levels. Climatic instability through most of the mid-nineteenth century contributed to the increasingly desperate competition for reliable food supplies.[8] On the plains, precipitation patterns oscillated between inundation and severe drought, undermining the predictability of bison movements. By the 1820s, the ascendancy of equestrian chase hunting over less disruptive harvesting practices such as pounding also undermined predictability.[9]

While plains populations were still reeling from the measles and whooping cough, word spread from the south that smallpox was raging along the Missouri River and that many of the Assiniboine had perished from the dreaded disease. In US territory, the Sioux, A'aninin, and Flathead in the plateau, along with other groups in the south, suffered terrible losses during the 1820s. West of the continental divide disease reportedly killed four-fifths of the population along the Columbia River.[10] Fortunately, smallpox did not become widespread in British territory. At Red River, the HBC vaccinated large numbers of people, halting spread of the disease[11] and providing the community with some immunity against the even more serious smallpox outbreak of 1837.

As inhabitants of the plains coped with epidemics and renewed warfare in the 1820s, the agricultural colony at Red River took root. The eventual success of the settlement was not achieved without great effort and considerable frustration. During the first decade of the HBC monopoly, the settlers endured a series of environmental setbacks that included shortages of bison meat, prairie fires, poor crops, a major flood, and in 1827 another epidemic of whooping cough.[12] The worst was the flood of 1826, which led many European settlers to abandon the struggling colony.[13]

Although settlers had established themselves less than a decade before, the country surrounding Red River had been under severe hunting pressure for decades before the 1820s. Since the re-establishment of the Montreal trade in the 1760s, the land between the forks of the Red and Assiniboine Rivers and Lake Winnipeg served as the hunting ground for both Canadian and English traders in addition to the aboriginal population of the area.

The Anishinabe, who migrated to the Red River area in the last decades of the eighteenth century, experienced severe depletion of game in the region even before establishment of the colony. By the time the Selkirk colonists arrived, the country along the Red was all but hunted out. The depletion of large game, along with mortality from epidemic disease and military conflict, contributed to territorial abandonment, which opened the region for settlement by the Anishinabe. Miles Macdonell, who oversaw establishment of the new community, said that the Anishinabe were eager for the settlers to arrive. Their long relationship with European traders had made them "quite dependent, their country being stripped of its most valuable furs." He added, "The Saulteaux are now quite afraid of being altogether abandoned by the traders & are pleased to see people of steady habits arrived who are to make permanent residence; acting toward them on fair and just principles and administering to their wants."[14] The Anglican missionary John West, touring his parish in 1820, recorded the hardship of the aboriginal population who had settled near the colony. During the winter of 1822–23, the scarcity of game and severity of the weather drove the Saulteaux chief Peguis and his people to eat their dogs and the remains of a horse that had succumbed to the cold.[15] The Saulteaux under Peguis were experienced farmers, but their expertise was probably no match for the harsh conditions of the early nineteenth century.

The situation among the Saulteaux foreshadowed the region-wide TB epidemic that came with the extermination of bison and the failure of agriculture half a century later. The strategic location of Red River, along the route from Canada to the northwest, spread tuberculosis as sick members of Canadian canoe brigades on tight schedules passed by communities along the waterway.[16] A recent scientific study asserted that a genetic lineage of tuberculosis traced to Quebec was spread by French Canadians during the fur trade period and persists in TB among isolated indigenous communities into the twenty-first century.[17]

Despite the hardships, the population of the Red River settlement continued to grow through the 1820s. Part of the increase was the result of corporate downsizing after the merger. The unemployed drifted to the colony, supplementing the trickle of agricultural immigrants from the east and Europe. Agrarian missions, such as St. Peter's under the tutelage of West in the early 1820s, were established to help displaced aboriginal employees become self-sufficient. Officials who sought to create an island of European settlement along the Red River saw the number of country-born people moving to the colony as a problem. By the mid-1820s, the HBC stopped granting its retirees land in the colony to control what it considered the wrong kind of growth – those who depended on corporate assistance or would not commit themselves fully to an agrarian lifestyle. By 1834, the company required its retirees to purchase a minimum of fifty acres to settle in the colony. A decade later it banned them from the settlement entirely.[18]

Because the HBC in monopoly served as the de facto government of the northwest, changes to corporate strategies had important consequences for the people of the region. Recognizing that the free flow of alcohol had created serious social problems during the decades of unrestrained competition, the company imposed what was essentially a prohibition on alcohol in some of its domain. In 1822, the Northern Department Council directed that the flow of alcohol to the interior be reduced by 50 percent. In isolated areas, it imposed a complete ban. In 1826, it prohibited the trade in alcohol in the districts of Athabasca, Mackenzie, and English River, eliminating the sanctioned flow of alcohol to fur producers and company employees beyond Cumberland House.[19] The policy was unpopular with fur producers: in 1824–25, Chief Factor James Leith at Cumberland House attributed the decline in his returns to restrictions on the trade in alcohol.[20] Along the southern and western boundaries of HBC territory, the official liquor trade continued as free traders and others undermined the jurisdictional realities of the charter. The illicit sale of alcohol by American traders on the southern margin of the country prompted many producers to shift their trade away from the HBC, which held the titular monopoly in the region.[21]

Game conservation was another issue that the company took on, imposing limits and even banning the harvest of certain species in depleted regions. In Athabasca, beaver had largely been extirpated by Iroquois trappers working for the North West Company, and by the 1820s large game such as moose, caribou, and bison were also rare.[22] On his inspection tour in 1823, George Simpson was "appalled" at the condition of the Nelson and lower Churchill districts, since "he did not see a solitary vestige of beaver and he could see no remedy save to forbid beaver-hunting there entirely for the next five years." His first policy directives banned any trade in summer beaver, prohibited the use of steel traps and castoreum, and put in place strategies to rehabilitate the Athabasca as a major source of low-value muskrat fur.[23]

Only where fur production could be realistically curtailed and the monopoly secured were controls placed on the depleted resource.[24] In the relatively isolated but game-depleted country surrounding Lesser Slave Lake, producers were coerced into leaving, as traders "threw out [the] visiting Beaver without even the common courtesy of providing them with a gift of tobacco."[25] The closure of posts was intended to nurture game, but the result was often hardship for the local indigenous population. Simpson himself acknowledged that the closing of Fort St. John "reduced the whole population of the upper Peace to the utmost distress" and led to the deaths of many from famine.[26]

In areas where the monopoly rang hollow, such as the plains and parklands, the company was faced with competition from free traders and American interests. Aboriginal producers were encouraged to trap areas out, leaving a fur-denuded buffer along the margins of HBC territory.[27] When a country-wide quota system on beaver was introduced in 1826, border areas such as the Rainy, Red, and Saskatchewan Rivers were exempted from the plan.[28] On the southwestern margin of HBC influence, Peter Skene Ogden's expedition to the Snake River was ordered "to hunt as bare as possible all the Country South of the Columbia and West of the Mountains."[29]

Aboriginal producers responded in a number of ways to the strictures. Some, such as the Dunneza of the Peace River area, protested the closure of their fort by turning on the traders. In the fall of 1823, five were killed.[30] Elsewhere in Athabasca, Anishinabe commercial trappers who had invaded the area a generation earlier abandoned the country around Lesser Slave Lake and shifted to the mixed economy of the parklands in the south. Other Anishinabe groups, such as those in the Cumberland House district, responded to the unpredictability of the muskrat trade by abandoning the region and becoming bison hunters.[31] As they withdrew from fur production and focused their attention on the plains, the Anishinabe increasingly became important participants in the cycle of warfare as allies of the Cree in opposition to the Niitsitapi and the Mandan along the Missouri.[32]

The Plains Cree recovered from their losses during the 1820s largely by migrating from the woodlands to the prairie and bison.[33] In shifting their focus west, the Cree (along with the Anishinabe) continued a pattern of migration that had endured for 500 years. The withdrawal, or at least retreat, of many groups from the diminished possibilities of the monopoly fur trade helped them to maintain their independence during what was considered the despotic rule of the HBC.[34] Rather than withdrawing from the economic relationship with Europeans altogether, those who moved from the forest responded to new market opportunities afforded by free trade and the bison hunt.

Fur producers isolated from the borders of HBC territory, particularly inhabitants of the boreal forest and the marginal lands at the edge of the tundra, did not fare so well. The company's new policy mandated that trappers trade at only one post, with authorization required from corporate officials for a transfer to a different region.[35] HBC censuses were part of a strategy to set production quotas appropriate to the sizes of post populations.[36] Corporate authorities strongly opposed the migration of displaced aboriginal producers from areas of restricted trade to other areas, including Red River. By the 1820s, the depletion of large game forced northern hunters to make wholesale changes in their subsistence strategies. For many, fish and hares became necessary, if precarious, food staples. To keep the aboriginal population in the game-depleted hinterland, the HBC used a number of measures, including the distribution of gratuities and the extension of credit.[37] Seasonal employment on York boat brigades was an inducement for those who chose to stay and trap during the winter in the overhunted fur country north of Norway House.[38] In the York district, bonuses were paid to trappers who did not hunt depleted species.[39]

In areas where conservation measures were imposed and local harvesters accepted them, producers who "trespassed" from other districts often hunted game illegally.[40] To circumvent differential prices decreed by the company, Chipewyan and Inuit groups exchanged furs before trading with Europeans at Churchill to maximize their returns.[41] Around

Cumberland House, the Cree simply ignored appeals for conservation.[42] Their refusal to comply was undoubtedly related to the presence of free traders who had congregated along the lower Saskatchewan River after the merger. To counter the threat to its monopoly, the HBC attempted to bar freemen from the hinterland.[43]

The growth of Red River led to significant changes in both the economy and the epidemiology of Rupert's Land. The colony served as a pool of seasonal labour for the vast transportation network of the monopoly organization. With a surplus of native-born workers at its inland entrepot and elsewhere in its territory, the HBC no longer had to import workers from the British Isles. Increasingly, the workforce was of mixed heritage. By 1830, 20 percent were country born. Thirty years later half of HBC employees were born in the northwest. Officers, many of them still from Great Britain, found them unmanageable.[44]

By the mid-1850s, the population of the colony was estimated to be 8,000.[45] The ever-increasing demand for meat was met by a burgeoning Métis-controlled hunting economy that had first developed during the competition era to supply the North West Company brigades. As other aboriginal societies focused on the herds, interethnic conflict grew. For a time, Anishinabe fought Métis hunters, though the two groups later cooperated in the context of wider competition for the resource. Sioux antagonism toward the Red River hunters festered until "a state of war" erupted in the 1840s.[46] As the herds declined, tensions grew between the colony's meat suppliers and the Plains Cree, escalating into open violence by the 1850s.[47] Alexander Ross said of the bison at mid-century, "They are now like a ball between two players."[48]

Demand for hides in the global market outstripped the expanding but essentially local market for meat. By 1865, 200,000 hides were being delivered annually to St. Louis. The hides ended up as "gun belts for British soldiers in India, drive belts for industrial machinery in Liverpool, and luxury furniture in Manhattan townhouses."[49] Meeting the world demand destroyed the provisioning economy, leaving Red River short of meat. As herds at the eastern margin of the plains were hunted to extinction in the 1850s, Métis supply lines became too long for hunters to return to Red River after the chase. They set up winter camps, known as *hivernants,* farther and farther west.[50] The HBC also had to move its pemmican-gathering stations west as herds declined. In 1829, Fort Pitt was built between Carlton and Edmonton to secure meat for the trade.[51] In 1830, Fort Ellice succeeded Brandon House as the chief source of supply. Within twenty years, even Fort Ellice was too far east, and the company opened outposts closer to the shrinking herds.[52]

The shift from a European to a largely indigenous workforce after the merger also brought significant changes to the disease ecology of the northwest. Most Europeans in the region had immunity from diseases that were endemic in their countries of origin but often deadly to the country-born who had not been exposed to them. With increasing frequency, contagious diseases spread along the transportation routes of the interior. The burgeoning population of Red River served to maintain infections for extended periods, often ensuring the spread of pathogens as brigades left for the hinterland every spring.[53]

Increasingly, the west came under the economic and microbial influence of eastern North America. Completion of the Erie Canal in the mid-1820s turned a trickle of immigrants to the American Midwest into a flood. In 1826, as many as 1,200 people a day passed through Buffalo on their way west.[54] As in the northwest decades later, large-scale economic development brought hardship and the inevitable emergence of tuberculosis among indigenous populations of upstate New York.[55] The introduction of steam-powered vessels during the period served to bring greater numbers of people and their germs with increased speed to the frontier.[56]

Along the Missouri, expanding American trade and the flow of pathogens that came with it contributed to the destruction of the sedentary horticultural societies south of the forty-ninth parallel. By 1830, the American Fur Company had established a number of "strong forts" along the waterway. Trade was invigorated by the participation of First Nations moving south in response to corporate downsizing in Rupert's Land. The new American establishments siphoned off a significant portion of beaver returns from HBC territory. Almost immediately, American traders along the Missouri displaced the Mandan, who had long controlled the aboriginal trade on the northern US plains. Soon the Mandan were isolated, with only the Hidatsa and Crow as their allies, and under attack by Cree, Saulteaux, and Assiniboine from the north and Sioux from the east.[57] By the mid-1830s, military and economic pressure, following decades of unpredictable harvests during particularly variable weather,[58] contributed to the emergence of tuberculosis among the besieged population of the Missouri villages. Whooping cough and cholera outbreaks during the early 1830s also damaged the health of Missouri villagers.[59] In a survey of pulmonary consumption (tuberculosis) published in 1837, Samuel Morton stated that the disease "occasions a large share of the mortality which annually occurs among the Mandans of the Upper Missouri."[60]

In 1831, smallpox swept across the central American plains, killing half of the Pawnee nation.[61] In response to a lobbying campaign led by Reverend John McCoy, the US government implemented a smallpox prevention program that conferred immunity to over 3,000 inhabitants of the lower Missouri River. Unfortunately for the communities upstream, the physicians could not complete their work during the summer of 1832. They asked to be sent to the unvaccinated region the following year but were refused. Mandan, Hidatsa, Arikara, Assiniboine, Cree, and Niitsitapi in US territory were not vaccinated.

Those nations were severely debilitated when smallpox broke out along the Missouri in 1837. The partial success of the vaccination campaign shaped the differential outcomes of that epidemic, which in turn had important consequences for the development of the American plains for decades. Most Sioux bands, through vaccination or avoidance, were spared the mortality endured by their neighbours, and their better health facilitated their subsequent territorial expansion.[62]

The epidemic of 1837–38 killed an estimated 17,000 people and turned the region into "one great graveyard."[63] The outbreak spread up the Missouri from a steamboat, the *St. Peters,* whose crew carried the infection. For the Mandan, the death blow came less than two years later. Weakened by mortality estimated as high as 90 percent,[64] the villages were overrun by the Sioux in January 1839.

The disease ravaged the Assiniboine and Niitsitapi, whose territories straddled the forty-ninth parallel. The epidemic spread to the former when they ignored the warnings of American traders to stay away from Fort Union.[65] At Edmonton, John Rowand estimated mortality among the two groups as high as 75 percent.[66] Evidence of the carnage was still visible a decade later. In 1848, Paul Kane saw "[t]he bones of a whole camp of Indians, who were carried off by that fatal scourge of their race, the small-pox, ... bleaching on the plains."[67]

The epidemic did not sweep through HBC territory unchecked, for the company delivered medical and other types of assistance to its producers in viable areas of its domain. Governor Simpson described each post as "an Indian Hospital, where those who are unable to follow the Chase during the Winter months, are fed, clothed, and maintained."[68] The company was motivated by more than a sense of altruism; traders offered assistance to women, the sick, and the elderly so that able-bodied men could continue the commercial hunt.

In the Swan River district, Dr. William Todd, known as "Picotte" because of his own disfigurement from smallpox, was largely responsible for stopping the epidemic in its tracks through extensive vaccination.[69] His work had important consequences for the demographic future of indigenous peoples on the Canadian plains. Ethnic boundaries were blurred as Cree, Saulteaux, and Assiniboine survivors joined together.[70] One effect of differential outcomes of the outbreak was the ascendancy of the Anishinabe or Saulteaux in the territory that they shared with the Cree and Assiniboine, especially south of the Assiniboine River.[71] Most of those who could obtain HBC vaccine did so; many groups travelled to Todd's post to request the procedure. A few, such as a band of Qu'Appelle Cree, agreed to vaccination after talking to Todd.[72]

Communities protected from the contagion augmented their territory in the aftermath of the outbreak. The Plains Cree and Saulteaux, vaccinated in large numbers, expanded their territory after 1837–38.[73] The opposite was true for the Assiniboine and Niitsitapi, who did not have the opportunity to be vaccinated and suffered high mortality rates.[74] Because of the high death toll among members of the Niitsitapi, as many as 6,000 individuals, groups such as the Siksika retreated from their northern frontier along the Battle River to what became their reserve at Blackfoot Crossing on the Bow River.[75] In 1841, Simpson reported that the Siksika "have been reduced by one half of late years by Small Pox and other causes." The Tsuu T'ina (Sarcee) were particularly hit hard. Simpson estimated that they were reduced from a population of 1,800 to a mere 250.[76]

Tribal historians have noted the role of the epidemic in the decline of the Assiniboine, once ubiquitous in the northwest. According to Chief Dan Kennedy, the group was "literally wiped out."[77] Even early chroniclers of the west recognized that the Assiniboine, whose bands tended to have larger population aggregates than their neighbours, were especially vulnerable to smallpox. In 1860, Dr. James Hector wrote that the disease "seemed to single them out for more severe visitation than any of the other tribes, till at length they were almost extirpated, the northern part of their country being occupied by the less mischievous Crees."[78]

Chief Kennedy believed that the surviving Assiniboine fled westward through enemy territory to the foothills of the Rockies, where their descendants today occupy the reserve at Morley, Alberta.[79] The idea that

Assiniboine survivors took refuge among the Stoney is plausible but not likely; linguistic evidence indicates that the two groups have been discrete for so long that Stoney is "on the verge of becoming a separate language" from other Sioux dialects, including Assiniboine.[80] Although losses from disease undoubtedly played a hand in displacement of the Stoney to the foothills, they had occupied the region since at least the late eighteenth century and traded with the HBC at Edmonton and Rocky Mountain House.[81] Whatever the losses among the Assiniboine in the 1837 outbreak, mortality from smallpox was a key factor in their precipitous decline over the nineteenth century. Their position was also undermined by their inability to maintain sufficient horse herds to compete in the bison hunt. By the mid-nineteenth century, they were described as "impoverished," with few horses.[82] The handful of reserves that they occupy today provide but a faint reminder of the influence they once held across the west.

In addition to the protection afforded by vaccination, numerous groups used the time-tested strategy of heading into the bush or onto the plains to diminish the chances of contagion. At Pelly, Dr. Todd reported that at least two bands, one along the Red Deer River (in Manitoba) and the other in the Beaver Hills, refused to come to the post for fear of infection. Both groups endured privation by subsisting on rabbits rather than risk infection on the plains, where bison were numerous.[83]

Vaccinations performed by Dr. Todd, other HBC servants, and even First Nations people instructed in the procedure were the most significant example of the HBC's medical assistance to aboriginal groups in the monopoly period. Todd sent one group of aboriginal producers to the "Strong Woods" with a lancet and medicine to counter any infection that they might find there, and he "took many pains in instructing them how to use it in vaccinating others."[84] Although smallpox was the most virulent pathogen at the time, prevention through the use of cowpox vaccine was relatively simple. Lewis and Clark took vaccine with them on their expedition.[85] In Rupert's Land, the value of immunization was recognized early on. In 1811, before the arrival of the first settlers, Lord Selkirk suggested a vaccination campaign for the aboriginal inhabitants of Red River. Two years later the procedure was performed at York Factory with serum supplied by the HBC. During the measles and whooping cough outbreaks of 1820, the company vaccinated the population of Red River in response to rumours spreading northward. In the mid-1820s, the procedure was performed at Cumberland House, Norway House, and along the Albany River. What can truly be called a comprehensive vaccination program, however, was not implemented by the company until after the smallpox outbreak of 1837.[86]

Orders sent to HBC posts to conduct a vaccination program six months prior to the outbreak along the Missouri were never implemented.[87] When the crisis was over, the company conducted a territory-wide vaccination program, the first large-scale public health campaign undertaken in the northwest.[88] Vaccine was distributed as far northwest as the Mackenzie River. A sad irony, however, is that, as the HBC sought to end the most virulent disease of the time with some success, its employees infected communities with influenza and other diseases, which kept mortality rates high.

The HBC worked in other ways to prevent disease. Within years of the merger, the London Committee urged George Simpson to implement sanitation regulations at York Factory to combat chronic health problems there.[89] The company posted surgeons to a number of locations, and by 1830 at least two doctors were practising at Red River.[90] Quarantine techniques were also used to halt the spread of pathogens. In 1844, isolation measures perhaps stopped the spread of scarlet fever from Red River to the population north of Lake Winnipeg.[91] The company's interest in public health in its domain was prompted by humanitarian concerns as well as protection of its enterprise in the face of an increasingly complicated environment of disease and trade.[92]

Beyond the epidemiological situation, or perhaps because of it, the 1840s saw the introduction of the first large-scale missionary work outside the Red River settlement. Simpson had no affection for missionaries, but deteriorating conditions in the 1830s led him to accept their increasing presence. His change of heart was due to exhausted fur lands, the uncontrolled migration of displaced or unemployed Indians, and the slump in the beaver trade resulting from the growing popularity of silk hats in Europe.[93] Cutbacks in the trade resulted in increased hardship and dependence of aboriginal producers on the company's stores. Missionaries, whatever their faith, provided the HBC with a cheap way to deliver assistance. The missions also served to anchor communities to territories that otherwise would have been abandoned. By the early 1830s, the number of Muskego Cree heading south to Red River was straining the supplies of St. Peter's mission.

Anchoring surplus suppliers to HBC territory was also the rationale for establishment of the Roman Catholic mission at Île-à-la-Crosse in 1846. Father Thibault was invited to the district to stop the movement of Cree hunters south to the plains bison hunt. The Lac Caribou mission on Reindeer Lake was built to draw the Denesuliné (Caribou Eater Chipewyan) south from their independent life on the barrens.[94] The presence of missions, particularly the agrarian settlements established by Protestants, aided the material well-being of many, though the arrival of Christian groups in the north proved to be a mixed blessing.

As Fathers Taché and Laflêche were on their way to their postings in the interior in the summer of 1846, they held a mass at Frog Portage, where the routes north to Reindeer Lake and west to Île-à-la-Crosse intersect. The service had deadly consequences. It spread a fatal epidemic of measles to those who had congregated, and as many as eighteen people died from the infection caught at the mass.[95] Later twenty-nine converts at the newly established Anglican mission at Lac la Ronge also succumbed to measles.[96] Many of the inhabitants of the bush blamed missionaries for the spread of infection and death. The murders of the Roman Catholic missionary and his assistant at The Pas in June 1844 were in retribution for their perceived role in the spread of a scarlet fever epidemic the previous winter. The rapid acceptance of Catholic missionaries among the struggling populations in isolated regions of the north was in sharp contrast to the resistance of plains people to the efforts of Christians among them.[97]

A major factor in this increasing complexity was the growth of the agricultural colony at Red River, stimulated by its growing trade with the Minnesota Territory. In the 1840s, American traders such as Norman Kittson conducted a lucrative though illegal trade with the colony.[98] Métis free traders who, by the mid-1840s, were agitating for the legal right to an open trade further developed the link between Red River and the American frontier. Opponents of HBC rule in England quickly took up a petition attacking the monopoly, signed by almost 1,000 residents of the colony.[99]

The most vocal English critic was actually a native of the northwest with experience in the fur trade. Alexander Kennedy Isbister submitted his critique of the HBC monopoly to an inquiry in the British House of Commons in February 1847.[100] He attacked the monopoly charter on a number of points. The first was that the HBC had "to the utter impoverishment, if not ruin, of the natives" acquired "a princely revenue" through its monopoly. The second charged that the company had undermined aboriginal societies through the trade in liquor, a "deadly and demoralizing poison." The third dealt directly with the connection between the fur trade and hunger among "the larger part" of producers. His submission also lashed out against the trading monopoly imposed by the HBC, which he described as "gross aggressions on the rights and liberties of the natives."[101] Central to Isbister's critique was the connection between the fur trade and difficulty in securing food. The unpredictable climate of the 1840s undermined the Athapaskan societies of the western subarctic.[102] In the mid-1840s, the ships *Erebus* and *Terror*, part of the ill-fated Franklin Expedition, were frozen in the ice, and their crews perished from starvation and exposure. The description of the famine among the Dene by English explorer Henry Lefroy ignited a controversy over the HBC's role in the far north.[103] Isbister's criticism of the HBC was eloquent and probably just, but it failed to persuade parliament to revoke the charter until the late 1850s, when the reality of the Northwest's integration into the world economy was too strong to ignore.

By the 1840s, pathogens delivered overland from the expanding American frontier increasingly threatened the inhabitants of Rupert's Land. The opening of the Oregon Territory to settlers in 1846 had serious medical consequences, even for populations as distant as York Factory. That year an entire English regiment, comprising almost 400 men,[104] travelled from York Factory to Red River. The force was sent to protect the colony against the threat of Americans, the result of the escalating conflict over the Oregon Territory.[105] Because the soldiers could not be maintained by the HBC at Hudson Bay, the company abandoned its usual quarantine protocol and moved them from the coast to the colony, where they could be sustained. Yet the hasty transfer of troops spread infection throughout the region. York boat crews dispatched from Red River to assist in the movement of troops were infected with measles, which greatly exacerbated the compound epidemics of influenza, measles, and dysentery. That same year, 1846, proved to be one of the most calamitous years in the history of Red River.[106] Aboriginal mortality in northern Manitoba was so severe that traditional mourning practices were abandoned.[107]

Another source of infection was the little-used route from the lakehead to Red River. Influenza spread from northern Ontario, where Charles Mackenzie reported that as many as 100 people had gathered at Lac Seul. The post, according to the trader, was "more a hospital than a kitchen."[108] Disease extended as far northwest as the Yukon.[109] As influenza blanketed the country, measles infected populations west from the eastern seaboard, possibly along the Oregon Trail and then north into HBC territory.[110] Dysentery was added to the deadly mix during the summer of 1846. At Red River, George Simpson estimated that, in a span of four weeks, 300 out of a population of 5,000 inhabitants died. He likened the mortality to the devastating cholera pandemic that had spread through Europe and eastern North America during the early 1830s. Simpson, who had seen the misery of the combined epidemics of 1819–20, reported that the outbreaks of 1846 "led to a greater mortality than at any former period within my recollection."[111] Alexander Ross, the first historian of Red River, described the suffering as a "pest" that spread "terror" in the colony: "From the 18th of June to the 2nd of August, the deaths averaged seven a day, or 321 in all; being one out of sixteen of our population. Of these one-sixth were Indians, two-thirds half-breeds, and the remainder whites. On one occasion, thirteen burials were proceeding at once."[112]

In the late 1840s, political and economic developments further undermined the monopoly of the HBC and the relative isolation of the inhabitants of Rupert's Land. The settlement of the Oregon question and the subsequent partition of the west coast between American and British interests led to the first large-scale influx of agricultural immigrants overland to the Pacific Northwest. The intensified interaction between Europeans and the indigenous population of the American west led to almost yearly epidemics of one sort or another.[113] Resolution of the Sayer trial in 1848 both opened trade with Minnesota and provided judicial acknowledgement that the HBC had a monopoly in title only. Before the end of the decade, gold was found in California. In 1849, 25,000 emigrants travelled through the plains at the height of the California Gold Rush, infecting the Sioux population along the route with smallpox, measles, and cholera.[114] Amid the gold fever, the HBC was forced to allow many of its employees leaves of absence for up to six months to prevent the wholesale desertion of its workforce.[115]

By 1850, the company's hold on the country was eroding at an ever-quickening pace. From within, labour strife threatened its complex, if precarious, transportation system as native boatmen "began to flex their collective muscle."[116] Agricultural settlers, "mostly Orkney halfbreeds," left Red River and headed west, adding to the largely unsanctioned mixed economy in the Qu'Appelle Valley that had begun a generation earlier.[117] By mid-century, the shift westward of mixed bloods was matched by corporate restructuring as provision posts were moved farther onto the plains to tap into the ever-decreasing bison herds.[118] South of the forty-ninth parallel, the ill-fated Turtle Mountain Treaty between the American government and the Ojibwa, negotiated in 1851 but never ratified, sparked a land rush along the border. The derailed treaty process dispossessed the Turtle Mountain Ojibwa.

Across the plains, tension increased as bison herds dwindled and European settlement loomed. In addition to an escalation of interethnic violence, aboriginal groups began to resist the encroachment of European interlopers. The Anishinabe of Lake of the Woods refused to cooperate with the Hind Expedition in 1857.[119] As Hind surveyed the eastern plains for agricultural potential, Chief Peguis petitioned the Aborigines Protection Society in London for assistance in completing a treaty since his people feared the hardships that would follow the imminent European invasion.[120] Hind met with a council of Plains Cree, led by the highly esteemed chief Mis-tick-oos. The council was firm in its resolve to resist the encroachment of both Europeans and Métis bison hunters.[121] The explorer was told that leaders of the Plains Cree had earlier agreed that, because so many promises had been broken in the past, "[t]hey wished to establish some sort of toll of tobacco and tea for permission to pass through their country, threatening that if it were not given they would ... stop us by force."[122] The council blamed Europeans and their weapons for the declining herds and the pathogens that had accompanied the traders and settlers for the loss of human life. Europeans were no longer seen as allies and neighbours but as "others" who, like the Métis, were threats to the Cree. James Hector, the physician with the Palliser Expedition, estimated the population of Plains Cree at 12,500; "They are, however, rapidly on the decrease, as the small pox and other disease annually sweep them off in great numbers."[123]

Diseases continued to attack plains populations through the 1850s. Early in the decade, influenza spread across the interior from York Factory, the sixth such outbreak in twenty years.[124] The onset of winter mitigated the outbreak somewhat, but it still appeared as far west as Fort Vermilion, where, it was reported, "as many as 50 souls including 24 of our best hunters hav[e] been carried off by influenza." In 1856–57, smallpox again spread sickness and death along the Missouri hinterland[125] and northward, where "again the Qu'Appelle Crees were smitten, so that, added to their incessant strife with the Blackfeet for possession of the buffalo hunting grounds and for horses, the tribe was nearly wiped out."[126] Two years later "hundreds" of people in the Qu'Appelle Valley were reported to have died from scarlet fever.[127] As with earlier outbreaks, vaccinations at Red River prevented the spread of sickness to the colony.[128]

Scarlet fever swept across the aboriginal no man's land at the elbow of the South Saskatchewan to the Niitsitapi.[129] Dr. Hector spent a week in the Kainai (Blood) camp, and in that time between twenty and thirty people died from the disease, a sign, according to him, of their inevitable extermination.[130] Scarlet fever, a disease related to the streptococcus bacterium, might have been spread through interpersonal contact, perhaps by Hind's expedition. The typhoidal symptoms, resulting from salmonella bacteria spread through contaminated food and water, might have been exacerbated by the protracted drought in the southwestern plains that began in the mid-1850s (and lasted until the late 1860s).[131] For the Niitsitapi, the threat of water contamination from drought might have been made worse by their recent abandonment of the centuries-old practice of maintaining fresh water supplies by conserving beaver stocks within their territory.[132]

The already tense situation on the plains was further complicated during the summer of 1858 when gold was discovered on the Fraser River, prompting large numbers of Americans and eastern Canadians to cross Rupert's Land on their way west.[133] In addition to straining the food supply at Edmonton, miners virtually ignored the authority that the HBC had grown accustomed to over the years. By the end of the decade, the company had been stripped of even its titular monopoly.[134]

Over the mountains, the tide of gold seekers flooding into Vancouver Island and the mainland prompted imperial authorities to grant the district colonial status to deal with the myriad problems arising from the arrival of as many as 30,000 people.[135] The invasion of so many of what Governor James Douglas termed "rowdies" was no less than a catastrophe for many aboriginal populations in British Columbia. Among the disasters resulting from the gold rush were the massacre of an unarmed band near Okanagan Lake by miners and other "indiscriminate killings" and starvation resulting from the destruction of fish habitat. In 1862–63, a smallpox outbreak killed a significant portion of the aboriginal population. Among the dead were "no fewer than 500" Tsimshian at Fort Simpson.[136] In the Caribou, the British adventurer Walter Cheadle reported that 300 people had died.[137]

On the eastern plains, the shift from the fur trade to agriculture became inevitable.[138] Minnesota was granted statehood in 1858, and with it came a population explosion, railway development, and, as was so often the case in the American context, an "Indian war." The violence that erupted in the new state led to the deaths of 500 settlers, the subjugation of the Dakota nation, and the arrival of 450 Sioux refugees at Red

River in 1862.[139] The Dakota also had a reputation for violence arising from their incessant struggles with the Anishinabe and later the Métis. By the spring of 1863, the presence of 2,000 Dakota was causing panic in the colony.

For a time, the violence in Minnesota slowed the pace of settlement and the looming changes that it meant for Red River. Although the first steamboat arrived at the colony before 1860, catching the inhabitants and especially the HBC off guard, it was a decade before the connection had a major effect on both the economy and the disease ecology of Canadian territory. The unsanctioned and unregulated flow of alcohol to the Indians in the colony was a serious problem, and calls were made for authorities to deal with it.[140] By 1862, the bison herds had disappeared from Red River altogether, and hunters had to travel farther west onto the plains to find them.[141] There were still herds near the elbow of the South Saskatchewan River, though hunting there was fraught with the risk of armed conflict. The HBC, which had used pemmican as a staple of its supply network for decades, contemplated "the immediate establishment of extensive farms in the Saskatchewan district."[142] Some aboriginal groups began cultivation on their own to supplement their hunts.[143] Even on the western plains, the bison were becoming scarce, increasing the demand on the limited crops grown in the territory. Throughout the decade, food shortages were common in the colony and on the plains.[144] In 1863, the sale of the Hudson's Bay Company itself to the International Financial Society sealed the fate of the northwest as a bastion of the fur trade.[145] A year later the Canadian government announced that the plains could sustain a large agrarian population.[146]

The stability of the fur trade was further eroded by the discovery of placer gold deposits near Fort Edmonton in the early 1860s. The gold strike proved to be unproductive, but the number of gold seekers, perhaps as many as 100, doubled the European population of what became the province of Alberta. William Gladstone, the errant HBC servant, noted that both Governor McTavish and the aboriginal inhabitants of the plains opposed the development of the gold fields.[147] Americans from Montana came north in ever-increasing numbers to work the gold fields in British territory. Among them were unemployed fur traders, and according to Gladstone at least seventy-five miners who were ordered out of Fort Benton. Before the end of the Civil War, gold discoveries in Montana contributed to its being granted territorial status in the fall of 1864. By the end of the war, Benton had a population of 1,500, including the infamous James brothers. Gladstone described the community as "hell on earth for a time."[148] Adding to the turmoil, hostilities flared between the Niitsitapi and the Cree-Assiniboine alliance.[149] Horse raiding and the shortage of food fuelled intertribal conflict. In their winter count, the Piikani (Peigan) described 1861 as the year "when they ate dogs" because of the scarcity of game.[150]

As was so often the case, disease and food scarcity created a synergy of hardship. Scarlet fever killed 1,100 members of the Niitsitapi Confederacy over the winter and spring of 1864–65.[151] The epidemic spread as far north as the Mackenzie District, where up to 800 people died of scarlet fever and measles in less than a month in 1865.[152] Tensions flared as diseases spread. At Rocky Mountain House, the trader there requested "assistance in men and arms" because Indians were blaming whites for the sickness and threatening to kill them. Along the Missouri, the Niitsitapi killed eleven American miners. In June 1865, they killed almost thirty Cree or Assiniboine, "principally women and children."[153]

As the death toll from disease and violence mounted throughout the northwest, the inhabitants of Red River faced a more immediate problem by the summer of 1868. Crops were destroyed by insects for four years in succession.[154] Starvation loomed as drought and grasshoppers turned crops into "a complete failure – even seeds having to be imported."[155] Governor McTavish estimated that as many as 2,346 people were in immediate need of assistance.[156] By mid-summer, the Council of Assiniboia allocated all of the funds available to it to relief. An international campaign was launched to assist those afflicted by the crisis.[157] The Canadian government pledged financial assistance for the colony, but no money was sent to Red River. Instead, the dominion concentrated its relief effort on construction of the road linking the community with Lake Superior. Canada's response to the agricultural crisis served as the pretext for its annexation of Rupert's Land.

As the era of monopoly came to an end, plains communities were on the precipice of a new economic and social order. George Simpson, the "Little Emperor," who ruled the entire northwest as a despot, had died in 1860. Chief Peguis, among the most influential aboriginal leaders of the early nineteenth century, and signatory to the Selkirk Treaty, had died four years later. On the eastern plains, the bison economy had run its course. The new Dominion of Canada was about to annex the west and make the plains its own agricultural hinterland. The shift in economic paradigms after Canada's dominion over the west would bring unparalleled changes to the aboriginal inhabitants of the plains.

NOTES

1 James W. Daschuk, "Expansion of Settlement and Erosion of Health during the HBC Monopoly, 1821–1869," *Clearing the Plains: Disease, Politics of Starvation and the Loss of Aboriginal Life* (Regina: University of Regina Press, 2013), 59–77.
2 J.C. Yerbury, *The Subarctic Indians and the Fur Trade, 1680–1860* (Vancouver: UBC Press, 1986), 92; James R. Gibson, *Farming the Frontier: The Agricultural Opening of the Oregon Country, 1786–1846* (Seattle: University of Washington Press, 1985), 9–27.
3 Arthur J. Ray, "Some Conservation Schemes of the Hudson's Bay Company, 1821–50: An Examination of the Problems of Resource Management in the Fur Trade," *Journal of Historical Geography* 1 (1975): 53.
4 Edith Burley, *Servants of the Honourable Company: Work, Discipline, and Conflict in the Hudson's Bay Company, 1770–1879* (Don Mills, ON: Oxford University Press, 1997), 6; D.B. Freeman and F.L. Dungey, "A Spatial Duopoly: Competition in Western Canadian Fur Trade, 1770–1835," *Journal of Historical Geography* 7 (1981): 268–70.
5 Carol Judd, "Native Labour and Social Stratification in the Hudson's Bay Northern Department, 1770–1870," *Canadian Review of Sociology and Anthropology* 17 (1980): 307. See also Glen Makahonuk, "Wage Labour in the Economy of the Northwest Fur Economy, 1760–1849," *Saskatchewan History* 41 (1988): 7–8; Ron Bourgeault, "The Indian, the Métis, and the Fur Trade: Class, Sexism, and Racism in the Transition from 'Communism' to Capitalism," *Studies in Political Economy* 12 (1983): 64.
6 *Minutes of Council, Northern Department of Rupert Land, 1821–1831*, edited by R. Harvey Fleming (Toronto: Champlain Society, 1940), 229.
7 Paul Hackett, *"A Very Remarkable Sickness": Epidemics in the Petit Nord, 1670 to 1846* (Winnipeg: University of Manitoba Press, 2002), 156.
8 Renée Fossett, *In Order to Live Untroubled: Inuit of the Central Arctic, 1550–1940*, Manitoba Studies in Native History (Winnipeg: University of Manitoba Press, 2001), 115, 140.
9 R. Grace Morgan, "Beaver Ecology/Beaver Mythology" (Ph.D. diss., University of Alberta, 1991), 156–57.
10 John MacLean, *McDougall of Alberta: A Life of Rev. John McDougall D.D., Pathfinder of Empire and Prophet of the Plains* (Toronto: F.C. Stephenson, 1927), 38; John West, *The Substance of a Journal during a Residence at the Red River Colony, British North America in the Years 1820–1823* (Vancouver: Alcuin Society, 1967), 37; Alfred Crosby, "Virgin Soil Epidemics as a Factor in the Aboriginal Depopulation in America," *William and Mary Quarterly* 33 (1976): 290–91.

11 Paul Hackett, "Averting Disaster: The Hudson's Bay Company and Smallpox in Western Canada during the Eighteenth and Early Nineteenth Centuries," *Bulletin of the History of Medicine* 78 (2004): 594–95.
12 Laura Peers, *The Ojibwa of Western Canada, 1780–1870* (Winnipeg: University of Manitoba Press, 1994), 130.
13 Burley, *Servants of the Honourable Company*, 127.
14 Donna G. Sutherland, *Peguis: A Noble Friend* (St. Andrews, MB: Chief Peguis Heritage Park, 2003), 38.
15 West, *The Substance of a Journal*, 117–19.
16 Laura Peers and Theresa Schenk, eds., *My First Years in the Fur Trade: The Journals of 1802–1804, George Nelson* (Montreal: McGill-Queen's University Press, 2002), 80–81.
17 Caitlin Pepperell et al., "Dispersal of *Mycobacterium tuberculosis* via the Canadian Fur Trade," *Proceedings of the National Academy of Sciences* (2011), 6526–6531.
18 Burley, *Servants of the Honourable Company*, 55–56.
19 A.S. Morton, *A History of the Canadian West to 1870–71* (Toronto: University of Toronto Press, 1973), 640; E.E. Rich, *A History of the Hudson's Bay Company, 1670–1870*, 3 vols. (London: Hudson's Bay Record Society, 1959), 2: 477–78.
20 Peers, *The Ojibwa of Western Canada*, 102; Paul Thistle, *Indian–White Trade Relations in the Lower Saskatchewan River Region to 1840* (Winnipeg: University of Manitoba Press, 1986), 91–92.
21 Peers, *The Ojibwa of Western Canada*, 101–02.
22 Shepard Krech III, "The Influence of Disease and the Fur Trade on Arctic Drainage Lowlands Dene, 1800–1850," *Journal of Anthropological Research* 39 (1983): 132–33; Gertrude Nicks, "Demographic Anthropology of Native Populations in Western Canada, 1800–1975" (Ph.D. diss., University of Alberta, 1980), 51.
23 Rich, *A History of the Hudson's Bay Company*, 2: 471–72.
24 Arthur J. Ray, "Periodic Shortages, Native Welfare, and the Hudson's Bay Company, 1670–1930," in *The Subarctic Fur Trade: Native Social and Economic Adaptations*, edited by Shepard Krech III (Vancouver: UBC Press, 1984), 6.
25 Nicks, "Demographic Anthropology of Native Populations in Western Canada," 31.
26 Robin Ridington, "Changes of Mind: Dunne-za Resistance to Empire," *B.C. Studies* 43 (1979): 68; Nicks, "Demographic Anthropology of Native Populations in Western Canada," 51.
27 Peers, *The Ojibwa of Western Canada*, 103.

28 Ray, "Some Conservation Schemes of the Hudson's Bay Company," 55–57.
29 Barry Cooper, *Alexander Kennedy Isbister: A Respectable Critic of the Honourable Company* (Ottawa: Carleton University Press, 1988), 72; Glyndwr Williams, "Introduction," in *Peter Skene Ogden's Snake Country Journals 1827–28 and 1828–29* (London: Hudson's Bay Record Society, 1971), xiv.
30 Knut Fladmark, "Early Fur-Trade Forts of the Peace River Area of British Columbia," *B.C. Studies* 65 (1985): 51–52; David V. Burley, J. Scott Hamilton, and Knut Fladmark, *Prophecy of the Swan: The Upper Peace River Fur Trade of 1794–1823* (Vancouver: UBC Press, 1996), 126, 129; Shepard Krech III, "The Banditte of St. John's," *The Beaver* 313 (1982): 36–41; Shepard Krech III, "The Beaver Indians and the Hostilities at Fort St. John's," *Arctic Anthropology* 20 (1983): 35–45.
31 Ray, "Some Conservation Schemes of the Hudson's Bay Company," 54–55.
32 Milloy, *The Plains Cree: Trade, Diplomacy, and Warfare, 1790–1870*, 65; Hugh Dempsey, *Big Bear: The End of Freedom* (Vancouver: Douglas and McIntyre, 1984), 12–15; Susan Sharrock, "Crees, Cree-Assiniboines, and Assiniboines: Interethnic Social Organization on the Far Northern Plains," *Ethnohistory* 21 (1974): 111–15.
33 Jody Decker, "Depopulation of the Northern Plains Natives," *Social Science Medicine* 33 (1991): 388–90.
34 Laura Peers, "Changing Resource-Use Patterns of Saulteaux Trading at Fort Pelly, 1821–1870," in *Aboriginal Resource Use in Canada: Historical and Legal Aspects*, edited by Kerry Abel and Jean Friesen (Winnipeg: University of Manitoba Press, 1991), 105–18.
35 E.S. Rogers, "Cultural Adaptations: The Northern Ojibwa of the Boreal Forest 1670–1980," in *Boreal Forest Adaptations: The Northern Algonkians*, edited by A.T. Steegmann (New York: Plenum Press, 1983), 108.
36 Marshall Hurlich, "Historical and Recent Demography of the Algonkians of Northern Ontario," in *Boreal Forest Adaptations: The Northern Algonkians*, edited by A.T. Steegmann (New York: Plenum Press, 1983), 170.
37 Ray, "Periodic Shortages, Native Welfare, and the Hudson's Bay Company," 10.
38 Judd, "Native Labour and Social Stratification in the Hudson's Bay Company's Northern Department," 307.
39 Morton, *A History of the Canadian West to 1870–71*, 698; Robert Brightman, "Conservation and Resource Depletion: The Case of the Boreal Forest Algonkians," in *The Question of the Commons: The Culture and Ecology of Communal Resources*, edited by Bonnie McCay and James Acheson (Tucson: University of Arizona Press, 1987), 137.
40 Brightman, "Conservation and Resource Depletion," 135.

41 Katherine L. Reedy-Maschner and Herbert D.G. Maschner, "Marauding Middlemen: Western Expansion and Violent Conflict in the Subarctic," *Ethnohistory* 46 (1999): 712.
42 Shepard Krech III, *The Ecological Indian: Myth and History* (New York: W.W. Norton and Company, 1999), 194; Thistle, *Indian–European Trade Relations in the Lower Saskatchewan River Region to 1840*, 88.
43 Martha McCarthy, *To Evangelize the Nations: Roman Catholic Missions in Manitoba, 1818–1870* (Winnipeg: Manitoba Culture, Heritage and Recreation, Historic Resources, 1990), 51.
44 Burley, *Servants of the Honourable Company*, 102, 107–08.
45 Aborigines' Protection Society, *Canada West and the Hudson's Bay Company: A Political and Humane Question of Vital Importance to the Honour of Great Britain, to the Prosperity of Canada, and to the Existence of the Native Tribes; Being an Address to the Right Honourable Henry Labouchere, Her Majesty's Principal Secretary of State for the Colonies* (London: William Tweedie, 1856), 3.
46 McCarthy, *To Evangelize the Nations*, 16. See also David McCrady, "Living with Strangers: The Nineteenth-Century Sioux and the Canadian–American Borderlands" (Ph.D. diss., University of Manitoba, 1998), 20–27; Milloy, *The Plains Cree*, 111; Ron Rivard and Catherine Littlejohn, *The History of the Métis of Willow Bunch* (Saskatoon: Apex Graphics, 2003), 58–68.
47 Milloy, *The Plains Cree*, 99; Ray, "Periodic Shortages, Native Welfare, and the Hudson's Bay Company," 5.
48 Frank G. Roe, *The North American Buffalo: A Critical Study of the Species in Its Wild State* (Toronto: University of Toronto Press, 1970), 396.
49 Jeffrey Ostler, *The Plains Sioux and U.S. Colonialism from Lewis and Clark to Wounded Knee* (Cambridge, UK: Cambridge University Press, 2004), 57–58.
50 John Foster, "Wintering, the Outsider Adult Male, and the Ethnogenesis of the Western Plains Métis," *Prairie Forum* 19 (1994): 1–15.
51 J.G. MacGregor, *John Rowand: Czar of the Prairies* (Saskatoon: Western Producer Prairie Books, 1978), 88–89.
52 Milloy, *The Plains Cree*, 105.
53 Hackett, *"A Very Remarkable Sickness,"* 172. See also Arthur J. Ray, "Diffusion of Diseases in the Western Interior of Canada, 1830–1850," *Geographical Review* 66 (1976): 139–57.
54 Hackett, *"A Very Remarkable Sickness,"* 161.
55 Samuel G. Morton, *Illustrations of Pulmonary Consumption: Its Anatomical Characters, Causes, Symptoms, and Treatment* (Philadelphia: E.C. Biddle, 1837), 312–13.
56 Hackett, *"A Very Remarkable Sickness,"* 162–63.

57 Milloy, *The Plains Cree*, 65.
58 Fossett, *In Order to Live Untroubled*, 140.
59 Michael K. Trimble, "Chronology of Epidemics among Plains Village Horticulturalists, 1738–1838," *Southwestern Lore* 54 (1988): 23.
60 Morton, *Illustrations of Pulmonary Consumption*, 312–13. The account hinted at the emergence of the disease in the British territory to the north.
61 Michael K. Trimble, "The 1832 Inoculation Program on the Missouri River," in *Disease and Demography in the Americas*, edited by John W. Verano and Douglas Uberlaker (Washington, DC: Smithsonian Institution Press, 1992), 260–63.
62 Ostler, *The Plains Sioux and U.S. Colonialism from Lewis and Clark to Wounded Knee*, 31.
63 Trimble, "The 1832 Inoculation Program on the Missouri River," 257. The epidemic of 1837 is probably the best-documented disease episode on the plains in the nineteenth century. In the American context, see Milo M. Quaife, ed., "The Smallpox Epidemic on the Upper Missouri," *Mississippi Valley Historical Review* 17 (1930–31): 278–99; Clyde D. Dollar, "The High Plains Smallpox Epidemic of 1837–38," *Western Historical Quarterly* 8 (1977): 15–38; Michael K. Trimble, "The 1837–1838 Smallpox Epidemic on the Upper Missouri," in *Skeletal Biology in the Great Plains: Migration, Warfare, Health, and Subsistence*, edited by Douglas Owsley and Richard Jantz (Washington, DC: Smithsonian Institution Press, 1994): 81–89; K.C. Tessendorf, "Red Death on the Missouri," *American West* 14 (1977): 48–53; R.G. Robertson, *Rotting Face: Smallpox and the American Indian* (Caldwell, ID: Claxton Press, 2001).
64 Ostler, *The Plains Sioux and U.S. Colonialism from Lewis and Clark to Wounded Knee*, 31.
65 Ray, "Diffusion of Diseases in the Western Interior of Canada," 155–56.
66 Arthur J. Ray, *Indians in the Fur Trade: Their Role as Trappers, Hunters, and Middlemen in the Lands Southwest of Hudson Bay* (Toronto: University of Toronto Press, 1974), 193n11.
67 Paul Kane, *Wanderings of an Artist among the Indians of North America, from Canada to Vancouver's Island and Oregon through the Hudson's Bay Territory and Back Again* (Edmonton: Hurtig, 1968), 90.
68 Hackett, *"A Very Remarkable Sickness,"* 447–48; Ray, "Periodic Shortages, Native Welfare, and the Hudson's Bay Company," 1–20.
69 Library and Archives Canada (hereafter LAC), MG 29 B 15, Robert Bell Papers, vol. 61, f. 34, Anonymous, "Reminiscences of One of the Last Descendants of a Bourgeois of the Northwest Company," n.d., 29; Arthur J. Ray, "Smallpox: The Epidemic of 1837," *The Beaver* 306 (1975): 9–11.

70 Peers, *The Ojibwa of Western Canada*, 142.
71 Patricia Albers, "Changing Patterns of Ethnicity in the Northeastern Plains, 1780–1870," in *History, Power, and Identity: Ethnogenesis in the Americas, 1492–1992*, edited by Jonathan Hill (Iowa City: University of Iowa Press, 1996), 104.
72 HBCA, B.159/a/17, Dr. Todd's Journal, 22–23 October 1837, 5; 15 November 1837, 8; 8 December 1837, 9b.
73 Decker, "Depopulation of the Northern Plains Natives," 388.
74 Dan Kennedy, *The Recollections of an Assiniboine Chief/Dan Kennedy (Ochankugahe)*, edited by James Stevens (Toronto: McClelland and Stewart, 1972), 72–73; Ray, *Indians in the Fur Trade*, 187–88.
75 Hugh A. Dempsey, "Smallpox: Scourge of the Plains," in *In Harm's Way: Disasters in Western Canada*, edited by Anthony Rasporich and Max Foran (Calgary: University of Calgary Press, 2004), 26; William Barr, "Lieutenant Aemilius Simpson's Survey: York Factory to Fort Vancouver, 1826," in *Selected Papers of Rupert's Land Colloquium 2000*, compiled by David G. Malaher (Winnipeg: Centre for Rupert's Land Studies, University of Winnipeg, 2000), 7.
76 Hugh A. Dempsey, ed., "Simpson's Essay on the Blackfoot," *Alberta History* 38 (1990): 3.
77 Kennedy stated that the Assiniboine population in 1947 was a mere 3,000, a tenth of what had been estimated at the beginning of the nineteenth century. SAB, Mary Weekes Papers, R-100, vol. 3, f. 40, Dan Kennedy to Mary Weekes, 9 December 1947.
78 James Hector and W.S.W. Vaux, "Notice of the Indians Seen by the Exploring Expedition under the Command of Captain Palliser," *Transactions of the Ethnological Society of London* 1 (1860): 251.
79 Kennedy, *The Recollections of an Assiniboine Chief*, 72–73.
80 Douglas R. Parks and Raymond J. DeMallie, "Sioux, Assiniboine, and Stoney Dialects: A Classification," *Anthropological Linguistics* 34 (1992): 248.
81 Ian A.L. Getty and Erik Gooding, "Stoney," in *The Plains*, edited by Raymond J. DeMallie, vol. 13, part 1, of *Handbook of North American Indians* (Washington, DC: Smithsonian Institution Press, 2001), 596.
82 Gary Doige, "Warfare Patterns of the Assiniboine to 1809" (MA thesis, University of Manitoba, 1987), 172.
83 HBCA, B.159/a/17:9b (8 December 1837), 16b (5 March 1838).
84 HBCA, B.159.a/17:3 (25 September 1837), 3b (5 October 1837).
85 E. Wagner Stearn and Allen E. Stearn, *The Effect of Smallpox on the Destiny of the Amerindian* (Boston: Bruce Humphries Publishers, 1945), 56–57; Hackett, "Averting Disaster," 591.

86 Hackett, "Averting Disaster," 593–606.
87 Arthur J. Ray, "William Todd: Doctor and Trader of the Hudson's Bay Company, 1816–51," *Prairie Forum* 9 (1984): 23.
88 Hackett, "Averting Disaster," 602–06.
89 Michael Payne, *The Most Respectable Place in the Territory: Everyday Life in the Hudson's Bay Service, 1788 to 1870* (Ottawa: Environment Canada, Parks Canada Service, National Historic Parks and Sites, 1989), 93–105.
90 Ibid., 104.
91 Hackett, *"A Very Remarkable Sickness,"* 189.
92 Ray, *Indians in the Fur Trade*, 189.
93 Fritz Pannekoek, "The Reverend James Evans and the Social Antagonisms of Fur Trade Society, 1840–1846," in *Religion and Society and the Prairie West*, edited by Richard Allen (Regina: Canadian Plains Research Center, 1974), 2–3.
94 McCarthy, *To Evangelize the Nations*, 133–40.
95 Ibid., 113.
96 SAB, R-E2033, Edward Ahenakew Papers, "Stanley Mission," 2.
97 Robert Jarvenpa, "The Hudson's Bay Company, the Roman Catholic Church, and the Chipewyan in the Late Fur Trade Period," in *Le Castor Fait Tout: Selected Papers of the Fifth North American Fur Trade Conference, 1985*, edited by B. Trigger, T. Morantz, and L. Dechêne (Montreal: Lake St. Louis Historical Society, 1987), 491–92; Ray, "Periodic Shortages, Native Welfare, and the Hudson's Bay Company," 10.
98 J.M. Bumsted, *Trials and Tribulations: The Red River Settlement and the Emergence of Manitoba, 1811–1870* (Winnipeg: Great Plains Publications, 2003), 97–99.
99 John S. Galbraith, "The Hudson's Bay Company under Fire, 1847–62," *Canadian Historical Review* 30 (1949): 322–35, and especially Cooper, *Alexander Kennedy Isbister*. See also A.A. den Otter, "The 1857 Parliamentary Inquiry, the Hudson's Bay Company, and Rupert's Land's Aboriginal People," *Prairie Forum* 24 (1999): 143–70.
100 Cooper, *Alexander Kennedy Isbister*, 107.
101 Ibid., 36, 108–10.
102 For a full discussion of the difficult climatic period in the Arctic, see Fossett, *In Order to Live Untroubled*, 149.
103 J.H. Lefroy to Anna (Lefroy), Fort Simpson, 29 March 1844, in *John Henry Lefroy, in Search of the Magnetic North: A Soldier–Surveyor's Letters from the North-West 1843–1844*, edited by G.F.G. Stanley (Toronto: Macmillan, 1955), 110–11; Morton, *A History of the Canadian West to 1870–71*, 821.
104 Bumsted, *Trials and Tribulations*, 103.

105 John S. Galbraith, *The Hudson's Bay Company as an Imperial Factor, 1821–1869* (Toronto: University of Toronto Press, 1957), 313–16, and especially Frederick Merk, *The Oregon Question: Essays in Anglo-American Diplomacy and Politics* (Cambridge, MA: Harvard University Press, 1967).
106 Hackett, *"A Very Remarkable Sickness,"* 154, 199–236.
107 Paul Hackett, "Historical Mourning Practices Observed among the Cree and Ojibwa Indians of the Central Subarctic," *Ethnohistory* 52 (2005): 522.
108 Hackett, *"A Very Remarkable Sickness,"* 193.
109 Shepard Krech III, "The Early Fur Trade in the Northwestern Subarctic: The Kutchin and the Trade in Beads," in *Le Castor Fait Tout: Selected Papers of the Fifth North American Fur Trade Conference, 1985*, edited by B. Trigger, T. Morantz, and L. Dechêne (Montreal: Lake St. Louis Historical Society, 1987), 264–65.
110 Hackett, *"A Very Remarkable Sickness,"* 199–211.
111 Ibid., 199.
112 Alexander Ross, *The Red River Settlement: Its Rise, Progress, and Present State. With Some Account of the Native Races and Its General History, to the Present Day* (Edmonton: Hurtig, 1972), 362–63.
113 John F. Taylor, "Sociocultural Effects of Epidemics on the Northern Plains: 1734–1850," *Western Canadian Journal of Anthropology* 7 (1977): 56.
114 Ostler, *The Plains Sioux and U.S. Colonialism from Lewis and Clark to Wounded Knee*, 32–33. Among the Brulé Lakota, 500 of a pre-epidemic population of 3,500 died in 1849.
115 Burley, *Servants of the Honourable Company*, 155.
116 Judd, "Native Labour and Social Stratification in the Hudson's Bay Company's Northern Department," 311.
117 Galbraith, *The Hudson's Bay Company as an Imperial Factor*, 61–62; William S. Gladstone, *The Gladstone Diary: Travels in the Early West*, edited by Bruce Haig (Lethbridge: Historic Trails Society of Alberta, 1985), 43; Peers, *The Ojibwa of Western Canada*, 176–79.
118 John Milloy, "Our Country: The Significance of the Buffalo Resource for a Plains Cree Sense of Territory," in *Aboriginal Resource Use in Canada: Historical and Legal Aspects*, edited by Kerry Abel and Jean Friesen (Winnipeg: University of Manitoba Press, 1991), 64; Roe, *The North American Buffalo*, 410.
119 See Henry Youle Hind, *Narrative of the Canadian Red River Exploring Expedition of 1857 and of the Assiniboine and Saskatchewan Expedition of 1858*, 2 vols. (Edmonton: Hurtig, 1971), 1: 99–100.
120 Rupert's Land Research Centre, *An Historical Overview of Aboriginal Lifestyles: The Churchill–Nelson River Drainage Basin* (Winnipeg: Rupert's

Land Research Centre, 1992), 133; Peers, *The Ojibwa of Western Canada*, 198; Sutherland, *Peguis*, 139–43.

121 Hind, *Narrative of the Canadian Red River Exploring Expedition of 1857*, 1: 361.

122 Irene Spry, "The Great Transformation: The Disappearance of the Commons in Western Canada," in *Man and Nature on the Prairies*, edited by Richard Allen, Canadian Plains Studies 6 (Regina: Canadian Plains Research Center, 1976), 27; Milloy, *The Plains Cree*, 107.

123 Hector and Vaux, "Notice of the Indians Seen by the Exploring Expedition under the Command of Captain Palliser," 251.

124 Ray, "Diffusion of Diseases in the Western Interior of Canada," 150.

125 Hurlich, "Historical and Recent Demography of the Algonkians of Northern Ontario," 161.

126 John MacLean, *McDougall of Alberta: A Life of Rev. John McDougall D.D., Pathfinder of Empire and Prophet of the Plains* (Toronto: F.C. Stephenson, 1927), 38.

127 Winona Stevenson, "The Journals and Voices of a Church of England Native Catechist: Askenootow (Charles Pratt), 1851–1884," in *Reading beyond Words: Contexts for Native History*, edited by Jennifer S.H. Brown and Elizabeth Vibert (Peterborough: Broadview Press, 1996), 309.

128 A vaccination campaign was undertaken by Dr. William Cowan in 1852. LAC, MG 29 E 8, Robert Bell Papers, Diary of William Cowan, Surgeon to Enrolled Army Pensioners at Fort Garry, 22.

129 Katherine Hughes, *Father Lacombe: The Blackrobe Voyageur* (New York: Moffat, Yard and Company, 1911), 71–72.

130 Hector and Vaux, "Notice of the Indians Seen by the Exploring Expedition under the Command of Captain Palliser," 258–59.

131 David Sauchyn and Walter Skinner, "A Proxy Record of Drought Severity for the Southwestern Canadian Plains," *Canadian Water Resources Journal* 26 (2001): 266.

132 David Smyth, "The Niitsitapi Trade: Euroamericans and the Blackfoot Speaking Peoples to the Mid 1830s" (Ph.D. diss., Carleton University, 2001), 529.

133 Richard T. Wright, *Overlanders: The Epic Cross-Canada Treks for Gold* (Williams Lake, BC: Winter Quarters Press, 2000).

134 Galbraith, "The Hudson's Bay Company under Fire," 333–35.

135 Margaret A. Ormsby, *British Columbia: A History* (Vancouver: Macmillan of Canada, 1958), 134–63; Robin Fisher, *Contact and Conflict: Indian–European Relations in British Columbia, 1774–1890* (Vancouver: UBC Press, 1977), 95–118.

136 Robert T. Boyd, "Demographic History, 1774–1874," in *Northwest Coast*, edited by Wayne Suttles, vol. 7 of *Handbook of North American Indians* (Washington, DC: Smithsonian Institution Press, 1990), 142; Edward Sleigh Hewlett, "The Chilcotin Uprising of 1864," *B.C. Studies* 19 (1973): 63.
137 W.A. Cheadle, *Cheadle's Journal of a Trip across Canada, 1862–63* (Edmonton: Hurtig, 1971), 222.
138 Galbraith, "The Hudson's Bay Company under Fire," 335; Doug Owram, *The Promise of Eden: The Canadian Expansionist Movement and the Idea of the West, 1856–1900* (Toronto: University of Toronto Press, 1980), 38–58.
139 Peers, *The Ojibwa of Western Canada*, 199. See also Cheadle, *Cheadle's Journal of a Trip across Canada*, 121.
140 See, for example, "The Liquor Nuisance," *The Nor' Wester*, 14 August 1860; LAC, MG 19 A 48, Fort Garry Correspondence, Letter to Lawrence Clarke, 9 November 1867, Letter 4, 2.
141 Milloy, *The Plains Cree*, 105.
142 James M. MacGregor, *Senator Hardisty's Prairies, 1849–1889* (Saskatoon: Western Producer Prairie Books, 1978), 68–69. In 1857, the HBC established the first "provisioning" farm at Red River. Carolyn Podruchny, "Farming the Frontier: Agriculture in the Fur Trade, a Case Study of the Provisional Farm at Lower Fort Garry, 1857–1870" (MA thesis, McGill University, 1990).
143 Wayne Moodie and Barry Kaye, "The Northern Limit of Indian Agriculture in North America," *Geographical Review* 59 (1969): 521; Sarah Carter, *Lost Harvests: Prairie Indian Reserve Farmers and Government Policy* (Montreal: McGill-Queen's University Press, 1990), 42–43; Hector and Vaux, "Notice of the Indians Seen by the Exploring Expedition under the Command of Captain Palliser," 248.
144 McCarthy, *To Evangelize the Nations*, 222; T.R. Allsopp, *Agricultural Weather in the Red River Basin of Southern Manitoba over the period 1800 to 1975*, Atmospheric Environment Report CLI-3-77 (Downsview, ON: Fisheries and Environment Canada, 1977), 11–12; Sauchyn and Skinner, "A Proxy Record of Drought Severity for the Southwestern Canadian Plains," 266.
145 Galbraith, *The Hudson's Bay Company as an Imperial Factor*, 387–90.
146 Owram, *Promise of Eden*, 69–80.
147 Gladstone, *The Gladstone Diary*, 68–72.
148 Ibid., 75–81; John S. Collins, *Across the Plains in '64: Incidents of Early Days West of the Missouri River – Two Thousand Miles in an Open Boat from Fort Benton to Omaha – Reminiscences of the Pioneer Period of Galena, General Grant's Old Home* (Omaha: National Printing Company, 1904), 21–23;

James Fisk, "Expedition from Fort Abercrombie to Fort Benton," US House of Representatives, 37th Congress, 1863, 22, 29.

149 Milloy, *The Plains Cree*, 114; Abel Watetch, "History of Piapot Reserve," SAB, microfilm 2.75, *School Histories of 35 Indian Reserves*, 1955; Paul M. Raczka, *Winter Count: A History of the Blackfoot People* (Brocket, AB: Oldman River Cultural Centre, 1979), 57.

150 Raczka, *Winter Count*, 55, 60.

151 Hugh A. Dempsey, *A Blackfoot Winter Count*, Occasional Paper 1 (Calgary: Glenbow Museum, 1965), 14; Raczka, *Winter Count*, 56.

152 Martha McCarthy, *From the Great River to the Ends of the Earth: Oblate Missions to the Dene* (Edmonton: University of Alberta Press, 1995), 197.

153 Milloy, *The Plains Cree*, 114.

154 G. Herman Sprenger, "The Métis Nation: Buffalo Hunting vs. Agriculture in the Red River Settlement (circa 1810–1870)," *Western Canadian Journal of Anthropology* 3 (1972): 167; Allsopp, *Agricultural Weather in the Red River Basin of Southern Manitoba over the Period 1800 to 1975*, 12–13.

155 Allsopp, *Agricultural Weather in the Red River Basin of Southern Manitoba over the Period 1800 to 1975*, 12; Bumsted, *Trials and Tribulations*, 178.

156 McCarthy, *To Evangelize the Nations*, 204.

157 Funds were raised in Minnesota, England, and by subscription in Canada. Bumsted, *Trials and Tribulations*, 180–83.

# Copyright Permissions

**5.1 Bonenfant**

Reprinted with permission from the Canadian Historical Association. From Jean-Charles Bonenfant, *The French Canadians and the Birth of Confederation,* Canadian Historical Association Historical Booklet, 21 (Hull: Leclerc, 1966), 3–20. © 1966 Canadian Historical Association.

**5.2 Groulx**

Reprinted with permission from *Revue d'histoire de l'Amérique française.* From Lionel Groulx, "French Canadians and the Founding of Confederation," a translation of "Les Canadiens français et l'établissement de la Confédération," *Revue d'histoire de l'Amérique française,* 21, 3a (1967), 677–694, material originally published in *Les Canadiens français et l'établissement de la Confédération* (Montreal: Bibliothèque de l'Action française, May–June 1927), 1–21. © 1967.

**5.3 Brouillet**

Reprinted with permission from Copibec. Cet extrait a été reproduit aux termes d'une licence accordée par Copibec. From Eugénie Brouillet, "Quebec Culture and Federalism in 1867: The Spirit and Letter of the Federal System," *The Negation of a Nation: The Quebec Cultural Identity and Canadian Federalism,* a translation of material from "La culture québécoise et le fédéralisme de 1867: l'esprit et la lettre du régime," *La Négation de la nation. L'identité culturelle québécoise et le fédéralisme canadien* (Quebec: Septentrion, 2005), 105–106, 122–135, 140–150, 396, 399–403. © 1995 Septentrion.

**5.4 Kelly**

Reprinted with permission from Les Éditions du Boréal. From Stéphane Kelly, *Canada and Its Aims, According to Macdonald, Laurier, Mackenzie*

*King and Trudeau,* a translation of material from *Les fins du Canada, selon Macdonald, Laurier, Mackenzie King et Trudeau* (Montreal: Boréal, 2001), 33–47, 261. © 2001 Boréal.

**5.5 Silver**

From A.I. Silver, "Introduction," in *The French-Canadian Idea of Confederation, 1864–1900* (Toronto: University of Toronto Press, 1997), 3–32. © University of Toronto Press Incorporated 1997. Reprinted with permission of the publisher.

**6.1 Waite**

Reprinted with permission from Robin Brass Studios and Access Copyright. Copied under licence from Access Copyright. Further reproduction, distribution or transmission is prohibited except as otherwise permitted by law. From P.B. Waite, *The Life and Times of Confederation, 1864–1867: Politics, Newspapers, and the Union of British North America.* 3rd ed. (Toronto: Robin Brass Studios, 2001), 209–247. © 2001 Robin Brass Studios.

**6.2 Wilson**

Reprinted with permission from University of Toronto Press (www.utpjournals.com). From George E. Wilson, "New Brunswick's Entrance into Confederation," *Canadian Historical Review,* 9, 1 (1928), 4–24. DOI: 10.3138/CHR-09-01-01. © University of Toronto Press.

**6.3 Buckner**

Reprinted with permission from University of Toronto Press (www.utpjournals.com). From Phillip Buckner, "The Maritimes and Confederation: A Reassessment," *Canadian Historical Review,* 71, 1 (1990), 1–30. DOI: 10.3138/CHR-071-01-01. © University of Toronto Press.

**6.4 Waite**

Reprinted with permission from University of Toronto Press (www.utpjournals.com). From P.B. Waite, "The Maritimes and Confederation: A Reassessment," *Canadian Historical Review* 71, 1 (1990), 30–35. DOI: 10.3138/CHR-071-01-01. © University of Toronto Press.

**6.5 Careless**

From J.M.S. Careless, "George Brown," from *Dictionary of Canadian Biography,* vol. 10, *1871–1880,* ed. Mary McD. Maude, Diane M. Barker,

Henri Pilon. © University of Toronto Press and Les Presses de l'Université Laval, 1972. 93–101. Available online http://www.biographi.ca/en/bio/brown_George_10E.html. Reprinted with permission of the publisher.

**6.6 Morton**

Reprinted with permission from the Canadian Historical Association. W.L. Morton, *The West and Confederation*. Centennial Historical Booklet 7 (Ottawa: Centennial Commission, 1967), 3–19. © 1967 Canadian Historical Association.

**6.7 Owram**

From Doug Owram, "A Means to Empire: Canada's Reassessment of the West, 1857–69," *Promise of Eden: The Canadian Expansionist Movement and the Idea of the West, 1856–1900* (Toronto: University of Toronto Press, 1992), 59–78. © University of Toronto Press Incorporated 1980, 1992. Reprinted with permission of the publisher.

**7.1 Gray**

Reprinted from John Hamilton Gray, "Chapter 1," *Confederation; or, The Political and Parliamentary History of Canada from the Conference at Quebec, in October, 1864, to the Admission of British Columbia, in July 1871,* 1 (Toronto: Copp, Clark, 1872), 2–20, 23–24, 28–31.

**7.2 Martin**

Reprinted from Chester Martin, "British Policy in Canadian Confederation," *Canadian Historical Review,* 13, 1 (1932), 3–19.

**7.3 Stacey**

Reprinted with permission from University of Toronto Press (www.utpjournals.com). From C.P. Stacey, "Britain's Withdrawal from North America, 1864–1871," *Canadian Historical Review,* 36, 3 (1955), 185–198. DOI: 10.3138/CHR-036-03-01. © University of Toronto Press.

**7.4 Roby**

Reprinted with permission from Yves Roby, *The United States and Confederation,* Centennial Historical Booklet 4 (Ottawa: Centennial Commission, 1967): 3–20. Permission granted by the Privy Council Office © Her Majesty the Queen in Right of Canada, 2017.

**7.5 Shi**

Reprinted with permission from the University of California Press. From David E. Shi, "Seward's Attempt to Annex British Columbia, 1865–1869," *Pacific Historical Review,* vol. 47, no. 2 (May 1978), 217–238. DOI: 10.2307/3637972. Published by the University of California Press. © 1978 The Pacific Coast Branch, American Historical Association.

**8.1 Ryerson**

Reprinted with permission from the Communist Party of Canada. From Stanley B. Ryerson, "Engineering a Federal Union," *Unequal Union: Roots of Crisis in the Canadas, 1815–1873* (Toronto: Progress Books, 1973), 342–357. © 1973 Communist Party of Canada.

**8.2 Perry**

Reprinted from Adele Perry, "Gender, Race, and Our Years on the Edge of Empire," *On the Edge of Empire: Gender, Race and the Making of British Columbia, 1849–1871* (Toronto: University of Toronto Press, 2001), 194–201. © University of Toronto Press Incorporated 2001. Reprinted with permission of the publisher.

**8.3 Dumont**

Reprinted with permission from Les Éditions du Boréal. From Fernand Dumont, "Development and Survival," *The Origins of Quebec Society,* a translation of material from chapter 6, *Genèse de la société québécoise* (Montreal: Boréal, 1993), 202–211, 235–236, 375. © 1993 Boréal.

**8.4 McKay**

Reprinted with permission from University of Toronto Press (www.utpjournals.com). From Ian McKay, "The Liberal Order Framework: A Prospectus for a Reconnaissance of Canadian History," *Canadian Historical Review,* 81, 4 (2000), 617–51. Toronto: University of Toronto Press. DOI: 10.3138/chr.81.4.616. © University of Toronto Press Incorporated.

**8.5 Daschuk**

Reprinted with permission from University of Regina Press. From James W. Daschuk, "Expansion of Settlement and Erosion of Health during the HBC Monopoly, 1821–1869," *Clearing the Plains: Disease, Politics of Starvation and the Loss of Aboriginal Life* (Regina: University of Regina Press, 2013), 81–99. © 2013 University of Regina Press.

# Contributors

**Jean-Charles Bonenfant** (1912–1977) was a journalist, librarian, and university professor. Several of his publications were on Confederation and the role of French Canadians: *The French Canadians and the Birth of Confederation* (Canadian Historical Society, 1966), and *La naissance de la Confédération* (Leméac, 1969).

**Eugénie Brouillet** is a professor of law and the dean of the Faculty of Law at the Université Laval. Her research interests include individual rights, Canadian federalism, and constitutional law. Her publications include *La négation de la nation. L'identité culturelle québécoise et le fédéralisme canadien* (Les Éditions du Septention, 2005); with Louis Massicotte (dir.), *Comment changer une constitution? Les nouveaux processus constituants* (Les Presses de l'Université Laval, 2011); with Louis-Philippe Lampron (dir.), *La mobilisation du droit et la protection des collectivités minoritaires* (Les Presses de l'Université Laval, 2013).

**Phillip Buckner** is a professor emeritus at the University of New Brunswick, where he was the founding editor of *Acadiensis: Journal of the History of the Atlantic Region* and the founder of Acadiensis Press. A past president of the Canadian Historical Association, he created the CHA Canada's Ethnic Groups Series. Most recently he has been the editor of (and contributor to) a series of books on Canada and the British World, including a volume in the Oxford History of the British Empire: *Canada and the British Empire*. He also has published four papers focusing on Confederation over the past three years in various journals and books.

**David R. Cameron**, a fellow of the Royal Society of Canada, is a professor of political science and dean of arts and science at the University of Toronto. His professional career has been divided between public service – in Ottawa and at Queen's Park, Ontario – and academic life. A long-time student of Canadian federalism, Quebec nationalism, and constitutional reform, in recent decades he has turned his attention to political change and constitution-making in conflict and post-conflict situations in Sri Lanka, Iraq, Somalia, the Western Sahara, and Jerusalem.

**J.M.S. Careless** (1919–2009) was a professor of history at the University of Toronto for forty-five years. One of the pre-eminent Canadian historians of his generation, he is best known for his survey of Canadian history, *Canada: A Story of Challenge* (1953), and for his two-volume biography of George Brown, *Brown of the Globe* (1963). Both books won the Governor General's Award for Non-Fiction. Among many honours, Professor Careless was admitted to the Royal Society of Canada (1962), the Order of Canada (1982), and the Order of Ontario (1987).

**James Daschuk** is an associate professor in the Faculty of Kinesiology and Health Studies at the University of Regina. His book, *Clearing the Plains: Disease, Politics of Starvation and the Loss of Aboriginal Life*, published by the University of Regina Press, has won numerous awards, including the 2014 Governor General's prize for scholarly work in history and was named as one of the twenty-five most influential Canadian books of the last twenty-five years by the *Literary Review of Canada*. The French version, *La Destruction des Indiens des Plaines: Maladies, famines organisées, et disparition du mode de vie autochtone*, won the Governor General's literary award for translation in 2016.

**Fernand Dumont** (1927–1997) was a professor of sociology at the Université Laval. He was a prolific writer who received prestigious awards, including the Governor General's Literary Award for Non-Fiction, la Médaille Parizeau, and le Prix scientifique du Québec. His publications include notably *Le sort de la culture* (1987), *Genèse de la société québécoise* (1993), *Raisons communes* (1995), *L'avenir de la mémoire* (1995), and *Une foi partagée* (1996).

**John Hamilton Gray** (1814–1889) received his BA from King's College in Nova Scotia in 1833 and was called to the bar of New Brunswick in 1836. He was active in New Brunswick politics, serving briefly as its premier (1856–7), and later went on to represent his constituents in the House of Commons in Ottawa. Gray was an umpire between Great Britain and the United States under the Treaty of Washington (1857–8) and was appointed to the Supreme Court of British Columbia in 1872. He authored one of the first books on the union of the British colonies, *Confederation; or, The Political and Parliamentary History of Canada* (1872) and is perhaps best remembered as one of the Fathers of Confederation who attended the 1864 Charlottetown and Quebec Conferences.

**Lionel Groulx** (1878–1967) was a priest, a political activist, and a historian at the Université de Montréal. From 1920 to 1928, he led *l'Action française*, a nationalist monthly publication. His teaching and publications shaped French-Canadian history and nationalism for several decades. His publications include *L'enseignement français au Canada* (1931–33), *Histoire du Canada français depuis la découverte* (1950–52), and *Notre grande aventure: l'empire français en Amérique du nord, 1535–1760* (1958).

**Stéphane Kelly** teaches at the Cégep de Saint-Jérome and at the Université de Montréal. His publications include *La petite loterie: Comment la couronne a obtenu la collaboration du Canada français après 1937* (Boréal, 1997), and *Les Fins du Canada selon Macdonald, Laurier, Mackenzie King et Trudeau* (Boréal, 2001).

**Jacqueline D. Krikorian** is an associate professor in political science and law & society at York University. She undertakes research in constitutional politics, international law, and legal history. Her publications include *Globalizing Confederation, Canada and the World in 1867* (forthcoming with co-editors Marcel Martel and Adrian Shubert) and *International Trade Law and Domestic Policy: Canada, the United States and the WTO* (2012). She has been a fellow at the Institute of International Economic Law at Georgetown University Law Center and held the Fulbright Visiting Research Chair in U.S.-Canada Relations at the Woodrow Wilson Center for International Scholars in 2014.

**Marcel Martel** is a professor and the holder of the Avie Bennett Historica Canada Chair in Canadian History at York University. He has published several journal articles and book chapters on public policy, minority rights, moral regulation, and identity. His most recent publications include *Globalizing Confederation: Canada and the World in 1867* (forthcoming with co-editors Jacqueline D. Krikorian and Adrian Shubert), *Canada the Good? A Short History of Vice since 1500* (2014), and *Langue et politique au Canada et au Québec* (with Martin Pâquet, 2010), which was translated as *Speaking Up: A History of Language and Politics in Canada and Quebec.*

**Chester (Baily) Martin** (1882–1958) was a graduate of the University of New Brunswick, and in 1904 received the first Rhodes scholarship awarded to a North American. He was a founding member of the Department of History at the University of Manitoba, where he taught from 1909 to 1929, and then went on to be the chair of the Department of History at the University of Toronto for twenty-three years before retiring in 1952. Professor Martin was a renowned scholar who published extensively, particularly on western Canada. His major works included *Lord Selkirk's Work in Canada* (1916), *Empire & Commonwealth: Studies in Governance and Self-Government in Canada* (1929), and *Foundations of Canadian Nationhood* (1955). Martin was active in his profession, participating on the Federal Resources Commission and the Canadian Historical Society, where he held its presidency in 1928. In 1920 he was elected a fellow of the Royal Society of Canada and received its J.B. Tyrrell Historical Medal in 1940.

**Andrew W. McDougall** is a lecturer in the Department of Political Science at the University of Toronto Scarborough. His research focuses on Canadian federalism, intergovernmental relations, and public law. He recently defended his dissertation, "Canadian Federalism, Abeyances, and Quebec Sovereignty." His most recent publication is *Collaboration and Unilateral Action: Recent Intergovernmetnal Relations in Canada* (with Grace Skogstad and Robert Schertzer, IRPP Study No. 62, December 2016).

**Ian McKay** is the R.L. Wilson Chair of Canadian History at McMaster University and director of the Wilson Institute. His most recent publications include *The Vimy Trap: How We Learned to Stop Worrying and Love the Great War* (Toronto: Between the Lines, 2016, with Jamie Swift); *Warrior Nation: Rebranding Canada in an Age of Anxiety* (Toronto: Between the Lines, 2012, with Jamie Swift); *In the Province of History: Tourism and the Romance of the Past in Twentieth-Century Nova Scotia* (Montreal and Kingston: McGill-Queen's University Press, 2010, with Robin Bates);

*The Quest of the Folk: Antimodernism and Cultural Selection in Twentieth-Century Nova Scotia*, 3rd ed. (Toronto: Carleton Library, 2009); and *Reasoning Otherwise: Leftists and the People's Enlightenment in Canada, 1890–1920* (Toronto: Between the Lines, 2008), winner of the Canadian Historical Association's John A. Macdonald Prize.

**W.L. Morton** (1908–1980) was a widely respected historian best known for his research on western Canada. He completed his undergraduate studies at the University of Manitoba prior to winning a Rhodes scholarship to Oxford and held several teaching and administrative appointments, most notably at the University of Manitoba and Trent University, where he was elected chancellor in 1977. Morton's publications were extensive and included *The Progressive Party in Canada* (1950), which won the Governor General's Award for Non-Fiction, and the *Kingdom of Canada* (1960). Active in many associations and organizations, Morton served as president of the Canadian Historical Association and was the executive director of the Canadian Centenary Series. He received numerous honours and awards, including the Tyrrell Medal of the Royal Society of Canada and the Queen Elizabeth II Silver Jubilee Medal. He was appointed as an officer to the Order of Canada in 1969.

**Doug Owram** is a professor emeritus of history from both the University of Alberta and the University of British Columbia. He has authored or edited eleven books and many articles, including *Promise of Eden: The Canadian Expansionist Movement and the Idea of the West, 1856–1900; The Government Generation*; and *Born at the Right Time: A History of the Baby Boom Generation*. In recognition of his scholarship he was made a member of the Royal Society of Canada (1990) and won the University of Alberta's research prize in 1995.

**Adele Perry** is professor of history and senior fellow at St. John's College at the University of Manitoba, where she has taught since 2000. She works on histories of colonialism, gender, and Western North America and is the author, most recently, of *Colonial Relations: The Douglas-Connolly Family and the Nineteenth-Century Imperial World* (Cambridge, 2015) and *Aqueduct: Colonialism, Resources, and the Histories We Remember* (ARP, 2016).

**Yves Roby** was a member of the History Department at the Université Laval. Before developing the Franco-American field of studies, Roby published award-winning books on the social history of Quebec. His book entitled *Histoire économique du Québec, 1851–1896* (with Jean Hamelin) received the Governor General's Award (études et essais de langue française) in 1972. His distinguished publications on Franco-Americans include *Les Franco-Américains de la Nouvelle-Angleterre, 1776–1930* (Septentrion, 1990) and *Les Franco-Américains de la Nouvelle-Angleterre, rêves et réalités* (Septentrion, 2000), which was translated as *The Franco-Americans of New England: Dreams and Realities* (McGill-Queen's University Press, 2004).

**Stanley Bréhaut Ryerson** (1911–1998) was a Canadian historian and active member of the Communist Party of Canada. He studied at the University of Toronto and the Sorbonne in Paris, and was a professor at l'Université du Québec à Montréal, where he taught history between 1970 and 1992. Ryerson contributed to the *National Affairs Monthly*, the *World Marxist Review*, and the *Marxist Quarterly*. He authored two books, *The Founding of Canada: Beginnings to 1815* and *Unequal Union: Roots of Crisis in the Canadas, 1815–1873.* Both works made a significant contribution to social history and Quebec's place in the Canadian federation.

**David E. Shi**, a native of Atlanta, Georgia, taught U.S. history for seventeen years at Davidson College in North Carolina before becoming the president of Furman University in South Carolina in 1994. He retired from the presidency in 2010. A specialist in intellectual and cultural history, Dr. Shi has written numerous books, including *Matthew Josephson, Bourgeois Bohemian; The Simple Life: Plain Living and High Thinking; In Search of the Simple Life; Facing Facts: Realism in American Culture; The Bell Tower and Beyond: Reflections on Life and Learning;* and *America: A Narrative History*, now in its tenth edition.

**A.I. Silver** is a noted Canadian historian who taught in the Department of History at the University of Toronto. His works include *The French-Canadian Idea of Confederation (1864–1900)*, a canonical book on the attitudes of the French-Canadian public towards Confederation in its first three decades. He has authored numerous journal articles on Canadian history, including in the *Canadian Historical Review*, and several publications on the public's evolving perceptions of Louis Riel.

**C.P. (Charles Perry) Stacey** (1906–1989) was a renowned historian who focused on Canadian military and foreign policy. Stacey was a member of the Canadian Forces between 1924 and 1959, and served as its official historian for the Second World War. He received his PhD from Princeton, where he taught history between 1933 and 1949, and later became a faculty member at the University of Toronto (1959–1975). His publications are extensive and include *Canada and the British Army, 1846–1871: A Study in the Practice of Responsible Government* (1936), *The Canadian Army, 1939–1945* (1948), which won the Governor General's Award for Literary Merit, and *A Very Double Life: The Private World of Mackenzie King* (1976). Numerous awards and honours were bestowed upon Stacey for his exceptional contributions: he was an officer of the Order of Canada, a fellow of the Royal Society of Canada, a member of the Order of the British Empire, and received the Canadian Forces Decoration.

**Robert C. Vipond** is professor of political science at the University of Toronto. He has published broadly in the area of Canadian political development and constitutional politics, notably *Liberty and Community: Canadian Federalism and the Failure of the Constitution* (SUNY, 1991). His most recent book is *Making a Global City: How One Toronto School Embraced Diversity* (University of Toronto Press, 2017).

**P.B. (Peter Busby) Waite** is one of Canada's foremost scholars on Confederation. A graduate of the universities of British Columbia and Toronto, Waite went on to teach in the History Department at Dalhousie University for thirty-seven years. He has published many books and articles on Canadian history, including *The Life and Times of Confederation 1864–1867* (1962), *Canada 1874–1896: Arduous Destiny* (1971), and *The Man from Halifax: Sir John Thompson, Prime Minister* (1985). Waite has received many honours and distinctions and is an officer of the Order of Canada and a member of the Royal Society of Canada.

**George E. Wilson** (1890–1973) attended Queen's University and Harvard University before moving to Halifax to embark on his academic career. Wilson was at Dalhousie University for fifty years and was a renowned educator, teaching both history and political economy. He served in a number of administrative positions, including dean of arts and science for ten years. In 1950, he became president of the Canadian Historical Association and in 1961 was appointed as a fellow to the Royal Society of Canada.

# Select Bibliography

Comprehensive bibliographies – which this is not – are art forms that rarely receive the acknowledgment they deserve. Those who capture a body of scholarship on a specific topic at a particular moment in time provide their successors with an indispensable research tool; they ensure research is not lost to history and allow those looking back to glean insights into the works and issues deemed important at a specific period in time. To this end, we want to recognize the important work of Patrick Allen, "Confédération canadienne – bibliographie sommaire," *Revue d'histoire de l'Amérique française* 21, no. 3a (1967): 695–719; and R.G. Trotter, "The Bibliography of Canadian Constitutional History," *Bibliographical Society of America* 22, no. 1 (1928): 1–12, which gave us a starting point for our research.

**Newspapers**

*Charleston Daily News* (Charleston, South Carolina)
*Daily Clarion and Standard* (Jackson, Mississippi)
*Daily Globe* (Toronto)
*The Free Press* (Burlington, Vermont)
*The Gazette* (Montreal)
*Globe* (Toronto)
*The Journal* (Coudersport, Pennsylvania)
*Le Devoir* (Montreal)
*New York Times*
*Saint John Globe* (New Brunswick)
*Toronto Daily Star*
*Yorkville Enquirer* (Columbia, South Carolina)

### Government Sources (Canada and Its Provinces)

Government of Canada, Library and Archives. http://www.bac-lac.gc.ca.

National Inquiry into Missing and Murdered Indigenous Women and Girls in 2016. http://www.mmiwg-ffada.ca.

*Parliamentary Debates on the Subject of the Confederation of the British North American Provinces*, 3rd Session, 8th Provincial Parliament of Canada. Quebec: Hunter Rose, 1865.

*Quebec and Confederation, Speech of Sir Lomer Gouin, K.C.M.G., Prime Minister of the Province of Quebec on the Francœur Motion, Delivered in the Legislative Assembly of Quebec on January 23, 1918*. Montreal: Librairie Beauchemin, 1918.

*Reference re. Secession of Quebec*, [1998] 2 SCR 217.

Royal Commission of Inquiry on Constitutional Problems. *Report of the Royal Commission of Inquiry on Constitutional Problems (Tremblay Report)*. Quebec, 1956.

Royal Commission on Aboriginal Peoples. *Report of the Royal Commission on Aboriginal Peoples*. Ottawa, 1996.

Royal Commission on Bilingualism and Biculturalism. *Report of the Royal Commission on Bilingualism and Biculturalism (Dunton-Laurendeau Report)*. Ottawa: Queen's Printer, 1965–1970.

Royal Commission on Dominion-Provincial Relations. *Report of the Royal Commission on Dominion-Provincial Relations (Rowell-Sirois Report)*. Ottawa, 1940.

Senate of Canada. *Report Relating to the Enactment of the British North America Act, 1867, Any Lack of Consonance between Its Terms and Judicial Construction of Them and Cognate Matters*. Ottawa, 1939.

Statistics Canada. http://www.statcan.gc.ca.

Truth and Reconciliation Commission of Canada. *Honouring the Truth, Reconciling for the Future* (2015). http://www.myrobust.com/websites/trcinstitution/File/Reports/Executive_Summary_English_Web.pdf.

### Government Sources (United States)

*A Memorial, from the French Canadians of the United States, in Opposition to the Scheme for the Confederation of the British Provinces of North America*, to the Senate of the United States. New York, February 6, 1867. RG46, Records of the U.S. Senate, 39th Congress, box no. 39, Committee on Foreign Relations, SEN 39A-H6.1 (December 10, 1866 to February 26, 1867). National Archives, Pennsylvania Avenue, Washington, DC.

Chamberlain, Joshua. "Address to the Senate and House of Representatives," n.d. *Acts and Resolves Passed by the Forty-Sixth Legislature of the State of Maine*. Augusta: Stevens & Sayward, 1867.
*Congressional Globe*.
H.R. 754, *A Bill For the Admission of the States of Nova Scotia, New Brunswick, Canada East, and Canada West, and for the organization of the Territories of Selkirk, Saskatchewan, and Columbia*, 39th Congress, 1st Session. July 2, 1866.

**Government Sources (United Kingdom)**

*A Bill for the Union of Canada, Nova Scotia, and New Brunswick, and the Government Thereof; and for Purposes Connected Therewith*. February 12, 1867.
*British North America Act, 1867* (UK), 30 & 31 Victoria c 3.
*Canada Act, 1982*, (UK), 1982, c 11.
*Hansard's Parliamentary Debates*.

**Secondary Sources**

Ajzenstat, Janet. *The Canadian Founding: John Locke and Parliament*. Montreal and Kingston: McGill-Queen's University Press, 2007.
Ajzenstat, Janet, Paul Romney, Ian Gentles, and William D. Gairdner, eds. *Canada's Founding Debates*. Toronto: Stoddart, 1999.
Anderson, Benedict. *Imagined Communities: Reflections on the Origin and Spread of Nationalism*. New York: Verso, 2016.
Angers, F.A. *Essai sur la centralisation*. Montreal: Beauchemin, 1960.
Arès, Richard. "Confederation: A Pact or a Law?" A translation of "La Confédération: Pacte ou Loi?" *L'Action Nationale* 34, no. 3 (1949): 194–230.
– *Dossier sur le pacte fédératif de 1867, La Confédération: pacte ou loi?* Montreal: Les Éditions Bellarmin, 1967.
– "La grande pitié des minorités françaises." *Relations* 267 (1963): 65–8.
– "Un siècle de vie française en dehors du Québec." *Revue d'histoire de l'Amérique française* 21, no. 3a (1967): 531–70.
Bailey, Alfred G. "The Basis and Persistence of Opposition to Confederation in New Brunswick." *Canadian Historical Review* 23, no. 4 (1942): 374–97.
– "Railways and the Confederation Issue in New Brunswick, 1863–1865." *Canadian Historical Review* 21, no. 4 (1963): 285–312.
Baker, William M. "Squelching the Disloyal, Fenian-Sympathizing Brood: T.W. Anglin and Confederation in New Brunswick, 1865–1866." *Canadian Historical Review* 55, no. 2 (1974): 141–58.

Ballantyne, Tony. *Webs of Empire: Locating New Zealand's Colonial Past*. Vancouver: UBC Press, 2012.

Beasley, Edward. *Empire as the Triumph of Theory: Imperialism, Information and the Colonial Society of 1868*. London: Routledge, 2005.

Beck, J.M. *Joseph Howe*. 2 vols. Montreal and Kingston: McGill-Queen's University Press, 1982, 1983.

Bélanger, Réal. "Bourassa, Henri," in *Dictionary of Canadian Biography*, 18. http://www.biographi.ca/en/bio/bourassa_henri_18E.html.

Bellavance, Marcel. *Le Québec et la Confédération: un choix libre? Le clergé et la constitution de 1867*. Quebec: Septentrion 1992.

Berger, Carl. *The Writing of Canadian History: Aspects of English-Canadian Historical Writing since 1900*. Toronto: University of Toronto Press, 1986.

Bergeron, Gérard. *Le Canada Français. Après deux siècles de patience*. Paris: Ed. du Seuil, 1967.

Bilodeau, Rosario. "Liminaire." *Revue d'histoire de l'Amérique française* 21, no. 3a (1967): 529.

Bitterman, Rusty, and Margaret McCallum. "Upholding the Land Legislation of a 'Communistic and Socialist Assembly': The Benefits of Confederation for Prince Edward Island." *Canadian Historical Review* 87, no. 1 (2006): 1–28.

Bolger, Francis W.P. "The Charlottetown Conference and Its Significance in Canadian History." *Canadian Catholic Historical Association Report* 27 (1960): 11–23.

Bonenfant, J.-C. "Cartier, Sir George-Étienne." *Dictionary of Canadian Biography*, 10. http://www.biographi.ca/en/bio/cartier_george_etienne_10E.html.

– *The French Canadians and the Birth of Confederation*. Canadian Historical Association Historical Booklet 21. Hull: Leclerc, 1966.

– "Le Canada et les hommes politiques de 1867." *Revue d'histoire de l'Amérique française* 21, no. 3a (1967): 571–96.

Borrows, John. "(Ab)Originalism and Canada's Constitution." *Supreme Court Law Review* 58 (2012): 351–98.

– *Canada's Indigenous Constitution*. Toronto: University of Toronto Press, 2010.

– "Tracking Trajectories: Aboriginal Governance as an Aboriginal Right." *University of British Columbia Law Review* 38 (2005): 285–314.

Bossé, Éveline. *Joseph-Charles Taché (1820–1894), un représentant de l'élite canadienne-française*. Quebec: Garneau, 1971.

Bourassa, Henri. *Le patriotisme Canadien-Français: ce qu'il est, ce qu'il doit être. Discours prononcé au Monument National, le 27 avril 1902*. Montreal: La Cie de Publications de la Revue Canadienne, 1902.

Bourinot, John G. *Canada under British Rule, 1760–1900*. Cambridge: Cambridge University Press, 1900.

Boyd, John. *Sir George Etienne Cartier, His Life and Times: A Political History of Canada from 1814 until 1873.* Toronto: Macmillan, 1914.

Brebner, John Bartlet. *North Atlantic Triangle: The Interplay of Canada, the United States and Great Britain.* New Haven: Yale University Press, 1949.

Brossard, Roger. "The Working of Confederation: A French-Canadian View." *Canadian Journal of Economics and Political Science* 3, no. 3 (1937): 335–45, 353–4.

Brouillet, Eugénie. *The Negation of a Nation: The Quebec Cultural Identity and Canadian Federalism,* a translation of material from *La Négation de la nation. L'identité culturelle québécoise et le fédéralisme canadien.* Quebec: Septentrion, 2005.

Brouillet, Eugénie, Alain-G. Gagnon, and Guy Laforest, eds. *La Conférence de Québec de 1864, 150 ans plus tard: Comprendre l'émergence de la fédération canadienne.* Quebec: Presses de l'Université Laval, 2016.

Brunet, Michel. *Canadians et Canadiens.* Montreal: Fides, 1954.

– *La présence anglaise et les Canadiens. Études sur l'histoire et la pensée des deux Canadas.* Montreal: Beauchemin, 1958.

Buckner, Phillip, ed. *Canada and the British Empire.* Oxford: Oxford University Press, 2010.

– "The Maritimes and Confederation: A Reassessment." *Canadian Historical Review* 71, no. 1 (1990), 1–30.

Burpee, Lawrence J. "Western Exploration, 1840–1867." In Shortt and Doughty, *Canada and Its Provinces,* vol. 5, *United Canada (1840–1867),* 295–328.

Cairns, Alan C. "The Charter: A Political Science Perspective." *Osgoode Hall Law Journal* 30, no. 3 (1992): 615–25.

– "The Judicial Committee and Its Critics." *Canadian Journal of Political Science* 4 (1971): 301–45.

– "The Governments and Societies of Canadian Federalism." *Canadian Journal of Political Science* 10, no. 4 (1977): 695–725.

– "The Living Canadian Constitution." In *Constitution, Government and Society in Canada,* ed. Douglas Williams, 27–42. Toronto: McClelland & Stewart, 1988.

Cairns, Alan, and Edwin Black. "A Different Perspective on Canadian Federalism." *Canadian Public Administration* 9, no. 1 (1966): 27–45.

Cameron, David R. "Not Spicer and Not the B and B: Reflections on the Pepin-Robarts Task Force on Canadian Unity." *International Journal of Canadian Studies* 7–8 (1993): 333–46.

– "Post-Modern Ontario and the Laurentian Thesis." In *Canada: The State, The Federation: 1994,* ed. Douglas Brown and Janet Hiebert, 109–34. Kingston: Queen's Institute of Intergovernmental Relations, 1994.

Cameron, David R., and Jacqueline D. Krikorian. "Recognizing Quebec in the Constitution of Canada: Using the Bilateral Constitutional Amendment Process." *University of Toronto Law Journal* 58 (2008): 390–420.
– "The Study of Federalism, 1960–99: A Content Review of Several Leading Canadian Academic Journals." *Canadian Public Administration* 45, no. 3 (2002): 328–63.
Cameron, David R., Jacqueline D. Krikorian, and Robert C. Vipond. "Revisiting the 1865 Canadian Debates on Confederation: Rights and the Constitution," in "Reconsidering the Debates over Canadian Confederation," special issue, *Canada Watch* (2016): 3–15.
Cameron, David R., and Richard Simeon. "Intergovernmental Relations in Canada: The Emergence of Collaborative Federalism." *Publius: The Journal of Federalism* 32, no. 2 (2002): 1–23.
– "Ontario in Confederation: The Not-so-Friendly Giant." In *The Government and Politics of Ontario*, ed. Graham White, 158–88. Toronto: Nelson Canada, 1997.
Cappon, James. "The Principle of Sectarianism in the Canadian Constitution." *Queen's Quarterly* 12 (July 1, 1904): 425–42.
Careless, J.M.S. *Brown of the Globe*, 2 vols. Toronto: Macmillan, 1959 and 1963.
– "Frontierism and Metropolitanism: Concepts Revisited." In *Frontier and Metropolis: Regions, Cities and Identities in Canada before 1914*, 35–67. Toronto: University of Toronto Press, 1987.
– "George Brown." *Dictionary of Canadian Biography*, 10:93–101.
– "'Limited Identities' in Canada." *Canadian Historial Review* 49, no. 1 (1968): 1–10.
Caron, Jean-François, and Marcel Martel, eds. *Le Canada français et la Confédération, Fondements et bilan critique*. Quebec: Presses de l'Université Laval, 2016.
Cauchon, Joseph. *Étude sur L'Union Projetée des Provinces Britanniques de l'Amérique du Nord*. Quebec: D'Augustin Coté, 1858.
– *The Union of the Provinces of British North America*. Trans. George Henry Macaulay. Quebec: Hunter Rose, 1865.
Chapman, J.K. "Arthur Gordon and Confederation." *Canadian Historical Review* 37, no. 2 (1956): 141–57.
Clement, W.H.P. *The Law of the Canadian Constitution*. Toronto: Carswell, 1892.
Cook, Ramsay, ed. *Confederation*. Toronto: University of Toronto Press, 1966.
– "Quebec and Confederation: Past and Present." *Queen's Quarterly* 71, no. 4 (1964): 468–84.
Cornell, D.G. *The Great Coalition*. Centennial Historical Booklet 8. Ottawa: Centennial Commission, 1967.

Cote-Meek, Sheila. "Post-secondary Education and Reconciliation." *Policy Options*. http://policyoptions.irpp.org/fr/magazines/fevrier-2017/post-secondary-education-and-reconciliation/.

Creighton, Donald. *The Commercial Empire of the St. Lawrence, 1760–1850*. Toronto: Macmillan, 1980.

– "Confederation: The Use and Abuse of History." *Journal of Canadian Studies* 1, no. 1 (1966): 5.

– "Conservatism and National Unity." In *Essays in Canadian History Presented to George MacKinnon Wrong for His Eightieth Birthday*, ed. R. Flenley, 154–77. Toronto: Macmillan, 1939.

– *John A. Macdonald: The Young Politician; The Old Chieftain*. Toronto: University of Toronto Press, 1998.

– *The Road to Confederation: The Emergence of Canada, 1863–1867*. Don Mills: Oxford University Press, 2012.

– "Sir John Macdonald and Canadian Historians." *Canadian Historical Review* 29, no. 1 (1948): 1–13.

– "The United States and Canadian Confederation." *Canadian Historical Review* 39, no. 3 (1958): 209–22.

Crépeau, P.A., and C.B. Macpherson, eds. *The Future of Canadian Federalism*. Toronto: University of Toronto Press, 1965.

Curthoys, Ann. "Distant Relations: Australian Perspectives on Canadian Federation." In *Globalizing Confederation: Canada and the World in 1867*, ed. Jacqueline D. Krikorian, Marcel Martel, and Adrian Schubert. Toronto: University of Toronto Press, forthcoming.

Daschuk, James W. *Clearing the Plains: Disease, Politics of Starvation and the Loss of Aboriginal Life*. Regina: University of Regina Press, 2013.

David, L.O. *L'Union des Deux Canadas, 1841–1865*. Montreal: Eusèbe Senécal, 1898.

Dawson, Robert MacGregor, ed. *Constitutional Issues in Canada, 1900–1931*. London: Oxford University Press, 1933.

Dent, John Charles. *The Canadian Portrait Gallery*, 4 vols. Toronto: John B. Magurn, 1881.

– *The Last Forty Years: Canada since the Union of 1841*, 2. Toronto: George Virtue, 1881.

Désilets, Andrée. *Hector-Louis Langevin, un père de la Confédération canadienne (1826–1906)*. Quebec: Presses de l'Université Laval, 1969.

Dick, Lyle. "'A Growing Necessity for Canada': W.L. Morton's Centenary Series and the Forms of National History, 1955–80." *Canadian Historical Review* 82, no. 2 (2001): 223–52.

Dickason, Olive Patricia, and William Newbigging. *A Concise History of Canada's First Nations*. Toronto: Oxford University Press, 2015.

Dumont, Fernand. *Genèse de la société québécoise.* Montreal: Boréal, 1993.
– *The Origins of Quebec Society*, a translation of material from *Genèse de la société québécoise.* Montreal: Boréal, 1993.
Dutil, Patrice, and Roger Hall, eds. *Macdonald at 200: New Reflections and Legacies.* Toronto: Dundurn, 2014.
Easterbrook, W.T., and Hugh G.J. Aitken. *Canadian Economic History.* Toronto: University of Toronto Press, 2002.
Elkins, Zachary, Tom Ginsburg, and James Melton. *The Endurance of National Constitutions.* New York: Cambridge University Press, 2009.
Fafard, Patrick, and François Rocher. "The Evolution of Federalism Studies in Canada: From Centre to Periphery." *Canadian Public Administratioin* 52, no. 2 (2009): 291–311.
Farr, David M.L. *The Colonial Office and Canada, 1867–1887.* Toronto: University of Toronto Press, 1955.
– *Great Britain and Confederation.* Centennial Historical Booklet 1. Ottawa: Centennial Commission, 1967.
Flanagan, Thomas. *Riel and the Rebellion, 1885 Reconsidered.* Toronto: University of Toronto Press, 2000.
Foley, Michael. *The Silence of Constitutions: Gaps, "Abeyances" and Political Temperament in the Maintenance of Government.* New York: Routledge, 2011.
Forbes, Ernest, and D.A. Muise, eds. *The Atlantic Provinces in Confederation.* Toronto: University of Toronto Press, 1993.
Foucher, Pierre. "L'Acadie du Nouveau-Brunswick et la Constitution Canadienne." *Revue de l'Université de Moncton* 26 (1995): 1–47.
Gibson, James A. "The Colonial Office View of Canadian Federation, 1856–1868." *Canadian Historical Review* 35, no. 4 (1954): 279–313.
– "The Duke of Newcastle and British North American Affairs, 1859–64." *Canadian Historical Review* 44, no. 4 (1963): 142–56.
Granatstein, Jack. *Canada 1957–1967: The Years of Uncertainty and Innovation.* Toronto: McClelland & Stewart, 1986.
Grant, W.L. "General Outlines, 1840–1867." In Shortt and Doughty, *Canada and Its Provinces*, vol. 5, *United Canada (1840–1867)*, 3–10.
Gray, John Hamilton. *Confederation; or, The Political and Parliamentary History of Canada from the Conference at Quebec, in October, 1864, to the Admission of British Columbia, in July, 1871*, 1. Toronto: Copp, Clark, 1872.
Groulx, Lionel. "Ce Cinquantenaire." *L'Action française* 1, no. 7 (1917): 193–203.
– "French Canadians and the Founding of Confederation," a translation of "Les Canadiens français et l'établissement de la Confédération." *Revue d'histoire de l'Amérique française* 21, no. 3a (1967): 677–94. This work was

originally published in *Les Canadiens français et la Confédération canadienne*. Montreal: Bibliothèque de l'Action française, 1927, 1–21.
– *La Confédération Canadienne, Ses origines*. Montreal: Imprimé au Devoir, 1918.
Hamelin, Jean. "First Years of Confederation." Centennial Historical Booklet 3. Ottawa: Centennial Commission, 1967.
Hamilton, C.F. "Defence, 1812–1912." In Shortt and Doughty, *Canada and Its Provinces*, vol. 7, *The Dominion: Political Development II*, 379–468.
Harvey, D.C. "Confederation in Prince Edward Island." *Canadian Historical Review* 14, no. 2 (1933): 143–60.
Hayday, Matthew, and Raymond B. Blake, eds. *Celebrating Canada*. Vol. 1, *Holidays, National Days, and the Crafting of Identities*. Toronto: University of Toronto Press, 2016.
Henderson, James [sákéj] Youngblood. "Empowering Treaty Federalism." *Saskatchewan Law Review* 58 (1994): 241–329.
Hertel, François. *Cent ans d'injustice? Un beau rêve: le Canada*. Montreal: Éditions du Jour, 1967.
Hobsbawm, Eric, and Terence Ranger, eds. *The Invention of Tradition*. Cambridge: Cambridge University Press, 2012.
Hodgins, Bruce W. "Democracy and the Ontario Fathers of Confederation." In *Profiles of a Province: Studies in the History of Ontario*, 83–91. Toronto: Ontario Historical Society, 1967.
– "John Sandfield Macdonald and the Crises of 1863." *Canadian Historical Association Report* 44, no. 1 (1965): 30–45.
Innis, Harold A. *The Fur Trade in Canada*. Toronto: University of Toronto Press, 1999.
Janhunen, Anne. "'Colonization Road' and Challenging Settler Colonialism in Canada." ActiveHistory.ca (2016). http://activehistory.ca/2016/11/colonization-road-and-challenging-settler-colonialism-in-canada/.
Jennings, Ivor. *The Approach to Self-Government*. Cambridge: Cambridge University Press, 1956.
Keith, Arthur Berriedale. *Responsible Government in the Dominions*. 3 vols. Oxford: Clarendon, 1912.
Kelly, Stéphane. *Canada and Its Aims, According to Macdonald, Laurier, Mackenzie King and Trudeau*, a translation of material from *Les Fins du Canada, selon Macdonald, Laurier, Mackenzie King et Trudeau*. Montreal: Boréal, 2001.
Kennedy, W.P.M. *The Constitution of Canada: An Introduction to Its Development and Law*. London: Oxford University Press, 1922.
– "The Interpretation of the British North America Act." *Cambridge Law Journal* 8 (1944): 146–60.

Kerr, Donald G.G. "Edmund Head, Robert Lowe, and Confederation." *Canadian Historical Review* 20, no. 4 (1939): 409–20.

Knox, Bruce A. "The Rise of Colonial Federation as an Object of British Policy, 1850–1870." *Journal of British Studies* 11, no. 1 (1971): 92–112.

Krikorian, Jacqueline D. "British Imperial Politics and Canadian Judicial Independence." *Canadian Journal of Political Science* 33, no. 2 (2000): 291–332.

Krikorian, Jacqueline D., and David R. Cameron. "The 1867 Union of the British North American Colonies: A View from the United States." In *Globalizing Confederation: Canada and the World in 1867*, ed. Jacqueline D. Krikorian, Marcel Martel, and Adrian Schubert. Toronto: University of Toronto Press, forthcoming.

Krikorian, Jacqueline D., Marcel Martel, and Adrian Schubert, eds. *Globalizing Confederation: Canada and the World in 1867.* Toronto: University of Toronto Press, forthcoming.

Kylie, Edward. "Constitutional Development, 1840–1867." In Shortt and Doughty, *Canada and Its Provinces*, vol. 5, *United Canada (1840–1867)*, 105–62.

Laforest, Guy. *Trudeau et la fin d'un rêve canadien*. Sillery, QC: Les Éditions du Septentrion, 1992.

Laforest, Guy, Eugénie Brouillet, Alain-G. Gagnon, and Yves Tanguay, eds. *Ces constitutions qui nous ont façonnés: Anthologie historique des lois constitutionnelles antérieures à 1867*. Quebec: Presses de l'Université Laval, 2014.

Lamonde, Yvan. *The Social History of Ideas in Quebec, 1760–1896*. Translated by Phyllis Aronoff and Howard Scott. Montreal and Kingston: McGill-Queen's University Press, 2013.

Langelier, Charles. *La Confédération, sa genèse, son établissement*. Quebec: Le Soleil, 1916.

LaSelva, Samuel V. "Federalism as a Way of Life: Reflections on the Canadian Experiment." *Canadian Journal of Political Science* 26, no. 2 (1993): 219–34.

– *The Moral Foundations of Confederation: Paradoxes, Achievements, and Tragedies of Nationhood*. Montreal and Kingston: McGill-Queen's University Press, 1996.

Laskin, Bora. "'Peace, Order and Good Government' Re-examined." *Canadian Bar Review* 25 (1947): 1054–87.

LeFevre, Tate A. "Settler Colonialism." *Oxford Bibliographies*. Last modified May 29, 2015. http://www.oxfordbibliographies.com/view/document/obo-9780199766567/obo-9780199766567-0125.xml.

Lefroy, A.H.F. *Canada's Federal System*. Toronto: Carswell, 1913.

– "The Federal Constitution." In Shortt and Doughty, *Canada and Its Provinces*, vol. 6, *The Dominion: Political Development I*, 209–67.

Legaré, Anne. "Towards a Marxist Theory of Canadian Federalism." *Studies in Political Economy* 8, no. 1 (1982): 37–58.

Lewis, John. *The Makers of Canada*. Toronto: Morang, 1910.

Loranger, T.J.J. *Lettres sur l'interprétation de la constitution fédérale, dite l'Acte de l'Amérique Britannique du Nord, 1867*. Montreal: A Périard, 1884.

Lower, Arthur R.M. *Colony to Nation: A History of Canada*. New York: Longmans, Green, 1946.

– "Two Ways of Life: The Primary Antithesis of Canadian History." *Report of the Annual Meeting of the Canadian Historical Association* 22, no. 1 (1943): 5–18.

Mackenzie, Alex. *The Life and Speeches of Hon. George Brown*. Toronto: Globe Printing, 1882.

Mackintosh, W.A. "Economic Factors in Canadian History." *Canadian Historical Review* 4, no. 1 (1923): 12–25.

MacMechan, Archibald. "Nova Scotia: General History, 1775–1867." In Shortt and Doughty, *Canada and Its Provinces*, vol. 13, *Atlantic Provinces I*, 213–302.

MacMullen, John. *The History of Canada from Its First Discovery to the Present Time*. Brockville: McMullen, 1868.

MacNutt, W.S. *The Maritimes and Confederation*. Centennial Historical Booklet 2. Ottawa: Centennial Commission, 1967.

Macphail, Andrew. "The History of Prince Edward Island." In Shortt and Doughty, *Canada and Its Provinces*, vol. 13, *Atlantic Provinces I*, 305–75.

Mallory, J.R. "Five Faces of Federalism." In *The Future of Canadian Federalism*, ed. P.A. Crépeau and C.B. Macpherson, 3–15. Toronto: University of Toronto Press, 1965.

Martel, Marcel. "An Example for the World? Confederation and French Canadians." "Reconsidering the Debates over Canadian Confederation." Special issue, *Canada Watch*, 7–9. Toronto: Robarts Centre, 2016.

– "Ils n'étaient pas à la table de négotiations: les francophones en milieu minoritaire et leur expérience concernant le pacte confédératif." In *Le Canada français et la Confédération, Fondements et bilan critique*, ed. Jean-François Caron and Marcel Martel, 55–79. Quebec: Presses de l'Université Laval, 2016.

– *Le deuil d'un pays imaginé. Rêves, luttes et déroute du Canada français. Les relations entre le Québec et la francophonie canadienne*. Ottawa: University of Ottawa Press, 1997.

Martin, Chester. "British Policy in Canadian Confederation." *Canadian Historical Review* 13, no. 1 (1932): 3–19.

– "The United States and Canadian Nationality." *Canadian Historical Review* 18, no. 1 (1937): 1–11.

Martin, Ged. *Britain and the Origins of the Canadian Confederation, 1837–67.* Vancouver: UBC Press, 1995.
– "Launching Canadian Confederation: Means to Ends, 1836–1864." *Historical Journal* 27, no. 3 (1984): 575–602.
Mather, Frederic G. "Confederation in Canada." *Atlantic Monthly*, July 1880, 56–67.
Mayo, H.B. "Newfoundland and Confederation in the Eighteen-Sixties." *Canadian Historical Review* 29, no. 2 (1948): 125–42.
McArthur, Duncan. "History of Public Finance, 1840–1867." In Shortt and Doughty, *Canada and Its Provinces*, vol. 5, *United Canada (1840–1867)*, 165–82.
McDougall, Andrew. "Canadian Federalism, Abeyances, and Quebec Sovereignty." PhD diss, University of Toronto, 2016.
– "The Challenges of Repatriating Aboriginal Cultural Property in Canada." *Canadian Journal of Native Studies* 32, no. 2 (2012): 51–75.
McDougall, Andrew, Grace Skogstad, and Robert Schertzer. "Collaboration and Unilateralism: Explaining Recent Dynamics of Intergovernmental Relations in Canada." *IRPP Insight Series* 62 (2016).
McKay, Ian. "The Liberal Order Framework: A Prospectus for a Reconnaissance of Canadian History." *Canadian Historical Review* 81, no. 4 (2000): 617–51.
McNally, David. "Staple Theory as Commodity Fetishism: Marx, Innis and Canadian Political Economy." *Studies in Political Economy* 6 (1981): 35–63.
McPherson, Kathryn. "Gender and the Confederation Debates." "Reconsidering the Debates over Canadian Confederation." Special issue, *Canada Watch*, 30–2. Toronto: Robarts Centre, 2016.
McRoberts, Kenneth. *Misconceiving Canada*. Toronto: Oxford University Press, 1997.
Merivale, Herman. *Lectures on Colonization and Colonies, Delivered before the University of Oxford in 1839, 1840, & 1841*. London: Longman, Green, Longman and Roberts, 1861. Merivale updated some of his lectures in 1861 by including appendixes.
Migneault, Gaétan. "French Canada and Confederation: The Acadians of New Brunswick," a translation of "Le Canada français et la Confédération: les Acadiens du Nouveau-Brunswick." In *Le Canada français et la Confédération, Fondements et bilan critique*, ed. Jean-François Caron and Marcel Martel. Quebec: Presses de l'Université Laval, 2016.
Mills, Sean. *The Empire Within: Postcolonial Thought and Political Activism in Sixties Montreal*. Montreal and Kingston: McGill-Queen's University Press, 2010.
Miquelon, Dale. *New France 1701 to 1744: A Supplement to Europe*. Toronto: McClelland & Stewart, 1987.

Mohr, Thomas. *Guardian of the Treaty: The Privy Council Appeal and Irish Sovereignty*. Dublin: Four Courts, 2016.
Molinari, Patrick A. "L'Équilibre du fédéralisme canadien dans la balance de l'interprétation judiciare." *La Revue juridique Thémis de l'Université de Montréal* 13, no. 1 (1978): 99–106.
Monière, Denis. *Le développement des idéologies au Québec, des origines à nos jours*. Montreal: Éditions Québec-Amérique, 1977.
Moore, Christopher. *1867: How the Fathers Made a Deal*. Toronto: McClelland & Stewart, 1997.
Morgan, Cecilia. *Commemorating Canada: History, Heritage, and Memory, 1850s–1990s*. Toronto: University of Toronto Press, 2016.
Morrison, J.L. "Parties and Politics, 1840–1867." In Shortt and Doughty, *Canada and Its Provinces*, vol. 5, *United Canada (1840–1867)*, 13–101.
Morton, W.L. *The Critical Years: The Union of British North America, 1857–1873*. Toronto: McClelland & Stewart, 1964.
– *The West and Confederation*. Centennial Historical Booklet 7. Ottawa: Centennial Commission, 1967.
Neatby, Hilda. *Quebec: The Revolutionary Age, 1760–1791*. Toronto: McClelland & Stewart, 1971.
Ormsby, W.G. "Letters to Galt concerning the Maritime Provinces and Confederation." *Canadian Historical Review* 34, no. 2 (1953): 166–9.
Owram, Doug. *Promise of Eden: The Canadian Expansionist Movement and the Idea of the West, 1856–1900*. Toronto: University of Toronto Press, 1992.
Panitch, Leo, ed. *The Canadian State: Political Economy and Political Power*. Toronto: University of Toronto Press, 1977.
– "Dependency and Class in Canadian Political Economy." *Studies in Political Economy* 6 (1981): 7–33.
Paquin, Stéphane. *The Invention of a Myth: The Pact between Two Founding Peoples*, a translation of material from *L'invention d'un mythe, Le pacte entre deux peuples fondateurs*. Montreal: VLB éditeur, 1999.
Perry, Adele. *On the Edge of Empire: Gender, Race and the Making of British Columbia, 1849–1871*. Toronto: University of Toronto Press, 2001.
Pope, Joseph, ed. *Confederation: Being a Series of Hitherto Unpublished Documents Bearing on the British North America Act*. Toronto: Carswell, 1895.
– *Memoirs of the Right Honourable Sir John Alexander Macdonald, G.C.B., First Prime Minister of the Dominion of Canada*, 2 vols. London: Edward Arnold, 1894.
Pryke, K.G. "The Making of a Province: Nova Scotia and Confederation." *Canadian Historical Association, Historical Papers* 3, no. 1 (1968): 35–48.
Rémillard, Gil. *Le Fédéralisme canadien. Éléments constitutionnels de formation et d'évolution*, 2 vols. Montreal: Québec Amérique, 1980 and 1985.

– "Les intentions des Pères de la Confédération." *Les Cahiers de Droit* 20 (1979): 797–832.
– "L'interprétation par le juge des règles écrites en droit constitutionnel au Canada." *La Revue juridique Thémis de l'Université de Montréal* 13, no. 1 (1978): 59–67.
Robitaille, Georges. "La Confédération canadienne." *Report of the Annual Meeting of the Canadian Historical Association* 6, no. 1 (1927): 62–6.
Roby, Yves. *The United States and Confederation*. Centennial Historical Booklet 4. Ottawa: Centennial Commission, 1967.
Rocher, François. "The End of the 'Two Solitudes'? The Presence (or Absence) of the Work of French-Speaking Scholars in Canadian Politics." *Canadian Journal of Political Science* 40, no. 4 (2007): 833–57.
Rogers, Norman McL. "The Compact Theory of Confederation." *Canadian Bar Review* 9, no. 6 (1931): 395–417.
– "The Confederate Council of Trade." *Canadian Historical Review* 7, no. 4 (1926): 277–86.
– "The Genesis of Provincial Rights." *Canadian Historical Review* 14, no. 1 (1933): 9–23.
– "The Political Principles of Federalism." *Canadian Journal of Economics and Political Science* 1, no. 3 (1935): 337–47.
Romney, Paul. *Getting It Wrong: How Canadians Forgot Their Past and Imperilled Confederation*. Toronto: University of Toronto Press, 1999.
Rudin, Ronald. *Making History in Twentieth-Century Quebec*. Toronto: University of Toronto Press, 1997.
Rumilly, Robert. *Histoire de la province de Québec*. 41 vols. 1940–69.
Russell, Peter H. *Canada's Odyssey: A Country Based on Incomplete Conquests*. Toronto: University of Toronto Press, 2017.
– *Constitutional Odyssey: Can Canadians Become a Sovereign People?* Toronto: University of Toronto Press, 2004.
– "High Courts and the Rights of Aboriginal Peoples: The Limits of Judicial Independence." *Saskatchewan Law Review* 61 (1998): 247–76.
– "The Politics of Law." *Windsor Yearbook of Access to Justice* 11 (1991): 127–42.
Rutherdale, Myra, and J.R. Miller. "It's Our Country: First Nations' Participation in the Indian Pavilion at Expo '67." *Journal of the Canadian Historical Association* 17, no. 2 (2006): 148–73.
Ryerson, Stanley B. *Unequal Union: Roots of Crisis in the Canadas, 1815–1873*. Toronto: Progress Books, 1973.
Sapir, E. "Indian Tribes of the Coast." In Shortt and Doughty, *Canada and Its Provinces*, 21:315–46.

Schneiderman, David. *Red, White and Kind of Blue? The Conservatives and the Americanization of Canadian Constitutional Culture*. Toronto: University of Toronto Press, 2015.

Scott, Duncan C. "Indian Affairs, 1763–1841." In Shortt and Doughty, *Canada and Its Provinces*, 4:695–725.

– "Indian Affairs, 1840–1867." In Shortt and Doughty, *Canada and Its Provinces*, 5:331–62.

– "Indian Affairs, 1867–1912." In Shortt and Doughty, *Canada and Its Provinces*, 7:593–626.

Scott, F.R. "The Development of Canadian Federalism." *Papers and Proceedings of the Annual Meeting of the CPSA* 3 (1931): 231–47.

– "Political Nationalism and Confederation." *Canadian Journal of Economics and Political Science* 8, no. 3 (1942): 386–415.

Shi, David E. "Seward's Attempt to Annex British Columbia, 1865–1869." *Pacific Historical Review* 47, 2 (1978): 217–38.

Shortt, Adam. "Economic History, 1840–1867." In Shortt and Doughty, *Canada and Its Provinces*.

Shortt, Adam, and Arthur G. Doughty, gen. eds. *Canada and Its Provinces: A History of the Canadian People and Their Institutions*, 23 vols. Edinburgh: T. & A. Constable, Edinburgh University Press, 1913–17.

Silver, A.I. *The French Canadian Idea of Confederation, 1864–1900*. Toronto: University of Toronto Press, 1997.

Simeon, Richard. *Federal-Provincial Diplomacy*. Toronto: University of Toronto Press, 1972.

– *Political Science and Federalism: Seven Decades of Scholarly Engagement*. Kingston: Queen's University Institute of Intergovernmental Relations, 2002.

Skelton, Oscar Douglas. *Life and Times of Sir Alexander Tilloch Galt*. Toronto: Oxford University Press, 1920.

Smiley, Donald V. *The Federal Condition in Canada*. Toronto: McGraw-Hill Ryerson, 1987.

– "The Rowell-Sirois Report: Provincial Autonomy, and Post-War Canadian Federalism." *Canadian Journal of Political Science* 28, no. 1 (1962): 54–69.

Smith, Andrew. *British Businessmen and Canadian Confederation: Constitution Making in an Era of Anglo-Globalization*. Montreal and Kingston: McGill-Queen's University Press, 2008.

Smith, David E. *The Canadian Senate in Bicameral Perspective*. Toronto: University of Toronto Press, 2003.

– *The Constitution in a Hall of Mirrors: Canada at 150*. Toronto: University of Toronto Press, 2017.

– *Federalism and the Constitution of Canada*. Toronto: University of Toronto Press, 2010.

Smith, Jennifer. "Intrastate Federalism and Confederation." In *Political Thought in Canada*, ed. Stephen Brooks, 258–77. Toronto: Irwin, 1984.

Smith, Miriam. *A Civil Society: Collective Actors in Canadian Political Life*. Peterborough: Broadview, 2005.

Smith, Peter J. "The Ideological Origins of Canadian Confederation." *Canadian Journal of Political Science* 20, no.1 (1987): 3–29.

Soucy, Emile. "Confédération ou 'fédéralisme coopératif'"? *L'action nationale* 54, no. 2 (October 1864): 168–73.

Stacey, C.P. "Britain's Withdrawal from North America, 1864–1871." *Canadian Historical Review* 36, no. 3 (1955): 185–98.

– *Canada and the British Army, 1846–1871: A Study in the Practice of Responsible Government*. Toronto: University of Toronto Press, 1963.

– "Fenianism and the Rise of National Feeling in Canada at the Time of Confederation." *Canadian Historical Review* 12, no. 3 (1931): 238–61.

Stanley, George F.G. "Act or Pact? Another Look at Confederation." *Report of the Annual Meeting of the CHA* 35, no. 1 (1956): 2.

Stembridge, Stanley R. "Disraeli and the Millstones." *Journal of British Studies* 5, no. 1 (1965): 122–39.

Stevenson, Garth. *Ex Uno Plures: Federal-Provincial Relations in Canada, 1867–1896*. Montreal and Kingston: McGill-Queen's University Press, 1993.

– "Federalism and the Political Economy of the Canadian State." In *The Canadian State: Political Economy and Political Power*, ed. Leo Panitch, 71–100. Toronto: University of Toronto Press, 1977.

Stewart, Alice R. "Sir Edmund Head's Memorandum of 1857 on Maritime Union: A Lost Confederation Document." *Canadian Historical Review* 26, no. 4 (1945): 406–19.

Storey, Kenton. *Settler Anxiety at the Outposts of Empire: Colonial Relations, Humanitarian Discourses, and the Imperial Press*. Vancouver: UBC Press, 2016.

Stuart, Reginald C. *United States Expansionism and British North America, 1775–1871*. Chapel Hill: University of North Carolina Press, 1988.

Swainson, D. *Ontario and Confederation*. Centennial Historical Booklet 5. Ottawa: Centennial Commission, 1967.

Swinfen, David B. *Imperial Appeal: The Debate on the Appeal to the Privy Council, 1833–1986*. Manchester: Manchester University Press, 1987.

Taché, J.C. *Des Provinces de l'Amérique du Nord et d'une Union Fédérale*. Quebec: Des Presses à Vapeur de J.T. Brousseau, 1858.

Teit, J.A. "Indian Tribes of the Interior." In Shortt and Doughty, *Canada and Its Provinces*, 21:283–312.

Trotter, R.G. "British Finance and Confederation." *Report of the Annual Meeting of the Canadian Historical Association* 6, no. 1 (1927): 89–96.

– *Canadian Federation: Its Origins and Achievements; A Study in Nation Building.* London: J.M. Dent, 1924.

Trudeau, Pierre Elliott. *Federalism and the French Canadians.* Toronto: Macmillan, 1968.

Trudel, Marcel. *The Beginnings of New France, 1524–1663.* Toronto: McClelland & Stewart, 1973.

Ullman, Walter. "The Quebec Bishops and Confederation." *Canadian Historical Review* 44, no. 3 (1963): 213–34.

Underhill, Frank H. "Edward Blake, the Supreme Court Act, and the Appeal to the Privy Council, 1875–6." *Canadian Historical Review* 19, no. 3 (1938): 245–63.

– *The Massey Lectures, 1963: The Images of Confederation.* Toronto: Hunter Rose for CBC, 1970.

Vallières, Pierre. *Nègres blancs d'Amérique: Autobiographie précoce d'un "terroriste" québécois.* Montreal: Éditions Partis Pris, 1968.

Veracini, Lorenzo. "Introduction: Settler Colonialism as a Distinct Mode of Domination." In *The Routledge Handbook of the History of Settler Colonialism*, ed. Edward Cavanagh and Lorenzo Veracini. London: Routledge, 2017.

– *Settler Colonialism: A Theoretical Overview.* London: Palgrave Macmillan, 2010.

Vipond, Robert C. "Constitutional Politics and the Legacy of the Provincial Rights Movement in Canada." *Canadian Journal of Political Science* 18, no. 2 (1985): 267–94.

– *Liberty and Community: Canadian Federalism and the Failure of the Constitution.* Albany: SUNY Press, 1991.

– "1787 and 1867: The Federal Principle and Canadian Confederation Reconsidered." *Canadian Journal of Political Science* 22, no. 1 (1989): 3–25.

– "Whatever Became of the Compact Theory? Meech Lake and the New Politics of Constitutional Amendment in Canada." *Queen's Quarterly* 96 (1989): 793–811.

Vipond, Robert C., Jacqueline D. Krikorian, and David R. Cameron. "Les Résolutions de Québec de 1864, et les idées délaissées." In *La Conférence de Québec de 1864 150 ans plus tard, Comprendre l'émergence de la fédération canadienne*, ed. Eugénie Brouillet, Alain-G. Gagnon, and Guy Laforest, 291–308. Quebec: Presses de l'Université Laval, 2016.

Wade, Mason. *The French Canadians, 1760–1945.* Toronto: Macmillan, 1956.

Waite, P.B. *The Charlottetown Conference.* Centennial Historical Booklet 6. Ottawa: Centennial Commission, 1967.

– "Edward Cardwell and Confederation." *Canadian Historical Review* 42, no. 1 (1962): 17–41.
– *The Life and Times of Confederation, 1864–1867*. Toronto: Robin Brass, 2001.
– "The Maritimes and Confederation." *Canadian Historical Review* 71, no. 1 (1990): 30–5.
Wallace, Carl. "Albert Smith, Confederation and Reaction in New Brunswick: 1852–1882." *Canadian Historical Review* 44, no. 4 (1963): 285–312.
Warner, Donald F. *The Idea of Continental Union: Agitation for the Annexation of Canada to the United States, 1849–1893*. Lexington: University of Kentucky Press, 1960.
Watkins, Melville H. "A Staple Theory of Economic Growth." *Canadian Journal of Economics and Political Science* 29, no. 2 (1963): 141–58.
Wheare, K.C. *Federal Government*. London: Oxford University Press, 1963.
Whelan, Edward, ed. *A Brief Account of the Several Conferences Held in the Maritime Provinces and in Canada, in September and October, 1864, on the Proposed Confederation of the Provinces, together with a Report of the Speeches Delivered by the Delegates from the Provinces on Important Public Occasions*. Charlottetown: Haszard, 1865.
Whitelaw, William Menzies. *The Maritimes and Canada before Confederation*. Toronto: Oxford University Press, 1934.
Wilson, David A. *Thomas D'Arcy McGee*, 2 vols. Montreal and Kingston: McGill-Queen's University Press, 2008, 2011.
Wilson, George E. "New Brunswick's Entrance into Confederation." *Canadian Historical Review* 9, no. 1 (1928): 4–24.
Wolfe, Patrick. "Settler Colonialism and the Elimination of the Native." *Journal of Genocide Research* 8, no. 4 (2006): 387–409.
Woolford, Andrew, and Jeff Benvenuto. "Canada and Colonial Genocide." *Journal of Genocide Research* 17, no. 4 (2015): 373–90.
Wrong, George M., John Willison, Z.A. Lash, and R.A. Falconer. *Federation of Canada, 1867–1917: Four Lectures Delivered in the University of Toronto in March 1917, to Commemorate the Fiftieth Anniversary of the Federation*. Toronto: Oxford University Press and University of Toronto Press, 1917.
Yack, Bernard. *Nationalism and the Moral Psychology of Community*. Chicago: University of Chicago Press, 2012.
Young, Brian. *George-Etienne Cartier*. Montreal and Kingston: McGill-Queen's University Press, 1981.
Zaslow, Morris. *The Northward Expansion of Canada, 1914–1967*. Toronto: McClelland & Stewart, 1988.
– *The Opening of the Canadian North, 1870–1914*. Toronto: McClelland & Stewart, 1971.

www.ingramcontent.com/pod-product-compliance
Lightning Source LLC
LaVergne TN
LVHW090757070826
844660LV00022B/1011

* 9 7 8 1 4 8 7 5 2 1 8 9 9 *